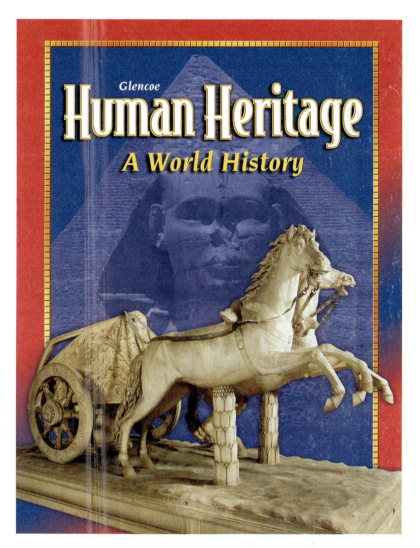

Glencoe
Human Heritage
A World History

Miriam Greenblatt
Peter S. Lemmo

 **Glencoe**

New York, New York   Columbus, Ohio   Chicago, Illinois   Peoria, Illinois   Woodland Hills, California

AUTHORS

Miriam Greenblatt is a writer, editor, and educational consultant who has traveled extensively in Asia, Africa, and Latin America. During the past 30 years, she has contributed to more than 50 elementary, junior high, and high school social studies texts and ancillaries, and has written almost two dozen history books for teenagers. A graduate of Hunter College of the City of New York and the University of Chicago, Greenblatt is a former teacher and a member of the National Association of Scholars and the Illinois Council for Social Studies. She is listed in *Who's Who in America 2005* and *Who's Who in the World 2005*.

Peter S. Lemmo is a former high school teacher who taught in the New York City school system for more than 30 years. A graduate of the City College of New York and the City University of New York, he has trained student teachers and contributed to several books. Lemmo has been instrumental in developing pilot instructional programs and curricula and was rated an exemplary teacher by the State Education Department of New York. He is also a member of the National Council for the Social Studies, the Association for Supervision and Curriculum Development, and other professional organizations, and he has traveled extensively in more than 55 countries.

The McGraw·Hill Companies

Copyright © 2006 by The McGraw-Hill Companies, Inc. All rights reserved. Except as permitted under the United States Copyright Act of 1976, no part of this publication may be reproduced or distributed in any form or by any means, or stored in a database or retrieval system, without the prior written permission of the publisher.

Printed in the United States of America

Send all inquiries to:
Glencoe/McGraw-Hill
8787 Orion Place
Columbus, OH 43240-4027

ISBN 0-07-869500-7 (Student Edition)

ISBN 0-07-869501-5 (Teacher Wraparound Edition)

2 3 4 5 6   071/043   10 09 08 07 06 05

ACADEMIC CONSULTANTS

Jerrold Green, Ph.D.
Director
Middle East Studies Center
University of Arizona
Tucson, Arizona

Al Naklowycz, Ph.D.
President
Ukrainian-American Academic
   Association of California
Carmichael, California

Joseph R. Rosenbloom, Ph.D.
Professor of Classics
Washington University
St. Louis, Missouri

FOLDABLES ™

Dinah Zike
Educational Consultant
Dinah-Might Activities, Inc.
San Antonio, Texas

TEACHER REVIEWERS

Rick Boeglin
Richardson North Junior High
   School
Richardson, Texas

Margaret Gray, Ph.D.
Vigo County School
   Corporation
Terre Haute, Indiana

Kathleen A. Grotto
West Orange Senior High
   School
West Orange, New Jersey

Dianne Hill
Muskogee Public Schools
Muskogee, Oklahoma

Nancy M. Kreeb
Central Junior High
Belleville, Illinois

Joseph Scheideler
Canton Junior/Senior High
   School
Collinsville, Connecticut

Janice H. Suddith
Paul Laurence Dunbar Middle
   School for Innovation
Lynchburg, Virginia

Sue A. Tillman Scoggins
Franklin Middle School
Springfield, Illinois

Contents

Unit 1 Place and Time

1 Geography and History 4
2 Prehistoric People 32
Around the World: Prehistoric Peoples of the Sahara 48
Standardized Test Practice 50

Unit 2 River Valley Civilizations

3 Mesopotamia 54
4 Egypt 66
5 Eastern River Valleys 82
Around the World: The Hittites 94
Standardized Test Practice 96

Unit 3 Ideas and Armies

6 The Phoenicians and the Hebrews 100
7 Military Empires 116
8 Africa and the Americas 128
Around the World: The Zhou 144
Standardized Test Practice 146

Unit 4 The Greeks

9 Beginnings 150
10 The City-States 162
11 Cultural Contributions 178
12 The Hellenistic Period 192
Around the World: The Nubians 202
Standardized Test Practice 204

Unit 5 The Romans

13 Beginnings 208
14 The Roman Republic 218
15 The Roman Empire 232
16 Christianity 246
Around the World: The Moche 258
Standardized Test Practice 260

Unit 8 The Late Middle Ages

24 Feudal Society — 366
25 The Church — 380
26 Rise of Trade and Towns — 398
27 Rise of Monarchies — 410
Around the World: Feudal Japan — 426
Standardized Test Practice — 428

Unit 6 The Early Middle Ages

17 The Germans — 264
18 The Franks — 274
19 The Irish and the Anglo-Saxons — 288
20 The Vikings — 298
Around the World: The Guptas — 310
Standardized Test Practice — 312

Unit 9 Beginning of Modern Times

28 The Renaissance — 432
29 The Reformation — 448
30 The Age of Discovery — 466
Around the World: The Swahili
Culture — 480
Standardized Test Practice — 482

Unit 7 Emergence of New Empires

21 The Byzantine Empire — 316
22 The Spread of Islam — 330
23 The Eastern Slavs — 346
Around the World: The Anasazi — 360
Standardized Test Practice — 362

Unit 10 The Changing World

31 Expansion Into the Americas — 486
32 Political Revolutions — 502
33 Rise of Industry — 522
Around the World: Russia — 538
Standardized Test Practice — 540

Unit 11 Nations and Empires

34 The Americas 544
35 Unrest in Europe 560
36 Rise of Imperialism 578
Around the World: Tibet 596
Standardized Test Practice 598

Unit 12 The Twentieth Century to Today

37 Conflict and Change 602
38 The Cold War Era 624
39 The World Since 1989 644
Around the World: Our Shrinking World 668
Standardized Test Practice 670

PRIMARY SOURCES
Library

Primary Sources Library 672

UNIT 1 African Origins 674
UNIT 2 The Pursuit of Justice 676
UNIT 3 The Empire of Mali 678
UNIT 4 Greek Society 680
UNIT 5 Eruption of Mount Vesuvius 682
UNIT 6 The Age of Viking Conquest 684
UNIT 7 Byzantine Women 686
UNIT 8 The Medieval Manor 688
UNIT 9 The Fall of the Aztec Empire 690
UNIT 10 The Iron Horse 692

UNIT 11 British India 694
UNIT 12 Equality and Peace 696

NATIONAL GEOGRAPHIC

Reference Atlas

World Political 700
World Physical 702
North America 704
South America 705
United States 706
Middle America 708
Europe 710
Asia 712
Middle East 714
Africa 716
Polar Regions 717
Pacific Rim 718

Glossary 720

Spanish Glossary 729

Index 738

v

Features

Map Skills

Understanding a Mercator Projection 17
Determining Relative Location 44
Identifying Physical Features 62
Reading Map Legends 75
Reading a Map Scale 108
Reading Latitude 135
Reading Longitude 156
Reading Physical Maps 165
Reading a Political Map 211
Understanding Inset Maps 284
Tracing Historical Routes 306
Analyzing Historical Maps 356
Determining Exact Location 394
Reviewing Map Legends 475
Reading a Military Map 511
Comparing Historical Maps 567
Reading a Demographic Map 651

Critical Thinking Skills

Understanding Cause and Effect 29
Distinguishing Fact From Opinion 60
Making Comparisons 111
Recognizing Bias 170
Identifying the Main Idea 242
Making Generalizations 321
Drawing Conclusions 461
Predicting Consequences 571

Technology Skills

Developing Multimedia Presentations 276
Evaluating a Web Site 390
Building a Database 516
Using an Electronic Spreadsheet 636

People in History

Mary Nicol Leakey 26
Lucy 36
Hammurabi 61
Tutankhamen 77
Wu 90
Moses 110
Darius 124
Mansa Musa I 133
Homer 158
Pericles 174
Aristotle 188
Demosthenes 194
Romulus 213
Julius Caesar 229
Diocletian 243
Saint Augustine 254
Theodoric the Great 267
Charlemagne 280
Alfred the Great 292
Canute 307
Constantine I 318
Muhammad 332
Ivan the Terrible 357
Trotula of Salerno 377
Eleanor of Aquitaine 392
Geoffrey Chaucer 407
Joan of Arc 417
Henry VIII 444
Elizabeth I 460
Ferdinand Magellan 474
Robert de La Salle 499
Marie-Antoinette 515
Robert Fulton 528
Toussaint-L'Ouverture 553
Otto von Bismarck 575
Liliuokalani 591
Joseph Stalin 611
Mohandas Gandhi 635
Nelson Mandela 659

Charts, Diagrams, and Illustrations

Major Landforms 10
The Earth's Structure 10
The Earth's Revolution 15
Alphabets 105
Phoenician and Hebrew Civilizations 111
Hebrew Prophets 113
Olympian Gods and Goddesses 181
Greek Scientists 189
Roman Floor Plan 237

A Roman Banquet Menu 239
Emperors During the *Pax Romana* 241
Norse Gods 304
Eastern Conquerors 341
Medieval Manor 375
Renaissance Manners 436
Renaissance People 442
Explorers 477
Native Americans 494
Scientists 524

Map Study

Tectonic Plates 11
Ice Ages 13
World Climate Zones 17
Archaeological Sites 27
Sites of Early People 44
Prehistoric Art in Africa 48
Mesopotamia 62
Ancient Egypt 75
Early India 84
Shang China 89
Hittite Empire 94
Phoenicia and the Hebrew Kingdoms 108
The Assyrian and Chaldean Empires 119
The Persian Empire 125
Early Africa 135
Early American Empires 141
Zhou Empire 144
The Early Aegean World 156
Elevation of Ancient Greece 165
Ancient Greece 173
The Empire of Alexander the Great 196
Ancient Nubia 202
Early Italy 211
The Expansion of the Roman Republic 228
The Expansion of the Roman Empire 235
The Spread of Christianity 251
Moche Civilization 258

Germanic Invasions 270
The Germanic Kingdoms 271
The Frankish Empire 284
England and the Danelaw 294
Viking Trade and Expansion 306
Gupta Empire 310
The Byzantine Empire Under Justinian 323
The End of the Byzantine Empire 327
Muhammad's Arabia 334
The Expansion of Islam 337
Kievan Rus 350
The Growth of Moscow 356
Anasazi Culture 360
The Crusades 394
Medieval Towns and Trade Routes 400
Europe in the Late Middle Ages 422
Japan 426
Renaissance Italy 438
The Religions of Europe 463
European Voyages of Discovery 475
Swahili Culture 480
European Colonies in the Americas 498
The English Civil Wars 504
American Revolution: North 511
American Revolution: South 511
Russian Empire 538
The Growth of the United States 549
Independence in Latin America 555
Napoleonic Europe 564
Europe After the Congress of Vienna 567
Imperialism 590
Tibet 596
Europe After World War I 607
Axis Expansion in Europe and Africa 617
Axis Expansion in the Pacific 619
African Independence 637
Commonwealth of Independent States 648
World Population 651
Afghanistan, 2001 663
Worldwide Internet Use 668

Be an Active Reader!

How Should I Read My Textbook?   Reading your social studies book is different than other reading you might do. Your textbook has a great amount of information in it. It is an example of nonfiction writing—it describes real-life events, people, ideas, and places.

Here are some reading strategies that will help you become an active textbook reader. Choose the strategies that work best for you. If you have trouble as you read your textbook, look back at these strategies for help.

 Before You Read

Set a Purpose
- Why are you reading the textbook?
- How might you be able to use what you learn in your own life?

Preview
- Read the chapter title to find out what the topic will be.
- Read the subtitles to see what you will learn about the topic.
- Skim the photos, charts, graphs, or maps.
- Look for vocabulary words that are boldfaced. How are they defined?

Draw From Your Own Background
- What do you already know about the topic?
- How is the new information different from what you already know?

If You Don't Know What A Word Means...
- think about the setting, or *context*, in which the word is used.
- check if prefixes such as *un, non,* or *pre* can help you break down the word.

As You Read

Question
- What is the main idea?
- How well do the details support the main idea?
- How do the photos, charts, graphs, and maps support the main idea?

Connect
- Think about people, places, and events in your own life. Are there any similarities with those in your textbook?

Predict
- Predict events or outcomes by using clues and information that you already know.
- Change your predictions as you read and gather new information.

Visualize
- Use your imagination to picture the settings, actions, and people that are described.
- Create graphic organizers to help you see relationships found in the information.

Reading Do's
Do ...
- ✔ establish a purpose for reading
- ✔ think about how your own experiences relate to the topic
- ✔ try different reading strategies

Reading Don'ts
Don't...
- 🚫 ignore how the textbook is organized
- 🚫 allow yourself to be easily distracted
- 🚫 hurry to finish the material

After You Read

Summarize
- Describe the main idea and how the details support it.
- Use your own words to explain what you have read.

Assess
- What was the main idea?
- Did the text clearly support the main idea?
- Did you learn anything new from the material?
- Can you use this new information in other school subjects or at home?

Place and Time

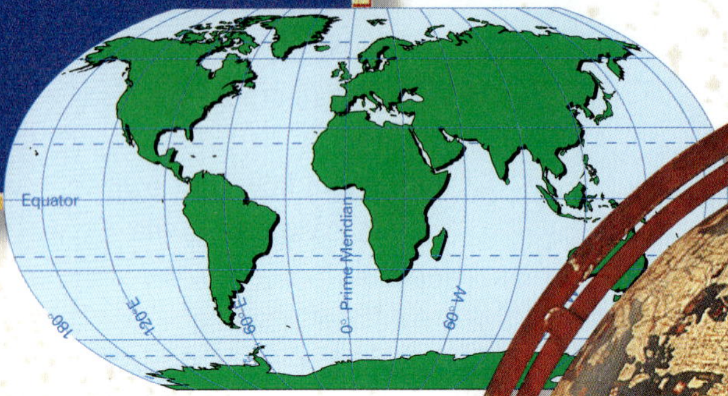

Equator
180°
120°E
90°E
60°W
0° Prime Meridian

Egyptian water clock ▼

▲ **An early globe**

c. **3,000,000** B.C.
Paleolithic Age begins

c. **1,500,000** B.C.
Homo habilis appears

c. **1,200,000** B.C.
Homo erectus appears

c. **250,000** B.C.
Homo sapiens appears

FOLDABLES™
Study Organizer

Summarizing Information Study Foldable *Make this foldable journal about geography and how it influenced history, and use it as a study guide.*

Step 1 *Fold a sheet of paper in half from top to bottom.*

Step 2 *Fold it in half again from side to side and label as shown.*

Place and Time

Reading and Writing *As you read the unit, use your "place and time journal" to describe how geography has affected early civilization settlements.*

PRIMARY SOURCES

Library

See pages 674–675 for another primary source reading to accompany Unit 1.

GO TO Read "The Iceman" from the **World History Primary Source Document Library CD-ROM.**

Journal Notes

When did people appear on the earth? What factors have influenced where and how people have lived? Note details as you read.

c. 100,000 B.C.
Cro-Magnons appear

c. 8000 B.C.
Neolithic Age begins

c. 6500 B.C.
Catal Hüyük established

Geography and History

3,000,000 B.C.–Present

▼ Celtic bronze plaque

Stonehenge ▶

| c. 1500 A.D.
Archaeology begins | 1719 A.D.
Archaeologists uncover Pompeii | 1799 A.D.
Rosetta Stone discovered | 1832 A.D.
Prehistory organized into periods | 1946 A.D.
Carbon 14 method of dating developed |

Chapter Focus

 Read to Discover

- How the six essential elements of geography help explain what a place is like and why.
- How geography has shaped history.
- How legends have been important to the study of history.
- How archaeology helps scientists learn about ancient civilizations.

Chapter Overview

Visit the *Human Heritage* Web site at <u>humanheritage.glencoe.com</u> and click on **Chapter 1—Chapter Overviews** to preview this chapter.

 Terms to Learn

landforms
tectonic plates
glaciers
river system
archaeology
artifacts

 People to Know

Gerardus
  Mercator
Mary Leakey
Frank Libby

 Places to Locate

Mount Everest
Nile River
Egypt
Pompeii

Why It's Important   Many scientists believe that people have been living on the earth for more than 2 million years. Where and how they lived was influenced greatly by the kind of land on which they lived. In many ways, the relationship between people and their environment has been the center of world history.

SECTION 1 Elements of Geography

Geography is the study of the earth and of the ways people live and work on it. Geography helps explain why people live the way they do. Geography also helps explain the past by answering questions about why certain events occurred where they did. Geographers use six essential elements to help explain what a place is like and why it is like that.

Reading Check
How does **geography** help explain the past?

The World in Spatial Terms   Geographers first look at where a place is located. *Location* serves as a starting point by asking "Where is it?" Knowing the location of places helps you to position yourself in space and to develop an awareness of the world around you.

There are two types of location: absolute and relative. **Absolute location** refers to the exact location of a place on the earth's surface. For example, the capital of Kenya—Nairobi—is located at one place and one place only. No other place on Earth has exactly the same location.

Reading Check
What does **absolute location** tell you about a place?

PLACES AND REGIONS   A place such as the Moi Avenue in Mombasa, Kenya, shown here can be described easily. It is the avenue with the huge crossed elephant tusks. **What other details could be included in a description of this place?**

✓ Reading Check
How do you determine a place's **relative location?**

Student Web Activity
Visit the *Human Heritage* Web site at **humanheritage.glencoe.com** and click on *Chapter 1— Student Web Activities* to find out more about the study of geography.

Relative location refers to the position of a place in relation to other places. Nairobi is located north of Mt. Kilimanjaro, west of the Indian Ocean, and southeast of Lake Turkana. Using this information, Nairobi can be found on a map of Africa if Mt. Kilimanjaro, the Indian Ocean, and Lake Turkana are located. A place may be described with many different relative locations.

Places and Regions   Geographers also look at places and regions. **Place** includes those features and characteristics that give an area its own identity or personality. These can be physical characteristics—such as landforms, climate, plants, and animals. Places can also be described by their human characteristics. These characteristics tell how many people live in a place, what language they speak, and what they do for a living. Knowing about a place's soil and about how its people make a living tells more about it than just its location. The physical and human characteristics of Nairobi, for example, make it a place that is different from Tokyo.

To make sense of all the complex things in the world, geographers often group places or areas into regions. **Regions** are areas that share one or more common characteristics. Regions can be defined by their physical features, such as the kind of land found there. The Sahara is a desert region. Regions can also be defined by their human features, such as the religion people practice, the language they speak, or the way they earn a living. A region that shares a common language, such as Quebec, where most people speak French, is such a region.

✓ **Reading Check**
What is a **region**?

Physical Systems
When studying places and regions, geographers look at how physical systems—such as volcanoes, glaciers, and hurricanes—act together to shape the earth's surface. They also look at *ecosystems,* or communities of plants and animals that are dependent upon one another and their particular surroundings for survival.

Human Systems
Geographers also examine human systems, or how people have shaped our world. They look at how boundary lines that divide countries and states are drawn and analyze why people settle in certain places and not in others.

An important theme in geography is the continual movement of goods, people, and ideas. Movement has brought the world's people closer together. Transportation—the movement of goods

Linking Across Time

Written Communication Ever since people wrote their first clay tablets more than 5,000 year ago (left), they have been looking for easier and quicker ways to write. Perhaps no invention has affected written communication more than the computer (right). **How has the computer helped the movement of ideas and information?**

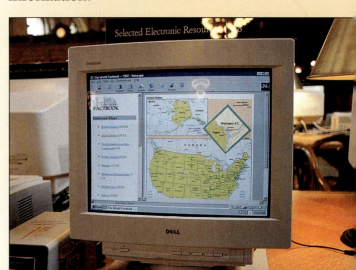

—allows people to use products made in places thousands of miles away. Transportation also provides for the movement of people, which increases the exchange of ideas and cultures. Communication—the movement of ideas and information—allows people to see or hear what is happening in their community or in another part of the world. Today, people receive almost instant information by radio, television, and computer.

Environment and Society   The study of geography includes looking at human/environment interaction, or how and why people change their surroundings. People respond to their environment in different ways. Sometimes they *adapt*, or adjust, to it. For example, people wear light clothing in hot places and warm clothing in cold places. At other times, people *modify*, or change, their environment. They may irrigate dry land to grow crops or build a dam to keep a river from flooding.

The Uses of Geography   People, businesses, and governments use geography and maps of all kinds on a daily basis. Geographic computer systems allow people to make better decisions about how to make the best use of places and regions. Understanding geography, and knowing how to use the tools and technology available to study it, prepares you for life in our modern society.

ENVIRONMENT AND SOCIETY   Many acres of American forests have been cut to supply lumber products to a growing nation. Many new trees are planted to replace those removed. **How do people respond to their environment?**

Section 1 Assessment

1. **Define:** geography, absolute location, relative location, place, region.
2. What six essential elements do geographers use to study the earth?
3. Why do geographers organize the world into regions?

Critical Thinking

4. **Making Comparisons** How does the element of the world in spatial terms differ from the element of places and regions?

Graphic Organizer Activity

5. Draw a diagram like this one, and use it to summarize information about each of the six essential elements of geography.

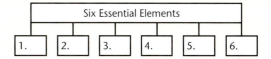

		Six Essential Elements			
1.	2.	3.	4.	5.	6.

SECTION 2 Land, Water, and Climate

Photographs of the earth taken from space show a contrast of water and land beneath huge swirls of white clouds. These photographs reflect three of the things geographers study: land, water, and climate.

Landforms Land covers about 30 percent of the surface of the earth. Land is made up of four main kinds of **landforms,** or natural features of the earth's land surface. These landforms are mountains, hills, plateaus, and plains. Geographers describe each landform by its **elevation,** or height above sea level, and its **relief,** or changes in height.

Mountains are the highest of the world's landforms. They rise at least 2,000 feet, or 610 meters, above sea level. One of the peaks in the Himalaya (him uh lā′ uh) Mountains in central Asia is Mount Everest, the world's highest mountain. It towers 29,035 feet, or 8,852 meters, above sea level. Other mountain ranges, like the Appalachians (ap uh lā′ chunz) in the eastern United States, are not as high. Mountains generally have high relief.

Hills are lower than mountains. They rise from 500 to 2,000 feet, or 152 to 610 meters, above sea level. They generally have moderate relief. Plateaus are raised areas of flat or almost flat land. Plateaus can vary in elevation from 300 to 3,000 feet, or 91 to 914 meters, above sea level. Most of them have low relief.

Plains are large areas of flat or gently rolling land. They generally rise less than 1,000 feet, or 305 meters, above sea level and have low relief. The world's largest plain is the North European Plain, which stretches for more than 1,000 miles, or 1,609 kilometers, from the western coast of France to the Ural Mountains in Russia.

✓ Reading Check

What are the four main kinds of **landforms?** How do geographers use **elevation** and **relief** to describe landforms?

Island Tips Some of the world's islands are really mountain summits—the tips of volcanoes that have risen from the sea. The highest summit in Hawaii, Mauna Kea, rises 13,796 feet, or 4,205 meters, above sea level. However, when measured from its base, Mauna Kea stands 32,000 feet, or 9,750 meters—taller than Mount Everest.

Surface Changes From Inside the Earth

The land surface of the earth is constantly changing. Most changes are caused by forces from deep within the earth, usually heat and pressure.

Heat and pressure are caused by the structure of the earth itself. The inside of the earth is made up of three separate layers. At the center of the earth is the **core.** The inner part of the core is solid rock, and the outer part of the core is made up of melted rock. Around the core is the **mantle,** which is made up mostly of hot, solid rock. Floating on the melted outer part of the mantle is a thin layer of rock, sand, and soil called the **crust.** The crust may be from 3 to 30 miles, or 5 to 49 kilometers, thick.

Heat from the core—the hottest part of the earth—causes the rock in the mantle to rise. This puts pressure on the crust and causes it to move. In recent years, scientists have come to believe that the crust does not move in one piece but in separate sections called **tectonic** (tek ton' ik) **plates.** These plates move very slowly, about 0.8 to 2 inches, or 2 to 5 centimeters, a year. Plates can move together, move apart, or slide past one another.

This movement of the plates explains what geographers call **continental drift.** Most geographers believe that about 220 million years ago, all the continents of the world formed one huge land mass named Pangaea (pan jē' uh). Over time, the plates

✓ Reading Check What is the composition of the earth's **core, mantle,** and **crust?**

✓ Reading Check What is the connection between **tectonic plates** and **continental drift?**

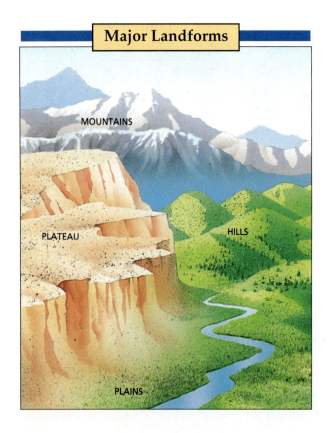

Major Landforms

MOUNTAINS

PLATEAU

HILLS

PLAINS

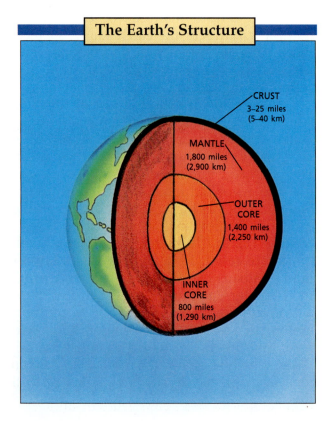

The Earth's Structure

CRUST
3–25 miles
(5–40 km)

MANTLE
1,800 miles
(2,900 km)

OUTER CORE
1,400 miles
(2,250 km)

INNER CORE
800 miles
(1,290 km)

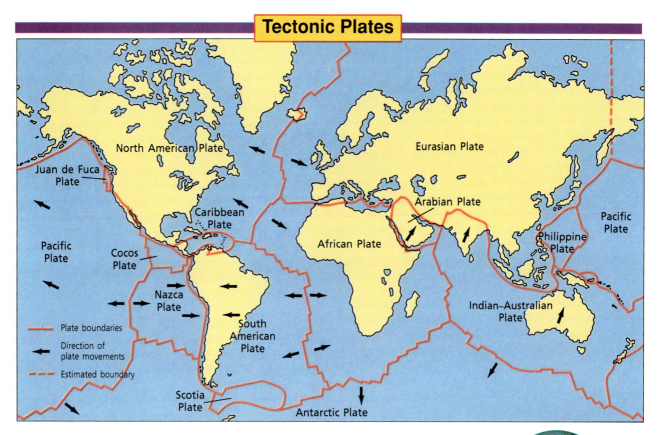

Tectonic Plates

North American Plate

Juan de Fuca Plate

Caribbean Plate

Pacific Plate

Cocos Plate

Nazca Plate

South American Plate

Eurasian Plate

Arabian Plate

African Plate

Pacific Plate

Philippine Plate

Indian–Australian Plate

Scotia Plate

Antarctic Plate

— Plate boundaries

← Direction of plate movements

--- Estimated boundary

moved and Pangaea split into seven continents. Some plates, such as the ones on which Africa and South America are located, moved apart. Other plates, such as the plates on which India and most of Asia are located, collided. The crust where these two plates met was squeezed upward to form the Himalayas.

Plate movement also creates **volcanoes.** These are cone-shaped mountains made when melted rock called magma flows up from the earth's mantle through cracks in the crust and then cools into solid rock. The Hawaiian Islands, for example, were formed by volcanoes that thrust up from the ocean floor.

Plate movements can also cause **earthquakes**, or sudden shifts in the earth's crust. These often happen when tectonic plates slide past one another. About 800,000 earthquakes occur each year with only about 50,000 of them strong enough for people to even feel them. A strong earthquake, however, can cause loss of life and serious property damage.

Both volcanoes and earthquakes are generally found along the edges of the earth's tectonic plates. They are so common around the Pacific Ocean that geographers call this area the "Ring of Fire."

The tectonic plates are still moving. Most geographers believe that thousands of years from now, California, which is on

MAP STUDY

PHYSICAL SYSTEMS
The idea that the continents were once joined and then slowly drifted apart is called the continental drift theory. **Which plate is colliding with the South American plate along the west coast of South America?**

Reading Check
How are **volcanoes** formed? What is a common cause of **earthquakes?**

EARTHQUAKE DISASTERS   Mexico has experienced many earthquakes that have caused terrible loss of life and property. These earthquakes most often occur without warning. **What causes an earthquake?**

a different plate from most of the United States, will be located far off the west coast of Canada.

Surface Changes From Outside the Earth   Forces from outside the earth also cause changes on its surface. Three main forces are wind, water, and ice. All three reshape the land by a process called erosion (i rō′ zhuhn), in which rock and soil are moved from one place on the earth's surface to another. These forces can either help or hurt people.

An example of helpful wind erosion can be found in the plains of northern China, where large amounts of wheat and other food crops are grown. The plains are covered with a thick, rich, yellowish soil called *loess* (les) which was carried there by winds blowing from deserts to the west. During the 1930s, however, winds blew away so much of the soil in the central part of the United States that the area became known as the Dust Bowl.

Water erosion that is helpful can be seen in the Mekong (may′ kawng) River of Southeast Asia. This river carries rich soil down from the mountains and spreads it over the lowlands, creating one of the most fertile areas in the world. Harmful water erosion occurs when the Huang Ho (hwong huh) in northern China overflows its banks and floods farms and homes.

Ice erosion has also caused changes on the earth's surface and in people's lives. Four times in the last 500,000 years, during what are called the Ice Ages, great ice sheets called **glaciers** spread out from the North and South poles. The ice drove people and animals away, smoothed hills into plains, created lakes, and dug new channels for rivers.

Landforms in History

Throughout history, landforms have played an important part in helping people decide where to live. People stayed away from mountainous areas where travel was difficult or where the air was so thin that it was hard to breathe. Instead, people settled mostly in plains and hilly areas where the soil was rich enough for crops to grow.

Landforms also have made a big difference in the political relationships of people. In ancient times the Greeks lived in many different city-states. One reason the Greeks did not join together to form a nation was that their communities were separated from one another by a landform—mountains.

Waterways

About 70 percent of the earth's surface is covered with water. The largest waterways in the world are the four oceans—the Atlantic, the Pacific, the Indian, and the Arctic.

Reading Check
How did **glaciers** affect human and physical geography?

MAP STUDY

PHYSICAL SYSTEMS
Scientists believe that glaciers covered large areas of the earth's surface during the Ice Ages. **What continents were affected the most by the Ice Ages?**

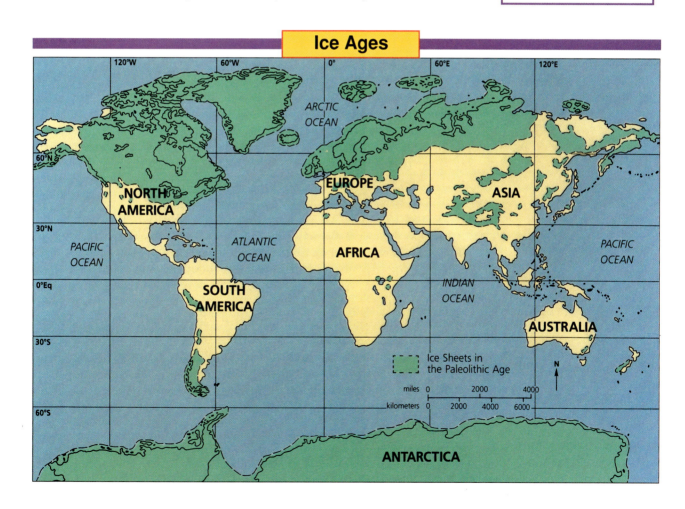

Ice Ages

Ice Sheets in the Paleolithic Age

Smaller bodies of salt water are known as seas. They are usually partly surrounded by land. Bodies of water that are completely surrounded by land are known as lakes. The world's largest fresh-water lake is Lake Superior in North America. It is about 350 miles, or 563 kilometers, long and 160 miles, or 257 kilometers, wide.

Waterways that empty into another body of water are known as rivers. Most rivers begin high in mountains or hills. A river and all the streams that flow into it make up a **river system.** The longest river system in the world is the Nile, which flows about 4,160 miles, or 6,693 kilometers, from its source in the highlands of central Africa to its mouth on the Mediterranean Sea.

Waterways in History Like landforms, waterways have played an important part in helping people decide where to live. People's earliest homes were along the banks of rivers and other waterways. These bodies of water provided them with a means for travel and trade, drinking water, and irrigation for crops as farming developed. Thus, river valleys were often sites for villages and cities. Animals also used waterways for food and drinking water, so the riverbanks were good hunting grounds.

Climate and the Sun The pattern of the weather of a place over many years is **climate.** The most important thing that shapes climate is the sun. The sun provides the earth with heat and light. All parts of the earth, however, do not receive the same amount of sunlight.

As the earth moves through space, it *rotates,* or spins like a top. Geographers say that it spins on its *axis,* an imaginary line that runs through the earth's center from the North Pole to the South Pole. It takes one day of 24 hours for the earth to spin around completely.

Besides rotating, the earth moves around the sun in an almost circular path called an *orbit.* This motion, known as a *revolution,* takes one year of 365¼ days to complete. It is the earth's revolution around the sun that causes the seasons.

Seasons vary from one part of the world to another. The earth's axis, instead of being straight up and down, is tilted at an angle. This means that places in the Northern Hemisphere are tilted toward the sun from March to September. As a result, these places have spring and summer at that time. During these same months, however, the Southern Hemisphere is tilted away from the sun. There it is fall and winter. Six months later, from September to March, conditions reverse, and the seasons are the opposite.

Climate Zones The amount of heat from the sun a place receives depends on its **latitude,** or distance north or south of the

---

Reading Check
What is the longest **river system** in the world?

Reading Check
How is **climate** shaped by movements of the earth?

Reading Check
How can a place's **latitude** help you predict temperatures in the area?

The Earth's Revolution

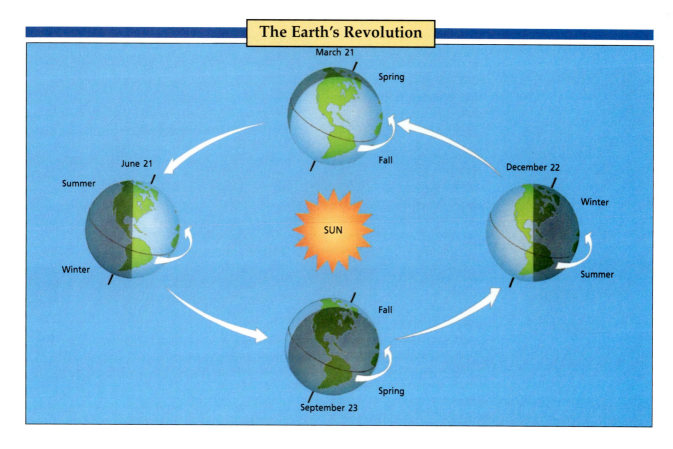

Equator. Rays from the sun are most direct at the Equator. Geographers often organize the earth into three climate zones based on latitude.

The **tropical zone,** also called the tropics, is the area between the Tropic of Cancer and the Tropic of Capricorn. The tropical zone always receives the most direct rays of the sun. Most places in the tropics are hot year-round.

The **temperate** (tem'puh ruht) **zone** is found in both the area between the Tropic of Cancer and the Arctic Circle in the Northern Hemisphere, and the area between the Tropic of Capricorn and the Antarctic Circle in the Southern Hemisphere. The sun's rays reach the temperate zone at a slant for part of the year and almost directly for the rest of the year. As a result, the weather in this zone is generally cold in winter and warm in summer.

The **polar zone** is the area north of the Arctic Circle and south of the Antarctic Circle. This area receives no sunlight at all during part of the year and only slanting rays during the rest of the year. As a result, the climate in the polar zone is very cold, and few people live there.

Reading Check
Where is the **tropical zone** located?

Reading Check
What type of weather is found in each **temperate zone?**

Reading Check
Why is the **polar zone** very cold?

Climate, Water, and Wind

In addition to the sun, climate is shaped by large bodies of water, which keep the temperature of a place from getting too hot or too cold. Water gains or

MONSOON Monsoons are very important to the agriculture of southern Asia. The wet, or summer, monsoons bring moisture necessary for farming to the area. Here, an Indian farmer struggles to plow his fields in the midst of monsoon winds and rain. **How do monsoons differ from prevailing winds?**

Reading Check
How did **prevailing winds** get their name? What are **ocean currents?**

loses heat more slowly than land. Also, air over a lake is cooler than air over the land.

Climate is also shaped by the movement of air and ocean water. Air that moves is called wind. Some winds are known as **prevailing** (pri vā′ lēng) **winds** because they blow from a certain direction almost all the time. Other winds are called monsoons because they change direction according to the season of the year. Monsoons often bring heavy rainfall. Ocean water that flows in a steady stream is called an **ocean current.** Both winds and ocean currents carry heat or cold and moisture all over the world. Ocean currents that flow from the Equator toward the poles warm the lands they pass. Currents that flow from the poles to the Equator cool the land they pass.

Reading Check
How do mountains affect **precipitation?**

Climate and Altitude   Climate is also shaped by altitude. The higher the altitude, the colder the climate. In the tropical zone, people often prefer living in highlands rather than lowlands because the highland temperatures are more comfortable. The ancient Incas settled in the Andes Mountains of Peru instead of along the Pacific coast for that reason. Mountains also affect **precipitation**—the falling of moisture such as rain or snow. As the air rises over mountains, it cools and drops its moisture.

Understanding a Mercator Projection

Because Earth is a sphere, no flat map can show its whole surface. Mapmakers use different **projections** (pruh jek´ shuhns), or ways of representing Earth on a flat surface.

One projection used often is a Mercator (muhr kāt´ uhr) projection. Named after Gerardus Mercator, a Flemish mapmaker of the 1500s, it is made by wrapping paper around a globe. A light shining from the center of the globe projects Earth's features onto the paper. This allows the map to be traced.

The parts of the map that are most like the earth are where the paper touches the globe, such as at the Equator. The parts that are most *distorted* (dis tort´ ed), or twisted out of shape, are where the paper does not touch the globe, such as near the poles.

Map Practice

1. Which of the earth's climate zones is shown most accurately?
2. Which is most distorted?
3. Is the shape of North America more accurate on this map or on a globe? Why?

World Climate Zones

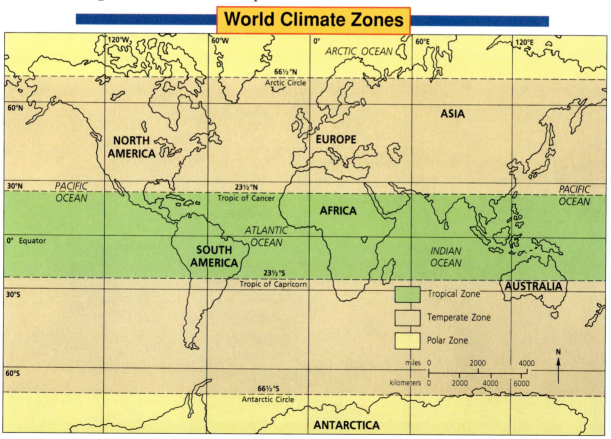

Climate Early Greeks classified climates based on what they knew about Greece and areas to the south and north. They called their own climate *temperate* because it posed few problems of shelter and clothing. They believed the area south of the Mediterranean Sea became hotter, so they called these lands *torrid.* Cold winds from the north led them to call that area *frigid.*

Climate in History

Climate, like land and waterways, plays an important part in shaping history. It helps determine where people live, what kind of clothes they wear, what kind of houses they build, and what crops they grow. It also affects the speed with which they work and the kinds of things they do for entertainment. Since climate is something humans cannot control, it has affected civilizations since prehistoric times.

Sometimes climate affects the way a country behaves towards its neighbors. Climate has also helped decide the outcomes of wars. For example, many of Russia's harbors stay frozen during much of the year. In the past, Russia has often gone to war with other countries in order to capture land for warm water ports. Climate was also one reason the Russians were able to stop the invasions of French ruler Napoleon Bonaparte (nuh pō′ lē uhn bō′ nuh part) in the 1800s and German ruler Adolf Hitler in the 1940s. The Russians were used to the bitter cold and snow of their country's winter, whereas the invaders were not.

COLD CLIMATE This buoy has become frozen in the St. Petersburg Harbor during the cold Russian winter. Such waterways have been important many times in Russia's history. **What has the lack of warm water ports and harbors caused Russia to do in the past?**

Section 2 Assessment

1. **Define:** landforms, elevation, relief, core, mantle, crust, tectonic plates, continental drift, volcanoes, earthquakes, erosion, glaciers, river system, climate, latitude, tropical zone, temperate zone, polar zone, prevailing winds, ocean current, precipitation.
2. What are some of the ways landforms and waterways have been important to history?
3. Into what climate zones do geographers often organize the earth?

Critical Thinking

4. **Making Generalizations** How does climate affect the way that you live?

Graphic Organizer Activity

5. Draw a diagram like this one, label it with the four kinds of landforms, and list examples of each landform in your community, state, or region.

SECTION 3 Natural Resources

Natural resources are materials found in nature. Some, such as air, are found everywhere. Others, such as oil, are found only in certain areas. Some places have many natural resources, while others have few.

Kinds of Natural Resources There are different kinds of natural resources. Some resources helpful to people include air, water, soil, sunlight, minerals, fossil fuels, forests, and animal life. Some of these—air, water, soil, and sunlight—are essential for any kind of life to exist. They are the most important natural resources.

Other natural resources, while not essential for life, are important because they enable people to live better. One such resource is **minerals,** or nonliving substances found beneath the earth's surface. Throughout history, people have used such minerals as iron, copper, tin, gold, and silver to make tools, weapons, jewelry, and money. Fossil fuels, such as coal, oil, and natural gas, provide the energy needed to heat homes and power machines.

Natural resources become valuable only when people learn how to use them. For example, during the 1200s Marco Polo left his native city of Venice, in present-day Italy, and traveled to

✓ Reading Check
What are some examples of **natural resources?**

✓ Reading Check
Why have **minerals** been important to people throughout history?

MINERALS   Some natural resources are found beneath the ground and are called minerals. Oil and coal are two minerals for which people drill and mine underground. The oil well shown here (left) is in the jungles of Nigeria. Coal mining in North Dakota is also shown (right). **What are other examples of minerals?**

Reading Check
How do **renewable resources** and **nonrenewable resources** differ from each other?

China. A few years after returning home, he wrote a book about the wonderful things he had seen on his journey. One of these was a black rock, now known as coal, which the Chinese dug out of the ground and burned to keep themselves warm. The Venetians (vi nē' shuhnz) doubted Marco Polo. They had not used coal as the Chinese had. People later changed their minds about coal when they began using it as a fuel to power steam engines and to process steel.

Some resources can be replaced as they are used. These are **renewable resources.** For example, American farmers who lived in the Dust Bowl of the 1930s were able to get back their once-rich soil. To do this they used better ways of farming and planted trees to keep the soil from being blown away. Other natural resources cannot be replaced as they are used. These are **nonrenewable resources.** For example, once fossil fuels and most minerals are used up, they will be gone forever.

In recent years, people have become more and more concerned about making better use of the world's natural resources. Some countries have passed laws to slow down the pollution of the air, water, and soil. Scientists also are trying to develop new sources of energy.

Natural Resources in History   Natural resources affected the location and growth of settlements throughout history. The sharing of these resources has also been important. Rich soil and plenty of water made farming possible and led to the rise of cities. Asians and Europeans came into contact with one another partly because Europeans wanted the silks and spices of Asia. Modern industry started in countries that had large amounts of coal and iron ore for making steel. During the 1800s, the discovery of gold in California, South Africa, Australia, and Alaska caused hundreds of thousands of people to move to those areas.

Section 3 Assessment

1. **Define:** natural resources, minerals, renewable resources, nonrenewable resources.
2. What resources are needed for life?

Critical Thinking

3. **Demonstrating Reasoned Judgment** Why do you think people have become more interested in making better use of the world's natural resources?

Graphic Organizer Activity

4. Create a diagram such as this one, and use it to show examples of how natural resources have helped shape history.

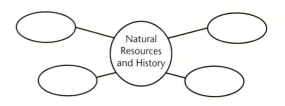

RENEWABLE RESOURCES   Soil is considered a renewable resource. Some human activities, like the strip mining of coal (left), use up the land. With careful management, however, such areas can be reclaimed, or made productive again (right). **What are some examples of nonrenewable resources?**

SECTION 4 Legends

Reading Check
What are the purposes of **legends?**

People have always been interested in learning about the past. Every group of people on the earth has **legends,** or folktales, that help to explain the past. These legends began as stories that were spoken or sung. People passed them down from generation to generation.

A Chinese Legend   The Chinese have a legend about the beginnings of China. It says that the universe was a huge egg. When the egg split open, the upper half became the sky, and the lower half became the earth. Out of the split egg came P'an Gu (pan gū), the first man. Each day for 18,000 years P'an Gu grew taller, the sky grew higher, and the earth grew thicker. Then P'an Gu died. His head split and became the sun and the moon. His blood filled the rivers and the seas. His hair became the forests and the meadows. His perspiration became the rain. His breath became the wind and his voice, the thunder.

An African Legend   The Africans have a legend about why the sun shines more brightly than the moon. It says that God created the Moon and then the Sun. Because the Moon was bigger and brighter, the Sun became jealous and attacked the Moon. They fought and wrestled until the Sun begged for mercy. Then they wrestled again. This time the Sun threw the Moon into the mud. Dirt splashed all over the Moon, and it was no longer as bright as before. To stop the fighting, God stepped in. He told the Sun that from then on it would be brighter than the Moon and would shine during the day for kings and workers. He told the Moon that from then on it would shine only at night for thieves and witches.

A Rumanian Legend   The Rumanians have a legend about the creation of mountains and valleys. It says that when God finished making the heavens, He measured them with a little ball of thread. Then He started to create the earth to fit under them. A mole came along and offered to help. So God let the mole hold the ball of thread while He created the earth.

STONEHENGE   Many legends have been told about the ancient ruins of Stonehenge in Great Britain, shown here. These stones are arranged in an unusual formation believed to date back to prehistoric times. **How do modern people learn about ancient legends such as the stories about Stonehenge?**

While God was weaving and shaping the earth, the mole let out the thread little by little. God was too busy to notice that, at times, the mole let out more thread than it should have. When God was finished, He was amazed to find that the earth was too big to fit under the heavens.

The mole, seeing what it had done, was afraid. It ran off and buried itself. God sent the bee to find the mole and ask it what should be done. But when the bee found the mole, it would not answer the question.

The bee hid in a flower, hoping the mole would think it was alone and start talking to itself. Soon, the mole thought out loud. It said that it would squeeze the earth so that the mountains would stick up and the valleys would sink down. Then the earth would be small enough to fit under the heavens. Upon hearing this, the bee buzzed off. The mole heard the buzzing and became angry. It put a curse on the bee, saying, "Henceforth, feed on yourself."

The bee told God what the mole had said. God squeezed the flat earth so that the mountains rose up, the valleys sank down, and the earth fit under the heavens. God then turned the mole's curse into a blessing. Ever since, the bee makes its own honey, while the mole lives underground and is afraid to come out.

Other Legends

These Chinese, African, and Rumanian legends are about the creation of the world. This is not true of all legends. Many are about the deeds of godlike men and women or about strange and wonderful lands. Other legends explain natural elements such as the placement of stars or why a maple tree has red leaves. Some even explain geographic features such as mountains and rivers.

After people developed writing more than 5,000 years ago, they wrote down their legends. Many came to be thought of as fact. In recent years, **archaeologists,** or scientists who study the remains of past human life, and **anthropologists,** or scientists who study the origin and development of humans, became curious about how much of certain legends was fiction and how much was fact. This led them to search out the truth of some of the legends.

Reading Check
What type of work is done by **archaeologists?** What do **anthropologists** study?

Section 4 Assessment

1. **Define:** legends, archaeologists, anthropologists.
2. How did people learn legends?

Critical Thinking

3. **Analyzing Information**
   What legends do you know?

What do they try to explain?

Graphic Organizer Activity

4. Draw a diagram like this one, and use it to show the order of events in one of the legends in this section.

EGYPTIAN ARTIFACTS   Archaeologists have uncovered many artifacts in Egypt. This spearhead (left), from about 15,000 B.C., is one of the oldest objects found in the region. The Rosetta Stone (right), from around 200 B.C., is one of the most famous archaeological finds. On it is carved a decree issued by Egyptian priests to honor a leader. **What kinds of objects can be considered artifacts?**

SECTION 5 Archaeology

Archaeology, or the study of the remains of past human life and cultures, began about 500 years ago. At that time, some Europeans dug up old marble statues and ornaments made by the ancient Greeks and Romans and sold them for a great deal of money. Scientists began to study these **artifacts,** or things made by people. They found they could learn from the artifacts how people lived long ago. People who lived in ancient times did not leave many written records.

Artifacts do not have to be works of art. They can be anything made by people such as weapons, tools, or pottery. The earliest artifacts are pieces of hard rock that were chipped into cutting or digging tools or into weapons.

Reading Check
How did **archaeology** get its start?

Reading Check
What information did scientists discover from the study of **artifacts?**

Mary Nicol Leakey
1913–1996

Paleoanthropologist

At age 11, Mary Nicol Leakey visited a cave filled with prehistoric paintings. The cave inspired her to become a paleoanthropologist—a person who studies prehistoric humans and prehumans. She later left England for East Africa. Here she discovered prehuman footprints more than 3.6 million years old! For more on this discovery, see pages 674–675.

Archaeological Finds

About 1700, some Italian farmers discovered they were living on top of an ancient Roman city named Herculaneum (huhr kyul lā′ nē uhm) that had been buried for more than 1,000 years. In 1719 archaeologists began uncovering the city. After more than 50 years, they uncovered not only Herculaneum but also another Roman city called Pompeii (pom pā′). These cities contained, among other things, fine houses, theaters, streets, and temples. More importantly, from what they found, the archaeologists learned exactly how ancient Romans lived.

The discovery of Herculaneum and Pompeii was followed in 1799 by one of the greatest of all archaeological discoveries. This was the finding in Egypt of the Rosetta Stone, a slab of stone on which are carved ancient Egyptian picture-writing and its Greek translation. Although scholars knew the Greek language well, they had not been able to *decipher,* or explain the meaning of, the ancient Egyptian language. The Rosetta Stone was a two-

POMPEII The Roman city of Pompeii was buried under the mud and lava from a volcanic eruption in 79 A.D. Discovered in the 1700s, the site has provided much information about Roman life and art, such as this wall painting from a home. **What other ancient Roman city was discovered in the 1700s?**

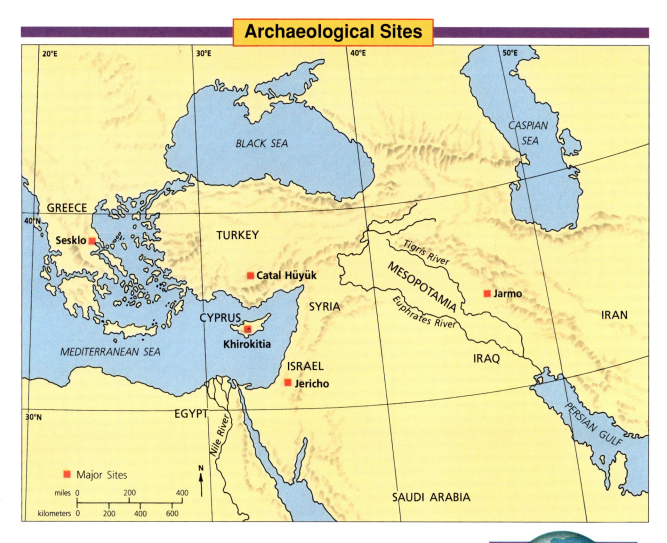

Archaeological Sites

BLACK SEA

CASPIAN SEA

GREECE

40°N

TURKEY

Sesklo

Catal Hüyük

Tigris River

MESOPOTAMIA

Jarmo

Euphrates River

SYRIA

IRAN

CYPRUS

Khirokitia

MEDITERRANEAN SEA

IRAQ

ISRAEL

Jericho

PERSIAN GULF

EGYPT

30°N

Nile River

Major Sites

N

miles 0   200   400

kilometers 0   200   400   600

SAUDI ARABIA

language dictionary that gave them the key to the meaning of Egyptian picture-writing. Now they could learn much more about the history of Egypt and its people.

A great many archaeological finds have been made since the discovery of the Rosetta Stone. For example, between 1850 and 1950 archaeologists uncovered five lost civilizations. In 1988 they discovered the oldest known piece of cloth, woven 9,000 years ago. Archaeologists continue to make discoveries in many parts of the world. This can be especially difficult because often only small pieces of artifacts are found. Thus, archaeologists have only hints or clues about people of past civilizations.

Dating Archaeological Remains

After archaeologists *excavate,* or dig into the earth, to uncover remains of the past, they have to *date,* or find the age of, the remains. In 1832 Christian J. Thomsen, a Danish archaeologist, divided early human history into three *ages,* or periods. These ages were based on the

MAP STUDY

PLACES AND REGIONS Archaeologists carefully piece together information gathered at archaeological sites. **What archaeological site is found near the Tigris and Euphrates rivers?**

material people used for making tools and weapons during them. Thomsen named these ages the Stone Age, the Bronze Age, and the Iron Age. Later, scientists also divided the Stone Age into three shorter periods of time—old, middle, and new. Scientists relied on common sense when unearthing artifacts. They assumed that older artifacts would be found beneath more recent ones.

Still later, archaeologists realized that the material used for tools and weapons was not as important as how people got their food. So they divided early human history into two general periods. During the first period, people were food gatherers. During the second period, they were food producers.

To tell the date of an archaeological find, scientists first used trees. Each year, trees form a new growth ring. Scientists counted the number of rings in a wooden object, such as a house beam, and compared the pattern with the rings of a tree whose age they knew. In that way, they could identify dates as far back as 3,000 years earlier.

ARCHAEOLOGICAL SITES Archaeological research is a major method of learning about ancient civilizations. Specialized techniques and tools are required for successful research. This archaeological excavation (left) is at the Agora in Athens, Greece. The archaeologist shown (right) is searching for artifacts with a metal detector. **What do bones, animal remains, and tools tell archaeologists about a people?**

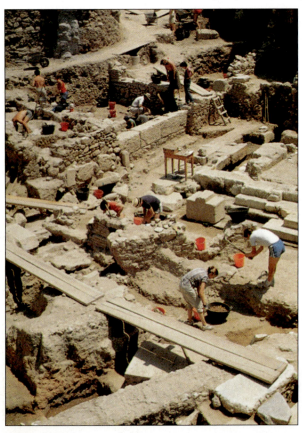

Understanding Cause and Effect

CRITICAL THINKING SKILLS

You know that if you watch television instead of completing your homework, you will receive poor grades. This is an example of a cause-and-effect relationship. This cause—watching television instead of doing homework—leads to an effect—poor grades.

When you look for why or how an event or chain of events took place, you are developing the skill of understanding causes and effects.

Learning the Skill A *cause* is any person, event, or condition that makes something happen. What happens as a result is known as an *effect*. These guidelines will help you identify cause and effect:

- Look for "clue words" that alert you to cause and effect, such as *because, led to, brought about, produced,* and *therefore.*
- Look for logical relationships between events, such as "She did this and then that happened."

In a chain of historical events, one effect often becomes the cause of other effects. The chart on this page shows such a chain of events.

CAUSES AND EFFECTS

CAUSES
- Europeans dig up artifacts for sale.
- Scientists study these artifacts.
- Artifacts provide information on the past.

↓

Start of Archaeology

↓

EFFECTS
- Lost civilizations are uncovered.
- Early human history is divided into periods.
- New methods of dating are devised.

Skill Practice

Study the cause-and-effect chart on this page. Then answer the questions below.

1. What were some of the causes of the start of archaeology?
2. What were some of the effects of archaeology upon history?
3. What effect do you think the discovery of lost civilizations has had upon our view of the past?

GO TO Glencoe's **Skillbuilder Interactive Workbook CD-ROM, Level 1,** provides instruction and practice in key social studies skills.

In 1946 an American scientist named Willard Frank Libby discovered that all living things contain a radioactive element called carbon 14. After plants, animals, and humans die, the carbon 14 gradually disappears. By measuring how much carbon 14 a skeleton or the remains of a wooden boat contain today, scientists can figure out about how old the object is as far back as about 30,000 years.

Section 5 Assessment

1. **Define:** archaeology, artifacts.
2. Why did scientists begin to study artifacts?
3. Why was the discovery of the Rosetta Stone important?

Critical Thinking

4. **Predicting Consequences** What would you like about being an archaeologist? What would you dislike?

Graphic Organizer Activity

5. Draw a diagram like the one below, and use it to show the three major periods in early human history.

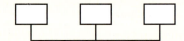

Chapter Summary & Study Guide

1. Geographers use six essential elements to study the earth: the world in spatial terms, places and regions, physical systems, human systems, environment and society, and the uses of geography.
2. Mountains, hills, plateaus, and plains make up 30 percent of the surface of the earth.
3. The surface of the earth is constantly undergoing change.
4. About 70 percent of the earth's surface is covered by water.
5. Climate is shaped by many factors, including winds, ocean currents, and altitude.
6. Geographers divide the earth into climate zones based on latitude.

7. Examples of natural resources include air, water, sunlight, minerals, fossil fuels, forests, and animal life.
8. Renewable resources can be replaced. Nonrenewable resources are gone forever when used up.
9. Legends have helped people explain the past.
10. Archaeologists study artifacts to learn how people lived long ago.
11. Since 1946, scientists have used the carbon 14 method of dating to identify the age of artifacts.

Self-Check Quiz

Visit the *Human Heritage* Web site at **humanheritage. glencoe.com** and click on *Chapter 1—Self-Check Quiz* to assess your understanding of this chapter.

Assessment

Using Key Terms

Imagine you are writing an explanation for a younger student of how geography has shaped history. Use the following words to describe in a simple way how landforms, waterways, and climate have influenced history.

landforms
climate
natural
  resources

tectonic plates
elevation
archaeology
erosion

glaciers
river system
artifacts

Understanding Main Ideas

1. What are the four major kinds of landforms?
2. What do geographers believe caused Pangaea to split into seven continents?
3. How has erosion both helped and hurt people?
4. Why did early people settle along the banks of waterways?
5. Why are air, water, soil, and sunlight important natural resources?
6. How have people's views about natural resources changed in recent years?
7. How is the carbon 14 test used as a dating tool?

Critical Thinking

1. In what climate zone would you prefer to live? Why?
2. "It is important to plan the use of the world's natural resources." What is your opinion of this statement? Explain.
3. Why is it important to identify the date of artifacts as exactly as possible?
4. How do ideas about the past change as more knowledge becomes available?

Graphic Organizer Activity

History Create a diagram like this one, and use it to show some of the archaeological finds that have changed history.

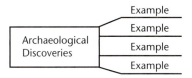

Geography in History

Physical Systems Look at the map on page 13 that shows how far ice sheets moved during the Ice Ages. What descriptive statements could you make about the movement of ice north of the Equator compared to south of the Equator?

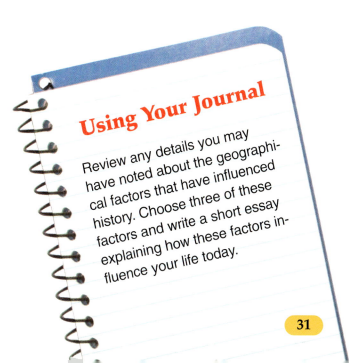

Using Your Journal

Review any details you may have noted about the geographical factors that have influenced history. Choose three of these factors and write a short essay explaining how these factors influence your life today.

Prehistoric People

8000 B.C.–3000 B.C.

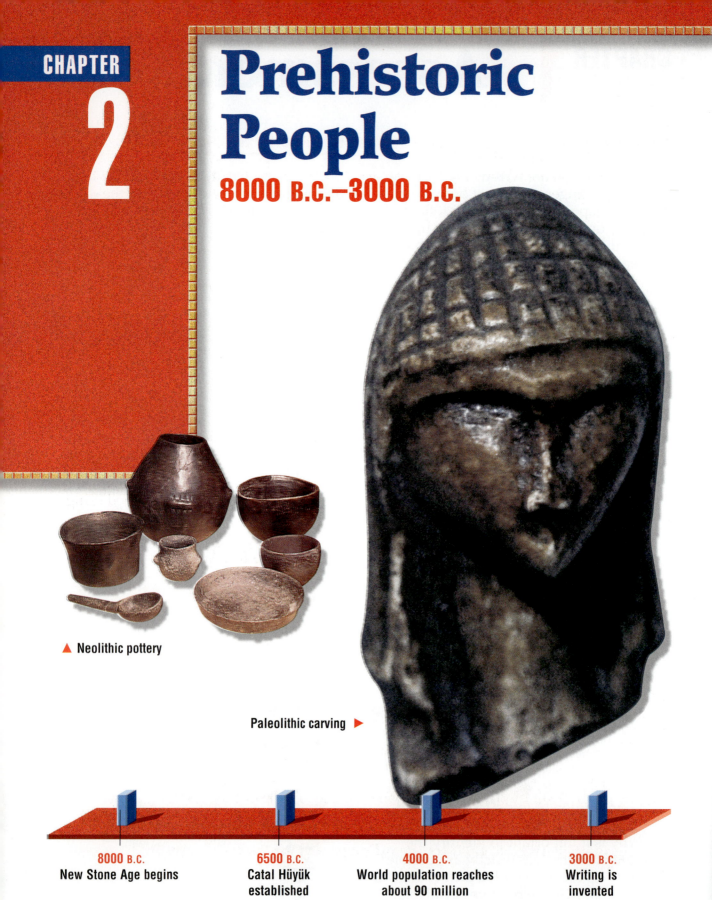

▲ Neolithic pottery

Paleolithic carving ▶

8000 B.C.
New Stone Age begins

6500 B.C.
**Catal Hüyük
established**

4000 B.C.
**World population reaches
about 90 million**

3000 B.C.
**Writing is
invented**

Chapter Focus

 Read to Discover

- How tools, language, clothing, and the discovery of fire helped early people advance.
- What Neanderthals and Cro-Magnons were like.
- How people changed from food gatherers to food producers.
- Why specialization, government, and religion were important in Neolithic societies.

Chapter Overview

Visit the *Human Heritage* Web site at humanheritage.glencoe.com and click on **Chapter 2—Chapter Overviews** to preview this chapter.

 Terms to Learn

prehistory
civilization
migrate
specialization

 People to Know

Lucy
Neanderthals
Cro-Magnons

 Places to Locate

Olduvai Gorge
Jericho
Catal Hüyük

Why It's Important Most archaeologists believe people have lived on the earth for millions of years. The period of time before the invention of writing is called **prehistory**. It lasted until about five thousand years ago, when people learned how to write. Through the use of artifacts, archaeologists have traced the milestones that paved the way from prehistory to the rise of **civilization**—a time when people progressed culturally and began to live in cities.

Reading Check
When did **prehistory** end? What helped bring about the rise of **civilization?**

SECTION 1   The Paleolithic Age

Although there were no written records during prehistory, scientists have learned a great deal about prehistoric people. They have learned how early human beings lived and what important discoveries were made. Scientists also think they know why people moved out of Africa to other parts of the world.

Many scientists believe that until about 1.75 million years ago, people lived only on the grasslands of eastern and southern Africa. Then the earth's climate changed—it became colder. Ocean water froze into huge glaciers that spread out from the North and South poles. As the ice sheets grew, the sea level fell and uncovered land that had been under water. Land bridges then connected Africa to both southern Europe and southwestern Asia.

Reading Check
How did early people **migrate** out of Africa?

People were able to **migrate**, or make their way, around the desert of northern Africa and across the land bridges. Between about 1.75 million and 700,000 years ago, people made their way into Europe and Asia. Much later, between about 40,000 and 15,000 years ago, they also migrated to the Americas.

Scientists call the first age in which people lived the Paleolithic (pā lē uh lith′ ik) Age, or Old Stone Age. It lasted from about 2.3 million years ago until 10,000 years ago. During this period, people obtained their food by hunting and gathering.

Reading Check
How did living in **bands** help people survive?

Obtaining Food   Paleolithic people lived in small **bands**, or groups, of about 30 members. When the food supply was good, the bands grew to about 40 or 50 members. Most of the group members lived to be no more than 20 or 25 years old. More than half of the children died from illnesses or were killed by animals before their first birthdays.

The people within a group lived and worked together and shared their food. They fed and cared for people who became injured or sick.

GROUP LIFE   Experts believe that most early people lived in groups made up of several families. Here, a group of hunters use stones to sharpen tools. Two men carry a large animal killed in a hunt, as a few women tend fires near their tents. **How did Paleolithic people use fire?**

EARLY TOOLS   For more than 2 million years, prehistoric people lived by hunting animals and gathering plants. They used tools made of wood and stone. The wooden tools have decayed. Archaeologists, however, have found many stone tools. **For what purposes did prehistoric people use stone tools?**

Each band searched for food within an area known as its **home territory.** This usually covered about two square miles, or five square kilometers, for every band member. There were campsites at various places throughout the home territory. The band stayed at a campsite until the available food supply was used up and then moved.

Women and children gathered berries, nuts, fruit, and eggs out of bird and turtle nests. They poked sticks into bee nests to get honey and into the ground to dig roots.

Men of the group obtained meat. They caught fish using their bare hands and hunted small animals with sticks and stones. Occasionally, they were able to kill a large animal that was too young, too old, or too badly hurt to run away. A good kill meant that the group would have enough meat to last for several days.

Making Tools

Life for hunters and gatherers became easier when they learned to make tools. At first the only tools people had were sticks and stones they found on the ground. Soon they learned to shape stones to make them more useful.

Reading Check
What were some of the features of a band's **home territory**?

Oldest Tools In 1995, archaeologists working in Ethiopia found stone spear points more than 2.6 million years old, making them the earliest tools found on Earth.

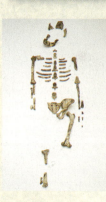

Lucy
c. 3,200,000 B.C.

Hominid Skeleton

Lucy made headlines in 1974 when two scientists—Donald C. Johanson and Tom Gray—discovered her skeleton in the deserts of Ethiopia. They named her after a popular Beatles song, "Lucy in the Sky with Diamonds." Although Lucy walked the earth 3.2 million years ago, her skeleton was nearly complete. She gave the world its first look at an early prehuman.

Among the earliest shaped stones are the *Olduvan pebble tools,* named after the Olduvai Gorge in eastern Africa where they were first discovered. Pebble tools were made from pebbles or stones about the size of a fist. The toolmaker hit one pebble with another, removing chips and creating a jagged cutting edge. This edge was sharp enough to cut the meat off of small animals' bones, split animal bones, and chop up plants.

Later people learned to knock long, sharp-edged chips, called flakes, from stones and use them as tools. Using flakes for knives, they could butcher, or cut up, animals as big as elephants quickly and efficiently. People also used flakes to scrape one end of a wooden branch into a sharp point for a digging stick or a meat skewer.

Making Fire

People also learned to make fire during the Paleolithic Age. The first fires they knew about were made by nature, such as those started by lightning. Eventually, people discovered how to make fire themselves. They created sparks by rubbing two sticks or stones together, or rapidly turning a stick in a hole in a dry log.

People used fire to keep themselves warm and dry. They also used it as a weapon, throwing burning sticks of wood at animals to drive them away. Sometimes they used fire to drive big animals into mudholes. The heavy animals would sink in the mud and people could then kill them.

People also used fire to clear out brush and undergrowth. Finally, people used fire to cook food. Cooked food was much easier to chew and digest than raw food. As a result, people spent less time eating and more time doing other things.

Seeking Shelter

Early people usually camped out in the open. They protected themselves from the wind by digging pits in the ground or by crouching in dry river beds. They also took shelter under an overhanging rock or piled up brush.

At first, early people used caves only for such emergencies as escaping from a sudden storm or a large animal. By about 100,000 years ago, however, people in China, western Europe, and southwestern Asia were living in caves most of the time.

Making Clothing

After hunters began killing large animals, they found that the animal skins could be used for protection and warmth. They scraped the skins clean and then laid them out in the sun to dry. Later, people discovered that pounding fat into the skin while it was drying would make it softer.

At first people wrapped the skins around themselves. Later, they learned how to fasten the skins together. Clothing made a big difference in where people lived. Before they had clothing, most people stayed in areas that were warm and dry. Once they

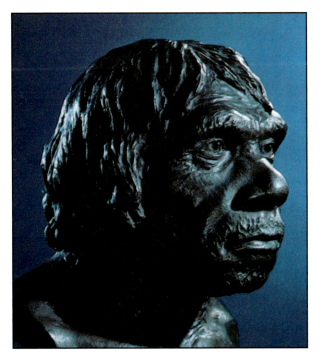

PREHISTORIC PEOPLE   There were two types of early *Homo sapiens,* Neanderthals and Cro-Magnons. From the remains of these two peoples, scientists have tried to reconstruct how they might have looked. These models show the facial features of the Neanderthal (left) and a Cro-Magnon (right). **In what areas of the world did the first people most likely live?**

had clothing to protect them from the weather, they were able to move into areas that were cooler and wetter.

Developing Language

In addition to learning to make tools, fire, and clothing, early people developed language. Before they learned to talk, early people simply made sounds or pointed to objects to express meaning. Hand signals were probably used for common things such as water, food, animals, and weapons. Gradually, because of new social needs, sounds and hand signals were no longer enough. The development of language was a great human achievement. It made it possible for people to work together, share ideas, and pass on their beliefs and stories. The younger generations could learn more easily from older generations, and greater progress was made in all areas of civilization.

The Neanderthals

The first people on Earth are known as *Homo habilis* (hō mō huh bil′ uhs), or "skillful man." Next came *Homo erectus* (hō′ mō ē rekt′ uhs), or "man who walks upright." Then, between about 300,000 and 200,000 years ago, came *Homo sapiens* (hō′ mō sāp′ ē uhnz), or "man who thinks."

Languages There may be 2,000 to 10,000 languages in the world today. Dialects, or variations within a language, range from about 20,000 to more than 50,000. The largest native language in the world is Chinese, but among the many dialects are Mandarin, Cantonese, Wu, Min, Xiang, Kan, and Hakka.

There are two kinds of *Homo sapiens*. The first is the Neanderthal (nē an' der tahl), named after the Neander River in Germany, where their remains were first discovered in 1856. Since then, other Neanderthal remains have been found throughout Europe and in parts of Asia and Africa. Scientists estimate that about 1 million Neanderthals were living at any one time.

Neanderthal people were good hunters. They used traps to catch birds and small animals. They used *pitfalls* to catch large animals like the rhinoceros and the elephant. A pitfall was a large hole that was covered with branches, leaves, and earth. As an animal ran across this hole, it crashed through the covering and fell into the pit. The hunters would then kill the animal with spears.

Neanderthals were also builders. In northern areas, for example, they made houses by covering a framework of mammoth bones with animal skins. More bones piled on the bottoms of the skins prevented them from being blown away. As many as 30 people lived in such a house during the cold months of the year. They improved cave dwellings by digging drainage ditches in caves and designing rock protection for entrances.

According to experts, Neanderthals were also the first people to bury their dead. Archaeologists have found graves of people from this time in which they discovered the remains of flowers, tools, and food.

Linking Across Time

The Aborigines Archaeologists have found spearheads and cave paintings showing that hunters traveled to Australia more than 40,000 years ago. Their descendants call themselves the Aborigines (ab uh rij' uh nēz) and live much as their ancestors did (far right). **Why does the study of traditional cultures provide valuable information about the past?**

PREHISTORIC HORSE   This prehistoric painting of a horse was found on the wall of a cave in Lascaux, France. Early art such as this always showed the animal's profile. **What can scientists learn about Cro-Magnon people from looking at their art?**

The Cro-Magnons

The second kind of *Homo sapiens* is the Cro-Magnon (krō mag′ nahn), named after a rock shelter in France where their remains were first discovered in 1868. Cro-Magnons appeared in North Africa, Asia, and Europe about 100,000 years ago. Archaeologists consider them the first modern human beings.

Cro-Magnons were very skillful toolmakers. They invented the *burin,* which resembles a chisel. By using the burin, people could make other tools and objects from antler, bone, ivory, and shell, as well as stone and wood.

Using new tools made Cro-Magnons better hunters, thus increasing their food supply. Points of antler or bone fastened to the end of wooden sticks could penetrate the hides of larger animals. People fashioned antler and bone into *spear throwers,* or devices that made spears fly through the air faster and farther. This allowed hunters to stay a greater distance from animals, making hunting less dangerous.

First Razors Cro-Magnons may have invented the first razors. Some Cro-Magnon cave paintings portray beardless men, and Cro-Magnon graves contain sharpened shells—the first razors. Later peoples hammered razors out of bronze or iron.

Another important tool that Cro-Magnons invented was the axe, which they used to cut down trees and hollow out the logs to make canoes. In southeastern Asia, they cut down stalks of bamboo and tied them together with vines to make rafts. Winds or ocean currents then carried the rafts to other lands. It is likely that this is how people reached Australia about 40,000 years ago.

Cro-Magnons also fashioned bone, ivory, and shell into body ornaments, such as necklaces and rings. They decorated their clothing with bone or ivory beads. They played music on flutes carved from long, hollow bones.

Cro-Magnons were artists as well as toolmakers. They carved statues out of ivory and bone or molded them out of clay. They covered the walls of some caves in western Europe, Africa, and South America with pictures painted brightly with paints made from minerals. The pictures show mostly animals, such as horses, bulls, and deer, but also show outlines and patterns of lines, dots, and curves.

Many anthropologists think cave paintings may have had religious significance. Cro-Magnons believed that animals had spirits. They thought that painting an animal's picture gave people power over its spirit and would help them find and kill the animal. Anthropologists think the cave paintings may have been a kind of textbook about Cro-Magnon ceremonies, traditions, or history.

Cro-Magnon bands cooperated, often hunting large animals together. This required them to jointly agree on rules and the first true leaders. Every year or so, they held social gatherings where they exchanged information about the movement of animal herds. They also traded materials such as amber and shells.

Section 1 Assessment

1. **Define:** prehistory, civilization, migrate, bands, home territory.
2. Why did early people begin to move out of Africa and into other parts of the world about 1 million years ago?
3. How did tools change in the Paleolithic Age?

Critical Thinking

4. **Analyzing Information** What do you think was the most important advancement made by early people? Explain.

Graphic Organizer Activity

5. Draw a diagram like this one, and use it to compare ways of life followed by the Neanderthals and Cro-Magnons. Be sure to include the accomplishments of each.

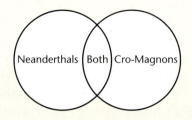

Neanderthals | Both | Cro-Magnons

DOMESTICATING ANIMALS   Early people painted scenes of their hunting and food-producing activities. Here, a cave painting from North Africa shows cattle being herded. Some cattle are tied to a rope, while women and children do chores. **What was the importance of learning to herd animals?**

Then... & Now

Early Art Paleolithic artists used three basic colors: black, red, and yellow. The pigments came from natural sources such as charcoal, clay, and minerals such as iron. They used these materials so skillfully that when Pablo Picasso, one of the masters of modern art, saw cave paintings in France, he reportedly exclaimed: "We have invented nothing!"

SECTION 2 The Neolithic Age

In the Neolithic (nē uh lith' ik), or New Stone Age, about 8000 B.C., people changed from food gatherers to food producers. Over several thousand years they began to obtain most of their food from farming. This brought about such great changes in the way they lived that experts call the beginning of farming the Neolithic Revolution.

Farmers and Herders   Two important discoveries brought on the Neolithic Revolution. One was learning to grow food. The other was learning to herd animals.

Experts believe that people discovered that seed from wild grains, such as wheat and barley, could be planted and harvested. This probably came about when they noticed that new shoots had grown from spilled grain. Scientists believe agriculture developed independently in different parts of the world. In southwestern Asia, early people grew wheat and barley, and in

HISTORY Online

Student Web Activity

Visit the *Human Heritage* Web site at **humanheritage.glencoe.com** and click on **Chapter 2— Student Web Activities** to find out more about the Neolithic Age.

eastern Asia, they grew millet, rice, and soy beans. In Mexico, they grew corn, squash, and potatoes, and they grew peanuts and a grain called sorghum in Africa.

People probably learned they could herd animals when a hunting band built fences to enclose a herd of wild animals they had chased into a ravine. The hunters killed one animal at a time, saving the rest for later. Soon captured animals began to lose their fear of people and became **domesticated,** or tamed, and the hunters became herders. In time, Neolithic people were breeding animals to improve the animals' qualities. People also began using certain animals such as donkeys, camels, and llamas as pack animals.

The Neolithic Revolution greatly increased people's food supplies. With more food available, the **population**, or number of people, began to grow. Experts think there were about 5 million people in the world in 8000 B.C. Within 4,000 years the population grew to about 90 million. People were also living longer.

Early Villages

Once people began to produce food, they were able to settle in one place. They built permanent shelters and formed villages of about 150 to 200 people in areas with a good soil and water supply.

✓ Reading Check
How did **domesticated** animals change the way some hunters lived?

✓ Reading Check
What caused the world's **population** to grow?

POTTERY MAKING   Neolithic people learned the art of baking clay pottery. Baked clay, unlike sun-dried clay, will not disintegrate in water. In this picture, men are covering the oven so that the pots inside will bake. **How did Neolithic people use pottery?**

EARLY VILLAGES   Archaeologists today continue to dig up artifacts of early people. These scientists have uncovered the sites of several ancient villages. **How do archaeologists know they have found the site of a prehistoric village?**

The earliest known villages in the world have been found in southwestern Asia. One of the oldest is Jericho (jer´ uh kō) in the West Bank between Israel and Jordan. It dates back to about 8000 B.C. Another is Abu Hureyra (ah bu hu rā´ rah) in Syria, which was founded about 500 years later. A third early village is Catal Hüyük (kat' uhl hū´ yūk) located in Turkey. People lived there from about 6500 to 5700 B.C.

Archaeologists know a great deal about Catal Hüyük because it was struck by a fire that blackened rather than destroyed wooden and cloth objects. The blackening helped preserve the objects. Evidence shows the houses in Catal Hüyük were made of sun-dried mud brick. They had flat roofs made of reeds plastered over with mud. The walls and roofs were supported by a *post-and-lintel,* or a horizontal length of wood or stone placed across two upright poles. The post-and-lintel was an important contribution to architecture because it enabled buildings to support weight above an open space.

As protection against attack, the houses in this village had two or three rooms and no doors. People went in and out of the houses through a hole in the roof by using a ladder. The houses were crowded together on the side of a hill. The floors were covered with rushes, or grasslike plants, and sleeping platforms were covered with mats.

First Farmers Many archaeologists believe that women invented the practice of agriculture. In societies of hunter-gatherers, women collected fruits, nuts, and seeds. As they did so, they probably noticed that plants sprouted where seeds fell. Only with the invention of the plow did men take over the job of farming.

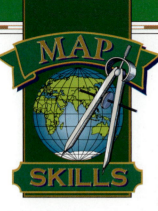

MAP SKILLS

Determining Relative Location

Most maps show direction, or the line or course along which something is pointing or facing. Understanding direction makes locating places, whether on a map or in a town, much easier.

All directions heading toward the North Pole are north (abbreviated N), and all directions heading toward the South Pole are south (S). When facing the North Pole, the direction to the right is east (E) and to the left is west (W). These four main directions are called **cardinal directions.**

There are also four other directions, which are known as intermediate directions. This is because they are located between the cardinal directions. The direction between north and east is northeast (NE) and between north and west is northwest (NW). The direction between south and east is southeast (SE) and between south and west is southwest (SW).

Map Practice

1. **What sites are located southwest of Neanderthal?**
2. **Which site is south of Broken Hill?**
3. **In which direction is Ngandong from Teshik-Tash?**

Sites of Early People

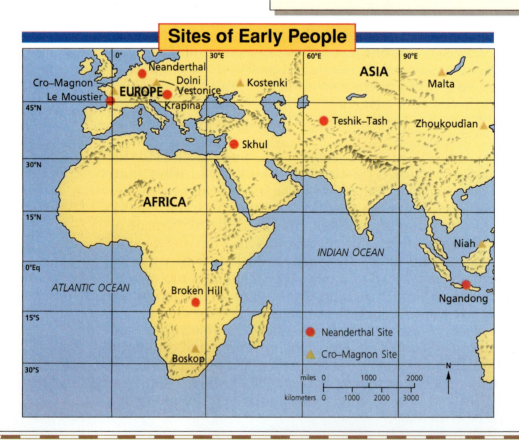

Among the houses stood open courtyards with large ovens for baking bread. Beyond the houses were vegetable gardens, apple orchards, fields of grain, and pastures where sheep and cattle grazed.

Specialization

A result of increased food supplies was **specialization,** or the development of occupations. Fewer people were needed to produce food so they began to do jobs that had nothing to do with food. They became potters, weavers, and metal workers. They exchanged the things they made for grain, fruit, and meat.

Specialization was aided by a number of developments. One was that people learned to make pottery by baking clay. They used pottery for carrying, cooking, and storing food. This enabled them to add such things as soups and stews to their diet.

In addition, people learned to weave cloth. People took wool from sheep, spun it into thread, and wove the thread into cloth on a loom, which was invented during the Neolithic Age. They dyed the cloth bright colors and used it for clothing.

Neolithic people also learned to work metals. They picked up lumps of copper, lead, gold, and silver that they found lying on the ground and hammered these metals into beads and jewelry. Soon they learned how to shape the metal into weapons. Because metals found on the ground were scarce, however, people continued to work mostly in stone, bone, and wood.

✔ Reading Check How did **specialization** develop in Neolithic times?

Government

Another development of Neolithic times was village government. It was more complex than government in earlier times due to land ownership. People's lives depended on the use of a given piece of land. As a result, people began to protect what they had. They set boundaries and passed their land on to their children.

Even so, disputes often arose over land ownership. To keep order in Neolithic villages, a single chief was chosen. Besides settling disputes, the chief, with the help of a small group of people, directed village activities.

Religion

Experts believe that the chiefs of most Neolithic villages were also priests. They handled religious duties for the village which included offering prayers for things people needed, such as rich soil, healthy animals, and water for crops.

At first, Neolithic people prayed to the forces of nature that they saw around them. After a time, they created gods and goddesses to represent these forces. The most important was the Earth Mother, the goddess of fertility. Many of the houses in Catal Hüyük, for example, had altars for this goddess.

Then... & Now

Religion Four out of five people in the world say they practice some form of religion. The five largest world religions are Christianity, Islam, Hinduism, Buddhism, and Judaism.

Archaeologists believe that more elaborate religious customs and ceremonies appeared at this time. Neolithic people began to build separate altars and other places of worship for their many gods and goddesses.

Section 2 Assessment

1. **Define:** domesticated, population, specialization.
2. What two important discoveries changed people from food gatherers to food producers?
3. What were two results of the increased food supply during the Neolithic Age?
4. What two roles did village chiefs play?

Critical Thinking

5. **Understanding Cause and Effect** How did learning to produce food lead early civilizations to develop villages?

Graphic Organizer Activity

6. Draw a diagram like this one, and use it to show the cause and effects of the development of farming.

Chapter Summary & Study Guide

1. Prehistoric time can be divided into the Paleolithic and Neolithic Ages.
2. During the Paleolithic Age, people lived in small hunting-and-food-gathering bands.
3. Over time, Paleolithic people learned to make tools and clothes, developed language, and discovered how to make fire.
4. Early *Homo sapiens* included the Neanderthal and the Cro-Magnon.
5. The shift from food gathering to food producing brought so many changes that it has been called the Neolithic Revolution.
6. Food production made it possible for people to settle in one place.
7. Increased food supplies in the Neolithic Age resulted in increased population and specialization.
8. Neolithic villagers learned to make pottery, weave on looms, and work with metals.
9. Neolithic village government was led by a chief who settled disputes and directed village activities.

Self-Check Quiz

Visit the *Human Heritage* Web site at **humanheritage. glencoe.com** and click on ***Chapter 2—Self-Check Quiz*** to assess your understanding of this chapter.

CHAPTER 2 Assessment

Using Key Terms

Write a short description of a day in the life of a person who lived during the Paleolithic or Neolithic ages. Use the following words in your description.

prehistory   civilization   migrate
bands   home territory   domesticated
population   specialization

Understanding Main Ideas

1. What is the main difference between the Paleolithic and Neolithic ages?
2. Why did Paleolithic people move from place to place?
3. How did early men and women share the work of getting food?
4. How did the discovery of fire affect people's lives?
5. What difference did clothing make in the way people lived?
6. Why did the Cro-Magnons produce cave paintings?
7. How did increased food supplies cause increased population?
8. Why did people in the Neolithic Age begin to take up different occupations?
9. How did people in the Neolithic Age change their form of government?

Critical Thinking

1. Do you think the development of farming should be called a revolution? Explain.
2. What would you have liked about living in Catal Hüyük? What would you have disliked?
3. How would you have organized work activities if you had been a village chief?

Graphic Organizer Activity

Economics Draw a diagram like this one, and use it to show the steps leading up to the rise of villages in the Neolithic Age. (Add steps as necessary.)

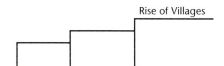

Rise of Villages

Geography in History

Environment and Society When early people began to build shelters, they used some geographic features to decide where they would build their homes. What features affected their choice of building sites? How might geography affect their choice of building materials?

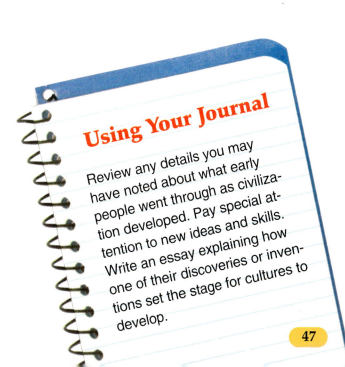

Using Your Journal

Review any details you may have noted about what early people went through as civilization developed. Pay special attention to new ideas and skills. Write an essay explaining how one of their discoveries or inventions set the stage for cultures to develop.

PREHISTORIC PEOPLES OF THE SAHARA

During the prehistoric era, the Sahara—the world's largest desert—looked nothing like it does today. Vast grasslands stretched across a broad open plain. Rivers and shallow lakes shimmered in the sun. The land was wet and green enough to support bands of hunters and some of the earth's earliest communities of herders.

Between 10,000 and 4,000 years ago, the area's climate changed. The rains stopped falling and the temperatures rose. The grasslands, rivers, and lakes disappeared. So did the prehistoric peoples who once lived there. However, they left behind a rich legacy of rock art that has kept their stories alive.

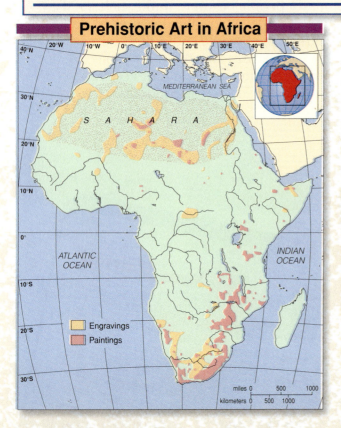

Prehistoric Art in Africa

Engravings

Paintings

▲ Africa has more prehistoric rock art sites than any other continent.

▲ In the dry desert of modern Libya, a life-size crocodile stretches across a rock. The engraving, carved about 9,000 years ago, captures a time when these giant reptiles soaked up the sun on the banks of ancient rivers.

the W🌐rld

▲ The camel arrived on the Sahara from Asia about 2,200 years ago. By then the grasslands of the past had nearly vanished. Today the Sahara is a vast sea of sand and rock, covering more than 3.5 million square miles.

Carved more than 7,000 years ago, this pair of giraffes grazed on the tall grasses that once covered the Sahara. Prehistoric people may have tried to domesticate, or tame, these animals. ▼

◄ Starting about 7,500 ▲ years ago, herding and farming emerged on the grassy northern plains of Africa. Paintings and carvings show the kinds of cattle raised by prehistoric peoples in this region.

Taking Another Look

1. In what parts of Africa is ancient rock art found?
2. What types of animals did prehistoric peoples of the region herd?

Hands-On Activity

Creating Art Design a postage stamp that one of the modern nations in the Sahara might create to celebrate its rock art.

Standardized Test Practice

Directions: Choose the *best* answer to each of the following multiple choice questions. If you have trouble answering a question, use the process of elimination to narrow your choices. Write your answers on a separate piece of paper.

1. **The ways that people build their homes can cause which of the following surface changes to the earth?**

   A Earthquakes

   B Volcanic eruptions

   C Erosion

   D Advancement of glaciers

   Test-Taking Tip: Always read the question and *all* of the answer choices carefully. Avoid answers that seem extreme. For example, it is very unlikely that the way people build their homes could *cause* the *advancement of glaciers.* Therefore, you can eliminate answer D.

2. **Some resources are nonrenewable, while others are renewable. Which of the following is an example of a renewable resource?**

   F Coal

   G Minerals

   H Plastic

   J Timber

   Test-Taking Tip: Think about the meaning of these terms. *Resources,* often referred to as "*natural resources,*" are materials found in nature. Renewable resources can be replaced as they are used. *Nonrenewable resources* CANNOT be replaced. It is a good idea to keep a vocabulary list of new words as you read each new chapter. The **glossary** of your textbook can help you define these unfamiliar words.

3. **Many early legends were created as ways to**

   A explain the creation of Earth

   B explain where archaeological remains came from

   C compare different societies

   D introduce children to a tribe's language

   Test-Taking Tip: Think of familiar examples to double-check your understanding of the question. Remember, sometimes more than one answer seems correct. For instance, though the telling of legends certainly helped children learn a tribe's language, that was not the primary reason they were created. Always choose the *best* answer.

4. **The discovery of the Rosetta Stone allowed scientists to**

   F understand the fall of the Roman Empire

   G understand the ancient Egyptian language

   H understand how Pompeii was destroyed

   J translate the ancient Greek language into English

   Test-Taking Tip: This question asks you to remember a *fact* about the Rosetta Stone. The Rosetta Stone served as a *language* dictionary. Only two answer choices discuss *languages,* so you can easily eliminate the others.

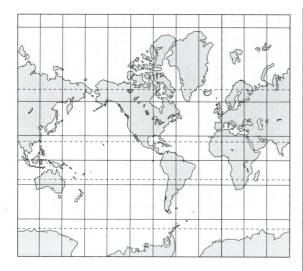

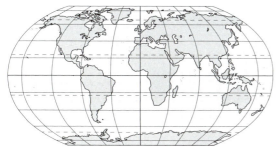

5. Which of the following CANNOT be shown on the map on the top?

A   True direction

B   Latitude and longitude

C   Bodies of water

D   The exact size of all continents

Test-Taking Tip: The map on the top is called a *Mercator projection*. Remember, a *map projection* is a way of representing a *round* earth on a *flat* piece of paper. What becomes distorted in a Mercator projection?

6. Which of the following is NOT considered an artifact?

F   A spearhead from ancient Egypt

G   A fossil of an extinct fish from the Paleolithic era

H   A clay water pitcher from the Shang dynasty

J   A silver bracelet from Pompeii

Test-Taking Tip: Another important term to remember is *artifact*. Artifacts are *things made by people.* Be careful when a question uses the words NOT or EXCEPT— overlooking these words is a common error. Look for the answer choice that does NOT fit.

7. During the Paleolithic Age, people lived in groups of 20 to 30 people. Increases in population within these bands were usually caused by

A   low average birth weight

B   discovery of safe migration routes

C   a stable food supply

D   frequent natural disasters

Test-Taking Tip: Eliminate answers that do not make sense. For example, answers A and D probably would probably cause a *drop* in population rather than an increase.

River Valley Civilizations

◄ Egyptian wood carving

Blue Nile hippopotamus ▼

5000 B.C.
Groups of people
begin migrating

3500 B.C.
Sumeria
established

2600 B.C.
Old Kingdom
begins in Egypt

2300 B.C.
Sargon I establishes
world's first empire

Compare and Contrast Study Foldable *Make this foldable to help you compare and contrast the river valley civilizations that developed in the Middle East, South Asia, and China.*

Step 1 *Fold a sheet of paper in half from side to side.*

Fold it so the left edge is about $\frac{1}{2}$ inch from the right edge.

Step 2 *Turn the paper and fold it into thirds.*

Reading and Writing *As you read the unit, write notes under each appropriate tab of your foldable. Keep in mind that you are trying to compare these civilizations.*

Step 3 *Unfold and cut the top layer only along both folds.*

This will make three tabs.

Step 4 *Label as shown.*

Mesopotamia | Egypt | Eastern River Valleys

RIVER VALLEY CIVILIZATIONS

PRIMARY SOURCES

Library

See pages 676–677 for another primary source reading to accompany Unit 2.

GO TO Read "The Epic of Gilgamesh" from the **World History Primary Source Document Library CD-ROM.**

Journal Notes

What was daily life like more than 5,000 years ago? Note details about it as you read.

1800 B.C.
Hammurabi establishes Babylonian Empire

1766 B.C.
Shang Dynasty begins in China

1600 B.C.
New Kingdom begins in Egypt

Mesopotamia
3500 B.C.–1700 B.C.

Sumerian man
and woman ▼

▲ Gold Sumerian
warrior's helmet

3500 B.C.
Sumeria
established

2300 B.C.
Sargon I creates the
world's first empire

1800 B.C.
Hammurabi conquers
Akkad and Sumer

1700 B.C.
Tales of
Gilgamesh started

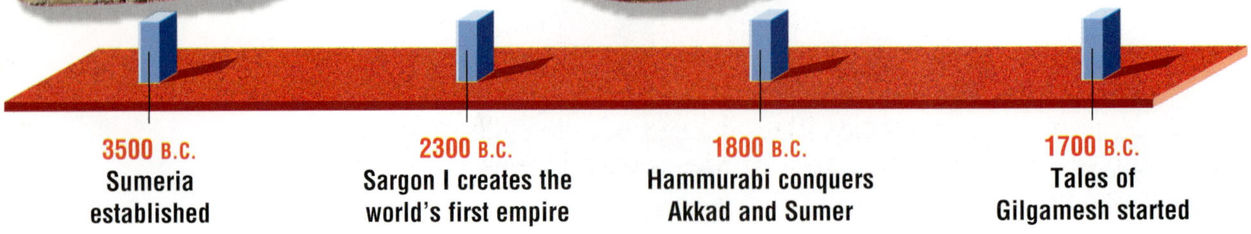

Chapter Focus

 Read to Discover

- How religion, family life, and government influenced the civilization of Sumer.
- Why Hammurabi and his reforms were important.
- How the developments of Mesopotamia contributed to other civilizations.

Chapter Overview

Visit the *Human Heritage* Web site at **humanheritage.glencoe.com** and click on *Chapter 3—Chapter Overviews* to preview this chapter.

 Terms to Learn

city-state
artisans
ziggurat
cuneiform
scribe
priest-kings
empire
culture
reform
reign

 People to Know

Gilgamesh
Sargon I
Hammurabi

 Places to Locate

Mesopotamia
Sumer
Ur
Babylon

Why It's Important   The earliest known civilizations developed along the Tigris and Euphrates rivers, which begin in the mountains of eastern Turkey. The twin rivers each flow more than 1,000 miles, or 1,600 kilometers, southeast across a great plain in an area known as the Middle East. Then, the waters join and empty into the Persian Gulf. Today, the land between the two rivers is part of the country of Iraq. In ancient times, the area was called Mesopotamia (mes uh puh tay′ me uh), "the land between the rivers."

Around 4000 B.C., groups of people began migrating, or moving, into Mesopotamia. They developed so many new ideas that the area has been called the "cradle of civilization." The influence of Mesopotamia left a lasting impact on the ancient world.

SECTION 1   The Rise of Sumer

The people who settled in southern Mesopotamia about 3500 B.C. were a short, stocky, black-haired people called Sumerians (sū mer′ ē uhnz). Their area of Mesopotamia was known as Sumer (sū′ mŭhr).

HISTORY Online

Student Web Activity

Visit the *Human Heritage* Web site at **humanheritage.glencoe.com** and click on **Chapter 3— Student Web Activities** to find out more about the Sumerian civilization.

Sumerian civilization is the earliest known on Earth. For the first time, people began to control their physical environment. The Sumerians knew they had to control the twin rivers. The rivers flooded each spring. When the waters went down, natural *levees* (lev' ēz), or raised areas of soil, remained behind. The Sumerians built the levees even higher and used them to keep back the floodwaters. During summer when the land became dry, they poked holes in the levees. The river water that ran through the holes made channels in the soil. The Sumerians made the channels larger until they became canals. They used the water in the canals to irrigate their crops. The chief crop of the Sumerians was barley. The Sumerians also grew wheat, sesame, flax, fruit trees, date palms, and many different kinds of vegetables.

A system of irrigation canals took much planning. People had to learn to work together. In time, they became more organized. They set up governments to make laws so they would know what was expected of them. As the population grew, they began to build cities.

There was no building stone and little timber in Sumer. The Sumerians had to find other materials to use for their houses and public buildings. They mixed mud from the river with crushed reeds to make bricks. They left the bricks out in the sun to bake and then used them to build their cities. One of the great cities of

Linking Across Time

Official Seals Around 3500 to 3400 B.C., officials in Mesopotamia started using cylinder seals (below) to mark goods and verify documents written in cuneiform on clay. Today governments around the world continue to use seals to mark documents such as the passports carried by United States citizens (right). **Why do you think governments stamp important documents with seals?**

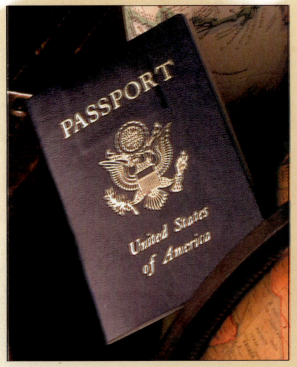

Sumer was Ur (uhr). The Sumerians were the first city-builders in this area of the world.

City-States

Each Sumerian city was considered a state in itself, with its own god and government. Each **city-state** was made up of the city and the farmland around it. Each city was surrounded by a wall of sun-dried brick. The wall had bronze gates that were opened during the day and closed at night to keep out lions and bandits.

Narrow, winding streets led from the gates to the center of the city. Near the center were the houses of the upper class—priests and merchants. These houses were two stories high with wooden balconies. The balconies looked out over courtyards around which the living quarters were built. The courtyards provided light and air for rooms. Outside walls were windowless to keep out heat from the sun and smells of the streets.

Behind the houses of the rich were the houses of the middle class—government officials, shopkeepers, and **artisans** (art' uh zuhnz), or skilled workers. These houses also were built around open courtyards but were only one story high. Farther out were the houses of the lower class—farmers, unskilled workers, and people who made their living by fishing.

The Sumerians were very proud of their cities. Often, one city-state would go to war with another city-state. They fought over boundary lines and to prove which city-state was stronger.

Religious and Family Life

At the center of each Sumerian city was a temple, called a **ziggurat** (zig' uh rat). The word "ziggurat" means "mountain of god" or "hill of heaven." Each ziggurat was made up of a series of square levels. Each level was smaller than the one below it. Great stairways led to the top of a ziggurat, which was believed to be the home of the city's chief god. Only priests could enter the home of the god.

Around the ziggurat were courts. The courts and the ziggurat were the center of Sumerian life. Artisans worked there. Children went to school there. Farmers, artisans, and traders stored their goods there. The poor were fed there. All great events were celebrated in this area.

The Sumerians believed that all the forces of nature, such as wind, rain, and flood, were alive. Because they could not control these forces, they viewed them as gods. In all, there were more than 3,000 Sumerian gods.

The Sumerians believed that at first there were only male gods. Then female gods appeared. The male gods found they had to work very hard to please the female gods. The male gods decided that they needed servants to do their work. So, from the mud of the rivers, they made humans who would be their servants. The Sumerians believed that they were on Earth only to

Reading Check What areas made up each Sumerian **city-state?**

Reading Check What are **artisans?**

Reading Check What was the purpose of a **ziggurat?**

SUMERIAN PRAYING STATUES   To honor their gods, Sumerians left statues of themselves within their temple. These statues, standing with their hands clasped, were meant to offer prayers when the people were not present. **In how many gods did the Sumerians believe?**

serve the gods. If the gods were unhappy with them, their crops would not grow and they would not live happy lives. Therefore, the goal of each Sumerian was to please the gods.

Only priests, however, could know the will of the gods. This made Sumerian priests very powerful. For example, all land was owned by a city's god. But priests controlled and administered the land in the god's name. The priests also ran schools.

Schools were only for the sons of the rich. Poorer boys worked in the fields or learned a trade. Schools were made up of rooms off the temple courtyards. They were known as tablet houses because their main purpose was to teach students how to write. Students sat in rows on brick benches. They wrote with sharp-ended reeds on clay tablets about the size of a postcard. Sumerian writing was called **cuneiform** (kyū nē′ uh form). It was made up of hundreds of markings shaped like wedges.

Writing developed because people had to keep track of business deals. When people lived in villages, they knew everyone and could remember what goods they exchanged with whom. When cities arose, there were too many people and goods to remember. At first, the Sumerians used pictures to represent objects. Later, they used pictures to represent ideas. Still later, they used pictures to represent syllables.

When a student graduated from school, he became a **scribe**, or writer. He worked for the temple, the palace, the government, or the army. Some scribes went to work for a merchant or set up their own businesses as public writers.

✓ **Reading Check**
What was **cuneiform?**

✓ **Reading Check**
What were some of the places a **scribe** might work?

Although only Sumerian males went to school, women did have rights. They could buy and sell property. They could run businesses and own and sell enslaved persons.

Although a woman handled her husband's affairs when he was away, the husband was the head of a household. He could divorce his wife by saying, "You're not my wife." If he needed money, he had the right to sell or rent his wife and children as enslaved persons for up to three years. He also arranged the marriages of his children.

Children were expected to support their parents when the parents became old and were also expected to obey older family members. All family members were to obey the gods and the priests.

Priests and Kings

At first, Sumerian priests were also kings of city-states. One of the most famous **priest-kings** was Gilgamesh (gil' ga mesh) of Uruk (ū' rūk). Tales told about Gilgamesh made him seem more like a god than a person. One tale, written about 1700 B.C., is the oldest known story in the world.

In the story, Gilgamesh and his friend Enkidu (en' ki dū) travel the world performing great acts of courage. When Enkidu dies, Gilgamesh searches for a way to live forever. He learns that only the gods can live forever. Part of the Gilgamesh story tells of a great flood that covered the whole world. The account of the flood is very much like the biblical story of Noah and the ark.

The Sumerian priest-kings received advice from an assembly made up of free men. When war broke out with another city-state, the assembly would choose one of its members to serve as military leader until the war was over. As time went on, these leaders stayed in charge even after peace returned. By about 3000 B.C., they took the place of priests as permanent kings. At the same time, kingship became *hereditary* (huh red' uh ter ē), or passed down from parent to child.

Then... & Now

Cuneiform Today only about 250 people know how to read the more than 1 million cuneiform signs that make up the written Sumerian language. To change this, a team of language experts at the University of Pennsylvania is working on an 18-volume Sumerian dictionary. The team expects the work to be done sometime in the 2000s.

✓ Reading Check
Who was one of the most famous Sumerian **priest-kings?**

Section 1 Assessment

1. **Define:** city-state, artisans, ziggurat, cuneiform, scribe, priest-kings.
2. How did the Sumerians gain control of the twin rivers?
3. What was the center of Sumerian life?

Critical Thinking

4. **Making Comparisons** How would you compare the lives of women in the time of Sumer to the lives of women in the modern world?

Graphic Organizer Activity

5. Draw a diagram like this one, and use it to show accomplishments of the Sumerians.

Accomplishments

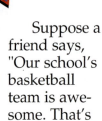

Distinguishing Fact From Opinion

Suppose a friend says, "Our school's basketball team is awesome. That's a fact." Actually, it is not a fact; it is an opinion. Are you able to tell the difference?

Learning the Skill A **fact** answers a specific question such as: What happened? Who did it? When and where did it happen? Why did it happen? Statements of fact can be checked for accuracy and proven. If your friend had said, "We have the highest-ranking team in the state," that could be a fact. We can look up the rankings of state teams and determine whether the statement is a fact.

An **opinion,** on the other hand, expresses beliefs, feelings, and judgments. Although it may reflect someone's thoughts, we cannot prove or disprove it.

An **opinion** often begins with phrases such as *I believe, I think, probably, it seems to me,* or *in my opinion.* It often contains words such as *might, could, should,* and *ought,* and superlatives such as *best, worst,* and *greatest.* Judgment words that express approval or disapproval—such as *good, bad, poor,* and *satisfactory*—also usually indicate an opinion.

To distinguish between facts and opinions, ask yourself these questions:

- Does this statement give specific information about an event?
- Can I check the accuracy of this statement?
- Does this statement express someone's feelings, beliefs, or judgment?
- Does it include phrases such as *I believe,* superlatives, or judgment words?

Skill Practice

Read each numbered statement. Then tell whether each is a fact or an opinion, and explain how you arrived at your answer.

1. Sumerian civilization is the earliest known on Earth.
2. The greatest accomplishment of the Sumerians was their system of irrigation.
3. A temple called a ziggurat formed the center of Sumerian life.
4. Women in Sumeria had terrible lives.
5. The priest-kings were better rulers than the military leaders who came into power.

GO TO Glencoe's **Skillbuilder Interactive Workbook CD-ROM, Level 1,** provides instruction and practice in key social studies skills.

SECTION 2 Later Mesopotamian Empires

About 2400 B.C., the power of Sumer started to fade. New civilizations began to develop in Mesopotamia as conquerors moved in from nearby areas.

Sargon I

Sargon I (sar' gon) was a ruler from an area in northern Mesopotamia known as Akkad (ak' ad). About 2300 B.C., he moved his armies south and began to conquer the city-states of Sumer one by one. He united the conquered city-states with Akkad and became known as king of Sumer and Akkad. Thus, Sargon I created the world's first **empire** (em' pīr), or group of states under one ruler. He extended this empire to include all of Mesopotamia.

Under Sargon I, Akkadian became the language of the people. Sumerian was used only for religious purposes. The Akkadians, however, worshiped the Sumerian gods. They also wrote their language in Sumerian cuneiform. Sargon I ruled his empire for more than 50 years. Shortly after his death, the empire fell.

Hammurabi of Babylon

Following the death of Sargon I, the separate city-states again rose to power. Then, about 1800 B.C., a new group of people called Amorites (am' uh rīts) entered the Tigris-Euphrates valley and built cities of their own. One of these cities was Babylon (bab' uh luhn). The king of Babylon, Hammurabi (ham uh rob' ē), conquered Akkad and Sumer and became ruler of a great new empire.

The people of Babylon took as their own many parts of the **culture,** or way of life, of the people they had conquered. For example, they took over the language of the city-states. They also worshiped the same Sumerian gods that the Akkadians had worshiped, but they gave those gods Babylonian names.

Hammurabi was a great conqueror. He extended his rule to the Mediterranean Sea. As ruler, he brought about many changes. He improved irrigation systems by building and repairing canals. He changed religion by raising the god of Babylon above all other gods. When the people began to worship this god as well as their own local god, they became more united. Hammurabi also reorganized the tax system and began a government housing program.

The **reform,** or improvement, for which Hammurabi became best known was a code of law. Each city-state had its own code. Hammurabi took what he believed were the best laws from each code. He put these together and then issued one code by which everyone in the empire was to live. Hammurabi wanted to make sure that his code was carried out fairly and justly. To do this, he

Reading Check
How did Sargon I build his **empire?** From what **culture** did the people of Babylon borrow? For what **reform** is Hammurabi best known?

Hammurabi
c. 1750 B.C.

Babylonian King

Hammurabi built an empire that stretched north from the Persian Gulf through the Tigris and Euphrates valleys and west to the Mediterranean Sea. He turned Babylon into one of the most powerful capitals of the ancient world.

Identifying Physical Features

Different physical features making up Earth's surface are often shown on maps. They include landforms, such as mountains, hills, plateaus, and plains. Physical features also include bodies of water, such as oceans, seas, lakes, and rivers.

Most maps use black boundary lines and color to point out water and land areas. Blue is generally used to show the size and shape of large bodies of water. For example, notice the Mediterranean Sea located west of Syria on the map below. Rivers, such as the Nile River in Egypt, are often shown by black lines. To distinguish rivers from boundaries, which are also shown by black lines, rivers are usually labeled.

Maps in this textbook use earth tone colors to point out land areas. Mountains are shown by shades of black. For example, there are mountains located where the Euphrates River begins but not where the river empties into the Persian Gulf.

Look at the map below, and answer the following questions.

Map Practice

1. **In addition to the Mediterranean, what seas are shown?**
2. **Besides the Nile, what rivers are shown?**
3. **How can you tell that the Persian Gulf coastline has changed over the years?**

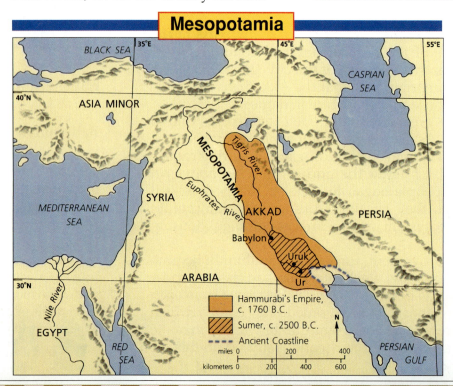

Mesopotamia

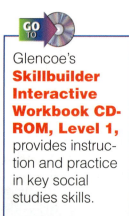

GO TO

Glencoe's **Skillbuilder Interactive Workbook CD-ROM, Level 1,** provides instruction and practice in key social studies skills.

appointed royal judges. Judges who were not honest and witnesses who did not tell the truth were punished.

Hammurabi's code covered almost everything in daily life. A person was believed innocent until proven guilty. Once proven guilty, a person was punished. Punishments ranged from fines to death. There were no prison sentences. Members of the upper class generally were punished more severely than members of the middle or lower classes.

During Hammurabi's rule, Babylon became an important trade center. Babylonians exchanged their *surplus*, or extra, products for money or for goods. People from other parts of the world came to trade, some from as far away as India and China. These traders paid gold and silver for the goods made by Babylonians.

Hammurabi ruled for more than 40 years. His **reign** (rān), or period of power, is known as the Golden Age of Babylon. After his death, however, the Babylonian Empire declined, and Mesopotamia was again divided into a number of small city-states.

Sculpture of a Sumerian Chariot

Reading Check
What did people call the **reign** of Hammurabi?

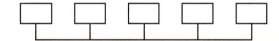

Section 2 Assessment

1. **Define:** empire, culture, reform, reign.
2. What happened to Sumer under Sargon I's rule?
3. How did Hammurabi come to power?

Critical Thinking

4. **Using Reasoned Judgment** What do you think Hammurabi would say about the court system in the United States today?

Graphic Organizer Activity

5. Draw a diagram like this one, and use it to show key events in the life of Hammurabi.

SECTION 3 Contributions

From the beginnings of Sumer until the death of Hammurabi, the influence of Mesopotamia on other civilizations was felt in many ways. Inventions, customs, and ideas of the Sumerian and Babylonian cultures were copied and improved upon by other peoples.

The Sumerians developed the earliest known civilization in the world. Mesopotamia has been called "the cradle of civilization." The oldest written records known are Sumerian. The Sumerians were the first people to write down their laws. Sumerian cuneiform became the model for other people's writing.

The Sumerians also invented many things such as the wheel, which helped transportation. Another was the plow, which made it possible for farmers to grow more food with less effort. Still another was the sailboat, which replaced muscle power with wind power.

The people of Mesopotamia developed a 12-month calendar based on the cycles of the moon. The calendar marked the times for religious festivals and planting.

From Mesopotamia also came contributions in the field of mathematics. The people developed a number system based on 60. From that came the 60-minute hour, 60-second minute, and 360-degree circle. The people of Mesopotamia also used a clock that was operated by controlled drops of water.

Section 3 Assessment

1. Why was Mesopotamia called "the cradle of civilization"?
2. What did the people of Mesopotamia contribute to the field of mathematics?

Critical Thinking

3. **Determining Cause and Effect** How have inventions by the people of Mesopotamia helped shape present-day life?

Graphic Organizer Activity

4. Draw a diagram like this one, and use it to show facts that support this statement: Mesopotamia was "the cradle of civilization."

Cradle of Civilization			
Fact	Fact	Fact	Fact

Chapter Summary & Study Guide

1. Civilization began in an area known as Mesopotamia, located between the Tigris and Euphrates rivers.
2. Sumer was the first known civilization in the world.
3. Sumerian civilization consisted of a series of city-states, the most important of which was Ur.
4. Each Sumerian city-state had its own chief god and government.
5. Sargon I of Akkad created the world's first empire in 2300 B.C.
6. About 1800 B.C., Hammurabi conquered Akkad and Sumer and established the Babylonian Empire.

7. Hammurabi unified the Babylonian Empire by setting up a single code of law and by raising the god of Babylon above all others.
8. Major contributions of the Mesopotamian civilizations include writing, the wheel, the plow, the sailboat, and a number system based on 60.

Self-Check Quiz

Visit the *Human Heritage* Web site at **humanheritage. glencoe.com** and click on *Chapter 3—Self-Check Quiz* to assess your understanding of this chapter.

Assessment

Using Key Terms

Imagine that you are a visitor to ancient Mesopotamia. Use the following words in a letter home in which you describe what you have seen and experienced during your visit.

artisans   culture   empire
ziggurat   priest-kings   scribe
reform   cuneiform   city-state
reign

Understanding Main Ideas

1. Why were the twin rivers important to Sumerian life?
2. Why was the ziggurat important to the Sumerians?
3. Who was Gilgamesh, and why was he important?
4. What did Sargon I accomplish?
5. What trading system did the people of Babylonia use?
6. What changes did Hammurabi bring to Mesopotamia?
7. What happened to people who broke Hammurabi's laws?
8. Why was the sailboat an important invention?

Critical Thinking

1. In what ways do you think your school is similar to or different from the schools in Sumeria?
2. What do you think would have happened to Sumer if it had suffered ten years of drought? How would the kingdom be affected?
3. Why do you think religion played such an important part in Sumerian life?

Graphic Organizer Activity

History Create a chart like this one, and use it to write newspaper headlines that tell the importance of each date to the history of Mesopotamia.

Date	Headline
3500 B.C.	Sumaria established
2300 B.C.	Sargon I creates the world's Empire
1800 B.C.	Hammurabi conquers Akkad & Sumer
1700 B.C.	Tales of Gilgamesh started

Geography in History

Human Systems Babylon became a major trading center. Refer to the map on page 62 and imagine that you are King Hammurabi. You must select the location for another settlement that you hope will also become a trading center. Where would you locate this settlement? Explain.

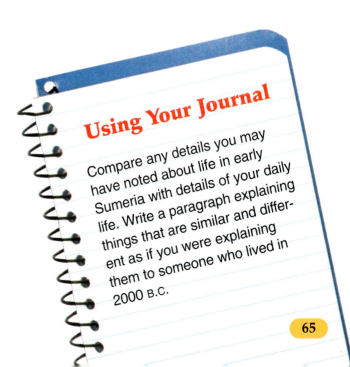

Using Your Journal

Compare any details you may have noted about life in early Sumeria with details of your daily life. Write a paragraph explaining things that are similar and different as if you were explaining them to someone who lived in 2000 B.C.

Egypt
3100 B.C.–671 B.C.

Tutankhamen's
gold mask ▶

▲ Wooden Egyptian sandals

2600 B.C.
Old Kingdom
established

2300 B.C.
Middle Kingdom
begins

1786 B.C.
Hyksos invade
Egypt

1550 B.C.
Ahmose founds
the New
Kingdom

671 B.C.
Assyrians take
over Egypt

Chapter Focus

 Read to Discover

- Why the Nile River was so important to the growth of Egyptian civilization.
- How Egyptian religious beliefs influenced the Old Kingdom.
- What happened during Egypt's Middle Kingdom.
- Why Egyptian civilization grew and then declined during the New Kingdom.
- What the Egyptians contributed to other civilizations.

 Terms to Learn

shadoof
pharaoh
pyramids
embalming
mummy
legend
hieroglyphic
papyrus

 People to Know

Narmer
Ahmose
Thutmose III
Hatshepsut
Amenhotep IV

 Places to Locate

Nile River
Punt
Thebes

Why It's Important   The Egyptians settled in the Nile River valley of northeast Africa. They most likely borrowed ideas such as writing from the Sumerians. However, the Egyptian civilization lasted far longer than the city-states and empires of Mesopotamia. While the people of Mesopotamia fought among themselves, Egypt grew into a rich, powerful, and unified kingdom. The Egyptians built a civilization that lasted for more than 2,000 years and left a lasting influence on the world.

HISTORY Online

Chapter Overview

Visit the *Human Heritage* Web site at **humanheritage.glencoe.com** and click on **Chapter 4—Chapter Overviews** to preview this chapter.

SECTION 1   The Nile

The Nile River flows north 4,145 miles, or 6,671 kilometers, from the mountains of central Africa to the Mediterranean Sea. The last 600 miles, or 960 kilometers, is in Egypt. There, the river cuts a narrow, green valley through the desert. Shortly before the Nile reaches the sea, it branches to form a fan-shaped area of fertile land called a *delta*. Most ancient Egyptians lived in this area. For a long time, they were protected from foreign invasions by the desert, the sea, and waterfalls called *cataracts* (kat' uh rakts).

NILE RIVER   Over thousands of years, the flooding of the Nile River has left rich soil all along its banks. The Nile River valley is only 3 percent of Egypt's land, yet most Egyptians live and work in this area. **What geographical features protected the Egyptians in the Nile River delta?**

The Egyptians had an advantage over the people of the other river valley civilizations. Every year, about the middle of July, the Nile overflowed its banks. The flood waters went down but left behind large amounts of rich soil good for growing crops.

Egyptian farmers planted their fields while the soil was still wet. To water their crops during the dry season, the Egyptians dug out *basins*, or bowl-shaped holes. They used a machine called a **shadoof** (shuh dūf') to lift water from the Nile to the basins. The Egyptians raised flax, wheat, barley, and grapes.

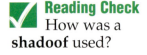

Reading Check
How was a **shadoof** used?

Section 1 Assessment

1. **Define:** shadoof.
2. Where did most Egyptians live?
3. How did the Egyptians control the Nile?

Critical Thinking

4. **Making Comparisons**   How did the Egyptians' use of the Nile River compare with the Sumerians' use of the Tigris and Euphrates rivers?

Graphic Organizer Activity

5. Draw a diagram like this one, and use it to show how the Nile River influenced Egyptian civilization. (Add more lines as needed.)

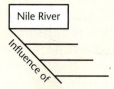

SECTION 2 The Old Kingdom

At first, Egypt was made up of two kingdoms. One was Upper Egypt, which lay in the southern part of the Nile River valley. The other was Lower Egypt, which lay in the north delta.

Narmer, also known as Menes (mē′ nēz), was a king of Upper Egypt. About 3100 B.C., he led his armies from the valley north into the delta. He conquered Lower Egypt and married one of its princesses, uniting the two kingdoms. He wore a double crown, the high white one of the south and the shallow red one of the north. Narmer had many titles. He was called "Lord of Upper and Lower Egypt," "Wearer of Both Crowns," and "Lord of the Two Lands." He set up a new capital at Memphis, a city on the border between Upper and Lower Egypt.

About 2600 B.C., the Old Kingdom started in Egypt. It lasted for nearly 500 years. During the period of the Old Kingdom, Egyptian cities became centers of religion and government. Kings, priests, government officials, and artisans lived there.

Most Egyptians, however, did not live in cities. They lived on large estates along the banks of the Nile. The rich Egyptians who owned these estates lived in wood and brick houses with beautiful gardens and pools. Walls were decorated with brightly

Then... & Now

Diets Change The diet of poor laborers and farmers in ancient Egypt consisted largely of bread, made of wheat and a grain called emmer. Today most villagers and poor city dwellers in Egypt eat a simple diet based on bread and fool, or broad beans. For a typical evening meal, each person dips bread into a large communal bowl of vegetable stew.

EGYPTIAN LIFE   Paintings from tombs offer much information about everyday life in ancient Egypt. Here, a wall painting shows a man and woman plowing and planting their fields. **How did the lives of the rich differ from those of the poor in Egypt?**

Linking Across Time

Harvesting Wheat   Both men and women harvested the wheat crops that helped fuel the growth of ancient Egypt (left). Today some Egyptian farmers still harvest this crop by hand with a sickle (right), much as their ancestors did more than 3,000 years ago. **What is the connection between the flooding of the Nile and the production of wheat?**

colored paintings that showed scenes of daily life. A household was made up of an owner's family, servants, and artisans. The artisans were hired to build boats, weave linen, and make tools and pottery.

Most Egyptians, however, were farmers who lived in villages on the estates. At first, their houses were made of reeds and mud. Later, they were made of sun-baked mud-brick. These houses generally had only one room with a roof made of palm leaves. They were built on high ground so that they would be safe from the yearly flood. Egyptian farmers worked in the fields and took care of the cattle. When they were not farming, they built monuments, dug ditches, and repaired roads.

The Pharaoh

The Egyptians believed that the strength and unity of their country came from having a strong ruler. At first, Egyptian rulers were called kings. Later, they were called **pharaoh** (fār′ ō), meaning "great house." To Egyptians, the pharaoh was a ruler, a priest, and a god. He was the center of Egyptian life and ruled on Earth the way other gods ruled in heaven.

The pharaoh owned all the land in Egypt, but he gave gifts of land to rich Egyptians and priests. To make sure the land produced well, the pharaoh saw to it that dams and irrigation canals were built and repaired. The pharaoh also ordered the building of brick *granaries*, or buildings for storing grain. These were used to store grain from good harvests so people would not starve in times of bad harvests.

✔️ **Reading Check**
How did the Egyptians view the **pharaoh?**

The pharaoh also chose all government officials. They made certain that taxes were gathered and building permits were given out. Trade with other lands was in the pharaoh's hands. The word of a pharaoh was law.

The Egyptians believed that what happened to Egypt depended on the pharaoh's actions. As chief priest, the pharaoh carried out certain rituals. For example, he made the first break in the irrigation dikes each year to open the land to the water. When the water went down, he drove a sacred bull around the capital city. The Egyptians believed this ritual would make the soil rich so they could grow good crops. The pharaoh was the first to cut the ripe grain. Egyptians believed this would bring a good harvest.

Pharaohs were treated with great respect. Whenever they appeared in public, people played music on flutes and cymbals. They also bowed and "smelled the earth," or touched their heads to the ground.

The Pyramids   Another way the people of the Old Kingdom showed how they felt about the pharaohs was by building them great tombs called **pyramids** (pir' uh midz). Because the sun sank in the west, these "Houses of Eternity" were built on the west bank of the Nile. They were designed to protect the pharaohs' bodies from floods, wild animals, and robbers. The Egyptians believed the pharaohs would be happy after death if they had their personal belongings. Therefore, they placed a pharaoh's clothing, weapons, furniture, and jewelry in the pyramids.

A Big Pyramid
The Pyramid of Khufu (see photo) contains more than 2 million stone blocks that average 2 1/2 short tons, or 2.3 metric tons, each. The pyramid originally stood 481 feet, or 147 meters, high. Today its base covers about 13 acres, or 5 hectares.

Reading Check
What was the purpose of the **pyramids?**

PYRAMIDS AT GIZA   The pyramids were built at Giza on the Nile River. The largest pyramid once enshrined the body of King Khufu. **What items were probably buried with the King?**

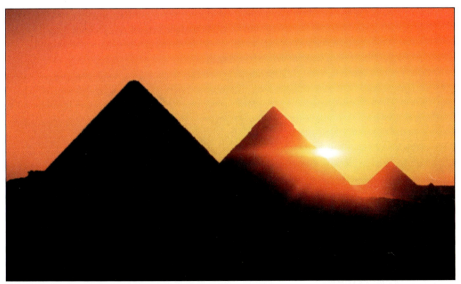

It took many people and much work to build the pyramids. Farmers worked on them during the three summer months that their fields were flooded. The workers used copper tools to cut huge granite and limestone blocks from quarries across the Nile valley or in Upper Egypt. The blocks of rock were tied with ropes onto wooden sleds, pulled to the Nile, placed on barges filled with sand, and floated across the river. Other workers then unloaded the blocks and pulled them to the place where the pyramids were being built. Huge mud and brick ramps were built beside each of the pyramids. The workers dragged the blocks up the ramps to each new layer of the pyramid.

Religious Beliefs

The Egyptians believed in many gods. Two of the most important gods were the river god Hapi (hop' ē) and the sun god Re (rā). The Egyptians depended on the river and the sun. The river brought them water and fertile soil, while the sun helped their crops to grow.

Another important god was Osiris (ō sī ris), god of the harvest and of eternal life. According to Egyptian legend, Osiris was an early pharaoh who gave his people laws and taught them farming. He and his wife Isis (ī'sis) ruled over the dead. The Egyptians believed that the souls of the dead went to the underworld. There, they were weighed on a scale. If a person had led a good life and knew certain magic spells, the scales balanced. Then, Osiris would grant the person life after death. To learn the correct magic spells, Egyptians studied a special book called the *Book of the Dead*.

EGYPTIAN GODS The god Osiris ruled over the Egyptian underworld. Here, he sits in judgment as other animal-headed gods weigh a dead man's soul and record the results. The scales have balanced, so the dead man may enter the underworld. **How did Egyptians prepare for life after death?**

The Egyptians also used a process called **embalming** (em balm' ēng) to preserve the bodies of the dead. At first, they used the process to preserve the body of the pharaoh because they believed the soul could not live without the body. It was important for a pharaoh's soul to live after death. In that way, the pharaoh would continue to take care of Egypt.

Later, embalming was used to preserve other people as well as the pharaoh. To embalm a body, the Egyptians placed it in a wooden box and covered it with a chemical called natron. Natron dried up the water in the body, causing it to shrink. After the shrunken body had dried, it was wrapped with long strips of linen. The wrapped body was known as a **mummy.** The mummy of a poor person was often buried in a cave or in the sand. The mummy of a rich person was placed inside a special case or coffin. The coffin was then placed in a tomb.

Reading Check
Why did the Egyptians develop the practice of **embalming?**

Reading Check
What is a **mummy?**

Section 2 Assessment

1. **Define:** pharaoh, pyramids, embalming, mummy.
2. How did most Egyptians live during the Old Kingdom?
3. What did the Egyptians believe happened to a person after death?

Critical Thinking

4. **Making Comparisons**   How were the pharaohs similar to and different from government leaders of the United States today?

Graphic Organizer Activity

5. Draw this diagram, and use it to compare the Egyptian burial practices for the rich and the poor.

Rich Both Poor

SECTION 3   The Middle Kingdom

About 2300 B.C., government officials, jealous of the pharaoh's power, took control of Egypt. Almost 200 years of confusion followed. Finally, new pharaohs brought peace and a new period called the Middle Kingdom.

Pharaohs had less power in the Middle Kingdom. After death, they were no longer buried in pyramids but in tombs cut into cliffs. Then the Egyptians began to trade with countries beyond the Nile valley.

The Middle Kingdom came to an end in 1786 B.C., when Egypt was invaded by the Hyksos (hik' sōs), a people from western Asia. The Hyksos crossed the desert in horse-drawn chariots and used weapons made of bronze and iron. Egyptians had always fought on foot with weapons made of copper and stone and were defeated.

Egyptian Bronze Art

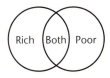

The Hyksos ruled Egypt for about 150 years. They copied some Egyptian customs but most Egyptians hated them. Around 1550 B.C., an Egyptian prince named Ahmose (ah mo' suh), using Hyksos weapons, led an uprising and drove the Hyksos out of Egypt.

Section 3 Assessment

1. How did the Middle Kingdom come about?
2. What ended Hyksos rule?

Critical Thinking

3. **Demonstrating Reasoned Judgment** Do you think the decrease in the pharaohs' power had a positive or negative effect on Egypt? Explain.

Graphic Organizer Activity

4. Draw a diagram like this one, and use it to compare the power of the pharaohs in the Old Kingdom and the Middle Kingdom.

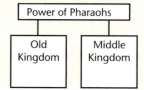

Power of Pharaohs

Old Kingdom — Middle Kingdom

SECTION 4 The New Kingdom

Ahmose founded another line of pharaohs and began the period known as the New Kingdom. During this time, Egypt became richer and its cities grew larger.

During the New Kingdom, most pharaohs were no longer content to remain within the Nile valley but marched their armies into lands to the east. It was during this period that the Egyptian empire was founded. One warrior-pharaoh, Thutmose III (thūt mō' suh), with an army of 20,000 archers, spear throwers, and charioteers, extended Egyptian control into Syria (sir' ē uh) and Palestine (pal' uh stīn).

One of the few pharaohs who was not interested in war and conquest was Hatshepsut (hat shep' sūt), Thutmose III's step-mother, who had ruled Egypt before her stepson. Her chief interests were trade and the building of temples. During her rule, Egyptian traders sailed along the coast of east Africa to the land of Punt. In the land of Punt, the Egyptians traded beads and metal tools and weapons for such things as ivory, a black wood called *ebony* (eb' uh nē), monkeys, hunting dogs, leopard skins, and *incense*, or material burned for its pleasant smell. The Egyptians had never seen most of these things. They welcomed the returning traders with a huge reception.

Religion   The Egyptians of the New Kingdom began to worship a new god. As the god of the city of Thebes, he had been called Amon. When Thebes became the capital of Egypt,

Statue of Hatshepsut

Reading Map Legends

In order to show information on maps, mapmakers use symbols. These are marks that stand for such things as places, directions, and features. Symbols include lines, dots, stars, and small pictures.

A list of symbols and what they stand for is called a **legend.** By reading legends, it is possible to identify empires, nations, religions, climates, and any other information that can be shown on a map.

For example, on the "Ancient Egypt" map below, notice that there are three symbols in the legend. Each symbol stands for the boundary of one of the Egyptian kingdoms. The broken line stands for the southern boundary of the Old Kingdom. The Middle Kingdom's boundary is shown by the dotted line. The area of the New Kingdom is shown in green.

Map Practice

1. **Which Egyptian kingdom included only the first cataract?**
2. **Which kingdom extended to the second cataract?**
3. **In which kingdom was Thebes located?**

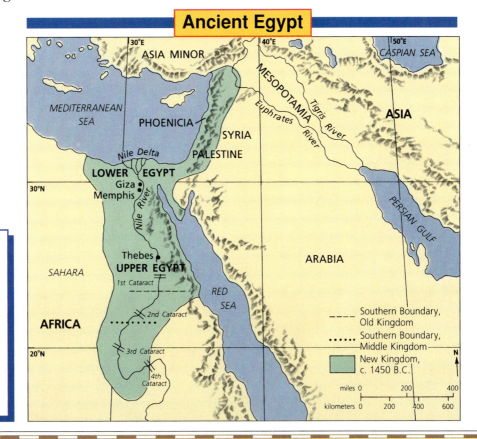

Ancient Egypt

GO TO

Glencoe's **Skillbuilder Interactive Workbook CD-ROM, Level 1,** provides instruction and practice in key social studies skills.

75

TEMPLE AT KOM OMBO   Warring pharaohs of the New Kingdom built large temples to honor their gods. The stone block in front of this temple shows Egyptian hieroglyphs. This temple has many statues and monuments. **Who provided the labor to build temples?**

The Best Dentist
Egyptians could have benefited from regular trips to the dentist. Everyone, rich and poor, suffered from cavities, inflamed gums, and infections. A physician in the Old Kingdom named Hesire won the title of "Chief of the Tooth-doctors."

however, the Egyptians combined Amon with the sun god Re. They called the new god Amon-Re (ah' muhn rā'). Amon-Re became the most powerful god of all. People built many temples in his honor. These were built, in part, by enslaved persons who had been captured by the warring pharaohs.

The temples were more than houses of worship. They were industrial centers. They gave work to sculptors and artisans who carved statues, built furniture, and made clothes for priests. They were treasuries, filled with copper, gold jewelry, glass bottles, bundles of grain, dried fish, and sweet-smelling oils. The temples were also schools—places where young boys were trained to be scribes. The right to become a scribe was passed on from father to son.

Scribes wrote religious works in which were spells, charms, and prayers. They kept records of the pharaohs' laws and lists of the grain and animals paid as taxes. They copied fairy tales and adventure stories and wrote down medical prescriptions.

There were several kinds of Egyptian writing. One was **hieroglyphic** (hī uhr uh glif′ ik), or a kind of writing in which pictures stand for words or sounds. The Egyptians carved and painted hieroglyphs, or picture symbols, on their monuments. However, scribes needed an easier form of writing to keep records. So, they developed two other kinds of writing in which hieroglyphs were rounded off and connected.

Decline of Egypt
Over time, the priests of Amon-Re gained much power and wealth. They owned one third of Egypt's land and began to play a major role in the government. As time passed, the pharaohs' power declined.

Then, about 1370 B.C., a new pharaoh named Amenhotep IV (ah muhn hō′ tep) came to the throne. He did not like the priests. He did not agree with them on what was good for Egypt. He wanted to return power to the pharaohs. Amenhotep IV closed the temples of Amon-Re and fired all temple workers. He set up a new religion that was different from the old religion because only one god was worshiped. This god was called Aton (ah′ tuhn). Amenhotep IV changed his name to Akhenaton (ahk nah′ tuhn), which means "Spirit of Aton." Only his family and close advisers, however, accepted the new religion.

HIEROGLYPHS Ancient Egyptians viewed hieroglyphs as gifts from the gods. The pictures were first used as a way of keeping records. Later, they represented the sounds of spoken language. Here, hieroglyphs are painted on a coffin lid. **How did hieroglyphs differ from cuneiform?**

Reading Check
What was **hieroglyphic** writing?

People in History

Tutankhamen
c. 1369 B.C.–1351 B.C.

Egyptian Pharaoh

Nicknamed the "boy king," Tutankhamen came to power at age 9. He pleased the priests by rejecting Akhenaton's religion. Although frail, he loved to race chariots and hunt animals. When he died at age 18, officials placed him in a treasure-filled tomb. The tomb's beautiful contents, discovered in 1922, made "King Tut" one of Egypt's most famous pharaohs.

After Amenhotep IV died, about 1360 B.C., his son-in-law Tutankhamen (tū tahng kah' muhn) became pharaoh. He was only nine years old. The priests made Tutankhamen return to the old religion. He died after ruling for only nine years.

Little by little, Egypt lost its power. One reason was the struggle between the priests and the pharaohs. Another was the pharaohs' attempts to keep neighboring countries under Egyptian control. Much energy and money was spent on war. Then, too, other peoples of the eastern Mediterranean were using iron weapons. Since Egypt had no iron ore, money was spent to bring in small amounts to make weapons.

By 1150 B.C., Egypt's empire was gone. Egyptian civilization kept growing weaker until Egypt was taken over by a people known as the Assyrians (uh sē' rē uhnz) in 671 B.C.

Section 4 Assessment

1. Define: hieroglyphic.
2. How did rulers of the New Kingdom expand trade?
3. Why did Egypt grow weak?

Critical Thinking

4. Drawing Conclusions   In your opinion, which of the following pharaohs contributed the most to Egyptian civilization: Thutmose III, Hatshepsut, Amenhotep IV, or Tutankhamen? Explain.

Graphic Organizer Activity

5. Draw this diagram, and use it to show important events in the history of the New Kingdom. (Add boxes as needed.)

SECTION 5   Contributions

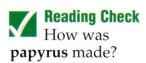
Reading Check
How was **papyrus** made?

The Egyptians made many contributions to other civilizations. One was a paper called **papyrus** (puh pī' ruhs). It was made from a reed also called papyrus. In order to write on papyrus, the Egyptians invented ink. The dry climate of Egypt preserved some writings so well that they can still be read today.

Papyrus had other uses. It was made into baskets and sandals. It was also tied in bundles to make columns for houses. Even rafts and riverboats were made of papyrus.

Other contributions of the Egyptians lay in the field of mathematics. They used a number system based on ten. They also used fractions and whole numbers. They used geometry to *survey*, or measure, land. When floods washed away the boundary markers that separated one field from the next, the Egyptians surveyed the fields to see where one began and the other ended.

The Egyptians knew the Nile flooded about the same time every year. They used this knowledge to make a calendar. The calendar had three seasons of 120 days each, and 5 special feast days for the gods.

The Egyptians also made contributions in the field of medicine. As dentists, eye doctors, animal doctors, and surgeons, Egyptian doctors were the first specialists in medicine. They were

HISTORY Online

Student Web Activity

Visit the *Human Heritage* Web site at **humanheritage.glencoe.com** and click on *Chapter 4— Student Web Activities* to find out more about Egyptian contributions.

MEDICAL PRACTICE IN ANCIENT EGYPT   Egyptian skill in medicine was highly valued in the Mediterranean area for 2,500 years. Here, an Egyptian doctor gives medicine to a patient. The doctor's assistant holds a scroll listing directions for treating the illness. **What kind of medical help did Egyptian doctors give their patients?**

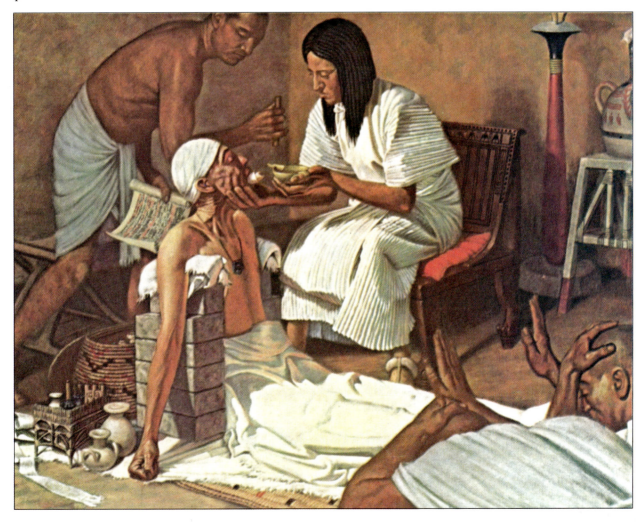

the first to use splints, bandages, and compresses. They were masters at sewing up cuts and at setting broken bones. The Egyptians also treated such problems as indigestion and hair loss. For indigestion, they used castor oil. For hair loss, they used a mixture of dog toes, dates, and a donkey hoof.

Section 5 Assessment

1. **Define:** papyrus.
2. What mathematical contributions did the Egyptians make to civilization?
3. What medical contributions did the Egyptians make to other civilizations?

Critical Thinking

4. **Demonstrating Reasoned Judgment** Which Egyptian contribution do you think has had the greatest impact on life in the United States today?

Graphic Organizer Activity

5. Draw a diagram like this one, and use it to rate Egyptian contributions from most important to least important. (Add lines as needed.)

Most

Least

Chapter Summary & Study Guide

1. Egyptian civilization began in the Nile River valley over 5,000 years ago.
2. About 3100 B.C., Narmer united Upper and Lower Egypt.
3. The Old Kingdom began about 2600 B.C. and lasted for nearly 650 years.
4. Kings of Egypt became known as pharaohs and were viewed by Egyptians as rulers, priests, and gods.
5. During the Old Kingdom, pyramids were built as tombs for pharaohs.
6. The Egyptians worshiped many gods.
7. The Egyptians placed great importance on life after death and created a process to preserve bodies as mummies.
8. The Middle Kingdom began about 1950 B.C. and lasted until the Hyksos invasion of Egypt in 1786 B.C.
9. The New Kingdom began after Ahmose drove the Hyksos out of Egypt about 1550 B.C.
10. During the New Kingdom, most pharaohs were interested in conquest.
11. During the New Kingdom, priests became very powerful.
12. Amenhotep IV tried to establish a religion based on one god, but he failed.
13. Toward the end of the New Kingdom, Egypt began to decline.
14. Egyptian contributions to later civilizations included the use of geometry, surveying, and papyrus.

HISTORY Online

Self-Check Quiz

Visit the *Human Heritage* Web site at **humanheritage. glencoe.com** and click on **Chapter 4—Self-Check Quiz** to assess your understanding of this chapter.

Using Key Terms

Use the following list of words to write a newspaper article describing the contributions of the Egyptians.

sadoof   pharaoh   pyramids
embalming   mummy   legend
hieroglyphic   papyrus

Understanding Main Ideas

1. What did the Egyptians borrow from the Sumerians?
2. What did the Nile River give to the Egyptian people?
3. Why did the Egyptians show such great respect for the pharaoh?
4. What role did the Hyksos play in the development of Egyptian civilization?
5. What role did religion play in Egypt during the Old Kingdom? During the New Kingdom?
6. What kinds of writing did the Egyptians have, and why were they used?
7. What problems did flooding of the Nile River create, and how did the Egyptians try to solve them?
8. How did the Egyptians use the papyrus reed?

Critical Thinking

1. Do you agree with experts who call Egypt "the gift of the Nile"? Explain.
2. How was the government of Egypt similar to that of Babylonia? How was it different?
3. Do you think Amenhotep IV was wise in opposing the priests of Amon-Re? Explain.
4. Would you have liked living in ancient Egypt? Why or why not?

Graphic Organizer Activity

History Create a chart like this one, and use it to compare characteristics of the Old Kingdom, Middle Kingdom, and New Kingdom of Egypt.

Old Kingdom	Middle Kingdom	New Kingdom

Geography in History

Environment and Society Note the area covered by ancient Egypt on the map on page 75. Why do you think the empire developed where it did, rather than expanding to the west or only to the south? Explain your answer.

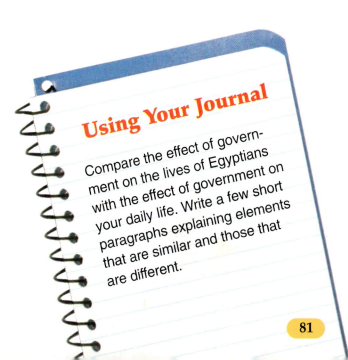

Using Your Journal

Compare the effect of government on the lives of Egyptians with the effect of government on your daily life. Write a few short paragraphs explaining elements that are similar and those that are different.

Eastern River Valleys

2500 B.C.–1000 B.C.

▼ Terra-cotta toy horse

▲ A Harappan necklace

2500 B.C.
Cities appear in Indus River valley

2000 B.C.
Cities appear in Huang Ho valley

1766 B.C.
Shang come to power in China

1200 B.C.
Aryans arrive in Indus River valley

1122 B.C.
Zhou invade Shang kingdom

Chapter Focus

Chapter Overview

Visit the *Human Heritage* Web site at **humanheritage.glencoe.com** and click on **Chapter 5—Chapter Overviews** to preview this chapter.

Read to Discover

- How the Indus River valley civilization developed.
- What has been learned from the ruins of Harappa and Mohenjo-daro.
- How religion influenced the Shang dynasty.
- Why the Shang dynasty declined.

 Terms to Learn

planned
  communities
citadel
dynasty
ancestors
oracle bones
nobles

 People to Know

Harappans
Aryans
Yü the Great
Wu

 Places to Locate

Indus River
Harappa
Mohenjo-daro
Huang Ho
  valley

Why It's Important   By 2500 B.C., cities started to appear in the Indus valley of South Asia. By 2000 B.C., they were being established in the Huang Ho (Yellow River) valley of China.

More isolated than the people of Mesopotamia or Egypt, the people of the eastern river valley civilizations were cut off from other parts of the world by high mountains, broad deserts, and large bodies of water. As a result, they became *self-sufficient*, or able to take care of nearly all their own needs. Compared to the Sumerians and the Egyptians, they did little trading with other parts of the world.

Because few artifacts have been found, much of what is known about the ancient eastern river valley civilizations comes from legends. Even so, available evidence points to unique and rich cultures that continue to interest archaeologists.

SECTION 1 The Indus River Valley

The Indus River flows through the countries known today as Pakistan and India. About 2500 B.C., a group of people called Harappans (huh rap' uhnz) settled in the valley of the Indus River. Although others had lived there before, the Harappans were the first to create a civilization. Harappan civilization extended about 1,000 miles, or 1,600 kilometers, from the foothills of the Himalayas to the Indian Ocean. This area was more than twice the size of either Mesopotamia or Egypt.

The lives of the Harappan people were shaped by the Indus River. The river fertilized the land and made its soil rich. When the river flooded, however, it swept away everything in its path. People had to control the Indus in order to settle near it. To do this, they built dikes and dams. They cleared land for farming and built irrigation systems to bring water to dry areas. They grew barley, wheat, peas, melons, and dates and fished in the river.

The Harappans were the earliest known people to grow cotton. They spun the cotton, wove it into cloth, and dyed it bright colors. They produced cotton cloth hundreds of years before anyone else.

The Indus River influenced the way the Harappans built their cities. To protect cities from floods, the Harappans built them on raised mounds. They used river mud to make bricks, which they baked in the sun. Then they went one step further. They *fired*, or baked, some bricks in *kilns*, or ovens. They used these kiln-dried bricks as a covering over the mud bricks. The fired bricks were stronger and lasted much longer than sun-dried ones. The Harappans used fired bricks for houses and public buildings.

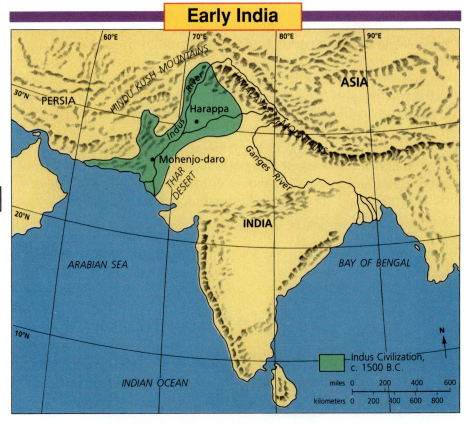

Early India

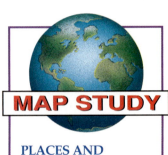

MAP STUDY

PLACES AND REGIONS India is part of the triangle-shaped peninsula that forms the southern part of the continent of Asia. **What geographic features would have helped to protect the people of the Indus River valley from enemies?**

THE GREAT BATH AT MOHENJO-DARO   The people of Mohenjo-daro may have washed themselves at the Great Bath. It measured 40 feet, or 12 meters, long and 23 feet, or 7 meters, wide. To make the Bath watertight, they used cement, tar, and four layers of brick. **What was the purpose of the Great Bath?**

HISTORY Online

Student Web Activity

Visit the *Human Heritage* Web site at **humanheritage.glencoe.com** and click on **Chapter 5— Student Web Activities** to find out more about Harappan civilization.

Harappa and Mohenjo-daro   Harappan civilization centered around two major cities, Harappa and Mohenjo-daro (mōhen′ jō dahr′ ō). These cities were about 400 miles, or 640 kilometers, apart. Many experts believe they were twin capitals.

Harappa and Mohenjo-daro are the oldest examples yet found of **planned communities,** or cities built to a definite plan. Both cities contained hundreds of small buildings. Some buildings served as homes, while others served as shops. The buildings were laid out on a planned street *grid,* or uniform network. The streets crossed each other at almost perfect right angles. The buildings that lined the streets were arranged in blocks of about the same size.

Most buildings were two stories high and were built around a courtyard, which opened into several rooms. Outer walls of buildings had no windows, and walls fronted on narrow lanes in such a way as to break the force of the wind. Almost every building had its own well, bathroom, and drains. The drains carried waste away from the houses and emptied it into drain holes lined with brick. These drains were cleaned often. This sanitation system helped protect the health of the Harappans.

The most important buildings of Harappa and Mohenjo-daro were built high above the houses and shops so as to be safe from neighboring peoples and floods. In each city, a **citadel** (sit′ uh duhl), or fortress, stood on a mound at least 40 feet, or 12 meters, high. It was surrounded by a thick brick wall. Inside the citadel at Mohenjo-daro was a huge watertight tank called the Great Bath. Some experts believe it was used for religious ceremonies. Next to

✓ Reading Check
What are **planned communities?**

✓ Reading Check
Where was a **citadel** located, and what did it look like?

the Great Bath stood a huge granary. Traders from other areas who stopped at Mohenjo-daro most likely left their goods there.

Harappa also had a series of huge granaries. The floor of each granary was supported on low walls. In the walls were air holes that allowed air to move around in the granary. This kept the grain dry and prevented it from spoiling. Nearby were circular brick platforms. Each had a scooped-out area in the center where grain could be pounded.

Decline of the Harappans
No one knows for certain how Harappan civilization came to an end. One reason may have been that the Harappans used up their natural resources. For example, the Harappan farmers may have tried to raise more and more crops on the same plots. This would have robbed the soil of nutrients needed to make it fertile enough to produce well. Without good harvests, there would not have been enough food to feed everyone, especially if the Harappan population was increasing.

Another reason may have been that the Harappans cut down too many trees to fuel their ovens. Without tree cover, floods would have swept away the soil and forced people to leave their cities and farming villages. It is known that parts of Mohenjo-daro had to be rebuilt several times because of floods. At first, the city was rebuilt carefully. As time went on, however, new buildings were not made as well, and older ones were patched up. Then, too, the Harappans may have gotten tired of rebuilding and decided to move somewhere else.

A third reason may have been that the Indus River valley was invaded and all the Harappans were killed. Unburied skeletons of groups of men, women, and children have been found in the streets of Mohenjo-daro's ruins. Every skeleton showed some kind of injury.

All that is certain is that Harappan civilization began to change about 1700 B.C. Not only were homes no longer built as well, but pottery was no longer made as carefully. By 1200 B.C., a group of people called Aryans (ār' ē uhnz) had taken over the Indus River valley. Harappan civilization ceased to be.

Evidence of a Lost Civilization
Very little is known about the Harappan people and their civilization. As yet, no one has been able to read Harappan writing. There is no record of the civilization's political history. No royal tombs have been discovered. All that is known about Harappan religion is that there was more than one god, and most Harappan gods were female.

Much of what is known comes from the ruins of Harappa and Mohenjo-daro. There, archaeologists have found jewelry made of gold and a blue stone called lapis lazuli (lap' uhs laz' uh lē), as

Sculpture of Harappan Priest-King

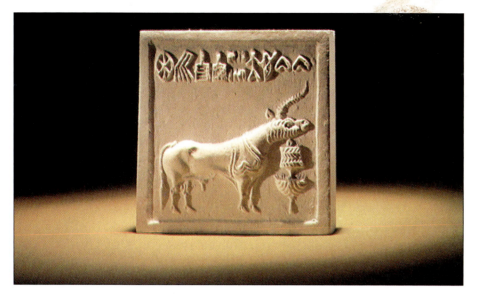

Bangles Today, many people in India and Pakistan wear bangles—ring-shaped bracelets and anklets. So did the Harappans. To find out how the Harappans made their bangles, archaeologists in the 1980s and 1990s turned to present-day bangle makers. Using traditional methods, they gave archaeologists insights into how the Harappan bangle makers might have worked.

HARAPPAN SEAL   This Harappan seal is 1 inch, or 2.5 centimeters, square. It shows a bull facing an incense burner. In eastern civilizations, the bull was a symbol of strength. The seal also shows Harappan writing. **What is unusual about Harappan writing?**

well as tools and weapons of stone, copper, and bronze. They have also found clay models of animals, rattles, dice, and toy carts with movable wheels.

One of the most important finds was a series of tiny seals made of soapstone. An animal and a line of writing were carved on each seal. The animals included tigers, elephants, rhinoceri, and crocodiles. This suggests that at one time much of the area was jungle. Most of the seals had a small hole in them and could be worn as necklaces or bracelets. The seals may have stated the names, titles, or trades of a person, family, or business. Experts believe the seals were used to stamp the wet clay that sealed packages of goods. Some Harappan seals have been found as far away as Sumer.

Section 1 Assessment

1. **Define:** planned communities, citadel.
2. How did the Indus River influence the Harappans?
3. What were some of the outstanding features of Harappa and Mohenjo-daro?

Critical Thinking

4. **Predicting Consequences** What do you think archaeologists would learn about the Harappans if they could read Harappan writing?

Graphic Organizer Activity

5. Draw a diagram like this one, and use it to summarize the accomplishments of the Harappans.

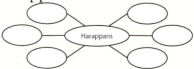

The Huang Ho Valley

About 2000 B.C., or 500 years after the Harappans settled in the Indus River valley, a civilization developed in the Huang Ho valley of northern China. There are no records of its beginnings, and no remains have been found. For this reason, much of what happened comes from legend.

According to Chinese legend, a man-god named Yü the Great drove out the serpents and dragons that lived along the Huang Ho. He drained the land so that people could live there and grow crops. Yü founded a kingdom called Xia (shē′ ah) and united most of northern China under his rule.

Many experts believe that the early settlers of China chose the Huang Ho valley for their home because it was fertile. The river flooded every year, bringing rich soil with it.

The valley was cut off from other civilizations. The people there developed their culture without borrowing from other civilizations. By 1800 B.C., there were villages and farms all along the river. The people farmed the land and used the river for travel and trade. They made clay ovens, cupboards, benches, and pottery. They built small round clay houses with thatched roofs.

Reading Check
What is a **dynasty?**

Cities of the Shang   The first records of Chinese civilization come from a **dynasty** (dī′ nuh stē), or ruling family, called Shang. The Shang came to power in 1766 B.C. They built the first Chinese

---

THE WISE MAN FU HSI   Chinese legends tell the stories of Yü and another man-god, Fu Hsi. Here, Fu Hsi points to eight geometric designs used to tell the future. **Why are legends important to historians studying early China?**

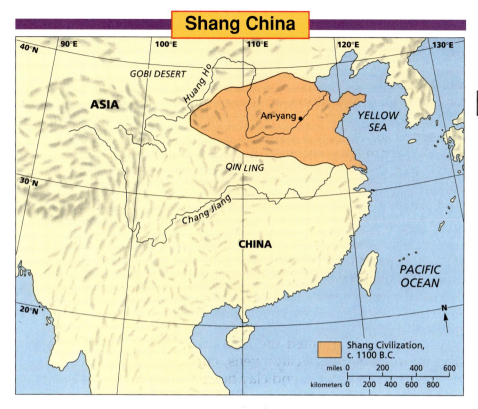

Shang China

GOBI DESERT
ASIA
Huang Ho
An-yang
YELLOW SEA
QIN LING
Chang Jiang
CHINA
PACIFIC OCEAN

Shang Civilization, c. 1100 B.C.

miles 0   200   400   600
kilometers 0   200 400 600 800

MAP STUDY

PLACES AND REGIONS The landforms of China contributed to the early isolation of the Chinese. **What geographical features would have discouraged the Shang people from movement to other lands or their contact with other people?**

cities. Most were designed in the same way. At the center stood a palace and a temple. Public buildings and the homes of high government officials were built around the palace. Within an outer district were workshops, burial grounds, and the homes of the workers.

Most of the Shang people, however, did not live in the city. The city was the home of the rich, the educated, and the skilled. Poorer people lived in the countryside. They were farmers who grew such grains as millet, wheat, and rice and raised cattle, sheep, and chickens. The farmers also produced silk, which was used to make clothes for the very rich. The Chinese produced silk hundreds of years before anyone else.

Spirits, Ancestors, and Kings   The Shang worshiped **spirits,** or supernatural beings, which they believed lived in mountains, rivers, and seas. The people believed they had to please the spirits. If the spirits became angry or unhappy, the people might suffer a poor harvest or lose a battle.

The Shang believed that **ancestors,** or those from whom one is descended, also influenced people's fortunes. So, they offered their ancestors food, wine, and special prayers. They hoped their ancestors would help them in time of need and bring them good fortune. Because of this respect for ancestors, family ties were very important to the Shang. They had rules about how family members should act toward one another. Children were taught to

Reading Check What role did **spirits** play in Shang religion?

Reading Check Why did the Shang respect their **ancestors?**

Reading Check
What were **oracle bones?**
Who were the **nobles,** and what role did they play in the Shang dynasty?

People in History

Wu
c. 1000 B.C.

Zhou King

Wu, the ruler of a former Shang territory, led the attack against the last Shang emperor. The emperor was so cruel that many soldiers gave up without a fight. Wu, known as "the Military King," believed the gods wanted the Zhou dynasty to rule China, and he became the first Zhou ruler.

obey their parents and to honor older people. Wives were trained to obey their husbands.

The Shang believed that their kings received their power from the spirits of nature and their wisdom from their ancestors. For this reason, religion and government were tied closely together. An important duty of kings was to contact the spirits of nature to make sure they provided enough water for farming.

Kings also asked the advice of their ancestors before making important decisions. To do this, kings had questions scratched on a flat, polished piece of bone. The bone had a hole drilled in it, and a hot bar was put in the hole. Heat from the bar produced a pattern of cracks on the bone. The cracks were believed to be the ancestors' replies to a king's questions. A special interpreter gave the king the meaning of the ancestors' replies. These bones are known as **oracle** (ōr′ uh kuhl) **bones.** The writing on them is the oldest known form of Chinese writing.

Under the king was a large class of **nobles,** or people of high rank in a kingdom. They spent much of their time hunting, both for pleasure and as preparation for war. Nobles often fought with each other about land. They joined together only when they had to fight other people who refused to accept Shang rule.

Nobles rode into battle in horse-drawn bronze chariots. They wore bronze helmets and armor made of buffalo or rhinoceros hide. They were skilled in the use of the bow and arrow. Their

ORACLE BONES   Shang rulers tried to learn the future by using oracle bones. Here, a turtle shell used for this purpose shows an early form of Chinese writing. **When did Shang rulers use oracle bones?**

arrows had sharp points of bone or bronze. Soldiers marched on foot behind nobles' chariots. These soldiers generally were poor peasants whom the nobles had forced to leave their farms and join the army.

Decline of the Shang There was a great gap between rich and poor during the rule of the Shang. Rich Shang lived in the cities in wooden houses. They owned bronze weapons and ornaments and wore linen, wool, fur, and silk clothes. Poor Shang lived in the countryside and worked with wooden or stone tools. Their houses were thatched or mud huts or caves scooped out of the ground. Neither group felt any loyalty toward the other.

Many experts believe that this gap between rich and poor weakened the Shang civilization. In 1122 B.C., a people known as Zhou (jō) invaded the Shang kingdom. The Shang were not united enough to hold off the invaders, and their civilization came to an end.

Linking Across Time

Metal Casting Shang metalsmiths perfected a form of casting to create some of the finest bronze works the world has ever known (below). Metalsmiths still use molds to create everything from artworks to machine parts (right). **What conclusions can you draw about Shang technology?**

The Shang left behind a great gift to the rest of the world in their works of bronze. These include sculptures, cups, vases, fancy vessels, and a variety of other items used for religious purposes. Many art experts believe these are among the finest works of bronze ever made.

Section 2 Assessment

1. **Define:** dynasty, spirits, ancestors, oracle bones, nobles.
2. What were some of the Shang religious beliefs?
3. What may have been the reason for the decline of the Shang civilization?

Critical Thinking

4. **Formulating Questions** If world leaders today could use oracle bones, what questions might they want answered before making decisions?

Graphic Organizer Activity

5. Draw a diagram like this one, and use it to show the structure of a typical Shang city.

Chapter Summary & Study Guide

1. The eastern river valley civilizations began in the Indus River valley about 2500 B.C. and in the Huang Ho valley about 2000 B.C.

2. The first people to build a civilization in the Indus River valley were the Harappans.

3. The Harappans are believed to have been the first people to produce cotton cloth, bake bricks in ovens, and build sanitation systems.

4. The Harappan cities of Harappa and Mohenjo-daro are the oldest known planned communities.

5. No one knows for sure how the Harappan civilization ended, but the Aryans moved into and took over the valley about 1200 B.C.

6. The legendary kingdom of Xia probably was established in China about 2000 B.C.

7. The Shang started the first recorded Chinese dynasty around 1766 B.C.

8. The Shang believed spirits and ancestors influenced their lives.

9. The Shang developed the form of writing found on oracle bones and a method of making beautiful bronze artworks.

10. Shang civilization ended with the Zhou invasion of 1122 B.C.

Self-Check Quiz

Visit the *Human Heritage* Web site at **humanheritage. glencoe.com** and click on *Chapter 5—Self-Check Quiz* to assess your understanding of this chapter.

Using Key Terms

Imagine you are preparing a feature film about the civilizations in the Indus River and Huang Ho valleys. Use the following words in a brief summary describing the facts you plan to present in your film.

planned communities   citadel
dynasty   spirits
ancestors   oracle bones
nobles

Understanding Main Ideas

1. Why is so little known about the early life of people in the Indus River and Huang Ho valleys?
2. Why were Harappa and Mohenjo-daro unique places in which to live?
3. What were some of the possible reasons for the decline of the Harappans?
4. What evidence suggests that there was trade between Harappa and Sumer?
5. Why were family ties important to the Shang people?
6. How did Shang kings use oracle bones?
7. Why did the gap between the rich and poor help weaken the Shang?
8. What cultural contribution did the Shang leave to the world?

Critical Thinking

1. Why did people in the eastern river valleys borrow little from people in other regions?
2. What do you think may happen to a civilization if it uses up its natural resources? Why?
3. Do you think people today hold ancestors in the same high regard as the Shang? Explain.

Graphic Organizer Activity

Citizenship Create a diagram like this one, and use it to show the flow of power and authority in the Shang government. Groups that should appear on the chart include: artisans, farmers, king, spirits, ancestors, and nobles. Which group appears at the top? At the bottom?

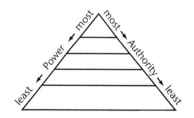

Geography in History

Places and Regions Refer to the map of early India on page 84. Note the location of the Indus civilization and the geographic features that may have affected its development. Describe what other area of this region is a likely place for other civilizations to develop. Explain why.

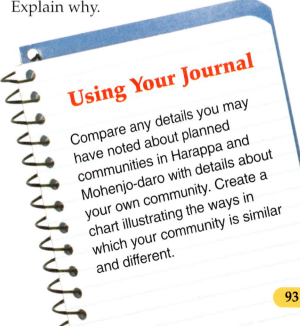

Using Your Journal

Compare any details you may have noted about planned communities in Harappa and Mohenjo-daro with details about your own community. Create a chart illustrating the ways in which your community is similar and different.

THE HITTITES

Around 2000 B.C., the Hittites moved into Asia Minor from an area somewhere beyond the Black Sea. Within the next 700 years, they built an empire that rivaled Egypt in size and power. Although the Hittites adopted many of the customs of the people they conquered, they developed ideas and inventions of their own. One of the most important of these was the Hittite battle chariot—the weapon that allowed the Hittites to challenge the civilizations of Mesopotamia and Egypt.

Hittite Empire

◄ Deeply religious, the Hittites used the fury of the gods to threaten people who broke laws or treaties. A Hittite artist armed this god with a thunder hammer and a handful of jagged lightning bolts.

▲ In 1595 B.C., Hittite armies plunged deep into Mesopotamia to capture the city of Babylon. Although a rebellion forced the Hittite king to return home, Babylon never recovered from the attack. The Hittites went on to take control of lands stretching from the Aegean Sea in the west to the upper Euphrates River in the east.

the World

◄ The Hittites preferred to rule by treaty rather than by force. They recorded the terms of these treaties on gold, silver, or iron tablets written in their own hieroglyphics or in cuneiform adopted from the Babylonians.

Some Hittite battle chariots carried two warriors—a driver and an archer. The larger and heavier battle chariots carried three—a driver and two armed soldiers. This allowed the Hittites to double their fighting power. ▼

The royal seal of a Hittite king was imprinted on this clay tablet. ◄

The Hittites considered the sun goddess, called Arinna, the giver of all life. Known as "Queen of Heaven and Earth," she was honored with works of gold such as this statue. ▶

Taking Another Look

1. Where did the Hittites build their empire?
2. What methods did they use to control their empire?

Hands-on Activity

Writing an Argument Write a list of arguments that an Egyptian soldier might have used to convince the pharaoh to adopt the all-new Hittite battle chariot.

Standardized Test Practice

Directions: Choose the *best* answer to each of the following multiple choice questions. If you have trouble answering a question, use the process of elimination to narrow your choices. Write your answers on a separate piece of paper.

1. **Sumerian society granted certain rights to women. Which of the following rights did Sumerian women have?**

   A They had the right to operate businesses.

   B They had the right to vote in city-state elections.

   C They had the right to attend the same schools as men.

   D They had the right to join the Sumerian army.

   > **Test-Taking Tip:** Eliminate answers that you know are incorrect. Since only the sons of the rich could attend school, you can eliminate answer C.

2. **Which of the following Mesopotamian inventions is still used in agriculture today?**

   F Ziggurats

   G Feed troughs

   H Cuneiform

   J Plows

   > **Test-Taking Tip:** Make sure that you read the question carefully. The question asks for an invention used in *agriculture* (farming). Since *cuneiform* is *Sumerian writing*, it cannot be the correct answer.

3. **The Code of Hammurabi was important because**

   A it punished unfair judges

   B it established one set of laws for all city-states

   C it protected confidential messages sent between judges

   D it required prison sentences for people convicted of crimes

   > **Test-Taking Tip:** Remember to read *all* the answer choices and pick the *best* answer. Although the Code of Hammurabi *did* punish unfair judges, this fact is not the *most important*. Which aspect of the Code was the most significant *change* from previous codes of law?

4. **A major accomplishment of the societies of Mesopotamia and ancient Egypt, which allowed these civilizations to flourish, was**

   F the building of pyramids to honor rulers

   G the teaching of English to children in school

   H the use of waterways to irrigate crops

   J the development of the 60-minute hour

   > **Test-Taking Tip:** The key phrase in this question is: *which allowed these civilizations to flourish*. Some of these accomplishments are certainly important—we still use the 60-minute hour today—but they did not all contribute to the *basic survival* of these two civilizations.

5. **The Mesopotamian, Egyptian, and Indus River valley civilizations arose where they did because**

   A of advice from their religious leaders about where to settle

   B there were so many hunting grounds in North Africa

   C the rivers they settled near provided a means of transportation

   D of the many renewable resources available nearby

   Test-Taking Tip: Think about what these three civilizations had in common (they all settled in river valleys). Why was this geographical feature so important to the development of these societies?

6. **The Egyptians made many contributions to other civilizations. Which of the following was NOT developed by the Egyptians?**

   F papyrus

   G a number system based on ten

   H medical splints and bandages

   J city-states

   Test-Taking Tip: Be careful—overlooking the words NOT or EXCEPT is a common error. Look for the answer that does NOT fit. Since the Egyptians *did* develop papyrus (a type of paper made from reeds), answer F is not the correct choice.

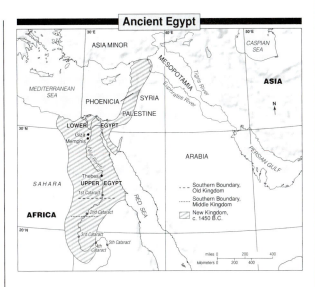
Ancient Egypt

7. **According to the map above,**

   A ancient Egypt did not include Thebes

   B the New Kingdom of Egypt included the Sahara

   C the southern boundary of the Old Kingdom was near the 1st Cataract of the Nile

   D Phoenicia was not part of the New Kingdom of Egypt

   Test-Taking Tip: Use the map's *legend*, or *key*, to help you understand what the map's symbols represent. Make sure your answer is supported by information *on the map*. Do not rely on your memory.

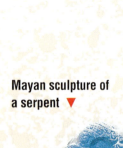

Mayan sculpture of a serpent ▼

◀ Mayan marble mask

3000 B.C.
Farming villages established in Americas

1800 B.C.
Abraham leads some Hebrews into Canaan

1500 B.C.
Phoenicians develop alphabet

522 B.C.
Darius reigns over Persia

200 A.D.
Ghana established

FOLDABLES™
Study Organizer

Comparing Information Study Foldable *Make this foldable to help you compare and contrast Middle Eastern and African and American civilizations.*

Step 1 *Fold one sheet of paper in half from side to side.*

Step 2 *Turn the paper and fold it into thirds.*

Reading and Writing *As you read, take notes about the different civilizations under the appropriate tab. When civilizations share the same characteristics, be sure to write the information under the "Both" tab.*

Step 4 *Cut the top layer only along both fold lines.*

Step 3 *Unfold and draw two overlapping ovals and label them as shown.*

Make the ovals overlap in the middle section.

This will make three tabs.

PRIMARY SOURCES
Library

See pages 678–679 for other primary source readings to accompany Unit 3.

 Read "Machu Picchu is Discovered" from the **World History Primary Source Document Library CD-ROM.**

Journal Notes

What contributions to the modern world were made by civilizations more than 3,000 years ago? Note details about these contributions as you read.

600 A.D.
Mayan civilization reaches its peak

1240 A.D.
Kingdom of Mali established

1438 A.D.
Incan Empire founded

6

The Phoenicians and the Hebrews

1200 B.C.–510 B.C.

▲ Ivory carving of a palm tree

◀ Israelites being led into captivity

1830 B.C.
Phoenician civilization develops

1800 B.C.
Abraham leads some Hebrews to Canaan

1200 B.C.
Hebrews escape enslavement in Egypt

814 B.C.
Carthage is founded

Chapter Focus

 Read to Discover

- How trade helped the Phoenicians and the Hebrews build their civilizations.
- What important cultural contributions were made by the Phoenicians and the Hebrews.
- What religious beliefs were held by the Hebrews.

 Terms to Learn

treaties
holy of holies
colonies
descendants
social justice
judge
psalms
prophets
sabbath

 People to Know

Abraham
Moses
Saul
David
Solomon

🌐 **Places to Locate**

Canaan
Carthage
Jerusalem
Israel
Judah

Why It's Important   At the eastern end of the Mediterranean Sea lies a piece of land shared today by Lebanon (leb' uh nuhn) and Israel. In ancient times, it was the bridge that connected Egypt and Mesopotamia, and it was known as Canaan (kā' nuhn). Soldiers, shepherds, and merchants who passed through Canaan carried new ideas and goods between Egypt and Mesopotamia.

Two groups—the Phoenicians and the Hebrews—settled in Canaan and formed small kingdoms. Each group was interested in trade and in learning. Through these peaceful activities, they made important contributions to later civilizations.

 **HISTORY Online**

Chapter Overview
Visit the *Human Heritage* Web site at <u>humanheritage.glencoe.com</u> and click on ***Chapter 6—Chapter Overviews*** to preview this chapter.

SECTION 1 The Phoenicians

The Phoenicians lived in the northern part of Canaan. Most of what is known about them comes from the Bible, the writings of other ancient peoples, and the ruins of their cities and ships.

The Phoenician people were part of a larger group known as the Canaanites (kā' nuh nīts). The Canaanites came from the desert south and east of Canaan. They were herders who wandered from pasture to pasture. Another group—the Philistines (fil' uh stēnz)—lived in southern Canaan along the Mediterranean coast. They came from the eastern Mediterranean near Greece. The Philistines were traders and shipbuilders.

The Growth of Trade

By 1200 B.C., the Phoenicians had built cities and towns along a narrow strip of land between the mountains and the sea. Although the land was rich, there was not enough to grow food for all of the people. For this reason, many Phoenicians turned to the sea to make a living.

The mountains near Phoenicia were covered with cedar forests. These forests provided wood that the Phoenicians used to build strong, fast ships. The Phoenicians started out as coastal traders. In time, they became widely traveled merchant shippers who controlled the trade of the Mediterranean. They exchanged cedar logs, cloth, glass trinkets, and perfume for gold and other metals. Many Phoenician ships were traveling workshops. Sailors who were also artisans carried their tools with them and worked onboard the ships.

Phoenician sailors and explorers plotted their courses by the sun and stars. They traveled to places where no one else dared to go. They brought Middle Eastern culture to unexplored areas of the western Mediterranean. Some experts believe the Phoeni-

Linking Across Time

Glass Making   Artisans along the Phoenician coast discovered the art of glassblowing in the 1st century B.C. (below). This revolutionary technique remained in wide use until the late 1800s A.D. and is considered an art form today (right). **What role did Phoenician trade play in spreading new ideas?**

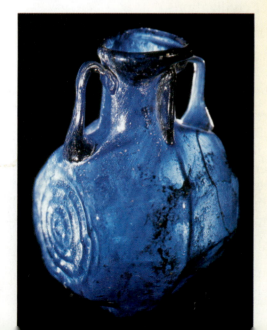

cians actually sailed around the west coast of Africa to India. They may even have sailed across the Atlantic Ocean to the Americas 2,000 years before Christopher Columbus.

From their business dealings, the Phoenicians learned the value of making agreements. They used the same idea to keep peace with their larger, more powerful neighbors. They signed peace **treaties,** or agreements between states or countries, in which they promised to supply free shipments of goods. In exchange for these shipments, the other countries agreed to guarantee Phoenician independence.

✅ **Reading Check**
How did the Phoenicians use **treaties** to keep the peace?

The Cities of Phoenicia

Phoenicia never became a united country. Mountains separated one group of Phoenicians from another. The only contact was through narrow mountain passes or by sea. As a result, Phoenicia remained a collection of independent city-states. The largest of these were Tyre (tīuhr), Byblos (bib' lus), Beirut (bā rūt'), and Sidon (sīd' uhn).

Though the people of all of these city-states spoke the same language and practiced the same religion, they did not always get along. The search for more profit from trade led to jealousy and quarrels among the city-states. The Phoenicians called themselves by the names of their city-states. Only people from other places called them Phoenicians.

At first, each city-state was ruled by a king who also served as high priest. In time, rich merchant families made the kings share their power with councils of merchants. Soon, the councils were telling the kings what to do.

Most Phoenician cities had stone walls around them for protection. Behind these walls stood the family-owned shops of merchants and artisans. Shopkeepers sold their goods outside their shops. Since wood was plentiful, many of the Phoenicians were carpenters and cabinetmakers. They were also very good at metalwork, which they learned from the Egyptians and the Mesopotamians.

Phoenician cities were very crowded. Streets were narrow and buildings were close together. Most buildings were made of stone or brick and had high narrow doors, windows, columns, and tiled roofs. Some houses had roof gardens.

Outside the walls of the city stood the port. It was the center of activity. Ships docked to load and unload goods. Phoenician merchants kept records of shipments of papyrus, gold, and linen from Egypt, pottery from Mesopotamia, and copper and hides from Cyprus (sī' pruhs). Goods were stored in great warehouses until they went to market in Phoenicia or were shipped overseas.

Phoenician cities were also important cloth-dyeing centers. The Phoenicians made an expensive purple dye that was in great demand. In fact, the name "Phoenician" means "of purple merchants." According to legend, a Phoenician god named

Book Names The name *Byblos* comes from a Greek word meaning "book." The Greeks gave the city its name because of the large amount of papyrus it exported. The English word *Bible* comes from the same term. The Bible, however, refers to Byblos by its original name—Gebal, a city inhabited since 7000 B.C.

PHOENICIAN TOMB   The Phoenicians offered human sacrifices to please their gods. Inside this underground burial chamber at Carthage are clay urns that hold the ashes of victims who were sacrificed. **Why were human and animal sacrifices made to the Phoenician gods?**

Melqart (mel' kart) was walking along the seashore with his girl-friend Tyrus (tī' rus) and a dog. When the dog picked up a shell-fish called *murex* (myuhr' eks) and bit into it, the dog's mouth turned purple. Tyrus liked the color so much that she said she would not marry Melqart unless he gave her a gown of that color. Melqart gave her the gown and started the dye-making trade in Phoenicia.

Gods and Goddesses   The Phoenicians believed in many gods who were closely tied to nature. Since they thought the gods met people only on hills and under trees, they worshiped only in these places at first. Later, they built temples. Each had an entrance hall, a main hall, and a **holy of holies,** or most sacred chamber, where the image or sacred stone of the god was kept. Sacrifices of wine, perfume, animals, and humans were made on a nearby stone altar. Only priests could offer these sacrifices. It was thought that this strengthened the power of the gods and kept them friendly toward people.

The Phoenicians believed in a life after death. At first, they buried their dead in clay *urns* (ernz), or ornamental vases. Later, influenced by Egyptian customs, they embalmed the bodies, wrapped them in linen, and placed them in stone coffins in hillside cemeteries.

Reading Check
What was the **holy of holies?**

Carthage   Some Phoenician sailors and traders set up trading posts along the coast of North Africa. Other Phoenicians built **colonies,** or permanent settlements, in these areas. These colonies soon turned into cities.

The most famous of these cities was Carthage (kar′ thij), founded in 814 B.C. in present-day Tunisia (tū nē′ zhē uh). Legend states the city was founded by a Phoenician princess named Dido (dī′ dō). At first Dido ruled the city of Tyre. Her brother, however, thought that he should rule Tyre. So, he killed Dido's husband and overthrew Dido. She fled to North Africa where she and her followers built Carthage.

Carthage soon became a Mediterranean power. It was a great trading city. Ships from Carthage may have traveled to the British Isles in search of tin, a metal highly valued by merchants.

The Alphabet   Through trade, the Phoenicians spread ideas as well as goods. Their most important gift was the idea of an alphabet. The Phoenicians did not invent the alphabet. They did, however, pass it on to other cultures.

At first, the Phoenicians used a system of picture writing. However, it was difficult to keep trade records this way. So, they looked for an easier writing system. They borrowed a simple version of Egyptian hieroglyphs from the people of the Canaanite towns that lay to the south. By the time the Canaanite system of writing reached Phoenicia, it had become an alphabet.

✓ **Reading Check**
Where did the Phoenicians build **colonies?**

HISTORY *Online*

Student Web Activity
Visit the *Human Heritage* Web site at humanheritage.glencoe.com and click on *Chapter 6—Student Web Activities* to find out more about Phoenician accomplishments.

ALPHABETS   This chart shows how different alphabets developed from the Phoenician alphabet. The characters of the alphabets closely resemble each other. **On whose system of writing did the Phoenicians base their alphabet?**

Modern Characters	Ancient Phoenician	Ancient Hebrew	Ancient Greek	Early Roman	Greek Names
A	∀ ∀	∀	⊿ A A	M Λ A	Alpha
B	⅂ 9	⅄ 9	⅃ Ɛ	ß B	Beta
G	⌐ ⌐	⌐ ⌐	⟨ Γ ⌐⌐	C G	Gamma
D	◁ ◁	◁ ◁	⊿ ◁ ᴘ	⊿ D	Delta
E	⅃	⅃	⅃ ᖴ Є	E	Epsilon
F	⌐	⅄	ᖴ ⅄ ⌐	F	Digamma
Z	Z	—	Ɩ	Z	Zeta
HE	⽥	E	⊟ H	H	Eta
TH	⊘	—	☉	—	Theta
I	⌐ ⌐	⅀	⌒ ⟨	Ɩ	Iota

The Canaanite system of writing had 22 symbols, or letters, from which any number of words could be formed. Since it was easy to use, the Canaanite system provided the writing system Phoenician traders needed for keeping records.

The Phoenicians made the Canaanite alphabet their own. They carried it to Europe, where the Greeks borrowed it and made a few changes. Later, the Romans borrowed it from the Greeks. Most western alphabets, including the English, are based on the Roman alphabet.

Section 1 Assessment

1. **Define:** treaties, holy of holies, colonies.
2. Why did the Phoenicians turn to trade to make a living?
3. How did the Phoenicians view their gods?

Critical Thinking

4. **Making Generalizations** Why is the alphabet a major contribution to civilization?

Graphic Organizer Activity

5. Draw a diagram like this one, and use it to show the causes and effects of the rise of Phoenician trade.

| Causes | → | Rise of Phoenician Trade | → | Effects |

SECTION 2 The Hebrews

Like the Phoenicians, the Hebrews, or Israelites, were a small group among the peoples of the ancient Middle East. Because of their religion, however, they have had a great influence on the world's civilizations. Their religion still exists today. It is called Judaism (jū′ dē iz uhm).

Most early Hebrews were *nomadic* (nō mad′ ik), or wandering, herders; some were traveling merchants. Leading long trains of donkeys loaded with goods, these merchants walked from one trading post to the next. The Hebrews followed a route that started from the city of Ur on the Euphrates River. There, Hebrew artisans made goods from gold, copper, and ivory. Hebrew merchants then stuffed the goods into bags, loaded them on donkeys, and started up the valley of the Tigris and Euphrates. At Harran (hah rahn′), a city near the Turkish mountains, they exchanged their goods for silver. Sometimes, merchants continued west and then south along the Mediterranean coast to trade with Egyptian, Phoenician, and Cretan (krēt′ uhn) merchants.

Israelite Ivory Box

ABRAHAM   Abraham taught the Hebrews to worship Yahweh. Here, Abraham is shown leading the Hebrews on their journey from Ur to Canaan. **Why did the Hebrews eventually leave Canaan?**

The God of Abraham

The story of the Hebrews and their god is written in the Bible. It states that Yahweh (yah′ wā), or God, made an agreement with Abraham. Abraham and his followers were to leave Ur and go to Canaan. There, they were to worship and obey Yahweh as the one true god. In exchange, Yahweh promised that they and their **descendants,** or offspring such as children, grandchildren, great-grandchildren, and so on, could always live in Canaan.

During ancient times, most people believed in many gods. These gods behaved like humans but were more powerful. The Hebrews, however, believed that Yahweh was different from humans. He did not get hungry or thirsty, marry, or have children. According to the Hebrews, Yahweh did only what was just and right, even though He was powerful and could do whatever He wanted.

Abraham and members of his household settled in Canaan around 1800 B.C. In Canaan, they raised flocks of sheep and grew wheat, figs, and olives. Abraham's grandson, Jacob, had 12 sons. Each son led a separate family group. These Hebrew groups later formed 12 Hebrew tribes. The Hebrews stayed in Canaan for about 100 years. Then, a drought came, and they went to Egypt where they could get food.

Reading Check
What did the agreement with Yahweh promise the **descendants** of Abraham's followers?

Reading A Map Scale

Maps provide many kinds of information. One thing maps can show is distance, or how far one point on a map is from another. To do this, most maps have a scale.

A map scale shows the relationship between the distances on the map and the actual distances on Earth. The length of a scale represents a certain number of miles or kilometers on Earth. Using this scale, it is possible to figure actual distances between any two points on this map.

For example, to figure the distance between the cities of Beirut and Tyre, use a ruler to measure how far apart they are. Now, compare this length with the map scale. Since Beirut and Tyre are about one-half inch, or 1.3 centimeters, apart on the map, the actual distance between them on Earth is about 50 miles, or 80 kilometers.

Map Practice

1. **What is the distance between Sidon and Damascus?**
2. **From north to south, how long is the Dead Sea?**
3. **How far is it from Jerusalem to Beirut?**

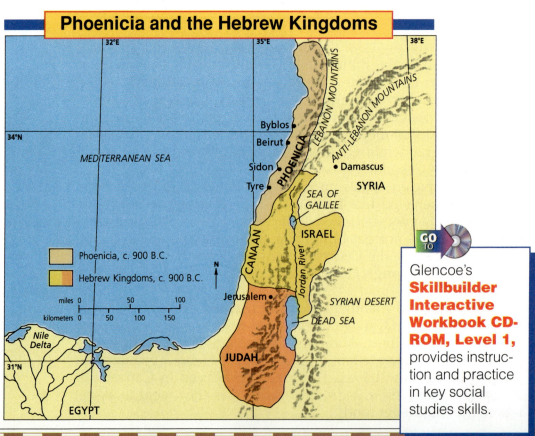

Phoenicia and the Hebrew Kingdoms

MOSES   According to the Bible, Yahweh allowed Moses and the Hebrews to pass through the Red Sea. The waters then closed again, drowning the pharaoh and his army. **What important set of laws did God give Moses on Mount Sinai?**

Moses and the Ten Commandments   After the Hebrews settled in Egypt, they were enslaved. About 600 years later, Moses, the Hebrew leader at the time, appeared before the pharaoh and told him to end Hebrew enslavement and let the Hebrews leave Egypt. The pharaoh at first refused but later agreed. Moses then led the Hebrews out of Egypt. The pharaoh again changed his mind and led his army in pursuit. According to the Bible, Yahweh parted the Red Sea to allow the Hebrews to cross and they escaped into the Sinai (sī′ nī) Desert. They called their escape the *Exodus* (ek′ suh duhs).

Life in the desert was hard, but Moses told the Hebrews not to give up. Moses led them to Mount Sinai. There, he climbed to the top of the mountain to receive a message from God. The Bible states that Yahweh told Moses that He would protect the Hebrews and lead them back to Canaan. In return, they were to renew the *covenant* (kuv′ uh nuhnt), or agreement, with Him. They were to promise to obey certain laws, the most important of which became the Ten Commandments.

The Ten Commandments stated that the Hebrews were to give their loyalty only to Yahweh. They were not to worship other gods or idols (ī′ dls). The Ten Commandments also taught that it was wrong to lie, steal, or murder, and that people should honor their parents and respect other people's property.

The Hebrews believed God was just, and they too should be just. They used laws to influence the way people behaved. Their

Ramses II No one knows for sure, but many scholars believe that Ramses II was the pharaoh who tried to stop the flight of Moses and the Hebrews out of Egypt. Ramses ruled Egypt for nearly 70 years and outlived a dozen of his sons.

Moses
C. 1300 B.C.–1200 B.C

Hebrew Prophet

During the Hebrew enslavement, the pharoah ordered the death of all Hebrew male infants. To save her son, Moses' mother put him in a papyrus basket and floated him down the Nile. Pharoah's daughter rescued the baby and raised him as her own. Moses later fled Egypt and worked as a shepherd until about age 80, when according to the Bible, Yahweh instructed him to free his people.

laws affected not only individuals but the whole community. The Hebrews believed in **social justice.** Everyone had a right to be treated fairly.

The Promised Land

Moses died shortly before the Hebrews reached Canaan. The Hebrews were afraid that without a strong leader they would not be able to enter Canaan. The people who already lived there had built many walled cities on hilltops. Soldiers in lookout towers guarded the cities against enemy attack. However, Joshua, a new leader and a good general, brought the Hebrews safely into the promised land.

Once they had settled in Canaan, the Hebrews became farmers and shepherds. They copied the Canaanites' tools and borrowed their alphabet. Canaan was rocky and dry. There was little water. So, during the two months of the rainy season, farmers collected and stored water in small caves or underground basins. During the dry season, they used what they had stored to irrigate their crops of olives, flax, barley, wheat, and grapes.

Most Hebrews lived in one-room houses. The room was divided in two, with one section slightly higher than the other. During the day, people cooked and did other household chores in the lower level. At night, donkeys and goats bedded down there, while the family slept on the upper level. The walls of the houses

HARVEST IN ANCIENT ISRAEL Hebrew writers called Canaan "a land flowing with milk and honey." This area, however, had a dry climate and little water. The Hebrews had to work hard to farm the land. Hebrew farmers and their workers gathering the harvest are shown in this painting. **What crops did the Hebrews grow in Canaan?**

Making Comparisons

CRITICAL THINKING SKILLS

Suppose you want to buy a portable compact disc (CD) player, and you must choose among three models. You would probably compare characteristics of the three models, such as price, sound quality, and size to figure out which model is best for you. In the study of world history, you often compare people from different cultures or regions. You might also compare people and events from one time period with those from a different time period.

Learning the Skill When making comparisons, you examine two or more groups, situations, events, or documents. Then you identify any similarities and differences. For example, the chart on this page compares the characteristics of two ancient civilizations.

When making comparisons, you first decide what items will be compared and determine which characteristics you will use to compare them. Then you identify similarities and differences in these characteristics.

PHOENICIAN AND HEBREW CIVILIZATIONS

CULTURAL CHARACTERISTIC	PHOENICIANS	HEBREWS
Homeland	*Canaan*	Canaan
Political organization	*city-states*	12 tribes
Method of rule	*kings/merchant councils*	kings/council of elders
Main occupations	*artisans, merchants, shippers*	herders, farmers, traders
Religion	*belief in many gods closely tied to nature*	belief in one all-powerful god
Main contribution	*spread of an alphabet*	idea of a single, just god

GO TO Glencoe's **Skillbuilder Interactive Workbook CD-ROM, Level 1,** provides instruction and practice in key social studies skills.

were made of mud-brick or stone plastered with mud and white-washed. Floors were made of beaten clay. Wooden beams supported a flat, thatched roof, which was covered with clay.

Kings

After Joshua died the 12 Hebrew tribes split apart. Each tribe was led by a council of elders. In times of crisis, a temporary leader called a **judge** settled disputes and led troops into battle.

In time, the Hebrews decided they needed a king to unite them. A warrior-farmer named Saul became their first king. He ruled well for several years. Toward the end of his reign, however, he lost the people's support. When Saul died in battle, David became the new king.

David reunited the Hebrews and defeated the Canaanites. He captured a Canaanite fortress and on that site established Jerusalem (juh rū' suh luhm), the capital of the Hebrew kingdom. A fine musician, David wrote many of the **psalms** (sahms), or sacred songs, found in the Bible.

After David died, his son Solomon (sahl' uh muhn) became king. Through trade and treaties with other lands, Solomon brought peace and made the Hebrew kingdom more powerful. He built a huge temple in Jerusalem out of limestone, cedar wood, and gold. It was designed and built by artisans from Phoenicia.

Solomon's wealth and wisdom became known all through the Middle East. Many Hebrews, however, were not happy with Solomon. They did not like working on his building projects or paying the high taxes he demanded. After Solomon died, the Hebrews in the northern part of the country set up their own separate kingdom called Israel. A southern kingdom, which was ruled from Jerusalem, became known as Judah. For nearly 200 years, the two kingdoms fought each other off and on. Gradually, both became weak enough for others to conquer.

The Prophets

Prophets, or persons claiming to have messages from God, appeared in the Hebrew kingdoms. They came from cities and villages. They were teachers, farmers, and shepherds. They criticized the way the Hebrews were living. The rich were mistreating the poor, and government officials were accepting bribes. The prophets reminded the Hebrews of their duty to God and to one another. They warned the Hebrews that Yahweh would punish them if they did not return to His ways.

Some prophets added a new meaning to the laws of Moses. They taught that Yahweh was the god not only of Hebrews, but of everyone.

The people refused to listen to the prophets' warnings. Then, it was too late. Powerful neighbors took over the Hebrew kingdoms. After 722 B.C., the Israelites, the people of the northern kingdom, disappeared. Although the Judeans survived, most were forced to move to Babylonia in 586 B.C.

✓ Reading Check What was the role of a Hebrew **judge**?

✓ Reading Check Who wrote many of the **psalms** found in the Bible?

✓ Reading Check Who were the **prophets**, and what message did they deliver?

While in Babylonia, the Judeans, or Jews, made changes in their religion. Having lost the great temple at Jerusalem, they had to find some other way to worship God. They began meeting in small groups on the **sabbath,** or day of rest. The groups would pray and talk about their religion and history. The Jews wrote down their laws, sayings, and stories of the past on scrolls. The study of these writings led the Jews to value learning, and their teachers became important leaders.

The Jews spent 70 years in Babylonia before they were allowed to return to their homeland. They rebuilt Jerusalem and the temple. Under a scribe named Ezra, they wrote down the laws of Moses in five books called the *Torah* (tor′ uh). Other writings were added later to make the Old Testament of the Bible.

✓ **Reading Check** What did Jews do on the **sabbath**?

HEBREW PROPHETS

Name	Teachings
Elijah c. 850 B.C.	Everyone should behave in a moral way.
Amos c. 755 B.C.	Prayers and sacrifices do not make up for bad deeds. Behaving justly is much more important than ritual.
Hosea 745-730 B.C.	God is a god of love and compassion who loves His people the way a father loves his children. God suffers when people turn from Him and do not follow His commandments.
Isaiah of Jerusalem 740-701 B.C.	People can have peace and prosperity only if they carry out God's will. The future depends on how justly one behaves in the present.
Micah 714-700 B.C.	Both rich and poor have to obey God's laws. It is important to "do justly, love mercy, and walk humbly with thy God."
Jeremiah 626-587 B.C.	Suffering is the result of wickedness. God will make a new covenant with the Jews in the future.
Ezekiel 593-571 B.C.	People are responsible for their own behavior.
Isaiah of Babylon c. 545 B.C.	God is the god of all people. God will free Israel and lead it back to the promised land.

Major Contributions   The Hebrews were the first people to believe in one god. At first, they believed God was concerned only about them. They expected other people to worship many gods. Later, some prophets said God cared about all peoples and all nations.

The Hebrews were the first to believe in a just god. They believed individuals and society should likewise be just. Their laws were designed to teach people to treat one another fairly.

Section 2 Assessment

1. **Define:** descendants, social justice, judge, psalms, prophets, sabbath.
2. Where did the Hebrews trade? What goods did they trade?
3. What new ideas did the Hebrews develop and contribute to later civilizations?

Critical Thinking

4. **Demonstrating Reasoned Judgment** How was the Hebrew belief in one god important to civilization?

Graphic Organizer Activity

5. Draw a diagram like this one, and use it to show milestones in the history of the Hebrews. (Add boxes as needed.)

Chapter Summary & Study Guide

1. Phoenician civilization began to develop about 1830 B.C.
2. Phoenicians earned a living from the sea and from trade items such as cedar and purple dye.
3. One of the most important Phoenician contributions was the spread of an alphabet.
4. The Phoenicians set up colonies along the North African coast, including Carthage, founded in 814 B.C.
5. According to the Bible, God made an agreement with Abraham whereby the Hebrews could always live in Canaan if they would worship Him alone.
6. About 1200 B.C., the Hebrews escaped Egyptian bondage and, under Moses' leadership, made a new covenant with God, promising to obey the Ten Commandments.
7. An important Hebrew contribution was the belief in a single just god and a just society.

HISTORY *Online*

Self-Check Quiz

Visit the *Human Heritage* Web site at **humanheritage. glencoe.com** and click on *Chapter 6—Self-Check Quiz* to assess your understanding of this chapter.

CHAPTER 6 Assessment

Using Key Terms

Imagine that you are a traveler to Canaan. Use the following words to write a letter home explaining the new ideas that you have learned about during your visit.

treaties   holy of holies   colonies
descendants   social justice   judge
psalms   prophets   sabbath

Understanding Main Ideas

1. Why were the Phoenicians successful long-distance sailors?
2. What were some of the features of a Phoenician city-state?
3. According to the Bible, what agreement did Yahweh make with Abraham?
4. Why did the Hebrews believe in social justice?
5. Why did the Hebrews make changes in their religion while living in Babylonia?

Critical Thinking

1. How can people who have very limited natural resources still manage to earn a living?
2. Why were language and religion by themselves not enough to unify the Phoenician people?
3. How does the idea that God is just affect the way people behave?
4. Explain the phrase, "Do justly, love mercy, and walk humbly with thy God."
5. Why do you think many people during this time believed that people should listen to prophets?

Graphic Organizer Activity

Culture Create a diagram like this one, and use it to compare Phoenician and Hebrew religious beliefs and practices.

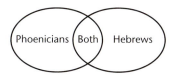

Geography in History

Places and Regions The Hebrews moved from place to place within the same region along the Mediterranean Sea. Choose one of their migrations and describe the geography and features of the land through which they passed. Then make a map showing the route and the geographic features of their migration.

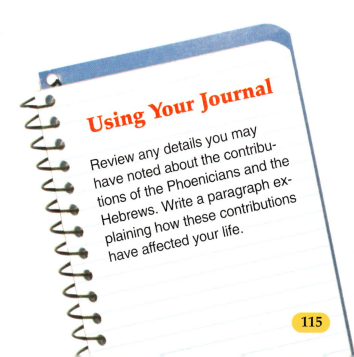

Using Your Journal

Review any details you may have noted about the contributions of the Phoenicians and the Hebrews. Write a paragraph explaining how these contributions have affected your life.

Military Empires

1400 B.C.–570 B.C.

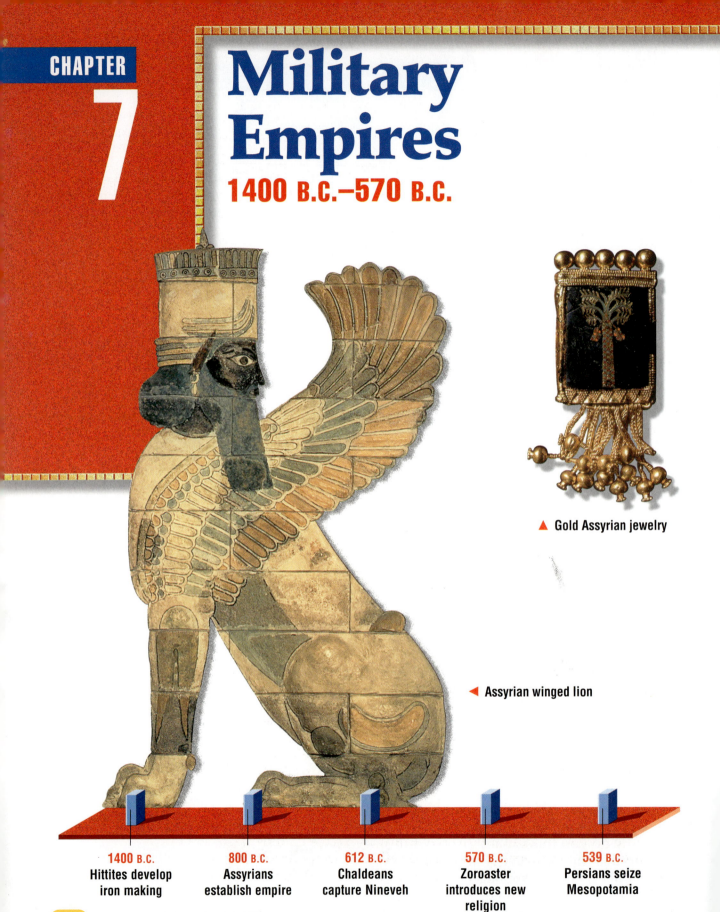

▲ Gold Assyrian jewelry

◀ Assyrian winged lion

1400 B.C.
Hittites develop
iron making

800 B.C.
Assyrians
establish empire

612 B.C.
Chaldeans
capture Nineveh

570 B.C.
Zoroaster
introduces new
religion

539 B.C.
Persians seize
Mesopotamia

Chapter Focus

 Read to Discover

- How the Assyrians established and maintained an empire in Mesopotamia.
- What the Chaldean city of Babylon was like.
- How the Persians were able to rule an empire that stretched from Egypt to India.

 **Chapter Overview**

Visit the *Human Heritage* Web site at **humanheritage.glencoe.com** and click on ***Chapter 7—Chapter Overviews*** to preview this chapter.

 Terms to Learn

empires
smelting
provinces
caravans
astronomers

People to Know

Ashurbanipal
Nebuchadnezzar
Cyrus
Darius
Zoroaster

 Places to Locate

Nineveh
Babylon
Persepolis
Lydia

Why It's Important While the Phoenicians and the Hebrews were developing their civilizations, powerful kingdoms rose and fell in Mesopotamia. Built by the Assyrians, the Chaldeans (kal dē´ uhns), and the Persians, these kingdoms were not content to stay where their civilizations began. Rulers raised large armies and expanded into neighboring lands. They developed new ways of organizing their **empires**—territories governed by a single ruler or nation. They also increased trade. Through conquest and trade, these three empire-builders spread their ideas and customs over a wide area.

 **Reading Check**
Which people used large armies to build powerful **empires** in Mesopotamia?

SECTION 1 The Assyrians

About 1,000 years after Hammurabi ruled, a people called Assyrians rose to power in Mesopotamia. Their country, Assyria, lay in the upper part of the Tigris River valley. The Assyrians spoke the same language and used the same writing system as the Babylonians.

The Assyrians were warriors. Experts believe their liking for war was influenced by geography. Assyria's rolling hills and rain-watered valleys did not provide protection against invaders. Assyrian shepherds and farmers had to learn to fight to survive. In time, fighting became a way of life.

The Assyrians built a powerful army. By 1100 B.C., they had defeated their neighboring enemies. By 800 B.C., they were strong enough to take over cities, trading routes, and fortresses throughout Mesopotamia.

ASSYRIAN SOLDIERS   Assyrian kings often celebrated their victories by decorating palaces and temples with scenes of warfare. Here, a wall sculpture shows Assyrian soldiers. **How was the Assyrian army organized?**

The Assyrian Army

The Assyrian army was well-organized. It was divided into groups of foot soldiers armed with shields, helmets, spears, and daggers. It also had units of charioteers, cavalry, and archers.

At first, the Assyrians fought only during summer when they did not have to be concerned about planting or harvesting crops. Later, as they took over more land, soldiering became a year-round job. When the Assyrians needed more soldiers, they hired them from other places or forced the people they had conquered to serve.

Assyrian power was due partly to their weapons, which were made of iron. Iron weapons are harder and stronger than weapons made of copper or tin. Iron had been used in the Middle East for many centuries. Until about 1400 B.C., however, it was too soft to be made into weapons. Then, a people called Hittites (hi' tītz) developed a process of **smelting.** They heated iron ore, hammered out its impurities, and rapidly cooled it. The Assyrians borrowed the skill of smelting from the Hittites.

The Assyrians were cruel warriors. For several hundred years, their armies spread death and destruction throughout the Middle East. They were especially skilled in attacking cities. They tunneled under walls or climbed over them on ladders. They used beams mounted on movable platforms to ram holes through city gates. Once they captured a city, they set fire to its buildings and carried away its citizens and goods.

Anyone who resisted Assyrian rule was punished. Those who did not resist had to pay heavy taxes. The Assyrians also

✓ **Reading Check**
How did the process of **smelting** work?

found a way to conquer people without fighting. They spread stories of their cruelty. Other people were so frightened by the stories that they would simply surrender.

Kings and Government   Assyria's kings were strong leaders. They had to be to rule an empire that extended from the Persian Gulf in the east to the Nile valley in the west. Assyrian kings spent much of their time fighting battles and punishing enemies. However, they were also involved in peaceful activities. A great Assyrian king, Ashurbanipal (osh uhr bon' uh pol), started one of the world's first libraries. It held 25,000 tablets of hymns, stories, and biographies.

Assyrian kings had to control many peoples spread over a large area. To do this, they divided their empire into **provinces,** or political districts. They then chose officials to govern each province. The officials collected taxes and made certain the king's laws were obeyed.

All provinces were connected by a system of roads. Although only roads near major cities were paved, all were level enough for carts and chariots to travel on. Over the roads moved the trade of the empire. Government soldiers were posted at stations along the

Reading Check
Why did the Assyrians divide their empire into **provinces**?

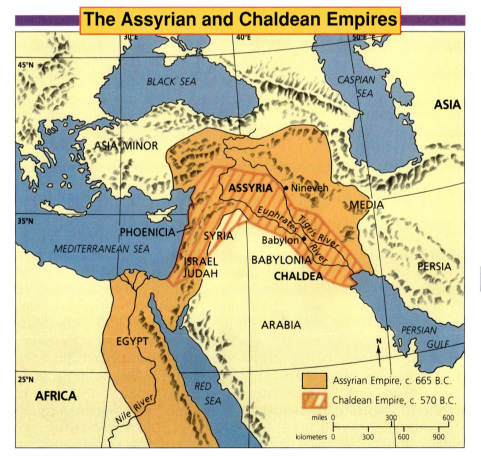

The Assyrian and Chaldean Empires

BLACK SEA

CASPIAN SEA

ASIA

ASIA MINOR

ASSYRIA • Nineveh

MEDIA

PHOENICIA

SYRIA

Euphrates River

Tigris River

MEDITERRANEAN SEA

Babylon •

ISRAEL
JUDAH

BABYLONIA

CHALDEA

PERSIA

ARABIA

PERSIAN GULF

EGYPT

N

AFRICA

RED SEA

Nile River

Assyrian Empire, c. 665 B.C.

Chaldean Empire, c. 570 B.C.

miles 0   300   600
kilometers 0   300   600   900

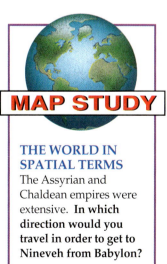

MAP STUDY

THE WORLD IN SPATIAL TERMS
The Assyrian and Chaldean empires were extensive. **In which direction would you travel in order to get to Nineveh from Babylon?**

roads to protect traders from bandits. Messengers on government business used the stations to rest and to change horses.

In time, the empire became too large to govern. After Ashurbanipal died, various conquered peoples worked to end Assyrian rule. One group was the Chaldeans. In 612 B.C., they captured Nineveh (nin' uh vuh), the Assyrian capital. The Assyrian Empire crumbled shortly after.

Section 1 Assessment

1. **Define:** empire, smelting, provinces.
2. How was Assyria governed?
3. Why did the Assyrian Empire fall?

Critical Thinking

4. **Forming Conclusions** Do you think ruling by fear is an effective way to govern? Why or why not?

Graphic Organizer Activity

5. Draw a diagram like this one, and use it to show the cause and effects of the Assyrian warrior way of life.

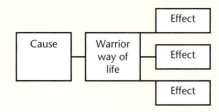

SECTION 2 The Chaldeans

Like the Assyrians, the Chaldeans were warriors who conquered many different peoples. Under their king Nebuchadnezzar (neb uh kuhd nez' uhr), they extended their empire's boundaries as far west as Syria and Palestine. The Chaldeans called themselves Babylonians. This was because most Chaldeans were descendants of the people who made up Hammurabi's empire about 1,200 years earlier. They built a new capital at Babylon in which nearly 1 million people lived.

Babylon was the world's richest city up to that time. It had its own police force and postal system. Huge brick walls encircled the city. The walls were so wide that two chariots could pass on the road on top. Archers guarded the approaches to the city from towers built into the walls.

In the center of the city stood palaces and temples. A huge ziggurat reached more than 300 feet, or over 90 meters, into the sky. When the sun shone, its gold roof could be seen for miles.

The richness of the ziggurat was equaled by that of the king's palace. The palace had "hanging gardens." These were layered beds of earth planted with large trees and masses of flowering vines and shrubs. They seemed to hang in mid-air. Nebuchadnezzar built the gardens to please his wife, who missed the mountains and plants of her native land.

Seven Wonders Historians of the time counted the Hanging Gardens of Babylon among the Seven Wonders of the World. Other wonders included: the pyramids of Egypt, the statue of Zeus at Olympia, the temple of Artemis (Diana) at Ephesus, the mausoleum at Halicarnassus, the Colossus of Rhodes, and the lighthouse at Pharos.

To please the people, Nebuchadnezzar built a beautiful street near the palace. It was paved with limestone and marble and lined by walls of blue glazed tile. Each spring, thousands of pilgrims crowded into Babylon to watch a gold statue of the god Marduk (mar′ duhk) being wheeled along this street. The Chaldeans believed that the procession would make their crops grow. They also believed it would help keep peace in the empire.

Outside the center of Babylon stood houses and marketplaces. There, artisans made pottery, cloth, and baskets. These were sold to passing **caravans,** or groups of traveling merchants. Traders came to Babylon from as far away as India and Egypt. Trade helped make Babylon rich.

Reading Check
How did **caravans** help Babylon grow rich?

ENTRANCE TO BABYLON   The Ishtar Gate was ancient Babylon's main entrance. It honored the goddess Ishtar and was covered with images of wild animals. **Why was Babylon surrounded by walls with gates?**

Babylon was also a center of science. Chaldean **astronomers,** or people who collect, study, and explain facts about the heavenly bodies, believed that changes in the sky revealed the plans of the gods. So, they studied the stars, planets, and moon. Once they knew the movement of heavenly bodies, they made maps that showed the positions of the planets and the phases of the moon. Chaldean astronomers made one of the first sundials. They also were the first to have a seven-day week.

Babylon was the center of a great civilization for many years. As time passed, though, the Chaldeans began to lose their power. They found it hard to control the peoples they had conquered. Then, in 539 B.C., Persians from the mountains to the northeast captured Babylon. Mesopotamia became just another part of the Persian Empire.

Section 2 Assessment

1. **Define:** caravans, astronomers.
2. What did the Chaldean astronomers contribute to science?
3. What led to the fall of the Chaldean Empire?

Critical Thinking

4. **Identifying Alternatives** Under whose rule—the Assyrians' or the Chaldeans'—would you have preferred to live? Explain.

Graphic Organizer Activity

5. Draw a diagram like this one, and use it to describe Babylon.

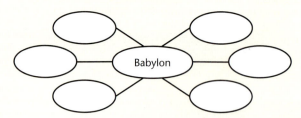

SECTION 3 The Persians

Originally, the Persians were part of the people known as Aryans. The Aryans were cattle herders from the grasslands of central Asia. About 2000 B.C., however, the Persians began to separate from other Aryans. They finally settled on a high plain between the Persian Gulf and the Caspian Sea, where they established Persia. Today, this region is called Iran (i ran'), or "the land of the Aryans." Modern Persians are Iranians (ir ā' nē uhnz).

The Persians lived peacefully in the highlands for over 1,000 years. They divided most of the country into large farms owned by nobles. The nobles spent most of their time riding horses and practicing archery. Their farms were worked by laborers.

There was little water on the hot plain. Farmers depended on streams that came down from the mountains. They dug underground tunnels from the springs to the fields. With water, farm-

Linking Across Time

Coins   The practice of showing portraits (below) or symbols on coins stretches back to the Lydians, who invented the use of coins, and the Persians, who spread their use. In 2000, the United States government issued a new one-dollar coin with the portrait of Sacajawea (far right). **Why do archaeologists and historians consider coins a valuable source of evidence about the past?**

ers were able to grow wheat and barley and to pasture flocks of fat-tailed sheep.

Army and Empire

About 600 B.C., the Persians were conquered by the Medes (mēdz), a neighboring people. The Medes, however, were soon overthrown by the Persians under King Cyrus (sī′ ruhs). Cyrus then organized an army to conquer new territory. The army grew until it numbered in the hundreds of thousands. Its officers were Persians, while its soldiers were either Persians or conquered peoples.

The best fighters in the Persian army were the Immortals. They earned this name because their number never fell below 10,000. When an Immortal became sick, was wounded, or died, another soldier took his place. The Immortals had the honor of leading the Persian army into battle.

Within a short time, the Persians ruled an empire that stretched from Egypt to India. The Persians were mild rulers who allowed their subjects to keep their own language, religion, and laws. The Persians believed loyalty could be won more easily with fairness than with fear or force. They wanted their subjects to pay taxes and to produce goods for trade. They felt these things would not be done if those under their rule were treated badly.

One of the strongest Persian kings was Darius (duh rī′ uhs). He wanted a monument to honor his military victories. So, he brought artisans from many lands to build a grand palace-fortress-treasury in the capital city of Persepolis (puhr sep′ uh luhs). Buildings with many columns were constructed on giant stone

HISTORY Online

Student Web Activity
Visit the *Human Heritage* Web site at **humanheritage.glencoe.com** and click on *Chapter 7— Student Web Activities* to find out more about Persian contributions.

Darius
c. 558 B.C.–486 B.C.

Persian King

Darius organized a vast empire. He wanted conquered people to pay taxes and to supply soldiers, but he respected their customs. He allowed the Jews to rebuild their temple in Jerusalem and consulted with Egyptian priests and Greek oracles in Asia Minor. However, he did not involve citizens in government. That innovation belonged to the Greek city-states that would challenge Darius near the end of his life.

platforms. In the gateways, workers carved figures that were half human and half beast. Persepolis became the most magnificent city in the empire.

Government Officials   The king did not govern alone. There were many officials to carry out his orders. They all spoke Aramaic (ar uh mā′ ik). This was the language used by Middle Eastern merchants.

The king chose a governor, a secretary, and a general for each of the 20 provinces of the empire. These officials collected taxes of gold, silver, sheep, horses, wheat, and spices and sent them to the royal treasury in Persepolis. These officials also settled local quarrels and protected the people against bandits. Each reported separately to the king. This helped keep them honest. If one was stealing tax money, for example, the others were sure to report it. The king would then remove the dishonest official from office.

Another group of officials was the inspectors. Called "the Eyes and Ears of the King," they traveled throughout the empire. They decided whether people were able to pay their taxes. They also checked on rumors of possible rebellion. The inspectors never warned provincial officials they were coming. This made provincial officials careful about doing a good job.

The last group of officials was the judges. They made sure that the king's laws were carried out properly.

Family Life   The Persians lived in houses with pointed roofs and porches that faced the sun. Poor families had one-room houses. Noble families had houses with one set of rooms for men and another for women and children.

Persian families were large. Fathers ruled their families in much the same way the king ruled the empire. A father's word was law. Poor children worked with their parents. The children of nobles, however, were cared for by their mothers until they were five years old. Then, they were raised by enslaved people. Often, they did not see their fathers until they reached adulthood. Boys were trained to ride horses and draw a bow. Girls were trained to run households and raise children.

Rich women lived very sheltered lives. They spent most of their time at home apart from the men. If they had to leave the house, they stepped into a closed *litter,* or a carriage without wheels that was carried by servants. Poor women had more freedom, but they had to work hard.

Religion   At first, the Persians worshiped many gods. Then, about 570 B.C., a religious leader named Zoroaster (zōr′ uh was tuhr) told the Persians about two gods. One god, Ahura Mazda (uh hūr′ uh maz′ duh), was wise and truthful. He created all good things in the world. The other god, Ahriman (ar′ i muhn), made all evil things in the world. Ahura Mazda and Ahriman were at war with each other all of the time.

Zoroaster said human beings had to decide which god they would support. Zoroaster then listed the good and bad deeds a person performed. Good deeds were keeping one's word, giving to the poor, working the land, obeying the king, and treating others well. Bad deeds included being lazy, proud, or greedy. Zoroaster could tell from the list which god a person had chosen. He believed that in the end Ahura Mazda would defeat Ahriman. People who supported Ahura Mazda would enjoy happiness after death. Those who supported Ahriman would be punished.

Trade   The Persians thought they should be warriors, farmers, or shepherds. They refused to become traders. They believed that trade forced people to lie, cheat, and be greedy. They did, however, encourage trade among all peoples they conquered.

The Persians improved and expanded the system of roads begun by the Assyrians. One road, the Royal Road, ran more than 1,600 miles, or more than 2,560 kilometers. A journey that took three months before the Royal Road was built took only 15 days after it was completed. The Persians also opened a caravan route to China. Silk was first brought west along this route.

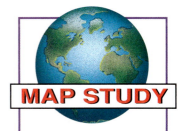

MAP STUDY

THE WORLD IN SPATIAL TERMS
The Persian Empire stretched from the Nile River to the Indus River, a distance of 3,000 miles, or 4,800 kilometers. Within this empire, the Persians ruled more than 50 million people. **Into what continents did the Persian Empire extend?**

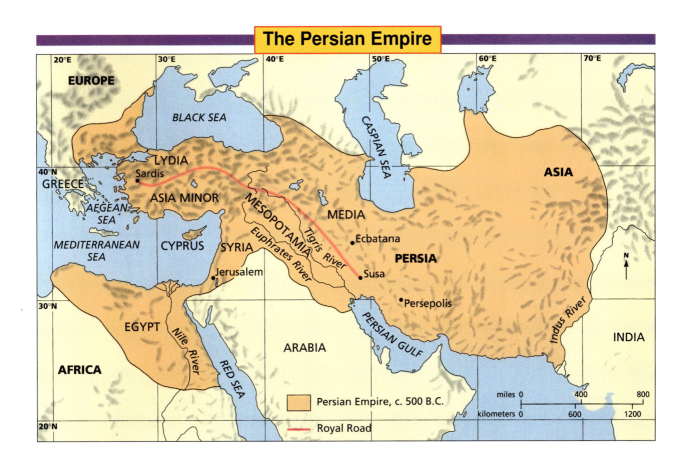

The Persian Empire

EUROPE
BLACK SEA
LYDIA
Sardis
GREECE
ASIA MINOR
AEGEAN SEA
MEDITERRANEAN SEA
CYPRUS
SYRIA
Jerusalem
EGYPT
Nile River
RED SEA
AFRICA
ARABIA
MESOPOTAMIA
Euphrates River
Tigris River
CASPIAN SEA
MEDIA
Ecbatana
PERSIA
Susa
Persepolis
PERSIAN GULF
ASIA
Indus River
INDIA

Persian Empire, c. 500 B.C.
Royal Road

miles 0   400   800
kilometers 0   600   1200

The Persians spread the idea of using coins for money. The first known coins had been made in Lydia (lid′ ē uh), a tiny kingdom in Asia Minor bordering on the Aegean Sea. After conquering Lydia, the Persian king decided to use gold coins in his empire. This helped to increase trade. It also changed the nature of trade. Merchants who had sold only costly goods began to sell everyday, cheaper things as well. They sold chickens, dried fish, furniture, clothing, and pots and pans. Since people could get more goods, they began to live better than they had before.

Section 3 Assessment

1. How did the Persians treat people they conquered?
2. What religious ideas did Zoroaster introduce to Persia?
3. In what ways did the Persians contribute to the growth of trade within their empire?

Critical Thinking

4. **Making Comparisons** How do the roles of government officials in the United States compare with the roles of government officials in Persia?

Graphic Organizer Activity

5. Draw a diagram like this one, and use it to describe the government, economy, and religion of the Persian Empire.

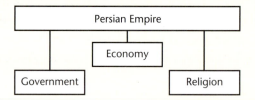

Chapter Summary & Study Guide

1. About 800 B.C., the Assyrians built an empire in Mesopotamia.
2. The Assyrians used the Hittite process of smelting to make strong iron weapons.
3. The Assyrian Empire was divided into provinces linked by roads.
4. In 612 B.C., the Chaldeans captured the Assyrian capital of Nineveh.
5. Under Nebuchadnezzar, the Chaldeans built a new capital at Babylon, which quickly became a center of trade and science.
6. Around 539 B.C., the Persians added Mesopotamia to their empire.
7. The Persians divided their empire into provinces, each governed by various groups of officials.
8. About 570 B.C., Zoroaster taught a new religion in which good and evil took the form of two gods who were constantly fighting each other.
9. Though the Persians did not become traders themselves, they encouraged trade within their far-flung empire.

Self-Check Quiz

Visit the *Human Heritage* Web site at **humanheritage. glencoe.com** and click on **Chapter 7—Self-Check Quiz** to assess your understanding of this chapter.

Assessment

Using Key Terms

Imagine you are writing a feature magazine article about the Assyrian and Chaldean empires. Use the following words in your article to describe some of the achievements made in these two empires.

empires   smelting   provinces
caravans   astronomers

Understanding Main Ideas

1. What do experts believe influenced the Assyrians to become warriors?
2. What made the Assyrians such feared fighters?
3. Why did the Chaldeans call themselves Babylonians?
4. What was the importance of the god Marduk to the Babylonians?
5. What was the relationship between the Persians and the Aryans?
6. In Persian government, who were "the Eyes and Ears of the King," and what did they do?
7. How was family life in Persia alike for both the rich and poor?
8. Why did the Persians refuse to become traders?

Critical Thinking

1. How can the reputation of a group like the Assyrians affect how others act toward that group?
2. How did the introduction of coins affect trade?
3. How would you describe the Persian attitude toward trade, and how wise was this policy?

4. In which of the empires discussed in this chapter would you have chosen to live? Explain.

Graphic Organizer Activity

Citizenship Create a diagram like this one, and use it to compare the governments of the Assyrian and Persian Empires.

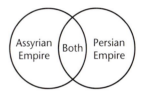

Assyrian Empire   Both   Persian Empire

 ## Geography in History

Environment and Society What changes in their environment did the Persians make that extended ideas started by the Assyrians and Chaldeans? Explain your answer.

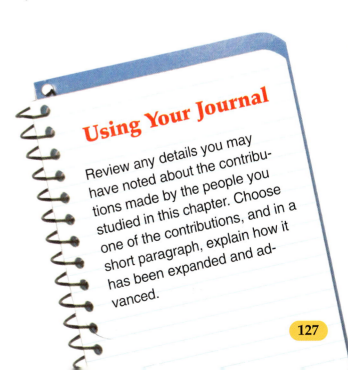

Using Your Journal

Review any details you may have noted about the contributions made by the people you studied in this chapter. Choose one of the contributions, and in a short paragraph, explain how it has been expanded and advanced.

Africa & the Americas

2000 B.C.–1500 A.D.

◀ Terra-cotta horse and rider from Mali

▲ Gold Ashanti disc from Mali

750 B.C.
Kushites conquer Egypt

500 B.C.
Mayan civilization begins

200 A.D.
Ghana founded

700 A.D.
Shona settle in Zimbabwe

1240 A.D.
Kingdom of Mali established

1400 A.D.
Aztec Empire prospers

Chapter Overview
Visit the *Human Heritage* Web site
at **humanheritage.glencoe.com**
and click on ***Chapter 8—Chapter
Overviews*** to preview this chapter.

Chapter Focus

 Read to Discover

- How the ancient African civilizations of Kush and Aksum passed along elements of their culture.
- How West African kingdoms and East African civilizations grew because of trade.
- How Native Americans developed farming and other skills.
- What kinds of civilizations developed in Mesoamerica.
- What life was like for the Inca of South America.

 Terms to Learn

silent barter
pilgrimage
population
  explosion
quipus

 People to Know

Kashta
Piankhi
Ezana
Sundiata Keita
Mansa Musa
Sunni Ali
Askia
  Muhammad
Montezuma II
Pachacuti

🌎 **Places to Locate**

Meroë
Timbuktu
Zimbabwe
Bering Strait
Tenochtitlán
Kilwa

Why It's Important While armies carved out empires in the Middle East, civilizations developed in Africa south of the Sahara and in the Americas. Through conquest and trade, Africans and early Americans built great kingdoms and empires that rivaled civilizations elsewhere in the world.

SECTION 1 Ancient African Kingdoms

Other civilizations besides Egypt flourished in ancient Africa. Archaeologists have discovered enough remains to know what these African civilizations were like.

Kush The first of these African civilizations was Kush. It lay south of Egypt on the Nile River in present-day Sudan (sūdan′). Its history began about 2000 B.C. At that time, the Kushites were nomadic cattle herders. They grazed long-horned cattle on a *savannah* (suh van′ uh), or grassy plain.

During the New Kingdom, Egyptian armies conquered Kush. Kush remained part of Egypt for almost 500 years. Over time, the Kushites learned many things from the Egyptians. They learned to worship the god Amon-Re. They learned how to work copper and bronze. They changed Egyptian hieroglyphs to fit their own language.

About 1160 B.C., Egypt's power declined. In time, the Kushites won back their independence. They set up a capital at Napata (nap' uht uh). From Napata, they sent caravans into Egypt. These caravans carried gold, ivory, ebony, and other goods to trade.

About 750 B.C., the Kushite king Kashta (kahsh' tuh) set out to conquer Egypt. He led his cavalry into Egypt and took some territory. His son Piankhi (pyahng' kē) completed the conquest and founded a dynasty that ruled Egypt for 70 years. However, during the 600s B.C., the Assyrians invaded Egypt. Armed with iron weapons, they drove the Kushites back to the south.

Despite their losses, the Kushites gained something from the Assyrians. They learned the secret of iron-smelting. Soon, Kushite farmers, using iron hoes, were growing large amounts of grain. Kushite blacksmiths were making iron knives and spears, which they exchanged for cotton textiles and other goods from India, Arabia, and China. Kush became a great trading nation.

Around 540 B.C., the Kushites moved their capital to Meroë (mār' ō ē). The city was on the Nile, which provided an avenue

A Brave Queen One warrior-queen of Meroë, Amanirenas, challenged the Romans who seized Egypt after the death of Cleopatra. The Romans eventually drove Amanirenas back into Meroë, but she fought valiantly and her deeds are recorded in Greek and Roman histories of the time.

KUSHITE PYRAMIDS The Kushites copied many elements of Egyptian art, language, and religion. The pyramids near the cities of Meroë and Napata are imitations of Egyptian pyramids. The Kushite pyramids are smaller, however, and have more steeply sloped sides. **What happened to the city of Meroë?**

for trade and transportation. Nearby were large deposits of iron ore and trees to fuel smelting furnaces. Meroë also lay in the center of good grazing land.

In Meroë, there was a huge temple dedicated to Amon-Re, with a long avenue of stone rams leading to its entrance. Sandstone palaces and houses of red brick filled the city. Walls of buildings were tiled in blue and yellow or covered with paintings. Small pyramids stood in the royal cemetery. Smelting furnaces poured forth huge columns of smoke, and around the furnaces lay heaps of shiny black *slag,* or waste from smelting.

Kush remained a great trading country for some 600 years, and then began to decline. As it declined, another kingdom rose to take its place. This was Aksum in present-day Ethiopia. About 350 A.D., Aksumite armies burned Meroë to the ground.

Aksumite Stone Monument

Aksum   Like Kush, Aksum was a trading country. Through ports on the Red Sea, Aksumite merchants served as middlemen for countries on the Mediterranean and in the Far East. They imported silks, spices, and elephants from India. They exported gold, ivory, and enslaved people from Africa. Jewish, Greek, and Arab merchants settled in Aksum.

It was most likely the Greeks who brought Christianity to Aksum. Emperor Ezana (ex zah' nuh), whose armies had destroyed Meroë, converted to Christianity in 324 A.D. This heritage was passed down to the present day.

Aksumites achieved many things. They developed a writing system. They learned to farm on *terraces* (ter' is uhz), or raised levels of land. They minted gold coins and built stone monuments 60 feet, or 18 meters, tall.

Over time, Aksum's power as a trading country began to decline. This was because other kingdoms began to interfere with Aksum's trade. After Arab armies swept across North Africa in the 600s A.D., the Aksumites retreated toward the *interior,* or inland areas, of their country. There, they lived in isolation for more than 1,000 years.

Section 1 Assessment

1. How did the Kushites and Egyptians influence each other?

2. Why did the Kushites choose Meroë as their capital?

Critical Thinking

3. Making Generalizations   How were the kingdoms of Kush and Aksum influenced by other cultures?

Graphic Organizer Activity

4. Draw a diagram like this one, and use it to show the effects of iron-smelting on Kush. (Add boxes as needed.)

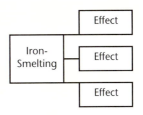

Several large trading kingdoms arose in West Africa after 400 A.D. Their rise was aided by the knowledge of iron-smelting. This was most likely brought to West Africa by *refugees,* or people who flee for safety, from Kush.

Ghana

The first of these trading kingdoms was Ghana (gah' nuh). Legend has it that Ghana was founded about 200 A.D. Around 350 A.D., the Ghanians learned how to smelt iron. With iron swords and lances, Ghanian warriors expanded the boundaries of their country. They also gained control over West Africa's major trade routes.

Along these trade routes, goods were carried by caravans of camels or donkeys. The most important goods were salt and gold. Caravans carried salt south from Taghaza (tuh gah' zuh) in present-day Algeria (al jir' ē uh). They returned north with gold from Wangara (wahn gar' uh), an area southwest of Ghana.

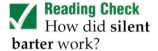

Reading Check
How did **silent barter** work?

Ghanian merchants and Wangara gold miners used a trading technique called **silent barter.** Ghanian merchants would travel to a trading site along a river in Wangara. They would place salt and other goods on the ground and beat drums to signal the gold miners. Then, they would withdraw. Next, the gold miners would appear, look at the goods, and leave some gold. Then, they would withdraw. If the Ghanians thought they had received enough gold, they would take it and leave. If not, they would withdraw and wait for the miners to leave more gold. When the exchange was over, the Ghanians would trade the gold to merchants from North Africa. Often, the gold was shipped to Europe and Asia for sale.

Only gold dust could be used in trade. Nuggets became the property of the king, who controlled the economy. Legend has it that one nugget was so heavy that it served as a hitching post for the king's horses.

In 1042 A.D., Arabs from North Africa started a war against Ghana. They destroyed the capital and made the Ghanians give them tribute. Ghana managed to regain its independence but was not strong enough to survive.

Photograph of Camel Caravan

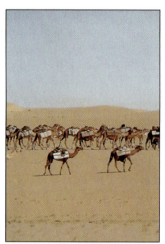

Mali

By 1240 A.D., Ghana was a part of Mali (mah' lē), a large trading kingdom in West Africa. The king of Mali, whose army had conquered Ghana, was Sundiata Keita (sūn dē ah' tuh kī ' tuh), or "Hungering Lion."

GOLD DESIGNS The gold mined in ancient Africa was often formed into intricate designs on jewelry and ceremonial ornaments. These pieces are elephant charms. **Who controlled most of the gold supply in ancient Ghana?**

Sundiata Keita did several things to make his kingdom strong. He reestablished the salt-gold trade, which the Arabs had disrupted. He organized a permanent army. He divided the kingdom into provinces, each headed by a general. The generals kept the peace and saw that there was enough food for the people. To strengthen ties with different groups in the kingdom, Sundiata Keita moved his capital from place to place.

Sundiata Keita wanted to impress the people with his power. When he appeared in public, trumpeters announced his arrival. He sat on an ebony throne under an arch made from large elephant tusks. He never spoke directly to people. Instead, requests were answered by servants standing at the foot of the stairs leading to the throne.

One of the most famous kings of Mali was Mansa Musa I (mahn' sah mū' sah), or King Moses I. One reason Mansa Musa was famous was because of a **pilgrimage** (pil' gruh mij), or religious journey, he made to Arabia in 1324–25. It took more than 14 months to cover the 3,000 miles, or 4,800 kilometers. Some 12,000 servants traveled with the king. Each carried a 4-pound, or 1.8-kilogram, gold bar. Mansa Musa gave many of these bars to poor

Reading Check
What is a **pilgrimage?**

people he met along the way. As a result of this trip, news of Mansa Musa and Mali reached as far as Europe.

In Arabia, Mansa Musa met a Spanish architect whom he brought back to Mali. There, the architect built a university in the trading city of Timbuktu (tim buhk tū'). It became a great center of learning and drew students from Europe, Asia, and Africa.

After 25 years, Mansa Musa's reign ended. The rulers who followed him were weak. Within 100 years after Mansa Musa's death, Mali lost its land to others.

Songhai   The kingdom that replaced Mali as the most powerful in West Africa was Songhai (song' hī). By the late 1400s, it controlled almost all the land that had been part of Mali. Songhai also conquered other lands and became the largest of the three trading kingdoms.

The Sultan Sunni Ali, in 1464, ruled Songhai from the city of Gao. He maintained a huge army equipped with armor, camels and horses. He also had a large navy that patrolled the Niger River. Following Sunni Ali's death, Askia Muhammad came to power in Songhai. He extended the empire even more and culture flourished. Sultan Askia welcomed teachers, doctors, poets, students, and religious leaders from Asia and Europe.

Songhai was more organized than the other two kingdoms. It was divided into provinces, with a governor for each. Everyone used the same weights and measures and the same legal system. Only members of the ruling Songhai could become political leaders or join the cavalry. Other groups had special jobs, such as caring for the army's horses or serving at the royal court. Most enslaved people, often prisoners of war, worked as farmers.

Despite its power, Songhai lasted only 100 years. In 1591 A.D., the ruler of Morocco sent an army across the Sahara to seize Songhai's gold mines. Though only half of the Moroccan soldiers survived the trip, they had guns. They defeated Songhai's soldiers, who were armed only with swords and spears.

Section 2 Assessment

1. **Define:** silent barter, pilgrimage.
2. What were two important trade goods in West Africa?
3. How was the kingdom of Songhai organized?

Critical Thinking

4. **Making Inferences**   Why do you think Ghanian merchants set up a system called silent barter?

Graphic Organizer Activity

5. Draw a diagram like this one, and use it to summarize the accomplishments of the three great West African kingdoms.

Reading Latitude

To measure distances north and south, mapmakers use imaginary lines on maps and globes. These are called lines of latitude and they run east and west around Earth. Lines of latitude are often called parallels because they never meet and remain the same distance from each other all the way around Earth.

Latitude is measured in degrees, as shown by the symbol °. The Equator, which is a line of latitude, is marked 0° because all other lines of latitude are measured from it. One degree of latitude equals about 69 miles, or 110 kilometers.

There are 90 lines of latitude from the Equator to each pole. Those lines north of the Equator are marked with an **N**. Those lines south of the Equator are marked with an **S**.

Map Practice

1. Which civilization was located closest to the Equator?
2. Which city, Timbuktu or Napata, was located closest to the 20°N line of latitude?
3. Which line of latitude runs through the center of the great trading civilization of Zimbabwe?

GO TO

Glencoe's **Skillbuilder Interactive Workbook CD-ROM, Level 1,** provides instruction and practice in key social studies skills.

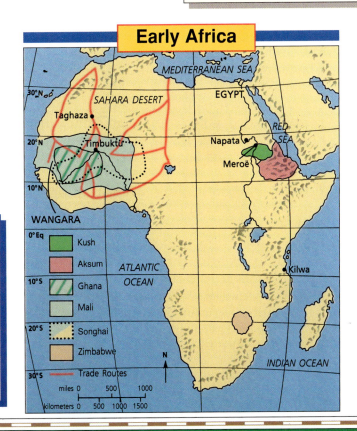

Early Africa

MEDITERRANEAN SEA

30°N
SAHARA DESERT
EGYPT
Taghaza
RED SEA
20°N
Timbuktu
Napata
Meroë
10°N
WANGARA
0° Eq
Kush
Aksum
ATLANTIC OCEAN
10°S
Ghana
Mali
Kilwa
20°S
Songhai
Zimbabwe
N
30°S
Trade Routes
INDIAN OCEAN

miles 0   500   1000
kilometers 0   500   1000   1500

SECTION 3 East African Civilizations

The growth of trading kingdoms in West Africa was matched by the rise of trading kingdoms and city-states in East Africa. Goods moved from the interior of East Africa to coastal markets, which, in time, became large city-states. Each of these had its own ruler and government.

Zimbabwe   One of the best-known trading kingdoms was Zimbabwe (zim bah′ bwā). The people of Zimbabwe speak a language known as Bantu (ban′ tū). Their ancestors, the Shona (shō′ nuh), once lived in present-day Nigeria (nū jir′ ē uh) in West Africa. About 100 A.D., a **population explosion,** or a large and sudden growth in population, took place. Since the land could not support the increased number of people, many Shona began to leave their homeland to look for new homes.

The Shona settled in Zimbabwe in East Africa about 700 A.D. There, they built towns using stones that were cut in such a way that they fit together without mortar. The capital had houses, a fort, and a temple. The fort stood on top of a hill and was surrounded by a huge wall. Besides the temple, the enclosed area contained the houses of the chief and his officials.

The people of Zimbabwe viewed their chief as a god-king. They approached him by crawling on their stomachs. Officials imitated him. If he coughed, they coughed. When he ate, they ate. The chief kept his throne as long as he was in good health. When he grew old, however, he was expected to take poison. Then, a younger man would become chief, and Zimbabwe could remain strong.

Another reason Zimbabwe remained strong was trade. Its people traded gold, copper, and ivory from the interior to merchants from cities along Africa's east coast. From these cities, trade was carried on with Arabia, Persia, India, and China.

Kilwa   Another important trading city-state in East Africa was Kilwa (kil′ wuh). From Kilwa, merchants sailed across the Red Sea and the Indian Ocean. The people of Kilwa collected heavy taxes from traders of other countries. They used their wealth to extend their power over neighboring city-states. They also used it to dress in fine cotton and silk and to fill their four-story houses with vases and hangings from India and China.

A culture known as Swahili (swah hē′ lē) developed in Kilwa and other East African city-states. Many Arab traders had settled in the coastal cities. For this reason, Swahili culture is a mix of

✓ Reading Check
How did a **population explosion** cause the Shona to leave their homeland?

Zimbabwe Ruins

Arabic and African cultures. The Swahili language is a combination of Bantu and Arabic.

Section 3 Assessment

1. **Define:** population explosion.
2. How did the people of Zimbabwe view their leader?
3. How did the people at Kilwa use their wealth?

Critical Thinking

4. **Understanding Cause and Effect** A population explosion among the Shona caused many of these people to leave their homeland. What are some of the events or conditions that might cause people to leave their homelands today?

Graphic Organizer Activity

5. Draw a diagram like this one, and use it to show features of Swahili culture.

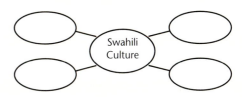

SECTION 4 Path to the Americas

Until about 25,000 years ago, there were no people in the Americas. Then, hunting-and-food-gathering bands began to cross into the Americas from Asia over a land bridge. This land bridge was formed during the last Ice Age. At that time, large amounts of ocean water were frozen into huge glaciers, and sea levels dropped. Today, this bridge is covered by the waters of the Bering Strait.

The bands came in search of food, following grass-grazing animals that had crossed earlier. The bands lived off their kill and also gathered wild plants. Over time, they spread all through the Americas. Experts believe people reached the southern tip of South America by about 9000 B.C.

About 7000 B.C., the last Ice Age ended. The climate became hotter and drier, and in many areas deserts took the place of grasslands. Large game almost disappeared. So, people had to find other ways of getting food.

By 6000 B.C., people in the Tehuacán (tā wah kahn') Valley south of present-day Mexico City had developed farming. By 3000 B.C., there were thousands of small farming villages all through the Americas. The most important crop was *maize* (māz), or corn.

Between 3000 B.C. and 1000 B.C., people developed such skills as weaving and pottery making. They grew peanuts, tomatoes, and potatoes. In a few areas, they built irrigation systems that helped support a growing population.

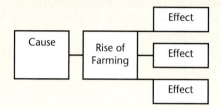
SECTION 5 Mesoamerica

As the number of people grew, societies became more complex. Several great civilizations rose in Mesoamerica, or Middle America, before 900 A.D. and others later.

The Olmecs   One of the earliest civilizations in Mesoamerica was that of the Olmecs (ōl' meks). It came into being around 1000 B.C. About 900 years later, it disappeared mysteriously. The Olmecs had a great influence on other peoples of the area and was called the "mother culture." They developed planned cities, hieroglyphic writing, and a calendar.

The Olmecs lived along the southern coast of the Gulf of Mexico. Part of the year, the people farmed. The rest of the year they built stone cities, which were chiefly religious centers. The cities stood on top of huge hills. They had temples; sacred pools; and houses for priests, artists, and architects. The people lived in nearby villages. They visited the cities on festival and market days.

Mayan Figure

The Mayas   Another great civilization, that of the Mayas (mī' uhz), began in Mesoamerica about 500 B.C. It reached its peak between 300 and 900 A.D. The Mayas lived in present-day southeast Mexico, Belize (buh lēz'), and Guatemala (gwah tuh mah' luh). Like the Olmecs, the Mayas lived in farming villages that surrounded religious cities. Mayan cities had temples and houses for priests and nobles.

The Mayas were great traders. Their cities, linked by roads paved with white cement, had busy marketplaces. Canoes handled local trade along the coasts.

Linking Across Time

Tortillas   Mayan women rose at dawn to boil and grind corn for making the dough for tortillas—thin, round, flat breads. They then worked the dough by hand (left) before baking. Tortillas remain a basic part of the Mayan diet today (right), with women making tortillas in much the same way as their ancestors. **Why was maize (corn) important to the development of civilization in the Americas?**

The Maya adapted their own hieroglyphs from the Olmecs. Mayan mathematicians came up with the idea of zero and a counting system based on 20. Mayan astronomers were able to predict when eclipses of the sun and the moon would take place. They developed a calendar, based on that of the Olmecs, with a year of 365 days. They also made cotton cloth and paper.

About 900 A.D., most Mayas abandoned their cities and disappeared. No one knows why. A plague may have broken out. Perhaps the soil could no longer produce enough food. War may have interfered with trade.

The Aztecs

Later, a third great civilization, that of the Aztecs, rose in Mesoamerica. About 1200 A.D., the Aztecs began moving south into the central valley of Mexico. Through military conquest, they expanded their empire to include all of central Mexico. By 1400 A.D., the Aztec Empire had 5 million people.

The Aztecs made the people they conquered pay tribute. This took the form of corn, clothing, rubber, and wood. It is believed that each year 2 million cotton cloaks alone were sent to the capital, Tenochtitlán (tā noch tē tláhn').

Tenochtitlán was built on an island in Lake Texcoco (teks kō′ kō). *Causeways*, or paved roads, connected the island to the mainland. The city had pyramid-temples, palaces, gardens, zoos, schools, and markets. About 300,000 people lived there. Some dressed in feathered capes and cloaks of many colors. Women wore flowers and feathers in their hair.

Busy Markets Markets played an important part in the economic and social life of the Aztec. The market at Tlateloco was the largest in the ancient Americas. About 60,000 people may have visited the market each day.

Painting of Aztec Farmer

To feed the people, the Aztecs had to create more farmland. They filled in parts of the lake and dug drainage canals. They planted crops in soil-filled reed baskets anchored in the lake. They also built *aqueducts* (ak' wuh dukts), or water channels, to bring fresh water to the city's reservoirs from mainland springs. Canoes delivered the water from the reservoirs to people's houses.

The Aztecs were a warlike people. War and religion were closely connected. The people worshiped two major gods. One was the rain god who stood for the peaceful life of farming. The other was the sun god who stood for war and expanding empire. The Aztecs believed that the sun god needed human sacrifices. The Aztecs felt that if they did not make them, the sun would not rise in the morning. Victims were generally prisoners of war.

The Aztec Empire reached its height in the early 1500s under Montezuma II (mahn tuh zū' muh). During his reign, however, Spaniards, who had guns and horses, attacked the Aztecs. Easily defeated by the Spaniards, the Aztecs lost their empire.

Section 5 Assessment

1. What were some of the accomplishments of the Maya?
2. How did the Aztec Empire come to an end?

Critical Thinking

3. **Drawing Conclusions** Why do you think Mayan civilization ended?

Graphic Organizer Activity

4. Draw a diagram like this one, and use it to summarize the accomplishments of the three great Mesoamerican civilizations.

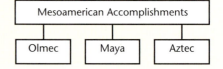

SECTION 6 The Incas

About the same time the Aztecs moved south into central Mexico, the Incas moved out from Peru. They established an empire that stretched along the west coast of South America for about 2,500 miles, or 4,000 kilometers. By the 1500s, there were 12 million people in the Inca Empire.

History   The Incas started out as farmers and shepherds. They built villages on the rocky slopes of the Andes Mountains. In the fertile valley below, they grew corn, potatoes, and other crops. On pastures above, they grazed alpacas (al pak' uhz) and llamas (lah' muhs).

In 1438, the Inca ruler Pachacuti (pah chuh kū' tē) conquered several neighboring peoples and founded the Inca Empire. He used several techniques to hold it together. He ordered

Student Web Activity

Visit the *Human Heritage* Web site at **humanheritage.glencoe.com** and click on *Chapter 8— Student Web Activities* to find out more about the ancient civilizations of the Americas.

conquered peoples to worship the Inca sun god in addition to their own gods. He made the Inca language of Quechua (kech' wuh) the official language. He moved people who had been living under Inca rule into newly conquered lands. They helped spread Inca culture and watched for signs of rebellion.

Pachacuti also had a huge system of stone-paved roads built. Rope suspension bridges crossed canyons and rivers. Way stations with food, weapons, and other supplies needed by the Inca army were set up on the roads. Only soldiers and government officials were allowed to use the roads.

Inca Way of Life A ruler, known as the Inca, determined the way of life. Land belonged to the ruler and not to the people who worked it. Villagers paid taxes to the empire in two ways.

Growing Grains The Aztecs and Incas grew high-protein grains called amaranth and quinoa. Today these grains, native to the Americas, have become important in parts of India, Pakistan, Nepal, and China. Amaranth and quinoa, in the form of flour and cereals, have become common in U.S. health-food stores.

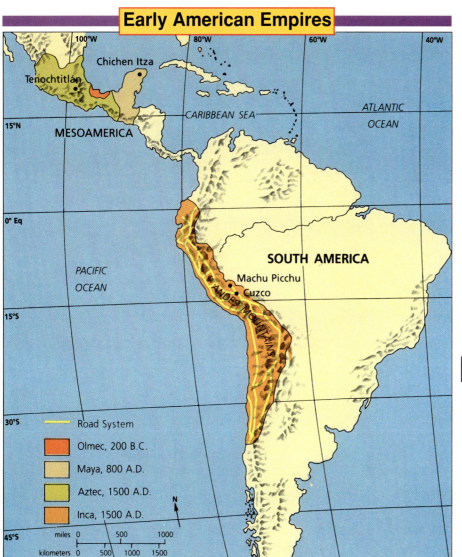

Early American Empires

- Road System
- Olmec, 200 B.C.
- Maya, 800 A.D.
- Aztec, 1500 A.D.
- Inca, 1500 A.D.

Chichen Itza
Tenochtitlán
MESOAMERICA
CARIBBEAN SEA
ATLANTIC OCEAN
SOUTH AMERICA
Machu Picchu
Cuzco
PACIFIC OCEAN
ANDES MOUNTAINS

100°W 80°W 60°W 40°W
15°N
0° Eq
15°S
30°S
45°S

miles 0 500 1000
kilometers 0 500 1000 1500
N

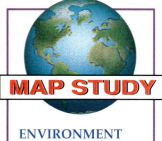

MAP STUDY

ENVIRONMENT AND SOCIETY The Inca developed engineering skills that enabled them to build a large network of roads. **How did the environment of the Inca make road building more difficult?**

They paid through their labor. This involved not only farming land, but also building roads and mining gold. In addition, they paid taxes in kind.

The Inca had to keep track of people and goods. Because there was no written language, special accountants used **quipus** (kē′ pūz), or counting devices, to do this. Quipus were made up of knotted strings of different colors. Each color represented a different item. The knots in each string stood for tens, hundreds, and so on. The spaces between the knots stood for zero.

The wealth of the Inca Empire was shown in the way the ruler lived. His palace was the size of a town. There were hundreds of rooms and thousands of servants. The Inca's bodyguards wore gold armor. The poles of the litter in which he was carried were covered with gold. A desire for this wealth was part of the reason the Spaniards destroyed the Inca Empire in the early 1500s.

Reading Check
What were **quipus,** and how did the Inca use them?

Section 6 Assessment

1. **Define:** quipus.
2. How big was the Inca Empire at its peak?
3. How did Pachacuti hold the Inca Empire together?

Critical Thinking

4. **Demonstrating Reasoned Judgment** Suppose the Inca had the choice of keeping Pachacuti as their leader or electing a new one. Which choice do you think they would have taken? Explain.

Graphic Organizer Activity

5. Draw a diagram like this one, and use it to show the changes that Pachacuti brought to the Incan way of life.

| Before | → | Rise of Pachacuti | → | After |

Chapter Summary & Study Guide

1. The Kushites and Egyptians influenced each other through conquest and trade.
2. The Aksumites destroyed Kush and later converted to Christianity.
3. The kingdoms of Ghana, Mali, and Songhai built West African empires based on a trade in salt and gold.
4. A population explosion led the Shona to build Zimbabwe in East Africa.
5. Kilwa and other coastal cities handled trade between Africa and Arabia, Persia, India, and China.
6. The Olmec and the Maya invented many new ideas, including forms of writing and a calendar.
7. The Aztec and the Inca built complex civilizations that lasted until the time of European arrival in the Americas.

HISTORY Online

Self-Check Quiz

Visit the *Human Heritage* Web site at **humanheritage. glencoe.com** and click on *Chapter 8—Self-Check Quiz* to assess your understanding of this chapter.

Using Key Terms

Imagine that you are putting together a photo display about ancient civilizations. You have found a photo that illustrates each of these terms:

silent barter   pilgrimage
population explosion   quipus

Use each term in a one-sentence caption describing what the photo shows.

Understanding Main Ideas

1. How did Ghana gain control of West African trade routes?
2. What was the effect of Mansa Musa's pilgrimage?
3. What was the main difference between the Mesoamerican civilizations that developed before and after 900 A.D.?
4. What did the Olmec contribute to other civilizations?
5. How did the Aztec treat the people they conquered?
6. Who directed and controlled the Incan way of life?

Critical Thinking

1. How do you think the development of African civilization might have been different if the Kushites did not develop iron-smelting?
2. Why was trade important to the growth of African civilization?
3. Which Mesoamerican civilization would you choose to live in? Why?
4. What contributions did early American civilizations make to present-day life in the United States?

Graphic Organizer Activity

History Draw two parallel time lines like the ones shown, and use them to compare important events in the early civilizations of Africa and the Americas. Sample events are provided to help you get started.

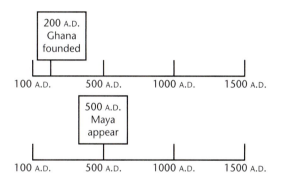

200 A.D. Ghana founded
100 A.D.   500 A.D.   1000 A.D.   1500 A.D.

500 A.D. Maya appear
100 A.D.   500 A.D.   1000 A.D.   1500 A.D.

Geography in History

The World in Spatial Terms Compare the maps of early empires found on pages 135 and 141. What similarities in locations of these civilizations can you find? What differences in locations are there between the two areas?

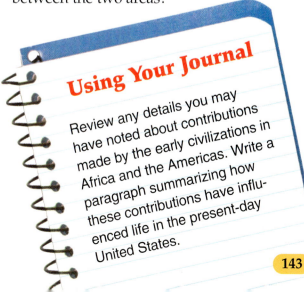

Using Your Journal

Review any details you may have noted about contributions made by the early civilizations in Africa and the Americas. Write a paragraph summarizing how these contributions have influenced life in the present-day United States.

THE ZHOU

The Zhou dynasty ruled for more than 800 years—the longest ruling dynasty in Chinese history. Zhou kings claimed they ruled according to a "mandate from heaven." However, this claim did not stop ambitious nobles from challenging their power. For the last 500 years of their rule, Zhou kings watched their empire crumble as warring states tried to seize control of China.

Despite the constant warfare, the Zhou dynasty oversaw many advancements. Achievements ranged from the development of new philosophies to the invention of new weapons.

Zhou Empire

The Zhou introduced many advances in farming, including the irrigation channels used by Chinese farmers today. These channels allowed farmers to flood the fields used to grow rice. Production of rice became increasingly important as the Zhou extended their power into China's great river basins. ▼

▲ The Zhou ruled from 1028 B.C. to about 256 B.C. Boundaries changed constantly throughout this period. This map shows the Zhou Empire around the height of its power.

the W🌐rld

▲ The Zhou created ornate metal statues, such as this winged dragon.

The Zhou kings considered the outside world uncivilized. They prided themselves on their cultural accomplishments. These chimes come from a Zhou orchestra, which included flutes, drums, wooden clappers, and more. The chimes consist of 64 bronze bells ranging in size from 8 inches to 5 feet. ▼

The Zhou had strong family ties and traditions. These mourning figures honor a family member who has died. ▶

Bronze work, such as this three-legged bowl and ladle, were crafted by the Zhou. ▼

Taking Another Look

1. When did the Zhou dynasty begin and end?
2. What advancement in farming did Zhou rulers introduce?

Hands-On Activity

Writing an Announcement Write an announcement for a CD of music played on the bronze chimes created during the Zhou dynasty.

Standardized Test Practice

Directions: Choose the *best* answer to each of the following multiple choice questions. If you have trouble answering a question, use the process of elimination to narrow your choices. Write your answers on a separate piece of paper.

1. **Which of the following statements about the Phoenicians is true?**

   A The Phoenicians invented the system of numbers we use today.

   B The Phoenicians introduced a written alphabet to Europe.

   C The Phoenicians lived under a single, unified government.

   D The Phoenicians used their navy to conquer and settle many distant lands.

   > **Test-Taking Tip:** This question requires you to remember an important *fact* about the Phoenicians. Since the Phoenicians did not have a *single, unified government,* you can eliminate answer C.

2. **In what unique way did the Phoenicians protect themselves from being conquered by other nations?**

   F They built a strong army that other nations feared.

   G They conquered other countries and took over foreign governments.

   H They signed peace treaties with neighboring countries.

   J They created a strong, unified central government in their country.

   > **Test-Taking Tip:** The important word in this question is *unique*. The Phoenicians certainly did not invent the idea of having a strong army (answer F). What *new idea* did they try?

3. **The Hebrews are thought to be the first people to**

   A devise a moral code

   B worship one god

   C live in the desert area known as Canaan

   D write down their religious legends

   > **Test-Taking Tip:** Make sure that you read the question and *all* the answer choices carefully. Think back to the other cultures and civilizations you have studied. Do you remember if, for instance, the Egyptians wrote down their religious legends? They did so in hieroglyphics. Though the Hebrews *did* write down their religious legends, they were not the *first* people to do so. Therefore, you can eliminate answer D.

4. **The Ten Commandments and the Code of Hammurabi are similar because they both**

   F say that people should respect each other and each other's property

   G established a regulated exchange system

   H lay out the proper punishments for different crimes

   J instruct people to worship only one god

   > **Test-Taking Tip:** This question asks you to make a *comparison*. Choose the answer that is true for *both* sets of laws. Eliminate any choice that is not true of either the Ten Commandments or the Code of Hammurabi.

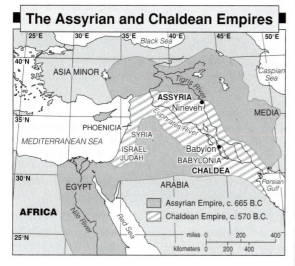

The Assyrian and Chaldean Empires

Assyrian Empire, c. 665 B.C

Chaldean Empire, c. 570 B.C.

Use the map above to answer questions 5 and 6.

5. **Approximately how far is it from Babylon to Nineveh?**

   A   100 miles

   B   150 miles

   C   300 miles

   D   450 miles

Test-Taking Tip: Use the *map scale* to determine the distance from one point to another. If you do not have a ruler, you can use a small piece of paper to copy the length of the scale. Hold the paper next to the area you want to measure to help you estimate the distance.

6. **Which of the following is east of Assyria?**

   F   The Black Sea

   G   Media

   H   Phoenicia

   J   Israel

Test-Taking Tip: Study the map carefully before you choose an answer. Which way is *east* on a map?

7. **What was something new and different about how the Persians traded?**

   A   They kept track of trades using a written alphabet.

   B   They traded pots and pans in exchange for cloth.

   C   They only traded within their own country.

   D   They did business by using coins for money.

Test-Taking Tip: Notice that the question asks you to identify what was *new and different* about the Persians' method of trading. Was trading pots and pans for cloth a *new and different* idea?

The Greeks

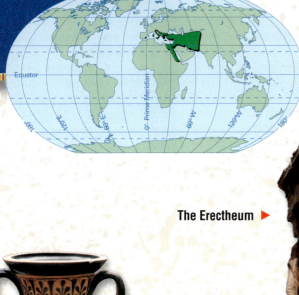

The Erectheum ▶

▲ A Greek urn

2800 B.C.
Minoan civilization begins

2000 B.C.
Mycenaeans move into Balkan Peninsula

1250 B.C.
Trojan War

750 B.C.
Homer writes the *Iliad* and the *Odyssey*

Organizing Information Study Foldable *Make this foldable to help you organize information about the history and culture of Greece.*

Step 1 *Mark the midpoint of the side edge of a sheet of paper.*

Draw a line along the midpoint.

Step 2 *Turn the paper and fold the outside edges in to touch at the midpoint. Label as shown.*

Reading and Writing *As you read the unit, organize your notes by writing the main ideas with supporting details under the appropriate tab.*

Step 3 *Open and label your foldable as shown.*

PRIMARY SOURCES

Library

See pages 680–681 for another primary source reading to accompany Unit 4.

GO TO Read "The Death of Socrates" from the **World History Primary Source Document Library CD-ROM.**

Journal Notes

What lasting ideas did the Greeks develop? Note details about these ideas as you read.

490 B.C.
Persian Wars begin

462 B.C.
Golden Age of Athens begins

434 B.C.
Peloponnesian War

Beginnings
2800 B.C.–750 B.C.

Mycenaean fresco
of women driving
a chariot ▼

▲ Mycenaean gold earrings

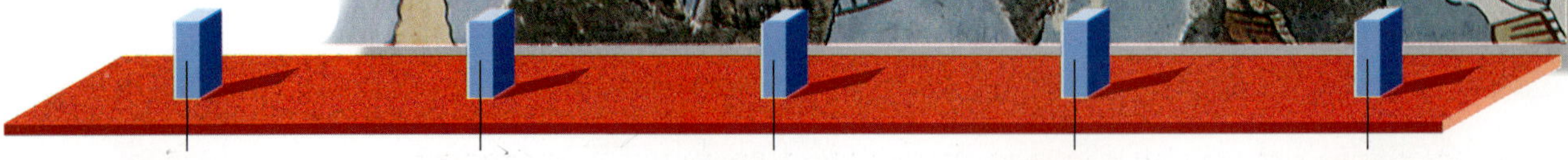

2800 B.C.	2000 B.C.	1400 B.C.	1250 B.C.	750 B.C.
Minoan civilization begins	Mycenaeans move toward Greece	Mycenaeans take control of Crete	Mycenaeans attack Troy in Asia Minor	Homer writes the *Iliad* and the *Odyssey*

Chapter Focus

 Read to Discover

- What life was like for the Minoans.
- How geography influenced the early peoples who lived on Crete and the Balkan Peninsula.
- What life was like for the Mycenaeans.
- How the "Dark Age" affected the Aegean world.

Chapter Overview

Visit the *Human Heritage* Web site at **humanheritage.glencoe.com** and click on **Chapter 9—Chapter Overviews** to preview this chapter.

 Terms to Learn

bull leaping
labyrinth
parchment
shrines
megaron
tenants
civil wars

 People to Know

Theseus
Homer
Odysseus
Helen

Places to Locate

Crete
Balkan Peninsula
Troy
Asia Minor
Ionia

Why It's Important   Greek civilization grew out of a combination of two earlier civilizations, Minoan (muh nō′ uhn) and Mycenaean (mīsuh nē′ uhn). Due to the geography of the land, both became great sea powers. Although their power was eventually destroyed, the Minoans and the Mycenaeans left an important *legacy* (leg′ uh sē) , or gift from the past, to the Greeks.

SECTION 1   The Minoans

Minoan civilization rose around 2800 B.C. on Crete (krēt), an island in the Mediterranean Sea. The Minoans, who were also known as Cretans, grew wheat, barley, grapes, and olives. When the olive groves and vineyards produced more than was needed, the Minoans traded the surplus for goods they could not grow or make on Crete.

Since there were many forests on Crete, the Minoans learned to work with wood and became good carpenters. They also learned to work with metal. They used their metalworking and carpentry skills to build ships and began to earn a living from trade instead of farming.

When pirates threatened them, the Minoans changed the way they built their ships so the ships could go faster. They made them slimmer, with two or three masts instead of one. The Minoans also put a deck over the heads of rowers to protect them.

Minoan Jar

They placed a wooden beam in the *prow,* or front part of the ship. This was used to smash a hole in enemy ships to sink them.

Over time, the Minoans drove off the pirates. By about 2000 B.C., Crete was the world's first important seafaring civilization. Minoan merchant ships traveled far to trade pottery, leather and bronze armor, and metal jewelry.

The People

The Minoans were a small people with bronzed skin and long dark hair. Men wore striped loincloths, long robes embroidered with flowers, or trousers that bagged at the knees. Women wore full skirts and short-sleeved jackets that laced in front. The Minoans had small waists and wore tight belts to show them off. They also wore jewelry, such as gold and silver earrings, necklaces, bracelets, and rings.

The Minoans spent their time in a variety of ways. Men farmed and fished. They raised cattle, long-horned sheep, and goats. They also served in the navy and the royal guard. Women performed household duties, attended sporting events, and went hunting in chariots.

The people of Crete loved sports. They built what was probably the world's first arena. It stood in the open air. Stone steps formed grandstands, where about 500 people could sit and watch the action. The king and the royal party had their own special box seats.

Boxing matches were held in the arena. **Bull leaping,** a form of bullfighting, was also held there. A young man and woman "fought" the bull together. The man would grab the bull's horns. As the bull raised its head to toss him, the man would do a somersault, landing on his feet on the bull's back. He would then do a back flip. Standing behind the bull, the woman would catch her partner as he landed. Many experts believe bull leaping was a religious ceremony as well as a sport.

Cities and Palaces

The Minoans built many cities, which were different from those of other ancient civilizations in two ways. At the heart of each Minoan city stood a palace rather than a temple. Also, Minoan cities did not have walls around them. Instead, people depended on the sea and navy for protection.

One of the largest cities of Crete was Knossos (kuh nahs′ uhs). It covered about 28 acres, or 11.2 hectares. About one-fifth of the area was taken up by a five-story palace that served as a government building, temple, factory, and warehouse. Its walls were built of stone and sun-dried brick framed with wooden beams. The Minoans decorated the inside walls with brightly colored *frescoes* (fres′ kōs), or watercolor paintings made on damp plaster. The palace had bathrooms with bathtubs and flush toilets. It also had hot and cold running water and portable fireboxes to heat rooms.

✓ Reading Check
What was **bull leaping?**

Student Web Activity
Visit the *Human Heritage* Web site at **humanheritage.glencoe.com** and click on *Chapter 9—Student Web Activities* to find out more about the Minoans.

The palace had several entrances. Passageways and rooms formed a **labyrinth** (lab' uh rinth), or a network of paths through which it is difficult to find one's way. Because labyrinth means "double ax," the palace was called the "House of the Double Ax." The palace was also called by that name because it was filled with pictures, carvings, and bronze models of a double ax.

Sea captains, merchants, and shipbuilders lived in houses around the palace. Past their houses stood those of artisans who made beautiful cups and vases and designed delicate jewelry.

Houses were built side by side around courtyards. Most were two stories high. Lower walls were made of stone, and the upper walls were made of sun-dried brick. The inside walls were painted with scenes from daily life. Each house also had its own well and drains.

Many early Minoan houses had no entrance from the street. A person went in or out through the roof and lowered a ladder over the side of the house. Later, wooden doors and windows made of oiled and tinted **parchment** (parch' muhnt), or thin animal skin, were added.

Reading Check
What is a **labyrinth?**

Reading Check
How did Minoans use **parchment** in building their homes?

BULL LEAPING   This painting from Knossos shows Minoans bull leaping. In the center, a man leaps over the bull's back. Another man grips the bull's horns so that it will lift its head and toss him. The woman behind the bull prepares to catch the leapers. **What other sporting event was held in a Minoan arena?**

Rulers and Religion

The rulers of Crete were priest-kings. They made the laws and represented the gods on Earth. The priest-kings would climb to the top of Mount Juktas (yūk′ tuhs) to look for a sign from heaven that would tell them the will of the gods. Then, they would tell their people what the gods wanted them to do.

The Minoans had many gods. The main god was the Great Goddess, Mother Earth. She made plants grow and brought children into the world. To honor her, the Minoans built **shrines**, or sacred places to worship, in palaces, on housetops, on hilltops, and in caves. The people believed that hilltops led to heaven, and caves led to the underworld.

Sacred horns made of clay and covered with stucco rested against the back wall of each shrine. A hole between the horns held a bronze double ax. Around the horns were clay models of animals. People left offerings of human hair, fruit, flowers, jewels, and gold at the shrines.

The Minoans believed that certain things were sacred. The lily was their sacred flower. The king wore a plumed crown of lilies and a lily necklace. The double ax was sacred. It stood for the power of Mother Earth and the authority of the king. The dove was sacred because it flew to the heavens.

Reading Check
Why did the Minoans build **shrines?**

MINOAN RELIGION   This Minoan fresco shows a religious ceremony. As a musician plays the harp, two women and a man carry offerings to a shrine. The double axes with birds sitting on them (left) are symbols of the Great Goddess. **What did Minoans believe about the Great Goddess?**

The Fall of the Minoans   No one is certain why Minoan civilization came to an end. What is certain is that about 1400 B.C., control of the sea and of Crete passed to the Mycenaeans.

Legend explains the fall of the Minoans with the story of Theseus (thee' see uhs) and the Minotaur (min' uh tauhr). A young Greek prince named Theseus was brought to Knossos. He was to be sacrificed to the Minotaur, a huge monster the king kept in the palace labyrinth. The Minotaur had the body of a man and the head of a bull and lived on human flesh. Theseus was put into the labyrinth. He fought the monster with a magical sword and killed it. When the Minotaur died, the power of the Minoans died too.

Section 1 Assessment

1. **Define:** bull leaping, labyrinth, parchment, shrines.
2. What kind of government did the Minoans have?
3. How did cities in Crete differ from cities in other ancient civilizations?

Critical Thinking

4. **Making Generalizations**   How did geography influence the development of the Minoan civilization?

Graphic Organizer Activity

5. Draw a chart like this one, and use it to fill in details on Minoan civilization.

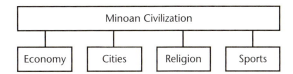

Minoan Civilization			
Economy	Cities	Religion	Sports

SECTION 2   The Mycenaeans

The Mycenaeans came from the grasslands of southern Russia. Around 2000 B.C., small groups started making their way west into Europe and then south through the Balkan (bol' kuhn) Peninsula. Finally, they settled in the lowlands of Greece.

The Mycenaean kings built fortress-palaces on hilltops. In times of danger or attack, the people in the villages outside the palace walls took shelter within the palace. Its chief feature was the **megaron** (meg' uh ron), or a square room with a fireplace in its center. The king held council meetings and entertained in the megaron.

Land was divided into estates that were farmed either by enslaved people or by **tenants,** or people who live on and work another person's land. Landowners gave the king horses, chariots, weapons, wheat, farm animals, honey, and hides in exchange for protection. Tenants labored to supply many of these items.

Reading Check
   How did Mycenaean kings use the **megaron?**
How did **tenants** earn a living?

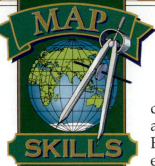

Reading Longitude

To measure distances east and west on Earth, mapmakers use imaginary lines on maps and globes. These are called lines of **longitude,** or **meridians** (muh rid′ ē uhnz), and they run from the North Pole to the South Pole.

Like lines of latitude, meridians are measured in degrees. All meridians are measured from the Prime Meridian, a line of longitude that runs through Greenwich, England. The Prime Meridian is marked 0°. Those lines east of the Prime Meridian are marked with an E, from 1°E to 180°E. Those lines west of the Prime Meridian are marked with a W, from 1°W to 180°W. Unlike lines of latitude, meridians are not always the same distance from one another. They are farthest apart at the Equator, and closest together at the poles.

Lines of longitude are often used to help specify location. For example, it is much easier to find Troy on the map below if one knows that it is located at about 26°E.

Look at the map below, and answer the following questions.

Map Practice

1. **Along which line of longitude was Knossos located?**
2. **Which early Aegean city was located closest to 20°E?**

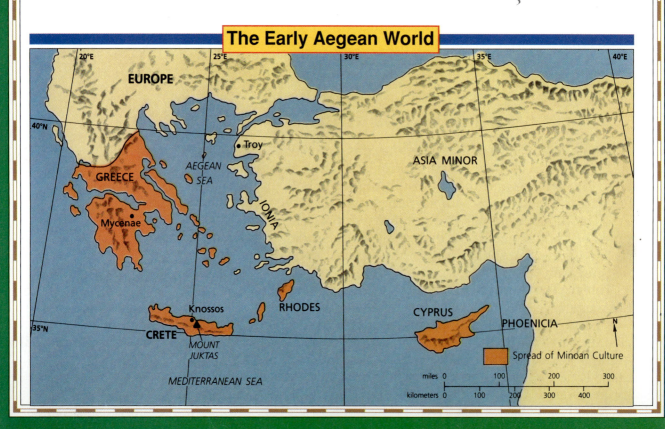

The Early Aegean World

Linking Across Time

Greek Shipping   The seafaring tradition has continued from Mycenaean times (below) into the present. Today Greece is among the top ten shipping nations in the world (right). **What does the size of this modern Greek ship tell you about Greek trade today?**

Although they kept large herds of cattle, the Mycenaeans relied on hunting to get more meat. They hunted rabbit, deer, boar, wild bulls, and game birds. Women rode with the men in chariots during the hunt. When hunters were after big game, they used greyhounds. The game was captured with nets or killed with spears, slings, or bows and arrows.

Traders and Pirates

Shortly after the Mycenaeans settled in the lowlands of Greece, they were visited by Minoan traders from Crete. The Mycenaeans began to imitate Minoan gold and bronze work. They adapted Cretan script to their own language. They copied Minoan fashions. Most important of all, they learned how to build ships and how to navigate.

The Mycenaeans also began to grow olives. They made presses to squeeze oil from the olives. They used the oil for cooking, as fuel for lamps, and to rub on their bodies. They sold plain oil in large clay jars and perfumed oil in painted vases. Sale of the oil made the Mycenaeans rich. It also led to the founding of trading stations and settlements on nearby islands.

Homer
c. 700s B.C.

Greek Poet

Homer remains a mystery. Nobody knows what he looked like or exactly when he lived. Ancient Greek *bards*, or poets, called him the "Ionian bard," so maybe Homer came from Ionia. Tradition says Homer was blind, but he was not blind to history. Archaeologists have proven that many of the stories told by Homer actually took place. That means his poems are more than good literature—they are also good history.

Despite their success in trade, the Mycenaeans were warriors at heart. In battle, they used large hide shields with wooden frames and fought with spears and swords. Their leaders wore fancy bronze armor. At first, the Mycenaeans fought one another. After they learned about shipbuilding and navigation, they outfitted pirate fleets and began to raid nearby lands. By about 1400 B.C., they had replaced the Minoans as the chief power of the Aegean world.

The Trojan War The Mycenaeans are famous for their attack on Troy, a major trading city in Asia Minor. This attack probably took place during the middle 1200s B.C. At the time, the Trojans (trō′ juhns) controlled the trade routes to the Black Sea. They made money by taxing the ships that carried grain and gold from southern Russia to Greece.

About 500 years after the Mycenaeans attacked Troy, a blind Greek poet named Homer (hō′ muhr) composed a long poem about the event. He called his poem the *Iliad* (il′ ē uhd). Homer also composed a poem called the *Odyssey* (ahd′ uh sē), which tells about the wanderings of Odysseus (ō dis′ ē uhs), a Mycenaean hero of the Trojan War. Homer drew his material for the two

THE TROJAN HORSE The first Greek myths came from the Mycenaeans. Later, the poet Homer gathered these legends and used them to write his works. Here, a painting of the Trojan horse from Homer's poem the *Iliad* is shown. **Where did Homer get his material for the *Iliad* and the *Odyssey*?**

poems from songs and legends that had been handed down by word of mouth. He then added his own descriptions and details of everyday life.

According to Homer's account in the *Iliad*, the Trojan War was fought over a woman. The king of Troy had a son named Paris, who fell in love with Helen, the wife of a Mycenaean king. When Paris took Helen to Troy, her husband became angry. He formed an army and sailed after them. However, the walls of Troy were so tall, thick, and strong that the Mycenaeans could not get into the city. They had to camp on the plain outside the city walls.

Mycenaean Goldwork

After ten years of fighting, the Mycenaeans still had not taken Troy. Then, Odysseus suggested a way they could capture the city. He had the soldiers build a huge, hollow wooden horse. The best soldiers hid inside the horse, while the rest boarded their ships and sailed away.

The Trojans saw the ships leave and thought they had won the war. They did not know the Mycenaean ships would return after dark. The Trojans tied ropes to the wooden horse and pulled it into the city as a victory prize. When they fell asleep, the Mycenaean soldiers hidden inside the horse came out. They opened the city gates and let in the rest of the Mycenaean army. The Mycenaeans killed the king of Troy and burned the city. Then, with Helen, they returned to their homes.

A "Dark Age" The Mycenaeans did not return to peaceful ways after crushing Troy. Instead, a series of **civil wars,** or wars between opposing groups of citizens, broke out. Within 100 years after the end of the Trojan War, almost no Mycenaean fortress-palaces were left. Soon after, a people called Dorians (dōr′ ē uhns) entered Greece and conquered the Mycenaeans. Their iron swords were not as well made as Mycenaean bronze swords. Nevertheless, Dorian swords were stronger. Thousands of Mycenaeans fled the Greek mainland and settled on Aegean islands and on the western shore of Asia Minor. These settlements later became known as Ionia (ī ō′ nē uh).

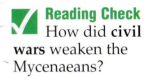

Reading Check How did **civil wars** weaken the Mycenaeans?

As a result of the civil wars and the Dorian invasion, the Aegean world entered a "Dark Age," which lasted until about 800 B.C. It was a time of wandering and killing. Overseas trade stopped. The people of the Aegean region forgot how to write and keep records. The skills of fresco painting and working with ivory and gold disappeared. The Aegean world was cut off from the Middle East, and the people had to create a new civilization on their own.

The people started over. Once again, herding and farming became the main ways of life. Local leaders ruled small areas. These leaders called themselves kings, but they were little more than chiefs. At first, the borders of the areas they ruled kept changing. In time, however, the borders became fixed, and each area became an independent community. The people of these communities began calling themselves Hellenes (hel' ēns), or Greeks. They worked hard to redevelop their culture and to learn new crafts and skills. The civilization they created flourished from about the 700s B.C. until 336 B.C.

Section 2 Assessment

1. **Define:** megaron, tenants, civil wars.
2. In what ways were the Mycenaeans influenced by Minoan culture?
3. According to Homer, how did the Mycenaeans finally win the Trojan War?
4. What happened in the Aegean world during the "Dark Age"?

Critical Thinking

5. **Demonstrating Reasoned Judgment** Why was the growing of olives such an important development for the Aegean world?

Graphic Organizer Activity

6. Draw a diagram like this one, and use it to show the causes and effects of the Trojan War on the Mycenaeans.

Causes	Trojan War	Effects

Chapter Summary & Study Guide

1. Minoan civilization began to develop on the Mediterranean island of Crete around 2800 B.C.
2. The Minoans started as farmers but eventually turned to trade.
3. Since the Minoans depended on the sea and their ships for protection, their cities were not walled.
4. The Minoans worshiped many gods, the most important of which was the Great Goddess, Mother Earth.
5. Around 1400 B.C., the Mycenaeans took control of the Mediterranean.
6. Instead of cities, the Mycenaeans built fortress-palaces on hilltops.
7. The Mycenaeans learned many things from the Minoans, including a writing script and the skills of shipbuilding and navigation.

8. The Mycenaeans fought a lengthy war against Troy, described in two long poems, the *Iliad* and the *Odyssey*.
9. After years of civil war, the Mycenaeans were conquered by the Dorians.
10. During the 300 years of the "Dark Age," the people of the Aegean area lost many of their skills and had to create a new civilization.

Self-Check Quiz

Visit the *Human Heritage* Web site at **humanheritage. glencoe.com** and click on **Chapter 9—Self-Check Quiz** to assess your understanding of this chapter.

Assessment

Using Key Terms

Imagine that you are living among the early Greeks. Use the following words to write a paragraph describing the life of the Minoans and the Mycenaeans.

bull leaping   labyrinth   parchment
shrines   megaron   tenants
civil wars

Understanding Main Ideas

1. What civilizations combined to form Greek civilization?
2. In what ways were the Minoan people able to gain control of the Mediterranean Sea?
3. What do experts believe about the sport of bull leaping?
4. Why didn't Minoan cities have walls around them?
5. What were some of the features of the palace at Knossos?
6. What did the Mycenaeans build instead of cities?
7. How was the Trojan War described in the *Iliad?*
8. Why did the people of Greece have to create a new civilization?

Critical Thinking

1. How well did the Minoans use their natural resources? Explain your answer.
2. What effect did being an island civilization have on the Minoans?
3. What role did religion play in Minoan daily life?
4. In what ways would the Mycenaean civilization have been different if the people had not learned to build and sail ships?

Graphic Organizer Activity

Culture Create a before-and-after chart like the one shown, and use it to show what the Mycenaean civilization was like before and after contact with the Minoans.

Before	Contact with Minoans	After

Geography in History

Places and Regions Refer to the map on page 156 as you think about the "Dark Age" of the Aegean region. What human actions and geographic factors made it possible for this period of history to last for 300 years?

Create a poster warning people about the events and geographic factors that led to the "Dark Age."

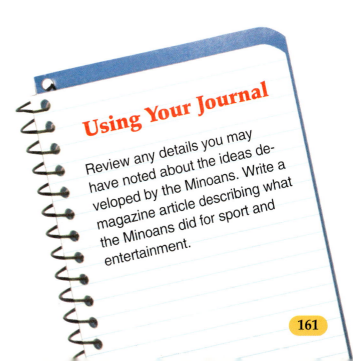

Using Your Journal

Review any details you may have noted about the ideas developed by the Minoans. Write a magazine article describing what the Minoans did for sport and entertainment.

The City-States
700 B.C.–335 B.C.

▲ Athenian silver coin

◀ Spartan soldier

700 B.C.
Greek city-states emerge

594 B.C.
Athens expands citizenship

507 B.C.
Sparta adopts constitution

490 B.C.
Persian Wars begin

404 B.C.
Sparta wins Peloponnesian War

338 B.C.
Philip II conquers Greece

Chapter Focus

Chapter Overview

Visit the *Human Heritage* Web site at <u>humanheritage.glencoe.com</u> and click on **Chapter 10— Chapter Overviews** to preview this chapter.

 Read to Discover

- Why the polis was the geographic and political center of Greek life.
- What life was like in the city-states of Sparta and Athens.
- How the Persian Wars affected Greece.
- How Athens controlled other city-states.
- Why the Greek city-states declined.

Terms to Learn	**People to Know**	**Places to Locate**
polis	Solon	Sparta
acropolis	Cleisthenes	Athens
agora	Darius	Ionia
aristocrats	Xerxes	Delos
oligarchy	Pericles	Thebes
constitution		
mercenaries		

Why It's Important   The geography of Greece—the mountains and the sea—separated communities from each other. Although these communities spoke the same language and shared many of the same customs, no single community had power over the others. Because of this, people developed a loyalty to the community in which they lived. These communities, known as city-states, became a feature of Greek civilization.

SECTION 1 The Polis

The **polis** (pah′ lis), or city-state, was the geographic and political center of Greek life. At first, each polis was made up of farming villages, fields, and orchards grouped around a fortified hill called an **acropolis** (uh krop′ uh lis). At the top of the acropolis stood the temple of the local god. At the foot was the **agora** (ag′ uh ruh). This was an open area used as a marketplace. As time passed, artisans, traders, and members of the upper class settled near the agora. By 700 B.C., this inner part of the polis had become a city. Together with the villages and farmland around it, it formed a city-state.

Each city-state had its own government and laws. The average city-state contained between 5,000 and 10,000 citizens. Workers born outside Greece, as well as women, children, and

Reading Check
Why was the **polis** important? What was the **acropolis?** How did the Greeks use the **agora?**

enslaved people, were not citizens. Only citizens could vote, own property, hold public office, and speak for themselves in court. In return, they were expected to take part in government and to defend their polis in time of war or conflict.

For Greek citizens in ancient times, civic and personal honor were one and the same. The polis gave them a sense of belonging. They put the good of the polis above everything else.

Two of the greatest Greek city-states were Sparta and Athens. Sparta had the strongest army in Greece, while Athens had the strongest navy. However, each developed differently with a different kind of government and a different way of life.

Section 1 Assessment

1. **Define:** polis, acropolis, agora.
2. What areas generally made up each city-state?
3. What rights and duties did Greek citizens have?

Critical Thinking

4. **Demonstrating Reasoned Judgment** Which of the requirements for citizenship in early Greece do you think were fair and which were not? Explain.

Graphic Organizer Activity

5. Draw a web like this one, and use it to show characteristics of most Greek city-states.

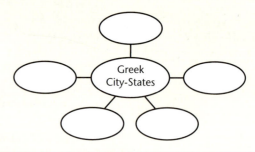

Greek City-States

SECTION 2 Sparta

Sparta was in the south-central region of Greece, in an area known as the Peloponnesus (pel ō puh nē' sus). By 500 B.C., it had become the greatest military power in Greece.

At first, Sparta was ruled by a king. About 800 B.C., **aristocrats** (uh rist' ō kratz), or nobles, took over the government. From that time on, Sparta had two kings who ruled jointly. Although they kept the title of king, they had little power. Their only duties were to lead the army and conduct religious services.

Only aristocrats could be Spartan citizens. All citizens over 20 years old were members of the Assembly, which passed laws and decided questions of war and peace. Each year, the Assembly chose five managers, known as *ephors* (ef' uhrs), to take charge of public affairs and guide the education of young Spartans. The Council of Elders helped the ephors. The Council was made up of men over 60 years old who were chosen for life. It suggested laws to the Assembly and also served as a high court.

Aristocrats, Helots, and Perioeci
The Spartans had little interest in farming. The land was worked by **helots** (hel' uhtz), or

Reading Check
Who were the **aristocrats?**

Reading Check
Who were the **helots?**

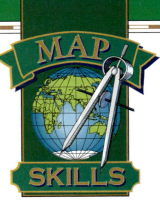

Reading Physical Maps

Physical maps are used to show something about the surface of Earth. The colors used on physical maps may show the rainfall of a certain area. They may also be used to show an area's temperatures or elevations. In the physical map below, the colors indicate elevation. Colors ranging from green to brown are used. The meaning of each color is explained in the legend.

Look at the map "Elevation of Ancient Greece" shown below. The legend says that light brown means above 5,000 feet, or above 1,500 meters. This means that any area on the map that is shaded light brown is at least 5,000 feet, or 1,500 meters, above sea level. Remember that having an elevation of above 5,000 feet does not necessarily mean that an area is covered with mountains. The area may actually be a plateau.

Map Practice

1. **What color shows an elevation of 1,000 to 2,000 feet, or 300 to 600 meters?**
2. **What elevation is shown by the color dark green?**
3. **What generalization can you make about the elevation of ancient Greece?**

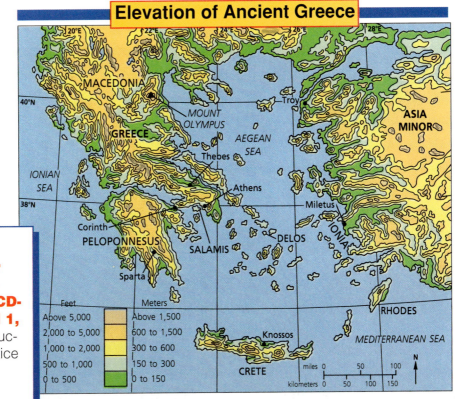

Elevation of Ancient Greece

Glencoe's **Skillbuilder Interactive Workbook CD-ROM, Level 1,** provides instruction and practice in key social studies skills.

enslaved people owned by the city-states. Helots had to turn over one half of their crops to the aristocrats who owned the land but lived in the center of the polis.

The Spartans were not interested in business or trade either. They left those fields to the **perioeci** (pār ē ē' sī), or merchants and artisans who lived in the villages. The perioeci were neither enslaved people nor citizens. Helots and perioeci worked, while aristocrats trained for the army and war.

By about 750 B.C., there were 20 times as many helots and perioeci as there were aristocrats. The aristocrats were now faced with a choice. They could make life better for their workers by letting them share in the government, or they could allow things to stay the way they were. To do that meant keeping the workers down by force. Since the aristocrats were afraid that any change would destroy their way of life, they chose to keep things the way they were.

Spartan Way of Life   The Spartans tried to become the strongest people in Greece. Newborn babies were examined to see if they were healthy. If they were, they were allowed to live. If they were not, they were left on a hillside to die.

Reading Check
How did the **perioeci** differ from the aristocrats of Sparta?

THE SPARTAN WAY OF LIFE   The life of a Spartan male centered on military training and physical fitness from the time he was seven years old. Here, a group of young warriors performs exercises on a Spartan racecourse. **What happened to unhealthy Spartan babies?**

When Spartan boys turned seven, they were sent to live in military camps. There, they were trained in groups under teenage leaders. They learned to read, write, and use weapons. The boys received only small amounts of food. They had to go barefoot and were given only one cloak to wear. They walked in silence, with their eyes to the ground, and spoke only when necessary. They slept outdoors without cover. Every ten days they were lined up and examined to make sure they were not getting fat.

Spartan men were expected to marry at 20 years of age. However, they could not have a household of their own. They had to live and eat in military barracks, where they shared expenses with other soldiers. They could retire from the army when they were 60 years old.

Sculpture of Spartan Girl

Spartan women had more freedom than the women of other Greek city-states. In the other city-states, women spent most of their time at home performing household duties. They did not go out without a chaperone. Then, they went out only to visit other women or attend religious festivals. They never spoke to men on the street or entertained their husbands' friends.

Spartan women, on the other hand, mixed freely with men. They enjoyed sports such as wrestling and racing. When Spartan women sent their men into battle, they told the men to come home with their shields or on them. If the men brought their shields home with them, it meant they had won the battle. Dead warriors were carried home on their shields.

The Spartans believed new ideas would weaken their way of life. Because of this, they tried to prevent change. When people of other Greek city-states began to use coins as money, for example, the Spartans kept using iron rods. Other city-states developed literature and art. Other city-states built up business and trade and improved their standard of living. Sparta remained a poor farming society that depended on the labor of slaves.

From its beginnings until its defeat in 371 B.C., Sparta had only one goal—to be militarily strong.

Section 2 Assessment

1. **Define:** aristocrats, helots, perioeci.
2. How did the lifestyles of Spartan women differ from other Greek women?
3. Why did Sparta try to prevent change?

Critical Thinking

4. **Making Comparisons** How was Sparta similar to other Greek city-states? How was it different?

Graphic Organizer Activity

5. Draw a chart like this one, and use it to weigh the pros and cons of living in Sparta.

Pros	Cons

SECTION 3 Athens

Northeast of Sparta, another city-state developed that had a very different philosophy about living than the Spartans. This polis, located on the Aegean coast, was Athens. Like Sparta, the location of Athens was strategic. Like all the other Greek city-states, Athens was first ruled by kings. However, about 750 B.C., some Athenian nobles, merchants, and manufacturers took over

ATHENS MARKETPLACE   The agora of Athens was a favorite meeting place of the people. These ruins show archaeologists the importance of this community area. **Why would the agora be located near the center of Athens?**

Student Web Activity

Visit the *Human Heritage* Web site at **humanheritage.glencoe.com** and click on *Chapter 10— Student Web Activities* to find out more about life in the Greek city-states.

the government. They set up an **oligarchy** (ol' uh gahr kē), or form of government in which a few people have the ruling power. Fights broke out between them and the farmers and artisans over land ownership. The upper-class Athenians did not want these fights to turn into an uprising against the government, so they agreed to make reforms. To do this, they had to change the government.

The first attempt to change the government was made by Draco (drā' kō), a noble. Draco, however, failed because his punishments were too harsh. Then, in 594 B.C., a rich merchant named Solon (sah' lon) was chosen to undertake the task.

Solon prepared a **constitution,** or a set of principles and rules for governing. This constitution broke the political power of the rich. Solon set a limit on how much land a person could own and gave landowners the right to vote in the Assembly. The Assembly was given the power to pass laws. Solon erased all debts. He freed all the people who had been forced into enslavement because of debt. Solon offered citizenship to artisans who were not Athenians, and he ordered every father to teach his son a trade.

Under Solon, more Athenians began to take part in government. Trade also increased. Still, many people were not happy. The rich thought Solon had gone too far, while the poor thought he had not gone far enough. By the time Solon had left office, he had lost much of his original popularity.

About 560 B.C., the government was taken over by another Athenian named Peisistratus (pī sis' trah tus). Peisistratus was supported by the lower classes. He divided large estates among farmers who owned no land. He stated that a person no longer had to own land to be a citizen. He also encouraged sculpture and other arts.

A Democratic Constitution

When Peisistratus died, his sons took over as leaders of the Athenian government. Not long after that, their government was overthrown by the Spartans.

In 508 B.C., the Spartans themselves were overthrown by a noble named Cleisthenes (klīs' thuh nēz). A year later, Cleisthenes put into effect the world's first constitution that was **democratic,** or favoring the equality of all people. For example, it gave Athenians the right of freedom of speech. The political reforms made by Cleisthenes lasted until the fall of Greece almost 300 years later.

Cleisthenes opened the Assembly to all males over 20 years old. Each year, the Assembly elected ten generals to run the Athenian army and navy and to serve as chief *magistrates* (maj' uh strātz), or judges. One of the generals was named commander-in-chief.

Reading Check
What type of government is an **oligarchy**?

Reading Check
What is a **constitution**?

Reading Check
What idea does a **democratic** government uphold?

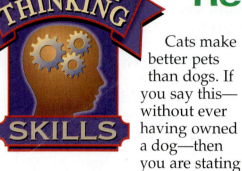

Recognizing Bias

Cats make better pets than dogs. If you say this—without ever having owned a dog—then you are stating a bias. A bias is a prejudice. It can prevent one from looking at a situation in a reasonable or truthful way.

Learning the Skill Most people have feelings and ideas that affect their point of view. This viewpoint, or *bias*, influences the way they interpret events. For this reason, an idea that is stated as a fact may really be only an opinion. Recognizing bias will help you judge the accuracy of what you read.

To recognize bias, follow these steps:

- Identify the author of the statement and examine his or her views and possible reasons for writing the material.
- Look for language that reflects an emotion or opinion—words such as *all, never, best, worst, might,* or *should.*
- Examine the writing for imbalances—leaning only to one viewpoint and failing to provide equal coverage of other possible viewpoints.
- Identify statements of fact. Factual statements usually answer the *Who? What? Where?* and *When?* questions.
- Determine how the author's bias is reflected in the work.

Skill Practice

Read the following excerpt in which a supporter of an oligarchy— a government by the few—evaluates how Athens dealt with members of the Delian League. Then answer the questions that follow.

[R]epresentatives of Athens come out, and . . . vent their hatred upon the better sort of people. . . . [T]he better sort of people are punished, . . . robbed of their money, driven from their homes, and put to death, while the lower classes are promoted to honor. . . .

[E]very single individual among the allies is forced to flatter the People of Athens . . . because he knows he will be tried . . . by the . . . People themselves, for such is the law and custom in Athens. He is forced to behave like a beggar in the courts of justice. . . . For this reason . . . the allies find themselves more and more . . . slaves to the people of Athens.

1. **Is the writer expressing a pro-Athens or anti-Athens bias?**
2. **What prejudice does the writer hold toward the lower classes?**
3. **What bias does the writer have toward the system of justice in Athens?**
4. **What bias does the writer hold toward democracy?**

GO TO Glencoe's **Skillbuilder Interactive Workbook CD-ROM, Level 1,** provides instruction and practice in key social studies skills.

The Council of Five Hundred handled the daily business of Athens. Members were chosen each year by lot. The names of 500 citizens were drawn from a large pot. No one could serve on the Council for more than two terms. Thus, every citizen had a chance to be a Council member.

There were two reasons why the Athenians preferred choosing council members by lot rather than by voting. First, they believed that in an election, people who had money or who could speak well would have an unfair advantage. Second, the Athenians believed that every citizen was smart enough to hold public office. The only exception was in times of war. Then, a skillful general was needed on the Council.

Under Cleisthenes, citizens were required to educate their sons. Since there were no public schools, boys either had a tutor or attended a private school. Starting when they were seven years old, boys studied writing, mathematics, and music. They also practiced sports and memorized the works of Homer and other noted Greek poets.

When they turned 18 years old, Athenian males became citizens. They went to the temple of the god Zeus (zūs) and took an oath of citizenship in front of their family and friends. In the oath, they promised to help make Athens a better place in which to live. They also promised to be honorable in battle, follow the constitution, and respect their religion.

Greek Helmet

The Persian Wars

About the time Athens was going through government changes, the Persians ruled the largest and most powerful empire in the western world. In 545 B.C., the Persians conquered Ionia—the Greek city-states in Asia Minor and on the Aegean islands. About 20 years later, the Ionians revolted. They asked the city-states on the Greek mainland for help. Athens and another polis responded by sending a few warships. After five years of fighting, however, the Persians put down the revolt. Although the Ionians were defeated, Darius, the Persian king, was not satisfied. He wanted to punish the mainland Greeks for helping the Ionians.

In 490 B.C., Darius sent a fleet of 600 ships and a well-equipped army to Greece. The Persians landed on the plain of Marathon about 26 miles, or 41 kilometers, northeast of Athens. After several days, the Persians decided to sail directly to Athens and attack it by sea. They began loading their ships. As soon as most of the Persian soldiers were aboard, Greek soldiers ran down in close order from the hills around Marathon. The remaining Persian troops were not prepared to meet this kind of attack and were defeated. A runner set off for Athens with news of the victory. Upon reaching Athens, he cried out *Nike!*, the Greek goddess of victory, and then died of exhaustion. Winning the Battle of Marathon gave the Greeks a great sense of confidence.

Then... & Now

The Marathon The runner Pheidippides (fi dip' uh dez) carried the news of the victory at Marathon back to Athens, about 26 miles away. He delivered his message and fell dead of exhaustion. Today, a *marathon* is a footrace of 26 miles, 385 yards. The term may describe any long-distance race.

Reading Check
What did Athenian **triremes** look like?

Shortly after the Battle of Marathon, rich silver mines were found near Athens. The Athenians spent their new wealth on **triremes** (trī' rēmz), or warships that had three levels of rowers on each side, one above the other. Soon, Athens had the largest navy in Greece. The Athenians planned to be prepared if the Persians returned.

The Persians did return. In 480 B.C., Darius's son Xerxes (zerk' sēz) sent 250,000 soldiers across the Aegean and conquered northern Greece. In order to stop the Persians from taking all of Greece, 20 Greek city-states banded together. The Spartans led the army, while the Athenians led the navy.

First, 7,000 Greek soldiers headed for the narrow pass of Thermopylae (ther mop' uh lē), about 100 miles, or 160 kilometers, from Athens. There, they held off the Persian army for three days. This gave the people of Athens time to flee to the island of Salamis (sal' uh muhs). Meanwhile, all but 300 Spartans and 700 other Greeks withdrew from Thermopylae. The Persians, helped by a traitor, found a way around the pass. They killed every soldier guarding the pass and then marched on Athens. Finding the city almost deserted, they set it on fire.

BATTLE OF SALAMIS   The Greek fleet, led by the Athenians, defeated the Persian navy in the Bay of Salamis. The faster Greek triremes were able to sail close to the Persian ships and attack with spears and arrows. **What happened to the Persians after the Battle of Salamis?**

Ancient Greece

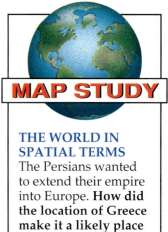

MAP STUDY

THE WORLD IN SPATIAL TERMS
The Persians wanted to extend their empire into Europe. **How did the location of Greece make it a likely place for a Persian attack?**

Then, the Greeks tricked the Persian fleet into sailing into the strait between Athens and Salamis. Since the strait was too narrow for all the Persian ships to enter at once, the Greeks could take them on a few at a time. Also, once the Persian ships were in the strait, their large size made them difficult to handle. With their lighter, faster ships, the Greeks defeated the Persian fleet.

Following the defeat, Xerxes returned to Asia. However, he left some troops behind. In 479 B.C., they were defeated by the Greeks in the Battle of Plataea (pluh tē′ uh). A few days later, Greek ships destroyed what was left of the Persian navy. The Persian Wars were over.

The Delian League and the Athenian Empire   The Persians had been driven from Greece, but they still ruled Ionia. Because of this, the Athenians suggested that the Greek city-states form a **defensive league,** or protective group. Since the league had its headquarters on the island of Delos, it was called the Delian (dē′ lē uhn) League. Sparta was one of the few Greek city-states that did not join the League.

Once a city-state became a League member, it could not withdraw unless all the other members agreed. The League had a common navy. Its ships were usually built and crewed by Athenians, but the other city-states paid the costs.

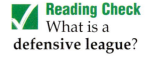

Reading Check
What is a **defensive league**?

People in History

Pericles
C. 495 B.C.–429 B.C.

Athenian General

As leader of Athens, Pericles turned the city-state into a center of learning. His influence was so great that historians call the period of his power the "Age of Pericles."

The League worked well for a while. As time passed, though, Athens gained more and more power. Other city-states had to ask Athens for permission to sail or to trade. Criminal cases were brought to Athens for trial. Athenian coins replaced other Greek money. Athenian soldiers interfered in the politics of other Greek city-states. In short, the Delian League had turned into the Athenian Empire.

The main leader of Athens at the time was a general named Pericles (per' uh klēz). Pericles was known as the "first citizen" of Athens. He had a dream of Athens as the most beautiful and perfect city of the time. To help make this dream come true, he rebuilt the palaces and temples on the Acropolis. It took 11 years to build the Parthenon (par' thuh non), the temple of the goddess Athena. Much of this building was done with money that belonged to the Delian League.

Pericles also built the Long Walls. These were two parallel, fortified walls with tile roofs. The Long Walls connected Athens with its seaport of Piraeus (pī rē' uhs) some five miles, or eight kilometers, away. Having the Long Walls meant Athens could get supplies even in times of war.

Linking Across Time

The Olive Tree According to Greek legend, the goddess Athena created the olive tree as her gift to human beings. Greek farmers have harvested olives for food and oil (below) for thousands of years. The olive tree continues to play an important part in the Greek economy today (right). **Why do you think Sparta burned the olive groves around Athens when it declared war on the city-state in 434 B.C.?**

Pericles led Athens for almost 30 years. During this period, art, philosophy, and literature reached new heights. Many people who came to Athens from other city-states settled there.

Decline of Athens

The more powerful Athens became, the more resentful other Greek city-states grew. Anti-Athenian feelings soon spread throughout Greece. When the Athenians attacked one of Sparta's allies, a group of city-states led by Sparta declared war on Athens. The war, which was called the Peloponnesian (pel uh puh nē′ zhuhn) War, lasted almost 30 years. It ended in 404 B.C. when Athens surrendered to Sparta.

Sculpture of Pericles

Between the war and a plague that struck during the war, Athens also lost more than one quarter of its people. Much of its land was ruined. Thousands of young Athenian men left home and became **mercenaries** (mer′ suh när ēz), or hired soldiers, in the Persian army.

When the Spartans took control of Athens in 404 B.C., they set up an oligarchy and chose 30 Athenian aristocrats to rule there. Not long after that, the Athenians successfully revolted and once more set up a democracy. However, Athens was never again as powerful as it had been before the Peloponnesian War.

✓ Reading Check
What type of jobs did Greek **mercenaries** seek in Persia?

Section 3 Assessment

1. **Define:** oligarchy, constitution, democratic, triremes, mercenaries.
2. What political reforms did Cleisthenes introduce?
3. What changes did Pericles bring to Athens?

Critical Thinking

4. **Understanding Cause and Effect** What were some of the causes and effects of the Peloponnesian War?

Graphic Organizer Activity

5. Draw a diagram like this, and use it to show how the Delian League affected both Athens and other city-states.

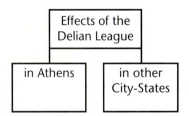

SECTION 4 Decline of the City-States

After the Peloponnesian War, most Greeks began to lose their sense of community. The war had lasted a long time and had cost a great deal of money. People became more interested in making money and having a good time. Soon, bitterness developed between the upper and lower classes within each polis.

After the war, Sparta ruled Greece. The Spartans were harsh rulers who angered the other Greeks. As a result, in 371 B.C., a group of city-states led by Thebes (thēbz) overthrew Spartan rule. The rule of Thebes, however, was no better than that of Sparta. It weakened the city-states even more. The Greeks were no longer strong enough or united enough to fight off invaders. In 338 B.C., Philip II of Macedonia (mas uh dō' nē uh) conquered Greece.

Section 4 Assessment

1. How did the Peloponnesian War help destroy the sense of community in most Greek city-states?
2. What were some of the reasons for the decline of the Greek city-states?

Critical Thinking

3. **Drawing Conclusions** Why might the Greeks have become more interested in making money for themselves rather than for the city-state after the Peloponnesian War?

Graphic Organizer Activity

4. Draw a flow chart like this one, and use it to trace the decline of the Greek city-states after the Peloponnesian War.

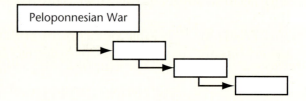

Peloponnesian War

Chapter Summary & Study Guide

1. Around 700 B.C., city-states became the center of Greek life.
2. The two greatest city-states were Sparta and Athens.
3. Sparta spent most of its time training its citizens for war.
4. Spartan women had more freedom than women in other city-states.
5. Spartans believed new ideas would weaken their way of life, so they tried to prevent change.
6. Between 750 and 507 B.C., Athens went through a series of reforms to broaden democracy.
7. In 507 B.C., Cleisthenes put into effect the first democratic constitution.
8. After several wars with Persia, Athens became Greece's leading polis.
9. Sparta defeated Athens in the Peloponnesian War, which was fought between 431 and 404 B.C.
10. The Peloponnesian War weakened the Greek city-states, leading to the conquest of Greece by Philip II of Macedonia in 338 B.C.

Self-Check Quiz

Visit the *Human Heritage* Web site at **humanheritage. glencoe.com** and click on *Chapter 10—Self-Check Quiz* to assess your understanding of this chapter.

Using Key Terms

Imagine you are living in Greece during the time of the Persian Wars. Use the following words to write a letter to a friend describing the organization and government of Sparta and Athens at that time.

polis   acropolis   agora
aristocrats   perioeci   oligarchy
helots   democratic   constitution
triremes   mercenaries   defensive
                                    league

Understanding Main Ideas

1. Why did Greek communities have little contact with one another?
2. What did the citizens of a polis consider most important?
3. Why was it important for Spartan women to be physically fit?
4. Why did Sparta remain a poor farming society?
5. Why was the Battle of Marathon important for the Greeks?
6. How did Athenians use the Delian League to build an empire?

Critical Thinking

1. Do you think that the Spartan emphasis on military training benefited Sparta? Why or why not?
2. What method of choosing members of the Athenian Council of Five Hundred would you have suggested? Explain your answer.
3. Why do you think some people in Athens might have objected to the title of "first citizen" for Pericles? Explain your answer.

4. What may happen to a community as a result of a long war? Why?

Graphic Organizer Activity

Culture Draw a Venn diagram like this one, and use it to compare Sparta and Athens at their height of power.

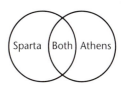

Sparta Both Athens

Geography in History

Places and Regions Note the location of the Greek city-states on the map on page 173. Why do you think these city-states developed in the places that they did, and what geographic features might have affected this development? Write a paragraph explaining the relationship between a city's location and the surrounding geographic features.

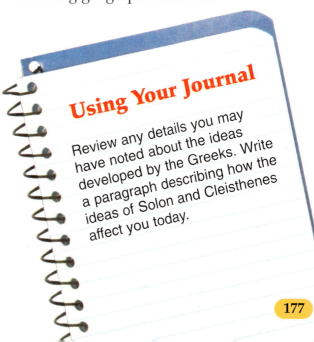

Using Your Journal

Review any details you may have noted about the ideas developed by the Greeks. Write a paragraph describing how the ideas of Solon and Cleisthenes affect you today.

Cultural Contributions

775 B.C.–338 B.C.

▲ Greek vase with women runners

◀ Statue of an Athenian girl

776 B.C.
First Olympic Games

585 B.C.
Thales predicts eclipse of sun

399 B.C.
Trial of Socrates

387 B.C.
Plato sets up Academy

322 B.C.
Aristotle dies

Chapter Focus

 Read to Discover

- How the Greeks honored their gods and goddesses.
- What contributions in athletics and the arts were made during the "Golden Age" of Greek culture.
- How Greek thinkers influenced the development of world civilization.

Chapter Overview

Visit the *Human Heritage* Web site at **humanheritage.glencoe.com** and click on **Chapter 11— Chapter Overviews** to preview this chapter.

 Terms to Learn

oracles
prophecy
pancratium
pentathlon
philosophia
Socratic
  method
hypothesis
syllogism

 People to Know

Herodotus
Socrates
Plato
Aristotle

 Places to Locate

Mount Olympus
Olympia

Why It's Important   The Greeks made many contributions to world civilization. Their accomplishments resulted, in part, because of an important religious belief. The Greeks felt their gods were honored if people tried to imitate them. The greater the skill the Greeks showed in thinking, athletic games, or the arts, the more the gods were honored. Greek efforts to do their best produced a "Golden Age" of learning. Many historians call this period the "Classical Age of Greece."

SECTION 1   Religious Practices

Although most Greeks held similar religious beliefs, there was no single Greek religion. Each city-state worshiped its own gods. Officials in each polis were in charge of public feasts and sacrifices. In their own homes, heads of families prayed and offered sacrifices to the gods.

Greek priests and priestesses often served as **oracles,** or persons who, it was believed, could speak with the gods. Many Greeks went to oracles for advice. The advice was generally given in the form of a **prophecy** (prof' uh sē), or a statement of what might

Reading Check
Why did many Greeks go to the **oracles?**
What is a **prophecy?**

THE DELPHIC ORACLE   The most popular oracle was a priestess in the temple at Delphi. The Greeks believed that Delphi was the center of the world, and they built many temples and other public buildings there (right). The painting of the Delphic oracle (left) shows her offering a prophecy to a Greek man. **Why was a prophecy from an oracle often confusing?**

happen in the future. Often, a prophecy could mean more than one thing. The person seeking advice had to decide what he or she believed to be the true meaning of the prophecy.

Gods and Goddesses of Mount Olympus

During the Golden Age, the Greeks worshiped the gods of Mount Olympus (ō lim' puhs). There were 12 major gods and goddesses. Each had specific duties to carry out.

Most ancient peoples feared their gods. They believed that people were put on Earth only to obey and serve the gods. The Greeks were the first people to feel differently. They placed importance on the worth of the individual. Because they believed in their own value, the Greeks had a great deal of self-respect. This allowed them to approach their gods with dignity.

The Greeks built temples to honor their gods. Inside each temple stood a statue of the god being honored. In front of the statue was an altar. Because the Greeks believed the temple was the god's home, they did not enter it. They worshiped outside, as a sign of respect.

Another way the Greeks honored their gods was with different kinds of festivals. Each showed the power of the god in whose honor it was given. Out of the festivals came two important contributions to western culture. These were the Olympic Games and the theater.

Student Web Activity

Visit the *Human Heritage* Web site at humanheritage.glencoe.com and click on **Chapter 11— Student Web Activities** to find out more about Greek contributions.

The Olympic Games   Every four years, in the middle of summer, a festival was held in Olympia (ō lim′ pē uh) to honor the god Zeus. Olympia was not really a town. It was a group of

OLYMPIAN GODS AND GODDESSES

Name	Realm
Zeus	ruler of Mount Olympus; king of the gods; god of the weather
Aphrodite	goddess of love and beauty
Apollo	god of the sun; patron of truth, archery, music, medicine, and prophecy
Ares	god of war
Artemis	goddess of the moon; mighty huntress and "rainer of arrows"; guardian of cities, young animals, and women; twin sister of Apollo
Athena	goddess of wisdom; city god of Athens; patron of household crafts; protectress in war of those who worshiped her; daughter of Zeus
Demeter	goddess of crops, giver of grain and fruit
Dionysus	god of fertility, of joyous life and hospitality, and of wild things
Hephaestus	god of fire and artisans; maker of Pandora, the first mortal woman; husband of Aphrodite
Hera	protectress of marriage, children, and the home; wife of Zeus
Hermes	god of orators, writers, and commerce; protector of thieves and mischief-makers; guardian of wayfarers; messenger to mortals; son of Zeus
Poseidon	god of the sea and earthquakes; giver of horses to mortals

temples and arenas built in fields. A 40-foot, or 12-meter, gold and ivory statue of Zeus stood in one of the temples.

The festival was known as the Olympic Games. It was the most important sporting event in Greece. While the games were going on, the Greeks would stop fighting any war in which they were involved. When the Spartans refused to call a truce during the Peloponnesian War to compete in the games, they had to pay a fine.

Athletes came from all over Greece and from Greek colonies in Africa, Italy, and Asia Minor to take part in the games. Individuals, rather than teams, competed. Only men were allowed to take part. Women were not even allowed to watch. Each athlete had to swear on the sacred boar of Zeus that he would follow the rules of the games. Those who broke the rules were fined.

The Olympics were made up of many events. One of the most exciting was the chariot race. It was held in the Hippodrome (hip′ uh drōm), which was an oval track with grandstands around it. The chariots had small wheels and were open in the back. At first, they were pulled by four horses. Later, only two horses were used. About 40 chariots started the race, but only a few could finish the 9 miles, or 14.4 kilometers. The driver of the winning chariot received a crown made from olive leaves.

WARRIOR'S RACE The first Olympic Games were mainly simple foot races. Later, other events were added. One of these additions was the warrior's race. In it, runners competed wearing full armor and carrying a shield. **What were some other events in the early Olympics?**

Another major event was boxing. Boxers did not use their fists. They wrapped their hands with strips of ox hide and slapped one another with the flat of the hand. There were no set rounds or points. A match between two boxers went on until one raised a finger in the air as a sign of defeat.

Another fighting event was the **pancratium** (pan krā′ shē uhm). This was a combination of boxing and wrestling in which no holds were barred between the two fighters. The only two things a fighter could not do were gouge an opponent's eyes or bite.

The winner of the **pentathlon** (pen tath′ luhn) was considered the best all-around athlete. The pentathlon itself was made up of five events. Those who took part had to run, jump, throw the discus (dis′ kuhs), wrestle, and hurl the javelin (jav′ luhn). Like other winners, the winner of the pentathlon was crowned with an olive-leaf wreath.

Olympic winners were heroes. Poets wrote about them. City-states held parades for them. Some city-states even gave them free meals for a year.

Between the different events at the games, poets read their works aloud. Herodotus (hi rahd′ uh tuhs), the "Father of History," first read his account of the Persian Wars at the Olympics. Greek historians even dated events by Olympiads (ō lim′ pē ads), or the four-year periods between games. The first recorded date in Greek history is the date of the first Olympic Games, which occurred in 776 B.C.

The Theater   The theater grew out of festivals given in honor of the god Dionysus (dī uh nī′ suhs). About 600 B.C., the Ionians began telling stories about Dionysus at festivals. A chorus chanted and danced each story to the music of a flute. At certain points, the chorus fell silent. The chorus leader then gave a *soliloquy* (suh lil′ uh kwē), or talk in which personal thoughts and feelings are expressed to the audience.

In time, the chorus became shorter and the soliloquies longer. Stories were then told about other gods and heroes. About the time of the Persian Wars, a Greek poet named Aeschylus (es′ kuh luhs) added an additional character to each story. Now, instead of singing or telling a story, it was acted out. Thus, Aeschylus created what came to be known as a play.

The first Greek plays were *tragedies* (traj′ uh dēz), or stories about suffering. All dealt with the past and with the relationships between people and gods. Not all of them had unhappy endings. Still, they all pointed out that though people suffered, most individuals were able to carry on despite their suffering.

Three of the great writers of tragedy were Aeschylus, Sophocles (sahf′ uh klēz), and Euripides (yū rip′ uh dēz). All three lived in Athens during its Golden Age. Aeschylus wrote about power and its effect on people. Sophocles showed that people

Reading Check
How did athletes compete in the **pancratium?** What five events made up the **pentathlon?**

Orchestra *Orchestra* is a Greek word from the verb "to dance." At first, it meant the space between the stage and the audience where the chorus performed. In modern times, the term designates both the area in front of the stage and the group of musicians who plays there.

Comedy and Tragedy Masks

suffered because of their sins and mistakes and that suffering could make someone a better person. Euripides tried to show that people suffered because they did bad things.

Soon after the development of tragedy, a second kind of play came into being. It was *comedy,* or a play with a happy ending. Unlike tragedies, Greek comedies were about the present. At first, they poked fun at certain politicians and other polis leaders, who often were in the audience. Later, comedies did away with the chorus. They also stopped poking fun at specific people. Instead, they poked fun at a certain kind of person, such as a son who wastes money or an enslaved person who plots against a master. One of the greatest writers of Greek comedy was Aristophanes (ar uh stahf' uh nēz). He found something funny about everyone.

Greek plays were performed only at community festivals. They began at sunrise and went on all day. Tragedies were presented in the morning and comedies in the afternoon. All the performers were men. Women were allowed to watch plays but could not act in them.

Each actor wore a huge canvas and plaster mask that showed the gender, age, and mood of the character. The mouth of the mask was shaped like a funnel. This helped carry the sound of the actor's voice to the entire audience. Actors also wore heavy padding under their robes and boots with thick soles. This made them seem larger than they really were.

Linking Across Time

Greek Theaters   The idea of having audiences sit around a stage to watch a play started with the Greeks (left). Today people go to theaters to watch everything from plays to movies to rock concerts (below). **How did the design of Greek theaters allow many people to attend a performance?**

Plays were given in open-air theaters. Anyone who did not have enough money to buy a ticket was admitted free. The audience sat on rows of stone benches set on the side of a hill. The benches were arranged in a semicircle around a stage that was level with the ground.

The Greeks believed support of the theater was a public responsibility. An official of each polis chose the plays to be performed. This official then assigned each play to a wealthy citizen to stage. A panel of citizens judged the plays at each festival.

Section 1 Assessment

1. **Define:** oracles, prophecy, pancratium, pentathlon.
2. How did the Greeks honor their gods and goddesses?
3. Who took part in the Olympics?

Critical Thinking

4. **Demonstrating Reasoned Judgment** Do you think support of the theater should be the responsibility of government or private groups? Explain.

Graphic Organizer Activity

5. Draw a diagram like this one, and use it to list events at the Greek Olympics. (Add additional answer lines as needed.)

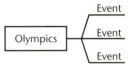

SECTION 2 Science

Among the things on which the Greeks placed great importance was *intellect* (in' tuh lekt), or the ability to learn and reason. The Greeks thought intellect should be used to its fullest. Because of this, they asked questions about many things and studied the laws of nature. To the Greeks, studying the laws of nature and loving wisdom were the same thing. They called it *philosophia* (fi la sō fē' ya). Today, people who search for such knowledge and wisdom are known as scientists and *philosophers*. Much of what they know is based on the thoughts of the Greeks.

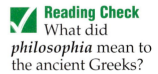

Reading Check
What did *philosophia* mean to the ancient Greeks?

Socrates In 399 B.C., a trial was held in Athens. The person on trial was Socrates (sok' ruh tēz), a 70-year-old Athenian philosopher who was interested in the thinking process. Socrates gave up private business so he could spend his time searching for truth. He believed people could discover truth if they knew how to think.

In his search for truth, Socrates walked throughout Athens trying to teach people how to think. He did this by asking questions. Each question was designed to make a person arrive

Rules for Life

Many quotes about ethical, or morally correct, living have been attributed to Socrates. These are two of the best known:

- "The unexamined life is not worth living."
- "I am a citizen, not of Athens or Greece, but of the world."

step-by-step at a final conclusion, or truth. This form of questioning is known as the **Socratic** (sō krat' ik) **method.**

All Athenians did not react in the same way to Socrates's teachings. Some were pleased because they learned how to examine their own beliefs and to think things out. Others saw Socrates's ideas as dangerous. They did not like self-examination, particularly when it pointed out their own mistakes. In time, they began to consider Socrates a threat to Athens. Finally, they accused him of denying the gods, corrupting the young, and trying to overthrow the government.

Socrates was tried before a jury of some 500 citizens. He defended himself by speaking about truth and goodness. He said, "Wealth does not bring goodness. But goodness brings wealth and every blessing, both to the citizen and to the polis." He also said he would not change his beliefs even to save his life.

The jury found Socrates guilty and sentenced him to death. The sentence was carried out by making Socrates drink poisonous hemlock juice. Later, the Athenians regretted having executed Socrates, so they put up a bronze statue in his honor.

DEATH OF SOCRATES Socrates faced death with self-control and dignity. Here, in an eighteenth-century painting, he is surrounded by his sorrowing friends as he prepares to drink poisonous hemlock juice. **How did the Athenians regard Socrates after his death?**

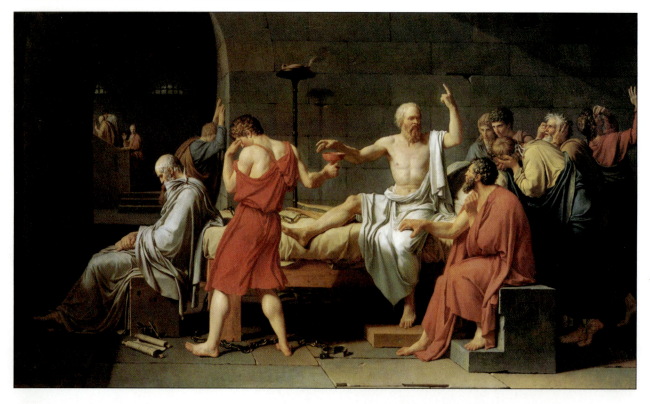

GREEK PHILOSOPHERS The ideas of Greek thinkers influenced the development of world civilization. Here, in a sixteenth-century European painting, Plato and Aristotle discuss the meaning of human achievement with their pupils. **What was the subject of Plato's *The Republic*?**

Plato Socrates left no writings. All that is known about him comes from one of his pupils, an Athenian aristocrat named Plato (plā' tō). Plato recorded the speeches Socrates made at his trial and just before his death.

Plato was 30 years old when Socrates died. Until then, Plato had wanted to become a politician. In 399 B.C., he changed his mind. He left Greece and traveled in Egypt and Italy for the next 12 years. When he returned, he set up a school outside Athens in the sacred grove of the hero Academus (ak uh dē' muhs). The school, where Plato hoped to train government leaders, was called the Academy. Plato taught there almost 40 years. The Academy itself lasted almost 900 years after Plato's death.

Plato's beliefs were contrary to the ideas that had made Athens great. Plato believed in order. He thought political liberty was disorder and did not approve of it. He thought only the wise and good should rule.

Plato set down his ideas about an ideal state in a book called *The Republic*. It is the first book ever written on **political science,** or the study of government. In it, Plato examined different kinds of government and explained how to avoid political errors.

Like Socrates, Plato believed in truth. He thought it could be found only after a long, hard search. In a work called *The Dialogues*

Reading Check
What is the subject of **political science?**

Sculpture of Aristotle

✓ **Reading Check**
What is the purpose of the **scientific method?** What is a **hypothesis?** How does a **syllogism** work?

People in History

Aristotle
384 B.C.–322 B.C.

Greek Scientist

After studying in Greece, Aristotle returned to Macedonia to teach the son of King Philip II. This boy, later known as Alexander the Great, would one day conquer many lands, including Greece. Thus, Aristotle's ideas came to influence an entire empire.

(dī′ uh logs), he showed how difficult it is to discover truth. *The Dialogues* consists of a series of discussions in which different people talk about such things as truth and loyalty. Socrates is the leading speaker in many discussions. Through these discussions, Plato brings out the self-questioning that goes on within a person troubled by such issues.

Aristotle

One of Plato's brightest pupils was Aristotle (ar′ uh stot l). Aristotle came to the Academy when he was 17 years old and stayed for 20 years. Before he died in 322 B.C., he founded his own school in Athens and wrote more than 200 books.

Aristotle was known as "the master of them that know." He believed in using one's senses to discover the laws that govern the physical world. He was the first to *classify*, or group together, plants and animals that resemble each other. His system, with some changes, is still used today. It has helped scientists handle a great amount of information in an orderly way.

Aristotle also added to the ideas of an earlier Greek scientist named Thales (thā′ lēz) of Miletus (mi let′ uhs). Thales developed the first two steps of what is known today as the **scientific method.** This is the process used by scientists to study something. First, Thales collected information. Then, based on what he observed, he formed a **hypothesis** (hī poth′ uh sis), or possible explanation. Aristotle provided a third step in the scientific method when he said that a hypothesis must be tested to see if it is correct.

Another important contribution Aristotle made was in *logic* (loj′ ik), or the science of reasoning. He developed the **syllogism** (sil′ uh jiz uhm). This is a method of reasoning that uses three related statements. The third statement is a conclusion based on the information given in the first two. For example:

Athenians are Greeks.
Socrates is an Athenian.
Therefore, Socrates is Greek.

Discoveries and Inventions

Greek scientists were not looking for ways to make life easier or better. They were trying to add to their store of knowledge. They had none of the tools scientists have today. There were no telescopes, microscopes, or scales that weigh small amounts. Even without these, however, the Greeks made important discoveries.

Their curiosity led Greek scientists to discover that natural events are not caused by the way gods behave. They also learned that the world is governed by natural laws that people can discover and understand.

There were many Greek scientists. The first was Thales of Miletus, who came from Ionia. Thales not only developed the first two steps of the scientific method, but he also correctly predicted

GREEK SCIENTISTS

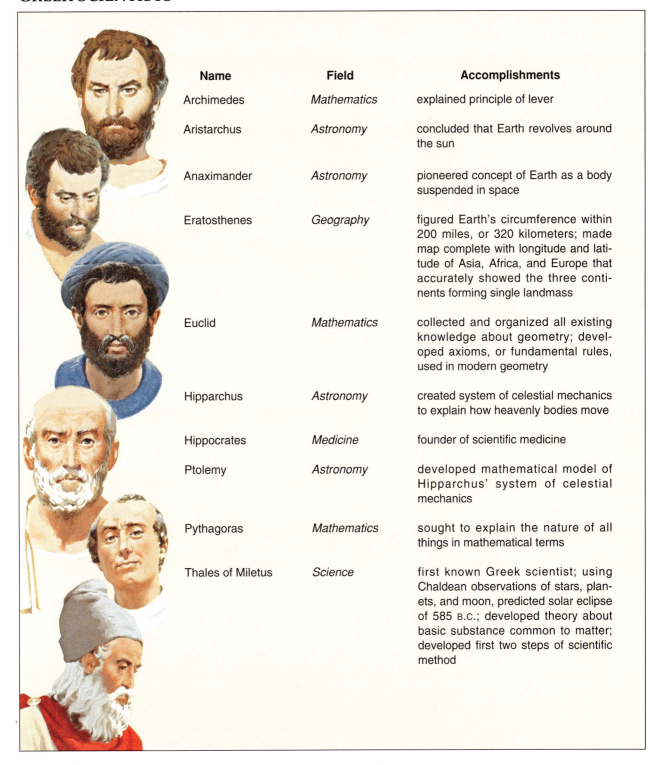

Name	Field	Accomplishments
Archimedes	*Mathematics*	explained principle of lever
Aristarchus	*Astronomy*	concluded that Earth revolves around the sun
Anaximander	*Astronomy*	pioneered concept of Earth as a body suspended in space
Eratosthenes	*Geography*	figured Earth's circumference within 200 miles, or 320 kilometers; made map complete with longitude and latitude of Asia, Africa, and Europe that accurately showed the three continents forming single landmass
Euclid	*Mathematics*	collected and organized all existing knowledge about geometry; developed axioms, or fundamental rules, used in modern geometry
Hipparchus	*Astronomy*	created system of celestial mechanics to explain how heavenly bodies move
Hippocrates	*Medicine*	founder of scientific medicine
Ptolemy	*Astronomy*	developed mathematical model of Hipparchus' system of celestial mechanics
Pythagoras	*Mathematics*	sought to explain the nature of all things in mathematical terms
Thales of Miletus	*Science*	first known Greek scientist; using Chaldean observations of stars, planets, and moon, predicted solar eclipse of 585 B.C.; developed theory about basic substance common to matter; developed first two steps of scientific method

an eclipse of the sun in 585 B.C. The contributions made by Thales and other Greek scientists were important to the growth of scientific thought.

Greek scientists also contributed to the field of medicine. The "Father of Scientific Medicine" was Hippocrates (hi pok' ruh tēz). Hippocrates was considered the perfect physician. He traveled throughout Greece diagnosing illnesses and curing sick people. He believed diseases came from natural causes. At the time, most other doctors thought diseases were caused by evil spirits entering the body.

Hippocrates drew up a list of rules about how doctors should use their skills to help their patients. His rules are known as the Hippocratic (hip uh krat' ik) Oath. The oath says that doctors should honor their teachers, do their best for the sick, never give poisons, and keep the secrets of their patients. Doctors all over the world still promise to honor the Hippocratic Oath.

Section 2 Assessment

1. **Define:** *philosophia*, Socratic method, political science, scientific method, hypothesis, syllogism.
2. What were Plato's beliefs about government?

Critical Thinking

3. **Drawing Conclusions**   Review the syllogism on page 188. Then write a syllogism to help you draw a conclusion about one of the Greek thinkers in this chapter.

Graphic Organizer Activity

4. Draw a diagram like this one. Use it to show the steps in the scientific method that Thales of Miletus and Aristotle developed.

Step 1   Step 2   Step 3

Chapter Summary & Study Guide

1. During the "Golden Age," the Greeks made many contributions in thinking, athletics, and the arts.
2. The Olympic Games, held every four years in honor of the Greek god Zeus, was the most important sporting event in Greece.
3. The theater, and eventually the play, developed out of a festival given in honor of the Greek god Dionysus.
4. Socrates, in his search for truth, developed a form of questioning known as the Socratic method.
5. Plato, who was one of Socrates's pupils, founded a school and wrote the first book on political science.
6. Aristotle developed a system of classification and provided a third step in the scientific method.

HISTORY Online

Self-Check Quiz

Visit the *Human Heritage* Web site at **humanheritage. glencoe.com** and click on **Chapter 11—Self-Check Quiz** to assess your understanding of this chapter.

Using Key Terms

Use the following words to make a chart that explains the ideas and contributions of the Greeks.

oracles
pancratium
philosophia
political science
hypothesis

prophecy
pentathlon
Socratic method
scientific method
syllogism

Understanding Main Ideas

1. What was the role of oracles in Greek religion?
2. What role did women play in the Olympic Games?
3. What was the relationship between Greek historians and the Olympic Games?
4. How did tragedies differ from comedies?
5. How did Athenians react to the teachings of Socrates?
6. Why did Plato set up the Academy?
7. How does the scientific method work?
8. In what subjects were Greek scientists most interested?
9. What was Euclid's most famous achievement?

Critical Thinking

1. What would you have done if it had been your decision whether or not to put Socrates on trial?
2. Why is the scientific method important to modern science?
3. How important was religion in ancient Greek civilization? Explain your answer.
4. Would you like being taught through the Socratic method? Why or why not?

Graphic Organizer Activity

History Draw a chart like this one, and use it to list four Greek ideas or inventions and to explain the effect each has had on your life.

Idea/Invention	Effect on My Life
1.	
2.	
3.	
4.	

Geography in History

Human Systems The Olympic Games drew contestants from all the areas under Greek control. What different methods of travel would athletes have used to reach Olympia where the games were held? Create a poster advertising transportation to the games.

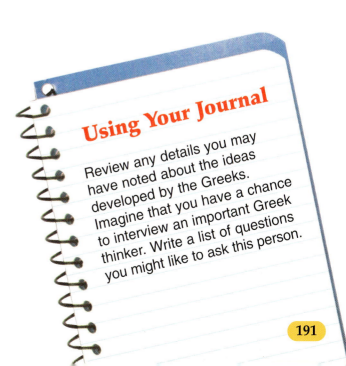

Using Your Journal

Review any details you may have noted about the ideas developed by the Greeks. Imagine that you have a chance to interview an important Greek thinker. Write a list of questions you might like to ask this person.

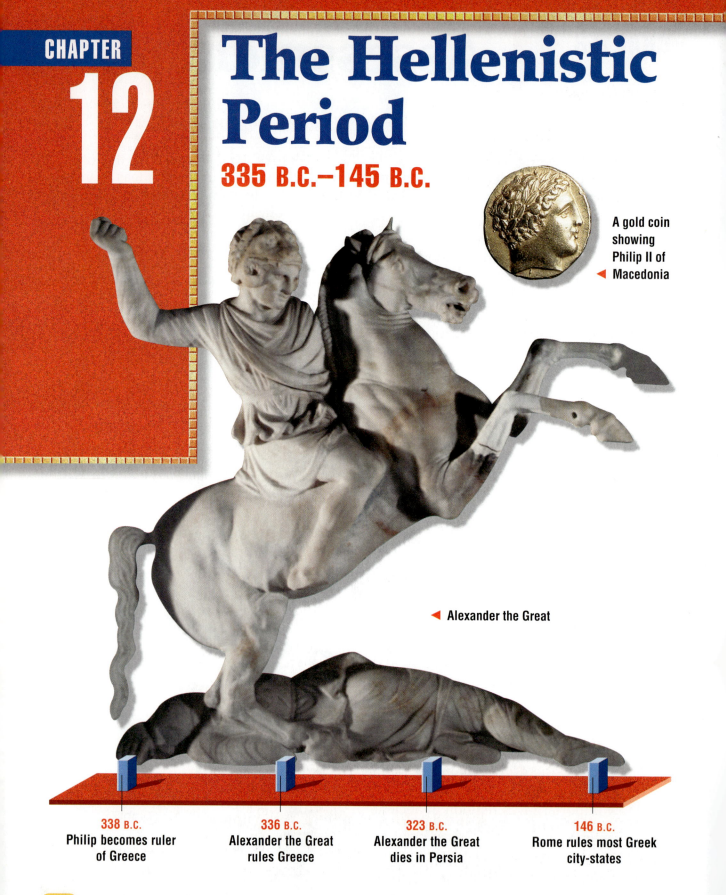

The Hellenistic Period

335 B.C.–145 B.C.

A gold coin showing Philip II of Macedonia ◄

◄ Alexander the Great

338 B.C.
Philip becomes ruler of Greece

336 B.C.
Alexander the Great rules Greece

323 B.C.
Alexander the Great dies in Persia

146 B.C.
Rome rules most Greek city-states

Chapter Focus

 Read to Discover

- How the spread of Greek culture influenced people from Gibraltar to India.
- How Philip II of Macedonia gained control of Greece.
- How Alexander attempted to bring unity to his empire.
- How Alexander's empire changed after his death.

Chapter Overview

Visit the *Human Heritage* Web site at <u>humanheritage.glencoe.com</u> and click on *Chapter 12— Chapter Overviews* to preview this chapter.

 Terms to Learn

hostage
phalanx
alliances
orator
barbaroi
factories
emigrated

 People to Know

Philip of
Macedonia
Demosthenes
Alexander the
Great

 Places to Locate

Macedonia
Persia
Alexandria

Why It's Important   After the Greek city-states lost their independence, many changes took place. The new rulers of Greece built empires and increased trade. At the same time, they spread Greek culture and customs. Before long, Greek ideas were influencing people from Gibraltar (juh brol' tuhr) to India.

The Greek language came to be spoken by many people. Greek architecture was copied for new buildings. Students studied Greek literature in school. People used Greek furniture in their homes. Greek plays became a popular form of entertainment. Business people took up Greek ways of banking.

The period in which all this took place has come to be called the Hellenistic (hel uh nis' tik) Age. The term "Hellenistic" means "like the Hellenes, or the Greeks."

SECTION 1   Philip II of Macedonia

By 338 B.C., Greece had a new ruler, Philip II of Macedonia. Macedonia was a small, mountainous country north of Greece. Most Macedonians were farmers. They cared little for the Greeks and had fought them in the Persian Wars. Macedonian kings, however, were of Greek descent and admired Greek culture.

Philip became ruler of Macedonia in 359 B.C. During his youth, he was a **hostage** (hos' tij), or a person held by an enemy until certain promises are carried out, for three years in Thebes. In those

 **Reading Check**
What is a **hostage**?

years, he learned to love Greek culture. However, he learned to dislike the weaknesses of the Greek form of government.

Philip believed it was his destiny to unify the Greek city-states and spread Greek culture. As soon as he became ruler of Macedonia, he set out to fulfill that destiny. It took him a little over 20 years.

Philip went about reaching his goal in many ways. For example, until his time, the Macedonian army was made up of volunteers, who fought only in the summer. Philip turned this part-time volunteer army into a year-round, well-organized, professional one.

Philip developed an infantry formation called a **phalanx** (fā' langks). Foot soldiers formed a solid body some 16 rows deep. Those in each line stayed so close together that their shields overlapped. This gave them added protection. The phalanx charged as a group, which gave it more striking power.

Philip also armed his soldiers with spears that were 14 feet, or over 4 meters, long. This was twice as long as ordinary spears. He

> **Reading Check**
> Why was a
> **phalanx** powerful?

People in History

Demosthenes
383 B.C.–322 B.C.

Greek Orator

Demosthenes, born into a wealthy Athenian family, was a great speaker and politician. He is most famous for a series of speeches called "Philippics," in which he warned the Greek people about King Philip of Macedonia. By 338 B.C., however, Philip had conquered Greece, and the city-states had lost their independence.

DEMOSTHENES   Demosthenes worked to preserve the freedom of the Greek city-states. He was known for his ability as a public speaker. It is said he trained himself by shouting above the roar of the ocean waves with his mouth full of pebbles. **What did Demosthenes try to tell the Greeks about Philip of Macedonia?**

added soldiers trained in the use of slingshots and bows and arrows. These soldiers could fight in hilly areas where the phalanx was not able to go.

Philip flattered local Greek officials and gave them gold. He found ways to cause disagreements among Greek city-states. Then, when city-states were weak from fighting each other, his army moved in and conquered them.

Philip made treaties with Greek leaders only to break them when the Greeks let down their guard. He saw marriage as a way of forming political **alliances** (uh lī' uhn siz), or partnerships. He married six or seven times for this reason.

Demosthenes (di mahs' thuh nēz), an Athenian **orator** (ōr' uh ter), or public speaker, tried to warn the Greeks that Philip was dangerous, but most would not listen. They were unhappy with their local governments and thought Philip would improve things.

When Philip led his soldiers into central Greece in 338 B.C., Thebes and Athens raised a small army to stop the invasion. The Greek army, however, was not strong enough and was defeated at the Battle of Chaeronea (ker uh nē' uh). Having gained control of Greece, Philip began preparing for a campaign against Persia. However, in 336 B.C., in the middle of his preparations, he was killed, and his son Alexander took over the throne.

Reading Check
How did Philip II use **alliances?** What is an **orator?**

Section 1 Assessment

1. **Define:** hostage, phalanx, alliances, orator.
2. Why was Philip able to defeat the Greek city-states?
3. Who was Demosthenes?

Critical Thinking
4. **Making Inferences** How do you think a Greek citizen living under the rule of Philip II would describe him as a ruler?

Graphic Organizer Activity
5. Use a web diagram like the one shown to list the achievements of Philip II.

Philip II

SECTION 2 Alexander the Great

Alexander took over Philip's throne at the age of 20. He had been a commander in the army since he was 16. Upon becoming a commander, he cut his shoulder-length hair and ordered his soldiers to shave their beards. This, he said, would keep enemy soldiers from grabbing them in close combat.

Alexander was physically strong and good-looking. He also had developed his mind. For three years, Aristotle had taught him literature, political science, geography, and biology. Because of this, Alexander included philosophers and scientists in his army.

The scientists collected plant and animal samples from newly conquered lands and sent them to Aristotle for examination.

Alexander was a great general who feared nothing. He crushed the Persian Empire and then marched as far east as northern India. He would have gone farther, but his troops refused. In the course of his conquests, Alexander covered more than 22,000 miles, or over 35,200 kilometers, from the Nile to the Indus rivers. Through all that territory, he never lost a battle.

Alexander's Empire

Alexander had a dream of a worldwide state in which all people would live together in peace. He wanted to bring unity and justice to his empire.

Alexander believed the only way to achieve his goal was to unite the Macedonians, the Greeks, and the Persians. He began by taking Persian soldiers into his army. Next, he married a Persian woman and had 80 of his leading army officers marry Persian women, too. Then, he began to dress in Persian fashion and to follow some Persian customs.

One custom was for rulers to claim they were gods. So, Alexander claimed he was a god and insisted that people treat him that way. The Macedonians and Greeks, however, refused to do so. The Greeks also objected to equal treatment for the Persians. They looked down on all people who did not speak Greek or

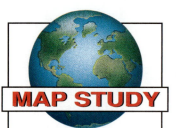

MAP STUDY

THE WORLD IN SPATIAL TERMS

At the time of his death, Alexander the Great ruled over much of the classical world. **Why do you think Alexander founded his capital, Alexandria, where he did?**

The Empire of Alexander the Great

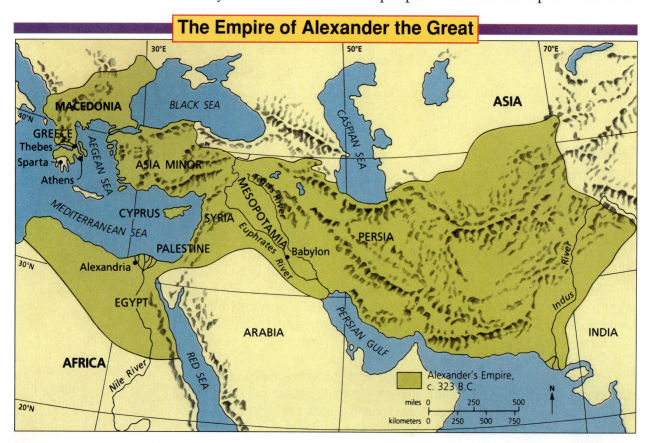

Alexander's Empire, c. 323 B.C.

LIGHTHOUSE OF ALEXANDRIA The lighthouse of Alexandria was one of the Seven Wonders of the Ancient World. It towered over Alexandria's two excellent harbors. A fire on top provided light to guide ships into port. **Why was Alexandria also considered a center for learning?**

follow Greek customs. They called such people *barbaroi* (bar' buh roi), from which the word "barbarians" comes. Because of such feelings, Alexander's attempt to achieve unity among the people in his empire was not successful.

Alexandria During his rule, Alexander founded about 70 cities, 16 of which were named Alexandria (al ig zan' drē uh) after himself. He encouraged Greeks and Macedonians to settle in the new cities, which were scattered throughout the empire.

The most noted Alexandria was in Egypt. Within 70 years after its founding, it had become a center of trade and learning. Greeks from throughout the eastern Mediterranean came there. They wanted to make the most of its economic opportunities and to be a part of its intellectual and social life.

Alexandria had two great harbors. They were protected by *breakwaters*, or barriers that break the force of waves. A lighthouse 400 feet, or about 122 meters, tall dominated the harbors. It is considered one of the Seven Wonders of the Ancient World.

Looking out over the chief harbor was a palace and a school with a library. The school was known as the Museum. It became a center for poets, writers, philosophers, and scientists. The library had the largest collection of books in ancient times. There, Euclid (ū' kluhd) wrote his geometry book. There, Eratosthenes (er uh

Reading Check
What English word is derived from *barbaroi?*

Student Web Activity
Visit the *Human Heritage* Web site at **humanheritage.glencoe.com** and click on *Chapter 12—Student Web Activities* to find out more about Alexandria.

ALEXANDER THE GREAT   Alexander conquered tremendous amounts of territory. His empire stretched from Greece to northern India. This painting of Alexander shows him leading his army ashore in Asia Minor and claiming all lands to the east as his own. **Why was Alexander unable to continue his conquests beyond India?**

tahs' thuh nēz) reasoned that a ship could reach India by sailing west from Spain. There, Archimedes (ar kuh mēd' ēz) and Hero (hē' rō) invented several machines.

End of the Empire

In 323 B.C., when Alexander was in Babylon, he became ill and died. He was 33 years old and had ruled for 13 years. His body was wrapped in gold and placed in a glass coffin in the Royal Tombs of Alexandria, Egypt. After his death, Alexander became a romantic legend. More than 80 versions of his life have been written in more than 20 languages.

After Alexander's death, fights broke out over who was to rule the empire. The areas Alexander had conquered in India returned to their original rulers. Three of Alexander's generals divided the rest of the empire among themselves. Antigonus (an tig' uh nuhs) became king of Macedonia. Ptolemy (tahl' uh mē) established the dynasty of the Ptolemies in Egypt. Seleucus (suh lū' kuhs) formed the Seleucid Empire in Persia. Athens and

Sparta again became independent city-states. Most other Greek city-states banded together into one of two leagues, but neither league had much power or importance.

Greek cultural influence, however, became stronger than ever after Alexander's death. The rulers who took Alexander's place adopted Greek as their language and used Alexander's titles. They even used his portrait on their coins.

Trade grew. From Africa and Asia came spices, ivory, incense, pearls, and rare woods. From Syria and Egypt came glass, metals, and linen. From Greece came olive oil, wine, and pottery. From Sicily and Egypt came wheat.

The cities that had been part of Alexander's empire now existed chiefly for trade and grew along with it. City officials made their laws, language, calendar, and coins Greek. Teachers brought Greek customs and ideas into schools. Merchants and bankers used Greek methods to run their businesses.

Fun Facts . . . .

Greek Discoveries
Greek scientists at Alexandria made several key discoveries. Eratosthenes calculated the earth's circumference to within 1 percent of its actual size. Archimedes invented a watering tool that Egyptian farmers used for nearly 2,000 years.

Linking Across Time

Hellenistic Influence The columns of an ancient Greek temple (left) influenced the style of this United States government building (right). **Why do you think the Hellenistic style of art and architecture is often used on present-day government buildings?**

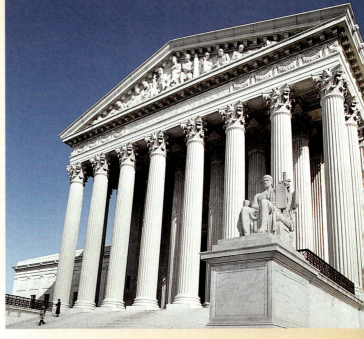

Reading Check
What are **factories?**
What happened to city-states when many young Greeks **emigrated?**

The Greek city-states, however, were never the same again. Although they kept their political independence, they could not gain back the power of the past. In time, economic conditions grew worse. Great **factories,** or places where goods are made, had been built in the new Hellenistic cities. Greek manufacturers now found they could not compete with these factories. Because of this, more and more young Greeks **emigrated** (em' uh grāt ed), or left one place to settle in another. Population in the Greek city-states fell. There were not enough people to work the land, and many farms once again became wilderness. By 146 B.C., most of the Greek city-states were under Roman control.

Section 2 Assessment

1. **Define:** *barbaroi*, factories, emigrated.
2. Who was Alexander the Great?
3. What conquests did Alexander make?
4. How did Greek influence continue to grow and spread after Alexander's death?

Critical Thinking

5. **Forming Conclusions**   How successful would Alexander's dream of uniting the world in peace be today? Explain.

Graphic Organizer Activity

6. Draw a time line like this one, and use it to show the major events in the life of Alexander the Great.

Chapter Summary & Study Guide

1. Philip II believed it was his destiny to unify the Greek city-states and spread Greek culture.
2. Philip II was able to conquer Greece in 338 B.C.
3. When Philip II died in 336 B.C., his son Alexander took over power.
4. Alexander was a great general whose conquests stretched from the Nile to the Indus.
5. Alexander tried without success to unite the Macedonians, the Greeks, and the Persians.
6. The most famous city founded by Alexander was Alexandria, Egypt.
7. After Alexander died in 323 B.C., his empire was divided among three of his generals.
8. Despite Alexander's death, Greek cultural influence became stronger.
9. Although the Greek city-states again became independent following Alexander's death, economic conditions in Greece grew worse.
10. Most Greek city-states were under Roman control by 146 B.C.

Self-Check Quiz

Visit the *Human Heritage* Web site at **humanheritage. glencoe.com** and click on *Chapter 12—Self-Check Quiz* to assess your understanding of this chapter.

CHAPTER 12 Assessment

Using Key Terms

Use the following words to write a short paragraph about how Philip II gained control of Greece. Then write a paragraph about what helped cause the end of the city-states.

hostage   phalanx   alliances
orator   *barbaroi*   factories
emigrated

Understanding Main Ideas

1. What changes did Philip II make in his army?
2. How did Philip II view marriage?
3. Why did the Greeks refuse to listen to Demosthenes' warnings?
4. What did Aristotle teach Alexander?
5. Why was Alexander unable to achieve unity among the people of his empire?
6. Why did many Greeks go to Alexandria, Egypt?
7. How did the physical features of Alexandria, Egypt, help trade?
8. What had happened to the Greek city-states by 146 B.C.?

Critical Thinking

1. Do you think Philip II was a successful military leader? Explain.
2. What other names might historians have given Alexander besides "the Great"?
3. What do you think Alexander could have done differently to achieve unity among the people in his empire? Explain.
4. In what ways can customs be spread without conquest?

Graphic Organizer Activity

Economics Create a cause-and-effect chart like this one, and use it to show reasons why the Greek city-states declined and the effects of their decline.

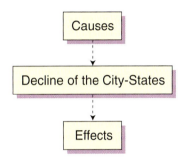

Causes

Decline of the City-States

Effects

Geography in History

Environment and Society What geographical features had an impact on the Greek economy? Note especially the development of manufacturing over farming and the Greeks' constant travel and trade.

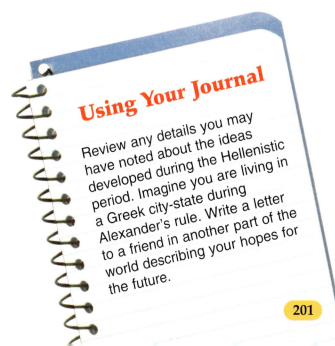

Using Your Journal

Review any details you may have noted about the ideas developed during the Hellenistic period. Imagine you are living in a Greek city-state during Alexander's rule. Write a letter to a friend in another part of the world describing your hopes for the future.

THE NUBIANS

Tales of Nubia—the vast land south of Egypt—fascinated the Greeks. They learned of its existence from stories told by the Egyptians or by the Nubians who lived in Egypt. However, few non-Africans visited Nubia until the rule of the Ptolemies, the Greek rulers of Egypt from 332 B.C. to 30 B.C. Under the Ptolemies, the Greeks got a firsthand look at one of the oldest civilizations in the ancient world.

Today, many archaeologists believe the Nubians may have developed their first culture around 8000 B.C. The Nubians also established a series of kingdoms in the area, such as Kush, that challenged the power of Egypt, Greece, and Rome. By the time Kush fell in 350 A.D., the Greek city-states had been under Roman rule for almost 500 years.

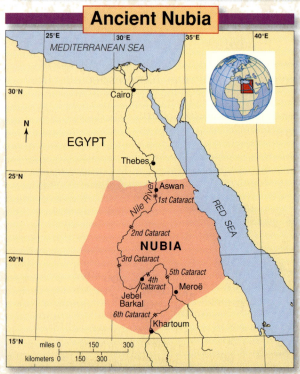

Ancient Nubia

◄ Nubian craftworkers excelled at creating fine works of art. This pendant is topped with a gold figure of a Nubian ruler.

▲ Geographical features, such as strong rapids and blazing deserts, protected the Nubians from unwanted visitors.

the W🌐rld

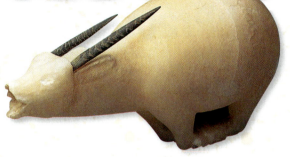

▲ The animals of inland Africa, such as lions, elephants, and giraffes, inspired Nubian artists. This bottle shows a bound oryx—a large African antelope prized by the Nubians for their beautiful long straight horns.

These figures of Nubian bowmen were found in the grave of a wealthy Egyptian buried around 2000 B.C. The Nubians were such skilled archers that the Egyptians ▲ called Nubia the "Land of the Bow." In times of peace, the Egyptians hired the Nubians as bodyguards.

The Nubians learned to work in bronze thousands of years ago. This statue of a Nubian king shows the skullcap and headband worn by the rulers of Kush. ▼

This bronze statue of a ▶ Nubian king, dating from about 700 B.C., was found in Cairo, Egypt, in 1929.

Taking Another Look

1. Where was Nubia located?
2. How did Nubia's location prevent the ancient non-African world from knowing much about its accomplishments?

Hands-On Activity

Creating an Advertisement Create a newspaper advertisement announcing a tour of Nubian artworks around the United States.

Standardized Test Practice

Directions: Choose the *best* answer to each of the following multiple choice questions. If you have trouble answering a question, use the process of elimination to narrow your choices. Write your answers on a separate piece of paper.

Greece and Persia

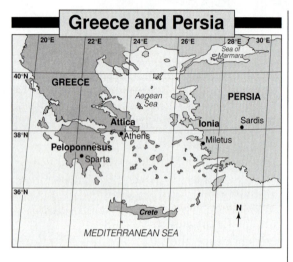

1. Along which line of longitude is Athens located?

A 22°E

B 24°E

C 38°N

D 36°N

Test-Taking Tip: *Lines of longitude*, or *meridians*, are used to measure distances <u>east</u> and <u>west</u>. They run from the North Pole to the South Pole. Be careful not to confuse *longitude* and *latitude*.

2. The Constitution of the United States has much in common with the constitution of ancient Athens. Which of the following provisions of the Athenian constitution is NOT part of the United States Constitution?

F Freedom of speech

G Choosing members of government by lottery

H Limits on the terms of elected officials

J Two separate bodies of government

Test-Taking Tip: Remember that the correct answer is true of the Athenian constitution but not true of the U.S. Constitution. Therefore, you can eliminate any answer that you know to be true of the U.S. Constitution. For instance, the United States Constitution *does* provide for freedom of speech, and so answer F cannot be the correct choice.

3. To protect themselves from attacks by the Persians, many Greek city-states joined the Delian League. This alliance allowed them to work together to defend themselves. Why did the Delian League eventually fall apart?

A The League suspended the voting rights of the Athenians.

B Most city-states decided that they would rather defend themselves alone.

C Athens took over the League, which made Athens too powerful.

D Athens stopped giving money to the League, so the League went bankrupt.

Test-Taking Tip: This question requires you to remember a *fact* about the Delian League. Make sure that you read the question and *all* of the answer choices carefully before selecting the *best* answer.

4. Socrates made several contributions to the fields of philosophy and science. Why was he sentenced to death in 399 B.C.?

   F Many people thought that he gave the rulers of Athens bad advice.

   G He designed a plan to overthrow the government of Greece.

   H He encouraged all people to leave their jobs and go in search of truth.

   J Many Athenians felt threatened by him because he pointed out their mistakes.

> **Test-Taking Tip:** Eliminate answers that do not make sense. Socrates was not interested in overthrowing the government; therefore, you can eliminate answer G.

5. The goal of early Greek philosophers was

   A to create new inventions to improve Greek society

   B to look for truths by using logic

   C to find ways to spread Christianity throughout the world

   D to redesign the military to be more effective

> **Test-Taking Tip:** It is important to remember what *philosophers* are. Although they are a type of scientist, their goal is not to *create new inventions* (answer A). The word *philosopher* means "lover of knowledge." Which answer choice fits best with this information?

6. Socrates' method of reaching a conclusion came to be called the Socratic method. However, this technique is not the only way to reach a conclusion. The scientific method is another way. How are the Socratic method and the scientific method similar?

   F Both require performing experiments with chemicals in a laboratory.

   G Both rely on following a step-by-step process to come to a conclusion.

   H Both place an emphasis on trusting instincts and ideas over physical evidence.

   J Both have been replaced by more advanced methods today.

> **Test-Taking Tip:** This question requires you to make a *comparison*. That means you must choose the answer that is true for *both* methods. Since the Socratic method does *not* use chemicals, and the scientific method *does* rely on physical evidence, you can rule out answers F and H.

7. Which of the following contributed to the end of the Greek empire?

   A Alexander the Great, a powerful and well-liked ruler, died.

   B People started moving out of Greek city-states, creating a shortage of workers.

   C There were conflicts about who would rule over the empire.

   D All of the above.

> **Test-Taking Tip:** Do not choose the first answer that "makes sense." Always read *all* of the answer choices before choosing the *best* one, especially when one of your choices is "all of the above" or "none of the above."

The Romans

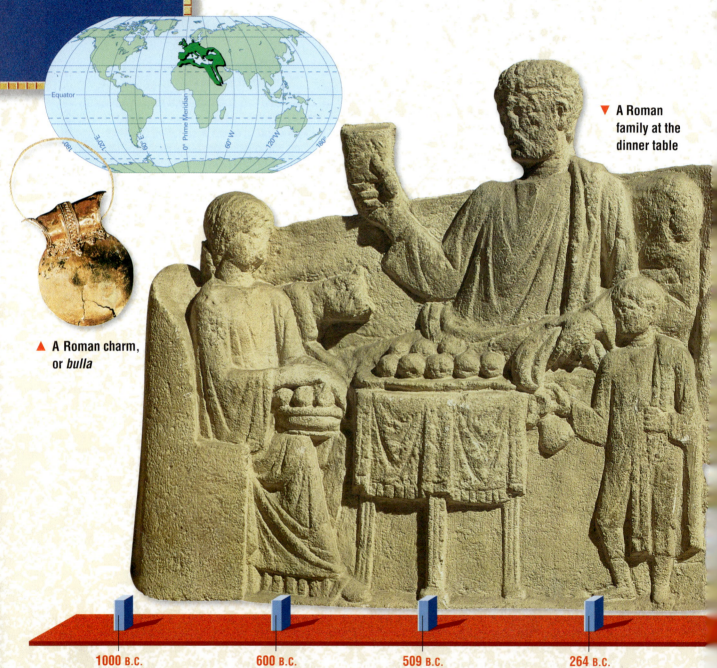

▼ A Roman family at the dinner table

▲ A Roman charm, or *bulla*

1000 B.C.
Latins settle on
Palatine Hill

600 B.C.
Etruscans rule
the central
Italian Peninsula

509 B.C.
Romans set up
republic

264 B.C.
Punic Wars begin

Categorizing Information Study Foldable *Make this foldable to help you organize your notes about the history of Rome.*

Step 1 *Fold a sheet of paper in half from side to side, leaving ½ inch tab along the side.*

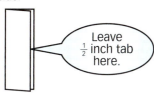

Leave $\frac{1}{2}$ inch tab here.

Step 2 *Turn the paper and fold it into fourths.*

Fold in half, then fold in half again.

Reading and Writing *As you read, identify the main ideas in each chapter. Write these ideas under the appropriate tab.*

Step 3 *Unfold and cut along the three fold lines.*

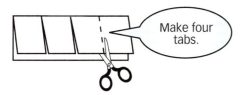

Make four tabs.

Step 4 *Label as shown.*

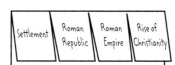

Settlement | Roman Republic | Roman Empire | Rise of Christianity

PRIMARY SOURCES
Library

See pages 682–683 for another primary source reading to accompany Unit 5.

 Read "Caesar is Assassinated" from the **World History Primary Source Document Library CD-ROM.**

46 B.C.
Julius Caesar is appointed dictator of Rome

27 B.C.
***Pax Romana* begins**

392 A.D.
Christianity becomes official religion of Roman Empire

Journal Notes

What contributions did the Etruscans and Romans make to world civilization? Note details about these people as you read.

Beginnings
1000 B.C.–500 B.C.

◄ Painting of an Etruscan woman

Rooster-shaped pottery ▶

1000 B.C.
Latins settle on Palatine Hill

800 B.C.
Rome is founded

616 B.C.
Etruscans conquer Rome

600 B.C.
Etruscans dominate all of northern Italy

Chapter Focus

Read to Discover

- How Rome was founded.
- What daily life was like for the Etruscans.
- What religious beliefs were held by the Etruscans.
- How Etruscans contributed to Roman civilization.

Chapter Overview

Visit the *Human Heritage* Web site at **humanheritage.glencoe.com** and click on **Chapter 13— Chapter Overviews** to preview this chapter.

Terms to Learn	**People to Know**	**Places to Locate**
soothsayers	Aeneas	Rome
omens	Romulus	Palatine
catacombs	Remus	Etruria
Forum		Lydia
fasces		
mundus		

Why It's Important   Italy extends south from Europe into the Mediterranean Sea. On the west coast is the mouth of the Tiber (ti´ buhr) River. Fifteen miles upstream is a group of seven hills. On the hill known as the Palatine (pal´ uh tīn), an early people founded a settlement later known as Rome. This settlement would become the center of a great empire, whose achievements still influence life today.

SECTION 1 Founding of Rome

Romans have a legend about the founding of their city. After the fall of Troy, the gods ordered a Trojan prince called Aeneas (uh nē´ uhs) to lead his people to a promised land in the West. When Aeneas's group reached Italy, they joined forces with a people known as Latins (lat´ nz).

About 800 B.C., a Latin princess gave birth to twin sons fathered by the god Mars. The princess had taken an oath never to have children. Because she broke her word, she was punished. Her sons, Romulus (rom´ ū luhs) and Remus (rē´ muhs), were taken from her and left to die on the bank of the flooding Tiber.

Romulus and Remus were found by a she-wolf, which fed and cared for them. One day a shepherd killed the she-wolf and discovered the babies. He took them to his home.

When the boys grew older, they decided to build a city on the Tiber. They decided to let the gods choose which brother should rule the city.

Each brother climbed to the top of a different hill to watch for a sign from the gods. Then 12 vultures flew over the Palatine. Since Romulus stood atop the Palatine, he claimed to be king. He and Remus then fought, and Remus was killed. Romulus became king of the city, which he named Rome.

Experts have learned that about 1000 B.C, groups of people with iron weapons began invading the lands around the Mediterranean. One group invaded Egypt and brought down the New Kingdom. Another group moved into the Balkan Peninsula. A third group, the Latins, settled on the Palatine. Romans belonged to this group.

The area where the Latins settled had a pleasant climate and fertile soil. Nearby were dense forests that supplied the Latins with timber. They built gravel roads to bring salt and other items from the coast.

By 776 B.C., the settlement on the Palatine had become a village of about 1,000 people. Most of the people were farmers who lived in wooden huts and worked the land. Their main crops were wheat and barley.

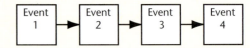

Section 1 Assessment

1. According to legend, how was Rome founded?
2. What natural resources existed in the area settled by the Latins?
3. How did the Latins live?

Critical Thinking

4. **Evaluating Information**   How true do you think the legend of Rome's founding is? Explain your answer.

Graphic Organizer Activity

5. Draw a diagram like this one, and use it to show the main events in the legend of Romulus and Remus. (Add more boxes, if necessary.)

Event 1 → Event 2 → Event 3 → Event 4

SECTION 2   The Etruscans

Etruscan Jewelry

Around 800 B.C., a people called Etruscans (ē truhs′ kuhnz) settled in Etruria (ē trur′ ē uh), the rolling hill country north of the Latin village on the Palatine. The Etruscans wrote in an alphabet borrowed from the Greeks. They spoke a language different from any other in the ancient world. Many historians believe they came from the kingdom of Lydia in Asia Minor.

The Etruscans dug tunnels and built dams to drain their marshy fields. High on hilltops, they built a number of cities, each surrounded by a thick wall.

The Etruscans were Italy's first highly civilized people. They were known as "the people of the sea." As pirates, they were

Reading A Political Map

In all parts of the world, people have created governments in order to live together. Maps that show areas ruled by particular governments are called **political maps.** Most people use political maps to find cities and countries.

Political maps use symbols to show the location of capitals and other cities. A star is usually used to show the capital of a country or state, and a dot is used to show other cities. Boundary lines mark where a country or state begins and ends. Boundaries may be shown by solid, dashed, or dotted lines. Colors often show the size and shape of countries and states. All these symbols, lines, and colors are not really on Earth's surface, but what they show exists.

On the map of "Early Italy" below, the three colors show the particular areas ruled by three peoples.

Map Practice

1. **Who controlled the southernmost part of Italy?**
2. **What two cities are shown?**
3. **What people controlled the smallest area?**

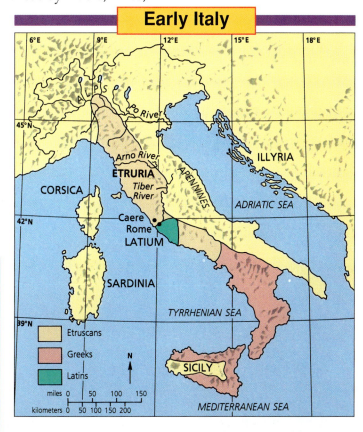

Early Italy

Legend:
- Etruscans
- Greeks
- Latins

GO TO

Glencoe's **Skillbuilder Interactive Workbook CD-ROM, Level 1,** provides instruction and practice in key social studies skills.

HISTORY *Online*

Student Web Activity

Visit the *Human Heritage* Web site at **humanheritage.glencoe.com** and click on **Chapter 13— Student Web Activities** to find out more about the historical roots of Rome.

feared and envied throughout the Mediterranean. As traders, they were admired and respected.

Etruscan farmers used mostly iron tools to grow barley, millet, wheat, grapes, and other fruits. They raised pigs, goats, sheep, ducks, chickens, and cattle. The farmers used cattle for food and to pull plows and wagons.

Etruscan miners dug copper, lead, iron, and tin. Etruscan metalworkers and sculptors turned these metals into weapons, utensils, and jewelry. Etruscan merchants exchanged both metals and finished goods for luxury items of gold, silver, and ivory from Syria, Greece, and other eastern Mediterranean countries.

The Etruscans had a strong army. The soldiers learned much about weapons and battle techniques from the Greeks. Their infantry formed a phalanx much like the one used by the Greeks. However, the Etruscans had one "weapon" no one else

Linking Across Time

Arches Etruscan engineers were among the first to use arches widely in their architecture. The semicircular stone arches could support great weight and allowed them to build gateways into fortified cities (below). Today the arch remains the symbol of a gateway, as illustrated by the stainless steel Gateway Arch in St. Louis, Missouri (right). The arch acts as a symbol of the door to the American West. **What types of buildings might be found in an Etruscan city?**

had—their shoes. They wore heavy leather shoes that laced firmly around the ankle. This gave them better footing than their enemies on rough or hilly ground.

Over time, the Etruscan cities grew in size and power. The Etruscans became rich. By 600 B.C., they dominated all of northern Italy, including the Latin village on the Palatine.

Daily Life   The Etruscans enjoyed bright colors, riches, and a good time. They gambled with ivory dice or played games similar to chess and backgammon. They often watched or took part in such sports as wrestling, running, boxing, and horse racing.

Most of all, the Etruscans loved music and dancing. Sounds from a double flute or a stringed lyre (līr) accompanied most of their activities. Much of their dancing was connected to religion. Dances were done to gain favor from the gods.

Both Etruscan men and women danced. Dancing was just one of the freedoms enjoyed by Etruscan women. Unlike Greek or Latin women, Etruscan women took part in public celebrations. They could also own property.

The Etruscans had a strong sense of **social order,** or the way groups of people are classed. At first, there were no great class differences among them. Only acrobats and enslaved people, who were captives of war, were thought inferior. Later, people were divided into three classes. The upper class consisted of wealthy landowners, nobles, and priests. The middle class had farmers, traders, and city workers. The lower class was enslaved people.

A few wealthy families owned most of the land. They also owned most of the enslaved people, who tended the land and did other work. The rich lived in rectangular, one-story homes made of sun-dried brick on a frame of heavy timbers. A pitched roof covered with clay tiles extended beyond the house. Stone-lined drains led from each house into the main drains that ran along the pebble-paved streets. Most homes also had broad, walled courtyards open to the sky. During the day, the center room was often used for talking about business. At night, it was the scene of entertainment.

Religious Beliefs   The Etruscans had many gods, most of whom were modeled after those of the Greeks. At first, the Etruscans worshiped their gods outdoors on platforms of stone or earth. Later, they built temples of wood, mud-brick, and clay on stone foundations. The temples had peaked, tiled roofs adorned with sculptures.

The Etruscans believed the universe was divided into provinces. Each province was ruled by different gods. Humans lived in the center of the universe, facing south towards the gods of nature and Earth. To the right lay the West, which was ruled by the gods of death and of the underworld. To the left lay the East,

✔ **Reading Check**
What three classes made up the Etruscan **social order** during later years?

which was ruled by the gods of the heavens. Because of this, Etruscans planned their cities and built their temples to face east.

The Etruscans also believed humans were powerless before the gods. More than anything else, the Etruscans wanted to please their gods. First, however, they had to discover what their gods willed. They did this through a priestly group of aristocrats called **soothsayers** (sūth' sā uhrz), or people who can predict events.

Soothsayers read certain **omens** (ō' muhnz), or signs of what is to happen. One group of soothsayers read omens from the livers of sacrificed animals. Another group of soothsayers explained the will of the gods by studying the direction and sounds of thunder and lightning and the flights of birds.

Reading Check
Why did the Etruscans go to **soothsayers**? What did **omens** reveal to the Etruscans?

Tombs of Gold

When an Etruscan noble died, a great banquet was held. At the banquet, two of the noble's slaves fought one another to the death. The spirit of the slave who was killed went with the noble's spirit to the underworld.

The dead were buried in tombs beneath the ground called **catacombs** (kat' uh kōmz). Much of what is known about Etruscan life comes from such tombs, whose inside walls were brightly painted with pictures of daily life. The tombs had chairs and beds. The bodies of the dead rested on the beds.

Reading Check
Why did the Etruscans build **catacombs**?

The Etruscans believed that life after death lasted longer and was more important than life on Earth. So, they carved their tombs out of natural rock, which would last for a long time. They filled the tombs with works of art and treasures of gold, silver, bronze, and ivory. Because of this, Etruscan tombs are known as "tombs of gold."

Outside each Etruscan city was a **necropolis** (nek rop' uh luhs), or cemetery, made up of acres of these tombs. The necropolis outside the city of Caere (sir' ē) is one of the largest Etruscan cemeteries. There, great mounds of soil are piled in the shape of a dome on top of a base. Some of the mounds measure 100 feet, or 30 meters, across.

Reading Check
What was a **necropolis**?

Section 2 Assessment

1. **Define:** social order, soothsayers, omens, catacombs, necropolis.
2. How did the Etruscan social order change over time?

Critical Thinking

3. **Making Comparisons** What similarities are there between the way the Etruscans treated their dead and the way modern people do?

Graphic Organizer Activity

4. Draw a diagram like this one, and use it to show the members of the three main Etruscan social classes.

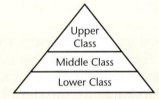

SECTION 3 Etruscans and Romans

Etruscan Gold Clasp

In 616 B.C., Lucius Tarquinius (lū′ shuhs tar kwin′ ē uhs) became the first Etruscan ruler of Rome. No one is certain whether Tarquinius took the throne from the Latin king by force or by cleverness. Nevertheless, his dynasty ruled Rome for more than 100 years.

The Etruscans were more culturally advanced than the Latins. They made many contributions to Roman civilization. In the area of architecture, the Etruscans taught the Latins how to use the arch in building bridges. The Etruscans also laid the foundations of Rome's first sewer system. They drained the swamp at the foot of the Palatine. This later became the place where Rome's **Forum** (fōr′ uhm), or the public square, was built. The Forum housed a palace, government buildings, and law courts.

The Etruscans made a contribution in the area of language as well. They borrowed the Greek alphabet and made some changes in it. The Romans, in turn, borrowed the Etruscan alphabet.

The Romans also borrowed some Etruscan customs. One was the fights of enslaved people held at Etruscan funerals. These were models for the **gladiatorial** (glad′ ē uh tōr ē uhl) **games** with which the Romans amused themselves. These games were fights between armed men, between men and animals, between women and dwarfs, and between animals. Another custom borrowed from the Etruscans was the **triumph** (trī′ uhmf), or the parade-like welcome given a Roman hero returning from battle.

In addition, the Romans borrowed Etruscan symbols of authority. One of these was the **fasces** (fas′ ēz), or a bundle of rods bound around an ax. It became the symbol of a Roman ruler's power to beat or execute other people.

The Etruscans also introduced the Romans to certain religious beliefs. These included soothsayers and gods with human forms. The Etruscans built the first temple on the Capitoline (kap′ uh tuh līn), one of the seven hills of Rome. Today, it is the center of Rome's **municipal** (myū nis′ uh puhl), or city, government.

The Romans founded their cities according to a ritual borrowed from the Etruscans. Soothsayers read omens that told where the city's boundaries should be. A ditch was dug to mark the boundaries. The plow used to dig the ditch had a bronze blade and was pulled by a white bull and cow yoked together. Workers then dug a trench at the center of the city. After each of the city's founders had tossed a handful of earth into the trench, the priests took over. They laid out the main street and determined the principal cross street. The place where the two streets met was marked by a stone.

✓ Reading Check What buildings were found at the Roman **Forum?**

✓ Reading Check What was the model for the Roman **gladiatorial games?** When did the Etruscans and the Romans hold a **triumph?**

✓ Reading Check What did the **fasces** symbolize during Roman times?

✓ Reading Check What is a **municipal** government?

The Etruscans believed that the stone covered a shaft leading to the underworld. Three times a year, an Etruscan priest lifted the stone to allow the souls of the dead to return to Earth. The Romans believed the place where the two streets met was the **mundus** (muhn' duhs), or the meeting point for the worlds of the living and the dead.

Etruscans were not the first to develop many of the ideas and practices that the Romans borrowed. The Etruscans were, however, the people who brought these ideas to the notice of the Romans. Thus, they played an important role in the development of Roman civilization.

Section 3 Assessment

1. **Define:** Forum, gladiatorial games, triumph, fasces, municipal, mundus.
2. What contributions did the Etruscans make to the Roman language?
3. How did the Etruscans and Romans establish their cities?

Critical Thinking

4. **Distinguishing Fact From Opinion** "The Latins benefited from Etruscan rule." What facts support this opinion?

Graphic Organizer Activity

5. Draw this diagram, and use it to show Etruscan contributions to the Romans.

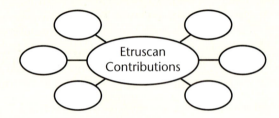

Chapter Summary & Study Guide

1. According to legend, Rome was founded by Romulus and Remus on the Palatine.
2. Some of the earliest farming settlements at Rome were built by the Latins.
3. The main occupation of the Latins was farming.
4. The Etruscans conquered Rome in 616 B.C. and took control of northern Italy.
5. The Etruscans enjoyed life and had a strong sense of social order.
6. The Etruscans were noted throughout the Mediterranean world as traders and pirates.
7. Religion was important to the Etruscans, and they went to soothsayers to find ways to please their many gods.
8. The Romans learned many things from the Etruscans, including use of the arch in building, an alphabet, and a ritual for establishing cities.

Self-Check Quiz

Visit the *Human Heritage* Web site at **humanheritage. glencoe.com** and click on *Chapter 13—Self-Check Quiz* to assess your understanding of this chapter.

Using Key Terms

Imagine you are an archaeologist studying the ruins of an Etruscan city for the first time. Use the following words to write a letter describing some of the exciting things that you have discovered.

social order	soothsayers	omens
catacombs	necropolis	Forum
gladiatorial games	triumph	fasces
municipal	mundus	

Understanding Main Ideas

1. What part of Italy did the Etruscans dominate?
2. How did the kind of shoes the Etruscans wore help them in battle?
3. What group of people owned most of the land in Etruria?
4. Why did the Etruscans build their temples to face east?
5. How have experts learned much of what they know about Etruscan life?
6. Who was the first Etruscan ruler of Rome?
7. What customs did the Romans borrow from the Etruscans?
8. What religious beliefs did the Etruscans intoduce to the Romans?

Critical Thinking

1. Compare the role of women in Etruria with their role in Greek civilization.
2. What role did religion play in Etruscan life? How did Etruscan religious ideas differ from those of the Greeks?
3. What would you have enjoyed the most about living in Etruria? Explain.
4. Was the Etruscan conquest of Rome good for the Romans? Explain.

Graphic Organizer Activity

Culture Draw a diagram like the one shown, and use it to compare the role of women in Etruria with the role of women in most Greek city-states.

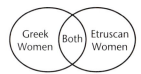

Geography in History

The World in Spatial Terms Look at the map on page 211. If the people of Etruria were attacked by another empire, from what direction and by what means would the attack come? What geographic feature might protect Etruria? Draw a map showing the most likely routes of a possible attack.

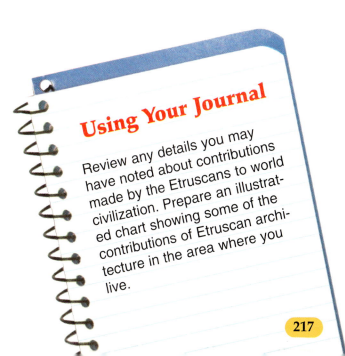

Using Your Journal

Review any details you may have noted about contributions made by the Etruscans to world civilization. Prepare an illustrated chart showing some of the contributions of Etruscan architecture in the area where you live.

The Roman Republic
509 B.C.–30 B.C.

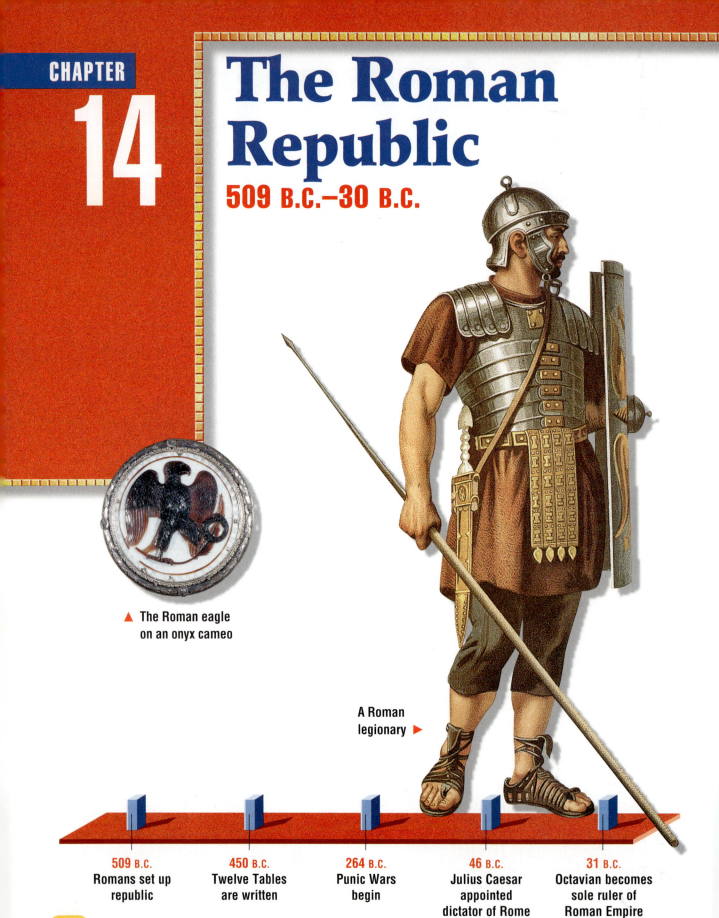

▲ The Roman eagle
on an onyx cameo

A Roman
legionary ▶

509 B.C.
Romans set up
republic

450 B.C.
Twelve Tables
are written

264 B.C.
Punic Wars
begin

46 B.C.
Julius Caesar
appointed
dictator of Rome

31 B.C.
Octavian becomes
sole ruler of
Roman Empire

Chapter Focus

Read to Discover

- How the government of the Roman Republic was organized.
- How the Roman Republic was able to expand its territory.
- How the effects of conquest changed the Roman economy and government.
- How reformers attempted to save the Roman Republic.

 Terms to Learn

republic
patricians
plebeians
consuls
legionaries
dictator
triumvirate

 **People to Know**

Tarquin the Proud
Hannibal Barca
Tiberius
 Gracchus
Julius Caesar
Mark Antony
Octavian

Places to Locate

Carthage
Sicily
Gaul
Corinth

Why It's Important   In 509 B.C., the Romans overthrew Tarquin (tar' kwin) the Proud, their Etruscan king, and set up a **republic.** Under this form of government, people choose their rulers. However, not everyone had an equal say in the Roman Republic. The **patricians** (puh trish' uhnz)—members of the oldest and richest families—were the only ones who could hold public office or perform certain religious rituals. Poorer citizens, known as **plebeians** (pli bē' uhnz), paid taxes and served in the army. Yet they could not marry patricians or hold office. If they fell into debt, they could be sold into slavery.

In later years, reformers would take steps to make the Roman Republic more democratic. The idea of a government chosen by the people would serve as a model for future generations, including the founders of the United States.

Chapter Overview

Visit the *Human Heritage* Web site at **humanheritage.glencoe.com** and click on ***Chapter 14— Chapter Overviews*** to preview this chapter.

Reading Check
What is a **republic?** Who were the **patricians** and the **plebeians?**

SECTION 1   The Government

At the head of the Roman Republic were two **consuls** (kon' suhlz) who were chosen each year. They were administrators and military leaders. Each had the power to **veto,** or say no to, the acts of the other. Both had to agree before any law was passed.

Next in importance was the Senate. It was made up of 300 men called senators who were chosen for life. The Senate handled the daily problems of government. It advised the consuls.

Reading Check
How long did the **consuls** hold power? How did the **veto** prevent a consul from becoming too powerful?

ROMAN SENATE   This painting shows the famous orator Cicero making a speech attacking a political opponent. **What duties did the Senate perform in the Roman Republic?**

Reading Check
What role did the **tribunes** play in Roman government?

It discussed ways to deal with other countries, proposed laws, and approved public contracts for building roads and temples.

Judges, assemblies, and **tribunes** (trib′ yūnz), or government officials who protected the rights of plebeians, were also part of the Roman government. All Roman citizens belonged to the assemblies, which could declare war or agree to peace terms.

Until about 450 B.C., Roman laws were not written down. In that year, laws were carved on 12 bronze tablets known as the Twelve Tables. These were placed in the Forum. The laws applied to both patricians and plebeians. Most were about wills, property rights, and court actions. The laws on the Twelve Tables became the foundation for all future Roman laws.

The election of tribunes and recording of laws were the first steps to a more democratic government. Later, more plebeian demands were met. By about 250 B.C., no one could be sold into slavery because of debt. Plebeians could hold public office.

Section 1 Assessment

1. **Define:** republic, patricians, plebeians, consuls, veto, tribunes.
2. What were some restrictions placed on the plebeians during the early years of the Roman Republic?

Critical Thinking

3. **Demonstrating Reasoned Judgment** Why do you think it was important for the Romans to have laws written down?

Graphic Organizer Activity

4. Draw this diagram, and use it to describe each part of Roman government.

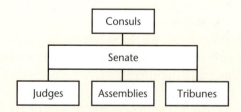

SECTION 2 Roman Expansion

Once the Romans had set up a republic, they worked to protect it. They were afraid that the Etruscans would try to regain control of Rome. To prevent this, the Romans crossed the Tiber River and conquered several Etruscan cities. Roman land now bordered that of other Italian people. To protect their new boundaries, the Romans either conquered their neighbors or made alliances with them. By 290 B.C., Rome was the leading power in central Italy. By 275 B.C., it ruled the whole peninsula. By 146 B.C., Rome ruled most of the Mediterranean world.

The Romans were able to gain territory because they had a strong army that was organized into **legions** (lē' juhnz). Each legion contained some 5,000 soldiers called **legionaries** (lē' juh ner ēz) and was divided into groups of 60 to 120 soldiers.

The legion had several advantages over the phalanx. The legion was smaller and could move faster. Soldiers in a phalanx fought as a group and attacked from only one direction. Each legionary depended on his own fighting ability. The groups within a legion could split off from the main body and attack from the sides and the rear as well as the front.

Then... & Now

Rank and File The basic unit of the Roman legion was the *maniple*—120 soldiers standing side by side in ranks of 10 and lined up one behind another in files of 12. The term *rank and file,* which refers to the ordinary members of an organization, comes from this military system.

✓ Reading Check
How did Roman **legions** differ from the phalanx? How many **legionaries** were in each legion?

Linking Across Time

Citizen-Soldiers During the early years of the Roman republic, all male citizens were required to serve in the army (below). Today military service continues to be an important responsibility of citizenship in democratic nations such as the United States (right). **Why did the use of citizen-soldiers help ensure the loyalty of legionaries to Rome?**

Roman Bronze Lamp

Legionaries were well trained. They spent hours practicing with their double-edged iron swords. They went on long marches every day. Before going to sleep, they had to build complete fortified camps, even when the legion would stay in an area only one night. They built roads out of lava blocks so soldiers and supplies could move forward more rapidly.

The Romans were mild rulers. At first, they did not tax the people they conquered. They let the conquered people keep their own governments and take care of their own affairs. Some were even allowed to become Roman citizens. In return, the conquered people were expected to serve in the Roman army and to support Rome's foreign policy. As a result, many enemies of Rome became loyal Roman allies.

Section 2 Assessment

1. **Define:** legions, legionaries.
2. Why were the Romans able to gain territory?
3. What was life like for a Roman legionary?

Critical Thinking

4. **Drawing Conclusions** How would you describe the way the Romans treated people they conquered, and do you think this was wise? Explain.

Graphic Organizer Activity

5. Draw a chart like this one, and use it to show the cause and effects of Roman conquest of Etruscan cities.

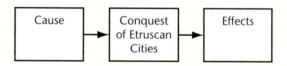

| Cause | | Conquest of Etruscan Cities | | Effects |

SECTION 3 The Punic Wars

By 264 B.C., the Romans had conquered some Greek city-states in southern Italy. This brought them into contact with the Phoenician city of Carthage. Carthage controlled most of North and West Africa, most of what is now Spain, and some islands off the coast of Italy. Carthage also ruled the western half of Sicily (sis' uh lē), a large island at the toe of the Italian "boot." The Romans felt threatened by the Carthaginians (kar thuh jin' ē uhnz). They also wanted Sicily's granaries.

The First Punic War   In 264 B.C., the Romans and Carthaginians clashed. The war that broke out lasted for 23 years. It was the first of three wars between Rome and Carthage that came to be known as the Punic (pyū' nik) Wars.

Carthage's military strength lay in its navy, while Rome's lay in its army. At first, the Romans had no navy. They built their first fleet to fight the Carthaginians. The Romans modeled their ships after a Carthaginian warship they found abandoned on a beach. They made one improvement on the Carthaginian model. They added a *corvus* (kor′ vuhs), or a kind of movable bridge, to the front of each ship. The Romans knew they could not outsail the Carthaginians, but believed they could outfight them. The corvus allowed soldiers to board an enemy ship and fight hand-to-hand on its decks. In a sense, it changed a sea war into a land war.

The Romans lost many ships and men in storms during the First Punic War. Yet, in the end, they defeated the Carthaginians. In 241 B.C., the Carthaginians agreed to make peace and left Sicily.

Hannibal and the Second Punic War

In 218 B.C., the Second Punic War began. At that time, the Carthaginians, led by General Hannibal Barca (han′ uh buhl bar′ ka), attacked the Roman army by land from the north. Hannibal and his troops surprised the Roman army by marching from Spain through southern Gaul (gol), or present-day France, and then crossing the Alps into Italy. They brought elephants with them across the snow-covered mountains to help break through the Roman lines.

Winning victory after victory, Hannibal's army fought its way to the gates of Rome. When the Carthaginian army got to Rome, however, it did not have the heavy equipment needed to

HANNIBAL Hannibal's army, with elephants, faced many dangers in its attack on Rome. The elephants had to be floated on barges across rivers and brought over the snow-capped Alps. **Why did Hannibal's attack on the city of Rome fail?**

Student Web Activity

Visit the *Human Heritage* Web site at humanheritage.glencoe.com and click on **Chapter 14—Student Web Activities** to find out more about the Punic Wars.

Hannibal began crossing the Alps with about 46,000 troops and 37 elephants. He emerged with 26,000 troops and almost no elephants. A Roman general proclaimed: "They are ghosts and shadows of men already half dead. All their strength has been crushed and beaten out of them by the Alpine crags." The general was wrong. The Gauls, who were enemies of the Romans, joined Hannibal and boosted his army to almost 50,000.

batter down the city's walls. It could not get more supplies because the Roman navy controlled the sea.

Unable to capture Rome, Hannibal and his troops roamed the countryside of southern Italy for 15 years. They raided and burned towns and destroyed crops. Then, the Romans attacked Carthage, and Hannibal was called home to defend it. Hannibal lost his first battle—and the war—at the town of Zama (zā′ muh). The power of Carthage was broken.

In 201 B.C., Carthage agreed to pay Rome a huge sum of money and to give up all its territories, including Spain. The Spanish resources of copper, gold, lead, and iron now belonged to the Romans.

The Third Punic War   Following the Second Punic War, there was peace for about 50 years. Then, Carthage began to show signs of regaining power. To prevent this, the Romans attacked in 149 B.C., the Third Punic War. They burned Carthage and plowed salt into its fields so nothing would grow. They killed the Carthaginians or sold them into slavery.

That same year, 146 B.C., the Greek city-state of Corinth (kor′ inth) and some of its allies refused to obey a Roman order. The Romans attacked Corinth and burned it to the ground. Rome already controlled Macedonia and Syria. Now, it added Greece to the areas under its rule. Thus, Rome became the leading power of the Mediterranean world.

Section 3 Assessment

1. What territory did Carthage control in 264 B.C.?
2. What happened to Carthage in the Third Punic War?
3. How did Rome become the leading power of the Mediterranean world?

Critical Thinking

4. **Predicting Consequences**   What might have happened to Rome if it had lost the Punic Wars?

Graphic Organizer Activity

5. Draw a chart like this one, and use it to summarize the outcome of each of the Punic Wars.

Punic Wars	Outcome
First	
Second	
Third	

SECTION 4   Effects of Conquest

The conquests and the wealth that came with them changed Rome's economy and government. Among the changes were the replacement of small farms with large estates, the use of enslaved people, a movement from farms to cities, and the decline of the Roman Republic.

Agricultural Changes

Rome's conquests brought changes in agriculture. One change was in the size and purpose of farms. Most Romans had been small farmers who believed in hard work and service to Rome. Now, the small farms were replaced by large estates called **latifundias** (lat uh fuhn' dē uhs). The small farms had grown wheat for food. Latifundias, on the other hand, produced crops, sheep, and cattle for sale at market. Some contained olive groves and vineyards. Because they no longer grew their own wheat, the Romans began to import wheat from such conquered areas as Sicily and North Africa.

The main reason for this change in Roman agriculture was Hannibal's invasion. While his soldiers were in Italy, they lived off the land. To prevent them from getting food, Roman farmers burned their fields and crops. By the time the Second Punic War was over, much of the land was ruined. Most Roman farmers did not have money to fix up their farms or restore the land. Only patricians and rich business people had that kind of money. They bought the small farms and combined them to make latifundias.

Another change in agriculture was in who worked the land. When Rome first began expanding, the Romans did not enslave the people they conquered. By 146 B.C., that was no longer true. The Romans were impressed by the wealth of Greece, Syria, and Carthage. Since those areas had widespread slavery, the Romans sent thousands of prisoners to Rome as enslaved people. Most lived and worked on latifundias.

From Farm to City

The farmers who had sold their land had few choices. They could stay and work the land for the new owners or move to the city. Almost all of them moved to Rome.

There the farmers crowded into wooden apartment buildings six or more stories high. Living conditions were terrible. The aqueducts that brought water to the city were not connected to apartment buildings. Neither were the sewers that carried away waste. Buildings often caught fire or collapsed. Diseases such as typhus (tī' fuhs) were common.

Most farmers could not earn a living in the city. Except for construction, Rome had almost no industry. Most businesses were staffed by enslaved people from Greece. About the only way the farmers could get money was by selling their votes to politicians.

Decline of the Roman Republic

As Rome's rule spread beyond Italy, the Romans began to demand taxes, as well as enslaved people, from the areas they conquered. Tax contracts were sold to people called **publicans** (pub' luh kuhnz). They paid Rome ahead of time for the contracts. Then, they collected taxes from the conquered people. The amount of taxes collected was supposed to be no more than 10 percent above the price paid for the contract. Most publicans, however, made extra money.

Reading Check
What was the purpose of the **latifundias?**

Sculpture of Roman Consul

Reading Check
Why did Rome sell tax contracts to the **publicans?**

ROMAN APARTMENTS   Wealthy Romans built brick and stone apartments. They decorated the floors with mosaics and the walls with paintings. These apartment dwellers owned only a few pieces of furniture, most of which were simple in design. **What sort of buildings did poor Romans live in during the Republic?**

By about 135 B.C., Rome was in a great deal of trouble. Because farmers had lost their land, they had also lost their economic and political independence. Merchants had become poorer because rich Romans could get luxuries elsewhere. Artisans had lost business because rich Romans wanted goods from Greece and Syria. Government officials were too busy getting rich to worry about solving the republic's problems.

The gap between rich and poor grew greater. The poor hated the rich for what the rich had done to them. The rich hated and feared the poor. Rome was no longer politically stable.

Section 4 Assessment

1. **Define:** latifundias, publicans.
2. How was Roman agriculture influenced by Hannibal?
3. What was life like in Rome during the decline of the republic?

Critical Thinking

4. **Identifying Central Issues** Why might a large gap between rich and poor present problems for an empire?

Graphic Organizer Activity

5. Draw this diagram, and use it to compare Roman agriculture before and after the rise of the latifundias.

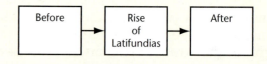

SECTION 5 Roman Leadership

Over the next 100 years, many different popular leaders tried to improve conditions in Rome. Some were reformers, while others were generals.

The Reformers   Tiberius Sempronius Gracchus (tī bir′ ē uhs sem prō nē uhs grak′ uhs) was the first reformer. He thought making small farmers leave their land had caused Rome's troubles.

When he became a tribune in 133 B.C., Tiberius Gracchus wanted to limit the amount of land a person could own. He wanted to divide up public lands and give them to the poor. Another tribune vetoed his idea. Tiberius Gracchus then talked the assembly into putting his idea into effect and getting rid of that tribune.

Tiberius Gracchus ran for a second term as tribune, although it was against the law. To stop him, the Senate staged a riot and had him and hundreds of his followers killed.

In 123 B.C., Tiberius Gracchus's younger brother Gaius (gī′ yuhs) Sempronius Gracchus was elected tribune. He thought moving the poor from the city back to the countryside was the answer to Rome's troubles.

Gaius Gracchus improved and extended the reforms of his brother. He had the government take over the sale of wheat and sell it to the poor below market price. Soon, however, wheat was being given away rather than sold. Nearly one out of every three Romans was receiving free wheat. Meanwhile, the Senate began to feel threatened by some of Gaius Gracchus's ideas and in 121 B.C. had him killed.

The Generals   After the reformers came the generals. In 107 B.C., General Gaius Marius (mar′ ē uhs), a military hero, became consul. The son of a day laborer, Marius was the first lower-class Roman to be elected to such a high office. He was supported by many ex-soldiers who felt the rich and the government had taken advantage of them. Many of the ex-soldiers had been farmers who had lost their farms when they left to serve in the army.

Marius thought he could end Rome's troubles by setting up a professional army. Until this time, only property owners could become legionaries. Marius opened the army to everyone. He convinced the poor to join by offering them pay, land, pensions, and *booty,* or things taken from the enemy in war. Marius's plan helped Rome by providing jobs for many out-of-work Romans. At the same time, it hurt the Roman Republic. Instead of giving loyalty to the government, the soldiers gave it to the general who hired and paid them.

Sculpture of Tiberius Gracchus

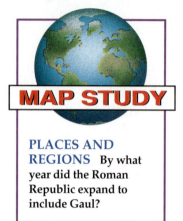

Reading Check
What power
does a **dictator** hold?
What kind of govern-
ment exists under a
triumvirate?

MAP STUDY

**PLACES AND
REGIONS** By what
year did the Roman
Republic expand to
include Gaul?

Marius was opposed by another general, Lucius Cornelius Sulla (kor nēl' yuhs suhl' uh). Sulla had been given a military command that Marius wanted. Marius tried to get the assembly to take the command away from Sulla and give it to him. An angry Sulla marched his army on Rome and seized the city. It was the first time a Roman commander had led his soldiers against the capital.

Civil war broke out. When it was over, Sulla made himself **dictator** (dik' tā tuhr), or absolute ruler, of Rome. Sulla believed the way to end Rome's troubles was to increase the power of the Senate. So, he doubled the Senate's size. He gave the senators more duties and weakened the power of the tribunes. At the same time, he stopped generals from holding the same army command for more than one year at a time.

Julius Caesar   When Sulla retired, a new group of generals fought for control of Rome. In 60 B.C., political power passed to a **triumvirate** (trī um' vuhr it), or a group of three persons with equal power. This First Triumvirate was made up of Marcus

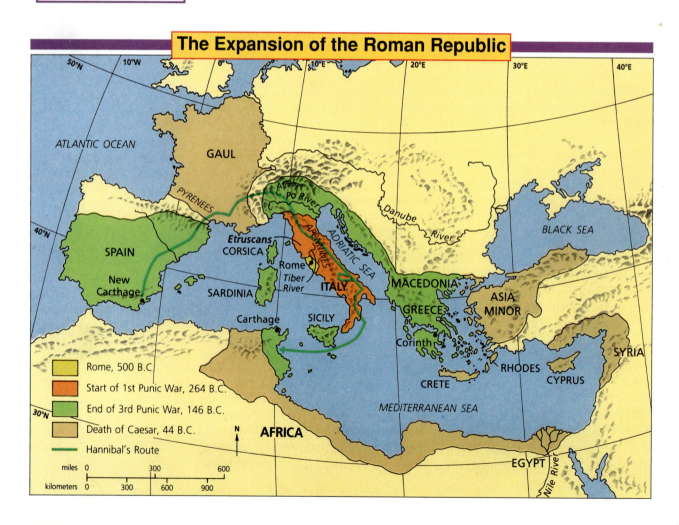

The Expansion of the Roman Republic

Rome, 500 B.C
Start of 1st Punic War, 264 B.C.
End of 3rd Punic War, 146 B.C.
Death of Caesar, 44 B.C.
Hannibal's Route

Licinius Crassus (mar′ kus luh sin′ ē uhs kras′ us), Gnaeus Pompeius (guh nā′ uhs pom pē′ uhs), and Julius Caesar (jūl′ yuhs sē′ zuhr). Pompeius, who was also known as Pompey (pom′ pē), and Caesar had different ideas about how Rome should be ruled. Pompey believed in a republic that was ruled by upper-class senators. Caesar believed in one-man rule.

After Crassus's death, the two remaining rulers fought for power. Caesar finally gained control after Pompey was murdered in 48 B.C. Caesar was a well-educated politician who had become a soldier. He had both military strength and strong family alliances to back him.

In 58 B.C., Caesar was named governor of a Roman province. There, he built up a large, strong army that was loyal to him. Within seven years, he conquered what is now northern France and Belgium (bel′ juhm) and invaded Britain. The Senate began to fear he was growing too strong. So, in 50 B.C., it ordered Caesar to break up his legions and return to Rome. Instead, Caesar entered the city at the head of his troops. By 46 B.C., he was dictator of Rome.

Caesar brought about many reforms. He redistributed state lands in Italy and founded new colonies overseas. This gave land to thousands of ex-soldiers who had none. He began public works projects such as building roads and buildings and draining the marshes around Rome. This gave jobs to thousands of Romans who had not been able to find work. He planned and paid for gladiatorial games that were free to the public. This kept the poor and the idle from turning into unhappy and angry mobs. He doubled the size of the Senate. Although this made each senator less powerful, it gave business people a chance to become senators. He cut back the activities of the publicans. He gave Roman citizenship to Greeks, Spaniards, and Gauls. He adopted a new calendar based on the Egyptian calendar. Called the Julian (jūl′ yuhn) calendar, a form of it is still in use today.

Caesar did a great deal for Rome and its people. Still, some Romans were afraid that Caesar planned to make himself king. About 60 men, most of them senators, worked out a plan to kill him. As he entered the Senate on the Ides (ī dz) of March, or March 15, 44 B.C., Caesar was stabbed to death.

End of the Republic   Angered by Caesar's death, the Roman people turned against those who had killed him. Political power passed to another triumvirate. Marcus Antonius (an tō′ nē uhs), or Mark Antony, Caesar's closest follower and a popular general, took command of Rome's territories in the East. Octavian (ok tā′ vē uhn), Caesar's grand-nephew and adopted son, took charge of the West. Marcus Aemilius Lepidus (uh mēl′ ē uhs lep′uhd uhs), one of Caesar's top officers, took over the rule of Africa. All three shared control of the Italian homeland.

For a while, the triumvirate worked. Then, fights broke out among the three leaders. When the fighting ended in 31 B.C., Octavian had won. Within four years, he became sole ruler of the Roman Empire.

Section 5 Assessment

1. **Define:** dictator, triumvirate.
2. Why did civil war break out in Rome?
3. Why did a group of Roman senators murder Julius Caesar?

Critical Thinking

4. **Demonstrating Reasoned Judgment** How effective do you think a triumvirate is as a form of government? Explain.

Graphic Organizer Activity

5. Draw this chart, and use it to summarize the reforms supported by popular leaders during the closing years of the Roman Republic.

Leader	Reform	Effect

Chapter Summary & Study Guide

1. In 509 B.C., the Romans overthrew the Etruscans and set up a republic.
2. About 450 B.C., leaders wrote down Roman laws in the Twelve Tables.
3. By 275 B.C., well-trained Roman legions had taken control of Italy.
4. Between 264 and 146 B.C., Rome and Carthage fought three wars known as the Punic Wars.
5. The organization of Roman lands into large estates forced many small farmers off the land and into the cities.
6. By 135 B.C., Rome faced many serious political and economic problems.
7. A series of reform-minded leaders tried various ways to improve conditions in Rome, but political rivalries prevented any leader from holding power for long.
8. After Julius Caesar was killed by Romans who feared he might become king, power was divided among three leaders.
9. Fights among the three-way rule of Mark Antony, Octavian, and Marcus Lepidus led to the collapse of the Roman Republic.
10. In 31 B.C., Octavian became the sole ruler of the Roman Empire.

Self-Check Quiz

Visit the *Human Heritage* Web site at **humanheritage.glencoe.com** and click on *Chapter 14—Self-Check Quiz* to assess your understanding of this chapter.

Using Key Terms

Imagine that you are writing a "Citizenship Handbook" for the new Roman citizens of 46 B.C. Write one sentence explaining the importance of each of the following terms.

republic   patricians   plebeians
consuls   veto   tribunes
legions   legionaries   latifundias
publicans   dictator   triumvirate

Understanding Main Ideas

1. What changes were made in Rome's government as a result of demands by the plebeians?
2. Why was the Roman legion so effective in battle?
3. Why did Rome decide to fight three wars against Carthage?
4. How were the Romans able to overcome the navy of Carthage?
5. What effect did latifundias have on Rome's small farmers?
6. Who won the struggle for political power after the death of Julius Caesar?
7. What effect did Marius's reforms have on the loyalty of the legionaries?
8. Why did the Senate order Julius Caesar to break up his legions?

Critical Thinking

1. How wise do you think the Romans were to enslave the people they conquered? Explain.
2. Do you think the Romans were wise or foolish to start taxing the people they conquered? Explain.
3. If you had lived in Rome after 135 B.C., what would you have done to solve its problems?

4. If you had lived when Caesar was killed, how would you have felt about his murder? Explain.

Graphic Organizer Activity

History Create a chart like this one, and use it to show steps in the decline of the Roman Republic.

Height of Republic

End of Republic

Geography in History

Human Systems Refer to the map on page 228. Imagine you are a government representative who must travel from Rome to Cyprus. Describe how you would travel and what route you would take. Then draw a map showing your route.

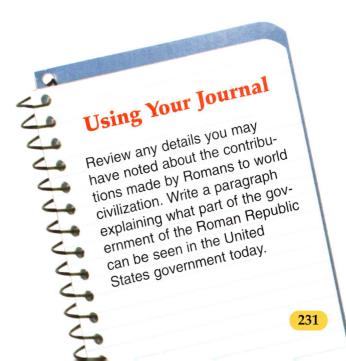

Using Your Journal

Review any details you may have noted about the contributions made by Romans to world civilization. Write a paragraph explaining what part of the government of the Roman Republic can be seen in the United States government today.

CHAPTER 15

The Roman Empire

27 B.C.–410 A.D.

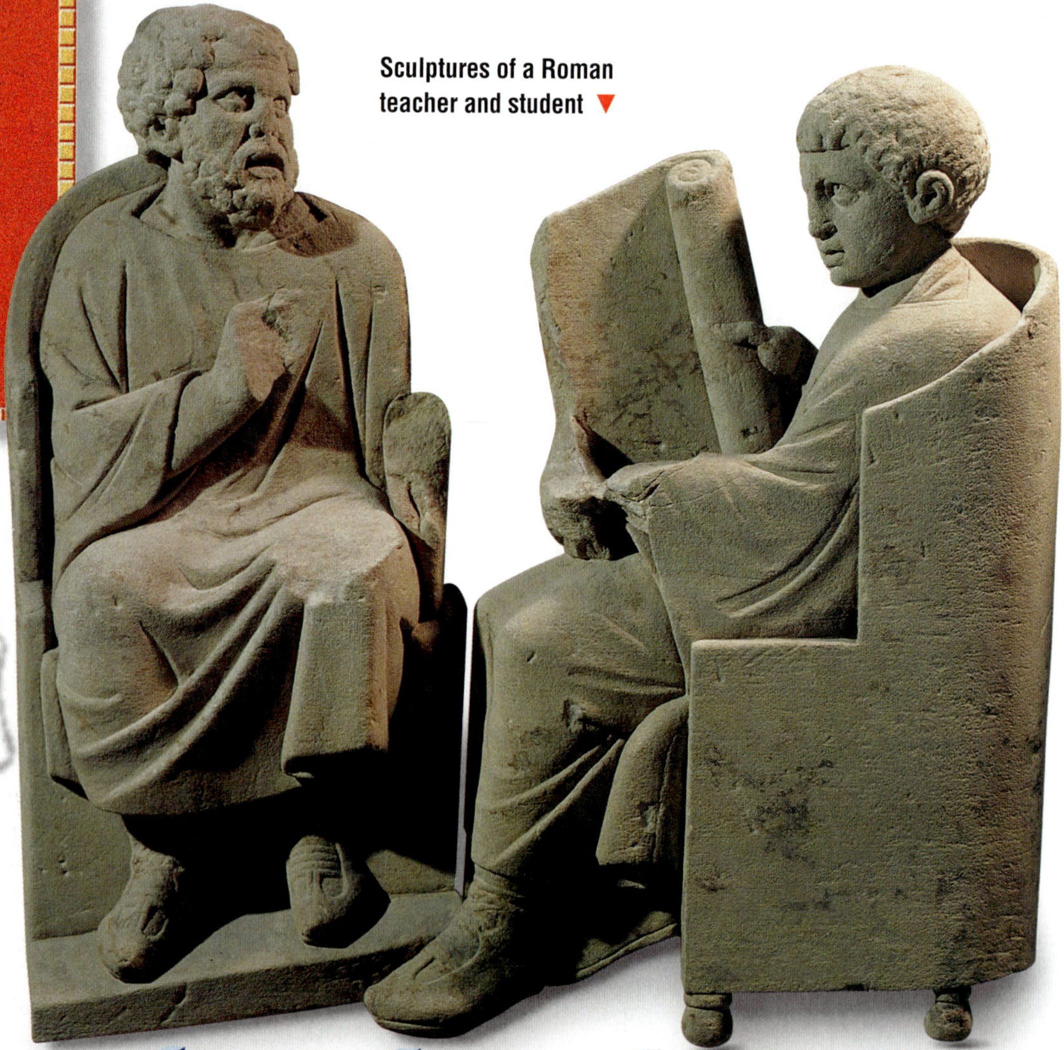

Sculptures of a Roman teacher and student ▼

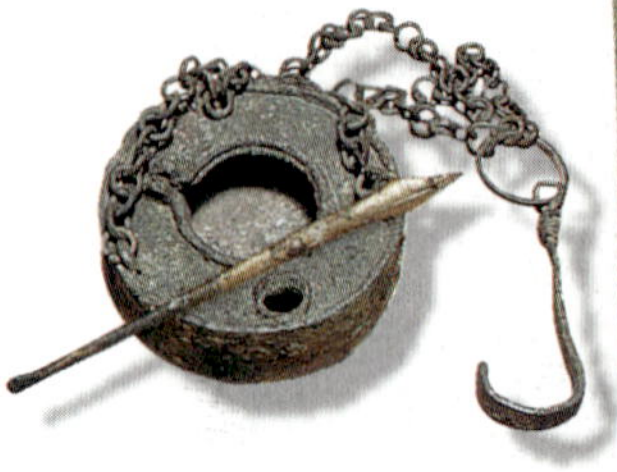

▲ Roman inkpot and pen

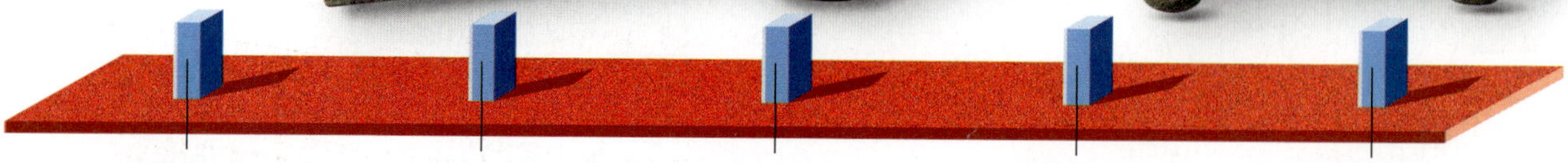

27 B.C.
Octavian becomes first Roman emperor
125 A.D.
Roman law is standardized
330 A.D.
Constantine I moves Roman capital to Constantinople
378 A.D.
Battle of Adrianople
410 A.D.
Rome falls to Germanic invaders

Chapter Focus

 Read to Discover

- How Augustus ruled the Roman Empire.
- What happened to trade and law during the *Pax Romana*.
- What daily life was like during the *Pax Romana*.
- Why the Roman Empire declined.

 Terms to Learn

emperor
census
tariffs
gladiators

 People to Know

Augustus
Marcus Aurelius
Diocletian
Constantine I
Alaric

 Places to Locate

Circus Maximus
Constantinople
Adrianople
Danube River

Chapter Overview

Visit the *Human Heritage* Web site at humanheritage.glencoe.com and click on **Chapter 15— Chapter Overviews** to preview this chapter.

Why It's Important   In 27 B.C., Octavian told the Senate that he had restored the republic, and he offered to resign as sole ruler of Rome. The Senate turned down the offer and gave him several titles. In the end, Octavian took for himself the title of Augustus (ah guhs' tuhs), or "revered one." That is what he is generally called in history books.

In practice, Octavian became the first Roman **emperor,** or absolute ruler of an empire. His policies paved the way for more than 200 years of peace. Even after the empire collapsed, Roman influence would survive in much of the world.

Reading Check
What is an **emperor?**

SECTION 1   The Rule of Augustus

Augustus was a clever politician. He held the offices of consul, tribune, high priest, and senator all at the same time. However, he refused to be crowned emperor. Augustus knew that most Romans would not accept one-person rule unless it took the form of a republic.

Augustus kept the assemblies and government officials of the republic. He was careful to make senators feel honored. He talked of tradition and the need to bring back "old Roman virtues."

At the same time, Augustus strengthened his authority in two ways. First, he had every soldier swear allegiance to him personally. This gave him control of the armies. Second, he built up his imperial household to take charge of the daily business of

Reading Check
Who were the **freedmen?**

government. He chose people because of their talent rather than their birth. This gave enslaved people and **freedmen,** or former enslaved people, a chance to be part of the government.

Augustus wanted boundaries that would be easy to defend. So, he rounded out the empire to natural frontiers—the Rhine (rīn) and Danube (dan' yūb) rivers in the north, the Atlantic Ocean in the west, and the Sahara in the south—and stationed soldiers there.

Augustus was not interested in gaining new territory for Rome. Instead, he worked on governing the existing empire. He gave provincial governors long terms of office. This allowed them to gain experience in their jobs. He also paid them large salaries. In this way, they would not feel the need to overtax the people or keep public money for themselves. To make sure that people did not pay too little or too much tax, Augustus ordered a **census** (sen' suhs), or population count, to be taken from time to time.

Reading Check
Why did Augustus order a **census?**

Augustus also made Rome more beautiful. He wrote strict laws to govern the way people behaved in public. He protected the city by setting up a fire brigade and a police force. He encouraged learning by building Rome's first library.

Augustus ruled for 41 years. During that time, he brought peace to Rome. He also gave the Romans a new sense of patriotism and pride. He made Roman citizenship available to people in the provinces. Most important, however, he reorganized the government of Rome so that it ran well for more than 200 years.

Section 1 Assessment

1. **Define:** emperor, freedmen, census.
2. Why did Augustus refuse to be crowned emperor?
3. How did Augustus try to make the Roman Empire like a republic?

Critical Thinking

4. **Demonstrating Reasoned Judgment** Which of Augustus's improvements do you think was the most important? Explain.

Graphic Organizer Activity

5. Draw this diagram, and use it to show the achievements of Augustus.

SECTION 2 Pax Romana

The peace that Augustus brought to Rome was called the *Pax Romana* (pahks rō mah' nah). It lasted for 200 years. Of course, revolts and other problems were not unknown during this time. For the most part, however, Rome and its people prospered. Civilization spread, and cultures mixed.

Trade With peace came increased trade. The same coins were used throughout the empire. There were no **tariffs** (tar' ifz), or taxes placed on goods brought into the country. Goods and money moved freely along the trade routes. The Mediterranean was cleared of pirates, making it safe for trade and travel. Shipping became a big business. Every summer, hundreds of ships carried grain from North Africa to Italy. Other ships bound for Rome were loaded with cargoes of brick, marble, granite, and wood to be used for building. Luxury items, such as amber from the north and silk from China, passed overland across Roman roads.

Increased trade meant more business for Romans. The city hummed. Shopkeepers grew richer. Wine and olive oil were the main items bought by other countries. Italy became a manufacturing center for pottery, bronze, and woolen cloth.

Law During the *Pax Romana*, Roman law went through major changes. Because the times were different, the laws first set down

Reading Check
What are **tariffs**?

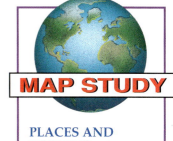

MAP STUDY

PLACES AND REGIONS The Roman Empire had been divided into two parts. **What empire did Greece belong to?**

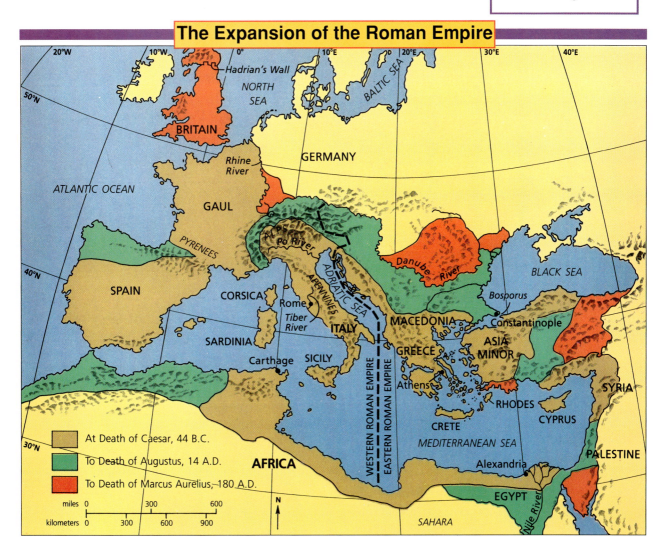

The Expansion of the Roman Empire

At Death of Caesar, 44 B.C.

To Death of Augustus, 14 A.D.

To Death of Marcus Aurelius, 180 A.D.

on the Twelve Tables were changed. When Rome conquered a new territory, Roman merchants had to do business with non-Romans. Roman judges had to write new laws that would be as fair to non-Romans as to Romans. The Roman judges were helped by special lawyers and legal writers called *juris prudentes* (jū' ruhs prū' duhntz).

✔ Reading Check
Who were the *juris prudentes,* and what were they supposed to do?

After a while, the judges and their helpers developed certain principles of law that were fair to everyone. A law was believed to be just because it was reasonable, not because the government had the power to make people obey it. Everyone was considered equal before the law. A person was innocent until proven guilty.

By about 125 A.D., Roman law was *standardized*. This meant that legal procedures were the same in all parts of the empire. This helped Rome govern a large area successfully. In later years, Roman legal principles formed the basis for the laws of most western countries and of the Christian church.

Section 2 Assessment

1. **Define:** tariffs, *juris prudentes*.
2. What happened to trade during the *Pax Romana*?
3. What happened to law during the *Pax Romana*?

Critical Thinking

4. **Evaluating Information** Do you think the term *Pax Romana* was a good term for this 200-year period in Roman history, or would you describe it with another term? Explain.

Graphic Organizer Activity

5. Draw this diagram, and use it to show the effects of the *Pax Romana*. (Add more lines as needed.)

Pax Romana	Effect
	Effect
	Effect
	Effect

SECTION 3 Daily Life

In the early years of the empire, about 1 million people lived in Rome. It suffered from many of the same problems as cities of today. There was too little housing. The air was polluted. There was crime in the streets. The cost of living was high. Many Romans could not find jobs and had to pay taxes on almost everything.

✔ Reading Check
What were some of the features of a Roman **domus?**

A rich person in Rome lived in a **domus** (dō' muhs), or house, with marble walls, colored stone floors, and windows made of small panes of glass. A furnace heated the rooms, and pipes brought water even to the upper floors.

Most Romans, however, were not rich. They lived in apartment houses called *islands* that were six or more stories high. Each island covered an entire block. At one time, there were 26

ROMAN FLOOR PLAN This is a typical floor plan of a *domus*. **What class of Romans would live in a house such as this?**

The Atrium Many shopping malls today have an atrium, a sky-lit central court. The idea for the atrium comes from ancient Rome. In a Roman house, the atrium was the central room. It was often open to the sky and had a pool to collect rainwater.

blocks of islands for every private house in Rome. The ground floor of most islands was given over to shops. These opened onto the street from large arched doorways.

Rents were high in Rome. They varied according to the apartment floor—the higher up the apartment, the lower the rent.

The Family In Rome, the family was all-important. The father was head of the household. His word was law. He arranged the children's marriages to improve social position or to increase wealth. Cousins were expected to help one another politically.

Until they were 12 years old, most Roman boys and girls went to school together. Then, the sons of poor families went to work, while the sons of rich families began their formal education. They studied reading, grammar, writing, music, geometry, commercial arithmetic, and shorthand. When they were 15 years old, they entered a school of *rhetoric* (ret' uhr ik), or speech and writing, to prepare for a political career. Some went to schools in Athens or Alexandria for philosophy or medicine.

Girls received a different kind of education. When they were 12 years old, their formal education stopped. Instead of going to school, the daughters of the rich were given private lessons at

Painting of Roman Couple

Linking Across Time

Stadiums   During Roman times, people filled stadiums such as the Colosseum (left) to watch gladiator fights and other public games. Stadiums remain popular today but are usually used for team sports such as baseball, football, or soccer (right). **Who staged the public games held at stadiums in Rome?**

home. As a result, many Roman women were as well as or better informed than Roman men. Some women worked in or owned small shops. Wealthy women had enslaved people to do their housework. This left them free to study the arts, literature, and fashions, or to ride chariots in the countryside for a day's *pigsticking,* or a type of hunt.

At Leisure

At home, the Romans enjoyed gambling with dice. They met friends at public bathhouses where they could take warm, cold, or steam baths. The bathhouses of Rome, however, provided more than baths. Some had gymnasiums, sports stadiums, and libraries. There, the Romans could watch or play games. They also could listen to lectures, see musical shows, exercise, or just sit and talk.

The Romans had no team sports to watch. Instead, they flocked to see free public games, which often ran from dawn to dusk. Under the republic, the games had generally been staged by politicians who were looking for votes. Under the empire, the games were staged by the government. The games included circuses, chariot races, and gladiatorial games. The most exciting chariot races were held at the Circus Maximus, an oval arena that could seat more than 200,000 people.

The people who fought animals and one another in arenas were called **gladiators** (glad' ē ā tuhrz). Most were enslaved people, prisoners of war, criminals, or poor people. They were

Reading Check
Which groups of people were trained as **gladiators?**

trained by managers who hired them out. A few gladiators were upper-class Romans who wanted excitement and public attention.

The night before they were to fight, gladiators would appear at a feast. There, they could be looked over by fans and gamblers who wanted to bet on the outcome of a match. When the gladiators entered the arena on the day of the games, they would walk past the emperor's box and say, "Hail Emperor, those who are about to die salute you."

Many gladiators did die. Those whose fighting pleased the crowd became idols of the people. A few won their freedom. Those who gave a poor performance were killed, even if they survived the fight.

All kinds of animals were used in the public games. Some animals pulled chariots or performed tricks. Most, however, fought one another or gladiators. Sometimes, as many as 5,000 wild animals were killed in a single day. In some cases, such as that of the Mesopotamian lion and the North African elephant, whole species were eventually wiped out.

HISTORY Online

Student Web Activity

Visit the *Human Heritage* Web site at **humanheritage.glencoe.com** and click on *Chapter 15—Student Web Activities* to find out more about early Roman life.

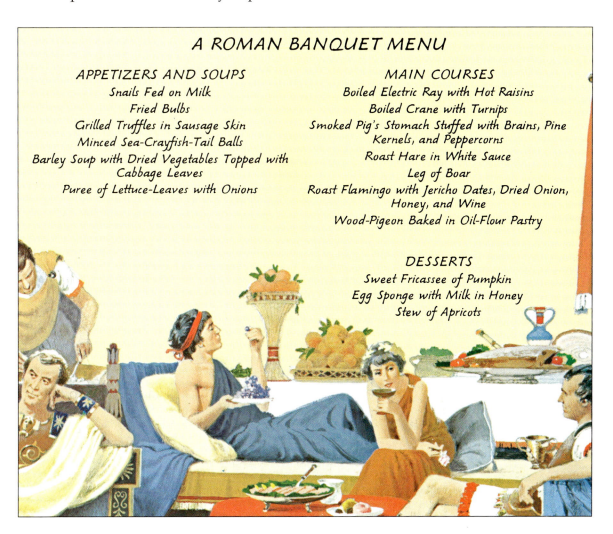

A ROMAN BANQUET MENU

APPETIZERS AND SOUPS
Snails Fed on Milk
Fried Bulbs
Grilled Truffles in Sausage Skin
Minced Sea-Crayfish-Tail Balls
Barley Soup with Dried Vegetables Topped with Cabbage Leaves
Puree of Lettuce-Leaves with Onions

MAIN COURSES
Boiled Electric Ray with Hot Raisins
Boiled Crane with Turnips
Smoked Pig's Stomach Stuffed with Brains, Pine Kernels, and Peppercorns
Roast Hare in White Sauce
Leg of Boar
Roast Flamingo with Jericho Dates, Dried Onion, Honey, and Wine
Wood-Pigeon Baked in Oil-Flour Pastry

DESSERTS
Sweet Fricassee of Pumpkin
Egg Sponge with Milk in Honey
Stew of Apricots

Section 3 Assessment

1. **Define:** *domus*, gladiators.
2. What kind of schooling did Roman children receive?
3. What did the Romans do for entertainment?

Critical Thinking

4. **Drawing Conclusions** What conclusions can you draw about Roman society based upon popular leisure activities?

Graphic Organizer Activity

5. Draw this diagram, and use it to compare family life in the United States with Roman family life during the *Pax Romana*.

Roman Families / Both / U.S. Families

SECTION 4 Fall of the Empire

The *Pax Romana* ended after about 200 years. From then on, conditions in the Roman Empire grew worse. By 476 A.D., there was no empire left. Instead, much of western Europe was a patchwork of <u>Germanic kingdoms</u>. The eastern part of the empire, however, lasted about 1,000 years longer as part of the Byzantine (biz' n tēn) Empire.

There are many reasons the Roman Empire fell. The first was political. The emperors had no written rule about who was to inherit the throne upon an emperor's death. Sometimes, the title was inherited by a son. Sometimes, an emperor adopted an heir to the throne. Between 96 and 180 A.D., all the emperors were adopted. The system worked well until 180 A.D.

Marcus Aurelius (ah rē' lē uhs) became emperor in 161 A.D. He was kind, intelligent, and devoted to duty. His son Commodus (kahm' uh duhs), however, was the opposite. He became emperor when Marcus Aurelius died in 180 A.D. He was so cruel and hated that in 192 A.D. he was strangled by the Praetorian (prē tōr' ē uhn) Guard, or the emperor's bodyguards. The Praetorian Guard then sold the throne to the highest bidder. This set a terrible example. For nearly 100 years, legion fought legion to put its own emperor on the throne. By 284 A.D., Rome had 37 different emperors. Most were murdered by the army or the Praetorian Guard.

The second reason for Rome's downfall was economic. To stay in office, an emperor had to keep the soldiers who supported him happy. He did this by giving them high wages. This meant more and more money was needed for the army payroll. As a result, the Romans had to pay higher taxes.

In addition to higher taxes, the Romans began to suffer from **inflation,** or a period of ever-increasing prices. Since there were

The Pantheon The "good emperor" Hadrian built the Pantheon in Rome as a temple to honor all the gods. Today the beautiful building is a national shrine, a church, and the burial place of two kings of Italy.

Reading Check
What is **inflation?**

no new conquests, gold was no longer coming into Rome. Yet, much gold was going out to pay for luxury items. This meant there was less gold to use in coins. As the amount of gold used in coins decreased, money began to lose its value. Prices went up. Many people stopped using money altogether. Instead, they began to **barter**, or exchange goods without using money.

The third major reason Rome fell centered on foreign enemies. While the Romans fought each other over politics and money, they left Rome's frontiers open to attack. Germanic hunters and herders from northern and central Europe began to raid Greece and Gaul. Trade and farming in those areas declined. Cities again began to surround themselves with protecting walls.

✓ **Reading Check**
Why did Romans begin to **barter?**

Diocletian and Constantine I   Two emperors, Diocletian (dī ō klē' shuhn) and Constantine I (kon stan tēn'), tried very hard to save the Roman Empire from collapse.

EMPERORS DURING THE *PAX ROMANA*

	Emperor	Reign	Accomplishments
	Augustus	27 B.C.–14 A.D.	first emperor of Roman Empire
			reorganized government of Rome; brought peace to Rome
	Tiberius	14 A.D.–37 A.D.	reformed taxes and improved financial state of government
	Caligula	37 A.D.–41 A.D.	repaired roads and began construction of two aqueducts
	Claudius	41 A.D.–54 A.D.	conquered most of England
			extended citizenship to many people outside Rome
			set up ministries to handle government administration
	Nero	54 A.D.–68 A.D.	rebuilt Rome after the fire of 64 A.D. and gave it a city plan
	Flavian Emperors Vespasian Titus Domitian	69 A.D.–96 A.D.	brought people from the provinces into the Senate
			secured frontier regions
			brought Rome new prosperity
			built the Coliseum
	Five Good Emperors Nerva Trajan Hadrian Antoninus Pius Marcus Aurelius	96 A.D.–180 A.D.	built aqueducts, bridges, and harbors
			extended citizenship to more provinces
			cut dishonesty in business and government

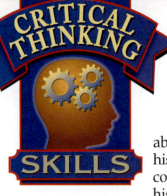

CRITICAL THINKING SKILLS

Identifying the Main Idea

As you read about world history, you come across historical dates, events, and names. These details are easier to understand and remember when they are connected to one main idea.

Understanding the main idea allows you to grasp the whole picture or story. The details then become more easily understood.

Learning the Skill Follow these steps to identify a main idea:

- Before you read the material, find out the setting of the article or document: the time, the place, and who the writer is.
- Read the material and ask, "What is the purpose of this information?"
- Study any photographs or illustrations that accompany the material.
- Ask, "What are the most forceful statements in this material?"
- Identify supporting details.
- Identify the main idea, or central issue.

GO TO Glencoe's **Skillbuilder Interactive Workbook CD-ROM, Level 1,** provides instruction and practice in key social studies skills.

Skill Practice

The passage that follows comes from a document issued by Diocletian, the emperor of Rome from 284 to 305 A.D. In it, he describes a plan for ending Rome's economic problems. Read this passage and answer the questions that follow.

In the commerce carried on in the markets or involved in the daily life of cities, high prices are so widespread that they are not lowered even by abundant supplies or good years. . . . There are men who try . . . to profit in good as well as poor years even though they have enough wealth to satisfy entire nations. . . . Prices have been driven so high that sometimes in a single purchase a soldier is deprived of his bonus and salary. . . .

We have decreed that there be established . . . maximum prices. . . . It is our pleasure, therefore, that the prices . . . be observed in the whole of our empire and the penalty for violating this law shall be death. . . . We urge obedience to this law, since it provides . . . against those whose greed could not be satisfied.

1. Why has Diocletian issued this document?
2. What main idea, or central issue, is discussed by the document?
3. What supporting details are used to support the main idea?
4. What forceful statement does Diocletian use to make sure people do not miss the seriousness of the central issue?

Diocletian, who was the son of a freedman, ruled from 284 to 305 A.D. He made many changes as emperor. He fortified the frontiers to stop invasions. He reorganized the state and provincial governments to make them work better. To keep prices from rising, he set maximum prices for wages and goods. To make sure goods were produced, he ordered workers to stay in the same jobs until they died. He also made city officials personally responsible for the taxes their communities had to pay.

One of the most important changes Diocletian made concerned the position of the emperor. Diocletian established the official policy of **rule by divine right.** This meant the emperor's powers and right to rule came not from the people but from the gods.

Diocletian realized the Roman Empire covered too much area for one person to rule well. So, he divided it into two parts. He allowed someone else to govern the western provinces, while he ruled the richer eastern provinces.

In 312 A.D., Constantine I became emperor. He ruled until 337 A.D. Constantine took even firmer control of the empire than Diocletian. To keep people from leaving their jobs when things got bad, he issued several orders. The sons of workers had to follow their fathers' trades. The sons of farmers had to stay and work the land their fathers worked. The sons of ex-soldiers had to serve in the army.

To escape government pressure and control, wealthy landowners moved to their *villas,* or country estates. Most villas were like small, independent cities or kingdoms. Each produced enough food and goods to meet the needs of everyone who lived on the estate.

Despite the changes made by Diocletian and Constantine, the Roman Empire continued to decline in the west. In 330 A.D., Constantine moved the capital from a dying Rome east to the newly built city of Constantinople (kon stan tuh nō′ puhl) in present-day Turkey.

End of the Empire

Both Diocletian and Constantine I worked hard to save the Roman Empire. However, neither emperor succeeded in the end.

German attacks increased, especially in western Europe. There, the Germans crossed the Danube River in order to escape from the Huns, nomadic herders who had wandered west from Outer Mongolia in Asia. In 378 A.D., a Germanic group defeated Roman legions at the Battle of Adrianople (ā drē uh nō′ puhl). One reason the Germans were able to defeat the Romans was because of an invention they borrowed from the Huns. This invention was the iron stirrup. Using iron stirrups made cavalry stronger than infantry, even the powerful Roman legions. This was because the force of the charging horse was added to the force of the weapon.

✔ **Reading Check**
What does **rule by divine right** mean?

Diocletian
245 A.D.–313 A.D.

Roman Emperor

Diocletian was born of humble parents in what is now Croatia, an area in eastern Europe ruled by the Romans. He rose to power as an officer in the Roman army, and it was his troops who proclaimed him emperor in 284 A.D. Diocletian's division of the empire into parts earned him the loyalty of powerful supporters such as Constantine I. In 305 A.D., he retired to a castle in present-day Split, Croatia.

By about 400 A.D., Rome had grown quite weak. In the winter of 406 A.D., the Rhine River froze. Groups of Germans crossed the frozen river and entered Gaul. The Romans were not able to force them back across the border.

In 410 A.D., the Germanic chief Alaric (al' uhr ik) and his soldiers invaded Rome. They burned records and looted the treasury. The Roman Senate told the people, "You can no longer rely on Rome for finance or direction. You are on your own."

Section 4 Assessment

1. **Define:** inflation, barter, rule by divine right.
2. How did wealthy landowners react to economic reforms by Diocletian and Constantine?
3. How did the Germans gain control of the Roman Empire?

Critical Thinking

4. **Identifying Alternatives** What do you think could have been done by either Diocletian or Constantine to save the Roman Empire?

Graphic Organizer Activity

5. Draw this diagram, and use it to summarize the causes for the fall of the Roman Empire.

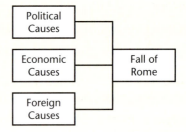

Chapter Summary & Study Guide

1. Octavian, better known as Augustus, became the first Roman emperor in 27 B.C.
2. Reorganization of the empire by Augustus introduced a 200-year period of peace, called the *Pax Romana.*
3. During the *Pax Romana,* trade increased, and Roman law became standardized.
4. During the *Pax Romana,* about one million people lived in Rome, where they suffered from such problems as overcrowding, pollution, crime, and unemployment.
5. Whether rich or poor, most Roman children went to school until age 12.

6. The Roman government staged free public games to entertain the people.
7. Reasons for the fall of Rome include the lack of a formal rule for inheriting the throne, inflation, and attacks by Germanic invaders.
8. Despite efforts by Diocletian and Constantine I to save the empire, Rome fell to Germanic invaders in 410 A.D.

Self-Check Quiz

Visit the *Human Heritage* Web site at **humanheritage. glencoe.com** and click on **Chapter 15—Self-Check Quiz** to assess your understanding of this chapter.

Using Key Terms

Imagine you are living in Rome around 400 A.D. Use the following words to write a letter to a friend explaining some of the reasons for the decline of the Roman Empire.

emperor	freedmen	census
juris prudentes	tariffs	*domus*
gladiators	inflation	barter
rule by divine right		

Understanding Main Ideas

1. How did Augustus make life safer for people living in Rome?
2. How did increased trade during the *Pax Romana* affect the Romans?
3. Why did the Romans change the laws set down in the Twelve Tables?
4. Why was it important to make Roman law standardized across the empire?
5. What happened to some animal species as a result of the public games?
6. How did the Praetorian Guard contribute to the empire's decline?
7. Why did Diocletian divide the Roman Empire in two?
8. What were the main reasons for the fall of the Roman Empire?

Critical Thinking

1. What were Augustus's strengths and weaknesses as a ruler?
2. Why would the absence of tariffs increase trade?
3. Would you have enjoyed living in Rome during the *Pax Romana*? Explain.
4. What happens to a government if it does not have rules for passing on power from leader to leader?

Graphic Organizer Activity

Culture Create this diagram, and use it to compare the education of Roman children with the education of children in the United States.

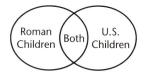

Geography in History

The World in Spatial Terms Refer to the map on page 235. Describe the general location of the Roman Empire according to its longitude and latitude. Also identify the location of the imaginary dividing line between the western and eastern empires.

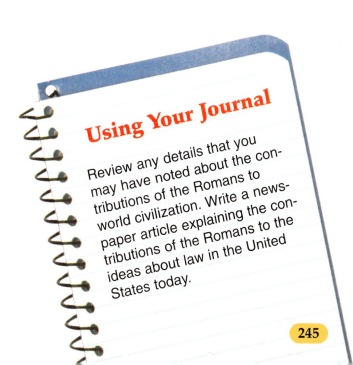

Using Your Journal

Review any details that you may have noted about the contributions of the Romans to world civilization. Write a newspaper article explaining the contributions of the Romans to the ideas about law in the United States today.

Christianity
1 B.C.–1054 A.D.

◀ Early Christian symbol

Jesus on his throne ▶

30 A.D.
Jesus is crucified
by Romans

64 A.D.
Romans ban
Christianity

312 A.D.
Constantine I
accepts
Christianity

392 A.D.
Christianity becomes
official religion of
Roman Empire

1054 A.D.
Latin and Greek
churches
separate

Chapter Focus

Chapter Overview

Visit the *Human Heritage* Web site at **humanheritage.glencoe.com** and click on *Chapter 16— Chapter Overviews* to preview this chapter.

 Read to Discover

- How Jesus' life and teachings formed the basis of Christianity.
- How Christianity spread throughout the Roman Empire.
- How the early Christian church was organized.
- What relationship existed between Christianity and Roman society before and after the time of Constantine I.
- What life was like for the early monks and nuns.

Terms to Learn	**People to Know**	**Places to Locate**
scriptures	Jesus	Bethlehem
messiah	Paul	Nazareth
gentiles	Constantine I	Jerusalem
missionary	Theodosius	
churches	Jerome	
apostles	Augustine	
priest		
bishop		
heresy		
monks		
nuns		

Why It's Important   Christians brought new ideas and important changes to the Roman Empire. Their religion, Christianity, started in Palestine among the Jews and later spread throughout the empire and the world. Despite cruel treatment, the early Christians clung to their faith, and by 400 A.D. most Romans had come to accept the religion as their own.

SECTION 1   The Beginnings

Christianity is based on the life and teachings of Jesus (jē' zuhs), who lived in Palestine during the reign of Augustus. After Jesus died, his teachings were spread by his followers. Christianity survived the fall of Rome and grew to be one of the major influences on western civilization.

The Life of Jesus   Jesus, born a Jew in the town of Bethlehem (beth' luh hem), grew up in Nazareth (naz' uhr uhth). There, he received a Jewish education. He studied the **scriptures**

 **Reading Check**
What are the **scriptures?**

Mosaic of Christian Symbol

(skrip' churz), or sacred writings, and learned prayers in the Hebrew language. Later, he went to work as a carpenter.

When he was about 30 years old, Jesus began to travel around Palestine preaching to people. Men and women came in large numbers from all over the country to see and hear him. Jesus taught that God created all people and loves them the way a father loves his children. Therefore, people should behave like God's children and love God and one another. Jesus said that God loves even people who have sinned. Jesus told people that if they were truly sorry and placed their trust in God, they would be forgiven.

Jesus spoke in the everyday language of the people. He presented his teachings in *parables* (par' uh buhlz), or stories, about persons and things that were familiar to his listeners. In this way, they could better understand the religious principles he was trying to teach. For example, in the parable of the Good Samaritan (suh mar' uh tuhn), Jesus told about a man from Jerusalem who was attacked by robbers. They beat the man severely and left him lying in the road. Two passers-by from Jerusalem saw him there but did nothing. Then came a man from the city of Samaria (suh mar' ē uh). He stopped, washed the man's wounds, and carried him to a nearby inn. The parable taught that people should not ignore wrong but should do something about it. The parable also taught that people should help everyone, not just those from their own community.

In 30 A.D., after about three years of preaching, Jesus and 12 of his disciples went to Jerusalem to celebrate Passover, the holiday that marks the exodus of the Jews from Egypt. At the time, there was much unrest in the city. Many Romans were angry because the Jews refused to worship statues of the Roman emperor. The Jews were tired of the high taxes they had to pay and of the pressure put on them by the Romans. They hoped and waited for a **messiah** (muh sī' uh), or someone who would save them.

When Jesus arrived in Jerusalem, many Jews greeted him as the messiah. This worried other Jews and Romans alike. Jesus was convicted of treason under Roman law and was *crucified* (krū' suh fīd), or executed on a cross, outside Jerusalem. Usually, only lower-class criminals were killed in this way.

The loss of their leader greatly saddened Jesus' disciples. Then, according to Christian tradition, Jesus rose from the dead. He remained on Earth for 40 days before going directly to heaven. His *resurrection* (rez uh rek' shuhn), or rising from the dead, convinced his disciples that Jesus was the Son of God who had become man. They believed that because Jesus had suffered death and had risen to life, he could forgive the sins of all people. They thought that anyone who believed in Jesus and lived by his teachings would know eternal life after death. From then on, the disciples called him Christ, after the Greek word *Christos* (khrēs tōs'), meaning "messiah."

Reading Check
Why did Jews await the arrival of a **messiah?**

Painting of Some of Jesus' Disciples

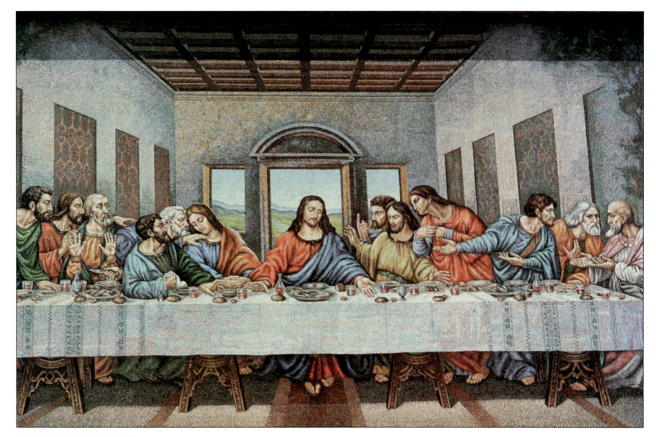

THE LAST SUPPER The night before he was crucified, Jesus met with his closest disciples for the meal that marks the start of Passover. At this meal, known as the Last Supper, Jesus set the guidelines for later Christian ceremonies. **Why did Jesus and his disciples go to Jerusalem?**

Paul

The disciples were among the first people to become Christians. After Jesus died, they tried to spread his *gospel*, or teachings, among the Jews in Palestine. They had little success, however. Most Palestinian Jews wanted a political messiah. They were not interested in a religious one. The disciples then began to spread their message to Jews who lived outside Palestine. Soon, small groups of people who believed in Christ were meeting in Antioch (ant' ē ahk), Corinth, Rome, and other trading cities of the Mediterranean area.

At about the same time, a Jew named Paul decided to teach Christianity to **gentiles** (jen' tīls), or non-Jews, as well as to Jews. Paul had once been a close follower of Judaism. Then, according to Christian tradition, while he was traveling on the road to Damascus (duh mas' kuhs), Paul was blinded by a bright light and heard Christ's voice. After he was able to see again, Paul became a Christian. He spent the rest of his life spreading the Christian message throughout the Roman world.

Reading Check
Who were the **gentiles?**

In each city where Paul preached, new Christian communities formed. Paul wrote letters to these groups to help guide the members. In his letters, he stated that gentiles who became Christians did not have to follow Jewish rituals and laws. All they needed was to have faith in Jesus. This appealed to many people.

Paul was very important to the growth of Christianity. He was its first **missionary** (mish' uh ner ē), or person who spreads religious beliefs to those who do not believe. After Paul's death, other Christian missionaries continued his work.

✔ Reading Check
Why is Paul considered the first Christian **missionary**?

Section 1 Assessment

1. **Define:** scriptures, messiah, gentiles, missionary.
2. Why did the Romans charge Jesus with treason?
3. What changes did Paul make in the Christian religion?

Critical Thinking

4. **Demonstrating Reasoned Judgment** Of the people you know about today, who could be called a Good Samaritan? Give examples.

Graphic Organizer Activity

5. Draw this diagram, and use it to show some of the Christian beliefs taught by Jesus.

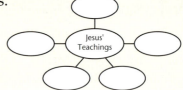

Jesus' Teachings

SECTION 2 Christianity and Rome

The Roman Empire helped Christianity spread. The *Pax Romana* allowed missionaries to move across Roman lands in safety. The Roman system of roads helped them go from one place to another quickly. Since most people spoke either Latin or Greek, the missionaries could talk with them directly.

Political Conditions Political conditions did not favor the spread of Christianity, however. Although all people in the Roman Empire were generally allowed to worship freely, the Romans expected everyone to honor the emperor as a god. The Christians, like the Jews, refused to do this. They claimed that only God could be worshiped. This made the Romans angry.

The Romans also did not like other Christian ideas. For example, Christians did not want to serve in the army or hold public office. They often criticized Roman festivals and games. They taught that all people would be equal in heaven if they followed Jesus' teachings.

Because of these differences, the Romans blamed and punished Christians for all kinds of disasters, such as plagues and famines (fam' uhnz). In 64 A.D., the Romans accused the Chris-

HISTORY Online

Student Web Activity

Visit the *Human Heritage* Web site at **humanheritage.glencoe.com** and click on *Chapter 16— Student Web Activities* to find out more about early Christianity.

tians of starting a fire that burned much of Rome. Christianity was then made illegal, and many Christians were killed.

Some officials paid no attention to the law that made Christianity illegal. However, Christians still had a hard time in most areas. In Rome, they were not allowed to use Roman burial places. They had to bury their dead in crowded catacombs.

The Spread of Christianity   Even with all of the hardships, Christianity spread. It was of more interest to the poor workers and enslaved people in the cities. They led very hard lives. They liked a religion that promised a happier life after death.

Over time, however, Christianity began to draw people from all classes. After 250 A.D., many Romans grew tired of war and

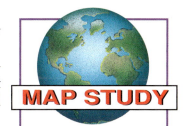

MAP STUDY

HUMAN SYSTEMS
By 1100 Christianity had spread throughout most of Europe and parts of Asia and North Africa. **How did Paul's journeys help the spread of Christianity?**

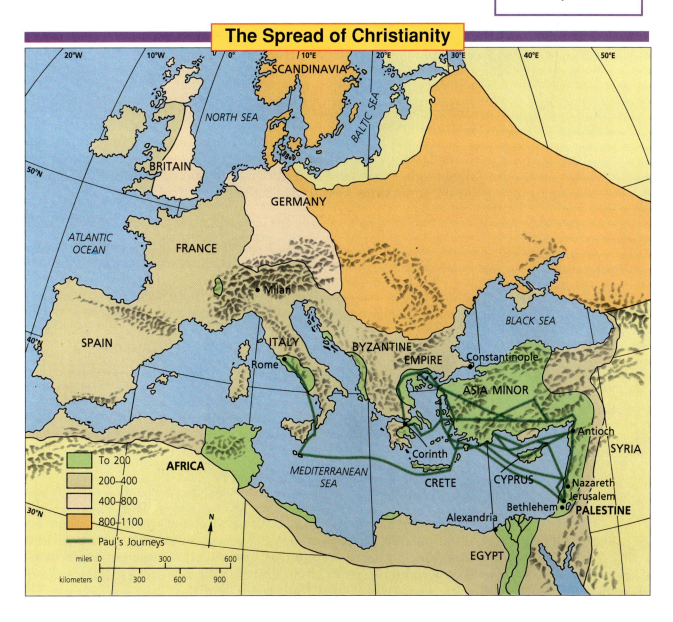

The Spread of Christianity

Map legend:
- To 200
- 200–400
- 400–800
- 800–1100
- Paul's Journeys

miles 0 — 300 — 600
kilometers 0 — 300 — 600 — 900

Map labels: SCANDINAVIA, NORTH SEA, BALTIC SEA, BRITAIN, GERMANY, ATLANTIC OCEAN, FRANCE, Milan, SPAIN, ITALY, Rome, BYZANTINE EMPIRE, BLACK SEA, Constantinople, ASIA MINOR, AFRICA, Corinth, MEDITERRANEAN SEA, CRETE, CYPRUS, Antioch, SYRIA, Nazareth, Jerusalem, Bethlehem, PALESTINE, Alexandria, EGYPT

feared the end of the empire. They began to admire the certainty and courage of the Christian missionaries. They wanted the love, kindness, and feeling of safety that Christianity offered. At the same time, many Christians started to accept the empire.

Constantine I and Theodosius

In 312 A.D., Constantine I, who was a general at the time, accepted Christianity. Legend says that as he was about to go into battle, Constantine saw a flaming cross in the sky. Written beneath the cross were the Latin words *in hoc signo vinces* (in hok sig′ nō win′ kās). This means, "In this sign thou shalt conquer." Constantine won the battle and with it the throne of the Roman Empire. Constantine believed God had helped him gain his victory. Because of this, he ordered his soldiers to paint crosses on their shields.

The following year, the Edict (ē′ dikt) of Milan (mi lan′) was issued. It gave religious freedom to all people. It also made Christianity legal. Constantine I did many other things to help Christianity grow. He had churches built in Rome and Jerusalem. He used government money to pay for Christian schools. He let church leaders enter government service and excused them from paying taxes.

The emperor who followed Constantine I continued pro-Christian policies. In 392 A.D., Emperor Theodosius (thē uh dō′ shē uhs) made Christianity the official religion of the Roman Empire. At the same time, he outlawed all other religions.

Section 2 Assessment

1. What factors brought about a change in attitude between Romans and Christians?
2. What did Christians believe would happen to people in heaven?

Critical Thinking

3. **Making Inferences** Why do you think the hardships put on Christians by the Romans could not stop the spread of Christianity?

Graphic Organizer Activity

4. Draw this diagram, and use it to show what life was like for Christians before and after the rule of Constantine I.

Before		Constantine I		After

SECTION 3 The Church

Reading Check
Why did early Christians form **churches**?

Early Christians thought the end of the world was near. At the time, they believed Jesus would return to set up God's kingdom on Earth. While they were waiting for this to happen, they lived together in small groups called **churches.** They shared their possessions and took turns leading worship services in homes and outdoors. Each group was in charge of its own affairs. **Apostles** (uh pos′ uhls), or those people Jesus chose to teach his gospel, visited the different groups. The apostles taught and gave advice. They also provided a sense of unity.

Church Structure

After the apostles died, Christians realized that Jesus was not going to return to Earth as quickly as they had expected. They looked for ways to hold their churches together. One way was by organizing the churches. They used the Roman Empire's structure of government as a model for this organization.

By 300 A.D., each church was called a **parish** (par′ ish). Each had a leader known as a **priest.** Several parishes were put together into larger groups. Each group was called a **diocese** (dī′ uh sis), a word that originally meant a Roman military district. A **bishop** headed each diocese. The most important bishops were called **archbishops.** They governed churches in larger cities. The five leading archbishops were called **patriarchs** (pā′ trē arks).

As time went on, the archbishop of Rome began to claim power over the other archbishops. By 600 A.D., he was called Pope. This comes from a Latin word meaning "father." Christians who spoke Latin saw him as the head of all the churches. Christians who spoke Greek, however, would not accept him as the leader of their churches. They turned instead to the archbishop of Constantinople. In 1054 A.D., the two church groups separated. The Latin churches as a group became known as the Roman Catholic Church. The Greek churches became known as the Eastern Orthodox Church.

The New Testament

At the same time Christians were developing a church organization, they were deciding what writings to put into the New Testament, or Christian scriptures. Jesus had left no written records. However, after his death, others wrote about Jesus' life and teachings.

Toward the end of the 300s A.D., four accounts were accepted as part of the New Testament. The accounts were believed to have been written by Matthew, Mark, Luke, and John. These men were four of Jesus' early followers. A number of letters written by Paul and other disciples were also accepted as part of the New Testament.

At about the same time, bishops met to discuss questions about Christian thinking. Decisions they reached at these meetings came to be accepted as official *doctrine* (dok′ truhn), or statements of faith. The points of view the bishops did not accept were declared to be **heresy** (her′ uh sē), or false doctrines.

Fathers of the Church

Between 100 and 500 A.D., different scholars wrote works that greatly influenced later Christians. These scholars became known as the "Fathers of the Church."

Reading Check
Who were the **apostles?**

Reading Check
What is a **parish?** What was the role of an early **priest?** What was the original meaning of **diocese?**

Reading Check
What was the role of the **bishop?** Who were the **archbishops** and **patriarchs?**

Reading Check
What did bishops consider as **heresy?**

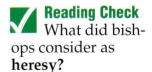

Religious Orders   The religious order that lived at the monastery at Monte Cassino (left) followed the teachings of Benedict and were known as Benedictines. In 1950, Mother Teresa, an eastern European nun, continued this tradition by founding the Missionaries of Charity, an order dedicated to helping the poor of India (right). **What rules did early members of the Benedictine order follow?**

People in History

Saint Augustine
354 A.D.–430 A.D.

Christian Scholar

Augustine was born in present-day Algeria. In 387 A.D., he embraced Christianity. As invaders poured into Rome, Augustine became one of the leading defenders of Christianity. After his death, church leaders declared him a saint.

One such scholar was Jerome (juh rōm′). He translated the Old and New Testaments into Latin. His translation was called the *Vulgate* (vul′ gāt). It became the official Bible used by the Roman Catholic Church.

Augustine (o′ guh stēn) was an important leader of Christian thought. His best-known work was *City of God.* In it, he defended Christianity against those who said that Rome would not have fallen if it had not accepted Christianity. Augustine said that Rome fell because it became rich and corrupt and persecuted Christians.

Monasteries   In the early years of Christianity, thousands of Christians left the cities to live and pray alone in isolated areas. Such people were known as *hermits.* In Egypt and Syria especially, thousands of hermits lived in the desert. They believed that this would help them grow closer to Christ.

A hermit was protected from the temptations of daily life. At the same time, however, such a person was not doing anything to improve the world. Near the end of the 300s A.D., a bishop named Basil (baz′ uhl) suggested a different way of life. He said that Christians should form religious settlements near cities. In this way, they would be protected from the evils of the world. At the same time, they could help other people by doing good deeds and by setting an example of Christian living. Many Christians took Basil's advice.

Christian men who did as Basil suggested were called **monks.** Their settlements, or communities, were known as **monasteries** (mon′ uh ster ēz). Christian women who did the same were called **nuns.** They lived in quarters of their own called **convents** (kon′ vents). Basil drew up a list of rules for these religious communities. This list, which is known as the Basilian (buh zil′ ē uhn) Rule, became the model for Eastern Orthodox religious life.

In the West, another set of rules called the Benedictine (ben uh dik′ tuhn) Rule was followed. It was drawn up about 529 A.D. by an Italian named Benedict (ben′ uh dikt). The monks who followed Benedict's rule promised to give up all their possessions before entering a monastery. They agreed to wear simple clothes and eat only certain foods. They could not marry. They had to obey without question the orders of the **abbot** (ab′ uht), or leader of the monastery. They had to attend religious services seven times during the day and once at midnight. They also were expected to work six or seven hours a day in the fields around the monastery. When they grew older, they did clerical work or worked as carpenters and weavers. They spent their whole lives serving Christ.

Reading Check
Why did **monks** build the first **monasteries?** Why did Christian women become **nuns** and live at **convents?**

Reading Check
What was the role of an **abbot?**

EARLY CHRISTIANS   Church leaders often dictated their thoughts as Pope Gregory is shown (left) doing. Those thoughts were studied by a church monk shown here (right) in order to improve his knowledge of Christianity. **Where did monks at this time live?**

By 800 A.D., monks were playing an important role in spreading Christianity throughout Europe. By preserving old Roman and Greek writings, they helped western civilization survive and progress.

Section 3 Assessment

1. **Define:** churches, apostles, parish, priest, diocese, bishop, archbishops, patriarchs, heresy, monks, monasteries, nuns, convents, abbot.
2. How was the early Christian church organized?
3. How did monks help western civilization survive?

Critical Thinking

4. **Making Generalizations** What general statement can you make about the main purpose of monastic life?

Graphic Organizer Activity

5. Draw this diagram, and use it to compare the lives of hermits with the lives of monks and nuns.

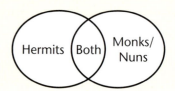

Hermits — Both — Monks/Nuns

Chapter Summary & Study Guide

1. Jesus' teachings angered Roman officials, who arrested and executed him around 30 A.D.
2. Paul preached Christianity to Jews and non-Jews alike, helping to make Christianity a world religion.
3. Some Romans, particularly the emperors, tried unsuccessfully to stop the spread of Christianity.
4. In 313 A.D., Christianity became legal in Rome. In 392 A.D., it became the empire's official religion.
5. By the end of the 500s A.D., early Christians had organized a church and decided which writings should appear in the New Testament.

6. By 600 A.D., most Latin-speaking Christians looked on the Pope in Rome as the head of the Church.
7. In 1054 A.D., most Greek-speaking Christians split from the Latin Church to form the Eastern Orthodox Church.
8. Religious scholars and monks helped preserve Greek and Roman writings and wrote works that greatly influenced later Christian thinkers.

Self-Check Quiz

Visit the *Human Heritage* Web site at **humanheritage. glencoe.com** and click on *Chapter 16—Self-Check Quiz* to assess your understanding of this chapter.

Using Key Terms

Sort the following words into these categories: *people, places,* and *other,* as they apply to the beginning of Christianity. Then write one sentence explaining each term you classified as *other.*

scriptures	messiah	gentiles
missionary	churches	apostles
parish	priest	diocese
bishop	archbishops	patriarchs
heresy	monks	monasteries
nuns	convents	abbot

Understanding Main Ideas

1. Where did Christianity start?
2. Why did Jesus teach in parables?
3. Why did the Romans blame and punish the Christians for many disasters?
4. What groups of people were first attracted to Christianity?
5. What legend is told about Constantine I?
6. Why did Christians develop a church organization?
7. Why did the Latin and Greek churches split into two groups?
8. What kinds of work did the monks do?

Critical Thinking

1. Why do you think people seemed to remember Jesus' teachings more when he used parables?
2. Do you think citizens should have religious freedom or be required to follow one official religion? Explain.
3. What do you think could have been done to prevent the split between the Latin and Greek churches?

Graphic Organizer Activity

Culture Create a chart like the one shown, and use it to show the organization of the early Church. From the top, arrange these religious offices in order of authority: monks and nuns, patriarchs, bishops, pope, archbishops, priests.

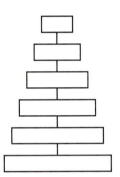

Geography in History

Places and Regions Refer to the map on page 251, noting Paul's journeys. Describe what geographic features and landscapes Paul would have seen as he traveled from Antioch to Corinth.

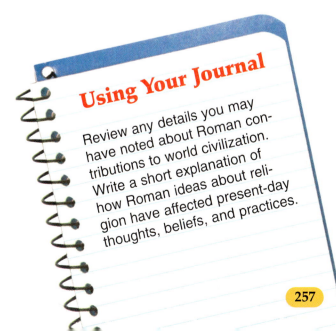

Using Your Journal

Review any details you may have noted about Roman contributions to world civilization. Write a short explanation of how Roman ideas about religion have affected present-day thoughts, beliefs, and practices.

Around

THE MOCHE

As the Roman Empire reached its height, a people named the Moche rose to power in the coastal deserts of present-day Peru. The Moche civilization lasted from roughly 100 A.D. to 800 A.D.

Although the Moche did not develop a written language, the story of their culture is told through the buildings and artwork that they left behind.

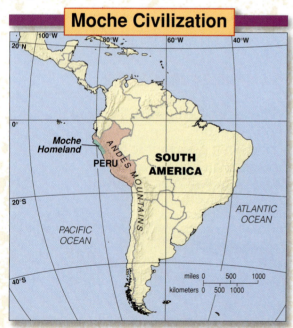

Moche Civilization

▲ A series of rivers runs out of the Andes Mountains and cuts through the dry deserts of Peru's northern coast. The Moche dug irrigation ditches and used water from these rivers to turn the deserts into farmland. They produced so much food that the population boomed. One river valley may have supported more than 10,000 people.

▲ One of the most powerful groups in Moche society was that of the warrior-priests—nobles who served as both military and religious leaders. A curved, gold headdress symbolized their power.

◄ When a warrior-priest died, the Moche filled his grave with a wealth of treasures to accompany him to the next life. Talented metal workers, Moche artists produced complicated designs. This gold-and-turquoise ear ornament shows what a Moche warrior-priest looked like.

The Moche built hundreds of flat-topped ► pyramids. Temples and platforms on the top of the pyramids made them religious and administrative centers. The biggest Moche pyramid— the Pyramid of the Sun—covered over 12.5 acres. It was the largest structure built in the ancient Americas.

Pottery often took the form of animals important ► to the Moche, such as the llama. The llama served as a pack animal for long-distance trips. It also provided meat for food and wool for weaving.

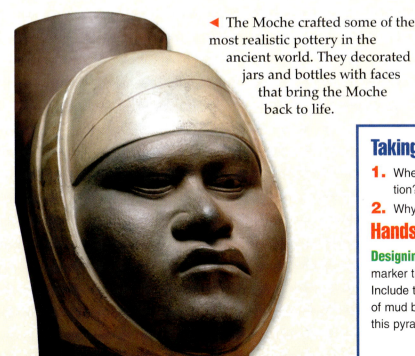

◄ The Moche crafted some of the most realistic pottery in the ancient world. They decorated jars and bottles with faces that bring the Moche back to life.

Taking Another Look

1. Where and when did the Moche build their civilization?

2. Why did the Moche experience a population boom?

Hands-On Activity

Designing a Historical Marker Design a historical marker that might be placed at the Pyramid of the Sun. Include this fact: The Spanish word for pyramids made of mud bricks is *huacas*. Thus the Spanish name for this pyramid is *Huaca del Sol.*

Standardized Test Practice

Directions: Choose the *best* answer to each of the following multiple choice questions. If you have trouble answering a question, use the process of elimination to narrow your choices. Write your answers on a separate piece of paper.

1. **Plebeians made up a majority of ancient Rome's total population. However, early Roman laws did not treat the plebeians fairly. Which of the following is an example of a law that was unfair to the plebeians?**

   A Senators in Rome held their positions for their whole lives.

   B Plebeians had to pay taxes but could not serve in the government.

   C There were only two consuls chosen to lead the Roman Republic each year.

   D Tribunes were set up to represent plebeians in Roman government.

   Test-Taking Tip: The important phrase in this question is *unfair to the plebeians.* Answer A may seem unfair, but was it specifically *unfair to the plebeians?*

2. **Early Romans believed that certain people, called *soothsayers,* could predict the future. Roman soothsayers were most similar to**

   F Greek oracles

   G modern-day priests

   H philosophers like Socrates

   J Egyptian pharaohs

   Test-Taking Tip: This question asks you to make a *comparison.* Although oracles, priests, philosophers, and pharaohs may have all been consulted for *advice,* they did not all *predict the future.*

Use the map on the top of the next page to answer questions 3 and 4.

3. **In 130 A.D., the Roman Empire surrounded which body of water?**

   A The Mediterranean Sea

   B The Atlantic Ocean

   C The North Sea

   D The Red Sea

   Test-Taking Tip: Make sure that your answer is supported by information *on the map.* Use the *map key,* or *legend,* to help you understand how the map is organized. Remember that all the different patterns and shades of gray in the key refer to the Roman Empire. They just help to differentiate it at different points during its expansion.

4. **In 146 B.C., which part of the Roman territory was west of the Prime Meridian?**

   F Great Britain

   G Syria

   H Italy

   J Spain

   Test-Taking Tip: This question requires you to remember the term *Prime Meridian.* The Prime Meridian is the line of longitude that divides *east* and *west.* What degree represents it?

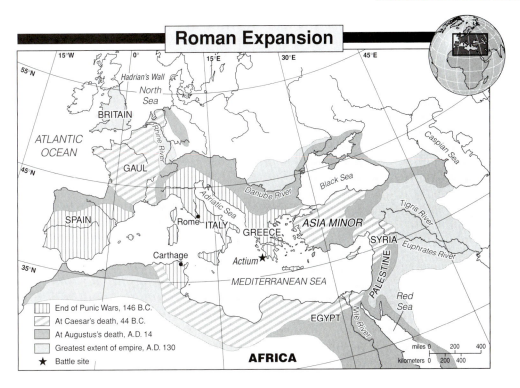

Roman Expansion

15°W · 0° · 15°E · 30°E · 45°E

55°N

Hadrian's Wall
North Sea
BRITAIN
ATLANTIC OCEAN
45°N
Rhine River
GAUL
Danube River
Caspian Sea
Adriatic Sea
Black Sea
SPAIN
Rome ITALY
GREECE
ASIA MINOR
Tigris River
SYRIA
Euphrates River
Carthage
Actium ★
PALESTINE
35°N
MEDITERRANEAN SEA
Red Sea
EGYPT
Nile River
AFRICA

Legend:
- ▯▯▯ End of Punic Wars, 146 B.C.
- ⬚ At Caesar's death, 44 B.C.
- ▨ At Augustus's death, A.D. 14
- ☐ Greatest extent of empire, A.D. 130
- ★ Battle site

miles 0 · 200 · 400
kilometers 0 · 200 · 400

---

5. During the *Pax Romana*, when Rome was at peace for 200 years, Augustus

A established the principle that laws must be fair to everyone

B focused on conquering other lands to increase trade opportunities

C paid pirates to patrol the trade routes that Roman merchants used

D failed to maintain a strong army, leaving Rome open to foreign attacks

> **Test-Taking Tip:** Eliminate answers that do not make sense. For example, if Rome was *at peace,* then Romans were probably not *conquering other lands* (answer B) or *open to foreign attacks* (answer D).

6. Which of the following was NOT a factor that facilitated the spread of Christianity through the Roman Empire?

F Missionaries spread the religion along the trade routes established by the Romans.

G Many people in the Empire understood the same languages, so Christians could spread their ideas.

H Christianity appealed to poor people by saying that there was a better life after death.

J People who became Christians were still allowed to worship Roman gods.

> **Test-Taking Tip:** Be careful when a question says NOT or EXCEPT. Look for the answer choice that does NOT fit. For instance, answer G, that people spoke the same languages, would be very helpful in communicating any ideas. Therefore, it was probably helpful in spreading Christianity, and you can eliminate it as a possible correct answer.

STOP

6

The Early Middle Ages

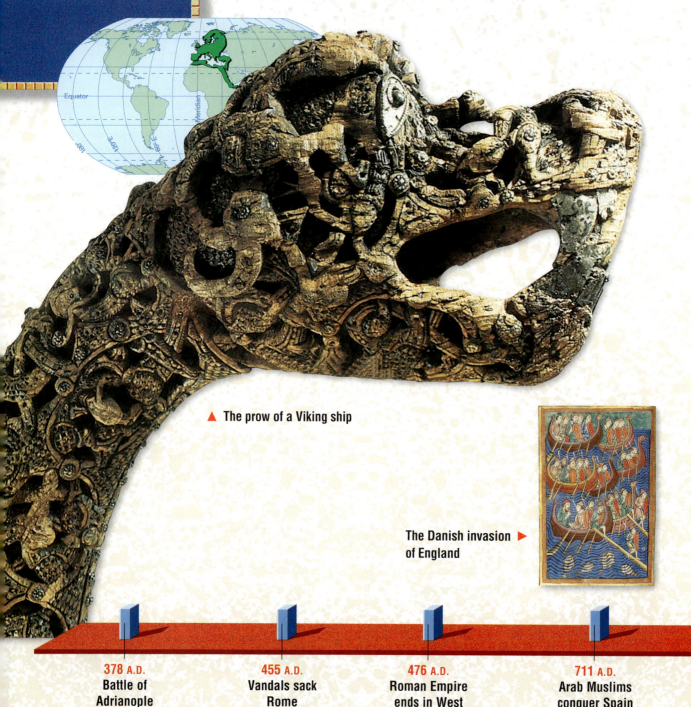

▲ The prow of a Viking ship

The Danish invasion ▶
of England

378 A.D.
Battle of
Adrianople

455 A.D.
Vandals sack
Rome

476 A.D.
Roman Empire
ends in West

711 A.D.
Arab Muslims
conquer Spain

Summarizing Information Study Foldable *Make this foldable to help you organize and summarize information about the western European civilization that developed during the early Middle Ages.*

Step 1 *Mark the midpoint of a side edge of one sheet of paper. Then fold the outside edges in to touch the midpoint.*

Step 2 *Fold the paper in half again from side to side.*

Reading and Writing *As you read the unit, write information under each appropriate tab. Be sure to summarize the information you find by writing only main ideas and supporting details.*

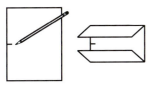

Step 3 *Open the paper and cut along the inside fold lines to form four tabs.*

Cut along the fold lines on both sides.

Step 4 *Label as shown.*

The Germans | The Franks
The Irish and Anglo-Saxons | The Vikings

PRIMARY SOURCES
Library

See pages 684–685 for other primary source readings to accompany Unit 6.

GO TO Read "Charlemagne Described" from the **World History Primary Source Document Library CD-ROM.**

732 A.D.
Battle of Tours

800 A.D.
Charlemagne is crowned emperor

911 A.D.
Normans settle in Normandy

Journal Notes

What was life like in Europe and other areas during the early Middle Ages? Note details about the changes taking place in government, the economy, and learning.

The Germans
300 A.D.–550 A.D.

▲ A Germanic brooch in
the shape of an eagle

The mausoleum ▶
of Theodoric
the Great

300 A.D.	378 A.D.	410 A.D.	455 A.D.	550 A.D.
Romans allow groups of Germans to cross their borders	Battle of Adrianople	Alaric captures Rome	Vandals sack Rome	Roman Empire is replaced by Germanic kingdoms

Chapter Focus

 Read to Discover

- What life was like in German villages.
- How the Germans' laws and love of battle influenced them.
- What role the Goths and Vandals played in the decline of the Roman Empire.
- What replaced the Roman Empire in the West.

Chapter Overview

Visit the *Human Heritage* Web site at **humanheritage.glencoe.com** and click on ***Chapter 17— Chapter Overviews*** to preview this chapter.

Terms to Learn

clans
chieftain
blood feuds
oath-helpers
ordeal
wergeld

 People to Know

Wodan
Thor
Atilla
Alaric
Odoacer
Theodoric

Places to Locate

Danube River valley
Valhalla

Why It's Important   During the first 400 years after the birth of Christ, the Germans left the forests and marshes of northern Europe in search of warmer climates and better grazing land for their cattle. They slowly drifted south toward the Roman Empire.

Attracted by Rome's wealth and culture, the Germans hoped to live peacefully within the empire's borders. However, the Romans considered them enemies and for many years fought to keep the Germans out of Rome. By 300 A.D., however, the empire had begun its long decline and could no longer turn back the Germans. So the Romans allowed groups of Germans to move into the Danube River valley, where a blending of German and Roman ways took place.

SECTION 1 Village Life

Although the Germans took part in Roman life, they also kept much of their own culture. They lived in villages surrounded by farmlands and pastures. Most of the homes were long thatched-roof huts with an open space around them. The family lived in one end of the hut and divided the other end into animal stalls.

GERMAN VILLAGE   The Germans built their villages just within the borders of the Roman Empire. There they became farmers. They lived in family groups that included parents, children, grandparents, aunts, uncles, and cousins. **What was a German home like?**

Student Web Activity

Visit the *Human Heritage* Web site at **humanheritage.glencoe.com** and click on *Chapter 17— Student Web Activities* to find out more about Germanic tribes.

The body heat of the animals helped to warm the hut during the cold winters. Wooden tables and benches placed along the walls of the hut were the only furniture. A few wealthier villagers added wall hangings or carpets.

German villagers made their living herding cattle, which provided food and clothing. They also traded cattle for Roman glass vessels, table articles, and jewelry. The Germans farmed as well. They grew barley, rye, wheat, beans, and peas. Most farm work was done by women, children, and enslaved people. When the women were not working in the fields or cooking, they spun wool and wove cloth on upright looms.

German dress was simple. The women wore long skirts made of different yarns, or one-piece sack-like dresses that extended from the shoulders to the feet. Sometimes, they wore scarves or shawls fastened with a bone pin. The men wore short woolen *tunics,* or coat-like garments, and close-fitting trousers. They covered the tunics with cloaks fastened on the right shoulder with a brooch.

The Germans believed in hospitality. So strong was this belief that it was against the law to turn away anyone who came to the door. Invited guests and strangers alike were welcomed, fed, and entertained. Feasting, drinking, and dancing were favorite German pastimes. Men also enjoyed gambling with dice. Sometimes, they took part in such organized sports as boxing and wrestling. In winter, they skated on frozen ponds and lakes using skates made of flat bone.

The Germans spoke a language that later became modern German. At first, they could not read or write because their language had no alphabet. However, some learned to speak and write Latin. Gradually, they began to use Roman letters to write their own language.

Warriors   German men were warriors. They spent most of their time fighting, hunting, or making weapons. They began training for war when they were young boys. When a male reached manhood, he was brought before a special gathering held in a sacred grove under a full moon. There, he received a shield and a spear, which he had to carry with him at all times. The loss of the shield and spear meant loss of honor.

The Germans were divided into **clans,** or groups based on family ties. At first, the Germans gave their greatest loyalty to their clan. After a while, however, they developed a strong feeling of loyalty toward a military leader called a **chieftain** (chēf' tuhn). A man had to fight well to become a chieftain. In the beginning, a chieftain was elected by a band of warriors. Later, this office became hereditary.

Chieftains gave their men leadership, weapons, and a chance for wealth and adventure. They also kept peace among their warriors. In some cases, they gave their warriors food and shelter. In return, warriors gave their chieftains complete loyalty. Some even gave their chieftains credit for the brave deeds they themselves did. In battle, chieftains fought for victory, and warriors fought for their chieftains.

German warrior bands did not have fixed plans of fighting. Each band was small and usually fought on its own, apart from other bands. The bands made surprise raids against their enemies. Warriors on foot and on horseback would charge wildly, yelling in loud voices to frighten their foes. They fought with daggers, short swords, and heavy axes made of metal and stone. They carried light wooden shields and wore suits of leather. A successful attack provided warriors with enslaved people, cattle, and other treasures.

The Germans' love of battle was closely linked to their religion. Germans had many gods who liked to fight and to hunt. The chief god, Wodan (wōd' n), was the god of war, poetry, learning, and magic. Another god of war was Wodan's

Reading Check
What are **clans?** How did a German leader become a **chieftain?**

Linking Across Time

Public Assemblies Germanic people picked leaders and decided laws in public assemblies. All freemen—except "cowards"—took part in these meetings (left). The Germanic conquest of the Roman Empire helped spread this practice. It became the basis of later democratic assemblies, including modern-day town meetings (right). **How did the Germans record their laws?**

son Thor (thōr), who was also the god of thunder. The Germans believed that the sound of thunder came from Thor's chariot wheels.

The Germans admired bravery. Like the Spartans, they expected their warriors to win in battle or to die fighting. The only German shields left on a battlefield were those of dead warriors. The Germans believed that goddesses carried the spirits of warriors who died in battle into the afterlife. There, in the hall of Wodan, called Valhalla (val hal' uh), the warriors would feast and fight forever.

Law The Romans believed that law came from the emperor. The Germans believed it came from the people. German rulers could not change a law unless the people approved.

The Germans based their laws on the customs of their ancestors. Instead of writing down the laws, the Germans memorized them and passed them from parent to child.

Reckless fighting, often caused by too much drinking, caused problems in German villages. The Germans wanted to keep such

German Shield

fights from becoming **blood feuds** (fyūds), or quarrels in which the families of the original fighters seek revenge. Blood feuds could go on for generations. To keep this from happening, the Germans set up courts. Judges listened to each side and tried to find a settlement that would bring peace to the village.

The Germans decided who was guilty or innocent in different ways. One way was by oath-taking. People accused of crimes would declare their innocence by oath. Then, they would be defended by **oath-helpers.** These were people who swore that the accused was telling the truth. The Germans believed that anyone who lied when taking an oath would be punished by the gods.

People accused of crimes could not always find oath-helpers to come to their aid. In such cases, guilt or innocence was decided by **ordeal** (ōr dēl'), or a severe trial. Accused persons had to walk barefoot over red-hot coals or put an arm into boiling water. The burns of the innocent were supposed to heal within three days. There was also ordeal by water. A person was tied hand and foot and thrown into a lake or river. The Germans viewed water as a symbol of purity. If a person sank to the bottom, he or she was innocent. If a person floated, he or she was guilty.

A person who was judged guilty was not always punished physically. Courts could impose fines called *wergeld* (wuhr' geld). The exact amount of the payment varied. For example, the wergeld for harming a chieftain was higher than the one for harming a warrior. In the same way, a fine for killing a young girl was greater than one for killing a woman too old to have children. Although courts could set these fines, they did not have the power to collect them. They had to depend on public opinion to make a guilty person pay the fine.

The German legal system did not treat all people fairly. A person's wealth and importance, rather than the seriousness of the crime, determined the penalty. German laws did, however, keep the peace.

Reading Check
How did Germans try to prevent **blood feuds?**

Reading Check
How did **oath-helpers** take part in German trials?

Reading Check
Why would an accused person be required to go through an **ordeal?**

Reading Check
What was a *wergeld?*

Section 1 Assessment

1. **Define:** clans, chieftain, blood feuds, oath-helpers, ordeal, *wergeld.*
2. What were some of the duties of a German chieftain?
3. What were some features of German religion?

Critical Thinking

4. **Making Inferences** Why do you think hospitality was so important to the Germans?

Graphic Organizer Activity

5. Draw this diagram, and use it to compare strengths and weaknesses of German law.

Strengths	Weaknesses

HUMAN SYSTEMS

In 472 A.D. Germanic people controlled about 20 percent of the western Roman Empire. **From which general directions did most of the Germanic people invade the western Roman Empire?**

SECTION 2 The Conquerors

The Goths (gahths) were a Germanic people who lived in the Balkan Peninsula of Europe. They were divided into two groups called Ostrogoths (ahs' truh gahths), or East Goths, and Visigoths (viz' uh gahths), or West Goths.

In the late 300s, both groups were attacked by the Huns led by Attila (at' uhl uh), or "Little Daddy." The Huns conquered the East Goths. The West Goths feared they would be next. So, they asked the Roman emperor for protection. He let them settle just inside the empire's frontier. In return, they gave up their weapons and promised to be loyal to Rome.

Before long, trouble broke out between the West Goths and Roman officials. The West Goths had to buy the empire's food at very high prices. The Romans also kidnapped many young West Goths and enslaved them.

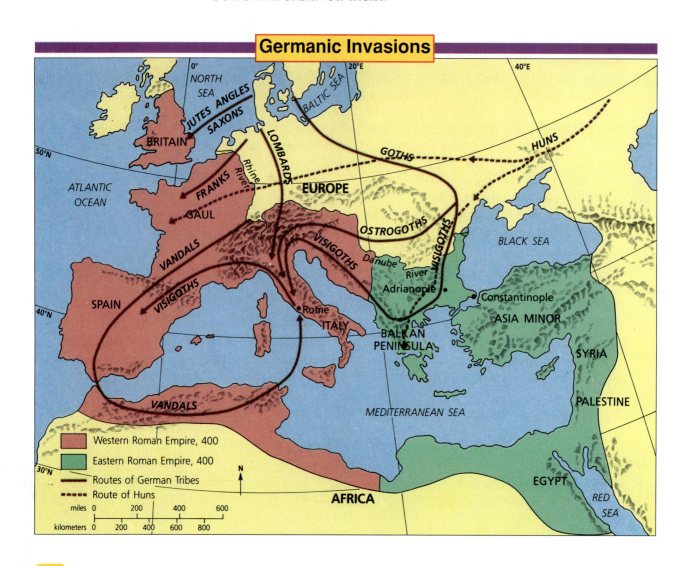

Germanic Invasions

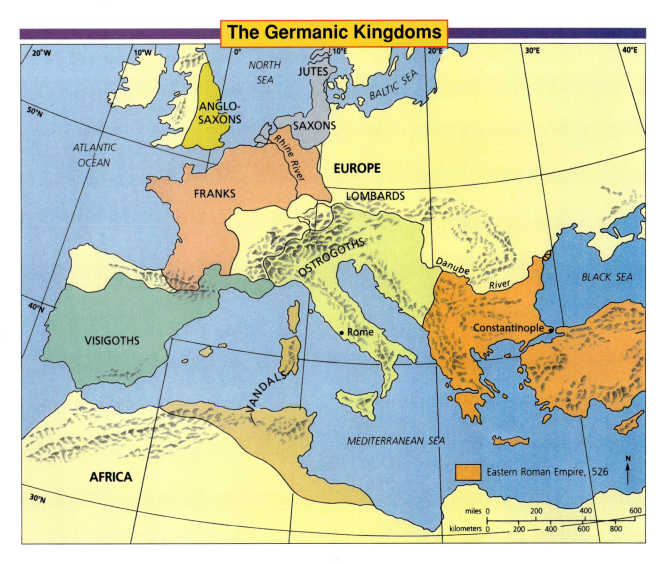

The Germanic Kingdoms

Finally, the West Goths rebelled against the Romans and defeated them at the Battle of Adrianople in 378. Then, in 410, led by the chieftain Alaric, they captured and looted Rome.

After the capture of Rome, the West Goths continued on to Gaul. Then, they moved into Spain, which was occupied by Romans and another Germanic group called Vandals (van' duhlz). The West Goths ended Roman rule in Spain, drove out the Vandals, and set up their own kingdom.

The Vandals in turn crossed the Mediterranean to North Africa. They became pirates and attacked cities along the Mediterranean coast. From these attacks came the English word "vandalism," meaning the willful destruction of property.

In 455, the Vandals attacked and burned Rome. They did, however, spare the lives of the Romans. Afterwards, the Vandals returned to North Africa. Like Rome's capture in 410 by the West Goths, this event shook the Roman world.

MAP STUDY

PLACES AND REGIONS The Visigoths defeated the Vandals, who were forced to settle in North Africa. **What advantage did the Vandals have because of their new location in the region?**

The Germanic invasions were one of the three main reasons the Roman Empire in the West began to fall. While the Roman Empire in the East prospered, generals in the West fought for control of Rome and Italy.

In 476, a German general named Odoacer (ŏd′ uh wā suhr) took control. He did not appoint an emperor. Instead, he ruled the western empire in his own name for almost 15 years. Then, a group of East Goths invaded Italy, killed Odoacer, and set up a kingdom under their leader Theodoric (thē ahd′ uh rik).

By 550, the Roman Empire in the West had faded away. In its place were six major and a great many minor Germanic kingdoms. Many Roman beliefs and practices remained in use, and would shape later civilizations.

Section 2 Assessment

1. What happened to the East Goths in the late 300s? What effect did this have on the West Goths?
2. What did the Vandals do after leaving Spain?
3. What replaced the Roman Empire in the West?

Critical Thinking

4. **Predicting Consequences** What do you think might have happened if Roman officials had treated the West Goths fairly? Explain.

Graphic Organizer Activity

5. Draw this diagram, and use it to describe important events in the fall of Rome. (Key dates are given.)

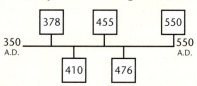

Chapter Summary & Study Guide

1. About 300 A.D., groups of Germans began settling in the Roman Empire.
2. German warriors were organized into bands headed by military chieftains.
3. The Germans' love of battle was closely linked to their religion.
4. The Germans determined a person's guilt or innocence through use of oath-helpers and by ordeal.
5. The Germans believed that law came from the people.
6. The Huns conquered the East Goths and forced the West Goths to turn to Rome for protection.
7. Harsh treatment of the West Goths by the Romans set off a chain of events leading to the capture of Rome in 410 A.D.
8. A Germanic chieftain took control of Rome in 476 A.D., and by 550 A.D., the Roman Empire had been replaced by a number of Germanic kingdoms.

Self-Check Quiz

Visit the *Human Heritage* Web site at **humanheritage. glencoe.com** and click on *Chapter 17—Self-Check Quiz* to assess your understanding of this chapter.

Using Key Terms

Write a short story describing the daily life of a person in one of the early Germanic groups. Use the following words in your story.

clans   chieftain   blood feuds
oath-helpers   ordeal   *wergeld*

Understanding Main Ideas

1. Why did the Germans begin to move south toward the Roman Empire?
2. Why were the Germans allowed to cross the borders of the Roman Empire?
3. How did German warriors show their loyalty to their chieftain?
4. What did the Germans believe the afterlife would be like for warriors?
5. According to German beliefs, from what source did law come?
6. What was the reason for the German ordeal by water?
7. Why did the West Goths want to enter the Roman Empire?
8. What happened to Rome after its capture by Odoacer in 476 A.D.?

Critical Thinking

1. What parts of Roman culture did the Germans adopt? What parts of their own culture did they keep?
2. Imagine you will soon become a Germanic chieftain. Explain what you would provide for your warriors.
3. What would you have liked and disliked about living in a German village?
4. Do you believe the penalty for a crime should depend on a person's wealth or importance? If not, on what should it depend? Explain.

Graphic Organizer Activity

Citizenship Create a diagram like the one shown, and use it to show German contributions to Western ideas about law and government.

German Contributions	1.
	2.
	3.

Geography in History

Places and Regions Refer to the map on page 271. Access to the sea played an important role in the economy of each Germanic kingdom. Which kingdom had the longest seacoast? About how many miles (km) long was it?

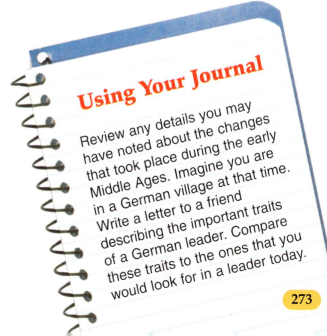

Using Your Journal

Review any details you may have noted about the changes that took place during the early Middle Ages. Imagine you are in a German village at that time. Write a letter to a friend describing the important traits of a German leader. Compare these traits to the ones that you would look for in a leader today.

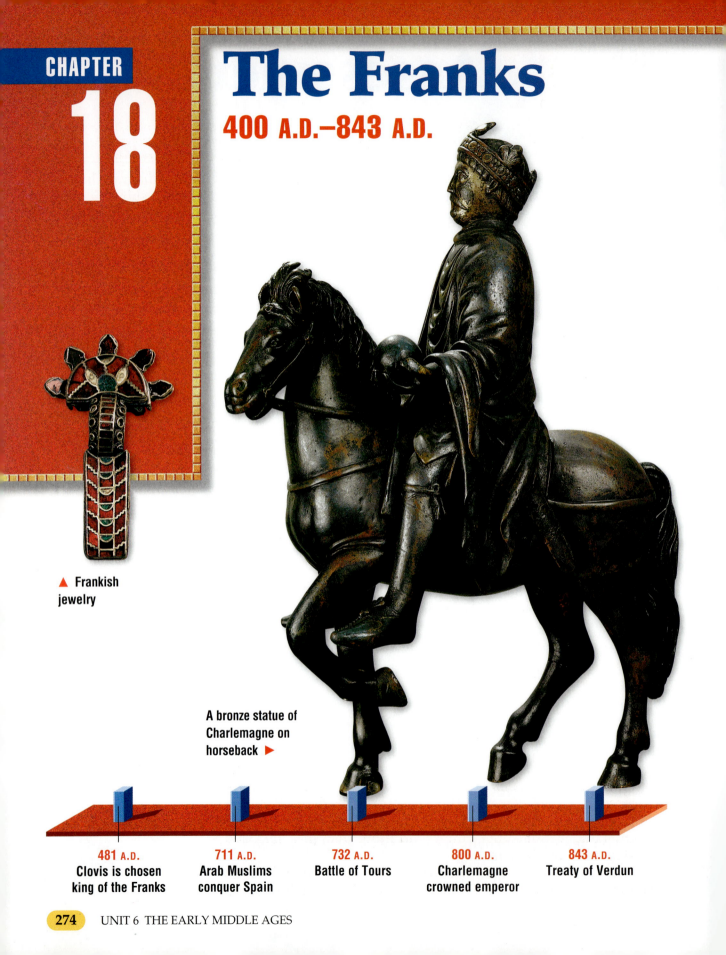

The Franks
400 A.D.–843 A.D.

▲ Frankish
jewelry

A bronze statue of
Charlemagne on
horseback ▶

481 A.D.
Clovis is chosen
king of the Franks

711 A.D.
Arab Muslims
conquer Spain

732 A.D.
Battle of Tours

800 A.D.
Charlemagne
crowned emperor

843 A.D.
Treaty of Verdun

Chapter Focus

 Read to Discover

- How Clovis united the Franks and brought them Christianity.
- How Charles Martel's defeat of the Arabs kept western Europe Christian.
- How Charlemagne brought all of western Europe under his rule.
- What life was like in Charlemagne's empire.
- Why Charlemagne's empire collapsed.

 Terms to Learn

converted
anointed
counts
lords
serfs
minstrels

 People to Know

Clovis
Charles Martel
Pepin
Charlemagne
Roland
Louis the Pious

🌎 **Places to Locate**

Paris
Tours
Aachen

Why It's Important   The decline of the Roman Empire led to disorder everywhere in western Europe. Many of the Germanic invaders were too weak to govern well. As a result, towns and villages fell into ruin. Roads and bridges were not repaired. Robbers roamed the countryside, making it unsafe for travelers. Trading and business slowed down, and there were shortages of food and other goods. People were no longer interested in learning, and many books and works of art were damaged or lost.

Chapter Overview

Visit the *Human Heritage* Web site at **humanheritage.glencoe.com** and click on ***Chapter 18— Chapter Overviews*** to preview this chapter.

SECTION 1 Clovis

During this period, a Germanic people called the Franks became very important. They began to build a new civilization, one that later developed into modern France and Germany. The Franks lived along the Rhine River in what is now Germany. They were more successful in governing than other Germans. One reason for this was that the area in which they lived was close to their homeland, and they felt fairly secure. Also, unlike the Goths and Vandals, the Franks did more than just fight and rule. They became farmers.

At first, the Franks were divided into separate groups without a common ruler. In 481, one Frankish group chose a man named

Developing Multimedia Presentations

You want to present a research report to your class, and you want to really hold their attention. How do you do it? Your presentation can be exciting if you use various forms of media.

Learning the Skill At its most basic, a multimedia presentation involves using several types of media. To discuss life under the Frankish kings, for example, you might show photographs of historic paintings. You could also record selections from *The Song of Roland* or ballads sung by minstrels. Or you might present a video of Charlemagne's life.

You can also develop a multimedia presentation on a computer. Multimedia as it relates to computer technology is the combination of text, video, audio, and animation in an interactive computer program.

In order to create multimedia productions or presentations on a computer, you need to have certain tools. These may include traditional computer graphic tools and art programs, animation programs that make still images move, and authoring systems that tie everything together. Your computer manual will tell you what tools your computer can support.

This chapter focuses on the growth of the Frankish empire in the early Middle Ages. Ask yourself questions like the following to create a multimedia presentation on the cultural and political developments of that era:

- Which forms of media do I want to include? Video? Sound? Animation? Photographs? Graphics? Other?
- Which of these media forms does my computer support?
- What kind of software programs or systems do I need? An art program? A program to create interactive, or two-way, communication? An authoring system that will allow me to change images, sound, and motion?
- Is there a "do-it-all" program I can use to develop the kind of presentation I want?

Skill Practice

Developing Multimedia Presentations

Keeping in mind the four guidelines given above, write a plan describing a multimedia presentation you would like to develop. Indicate what tools you will need and what steps you must take to make the presentation a reality.

Clovis (klō′ vis) as king. Although he was cruel and greedy, Clovis was a good general and an able king. He eventually brought all the Franks under one rule. Part of Clovis's kingdom later became France, which took its name from the Franks.

Clovis was the first Germanic king to accept the Catholic religion. Clovis was not happy with the Frankish gods. Although he prayed to them faithfully, they failed to help him win battles. Clovis decided that if he defeated the enemy, he would become a Christian. Clovis's army won its next battle. Clovis and some 3,000 Frankish soldiers, still in full battle dress, immediately **converted** (kuhn ver′ tuhd), or changed religion, to Christianity. It was not long before all the Franks followed his example.

When Clovis became a Christian, he gained the support of the Romans in his kingdom. Before long, the Franks began speaking a form of Latin that later became the modern French language. Now, all the people in Clovis's kingdom practiced the same religion, spoke the same language, and felt united.

The Pope and other church officials gave Clovis their support. Priests served in his government. In return for the Church's help, Clovis was expected to protect the Church against all non-believers.

Clovis extended his rule over what is now France and western Germany and set up his capital in Paris. He admired the Roman Empire. He wore purple robes similar to those of the Roman emperors and made Latin the official language of the court.

✓ Reading Check
What happened after Clovis **converted** to Christianity?

Section 1 Assessment

1. **Define:** converted.
2. What modern nations developed out of the civilization built by the Franks?
3. Why were the Franks more successful at governing than other Germanic peoples?

Critical Thinking

4. **Drawing a Conclusion** Why was it important for Clovis to have the Pope's blessing and the support of the Church?

Graphic Organizer Activity

5. Draw this diagram, and use it to show the cause and effects of Clovis's conversion to Christianity.

| Cause | → | Clovis Converts | → | Effects |

SECTION 2 Charles the Hammer

The Frankish kings who followed Clovis were weak rulers. Instead of keeping the kingdom united, they divided it among their sons. The sons often fought over their shares of land. They

spent so much time and energy fighting that they lost much of their power to local nobles.

It was not long before the Franks began to accept the leadership of a government official known as the "Mayor of the Palace." The Mayor was a noble and the most important official in the king's household. As the Frankish kings grew weaker, the Mayors took over many of their duties. In time, the Mayors were conducting wars, giving out land, and settling disputes. Of all the Mayors, the most powerful was Charles Martel (mahr tel'). He wanted to reunite all the Frankish nobles under his rule. Before long, Charles Martel had gained the support of the Church.

Charles Martel became known as "The Hammer" because of his strength in battle. In 732, he led the Franks in the Battle of

BATTLE OF TOURS   Charles Martel (shown center in this painting) leads his army against the Muslims at the Battle of Tours. The Frankish victory halted the Muslim advance into western Europe. It also helped the Frankish rulers to build a strong kingdom. **Why were the Muslims invading western Europe?**

Tours (tūrz), one of the most important battles in European history. The Franks defeated an army of Arabs and Berbers who had conquered Spain in 711. The Arabs and Berbers were Muslims, who hoped to spread their religion of Islam everywhere. The Franks' victory at the Battle of Tours enabled Christianity to survive in western Europe.

When Charles Martel died, his son Pepin (pep' in) became Mayor of the Palace. With the help of the Pope and most Frankish nobles, Pepin removed the king and started a new dynasty. Pepin was the first Frankish king to be **anointed** (uh noin' tuhd), or blessed with holy oil, by the Pope. In return for the Church's support, Pepin helped the Pope when he was threatened by a group of Germans known as Lombards (lahm' bahrdz). Pepin led an army into Italy, defeated the Lombards, and gave the land they held in central Italy to the Pope. This gift made the Pope the political ruler of much of the Italian Peninsula.

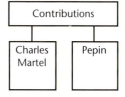

Reading Check
Who **anointed** Pepin, and why was this an important event?

Section 2 Assessment

1. **Define:** anointed.
2. Why was the Battle of Tours a turning point in history?
3. How did Pepin help the Pope?

Critical Thinking

4. **Predicting Consequences** What might western Europe have been like if the Arabs and Berbers had won the Battle of Tours?

Graphic Organizer Activity

5. Draw this diagram, and use it to compare the accomplishments of Charles Martel and his son Pepin.

```
           Contributions
           ┌──────┴──────┐
       Charles        Pepin
       Martel
```

SECTION 3 Charlemagne

When Pepin died in 768, his kingdom was divided between his two sons. His son Carloman died within a few years. Pepin's other son Charles then became king of the Franks. He is best known by his French name Charlemagne (shar' luh mān), which means "Charles the Great."

A powerful leader, Charlemagne wanted to bring all of western Europe under his rule. He also wanted all the Germanic people to become Christian. To achieve these goals, he waged a series of wars.

First, Charlemagne went to Italy and defeated the Lombards. Next, Charlemagne attacked Saxons (sak' suhnz), who lived in what is now northern Germany. For years, the Saxons had been raiding towns and monasteries inside the Frankish border. He

HISTORY Online

Student Web Activity
Visit the *Human Heritage* Web site at
humanheritage.glencoe.com
and click on *Chapter 18—Student Web Activities* to find out more about Charlemagne.

Charlemagne
c. 742 A.D.–814 A.D.

Christian Emperor

Charlemagne continued the German warrior tradition, spreading the Christian religion at the tip of a sword. In building his empire, he brought together the German, Roman, and Christian cultures that became the basis for European civilization.

sent thousands of captured Saxons into Frankish territory and then moved many Franks onto Saxon lands. Eventually, the Saxons accepted Christianity.

Charlemagne also led his armies in several campaigns across the Pyrenees (pēr′ uh nēz) Mountains to fight the Muslims in Spain. A mountain people known as Basques (basks) did not want the Frankish armies to cross their territory. When Charlemagne was returning home from one of his Spanish campaigns, Basque warriors attacked the rear guard of his army in a narrow mountain pass. The rear guard was led by Roland, a fine warrior. Since Roland had far fewer soldiers than the Basques, he lost the battle. Even so, the fight was remembered, told, and retold throughout Europe. Over time, it became legend and was written down in French as a poem called *The Song of Roland.*

By 800, Charlemagne had created a large empire. It included most of the Germanic peoples who had settled in Europe since the early 400s. Charlemagne also fought against non-Germanic peoples in northern and eastern Europe. Although they managed to keep their freedom, they agreed to respect Charlemagne's power and not fight against his army.

CROWNING OF CHARLEMAGNE   In 800, Charlemagne became emperor of a new Christian Roman Empire. Here, Charlemagne is crowned "Emperor of the Romans" by the Pope. **How did Charlemagne aid the Church?**

A Christian Empire

Charlemagne became the most powerful leader in western Europe. The people considered him as important as any Roman emperor. Charlemagne wanted to keep close ties between the Church and the government. Church officials kept records and helped Charlemagne run the country. In turn, he appointed the bishops and regarded any act against the Church as a sign of disloyalty to him.

Both Charlemagne and the Pope wanted a new Christian Roman Empire in western Europe. Charlemagne's conquests had brought him closer to their goal. On Christmas day in 800, Charlemagne was worshiping in St. Peter's Church in Rome. When the religious ceremony was over, the Pope placed a crown on Charlemagne's head. The Pope then declared that Charlemagne was the new Roman emperor. Although Charlemagne accepted the title, he was not pleased that the Pope had crowned him. This made it seem as if the emperor's right to rule came from the Pope rather than directly from God.

Charlemagne was a wise and just ruler who issued many laws. To make sure these laws were obeyed, he set up law courts all through the empire. Charlemagne chose officials called **counts** to run the courts. The counts took care of local problems, stopped feuds, protected the poor and weak, and raised armies for Charlemagne.

Charlemagne often had trouble keeping the counts under his control because of poor transportation and communication. So, he sent royal messengers all through the empire to check on them. These messengers reported to Charlemagne how well the counts were doing their jobs. Once a year, Charlemagne called his counts and warriors together. They reported troubles and talked over new laws for the empire. The final decision on what new laws to issue, however, was made by Charlemagne.

Charlemagne ruled his empire from Aachen (ah' kuhn), known today as Aix-la-Chapelle (āks' lah shah pel'). However, he did not always stay in the capital. He journeyed throughout the empire with his advisers and servants. The royal party would stop and rest at different palaces or homes. Wherever the king and his officials went, they were given food and entertained by the people. Such royal visits ensured the loyalty of local officials and people to Charlemagne's government.

Education

Most people in Charlemagne's empire could neither read nor write. Charlemagne, however, appreciated learning. Unlike earlier Frankish rulers, he believed in education and was proud of his own ability to read Latin. He kept a slate and copybook next to his bed so that he could practice writing.

Charlemagne wanted his people to be educated also. He worked hard to push back the darkness that had followed the fall of the Roman Empire. He encouraged churches and monasteries

Reading Check
What role did **counts** play in Charlemagne's government?

Frankish Officials
Officials in Charlemagne's court had specific duties. His *chaplain* advised the emperor on matters of conscience and supervised official documents. The *count of the palace* judged court cases that were not handled by Charlemagne and managed the palace in the emperor's absence. The *chamberlain* took care of the royal bedroom and treasury. The *seneschal* kept the palace supplied with food, wine, and servants. The *constable* cared for the horses.

CHARLEMAGNE'S SCHOOL   Charlemagne often visited his palace school, which was attended by children of the court. Directed by the monk Alcuin, the school also provided a place where scholars could gather to share their knowledge and to inspire one another. **Why was Charlemagne interested in learning?**

Deep Sleep Many legends spread about Charlemagne. According to one legend, he did not die but was only sleeping, and would awaken at the hour of his country's need.

to found schools. He had a scholar named Alcuin (al' kwin) start a school in one of the palaces to train the children of government officials to serve in the Church or in the royal household. The children studied such subjects as religion, Latin, music, literature, and arithmetic.

Scholars came from all over Europe to teach in Charlemagne's school. One of their many tasks was to copy manuscripts. This led to the development of a new form of writing. The Roman writing the scholars used contained only capital letters. These letters took up a lot of space on a page. So, the scholars began to write with small letters instead of capital ones. The new letters not only took up less space, but they were also easier to read. The new letters became the model for the lower-case letters used today.

Under Charlemagne, the arts began to flower again. Painters, sculptors, and metalworkers developed their talents. They built palaces and churches around a large courtyard as the Romans did. Artists covered palace and church walls with pictures showing stories from the Bible. They made book covers and ornamental weapons, and they decorated the manuscripts copied by scholars.

Estate Life   Lords, or nobles, were the most powerful people in Charlemagne's empire. They were the descendants of Frankish warriors and Roman landowners. Most of the lords' wealth came from goods grown or made on their estates. As there was little trade in Charlemagne's empire, each estate took care of its own needs. There were shoemakers, carpenters, and blacksmiths on each estate. There were also artisans who made weapons, cooking vessels, and jewelry.

Lords lived in stone farmhouses. Wooden *stockades* (stah kādz′), or fences, often were built around the houses. Each farmhouse had a banquet hall, sleeping quarters, cellars, stables, storage places, and a small chapel.

Farmers lived in simple wooden houses in small villages on the estates. They worked in the fields, vineyards, orchards, and forests around their villages. The fields were owned by the lords, but the farmers worked them three days a week. The rest of the time they worked small pieces of land the lords had given them.

Reading Check
Who were the **lords,** and from where did they get their wealth?

Linking Across Time

Writing in Minuscule   Today the word *minuscule* means "extremely small." However, during the rule of Charlemagne, it referred to small letters used in writing (below). The use of small letters replaced the all-capital letters used by the Romans. This writing style later developed into the capital and lowercase letters used in all Western languages (right).
What subjects did the children of government officials study?

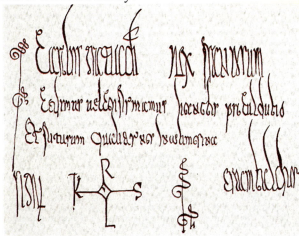

MAP SKILLS

Understanding Inset Maps

Sometimes, there is not enough space on a map for information to be shown clearly. Mapmakers have solved this problem by using **inset maps,** or small maps that are set within larger ones. Often placed in a corner of the main map, inset maps may have their own scales and legends.

Inset maps are used for two reasons. One is to show parts of the main map enlarged and in greater detail. Maps of countries or states often include inset maps showing individual cities.

Another reason inset maps are used is to show in a different way an area on the main map. For example, on the map below, the main map shows the Frankish Empire from Clovis through Charlemagne. The inset map in the upper right shows what happened to the same territory after the death of Charlemagne.

Map Practice

1. **What two cities were in the kingdom of Charles?**
2. **Who controlled Rome after the Treaty of Verdun?**
3. **Through which kingdom did the Danube River flow?**

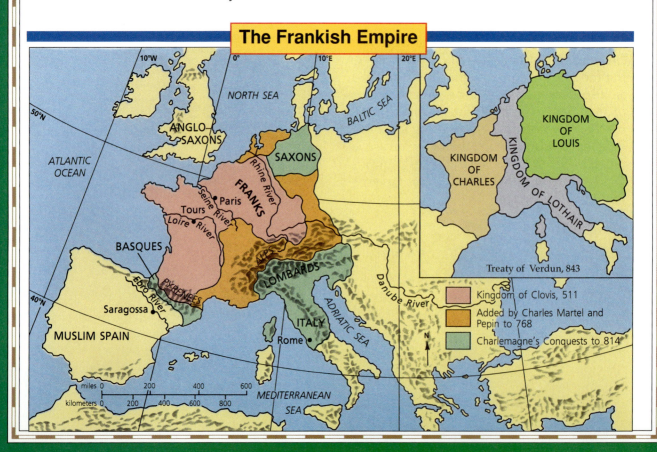

The Frankish Empire

Treaty of Verdun, 843

Kingdom of Clovis, 511
Added by Charles Martel and Pepin to 768
Charlemagne's Conquests to 814

The farmers divided the land into three sections. They let one section lie *fallow* (fal' ō), or not planted. On the other two sections, they used heavy metal plows to prepare the hard but fertile soil. In autumn, they planted wheat or rye in one section. In spring, they planted oats or barley in the other section. Each year, the farmers *rotated* (rō' tā tuhd), or changed by turns, the kind of crops they grew in each section. They also let a different section lie fallow. These changes helped them grow larger crops.

Besides working the land, the farmers had to give the nobles food and animals. The farmers had to perform many services for the nobles, too. Men repaired buildings on the estates, cut down trees, carried loads, gathered fruits, and served in the army. Women worked as hard as men. They looked after the children and small animals, wove cloth, and sewed clothing copied from earlier Roman styles. The farmers gradually did more for the nobles and less for themselves. They were becoming **serfs**, or people bound to the land.

Neither the nobles nor the farmers had much time to learn to read or write or to think about religion. Both groups accepted Christianity, but the new religion had little to do with their daily lives. However, on religious holidays, both rich and poor sang, danced, and feasted. They listened to traveling musicians called **minstrels** (min' struhlz). The minstrels journeyed from place to place singing the praises of Charlemagne and his empire.

The Collapse of the Empire

The glory of the empire did not last long after Charlemagne's death in 814. The empire needed a strong and able ruler. Charlemagne's heirs were neither. Many counts and lords became increasingly independent. They cared more about their own estates than about the good of the empire. They refused to obey Louis the Pious (pī' uhs), Charlemagne's son.

Louis the Pious unknowingly weakened the empire further when he divided it among his three sons. After he died, they began fighting among themselves over their shares. Lothair (lō thahr'), Louis's oldest son, received the title of emperor. His younger brothers, Charles and Louis, were jealous of Lothair.

In 843, the brothers agreed to a new and different division of the empire. Under the Treaty of Verdun (ver duhn'), Lothair kept the title of emperor, but he ruled only a narrow strip of land that stretched from the North Sea to the Italian Peninsula. Louis received the area to the east. Called the East Frankish Kingdom, it later became the nation of Germany. Charles received the area to the west. Called the West Frankish Kingdom, it later became France.

The brothers were weak rulers who allowed the counts and nobles to have most of the power. Once again, a united western Europe was divided into smaller territories.

Painting of Minstrel

✔ Reading Check
How did farmers gradually become **serfs**?

✔ Reading Check
How did **minstrels** increase Charlemagne's popularity?

Section 3 Assessment

1. **Define:** counts, lords, serfs, minstrels.
2. Why did Charlemagne object to the Pope crowning him emperor?
3. What did Charlemagne do to encourage learning?

Critical Thinking

4. **Identifying Alternatives** What might have prevented the collapse of Charlemagne's government?

Graphic Organizer Activity

5. Draw this diagram, and use it to summarize Charlemagne's political, educational, and cultural accomplishments.

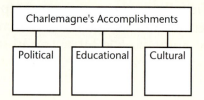

Chapter Summary & Study Guide

1. During the late 400s, the Franks began to build a civilization that would later develop into the modern nations of France and Germany.
2. Clovis united the Franks and was the first Germanic king to accept the Catholic religion.
3. Clovis gained the support of the Romans in his kingdom and made Latin the official language of the royal court.
4. A series of weak kings followed Clovis, and leadership gradually came into the hands of a government official known as the "Mayor of the Palace."
5. In 732, a Mayor of the Palace named Charles Martel defeated the Muslim army at the Battle of Tours. This kept western Europe Christian.
6. Charles Martel's son Pepin started a new dynasty and became the first Germanic king to be anointed by the Pope.
7. Pepin's son Charlemagne brought all of western Europe under his control.
8. In 800, the Pope crowned him the new Roman emperor.
9. Charlemagne was a wise and just ruler who wrote new laws.
10. Charlemagne was very interested in learning and encouraged the founding of schools in his empire.
11. During the rule of Charlemagne, powerful lords grew wealthy from goods grown or made on their estates.
12. Louis the Pious divided the Frankish Empire among his three sons, which led to its final collapse.

Self-Check Quiz

Visit the *Human Heritage* Web site at **humanheritage. glencoe.com** and click on *Chapter 18— Self-Check Quiz* to assess your understanding of this chapter.

Using Key Terms

Write a paragraph about the Franks and their rule in western Europe. Highlight one of the people mentioned in the chapter in your paragraph. Use the following words.

converted   anointed   counts
lords   serfs   minstrels

Understanding Main Ideas

1. What happened to western Europe after the decline of the Roman Empire?
2. How did Clovis help people within his empire feel united?
3. What was the relationship between the Church and Clovis?
4. Why did the Mayor of the Palace become important?
5. What were Charlemagne's main goals when he became king of the Franks?
6. How did Frankish farmers become serfs?
7. What happened to western Europe after Charlemagne's heirs came to power?

Critical Thinking

1. Do you think that Charlemagne's traveling all over the empire was a wise idea? Why or why not?
2. Why was the title "the Great" good for Charlemagne? What other title might have been better? Why?
3. What parts of life in Charlemagne's empire would you have liked? What parts would you have disliked?
4. What do you think Louis the Pious could have done with the Frankish Empire instead of dividing it among his three sons?

Graphic Organizer Activity

Economics Create a diagram like the one shown, and use it to show details that support this main idea: "Life in the Frankish Empire centered around the estates of lords."

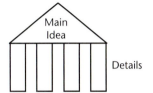

Main Idea

Details

Geography in History

Places and Regions Refer to the map on page 284 and compare the locations of Saragossa, Paris, and Rome. Each of these was an important city in the Frankish Empire. What geographic similarities and differences can you see in these places?

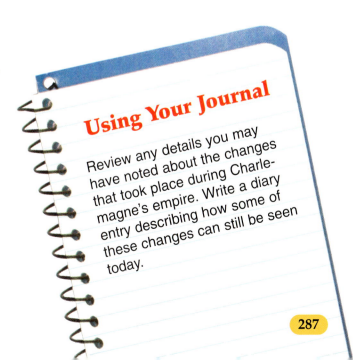

Using Your Journal

Review any details you may have noted about the changes that took place during Charlemagne's empire. Write a diary entry describing how some of these changes can still be seen today.

The Irish and the Anglo-Saxons

55 B.C.–911 A.D.

▲ The Alfred jewel

The helmet of an Anglo-Saxon king ▶

410 A.D.
Roman legions leave Britain

597 A.D.
Pope Gregory I sends monks from Rome to England

c. 700 A.D.
Beowulf is written

835 A.D.
Danes begin raiding England

Chapter Focus

 Read to Discover

- How Rome influenced the area known today as the British Isles.
- What life was like in Celtic Ireland.
- How Christianity developed in Ireland and England.
- Why the Anglo-Saxons united under Alfred the Great.
- What life was like in Anglo-Saxon England.

Chapter Overview

Visit the *Human Heritage* Web site at **humanheritage.glencoe.com** and click on *Chapter 19— Chapter Overviews* to preview this chapter.

Terms to Learn	**People to Know**	**Places to Locate**
coracles	Saint Patrick	British Isles
shires	Saint Columba	Kent
sheriff	Pope Gregory I	Wessex
king's peace	Ethelbert	Daneland
witenagemot	Bede	
witan	Alfred the Great	

Why It's Important   Off the west coast of Europe lies a group of islands that never became part of Charlemagne's empire. Known today as the British Isles, they consist of Great Britain, Ireland, and many smaller islands.

Roman legions led by Julius Caesar invaded Britain in 55 B.C. The Romans eventually conquered much of the island and ruled it for almost 400 years. The Romans had difficulties ruling some of the area. A conquered people called Celts (kelts) were not interested in or influenced by Roman culture.

During the 300s A.D. Roman soldiers were called home to defend the empire's borders against the Germanic invasions. After 410 A.D., the island was overrun by groups from northern Germany and Denmark, called Angles, Saxons, and Jutes. These groups united to become the Anglo-Saxons. They built settlements and set up several small kingdoms. The southern part of Britain soon became known as Angleland, or England. The people became known as the English.

SECTION 1   Celtic Ireland

With the coming of the Anglo-Saxons, most of the Celts who lived in Britain fled to Ireland. In time, Ireland became the major center of Celtic culture. Ireland had no cities. The people were divided into clans that lived in small villages. Most farmed and

Reading Check
How did the Irish use boats called **coracles**?

Student Web Activity
Visit the *Human Heritage* Web site at **humanheritage.glencoe.com** and click on **Chapter 19— Student Web Activities** to find out more about the work of Irish monks.

raised cattle. The more cattle a person owned, the wealthier that person was considered to be.

The Irish were a seafaring people, too. They made boats called **coracles** (kor' uh kuhls) by stretching cow hides over a wooden frame. Some coracles were large enough to hold as many as 30 people. The boats handled well at sea and were used for travel, trade, and fishing.

The Irish were able to remain free of Germanic attacks because their island was located farther out in the Atlantic Ocean than Britain. Scholars, artists, merchants, and monks from many parts of Europe came to Ireland because of its peace and safety.

Irish scholars and artists were influenced by Christianity. The Irish Church was founded by Saint Patrick. Born in Britain in the 400s A.D., Saint Patrick was kidnapped when he was young and taken to Ireland by Irish pirates. Later, he escaped to Europe, where he studied to be a priest. After becoming a bishop, he returned to Ireland and converted the people to Christianity. He spread his message all through the island and set up many new churches.

Ireland lost contact with Rome during the Germanic invasions of the Roman Empire. This meant the Pope could no longer lead the Irish Church. So, the Church turned to its abbots. Many were related to the heads of the different clans. Each clan supported its own monastery.

The monasteries became centers of Irish life, although many were in places that were not accessible—on rocky coasts or steep hills. Most monasteries were made up of a group of huts with a wooden stockade around them. Later, some monasteries were built of stone. Because of poor transportation and communication, church organization was weak. So, each monastery took charge of its own affairs. Irish monks soon began to follow practices different from those of the Roman Church. They wore their hair in a different way and celebrated Easter on a different day. Their rituals were not the same as those of the Romans.

Irish monasteries set down few rules. A monk was free to move from one monastery to another. Many monks chose to be hermits. Others set up schools to teach Christianity. Still others became missionaries. They sailed the North Atlantic and the Irish Sea seeking new converts and looking for islands on which to build new monasteries.

One of the best-known monks was Saint Columba (kuh luhm' buh). He set up a monastery on Iona (ī ō' nuh), an island off the west coast of Scotland. From his base on Iona, Saint Columba did missionary work among the many non-Christian Celts along the coast.

Monks from Iona went to northern England to preach to the Anglo-Saxons. Other Irish monks went to northern Europe,

IRISH MONASTERY   Irish Christian monks established monasteries throughout the British Isles and Europe. Many of their stone living quarters, like the ones shown here, still stand today along the rocky coast of western Ireland. **What attracted monks to Ireland?**

where they built monasteries and churches. Many Irish scholars became part of Charlemagne's palace school. They helped spread Christianity and learning throughout his empire.

Section 1 Assessment

1. **Define:** coracles.
2. How did the Irish earn a living?
3. Why did Irish monasteries take charge of their own affairs?

Critical Thinking

4. **Predicting Consequences** What might have happened in Britain if the Romans had not left in 410 A.D.?

Graphic Organizer Activity

5. Draw this diagram, and use it to show the cause and effects of Irish isolation from Germanic invasions.

SECTION 2   Christianity

Ireland was Christian, but the Anglo-Saxon kingdoms of Britain were not. They followed the Germanic religions. Then, Pope Gregory I decided to convert the Anglo-Saxons to Christianity. Legend has it that he saw some Anglo-Saxon boys waiting in the marketplace of Rome to be sold into slavery. Gregory noticed their light skin, handsome faces, and blonde hair and asked where their home was. When he learned that the boys were Angles, he said they had the faces of angels and should be Christians.

Therefore, in 597 A.D., Pope Gregory sent a mission of 41 monks from Rome to England under the leadership of Augustine. The missionaries landed in the small kingdom of Kent in southern England. Kent's queen, Bertha, was already a Christian, but its king, Ethelbert (eth' uhl bert), was not. At first, Ethelbert was very suspicious of Augustine and the other monks. He would meet with them only in the open air where their "magic" could not hurt him. Within a year, however, Ethelbert became a Christian. He allowed Augustine to build a church in the town of Canterbury (kant' uhr ber ē) and to teach the people about Christianity.

The Anglo-Saxons were quick to accept the new religion, and by 700 A.D. all England was Christian. The Pope was head of the Church. Monasteries were built throughout England. As in Ireland, they became centers of religion and culture.

One monk, Bede (bēd), was a great scholar. He wrote the first history of the English people. He also brought to England the Christian way of dating events from the year of Jesus' birth.

Although they accepted Christianity, the Anglo-Saxons kept much of their old culture. They told old legends about brave warriors fighting monsters and dragons. One such legend was about a warrior named Beowulf (bā' uh wulf). *Beowulf*, one of the earliest known tales, is an epic poem of almost 3,200 lines. Created by an unknown poet in about 700, it was passed along by oral tradition for two centuries. Finally, in the 900s, the work was written down. In colorful verses it describes how the hero warrior Beowulf goes from place to place fighting wicked people and ferocious animals. His greatest battle is when he defeats a horrible monster named Grindel. The language in which *Beowulf* was written is a form of English called Old English. This poem is one of the most important works of Anglo-Saxon literature.

During this time, stories, tales, and historical events were told orally, sung, or recited. *Beowulf* and other early literature became the source of later Anglo-Saxon poetry and music. With the increased influence of the Christian Church in western

Europe, religion would also provide the subjects for much early literature. This literature reflected the lives of the people of the time and their culture.

Alfred the Great

About 835 A.D., bands of Danes began attacking the coast of England. Before long, they were making permanent settlements in conquered areas. The English kingdoms decided to resist the invaders. They chose as their leader Alfred, King of Wessex (wes' iks). Alfred later became known as Alfred the Great, one of England's best-loved rulers.

Alfred knew the Anglo-Saxons were not yet strong enough to drive out the Danes. To gain time to build a stronger army, he paid the Danes a sum of money each year to leave England alone. When he felt his army was strong enough, he refused to make any more payments. The Danes invaded England and defeated the

Linking Across Time

Keeping the Peace

In Anglo-Saxon times, the job of peacekeeping fell to local nobles known as sheriffs (below). In the United States, the job of sheriff now belongs to a paid public official (right). **What conditions in England made it necessary for nobles to enforce the law?**

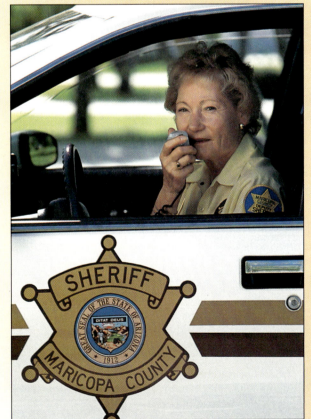

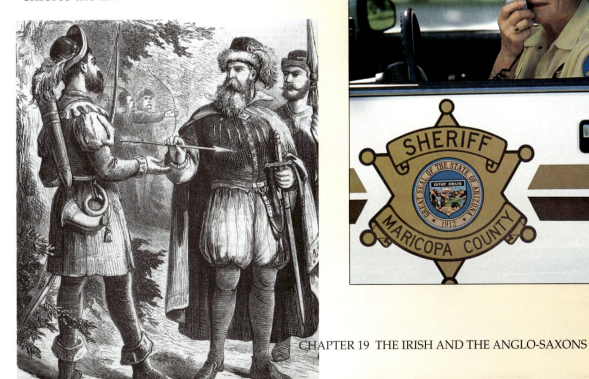

Anglo-Saxons. The next year, Alfred again gathered his army and met the Danes in battle. This time, the Danes were defeated.

Alfred continued to strengthen his army. He built the first English fighting ships and constructed fortresses throughout England. The entire country rallied behind him. He was no longer just King of Wessex but King of England.

Alfred never became strong enough to drive the Danes completely out of England. So, he signed a treaty with them. The treaty recognized the right of the Danes to rule the northeast part of England, an area that became known as the Danelaw (dān' lah). In return, the Danes promised to remain inside the Danelaw and not try to conquer more English land. In later years, the English took control of the Danelaw and made it part of their kingdom.

The Danes had destroyed part of the English city of London. Alfred had it rebuilt. Before long, it became the country's leading city. To gain the continued loyalty and obedience of the people, Alfred set forth new laws based on old Anglo-Saxon customs. These customs protected the weak against the strong and stressed honesty in making agreements.

MAP STUDY

THE WORLD IN SPATIAL TERMS

The Danes had conquered an area north of the Thames River and established permanent settlements there. **What bodies of water bordered Danelaw? What two cities were located south of Danelaw?**

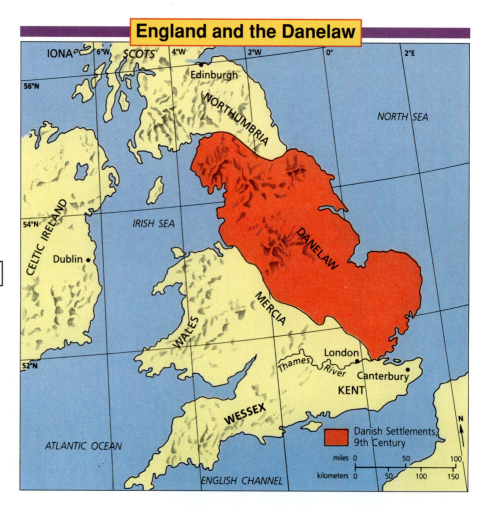

England and the Danelaw

Danish Settlements, 9th Century

miles 0   50   100

kilometers 0   50   100   150

Alfred was well-educated and interested in learning. He did much to educate the English. Like Charlemagne, Alfred started a palace school to train nobles' sons for government posts. At that time, books were generally written in Latin, a language most English church and government officials did not know. Alfred's scholars translated the books into English. So that the people would become familiar with their history, Alfred had monks begin a record of English history starting with Roman times.

The Government

The government of Anglo-Saxon England centered on the king. A council of lords generally elected kings from among members of the royal family. After 700 A.D., the Church usually crowned the new rulers. The king directed the central government, which was made up of royal servants and advisers. They handled the king's needs and wishes.

The central government, however, was too weak to govern the whole country. So, the king set up local governments. England was divided into districts called **shires** (shīrz). Each was run by a **sheriff,** who was a local noble chosen by the king. The sheriff collected money, enforced the law, called out soldiers when needed, and told the king what was happening in the shire.

The king and his household moved around instead of remaining in a capital city. Whatever area the royal household was in was under the **king's peace,** or royal protection. Lawless acts were not allowed. Anyone who committed a crime was punished under the king's laws rather than local laws. In time, the king's peace spread to all areas of the kingdom, whether the king was there or not. This helped unite Anglo-Saxon England.

Nobles and church officials gave the king advice on how to run the country. They could not, however, order a king to act against his will. A group of nobles and church leaders, known as the **witenagemot** (wit uhn uh' guh mōt), met with the king to talk over problems. Each member of the group was known as a **witan** (wi' tuhn), or wiseman. The group approved laws drawn up by the king and his household. It also acted as a court.

The People

The people in Anglo-Saxon England were generally divided into two classes. One was the nobles. An Anglo-Saxon became a noble by birth or as a reward for special service to the king. Nobles had to attend the witenagemot, keep peace in local areas, and serve the king in war. Noblemen wore pants and tunics covered by silk or fur cloaks. Noblewomen wore tunics and long cloaks held in place on each shoulder by a brooch.

The king rewarded many nobles with gifts of gold, silver, horses, and weapons. He also gave them estates throughout the kingdom. As a result, nobles spent a great deal of time moving from place to place with their families and servants. A noble's house had a large hall where meals were served and guests

Reading Check
Why did early English kings divide the country into **shires?** What were some of the jobs of the **sheriff?**

Reading Check
How did the **king's peace** help unite England?

Reading Check
What was the purpose of the **witenagemot?** Who might become a **witan?**

entertained. Its walls were covered with *tapestries* (tap' uh strēz), or woven hangings with pictures on them. Tables and benches were the hall's only furniture. The bedrooms of nobles and their families were next to the hall or in a separate building.

The other class of people in Anglo-Saxon England was the peasants. They lived in small villages on or near a noble's estate and led a hard life. Most did not own their own land but worked fields belonging to the noble. Every year, the noble redivided the land, and each peasant received different strips. This was done to make sure that peasants would be treated equally. They helped each other farm the land by sharing tools and oxen. The peasants kept part of the crop for food and gave part to the noble. In return, the noble protected his peasants from enemy attacks.

Peasants lived in one-room wood and plaster huts. Both the family and the animals shared the same room. An open fireplace, which provided heat during winter, stood in the center. Smoke from the fire escaped through a hole in the straw roof.

Section 2 Assessment

1. **Define:** shires, sheriff, king's peace, witenagemot, witan.
2. How did Christianity come to the Anglo-Saxon kingdoms of England?
3. What did Alfred do to unite Anglo-Saxon England?

Critical Thinking

4. **Drawing Conclusions** Why do you think Alfred was given the title of "the Great"?

Graphic Organizer Activity

5. Draw this diagram, and use it to record the things that nobles and peasants gave to each other.

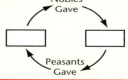

Nobles Gave

Peasants Gave

Chapter Summary & Study Guide

1. After Roman legions left Britain in 410 A.D., it was overrun by the Angles, Saxons, and Jutes, who united to become the Anglo-Saxons.
2. After the Anglo-Saxons drove most of the Celts from Britain, Ireland became a center of Celtic culture.
3. Monasteries became centers of Irish life.
4. In 597 A.D., Pope Gregory I sent monks to England, and by 700 A.D. England had become Christian.
5. When bands of Danes began raiding England in the 800s, the Anglo-Saxons united behind Alfred the Great.
6. English kings directed the central government, but they relied on help from local governments, nobles, and church leaders.

HISTORY *Online*

Self-Check Quiz

Visit the *Human Heritage* Web site at **humanheritage.glencoe.com** and click on *Chapter 19—Self-Check Quiz* to assess your understanding of this chapter.

Using Key Terms

Write a paragraph to be used in a book on the Celts and Anglo-Saxons describing one part of their lives. Use the following words in your paragraph.

coracles   shires   sheriff
king's peace   witenagemot   witan

Understanding Main Ideas

1. Why did the Romans have trouble ruling Britain?
2. Why did Roman rule in Britain crumble during the 300s A.D.?
3. What happened to Britain when the Roman legions left?
4. What country became the major center of Celtic culture?
5. Why did the Irish church turn to its abbots for leadership?
6. Why did Alfred the Great pay the Danes to leave England alone?
7. Why did the king set up local governments in England?
8. What were the duties of nobles?

Critical Thinking

1. What effect did the Germanic invasions of the Roman Empire have on the history of England?
2. How did Ireland's location affect the development of Celtic culture? Explain your answer.
3. Would you agree or disagree that the king had too much power in Anglo-Saxon England? Explain.
4. What parts of an Anglo-Saxon noble's life would you have liked? What parts would you not have liked?

Graphic Organizer Activity

Culture Create a diagram like this one, and use it to compare the development of Christianity in Ireland and in the Frankish Empire.

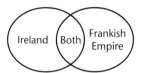

Ireland Both Frankish Empire

Geography in History

The World in Spatial Terms Refer to the map on page 294, and determine the most direct route from Edinburgh to London. How far would a person using this route have to travel? How much farther would that person have to travel to meet with priests of the church in Canterbury?

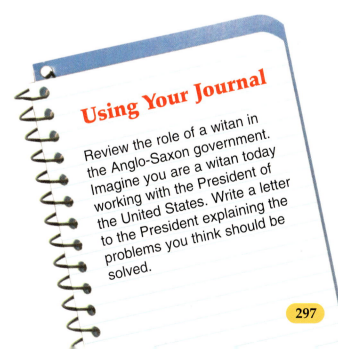

Using Your Journal

Review the role of a witan in the Anglo-Saxon government. Imagine you are a witan today working with the President of the United States. Write a letter to the President explaining the problems you think should be solved.

The Vikings
900 A.D.–1035 A.D.

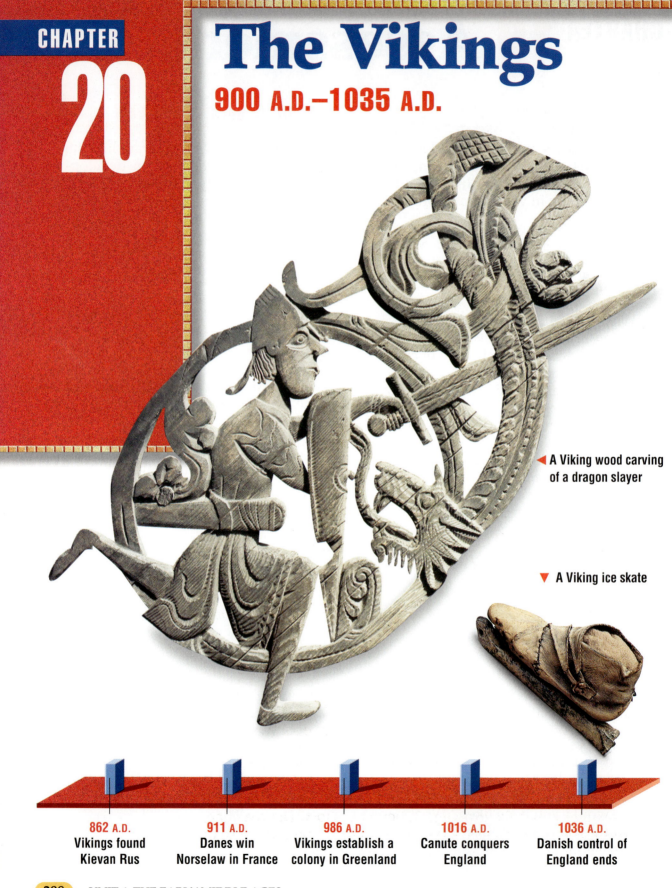

◀ A Viking wood carving
of a dragon slayer

▼ A Viking ice skate

862 A.D.
Vikings found
Kievan Rus

911 A.D.
Danes win
Norselaw in France

986 A.D.
Vikings establish a
colony in Greenland

1016 A.D.
Canute conquers
England

1036 A.D.
Danish control of
England ends

Chapter Focus

 Read to Discover

- How the Vikings earned a living.
- What daily life was like for the Vikings.
- How Viking warriors and adventurers traded and raided.
- What role the Danish Vikings played in the histories of England and France.

 Terms to Learn

jarls
berserkers
Eddas
runes

 People to Know

Rurik
Erik the Red
Leif Eriksson
Canute
Rollo

 Places to Locate

Scandinavia
Jutland
Vinland
Norselaw

Why It's Important   During the 900s, Charlemagne's empire and Anglo-Saxon England were attacked by new invaders known as Norseman, or Vikings (vī′ kēngs). They came from the far northern part of Europe now called Scandinavia (skan duh nā′vē uh). They spread fear and destruction throughout western Europe. However, they opened up new trade routes and taught seafaring skills to other Europeans.

The Vikings captured parts of Britain and France. They ruled cities in Russia and set up colonies on islands in the North Atlantic. They even traveled to North America. Those who went abroad married the people they conquered and accepted a new religion and new customs. Others stayed in Scandinavia and set up the kingdoms of Norway, Sweden, and Denmark.

SECTION 1   The Land

The Viking homeland of Scandinavia was an area made up mostly of forests and long, rugged coastlines. The southern part, known as Jutland (juht′ luhnd), or Denmark, had many natural harbors and was well suited for farming. It had large plains where the Vikings grew grains and pastured their cattle, sheep, and pigs.

The rest of Scandinavia was not as well suited to farming. The soil was rocky, and the growing season was short. The coastline, however, had many *fjords* (fē yōrdz′), or narrow bays. Because of this, the people turned to the sea to make a living.

Ships and Trade

The Vikings built ships with timber from the dense forests. These ships were large and well suited for long voyages. The bodies were long and narrow. The sides, where a single row of 16 oars was placed, were usually decorated with black or yellow shields. The tall bows were carved in the shape of a dragon's head. This was supposed to frighten both enemies and the evil spirits of the ocean. The strongly sewn sails were square and often striped red and yellow. The ships bore names like "Snake of the Sea," "Raven of the Wind," and "Lion of the Waves."

An awning in the forepart of the ship protected sailors from bad weather. They slept in leather sleeping bags and carried bronze pots in which to cook meals. Whenever possible, they cooked meals ashore to avoid the danger of a fire onboard ship.

The Vikings plotted their courses by the positions of the sun and the stars. They sailed far out into the North Sea and the Atlantic Ocean in search of good fishing areas and trade. They did most of their traveling and trading in spring after their fields were sown or in fall after their crops were harvested. They spent the long winters repairing their boats and weapons.

The Vikings were as successful in trade as the Phoenicians. Viking traders carried furs, hides, fish, and enslaved people to western Europe and the Mediterranean. They returned from these areas with silk, wine, wheat, and silver.

VIKING TRADE The Vikings traveled very far in order to trade. They sailed to the Mediterranean and traded for Arabic silver coins. The Vikings then melted down the coins and used the silver to make jewelry. **What other items did the Vikings trade for?**

Then...& Now

Berserk Of the many words that entered English from Old Norse, one of the most threatening is *berserk*. It comes from the Viking warriors known as *berserkers*, who rushed headlong into battle shrieking, leaping, and seemingly unaware of pain.

Towns, Villages, and Jarls Trade led to the growth of market towns in Scandinavia. These towns generally had two main streets that ran along the water's edge. Buyers and sellers set up booths along these streets where they showed their wares. The towns were protected on their land side by mounds of earth surrounded by wooden walls with towers.

Most Vikings lived in villages scattered all through the country. Their houses were made of logs or boards. The roofs, which were made of sod-covered wood, slanted deeply to shed the heavy winter snows. Carved dragons decorated the roofs at either end. Each house had a small porch at its front that was held up by carved pillars.

Distance and the cold winters isolated the people of one village from those of another. Because of this, there was no central government. The people were divided into groups ruled by military chiefs called *jarls* (yahrlz). Some jarls were elected, while others inherited their position. Sometimes, a jarl became strong enough to take over neighboring lands. When a jarl had enough land under his rule, he was looked upon as a king.

Reading Check
Who were the *jarls*, and how were they selected?

Section 1 Assessment

1. **Define:** *jarls*.
2. How did people in Scandinavia make a living?
3. What were some of the features of Viking towns?

Critical Thinking

4. **Making Generalizations** How did the Vikings use their natural resources?

Graphic Organizer Activity

5. Draw this diagram, and use it to describe geographic features of the Viking homeland.

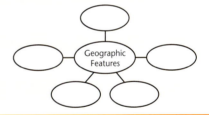

Geographic Features

SECTION 2 Daily Life

Family life was important to the Vikings. Most households had 20 to 30 members, including parents, grandparents, married children, and grandchildren. Families often fought bloody feuds to defend their honor. The payment of fines later ended such feuds.

The People Viking warriors were called *berserkers* (ber zerk' erz). They believed in a life of action and valued deeds that called for strength and courage. They fought to gain wealth, honor, and fame. They believed that a liking for war brought special honors from the gods.

To call their warriors to battle, the Vikings lit bonfires on the tops of mountains. Those who saw a fire would light a new one to

Reading Check
Who were the Viking *berserkers*, and why did they fight?

Viking Sword Hilt

spread the message. Warriors fought with battle axes, swords, and spears. Metal helmets decorated with animal figures protected their heads. Shirts made of iron rings and covered by a large cloth protected their bodies. Warriors preferred to die by their own hand rather than give their enemies the satisfaction of capturing or killing them.

The women encouraged their men to fight. A Viking groom bought his wife from her family on their wedding day. If he was not pleased with her, he could sell her. Yet, the position of Viking women was quite high. They took complete charge of the home. They could attend public meetings and talk with men other than their husbands. They could own property and get a divorce. Many Viking women grew herbs that were used as medicine.

Both men and women liked fine clothes. Men usually dressed in trousers and woolen shirts covered by knee-length tunics. Broad leather belts held the clothing in place. Sheepskin hoods and caps kept their heads warm. For special events, men wore red cloaks with brooches and carried decorated swords and daggers. Women also wore tunics held in place by a belt. They covered their heads with woolen or linen caps and wore large brooches, pins, and bracelets. Both men and women wore their hair long. The men took great pride in their mustaches and beards. Calling a

VIKING ADVENTURES   This painting of Vikings at sea shows the detail and decoration these north people put into their ships. The bows of their ships were usually elaborately carved. **Why did many Viking ships display the head of a dragon on the bow?**

Viking man "beardless" was an insult that could be wiped out only by death.

The Vikings had no schools. Girls were taught household skills, such as spinning, weaving, and sewing, by their mothers. Boys were taught to use the bow and arrow and to be good fighters by their fathers. Boys also memorized tales of heroes and gods and competed in games that tested their strength and endurance.

Religion   The Vikings worshiped many gods that at first were similar to the Germanic gods. Over time, they changed their gods to suit the hard life of Scandinavia. The Vikings believed that the gods were responsible for the weather and for the growth of crops. Since the gods liked to hunt, fish, and play tricks on one another, the Vikings viewed them as extra-powerful humans.

The Vikings bargained with their gods to get what they wanted. Priests offered sacrifices of crops and animals for the whole village. Most Vikings also had small shrines in their homes where they could pray or offer sacrifices.

The Vikings were proud of their gods and told stories of the gods' great deeds. These stories later became written poems called *Eddas* (ed' uhz). The Vikings also made up *sagas* (sah' guhz), or long tales. At first, storytellers used to recite them at special feasts. One such tale took 12 days to recite. After 1100, the Vikings wrote down their sagas. With the coming of Christianity, however, the people lost interest in them. Many were forgotten or were forbidden by the Church. Only the people on the isolated island of Iceland passed on the old tales.

Early on, the Vikings spoke a language similar to that of the Germans. In time, the one language developed into four—Danish, Norwegian (nor wē' juhn), Swedish, and Icelandic. These languages were written with letters called *runes* (rūnz), which few people except priests could understand or use. The Vikings used the runes as magic charms. They wrote the runes in metal and carved them in bone in the hope that they would bring good luck. When the Vikings accepted Christianity, they began to write their languages with Roman letters.

Viking Rune Stone

Reading Check
What were the *Eddas?*

Reading Check
What were some of the ways that the Vikings used *runes?*

Section 2 Assessment

1. **Define:** *berserkers, Eddas, runes.*
2. What kind of education did Viking children receive?
3. How did the Vikings view their gods?

Critical Thinking

4. **Demonstrating Reasoned Judgment** What might have been some of the advantages and disadvantages of living in the large Viking households?

Graphic Organizer Activity

5. Draw this diagram, and use it to compare the role of Viking women with the role of women in the United States today.

Viking Women | Both | Women Today

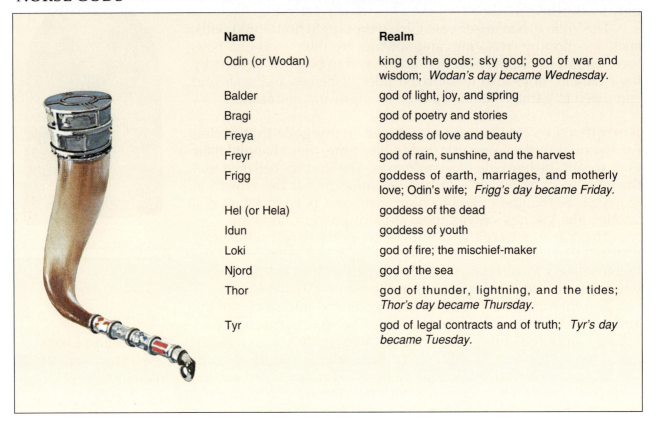

Name	Realm
Odin (or Wodan)	king of the gods; sky god; god of war and wisdom; *Wodan's day became Wednesday.*
Balder	god of light, joy, and spring
Bragi	god of poetry and stories
Freya	goddess of love and beauty
Freyr	god of rain, sunshine, and the harvest
Frigg	goddess of earth, marriages, and motherly love; Odin's wife; *Frigg's day became Friday.*
Hel (or Hela)	goddess of the dead
Idun	goddess of youth
Loki	god of fire; the mischief-maker
Njord	god of the sea
Thor	god of thunder, lightning, and the tides; *Thor's day became Thursday.*
Tyr	god of legal contracts and of truth; *Tyr's day became Tuesday.*

SECTION 3 Raiders and Adventurers

Scandinavia's population kept increasing. By the end of the 800s, many Viking villages were overcrowded, and there was not enough food for everyone. Since there was no central government, the kings constantly fought one another and made life difficult for their enemies. Before long, many Viking warriors began to seek their fortunes in other lands. They set sail on their long, deckless ships that were propelled through the water with oars. On them, the Vikings could safely sail the deep water of the Atlantic Ocean or the shallow rivers of Europe.

From East Europe to North America   Viking adventurers traveled to and raided areas from east Europe to North America. Swedish Vikings crossed the Baltic Sea and traveled down the rivers toward what is now Belarus, Ukraine, and Russia. They established a trade water route from the Baltic to the

Black Sea and on to the wealthy city of Byzantium (bi zan' tē uhm). This water route became known as the Varangian (vah rahng ē'uhn) Route. In 862, a Swedish chief named Rurik (r ū' rik) founded a Viking settlement that became the Kievan Rus state.

Norwegian Vikings set up trading towns in Ireland, explored the North Atlantic, and founded a colony on Iceland. Led by an adventurer named Erik the Red, they founded a colony on the island of Greenland in 986. Then, Erik's son, Leif Eriksson (lēf er' ik suhn), landed on the northeast coast of North America. He and his followers named the spot where they landed Vinland because of the wild grapes they found growing there. Today, the area is called Newfoundland (nū' fuhn luhnd). The Vikings did not set up a colony in Vinland because it was so far away from home and because they were repeatedly attacked by Native Americans.

Most Viking adventurers, however, went to western and southern Europe in search of food and valuables. They disguised their ships to look like wooded islands by covering them with tree branches. Then they traveled far up the rivers to make surprise

Linking Across Time

Iceland   Around 930, the Vikings drew up a constitution that provided for a legislative assembly called the Althing (left). The Althing still meets today (right), making it the oldest practicing legislative assembly in the world. **What conditions in Scandinavia led the Vikings to settle in Iceland?**

Tracing Historical Routes

Lines on maps generally show boundaries or rivers. On some maps, however, lines may show other things, such as **historical routes.** These are roads or courses over which people or goods have traveled all through history.

Such routes are often colored to make the map easier to read. A colored line may have arrows to point out the direction taken by people or goods. If there is a legend on the map, it may provide clues to the meaning of the different lines and colors.

For example, on the map of "Viking Trade and Expansion" below, the legend shows that the brown line is the Varangian Route. The two arrows along the line point out that the route began in Sweden and ended in Byzantium.

Map Practice

1. **What were some places visited by Vikings along their trade routes?**
2. **Which routes ran through the largest area of Viking settlement?**
3. **What two cities lay along Viking invasion routes?**

Viking Trade and Expansion

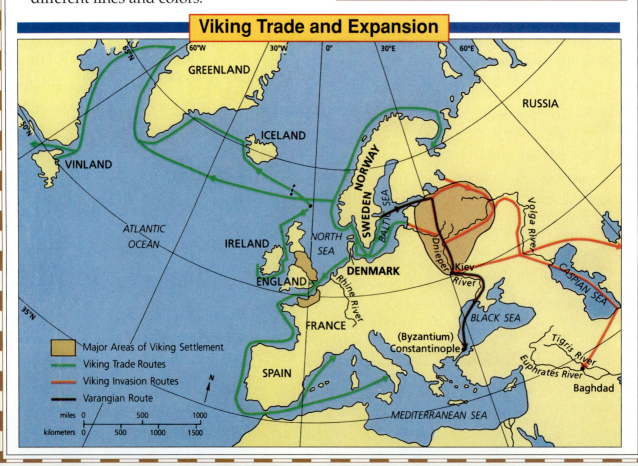

VIKING SHIPS The Vikings were among the best shipbuilders of their time. At sea, the Vikings depended on the wind and sails for power. On a river, rowers powered the ship. The Viking ships in this painting pursue enemy trading ships. **How did Vikings disguise their ships on rivers?**

attacks. They stole goods, destroyed homes, burned churches, and killed or enslaved people they captured. All Europe feared the Vikings. In their churches, the people prayed, "From the fury of the Norsemen, Good Lord, deliver us!"

The Danes The Danes were among those Vikings who raided western and southern Europe. One group invaded England and set up settlements there in the Danelaw. Their right to rule this area had been recognized by Alfred the Great. In 954, an heir of Alfred the Great forced the Danes to leave. In 978, Ethelred (eth' uhl red), nicknamed the Unready, became king of England. The Danes saw their chance and began raiding England again. At first, Ethelred was able to buy them off with silver. In 1016, however, a Danish king called Knut, or Canute (kuh nūt'), conquered England and made it part of his North Sea Empire. Canute was a powerful and just ruler. He converted to Christianity and brought peace and prosperity to England. Soon after his death in 1035, however, Danish control of the country came to an end. Some Danes left England. Those who remained became a part of the English people and culture.

Another group of Danes tried to take the city of Paris in France, but the French managed to fight them off. In 885, the

Danes tried again. The people of Paris held them off for ten months. Finally, the French king paid the Danes gold to abandon their attack.

Led by a warrior named Rollo (rahl' ō), the Danes began settling along the French coast opposite England. In 911, the French king signed a treaty with Rollo. He gave the Danes this land. In return, the Danes became Christians and promised to be loyal to the French king. The region in which the Danes settled became known first as the Norselaw and then as Normandy (nōr' muhn dē). The people became known as Normans.

Section 3 Assessment

1. Why did many Vikings leave Scandinavia?
2. Why did Europeans fear the Vikings?
3. What happened to the Danes who settled in England?

Critical Thinking

4. **Predicting Consequences** How might life have been different for the Vikings if there had been a central government in Scandinavia?

Graphic Organizer Activity

5. Draw the following diagram, and use it to summarize key dates in Viking history.

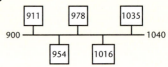

Chapter Summary & Study Guide

1. The Vikings lived in northern Europe in an area called Scandinavia.
2. The geography of the Viking homeland led people to become excellent sailors who earned their living through fishing, trading, and raiding.
3. The Vikings worshiped many gods and often told stories about them.
4. When the Vikings accepted Christianity, they stopped writing their languages in runes and began using Roman letters.
5. Overpopulation in Scandinavia in the 800s led many Vikings to establish settlements elsewhere, including Kievan Rus and Greenland.
6. In 1016, a Danish king called Canute conquered England, but after his death, Danish control of the country came to an end.
7. After besieging Paris, Danish Vikings settled along the French coast in an area known as Norselaw.

Self-Check Quiz

Visit the *Human Heritage* Web site at **humanheritage.glencoe.com** and click on ***Chapter 20—Self-Check Quiz*** to assess your understanding of this chapter.

Using Key Terms

Imagine you are a journalist writing a magazine article about Scandinavia. Use the following words to write a paragraph describing the Viking way of life.

jarls   *Eddas*
runes   *berserkers*

Understanding Main Ideas

1. Why did many Vikings turn to the sea to make a living?
2. How did the Vikings plot the courses of their voyages?
3. How were Viking houses protected from the winter?
4. Why was there no central government in Scandinavia?
5. How did a *jarl* become a king?
6. What role did women play in Viking society?
7. What were Viking stories about?
8. How did the Vikings use *runes*?
9. What effect did the Vikings have on Kievan Rus?
10. Why did the Vikings decide not to set up a colony in North America?

Critical Thinking

1. What effect did Christianity have on Viking life?
2. What would you have liked about being a Viking? What would you have disliked?
3. What do you think might have happened in Scandinavia if many Viking warriors had not left the area during the 800s?
4. What effect did Vikings have on the development of Europe during the Middle Ages?

Graphic Organizer Activity

Culture Create a diagram like the one shown, and use it to compare Viking culture before and after the arrival of Christianity in Scandinavia.

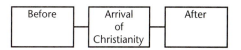

| Before | Arrival of Christianity | After |

Geography in History

Places and Regions Look at the map on page 306. The Vikings settled in areas beyond the Scandinavian region. What geographic features of Scandinavia may have contributed to the Vikings' expansion and movement? Write a paragraph showing how geographic features affected the Vikings' movement.

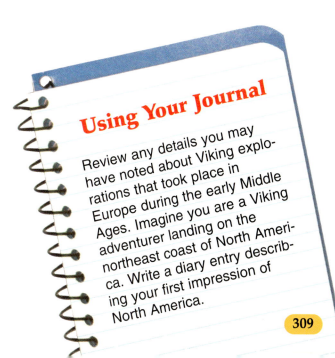

Using Your Journal

Review any details you may have noted about Viking explorations that took place in Europe during the early Middle Ages. Imagine you are a Viking adventurer landing on the northeast coast of North America. Write a diary entry describing your first impression of North America.

THE GUPTAS

As the Roman Empire crumbled, the Gupta (gup' tuh) Empire in what is now northern India entered a Golden Age. Beginning around 310 A.D., the Guptas began a period of great achievement and expansion.

Among the Gupta's contributions are many folktales and stories. In mathematics, the Gupta invented the concept of zero and developed symbols for the numbers 1 through 9. These symbols were carried to the West by traders and came to be called "Arabic numerals."

The empire lasted until about 600 A.D., when it dissolved into a collection of small states much like Europe.

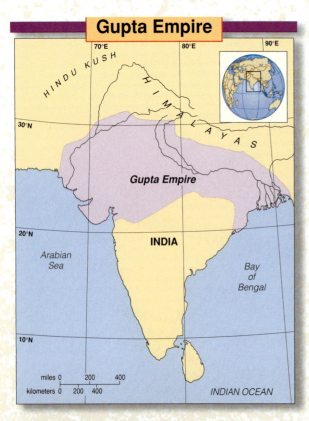

Gupta Empire

The Gupta Empire covered much of India and reached into parts of southwest Asia.

► The Guptas practiced Hinduism, but they tolerated other religions, especially Buddhism. Buddhism was founded about 563 B.C. by Siddartha Gautama (si dahr' tuh gow' tuh muh), who later became known as the Buddha. The Buddha, meaning the "Enlightened One," became the subject of many huge Gupta sculptures.

the World

◀ Despite the continued influence of Buddhism, Hinduism became the dominant religion of the Gupta Empire. During this period, rulers ordered the construction of stone or brick temples to honor Hindu gods and goddesses.

The great Gupta conqueror Samudra Gupta (suh mu' druh gup' tuh) minted his own coins. Ruling from about 335 A.D. to 375 A.D., he took over much of northern India and expanded trade as far south as islands in the Indian Ocean. The Sanskrit inscription on this coin describes Samudra Gupta as "the unconquered one, whose victory was spread in hundreds of battles, having conquered his enemies, conquers heaven." ▶

◀ Under the Guptas, Buddhist monks decorated the inside of caves, which were used as temples and monasteries, with paintings, statues, and carved pillars. Most paintings illustrated stories from the life of Buddha. Some paintings, however, show Gupta rulers and scenes from daily life, such as this woman.

Taking Another Look

1. During what years did the Gupta Empire flourish?
2. How did Gupta rulers try to unify their empire?

Hands-On Activity

Writing a Speech Write a one-minute speech in which you recommend that the phrase "Arabic numerals" be changed to "Gupta numerals."

311

Standardized Test Practice

Directions: Choose the *best* answer to each of the following multiple choice questions. If you have trouble answering a question, use the process of elimination to narrow your choices. Write your answers on a separate piece of paper.

Use the map below to answer question 1.

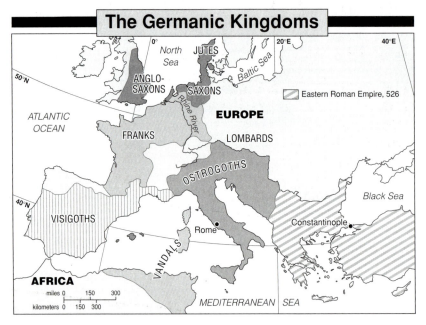

The Germanic Kingdoms

1. **This type of map is called a**

   A political map
   B physical map
   C military map
   D demographic map

   Test-Taking Tip: Even though this map does show some landforms, such as rivers, it is *not* primarily a physical map (answer B). What is the map's *main purpose*? A map's title—or legend (if there is one)—can give you clues.

2. **The legend of the Norse god Thor was used to explain**

   F why the Vikings were such good warriors
   G the sound of thunder
   H the story of Adam and Eve
   J the origins of language

   Test-Taking Tip: Eliminate answers that you know are incorrect. For example, the story of Adam and Eve (answer H) is a Bible story, and it is not related to the Vikings' religion.

3. The early Dark Ages were characterized by

A the development of strong trade routes in eastern Europe

B the failure of Christianity to spread to most parts of Europe

C a darkening of the sky due to air pollution around Europe

D an emphasis on war and conquest over education and trade

Test-Taking Tip: This question asks you to make a *generalization* about the Dark Ages. A generalization is a type of conclusion based on facts. Which of the answer choices *best* summarizes the Dark Ages? If you cannot remember any specific facts about the Dark Ages, ask yourself if it sounds like it was a positive or a negative time. In other words, what does the word *dark* suggest? Are there any answer choices you can eliminate as a result?

4. The battles waged by Charlemagne were different from earlier battles because

F for the first time, the purpose of war was to convert people to Christianity

G for the first time, wars were fought primarily on the water

H legends were written about the battles and Charlemagne's military leaders

J Charlemagne was the first to fight a war against the Pope

Test-Taking Tip: Always read the question and *all* the answer choices carefully. For example, Charlemagne fought *for* the Pope, not *against* the Pope, so you can eliminate answer J.

5. The Roman Catholic Church lost control of the Irish Church during the Germanic wars. What do you think was the reason for this?

A Ireland was far away, isolated, and relatively unimportant to Rome.

B Irish monks refused to follow the laws set by the Pope.

C Irish nobles refused to pay the taxes demanded by the Pope.

D The Irish refused to accept Christianity and kept worshiping their Celtic gods.

Test-Taking Tip: Make sure that you know where the major European countries are located on a map. How far was Ireland from Rome? Eliminate answer choices that do not make sense. If the Irish were already part of the Church, they must have accepted Christianity. Therefore, you can eliminate answer D.

6. After their encounters with the Germanic people in Europe, the Vikings stopped writing down their *sagas,* or long stories, about their gods. Why?

F They decided that they no longer had time to recite the long sagas.

G The Germanic people convinced the Vikings that stories were only for children.

H The Vikings were no longer interested in tales of warriors and exciting battles.

J The Vikings accepted Christianity, which outlawed stories about other gods.

Test-Taking Tip: For this question, you will have to think about the *influence* of the Germans on the Vikings. Since it is unlikely that the Vikings simply lost interest in these stories, you can get rid of answer H.

STOP

Emergence of New Empires

▲ A mosaic of a Byzantine woman

A gold Byzantine ▶ incense burner in the shape of a church

330 A.D.
Constantinople becomes capital of Roman Empire

527 A.D.
Justinian I becomes emperor of Byzantine Empire

622 A.D.
Hijrah

750 A.D.
Abbasids become new rulers of Arab Empire

FOLDABLES™
Study Organizer

Organizing Information Study Foldable *Make the following foldable to help you organize information about how empires in the Middle East and eastern Europe influenced other civilizations.*

Step 1 *Fold a sheet of paper in half from side to side.*

Fold it so the left edge is about $\frac{1}{2}$ inch from the right edge.

Step 2 *Turn the paper and fold it into thirds.*

Step 3 *Unfold and cut the top layer only along both folds.*

This will make three tabs.

Step 4 *Label as shown.*

EMERGENCE OF NEW EMPIRES
| The Byzantine Empire | The Spread of Islam | The Eastern Slavs |

Reading and Writing *As you read the unit, use your foldable to help you organize information about how empires affected other civilizations. Write the main ideas about each empire under the appropriate tab of your foldable.*

PRIMARY SOURCES

Library

See pages 686–687 for another primary source reading to accompany Unit 7.

 GO TO Read "The Fall of Constantinople" from the **World History Primary Source Document Library CD-ROM.**

Journal Notes

In what ways did the new empires that developed in the Middle East and in the eastern part of Europe influence other civilizations? Note details about these empires as you read.

1243 A.D.
Mongols defeat Seljuq Turks

1453 A.D.
Ottoman Turks capture Constantinople

1500 A.D.
Moscow becomes political center of Rus

CHAPTER 2

The Byzantine Empire

330 A.D.–1455 A.D.

◀ A gold Byzantine crown

▲ A Byzantine wedding ring

330 A.D.
Constantinople becomes capital of Roman Empire

527 A.D.
Justinian I rules Byzantine Empire

726 A.D.
Emperor Leo III bans icons

1054 A.D.
Eastern Orthodox and Roman Catholic churches separate

1453 A.D.
Turkish armies capture Constantinople

HISTORY
Online

Chapter Overview
Visit the *Human Heritage* Web site at <u>humanheritage.glencoe.com</u> and click on **Chapter 21— Chapter Overviews** to preview this chapter.

Chapter Focus

 Read to Discover

- Why the Byzantine Empire survived and prospered for 1,000 years.
- Why Constantinople was important to the empire.
- What role the Eastern Orthodox Church played in the Byzantine Empire.
- What forces helped bring about the decline of the Byzantine Empire.

Terms to Learn	People to Know	Places to Locate
relics	Constantine I	Constantinople
theology	Justinian	Byzantium
Greek fire	Theodora	Hagia Sophia
icons	Leo III	

Why It's Important   Emperor Constantine I moved the capital of the Roman Empire from Rome to Constantinople in about 330. About 100 years later, the Roman Empire in the West fell. The Roman Empire in the East, however, survived and prospered. It became known as the Byzantine Empire. Its people were called Byzantines. The Byzantines built a civilization based on a blend of Greek, Roman, and Christian ideas.

The empire in the East survived for several reasons. Constantinople was a mighty fortress that needed few soldiers to defend it. This freed soldiers to protect other areas of the empire. The empire's wealth supported a large army and was used to pay invaders to move farther and farther west.

SECTION 1 Constantinople

When Constantine first chose the old Greek city of Byzantium as the place for his new capital, he was aware of its advantages. The Roman Empire depended on trade, and the great centers of trade lay to the east. Byzantium was on the waterway between the Black and Aegean seas. Its harbor offered a safe haven for fishing boats, merchant ships, and warships. The city sat at the crossroads of the trading routes between Europe and Asia. Its location gave it control of the sea trade between Kievan Rus and the Mediterranean area. One of the most important east-west land routes passed through the city, too.

Constantine I
C. 288 A.D.–337 A.D.

Roman Emperor

Born in what is now Serbia, Constantine grew up the son of a Roman army officer. In 305 A.D., he became the co-emperor of Rome, but he continued to fight alongside the troops. During one battle, he saw a vision that convinced him to become the first Roman Emperor to accept Christianity. In 324 A.D., he triumphed as sole ruler of Rome and ordered a new capital city built at Byzantium. His rule helped ensure the eastward spread of Christianity.

The location also favored the city's defense. The sea protected it on three sides, and a huge wall protected it on the fourth side. Later, a huge chain was even strung across the city's north harbor for greater protection. Invaders would not easily take the new capital, which was renamed Constantinople.

It took more than four years to build Constantinople. Constantine modeled it after Rome. The city stood on seven hills. Government buildings and palaces were designed in the Roman style. Streets were narrow and apartment houses crowded. Constantinople even had an oval arena like the Circus Maximus where races and other events were held.

The city's political and social life was patterned on that of Rome, too. The emperor operated under Roman laws and ruled with the help of highly trained officials, who took charge of building roads, bridges, wells, and caravan shelters. The army followed Roman military customs. The poor people of Constantinople received free bread and enjoyed circuses and chariot races put on by the government. The wealthy people lived in town or on large farming estates. In fact, Constantine convinced many of the wealthy Romans to move to Constantinople by offering to build them palaces.

CONSTANTINOPLE   Constantinople's location made it an important center for trade. The wealth from this trade was used to make Constantinople an ornate and beautiful city. Citizens shown in this painting gather to watch a royal procession. **Why was Constantinople called the "new Rome"?**

The family was the center of social life for most Byzantines. The majority of them made their living through farming, herding, or working as laborers. There was, however, one important difference between Constantinople and Rome. From the beginning, Constantinople was a Christian city. It had been dedicated to God by Constantine, who viewed it as the center of a great Christian empire. Church leaders were consulted about all important events of everyday life and had great influence over the people. For a young man of Constantinople, a career in the church was considered a very high goal.

Byzantine Coins

Constantinople had many Christian churches. Constantine saw to it that they were the most magnificent buildings in the city. Government and church leaders gathered **relics** (rel' iks), or valued holy objects from the past, from throughout the Christian world. These were placed in public monuments, palaces, and churches. The bodies of saints rested in beautiful shrines. Thousands of people came to these shrines to pray to God for cures for their ills.

The city's Christian values could be seen in the way needy people were treated. The Byzantines believed that each Christian was responsible for the well-being of other Christians. Wealthy Byzantines formed organizations to care for the poor, the aged, and the blind. Even members of the emperor's household took great pride in founding and supporting good causes.

About 600,000 people lived in Constantinople during Constantine's rule. There were Greeks, Turks, Italians, Slavs, Persians, Armenians, and Jews. They spoke Greek among themselves but used Latin, the official language, for government business. Most people became Christians, and all called themselves Romans. Byzantine nobles and rulers continued to boast of their ties to Rome for the next 1,100 years.

✔ **Reading Check**
What are **relics,** and why did they attract thousands of people to Constantinople?

Student Web Activity
Visit the *Human Heritage* Web site at **humanheritage.glencoe.com** and click on *Chapter 21— Student Web Activities* to find out more about the city of Constantinople.

Section 1 Assessment

1. **Define:** relics.
2. Why did Constantine choose Byzantium as the site for the empire's new capital?
3. How could the influence of Christianity be seen in the city?

Critical Thinking

4. **Demonstrating Reasoned Judgment** In your opinion, what were some of the good things about living in Constantinople?

Graphic Organizer Activity

5. Draw this diagram, and use it to compare the cities of Rome and Constantinople.

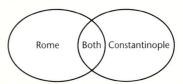

SECTION 2 Justinian I

After Constantine died, his sons ruled the empire. They were followed first by a general named Julian and then by a series of other emperors. Finally, in 527, a Macedonian named Justinian (juh stin' ē uhn) came to the throne. He was a strong ruler who came to be considered the greatest Byzantine emperor.

Justinian had served in the army and was a good general. He was well trained in law, music, architecture, and **theology** (thē ol' uh jē), or the study of religion. The people who served him were chosen for their abilities rather than for their wealth or social positions.

As emperor, Justinian controlled the army and navy, made the laws, headed the Church and the government, and was supreme judge. He could declare war or make peace. The Church taught that the emperor's acts were inspired by God. Therefore, what Justinian did could not be questioned. Those who came into contact with him were expected to bow down before him and kiss his feet and hands.

Theodora   Justinian's wife, the empress Theodora (thē uh dor' uh), was a great help to him. Theodora's family had been poor, and she had worked as an actress before meeting Justinian.

Reading Check
What is **theology?**

Fun Facts . . . .

Theodora Although Theodora was the daughter of a bear-keeper with a traveling circus, her strong will took her as far as the royal court. Justinian's court historian commented: "She never did anything at any time as the result of persuasion. . . . She claimed the right to govern the whole Roman Empire."

JUSTINIAN AND THEODORA   Theodora had a much greater influence on Byzantine government than other empresses. In this painting she urges Justinian to take action against a revolt. **What problems did Justinian face in marrying Theodora?**

Making Generalizations

If you say, "We have a good soccer team," you are making a generalization, or general statement, about your team. If you go on to say that the team has not lost a game this season and is the top-rated team, you are providing evidence to support your generalization. When studying history, it is often necessary to put together pieces of information—supporting statements—to arrive at a full picture.

Learning the Skill In some cases, authors provide only supporting statements, and you will need to make generalizations on your own. To make generalizations, follow these steps:

- Identify the subject matter and gather facts and examples related to it.

- Identify similarities or patterns among these facts.

- Use these similarities or patterns to form general ideas about the subject.

Read the passage about Hagia Sophia, a cathedral built by Justinian, and study the picture on this page. Then answer the questions that follow.

Hagia Sophia is the fourth largest cathedral in the world. Only St. Paul's Cathedral in England and St. Peter's Cathedral and Milan Cathedral in Italy are larger.

The building's huge round dome can be seen from everywhere in the church. The dome rests on four arches and four gigantic piers. It measures 102 feet (31 m) in diameter and stands 184 feet (56 m) high. A series of 40 arching windows flood the interior with light and draw the visitor's eyes upward.

GENERALIZATIONS:

a. It took great engineering skills to build Hagia Sophia.
b. Hagia Sophia made Constantinople the center of the Christian world.
c. Hagia Sophia is one of the world's greatest churches.
d. The arching windows are Hagia Sophia's most impressive feature.

Skill Practice

1. **Which of the generalizations above are supported by details in the passage?**
2. **Which of the generalizations are not supported by the passage?**
3. **Read Section 2 on pages 320–324. Write two generalizations about Justinian's wife, Theodora.**

GO TO Glencoe's **Skillbuilder Interactive Workbook CD-ROM, Level 1,** provides instruction and practice in key social studies skills.

The people of the empire had a low opinion of actresses. There was even a law forbidding marriages between them and high government officials. Justinian, however, wanted to marry Theodora. After he became emperor, he abolished the law and made Theodora his empress.

At first, Theodora only entertained guests and attended palace ceremonies. Gradually, however, she began to take an interest in politics. Soon she was helping Justinian fill government and church offices. She also convinced Justinian to allow women more rights. For the first time, a Byzantine wife could own land equal in value to her **dowry** (dow' rē), or the wealth she brought with her when she married. A widow could raise and support her young children without government interference.

In 532, Theodora made her most important contribution. A group of senators had organized a revolt to protest high taxes. They were able to gain much support from both the poor and the rich. The poor were angry because they were receiving less free food and entertainment. The rich were angry because, for the first time, they had to pay taxes. The leaders of the revolt were prepared to crown a new emperor. Justinian's advisers urged him to leave the city. Theodora, however, urged him to stay and fight. Justinian and his supporters took Theodora's advice. They stayed in Constantinople, trapped the rebels, killed 300,000 of them, and crushed the uprising. As a result, Justinian kept control of the government and became an even stronger ruler.

Law and Public Works

Justinian was very interested in law and spent much time reading the laws made by other emperors. He decided that the old legal system was too complicated and disorganized. He chose ten men to work out a simpler and better system. This group was headed by a legal scholar named Tribonian (tri bō' nē ahn).

Tribonian and the others studied the existing laws. They did away with those that were no longer needed. They organized and rewrote those laws that remained. In six years, they had developed a legal code that became the law of the land.

This code came to be known as the Justinian Code. It is considered one of Justinian's greatest achievements. It provided a summary of Roman legal thinking. It also gave later generations insight into the basic ideas of Roman law. It has had a great influence on the legal systems of almost every western country.

Justinian was as interested in public works as he was in law. He was almost always busy with some building program. He built churches, bridges, monasteries, and forums. He also built a system of forts connected by a large network of roads. When an earthquake destroyed Antioch, he had the whole city rebuilt.

One of Justinian's greatest accomplishments was the church called Hagia Sophia (hag'ē ī sō fē' uh), or "Holy Wisdom."

Reading Check
What is a **dowry,** and what did Theodora say it should be used to measure?

Then...&Now

Hagia Sophia Hagia Sophia, first built in the reign of Constantine, was twice destroyed by fire. When Justinian rebuilt the church, he ordered it be made fireproof. Earthquakes caused the dome to collapse in 559, but it too was rebuilt. The building became a mosque in 1453, and today it is a museum.

Nearly 10,000 workers, watched over by 200 supervisors, labored in shifts to build the church. It was built exactly as Justinian planned. The church had a gold altar and walls of polished marble. Gold and silver ornaments, woven cloth, and colorful **mosaics** (mō zā′ iks), or pictures made up of many bits of colored glass or stone, were everywhere. Figures of Justinian and Theodora were among the angels and saints that lined the walls.

Most impressive was the huge dome that rose high over the central part of the church. It was the first time such a huge circular dome had been set atop a rectangular opening. During the day, sunlight poured through the many windows in the dome. At night, thousands of oil lamps turned the building into a beacon that could be seen for miles.

Hagia Sophia was later called St. Sophia. For more than 900 years, it served as the religious center of the Byzantine Empire. It still stands today.

Conquest   Justinian wanted to reunite the eastern and western parts of the empire and restore the glory and power that was Rome's. To do this, he needed to conquer the German kingdoms in western Europe and North Africa. He appointed an officer named Belisarius (bel uh sar′ ē uhs) to reorganize and lead the Byzantine army.

Reading Check
What are **mosaics**?

MAP STUDY

THE WORLD IN SPATIAL TERMS
Justinian conquered parts of Italy, North Africa, and Spain.
About how many miles (km) did the Byzantine Empire under Justinian extend from its most eastern to its most western points?

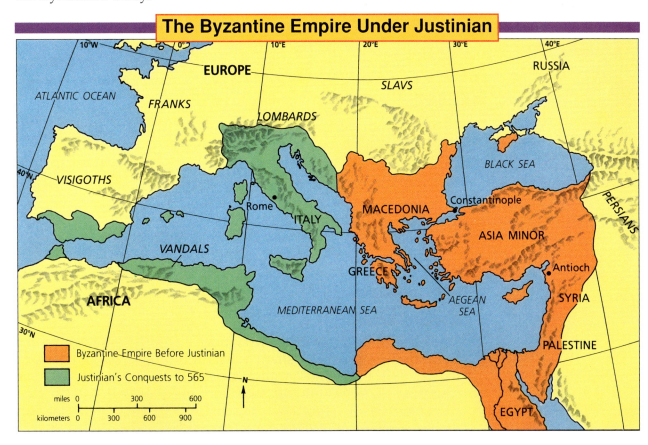

The Byzantine Empire Under Justinian

Byzantine Empire Before Justinian

Justinian's Conquests to 565

Until that time, the cavalry had been divided into groups of private soldiers hired by landowning nobles. Each group had its own commanders. Foot soldiers, who made up the largest part of the army, were called up when needed and then sent back to their homes. As a result, they felt little loyalty toward their officers.

When Belisarius took command, he set up a basic group of loyal and heavily armed cavalry soldiers. The group was so strong that the other soldiers willingly obeyed its orders. Then, Belisarius developed a series of battle moves that greatly strengthened the army's striking power.

During this time, the Byzantine navy was also improved, and the first secret weapon in history was developed. It was called **Greek fire,** a chemical mixture that ignited when it came into contact with water. Greek fire burned a person's skin and was hard to put out. The Byzantines guarded their secret so carefully that its exact formula is still unknown.

With these improvements, the Byzantines were able to control more of the Mediterranean. They were also able to win back much of Italy and North Africa. They defeated the Persians, and ensured the security of the empire's eastern borders. Most of the western provinces Justinian regained, however, were lost again a generation or so after his death.

Reading Check
Why was **Greek fire** the Byzantines' "secret weapon"?

Section 2 Assessment

1. **Define:** theology, dowry, mosaics, Greek fire.
2. How did Justinian feel about the old system of Roman laws? What did he do about it?
3. What was Justinian's goal for the Byzantine Empire?

Critical Thinking

4. **Making Inferences** What do you think Justinian would say about the state of the American legal system today? Explain.

Graphic Organizer Activity

5. Draw this diagram, and use it to write and support a generalization about improvements made to the Byzantine army.

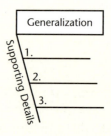

SECTION 3 The Church

Church and government worked closely together in the Byzantine Empire. Christianity was the official religion, which meant that everyone in the empire was supposed to be a Christian. The Byzantines believed the emperor represented Christ on Earth. Thus, the emperor was not only the head of the government but also of the Church.

Linking Across Time

Mosaics Byzantine artists excelled in the use of glass mosaics, especially in the design of icons (right). Today mosaics are still an important art form in Mexico (far right), continuing a tradition started by ancient peoples such as the Maya and Aztec. **Why did the Byzantines argue over the use of icons?**

The leader of the Church in Constantinople was called the Patriarch. He was chosen by the emperor. Under him were the **metropolitans** (met ruh pol' uh tuhns), or church officials in charge of the empire's important areas. Under them were the bishops and priests. Most priests were married. All higher Church officials, however, came from monasteries and were not married.

The monasteries played an important role in the Byzantine Empire. They helped the poor and ran hospitals and schools for needy children. They sent missionaries to neighboring lands to help keep the peace. These missionaries translated parts of the Bible and some religious services into several eastern European languages. They believed more people would become Christians if the Bible and Church ceremonies were in their own language.

Some missionaries, including a man named Cyril (sir' uhl), traveled among the Slavs, a people who had settled in eastern Europe. These missionaries gave the Slavs a new alphabet. It was based on the Greek alphabet and was called the Cyrillic (suh ril' ik) alphabet in honor of the man who had helped create it.

Religion was very important to the Byzantines. They often argued about religious matters. One point divided the Byzantines for more than 100 years. It centered on whether or not **icons** (ī' konz), or religious images, should be used in worship.

Many Byzantines honored icons. They covered the walls of their churches with them. Monasteries owned icons that were

Reading Check
What was the role of the **metropolitans** in the Byzantine Church?

Reading Check
What are **icons?**

CHAPTER 21 THE BYZANTINE EMPIRE **325**

Painting of Cyril

believed to work miracles. Some Byzantines, however, wanted an end to the use of icons. They thought honoring them was a form of idol worship forbidden by God.

In 726, Emperor Leo III ordered a stop to the use of icons in religious worship. He did not approve of icons, and he wanted to prevent church officials who favored them from gaining too much power. Leo and the church leaders argued over this. Most people refused to give up their icons. In 843, the emperor realized the cause was lost and once again allowed their use.

The fight over icons damaged the empire's relations with western Europe. Because so few people in the West could read, church leaders there used images instead of the written word to explain Christian teachings. When Leo decided to do away with icons, the Pope called a council of bishops. The council declared that Leo and his supporters were no longer Church members.

An argument also developed between the Pope and the Patriarch. The Patriarch would not recognize the Pope as head of the Church. The Pope broke his ties with the Byzantine emperor and turned to the Frankish kings for military protection. When the Pope crowned Charlemagne "Emperor of the Romans" in 800, the Byzantines were very angry. They believed this title belonged only to their emperor. These disputes helped pave the way for the break between Western and Eastern Christianity in 1054.

Section 3 Assessment

1. **Define:** metropolitans, icons.
2. What role did Christianity play in the Byzantine Empire?
3. What were some of the contributions of monasteries to Byzantine society and culture?

Critical Thinking

4. **Making Inferences** Why do you think the Slavs needed an alphabet that was different from the one used in the Byzantine Empire?

Graphic Organizer Activity

5. Draw this diagram, and use it to show the causes and effects of conflicts between the Pope in Rome and the Patriarch of Constantinople.

Causes	Religious Conflicts	Effects

SECTION 4 Decline of the Empire

The Byzantine Empire lasted for about 1,100 years. Its capital was the largest, richest, and most beautiful city in Europe. Its people were among the most educated and creative of that time. They preserved Greek culture and Roman law for other civilizations. They also spread Christianity to peoples in the East. The empire did much to help the growth of trade. It also gave the world new techniques in the fine arts. Even with all of these achievements, however, forces from both inside and outside the empire weakened it and led to its downfall.

Early Byzantine emperors had counted on farmers to make up the army. In return for their services, these farmers were given land. By the 1100s, however, the empire's borders were safe, and not as many soldiers were needed. The emperor decided to cut costs by changing the policy toward the farmers. Once they had lost their land, the farmers found little reason to remain loyal to the empire.

The empire also began to have problems with trade. When the Vikings conquered Byzantine lands in southern Italy in 1080, they threatened to attack Constantinople. The Byzantines no longer had enough soldiers to fight them. So, they turned for help to the Italian city-state of Venice. The Venetians defeated the Vikings. In return, the Byzantine emperor gave them the right to do business tax-free in all the empire's cities. Venetian ships and merchants soon controlled most of the empire's trade. This meant a great loss of income for the Byzantines.

Meanwhile, Christians from the West and Muslims from the East attacked the empire. Asia Minor was lost to these invaders. This greatly weakened the empire, which had depended on Asia Minor for food and materials as well as soldiers. One by one, the invaders took over more lands. Before long, the Byzantine Empire was reduced to a small area around Constantinople.

The End of the Byzantine Empire

Lands of Ottoman Turks, 1453

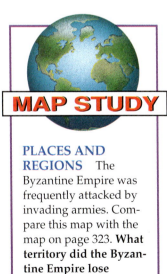

MAP STUDY

PLACES AND REGIONS The Byzantine Empire was frequently attacked by invading armies. Compare this map with the map on page 323. **What territory did the Byzantine Empire lose between 565 and 1453?**

The population dropped to less than 100,000. Docks and marketplaces stood empty. Even the emperors were poor. When Turkish armies with guns and gunpowder attacked Constantinople in 1453, they easily conquered the Byzantines.

Section 4 Assessment

1. What problems within the Byzantine Empire helped bring about its decline?
2. What outside forces helped cause the empire's downfall?

Critical Thinking

3. **Demonstrating Reasoned Judgment** Do you think the Byzantine emperor was wise in asking Venice for help against the Vikings? Why or why not?

Graphic Organizer Activity

4. Draw this diagram, and use it to show Byzantine contributions to world civilization.

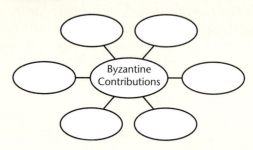

Chapter Summary & Study Guide

1. Around 330, Constantine moved the capital of the Roman Empire to Constantinople, the site of the old Greek city of Byzantium.

2. After the fall of Rome, the Roman Empire in the East became known as the Byzantine Empire.

3. Although Constantine patterned much of life in Constantinople after Rome, his acceptance of Christianity also helped shape the city.

4. When Justinian became emperor in 527, he was influenced in some of his decisions by the empress Theodora, who favored increased women's rights.

5. Two of Justinian's greatest achievements were development of a system of law known as the Justinian Code and construction of Hagia Sophia.

6. Under Justinian, Belisarius reorganized the Byzantine army and expanded the empire's borders.

7. Relations between the Pope and the Patriarch were weakened by the argument over icons, by the Patriarch's refusal to recognize the Pope as the head of the Church, and by the Pope's crowning of Charlemagne as emperor.

8. Both internal problems and outside forces weakened the Byzantine Empire, which was conquered by Turkish armies in 1453.

Self-Check Quiz

Visit the *Human Heritage* Web site at **humanheritage. glencoe.com** and click on *Chapter 21—Self-Check Quiz* to assess your understanding of this chapter.

Using Key Terms

You live in ancient Byzantium and are asked to write a paragraph describing your culture. Your paragraph is to be put in a time capsule to be opened by a future generation. Write your paragraph, including the following words.

relics   theology   dowry
mosaics   Greek fire   metropolitans
icons

Understanding Main Ideas

1. Why did the Roman Empire in the East survive the fall of Rome?
2. How did Constantinople's location help it become a great trading center?
3. How did Christianity affect Byzantine attitudes toward the care of needy people?
4. How did Theodora help women within the Byzantine Empire?
5. What led to the separation of the Eastern Orthodox Church and the Roman Catholic Church in 1054?
6. Why did Byzantine farmers gradually lose their loyalty to the empire?

Critical Thinking

1. What is your opinion of the following statement: "Constantine was wise to model Constantinople after Rome"?
2. What are the advantages for a government to have an offical religion? What are the disadvantages?
3. What do you think had the most to do with the decline of the Byzantine Empire? Explain.
4. What contribution made by the Byzantines do you think was the most important? Explain.

Graphic Organizer Activity

Citizenship Create a chart like the one shown, and use it to show the causes and effects of Justinian's decision to draw up a new code of laws.

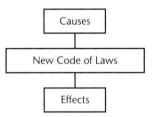

Causes

New Code of Laws

Effects

Geography in History

Human Systems Justinian expanded his empire greatly. Refer to the map on page 323. If you had been Justinian, in which direction would you have sent troops next to gain new territory? Why?

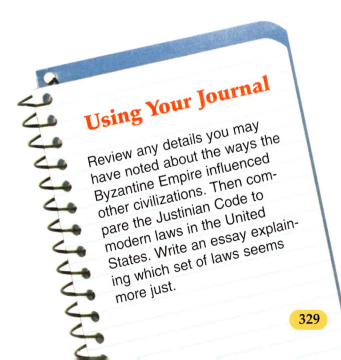

Using Your Journal

Review any details you may have noted about the ways the Byzantine Empire influenced other civilizations. Then compare the Justinian Code to modern laws in the United States. Write an essay explaining which set of laws seems more just.

The Spread of Islam

500 A.D.–1300 A.D.

▲ A page from the Quran

A highly decorated ► Islamic ceramic lamp

570 A.D. Muhammad born	**622 A.D.** Muhammad flees from Makkah to Yathrib	**710 A.D.** Moors invade Spain	**750 A.D.** Abbasids become rulers of Arab Empire	**c. 1290 A.D.** Ottoman dynasty founded in Asia Minor

Chapter Focus

 ## Read to Discover

- How Islam developed around the teachings of Muhammad.
- What religious beliefs are held by Muslims.
- How Islam spread beyond the Arabian Peninsula.
- What early Islamic life was like.
- What the Arab Empire contributed to science, mathematics, medicine, and the arts.

Chapter Overview
Visit the *Human Heritage* Web site at **humanheritage.glencoe.com** and click on **Chapter 22—Chapter Overviews** to preview this chapter.

 Terms to Learn   **People to Know**   **Places to Locate**

Terms to Learn	People to Know	Places to Locate
pillars of faith	Muhammad	Makkah
mosque	al-Idrisi	Madina (Yathrib)
imam	ar-Rāzi	Damascus
hajj	Omar Khayyám	Baghdad
alchemists	Ibn Khaldum	

Why It's Important   Between the northeast coast of Africa and central Asia lies the Arabian Peninsula. The people who live there are known as Arabs. At one time, most were Bedouins (bed' uh wuhnz). They were herders who roamed the desert in search of grass and water for their camels, goats, and sheep. They lived in tents woven from camel or goat hair.

Bedouin warriors during the 600s raided other peoples and fought one another over pastures and springs. They valued their camels and swords above all else. They enjoyed poetry and music. They believed in many gods.

In the 600s, a religion called Islam (is' luhm) began in the mountainous area of western Arabia known as the Hejaz (hej az'). Within 100 years, an Arab empire based on Islamic beliefs had developed. It controlled an area larger than that of the Roman Empire.

SECTION 1   Islam

The word "Islam" is an Arabic word. It means "the act of *submitting,* or giving oneself over, to the will of God." The Islamic faith was founded by an Arab merchant named Muhammad (mō ham' id). Muhammad came to be known as the prophet of Allah (ahl' uh). The word "Allah" is an Arabic word meaning "the God." Muhammad called those who followed his faith Muslims, which means "followers of Islam."

Islam shook the foundations of Byzantium and Persia, the two most powerful civilizations of the time. It brought into its fold people from different races and continents. It came to shape a way of life for one of every seven persons on Earth.

Makkah (Mecca)

By the middle of the 500s, three major towns had developed in the Hejaz. They were Yathrib (yath' ruhb), Taif (tah' if), and Makkah (mak' uh). Of the three, Makkah was the largest and the richest.

Makkah was supported by trade and religion. Traders stopped there for food and water on their way north to Constantinople. Arab **pilgrims,** or travelers to a religious shrine, came there to worship. Arabia's holiest shrine, the *Ka'bah* (kah' buh), stood in the center of Makkah. It was a low, cube-shaped building surrounded by 360 idols. A black stone believed to have fallen from paradise was set in one of its walls. Nearby was a holy well.

Muslims believe that the Ka'bah was first built by Adam. Later, Abraham and his son, Ishmael, rebuilt it. They had dedicated it to the worship of the one God. Later, however, people filled it with idols that represented the gods and goddesses of different tribes.

Muhammad

In 570, Muhammad was born to a widow of a respectable clan in Makkah. When he was six years old, his mother died, and he went to live with an uncle. When he reached his teens, he began working as a business person. At the age of 25, he married a rich 40-year-old widow named Khad'juh (kahd' yuh).

Muhammad was very successful in the caravan business. He was troubled, however, by the drinking, gambling, and corruption in Makkah. He began spending much time alone in a cave on a hillside outside the city. There, he thought and fasted. He decided that the people of Makkah had been led into evil by their belief in false gods. He concluded that there was only one God, Allah, the same god as the God of the Jews and the Christians.

In 610, Muhammad had a *revelation*, or vision. It is said that, when he was meditating in the cave, an angel appeared and ordered him to read some writing. According to Muslim tradition, he heard the voice of the angel Gabriel (gā' brē uhl) telling him to preach about God. Muhammad told Khad'juh what had happened. She went to see a holy man, hoping he could explain the meaning of Muhammad's story. The holy man told her that the heavenly visitor was the same one who had visited Moses and other prophets and that Muhammad was to be the prophet of his people.

✓ **Reading Check**
Why did Arab **pilgrims** travel to Makkah?

People in History

Muhammad
570 A.D.–632 A.D.

Prophet of Islam

Muhammad is one of the great figures in world history. His revelations and teachings form the basis of Islam, a faith that now claims more than one billion followers. While living in Yathrib (Madina), he established a model for future Islamic states in which religious leaders oversee government. His appeal for Islamic unity helped Muhammad to extend his Islamic state to the entire Arabian Peninsula.

HISTORY Online

Student Web Activity

Visit the *Human Heritage* Web site at **humanheritage.glencoe.com** and click on **Chapter 22— Student Web Activities** to find out more about the Islamic faith.

KA' BAH SHRINE   Modern Muslim pilgrims travel to Makkah to pray facing the shrine called the Ka' bah. It is considered a very holy place. **Who do Muslims believe first built the Ka' bah?**

In 613, Muhammad began to preach to the people of Makkah. He told them that there is only one God, Allah, before whom all believers are equal. He urged the rich to share with the poor. Muhammad saw life as a preparation for the Day of Judgment, or the day on which people would rise from the dead to be judged for their actions on Earth.

At first, the rich leaders of Makkah laughed at Muhammad. As he continued to preach, however, they began to feel threatened. They were afraid that people would stop coming to Makkah to worship at the Ka'bah. When pilgrims visited Makkah, they spent money on meals and clothing. The leaders thought that if fewer pilgrims came to Makkah, the city's economy would be ruined. Then, the leaders would no longer be rich. Because of this fear, they started persecuting Muhammad and his followers.

In 620, Muhammad preached to a group of pilgrims from Yathrib. They invited him to come there and be their leader. During the summer of 622, he and several hundred of his followers fled from Makkah to Yathrib. The year 622, called *Anno Hijrah* (an' ō hi jī' ruh), or "Year of the Migration," became the first year of the Muslim calendar. The city of Yathrib was renamed Madinat al-Nabi, "the city of the prophet," or Madina.

In Madina, Muhammad proved himself an able leader. He gave the people a government that united them and made them

Calendars The Islamic calendar, started in 622, is a lunar calendar with 354 days divided into 12 months. The Muslim Era, which counts years from the *Hijrah*, is used officially in Saudi Arabia, Yemen, and the Persian Gulf states. Even in Muslim countries that officially use the Gregorian calendar, many people follow the Muslim calendar at home.

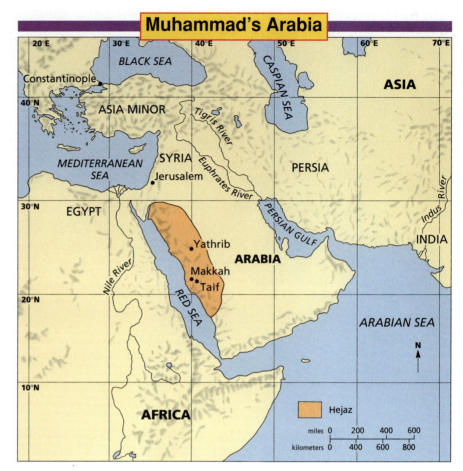

Muhammad's Arabia

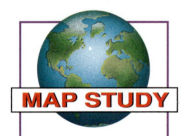

MAP STUDY

THE WORLD IN SPATIAL TERMS

Yathrib was an oasis of farms, Taif was a mountain refuge, and Makkah was a crossroads for trade. **About how many miles (km) inland from the Red Sea was Makkah located?**

The Quran As Muhammad preached, his followers wrote down or memorized his teachings. After Muhammad's death, his successor Abu Bakr ordered Muslims to retrieve those teachings wherever they could be found. It took 20 years to compile the teachings into the Quran, the Muslim scriptures followed today.

proud of their new faith. The people of Makkah were very angry with Muhammad's success in Madina. With far superior armies, they invaded Madina several times to crush the newly established Muslim community. The Muslims defended their city with great courage every time. In 628, Muhammad signed a peace treaty with the people of Makkah, which they violated in 630. It was in that year that Muhammad and his companions triumphantly entered their home city, Makkah. Their conquest was peaceful. Muhammad issued general forgiveness to all who had persecuted and opposed him. Within two years, all the tribes of Arabia declared their faith in Islam and their loyalty to Muhammad. In 632 Muhammad died.

The Quran

At the heart of Islam is the Quran (ko ran'), or Muslim scriptures. Muslims believe it is the direct word of God as revealed to Muhammad. For this reason, they feel they should follow it exactly.

The Quran is written in Arabic. It tells how good Muslims should live. They should not eat pork, drink liquor, or gamble. The Quran also gives advice on marriage, divorce, inheritance, and business.

The Quran describes the **pillars of faith,** or the five duties all Muslims must fulfill. The first duty is the confession of faith. All Muslims must recite the Islamic creed that states, "There is no God but Allah, and Muhammad is his prophet."

The second duty deals with prayer. Muslims must pray five times a day, facing Makkah each time. The prayers are said at dawn, noon, late afternoon, sunset, and evening. The prayers can be said anywhere. The only exception is the Friday noon prayer. It is usually recited at a **mosque** (mosk), or Muslim house of worship. There, believers are led by an **imam** (i mam'), or prayer leader.

The third duty has to do with the giving of *zakah,* or charity. This is a donation that every Muslim has to give at the rate of 2.5 percent of his or her annual savings. It can be given to needy people or to institutions that are involved in education and social services.

✔ **Reading Check**
What are the **pillars of faith?**

✔ **Reading Check**
What is a **mosque,** and what does an **imam** do there?
What action is called for in the giving of *zakah?*

ISLAMIC FAITH   Muslims learn the teachings of the Quran at an early age. A child in the photograph (left) studies passages from the Quran. From the prayer tower (right) of each mosque, announcers call the people to prayer. **What are the five duties that all Muslims must fulfill called?**

The fourth duty deals with fasting. The young, sick people, pregnant women, and travelers do not have to fast. Everyone else, however, must fast each year during the daylight hours of the holy month of Ramadan (ram' uh dahn).

The fifth duty involves a pilgrimage. Each able Muslim, at least once in his or her lifetime, must travel to Makkah two months after Ramadan. The journey is called the *hajj* (haj). For three days, Muslims from all over the world come together for ceremonies and sacrifice.

The Quran promises that all believers who fulfill their duties will go to Paradise, which has shade, fruit trees, beautiful flower gardens, cold springs, and singing birds. Hell is a flame-filled pit where drinking water comes from a salty well and where food is a strong-smelling plant that causes hunger.

Reading Check
What religious duty is performed in the *hajj?*

Section 1 Assessment

1. **Define:** pilgrims, pillars of faith, mosque, imam, *zakah, hajj.*
2. According to Muslim tradition, what caused Muhammad to begin his preachings?
3. What does the Quran say will happen after death?

Critical Thinking

4. **Identifying Cause and Effect** What effect did the rise of Islam have on Byzantium and Persia?

Graphic Organizer Activity

5. Draw this diagram, and use it to summarize the five pillars of faith.

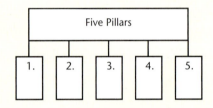

Five Pillars

| 1. | 2. | 3. | 4. | 5. |

The Arab Empire

When Muhammad died in 632, his followers needed a new leader. Without someone to guide them, the community could have broken up, and the faith could have been lost. A group of Muslims chose a new leader whom they called *khalifa*, or **caliph** (kā′lif), which means "successor."

Reading Check
What is a **caliph**, and who was the first caliph chosen?

The Rightly Guided Caliphs

The first caliph was Abu Bakr (uh bū′ bak′ uhr), Muhammad's father-in-law and close friend. Bakr and the next three caliphs were elected for life. These caliphs ruled from Madina. They kept in close touch with the people and asked advice of their most trusted friends. For this reason, they were called the Rightly Guided Caliphs.

The Rightly Guided Caliphs honored Muhammad's wish to carry Islam to other peoples. They sent warriors into Palestine, Syria, Iraq, Persia, Egypt, and North Africa. Throughout all these places, the Arabs were victorious.

The Arabs were successful for many reasons. Islam held them together. They were united in striving for a common goal which they considered holy—to carry Islam to other people. Their religious beliefs helped them fight against the enemies of their religion. Arab warriors believed that struggling on behalf of Islam earned them an eternal place in Paradise if they died in battle. Arab leaders were mentally and physically tough. They planned and carried out attacks. They also handled their camels and horses with great skill.

The Arab way of treating the people they conquered also contributed to their success. Those who gave in without a fight had to pay taxes. In return, the Arabs protected them and allowed them to keep their land. Those who fought and were defeated not only had to pay taxes, but also lost their land.

The Umayyads

Ali, Muhammad's son-in-law and the last of the Rightly Guided Caliphs, was killed in 661. Mu'awiya (mū uh' wi yuh), the new caliph, moved the capital from Madina to Damascus and founded the Umayyad (ū mī' yuhd) Dynasty. From that time on, the title of caliph was hereditary.

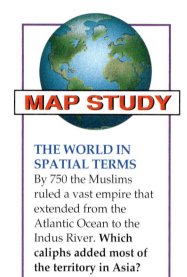

MAP STUDY

THE WORLD IN SPATIAL TERMS

By 750 the Muslims ruled a vast empire that extended from the Atlantic Ocean to the Indus River. **Which caliphs added most of the territory in Asia?**

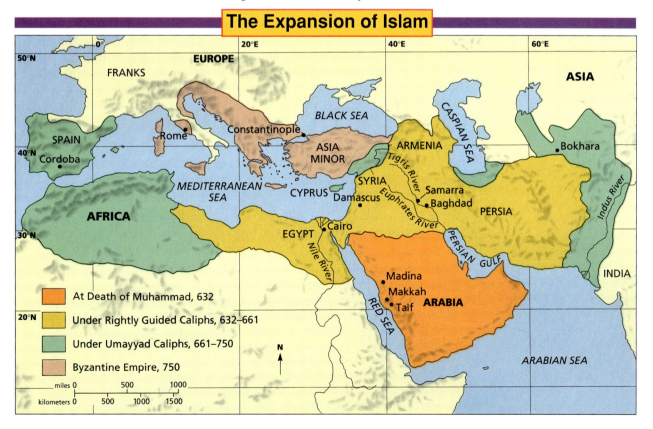

The Expansion of Islam

- At Death of Muhammad, 632
- Under Rightly Guided Caliphs, 632–661
- Under Umayyad Caliphs, 661–750
- Byzantine Empire, 750

miles 0 · 500 · 1000
kilometers 0 · 500 · 1000 · 1500

The Bazaar Muslim merchants traded their wares in the *bazaar*, originally the term for Persian public markets. The name came to be used for colorful outdoor marketplaces throughout the Middle East and North Africa. In English today, *bazaar* means a store that sells many kinds of goods.

The Umayyads ruled more like kings than religious leaders. They reorganized the government and made Arabic the official language. They minted the first Arab money. They set up horseback postal routes. They repaired and maintained irrigation canals. They also built beautiful mosques and encouraged the arts.

Many of these changes helped the people of the empire. However, the Umayyads had social and economic troubles that, in the end, led to their downfall. The conquered people who became Muslim complained that they were not treated the same as those who were born Muslim. They received less money for serving in the army. They also had to pay higher taxes.

The Muslims themselves divided into two groups. The smaller group was called the Shi'ah (shē' ah). Its followers, called Shi'ites (shē' īts), believed the office of caliph should be held only by descendants of Ali. The larger group, called the Sunni (sūn' nē), followed the Rightly Guided Caliphs and the caliphs after them. After a while, war broke out between the Umayyads and a group of Muslims called Abbasids (uh' bas uhdz). In 750, the Abbasids defeated the Umayyads. They then became the new rulers of the Arab Empire.

The Abbasids

The Abbasids ruled the Arab Empire from 750 to 1258. Their first 100 years in power was known as the Golden Age of Islam.

The Abbasids built a new capital called Baghdad (bag' dad) on the east bank of the Tigris River. The city was designed by a Jewish astronomer and a Persian engineer. Over 100,000 people worked four years to build it.

Baghdad was built in the shape of a circle. Around it were three huge, sloping brick walls and a deep *moat*, or wide ditch filled with water. Each wall had four large gates linked together by two highways that crossed in the center of the city. At that point stood the great mosque and the caliph's magnificent palace. A number of public officials had luxurious homes there also. The highways divided Baghdad into four pie-shaped sections. From the gates, each highway led to a different part of the empire.

Under the Abbasids, all that remained of Arab influence was the Arabic language and the Islamic religion. The name Arab no longer meant only a person from Arabia. It meant any subject of the empire who spoke Arabic.

The Abbasids created the government post of **vizier** (vi zir'), or chief adviser. The person serving as vizier stood between the throne and the people. He took charge of running the empire and chose the governors of the provinces.

The Abbasids did not try to conquer new lands. Instead, they made Baghdad one of the major trading centers of the world. Improved trade between countries led to a fresh

✔ Reading Check
What was the role of the **vizier**?

Linking Across Time

Carpets   Arab carpets were among the most sought-after items in the markets of the Islamic Empire. Carpets adorned the floors of mosques, palaces, and the tents of shepherds (below). Today, skilled Islamic weavers (right) continue to make some of the world's most prized carpets, including the prayer rugs used for kneeling in daily prayers. **What effect did the growth of trade have upon daily life in the Islamic Empire?**

exchange of ideas. Many writers and philosophers flocked to Baghdad. The Syrian Christians and Jews were instructed by the caliph to translate Greek writings into Arabic. Other scholars translated Indian literature into Arabic. The world's store of knowledge advanced greatly. Mathematical and scientific achievements were recorded. Mathematicians adapted numeric systems developed by the Guptas of India which are still in use today. Practical applications of this mathematics were used.

Life in the empire changed. Advanced farming methods were used to produce wheat, rice, beans, melons, cucumbers, celery, and mint. Orchards provided almonds and olives. Trade made many Arabs rich. They desired so many luxury goods that Arab artisans began producing some themselves. As trade grew, more records had to be kept. This led to the opening of banks. People had time to play games like polo and chess. Men stopped wearing the traditional Arab robe and began wearing pants. Meals were now served on tables instead of on the floor.

The empire soon became too large for one caliph to control. It began to break up into independent kingdoms. In 836, the caliph moved to a new capital city called Samarra. He returned to Baghdad in 892 and tried to regain power. By then, however, it was too late. In 945, the Persians took control of Baghdad.

The Golden Age of Muslim Spain

The Muslim Arabs who conquered North Africa intermarried with the Berbers and became known as Moors (mūrz). In 710, they invaded Spain. With the help of Spanish Jews, they defeated the West Goths, who had taken the country from the Romans. Then, the Moors set up a kingdom that allowed religious freedom.

For the next 400 years, a rich culture flourished in Spain. Many beautiful buildings, such as the Alhambra (al ham' bruh) in Granada, were built all through the country. Schools were founded in which Muslims, Jews, and Christians studied medicine and philosophy together.

During this time, Jews traveled to and traded in every part of the Arab Empire and beyond. In southeastern Rus, they met the Khazars (kuh zarz'), a half-Mongolian people who had converted to Judaism. From India and China, they brought back spices and silks to Spain.

Then... &Now

Cordoba By the 900s, Cordoba, the capital of Muslim Spain, was the largest city in Europe and a cultural center for scholars, musicians, and artisans. Cordoba was known especially for its fine leatherwork, woven silk and brocades, and gold and silver jewelry. Visitors to Cordoba today can still see the Great Mosque, completed about 976.

THE ALHAMBRA   Under Islamic rule, many beautiful buildings were built in Spain. The Alhambra, a palace in Granada, is considered the finest example of Islamic architecture in Europe. **What Islamic group invaded Spain in 710?**

EASTERN CONQUERORS

Seljuq Turks *c. 900-1258*

Seljuq *c. 900* chief from central Asia; settled with a group of followers near city of Bokhara and became Muslim

Toghril *c. 1055* grandson of Seljuq, conquered Baghdad; took title al-sultan, meaning "he with authority"; set up Muslim kingdom in western Asia

Mongols *c. 1206-1300*

Genghis Khan
c. 1220 united central Asian nomads; conquered Arab territory and created empire that covered most of Asia and eastern Europe

Hulagu *c. 1258* grandson of Genghis Khan; led attack on Baghdad in 1258; became first khan, or overlord, of a kingdom that stretched from Syria to India

Genghis Khan

Mamelukes *c. 1250-1517*

Shajar *c. 1250* freed slave who became first Mameluke ruler of Egypt; only Muslim woman to rule a country

Baybars *c. 1260* seized throne of Egypt; restored caliphate in Cairo; created Mameluke dynasty

Ottoman Turks *c. 1290-1922*

Osman
c. 1290-1326 founded Ottoman dynasty in Asia Minor

Muhammad II
c. 1451-1481 captured Constantinople in 1453; established Ottoman Empire

Muhammad II

Islamic Jug

Islamic Life

Islam was born in a society where men could have an unlimited number of wives and the killing of female children was common. Islam attempted to correct this situation.

Muhammad taught that raising a female child guaranteed a reward in Paradise for her parents. Before Islam, women could not inherit property from their parents. Islam, however, entitled them to half the share of their husband's wealth. Islam recognized a woman's right to an inheritance. In Islam, only under extreme circumstances is a man allowed to have up to four wives. One condition of this is that a man must be able to afford to provide equal treatment to each of his wives.

Both men and women were obligated to seek knowledge. Islamic society produced some women of great knowledge and power. At the time of the birth of a Muslim baby, the call for prayer was recited into the baby's ears. By doing this, the child was brought into a life of Islamic culture. Reciting and memorizing the Quran was an important requirement in education. The mosques served as neighborhood schools. The boys were sent for higher education to institutions in major cities. People would travel from country to country within the Muslim world seeking more knowledge. There was tremendous interest in traveling and exploration.

Section 2 Assessment

1. **Define:** caliph, vizier.
2. What were some of the accomplishments of the Umayyads?
3. How did the Arab Empire change under the Abbasids?

Critical Thinking

4. **Drawing Conclusions** Why were the years from 710 to around 1300 called the Golden Age of Muslim Spain?

Graphic Organizer Activity

5. Draw this diagram, and use it to show how the teachings of Islam tried to improve the treatment of women in Arab society.

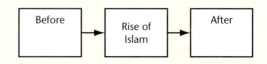

SECTION 3   Arab Contributions

Between the 770s and the 1300s, Arab scholars helped preserve much of the learning of the ancient world that otherwise would have been lost. They also made many other contributions to the modern world. The use of Arabic as a common language helped unite scholars and promote the sharing of knowledge. The Quran being written in Arabic contributed to this advancement.

Many Arab scientists tried to turn base metals, such as tin, iron, and lead, into gold and silver. These scientists, called **alchemists** (al' kuh mists), used both chemistry and magic in their work. The word "chemistry" comes from the Arabic word "Al-Chemist." Alchemists were never able to turn base metals into gold and silver. However, their work led to the practice of making experiments and keeping records of the results. The Arabs are considered the founders of modern chemistry.

Arab astronomers studied the heavens. They gave many stars the names they still carry today. They correctly described the eclipses of the sun. They also proved that the moon affects the *tides*, or the rise and fall of the oceans. The astronomers worked with Arab geographers to determine the size of Earth and the distance around it. From their studies, they decided that Earth might be round. The astronomer-geographer al-Idrisi (al i drē' si) drew the first accurate map of the world.

Arab mathematicians invented algebra and taught it to Europeans. Arab mathematicians also borrowed the numerals 0-9 from Gupta mathematicians and passed them to Europeans.

The Arabs gave much to the field of medicine. Unlike doctors in most other countries, Arab doctors had to pass a test before they could practice medicine. The Arabs set up the world's first school of pharmacy. They also opened the world's first drugstores. They organized medical clinics that traveled all through the empire giving care and medicines to the sick.

Arab doctors were the first to discover that blood *circulates*, or moves, to and from the heart. They were the first to diagnose certain diseases. The Persian doctor ar-Razi (al rā sē') discovered differences between measles and smallpox. Another Persian, Avicenna (ä vä sēn ä), was the first to understand that tuberculosis is *contagious*, or can be passed from person to person.

Arab doctors informed the scientific community about their discoveries by publishing their findings. Avicenna's *Canon of Medicine,* an encyclopedia of medicine, was used in European medical schools for 500 years.

The Arabs also made many contributions to the arts. One of their best known writings is *The Arabian Nights,* a collection of tales put together from Persian stories. The tales paint an exciting picture of Islamic life at the height of the empire. The Persian poet Omar Khayyám's (ō' mahr kī yahm') *Rubáiyát* (rū' bē aht) has been translated into many languages. It is considered one of the finest poems ever written.

Islamic art is distinct and full of color. It is used on walls, books, rugs, and buildings. It differs from most other art because of the Muslim belief that Allah created all living creatures. Islamic artists think it is a sin to make pictures of Allah's creations. As a result, most of their art is made up of geometric designs entwined with flowers, leaves, and stars.

Reading Check
Why are Arab **alchemists** considered the founders of modern chemistry?

Fun Facts....

Arabic Numerals
Europeans resisted the use of Arabic numerals well into the 1400s. An Italian bookkeeping manual insisted that Roman numerals "cannot be falsified as easily as those of the new art of computation, of which one can, with ease, make one out of another, such as turning the zero into a 6 or a 9."

Islamic Medical Diagram

Much of what is known about this time comes from Arabs who wrote down the history of Islam. They began to write about events centered around rulers and peoples. This is how most historians present history today. The Muslim historian Ibn Khaldun (ib' uhn kal dun') wrote about the Arabs, the Berbers, and the Persians. His writings were the first to take into account the influence of geography and climate on people.

Section 3 Assessment

1. **Define:** alchemists.
2. How did the use of the Arabic language promote learning?
3. What are two of the best-known Arab writings?

Critical Thinking

4. **Drawing Conclusions** Do you think the numerals 0 through 9 should be called Arabic or Gupta numerals? Explain.

Graphic Organizer Activity

5. Draw this diagram, and use it to show Arab contributions to science, math, and the arts.

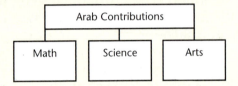

Chapter Summary & Study Guide

1. Muhammad was born in Makkah in 570.
2. In 613, Muhammad began to preach that the only god is Allah. This was the start of the Islamic religion.
3. In 622, Muhammad and his followers went from Makkah to Yathrib, where they organized a new government and army.
4. In 630, Muhammad led his followers into Makkah and dedicated the Ka'bah to Allah.
5. In 631, delegates throughout Arabia declared their loyalty to Muhammad and their belief in teachings such as the five pillars.
6. After Muhammad's death in 632, his followers chose a new leader, known as a caliph, and began building a huge empire.
7. In 661, the capital of the Arab Empire was moved to Damascus and the Umayyad Dynasty began.
8. In 750, the Abbasids took control of the Arab Empire and concentrated on trade rather than war.
9. The Moors in Spain combined Arab and Jewish cultures and allowed religious freedom.
10. The Arabs made many contributions to modern civilization, especially in science, math, and the arts.

Self-Check Quiz

Visit the *Human Heritage* Web site at **humanheritage. glencoe.com** and click on *Chapter 22—Self-Check Quiz* to assess your understanding of this chapter.

CHAPTER 22 Assessment

Using Key Terms

Imagine you are a traveler in the Arab Empire. Use the following words to write a journal entry describing your impressions of the empire.

pilgrims   pillars of faith   mosque
imam   *zakah*   *hajj*
caliph   vizier   alchemists

Understanding Main Ideas

1. How did Bedouins earn a living?
2. Why did Muhammad begin to spend time alone in a cave outside Makkah?
3. Why did Makkah's leaders persecute Muhammad and his followers?
4. What is the Islamic creed?
5. In what direction do Muslims face when they pray?
6. What does the Quran promise all believers who fulfill their duties?
7. What brought about the downfall of the Umayyad Dynasty?
8. What did the name "Arab" mean under the Abbasids?
9. What discoveries did Arab doctors make?

Critical Thinking

1. What role did religion play in Arab life?
2. How did the Moorish kingdom in Spain show it had been influenced by different cultures?
3. Which Arab contribution do you think has most affected other civilizations? Explain your choice.
4. What parts of life in the Arab Empire would you have liked? What parts would you have disliked?

Graphic Organizer Activity

History Create a time line like the one shown, and use it to summarize the main events in Muhammad's life. (Dates have been provided to help you get started.)

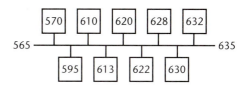

Geography in History

The World in Spatial Terms Islam spread across a wide area, as seen on the map on page 337. It included most of the area from the western edge of the Mediterranean Sea to the eastern shores of the Arabian Sea. What longitude and latitude lines mark the approximate location of this area?

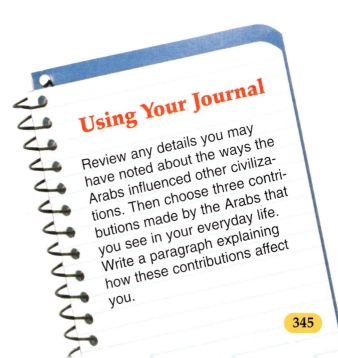

Using Your Journal

Review any details you may have noted about the ways the Arabs influenced other civilizations. Then choose three contributions made by the Arabs that you see in your everyday life. Write a paragraph explaining how these contributions affect you.

The Eastern Slavs

500 A.D.–1035 A.D.

▲ A Russian icon, the
archangel Michael

The spires of St. ▶
Basil's Cathedral,
Moscow

500 A.D.
Eastern Slavs settle
near the Volga River

988 A.D.
Kievan Rus adopts
Eastern Orthodoxy

1147 A.D.
Moscow is
founded

1240 A.D.
Mongols invade
eastern Europe

1552 A.D.
Ivan the Terrible
leads armies against
the Mongols

Chapter Focus

Read to Discover

- What life was like for the earliest Eastern Slavs.
- How early Rus states developed around Kiev.
- How Eastern Christianity influenced the people of Rus.
- What changes the Mongols brought about in Rus life.
- How Moscow became powerful.
- How the czars affected life in Muscovy.

Chapter Overview

Visit the *Human Heritage* Web site at **humanheritage.glencoe.com** and click on *Chapter 23— Chapter Overviews* to preview this chapter.

Terms to Learn
izbas
boyars
veche
khan
kremlin
czar

People to Know
Rurik
Vladimir I
Ivan the Great
Ivan the Terrible

Places to Locate
Volga River
Kiev
Dnieper River
Moscow

Why It's Important   North of the Byzantine Empire lived a people that historians today call Slavs. All that is known about their origins is that they were Indo-Europeans, like the Aryans who entered the Indus Valley and the Dorians who conquered the Mycenaeans. About 500 A.D., the Slavs began to develop well-organized settlements in eastern Europe in the areas now known as eastern Poland and western Ukraine.

SECTION 1   Early Eastern Slavs

About 500 A.D., a group of Eastern Slavs began to move eastward toward the Volga (vol' guh) River. They were hunters and farmers who were the ancestors of Ukrainians, Belarussians, and Russians. They settled in villages made up of about 25 related families. Each family owned a house that was built partly underground to provide warmth during the cold winter months. The land, animals, tools, and seed belonged to the village.

The oldest male governed the village with the help of a council. He assigned villagers different farming tasks and judged quarrels. During attacks, he acted as military leader.

By the 600s, the Eastern Slavs controlled all the land as far east as the Volga River. To clear this heavily forested land for farming, farmers used a method called *slash-and-burn*. They cut down trees, which they burned for fertilizer. On the cleared land, they planted crops such as barley, rye, and flax. After a few years, when the wood fertilizer in the soil had been used up, the farmers moved to a new place. There, they repeated the process.

The forests provided the East Slavs with all the timber they needed. The East Slavs soon became skilled in building with wood. They made musical instruments out of wood and used logs to make boats and *izbas* (uhz bahs'). An izba was a one-room log cabin with a gabled roof and wooden window frames. The whole family lived, worked, ate, and slept in the single room. Although each izba had a fireplace, some did not have a chimney. Smoke from fires had to escape through shutters that covered the windows.

The villagers worshiped many gods and honored nature, spirits, and ancestors. The most popular gods were Volos (vō' lōs), who protected cattle and sheep; Perun (pār' uhn), the god of thunder and lightning; and the Great Mother, the goddess of the land and harvest. The people built wooden images of their favorite gods on the highest ground outside the villages.

There were many slow-moving rivers in the area west of the Volga. At first, the East Slavs used them as roads between their villages. Before long, they began using them for trade as well. They set up a trade route that ran from the Baltic Sea in the north to the Caspian Sea in the south.

Reading Check
What did Eastern Slavic *izbas* look like?

Slavic Peoples Descendants of the West Slavs include the people of Poland, the Czech Republic, and Slovakia. Descendants of the South Slavs include Serbs, Croats, Slovenes, and Bosnians. Most West Slavs follow the Roman Catholic Church. South Slavs generally follow Eastern Orthodox Christianity, except for those Bosnians who follow Islam.

RUS CABIN   Houses in early Rus towns and villages were made of wood from the surrounding thick forests. Here, a modern Russian cabin is shown that is a good example of decorative styles passed on from early Rus artisans. **What was the inside of an izba, or Rus log cabin, like?**

By the end of the 800s, the East Slavs had built many trading towns along the riverbanks. During the five months of winter, merchants who lived in the towns gathered furs, honey, and other forest products from the people in neighboring villages. In spring, when the ice on the rivers had melted, the merchants loaded their goods on boats and floated south to Byzantium. There, they traded their goods for cloth, wine, weapons, and jewelry. Trade helped the East Slavs to live more comfortably and to develop their civilization.

Drawing of Rus Sled

The Eastern Slavs, to protect their trade route, relied on Viking warriors from Scandinavia. These men were known as Varangians, and the route was called the Varangian Route or the route from the Varangians to the Greeks. Eventually, the Varangians became part of the larger Slav population.

Section 1 Assessment

1. **Define:** *izbas.*
2. How were early Eastern Slavic villages governed?
3. Why were rivers important to the Eastern Slavs?

Critical Thinking

4. **Making Inferences** Why do you think the Eastern Slavs chose the Vikings to protect their trade routes?

Graphic Organizer Activity

5. Draw this diagram, and use it to show details about early Eastern Slavic life.

Eastern Slavic Life

SECTION 2 Kievan Rus

In 862, a Varangian named Rurik became the prince of Novgorod (nahv′ guh rahd), a northern town on the East Slav trading route. About 20 years later, Rurik's Varangian friend Oleg (ō′ leg) established the state of Kievan Rus. The term "Rus" meant "warrior band." He set up his capital at Kiev (kē ev′).

Kiev stood on a group of hills overlooking the main bend in the Dnieper (nē′ puhr) River. It was the southernmost town on the Varangian trading route. Whoever ruled Kiev controlled trade with Byzantium. Kiev also lay close to where the Ukraine forest turned into a *steppe* (step), or grassland. For hundreds of years, this steppe had served central Asian warriors as a highway into Europe. Because of this, Kiev was in a good location to protect merchant ships from attack.

The Kievan Rus state that Oleg established was really a group of small territories. The main ruler was the Grand Prince of Kiev. He was helped by local princes, rich merchants, and

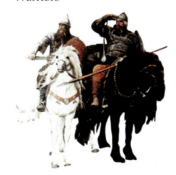
Painting of Eastern Slav Warriors

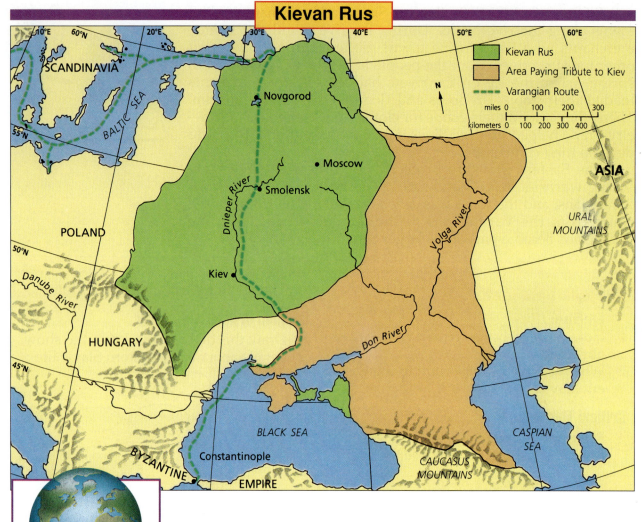

Kievan Rus

Legend:
- Kievan Rus
- Area Paying Tribute to Kiev
- Varangian Route

miles 0 100 200 300
kilometers 0 100 200 300 400

Places labeled: SCANDINAVIA, Novgorod, Moscow, Smolensk, POLAND, Kiev, HUNGARY, Constantinople, BYZANTINE EMPIRE, BLACK SEA, CASPIAN SEA, CAUCASUS MOUNTAINS, ASIA, URAL MOUNTAINS, BALTIC SEA, Dnieper River, Volga River, Don River, Danube River

MAP STUDY

PLACES AND REGIONS Along what bodies of water did the Varangian Route extend?

Reading Check
Who were the **boyars?**
What daily matters were handled by the *veche?*

boyars (bō yahrs′), or landowning nobles. The Grand Prince collected tribute from the local princes who in turn collected it from the people in their territories.

A *veche* (ve′ chuh), or assembly, handled the daily matters of the towns. It did everything from settling business differences to accepting or removing a prince. Any free man could call a meeting of the veche by ringing the town bell.

Vladimir I and the Eastern Orthodox Church
One of the most important princes of Kiev was Vladimir I (vlad′ uh mēr), a good soldier and a strong ruler. He spent the early years of his reign expanding Kievan Rus territory. His armies pushed the country's borders west into Poland and north along the stormy Baltic coast.

In 988, Vladimir chose Eastern, or Byzantine, Christianity as the country's official religion. The story is told about Vladimir's long search for a new faith that would unite the people. Vladimir sent a number of people to other countries to observe different religions. Those sent were not impressed with what they saw in Islamic, Jewish, or Roman Catholic worship. Then, in Byzantium's Hagia Sophia, they saw Eastern Orthodox worship. They were stunned by its beauty. When they returned to Kievan Rus, Vladimir accepted Eastern Orthodoxy as the official religion.

The Eastern Orthodox Church brought Byzantine culture to Kievan Rus. Priests from Byzantium taught the people religious rituals and the art of painting icons. They learned to write their language in the Cyrillic alphabet. Sons of boyars and priests were sent to newly built schools. The look of Kievan Rus towns changed as stone churches with domes and arches rose among the wooden buildings. Monasteries appeared.

Eastern Orthodoxy gave the Kievan Rus people a sense of belonging to the civilized world. However, it separated them

RELIGIOUS LIFE   Eastern Orthodoxy inspired art and architecture in Kievan Rus. These later Russian icons (left) closely resembled Byzantine examples. Stone churches with ornate, tiled domes (right) were built in Rus towns. **How did Eastern Orthodoxy separate Kievan Rus from the culture of western Europe?**

Fur-lined Crown

from western Europe. Since Kievan scholars had books in their own language, they had developed their own body of learning separate from that of the West.

Yaroslav the Wise

Another important ruler of early Rus was Yaroslav (yuh ruh slahf'), son of Vladimir I. Yaroslav became the Grand Prince of Kiev in 1019, after a long struggle with his brothers. Yaroslav was very interested in learning. He invited scholars from Byzantium to live in Kiev, and he was called Yaroslav the Wise.

Yaroslav encouraged artisans to practice their skills. The artisans built magnificent brick churches covered with white plaster and decorated with gold. Artists covered the walls of Yaroslav's palace in Kiev with scenes of music and hunting.

Under Yaroslav's rule, Kievan Rus enjoyed a golden age of peace and prosperity. Kiev grew until the city was larger than either Paris or London. Yaroslav developed closer ties with western Europe by family marriages.

Yaroslav also organized Kievan Rus laws based on old Slavic customs and Byzantine law. Under Yaroslav's code, crimes against property were thought to be more serious than those against people. There was no death penalty. In fact, criminals usually were not punished physically but had to pay a fine.

Decline of Kievan Rus

Kievan Rus began to decline around 1054. After Yaroslav's death, the princes of Kiev began to fight over the throne. People from the steppe took advantage of this fighting and attacked Kievan Rus's frontiers. This upset the trade flow which meant the loss of Kiev's major source of wealth. Kievan Rus became more isolated. In 1169 Kiev was attacked and plundered by Andrei Bogoliubsky, who wanted Kiev destroyed. The area never recovered.

Gradually, Kievan Rus changed from a trading land of towns into a farming land of peasants. To escape the invaders from the steppe, many of its people fled to the north and settled in the dense forests along the upper Volga.

Then... & Now

Pravda The Russian word *pravda* means "truth," but during Yaroslav's reign it also meant "justice." The Kievan legal system that Yaroslav organized was called *Russkaya Pravda*. In modern times, the word became familiar to the West as the name of a Moscow newspaper.

Section 2 Assessment

1. **Define:** boyars, *veche*.
2. Why was Kiev a good location to build a city?
3. How did the decline of Kiev affect the area and people?

Critical Thinking

4. **Demonstrating Reasoned Judgment** How would you have felt about Yaroslav's code of laws and his ways to punish criminals? Explain.

Graphic Organizer Activity

5. Draw this diagram, and use it to show the causes and effects of Vladimir I's acceptance of Eastern Orthodoxy as the official religion of Kievan Rus.

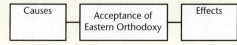

Causes	Acceptance of Eastern Orthodoxy	Effects

The Mongol Conquest

About 1240, a group of different but united tribes known as Mongols (mon' guhls) swept out of central Asia and took control of Rus principalities, or states. They destroyed villages and towns and killed many people. They made the Rus people pay tribute to the **khan** (kahn), or Mongol leader. They also made the Rus citizens serve in the Mongol armies.

The Church   The Eastern Orthodox Church remained strong during the Mongol invasion. Priests continued to preach and to write. They encouraged the people to love their land and their religion.

During this time, monks began to found monasteries deep in the northern forests. They were followed by Rus farmers searching for new land. Soon, towns and villages began to grow up around the monasteries. Although the Mongol rule caused Rus people to cling more to their religion, it also made them distrustful of ideas and practices from other countries.

Reading Check
What duties did the Rus people have to perform for the **khan**?

Fun Facts....

A Lone Cathedral Mongol invaders completely destroyed Kiev. The only building left standing was the cathedral of Saint Sophia, which contains the tomb of Yaroslav.

Linking Across Time

Easter Eggs   The Eastern Orthodoxy practiced by the Rus people included elements of early Eastern Slavic religions. Painted clay eggs (below) associated with springtime became the models for the eggs associated with the Christian festival of Easter. In the late 1800s and early 1900s, Russian goldsmith Carl Faberge elevated these eggs into what are now priceless works of art (right) housed in museums around the world. **How did the Mongol conquest strengthen the Rus Church?**

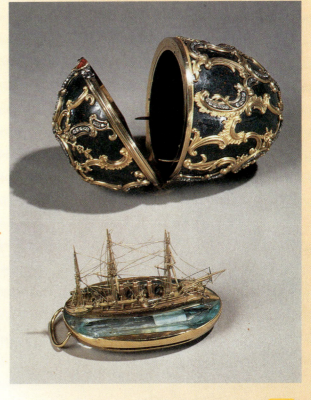

Church Vestment

The Mongol conquest somewhat isolated the Rus Church from other Christian churches. Because of this, the Church developed local rituals and practices. This united the people and made them proud of their own culture.

Daily Life   Even under Mongol rule, differences between the lives of the rich in Rus and the lives of peasants remained. The wealthy sometimes entertained guests with feasts of deer and wild pig. Peasants, on the other hand, rarely ate meat. Instead, they ate dark rye bread, cabbage, salted fish, and mushrooms.

The few pleasures the peasants had came from visiting one another. They told stories that praised the brave deeds of their warriors and other heroes. The stories were passed from old to young and became part of the Rus heritage.

Common dress for peasant men was white tunics, wide linen trousers, and heavy shoes woven from long strips of tree bark. They tied rags around their legs and feet instead of stockings to keep out the cold. Rich merchants and boyars wore tall fur hats and *caftans* (kaf' tanz), or long robes tied at the waist with a sash.

Rus women of all classes wore blouses or smocks, skirts, and long shawls. On holidays, they added headdresses with decorations that indicated the region from which a woman came and if she was married.

Section 3 Assessment

1. **Define:** khan.
2. Where did the Mongols come from?
3. What did the Mongols do to the Rus people when they invaded Rus lands?

Critical Thinking

4. **Predicting Consequences**   How might life have been different in the Rus states if the Mongols had not conquered these lands?

Graphic Organizer Activity

5. Draw this diagram, and use it to compare the lives of the rich and the lives of the peasants in Rus during Mongol rule.

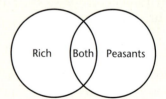

Rich — Both — Peasants

SECTION 4   The Rise of Moscow

Reading Check
What was the **kremlin**?

At the time of the Mongol conquest, Moscow (mos' kō), or Muscovy, founded in 1147, was a small trading post on the road from Kiev to the forests in the north. As more Rus people moved north to escape the Mongols, many artisans settled in or near Moscow's **kremlin** (krem' luhn), or fortress.

The princes of Moscow were bold and ambitious. They learned to cooperate with the Mongols and even recruited Muscovy soldiers for the Mongol army. In return, the Mongols gave the princes of Moscow the power to collect taxes throughout the country. If a Rus territory could not provide soldiers or tax money for the Mongols, Moscow's princes took it over. In this way, Moscow, the principality of Muscovy, began to expand.

As Moscow grew in size, it became stronger. The princes passed their thrones from father to son. Thus, there was no fighting over who the next ruler would be, and the people remained united.

The Muscovite metropolitan lived in Moscow. This created a second center for the Eastern Orthodox Church outside of Kiev. The metropolitan blessed the princes for their efforts to make Moscow a great city. The people obeyed the prince as a ruler chosen and protected by God.

Meanwhile, Mongol chiefs started fighting among themselves. As a result, they grew weaker, while Moscow grew stronger. In 1380, an army formed by Dmitry (duh mē' trē), the prince of Moscow, attacked and defeated the Mongols. The Mongols still remained powerful but no longer were feared or obeyed as they had been in the past.

Ivan the Great   In 1462, Ivan III (ī' vuhn), known as Ivan the Great, became prince of Moscow. In 1480, he ended Mongol control of Muscovy. He also expanded its boundaries to the north and west.

A few years before Mongol rule ended, Ivan married Sophia, a niece of the last Byzantine emperor. The Muscovite people felt this marriage gave Ivan all the glory of past Byzantine emperors. The Church believed it meant that Moscow had taken Byzantium's place as the center of Christianity.

Ivan began living in the style of the Byzantine emperors. He used the two-headed eagle of Byzantium on his royal seal. He brought Italian architects to Moscow to build fine palaces and large cathedrals in the kremlin. He raised the huge walls that still guard the kremlin. He called himself **czar** (zahr), or emperor. This later became the official title of the emperor.

Ivan died in 1505. By then, the people were convinced that their ruler should have full and unquestioned power over both Church and state.

Ivan the Terrible   In 1533, Ivan IV, the three-year-old grandson of Ivan III, became czar of Muscovy. He was not crowned until 1547, however. While he was growing up, a council of boyars governed the country for him. The boyars, however, wanted more power. To frighten Ivan into obeying

Painting of Ivan the Great

Reading Check What did the official title of **czar** mean?

MAP SKILLS

Analyzing Historical Maps

Some maps show how a certain country expanded and changed its boundaries over time. Maps that show boundary changes are called **historical maps**.

The map of "The Growth of Moscow" below shows the changes in Moscow's borders from 1300 to 1584. The color used to shade a certain area shows when that land became part of Moscow. It also shows the exact location of the land that was added. For example, green is the color used to show the land acquired by the time of Ivan IV's death. The shading on the map indicates that this land extended to the Caspian Sea in the southeast and to the Black Sea in the southwest.

Map Practice

1. **By what year did Moscow include part of the Don River?**
2. **By what year had Moscow acquired territory bordering on the Arctic Ocean?**
3. **Under which czar did Moscow control the largest amount of territory?**

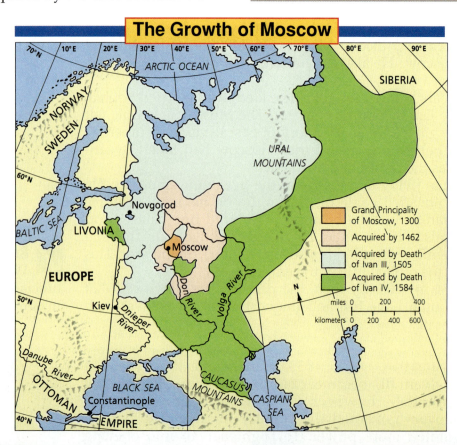

The Growth of Moscow

Legend:
- Grand Principality of Moscow, 1300
- Acquired by 1462
- Acquired by Death of Ivan III, 1505
- Acquired by Death of Ivan IV, 1584

miles 0 200 400
kilometers 0 200 400 600

them, they began to mistreat him. Ivan came to hate the boyars. He did, however, adopt their cruel habits. By the time he was a teenager, he was killing people just for going against his wishes.

When Ivan IV was 16 years old, he was crowned czar and began to rule in his own right. He ignored the boyars and turned to merchants and close friends for advice. He gave his advisers gifts of land and jobs as officials. To make sure that the officials' country estates were farmed while the officials themselves were in Moscow with him, Ivan ordered peasants not to leave their land. In this way, he took the first step in turning free peasants into serfs.

In 1552, Ivan led his armies against Mongol territories on the Volga. By this time, the Muscovites had learned the use of gunpowder from western Europe. The Mongols, however, still depended on bows and arrows. Within six years, Ivan conquered most of the Mongol territories. Muscovite settlers began to move east. Some, called Cossacks (kos' aks), began to farm along the Volga.

In 1558, Muscovite armies attacked Livonia (luh vō' nē uh), a land on the Baltic Sea. Livonia's neighbors sent troops to fight the Muscovite armies. In 1562, these troops defeated the Muscovite soldiers and took over much of their Baltic territory. Ivan blamed the boyars for his terrible defeat.

In 1564, Ivan suddenly left Moscow and went to live in a small monastery in the country. A month later, he announced that he was giving up the throne because of the boyars. Afraid that without Ivan the empire would fall, the people begged him to change his mind. They told Ivan that if he came back, he could have full authority to punish traitors and to take over their lands.

Ivan returned to Moscow, took over boyar lands, and gave the land to 5,000 of his most loyal supporters. In return, they formed the *Oprichnina* (ah prich' nē nuh), or secret police or soldiers of terror. Members of the Oprichnina dressed in black and rode black horses through the countryside. They scared the czar's enemies and carried brooms to show their desire to sweep treason from the land. They killed thousands of people. Finally, when the Oprichnina had defeated the boyars and returned control of the empire to Ivan, he broke up the group.

Ivan came to be called Ivan the Terrible. This is because the English translated the word meaning "awesome" as "terrible." To the Muscovites, however, Ivan was a great ruler who protected their country from enemies.

Ivan encouraged art and learning. He brought artists, scholars, and engineers from western Europe to teach the Muscovites new skills. He established a link between Moscow and England and Holland. He also increased the czar's power.

Painting of Ivan the Terrible

People in History

Ivan the Terrible
1530–1584

Russian Czar

Ivan was the first Russian ruler to be officially crowned as czar. He built a strong central government and was the first ruler to ever call a national assembly. He began Russian expansion eastward, conquering Siberia, and he began trade with England. His undoing was his fearful temper, which fell on enemies and friends alike.

When he died in 1584, however, Ivan left no suitable heir. He had killed the oldest of his three sons in a fit of rage. His middle son was feeble-minded, and his youngest son was still a baby. As a result, for some 25 years after Ivan's death, Muscovy was in confusion and disorder.

Section 4 Assessment

1. **Define:** kremlin, czar.
2. Why did Moscow become powerful?
3. What happened to Muscovy after Ivan the Terrible's death?

Critical Thinking

4. **Drawing Conclusions**   Which name do you think most accurately describes Ivan IV—Ivan the Awesome or Ivan the Terrible? Explain.

Graphic Organizer Activity

5. Draw this chart, and use it to compare the accomplishments of Dmitry, Ivan the Great, and Ivan the Terrible.

Dmitry	Ivan the Great	Ivan the Terrible

Chapter Summary & Study Guide

1. Between 500 and 800 A.D., groups of Eastern Slavs settled in lands west of the Volga River.
2. The early Eastern Slavs relied on Viking warriors known as the Varangians to protect a trade route running from the Baltic Sea in the north to the Caspian Sea in the south.
3. In 882, a Viking warrior named Oleg built the first Kievan Rus state.
4. In 988, Eastern Orthodoxy became the official religion of Kievan Rus.
5. The Eastern Orthodox Church brought Byzantine culture, including the Cyrillic alphabet, to Kievan Rus.
6. After 1054, Rus trade declined and people shifted to farming.
7. Around 1240, the Mongols conquered Rus, forcing many Rus people to flee. Many settled near Moscow in the north.
8. Moscow gradually became the center of economic and religious life.
9. In the late 1400s, Ivan the Great ended Mongol control of Muscovy and took the title of czar.
10. Beginning in 1552, Ivan the Terrible conquered most of the Mongol territories, and many Muscovites began moving eastward.
11. In 1584, Ivan the Terrible died without leaving a capable heir. Muscovy then entered a 25-year period of disorder.

HISTORY *Online*

Self-Check Quiz

Visit the *Human Heritage* Web site at **humanheritage. glencoe.com** and click on *Chapter 23—Self-Check Quiz* to assess your understanding of this chapter.

Using Key Terms

Imagine what a photograph illustrating each of the following words might look like. Write a sentence describing each picture, using the vocabulary word.

izbas   boyars   *veche*
khan   kremlin   czar

Understanding Main Ideas

1. How did the houses of the Eastern Slavs provide warmth?
2. Why did the early Eastern Slavs invite the Vikings into their lands?
3. How was the Rus state established by Oleg organized?
4. Why did Vladimir choose the Eastern Orthodox Church as the official church of the state?
5. How did Yaroslav develop closer ties with western Europe?
6. How did the Muscovites view the princes of Moscow?
7. What did Ivan III do for Muscovy?
8. Why did many Muscovites think Ivan the Terrible was a great ruler?
9. Between what European countries and Moscow did Ivan IV develop a link?

Critical Thinking

1. Why do you think trade with other cities is one of the first activities of successful cities such as Kiev?
2. What are the advantages and disadvantages of passing power from father to son, such as the czars did?
3. Do you think the word "terrible" describes Ivan IV? What other word or term might describe him better?

Graphic Organizer Activity

History Create a diagram like this one, and use it to summarize reasons for the rise and decline of Kievan Rus.

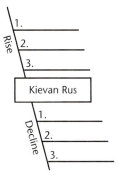

Rise
1.
2.
3.

Kievan Rus

Decline
1.
2.
3.

Geography in History

Human Systems Refer to the map on page 356. Imagine the czar has asked you to choose the location of a new settlement in the area acquired by the death of Ivan IV. Where would you locate the settlement and why? What geographic features affected your decision?

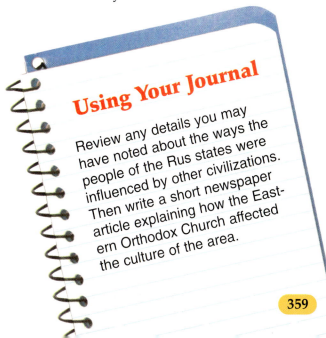

Using Your Journal

Review any details you may have noted about the ways the people of the Rus states were influenced by other civilizations. Then write a short newspaper article explaining how the Eastern Orthodox Church affected the culture of the area.

THE ANASAZI

The Anasazi (a' na sa' zē) built one of the most advanced cultures in North America outside of Mexico. From roughly 200 A.D. to 1300 A.D., they established thousands of settlements throughout the present-day southwestern United States. A network of trails and roads—some more than 30 feet wide—connected many of these settlements. Artifacts found at Anasazi sites show that these people traded far and wide, including with the ancient civilizations of Mexico and Central America. Today many Native Americans who live in this region, such as the Pueblo (pweb' lō), trace their roots to the Anasazi.

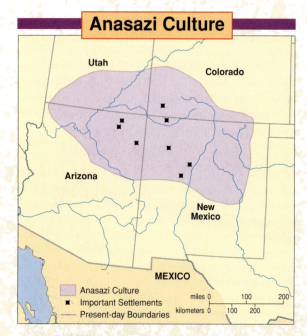

Anasazi Culture

Utah

Colorado

Arizona

New Mexico

MEXICO

Anasazi Culture
■ Important Settlements
— Present-day Boundaries

miles 0   100   200
kilometers 0   100   200

▲ The Anasazi lived in the area known as the Four Corners—the meeting place of the present-day states of Utah, Colorado, Arizona, and New Mexico. Like other desert cultures, they learned to farm the land by digging irrigation ditches to catch the rain and to channel water from rivers.

▲ The Anasazi never developed a written language. However, archaeologists think they may have left messages in the form of pictures painted or scratched into rocks throughout the Four Corners area. The meanings of many of these pictures remain unknown to this day.

the W🌐rld

▼ The Anasazi used turquoise as a trade item. At Chaco (cha'kō) Canyon, New Mexico, over 500,000 pieces of turquoise have been found. The Anasazi fashioned turquoise into beads for necklaces or used it to decorate everyday objects.

Nearly all Anasazi villages included large circular underground chambers known as *kivas* (kē'vas). Scholars believe that the Anasazi used the kivas as religious centers and as clubhouses. They also believe that the kivas were restricted to men, with women entering the kivas only on special occasions. ▼

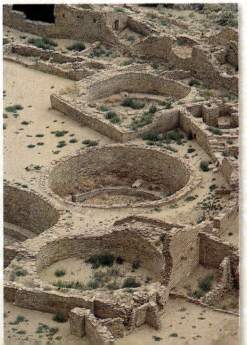

The Anasazi moved into the cliffs and canyons of the Southwest and built houses made of mud bricks. Perhaps 1,000 people lived in what is known as the Cliff Palace. Located in Mesa Verde, Colorado, the Cliff Palace had about 200 rooms and looked something like a modern apartment complex. When Spanish explorers first saw these houses, they called them *pueblos*—the Spanish word for "villages." ▼

Taking Another Look

1. What was the purpose of the kivas?

2. What were the main economic activities of the Anasazi?

Hands-on Activity

Designing a Postcard Design a postcard that you might send from the Four Corners area that shows a picture of an Anasazi artifact. On the back, include a description of your experiences.

Standardized Test Practice

Directions: Choose the *best* answer to each of the following multiple choice questions. If you have trouble answering a question, use the process of elimination to narrow your choices. Write your answers on a separate piece of paper.

1. **How was Justinian's wife, Theodora, different from the wives of previous emperors?**

   A She bore a male heir to the emperor's throne.

   B She was the first female to serve as emperor.

   C She fought as a member of the army to defend her husband.

   D She played a large role in shaping law and public policy.

   Test-Taking Tip: Eliminate answers that do not make sense. Since it is unlikely that Theodora was the first emperor's wife to give birth to a son (answer A), you can easily eliminate this answer choice.

2. **The Eastern Orthodox Church split from the Roman Catholic Church because of a disagreement over**

   F the content of the Old and New Testaments

   G what kinds of work missionaries should perform

   H who the leader of the Christian church should be

   J the role of women in the church

   Test-Taking Tip: This question requires you to remember a *fact* about the Eastern Orthodox Church. Make sure that you read the question and *all* of the answer choices carefully before selecting the *best* answer.

3. **In which of the following ways were Muhammad and Jesus similar?**

   A Both were born in Palestine.

   B Both were seen as threats to the existing governments.

   C Both stopped gaining followers after their deaths.

   D Both required their followers to accept the power of the Pope.

   Test-Taking Tip: This question asks you to make a *comparison* between these two leaders. Since Islam and Christianity are still gaining followers today, answer C is an unlikely choice.

4. **Like the Catholic Church, the Muslims split into two groups. How were the Sunni different from the Shiites?**

   F They believed that Islamic rulers did not have to be descendents of Ali.

   G They wanted the religious center of Islam to be Constantinople.

   H They were opposed to the use of religious icons as a part of ceremonies.

   J They wanted to recognize the Pope as their religious leader.

   Test-Taking Tip: This question also asks you to make a comparison, but this time it asks for a *difference* rather than a *similarity.* Be careful: even though the question mentions the split in the Catholic Church, it is *not* asking for a comparison between Catholicism and Islam. Therefore, you can eliminate any answers that have to do with the Catholic Church, like answer J.

The Growth of Moscow

Grand Principality
of Moscow, 1300

Acquired by 1462

Acquired by Death
of Ivan III, 1505

Acquired by Death
of Ivan IV, 1584

5. **Based on the map above, what important contribution to Moscow's potential for trade was made by the time of Ivan IV's death?**

   A Moscow gained access to the Ottoman Empire through the Volga and Don rivers.

   B Moscow gained access to trade routes to Norway and Sweden through the Baltic Sea.

   C Moscow gained access to western Europe through the Danube River.

   D Moscow gained control of land reaching to the Arctic Ocean.

   Test-Taking Tip: Use the *map key*, or *legend*, to help you understand how the map is organized. Make sure that your answer is supported by information on the map.

6. **The distance between Moscow and Novgorod is approximately**

   F 200 kilometers

   G 400 kilometers

   H 600 kilometers

   J 700 kilometers

   Test-Taking Tip: The map's *scale* will help you answer this question. If you do not have a ruler, you can copy the scale onto a small piece of paper to measure the distance. Notice that the answer choices are given in *kilometers,* not miles. The scale shows both: miles on the top, and kilometers below.

STOP

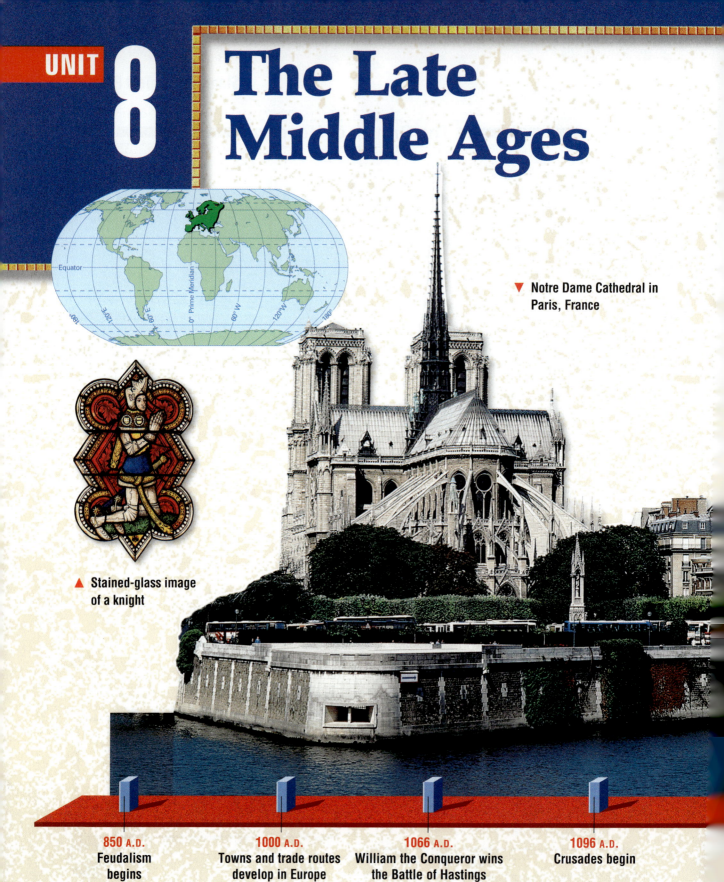

8 The Late Middle Ages

▼ Notre Dame Cathedral in Paris, France

▲ Stained-glass image of a knight

850 A.D.
Feudalism begins

1000 A.D.
Towns and trade routes develop in Europe

1066 A.D.
William the Conqueror wins the Battle of Hastings

1096 A.D.
Crusades begin

Organizing Information Study Foldable *Make the following foldable to help you organize information about the changes that occurred during the late Middle Ages.*

Step 1 *Fold two sheets of paper in half from top to bottom.*

Fold both sheets to leave $\frac{1}{2}$ inch tab on top.

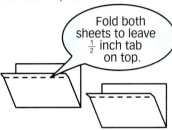

Step 2 *Place glue or tape along both ½ inch tabs.*

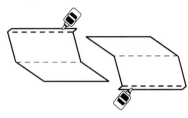

Reading and Writing *As you read the unit, list the developments that occurred in western Europe during the late Middle Ages. Write the developments under the correct foldable category.*

Step 3 *Fit both sheets of paper together to make a cube as shown.*

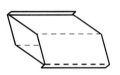

Step 4 *Turn the cube and label the foldable as shown.*

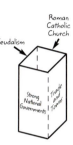

Roman Catholic Church

Feudalism

Strong National Governments

Trade and Towns

PRIMARY SOURCES

Library

See pages 688–689 for other primary source readings to accompany Unit 8.

 Read "Plan for a Crusade" from the **World History Primary Source Document Library CD-ROM.**

Journal Notes

What was life like during the late Middle Ages? Note details about it as you read.

1152 A.D.
Frederick I becomes Holy Roman Emperor

1215 A.D.
Magna Carta is signed

1337 A.D.
Hundred Years' War begins

Feudal Society
700 A.D.–1200 A.D.

A drinking vessel used by peasants ▶

◀ Peasant woman carrying sack of wheat

814 A.D.
Charlemagne dies

900 A.D.
Nobles defend themselves against the Vikings

1000 A.D.
Western Europe is divided into feudal territories

1100s A.D.
Most nobles live in stone castles

Chapter Focus

 Read to Discover

- Why feudalism developed in western Europe.
- What roles were played by lords and vassals.
- What the duties of a knight were.
- What life was like on a manor.

 Terms to Learn

feudalism	castles	tournaments
clergy	keep	joust
fiefs	ladies	manors
vassal	code of chivalry	seneschal
act of homage	page	bailiff
knight	squire	freemen
	dubbing	

Why It's Important Central government collapsed after the death of King Charlemagne. As the Vikings invaded western European kingdoms, local nobles took over the duty of raising armies and protecting their property. Power passed from kings to local lords, giving rise to a system known as **feudalism** (fyoo' dul ih zum). Under feudalism, landowning nobles governed and protected the people in exchange for services, such as fighting in a noble's army or farming the land.

The **clergy,** or religious leaders, also owned land and held power. Members of the clergy taught Christianity, helped the poor and sick, and advised the nobles who belonged to the Church. With western Europe divided into thousands of feudal territories, the Church served as a unifying force and exerted a strong influence over the culture of the Middle Ages.

 **Chapter Overview**

Visit the *Human Heritage* Web site at **humanheritage.glencoe.com** and click on *Chapter 24— Chapter Overviews* to preview this chapter.

 **Reading Check**
What was **feudalism?**

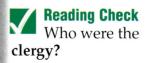 **Reading Check**
Who were the **clergy?**

SECTION 1 Land and Government

During feudal times, power was based on the ownership of land. Before feudalism, kings owned all the land within their territories. Then Charles Martel, the Frankish leader, began giving his soldiers **fiefs** (fēfs), or estates, as a reward for their service and loyalty. From their fiefs, the soldiers got the income they needed to buy horses and battle equipment. After 800, the kings of Europe followed Martel's example. From that time on, land ownership was tied to military service. With land ownership went power and wealth, giving soldiers a base from which to rule Europe.

Reading Check
Why did soldiers receive **fiefs** during the Middle Ages?

The Rise of Feudal Territories

After Charlemagne's death in 814, Europe had no central government. The kings who followed Charlemagne were so weak they could not even rule their own kingdoms well. They ignored their responsibilities and spent most of their time traveling from one royal estate to another. Before long, they began to depend on the nobles for food, horses, and soldiers. Some nobles grew more powerful than the king and became independent rulers. They gained the right to collect taxes and to enforce the law in their areas. Many nobles raised armies and coined their own money.

Around 900, the nobles took on the duty of protecting their lands and people from the Vikings. They built fortresses on hilltops and fenced their lands. The peasants asked these powerful nobles to protect them. In return, the peasants gave their lands to nobles and promised to work for them in the fields. However, most peasants ended up giving the nobles not only their land but also their freedom.

By 1000, the kingdoms of western Europe were divided into thousands of feudal territories. Each was about the size of an ancient Greek city-state. Unlike the polis, however, a feudal territory had no central city. The noble who owned the land also had the political power. He made the laws for his fief, and the people obeyed them. Peasants, unlike Greek citizens, had no say in the government.

Although the peasants and townspeople made up the largest group, they had fewer rights than the clergy and nobles. Almost everyone believed that God wanted it that way. As a result, few people tried to improve society or change their own way of life. Most people remained in the group into which they were born.

Lord and Vassal

Feudalism was based on ties of loyalty and duty among nobles. Nobles were both lords and vassals. A **vassal** (vas' uhl) was a noble who served a lord of higher rank and gave him loyalty. In return, the lord protected the vassal. All nobles were ultimately vassals of the king, who might even be the vassal of another king.

The tie between lord and vassal was made official in a special ceremony known as the **act of homage** (om' ij). The vassal, his head bare to show respect, knelt on one knee and placed his hands between those of the lord. He promised to serve the lord and to help him in battle. The lord accepted the promise, helped the vassal to his feet, and kissed him.

In return for the promise of loyalty and service, the lord gave his vassal a fief. Since there were few written agreements in the Middle Ages, the lord gave his vassal a glove, a stick, or a stone. This was to show that the lord's word could be trusted. He also gave the vassal the right to govern the people who lived on the

✔ Reading Check
What were the duties of a **vassal**? What took place during an **act of homage**?

fief. The lord promised to protect his vassal from enemy attacks. If the lord failed in this, the vassal no longer owed him loyalty.

Vassals had certain duties to perform. Their most important duty was to help the lord in battle. Vassals had to bring their own knights with them. They themselves were expected to take part in military service 40 to 60 days a year.

Vassals had to make payments to their lord. When a lord's daughter married, or his son became a **knight,** or a warrior on horseback, his vassals had to give the lord money. If a lord were captured in battle, his vassals either became prisoners in his place or paid his *ransom.* This is a sum of money given in exchange for a person's release.

Another duty of vassals was to attend the lord's court. Vassals were also expected to provide food and entertainment when their lord visited them. If a vassal failed in his duties to his lord, the lord had the right to take away the vassal's fief. When a vassal died, his fief usually passed on to his oldest son. The son then performed the act of homage.

Reading Check
What was a **knight?**

Section 1 Assessment

1. **Define:** feudalism, clergy, fiefs, vassal, act of homage, knight.
2. How did land ownership become tied to military service?
3. How did nobles become so powerful?
4. What were some duties of a vassal?

Critical Thinking

5. **Demonstrating Reasoned Judgment** What were the advantages of being a vassal? What were the disadvantages?

Graphic Organizer Activity

6. Draw this diagram, and use it to show some of the causes of feudalism.

SECTION 2 The Nobility

Life was not always easy or pleasant for nobles during feudal times. They did, however, enjoy more benefits than the common people.

From the 800s to the 1000s, nobles and their families lived in wooden houses surrounded by *palisades* (pal uh sāds'), or high wooden fences built for protection. In case of attack, people from nearby villages sought shelter inside the palisade.

The house consisted of one room with a high ceiling and a straw-covered floor. All activity took place in that one room. There, nobles met with vassals, carried out the laws, and said their prayers. The nobles, their families, servants, and warriors

NOBLE'S FEAST   Nobles celebrated special occasions with elaborate feasts. Such meals often included many courses of meats, fruits, and vegetables. In this painting a noble sits down to dinner while his many servants bring out more food. **Where were meals for nobles held?**

also ate and slept in that room. At mealtime, wooden tables were set up and piled high with meat, fish, vegetables, fruits, and honey. People ate with their fingers and threw scraps of food on the floor for the dogs. The straw got so dirty with mud, bones, and food that every few months it had to be swept outdoors and burned.

The fires that cooked the meals were also used to heat the house. Actually, the fires did little to keep out the cold. Smoke from them often stung the eyes and darkened the walls and ceiling.

Reading Check
What did **castles** look like?

The Castle   By the 1100s, nobles were living in stone houses called **castles.** Because they were designed as fortresses, the castles made nobles secure and independent. Castles had thick stone walls, one within another. Each corner had its own lookout tower with archers in it. Some castles were further protected by a moat with a soft and muddy bottom that stopped attackers from using ladders to climb over the outer walls. To cross the moat, a person had to use the castle's drawbridge, which could be raised to prevent entry. The drawbridge led to the *portcullis* (pōrt kul′ is), an iron gate that often served as the entrance to the castle.

Within the castle walls was a large open area. In the middle of this area was a **keep,** or tall tower with thick walls. It contained a great hall, many rooms, and a dungeon. The people of the household lived in the keep, which could be defended even if the rest of the castle fell to attackers. Shops, kitchens, stables, and rooms for troops and guests were also built inside the castle walls.

Many people, including the noble's servants and officials, lived in the castle. Since the noble was away fighting most of the time, the servants and officials were responsible for the castle's care and defense. Most castles had enough space to store a large supply of food and drink. As a result, people inside a castle could hold out against attackers for as long as six months.

✓ Reading Check
Why did the people of a household live inside the **keep?**

Student Web Activity
Visit the *Human Heritage* Web site at **humanheritage.glencoe.com** and click on ***Chapter 24—Student Web Activities*** to find out more about castles.

CASTLE   A castle was both a noble's home and a military fortress. During enemy attack, people from the surrounding area sought protection within the castle walls. Here, the moat and entrance of an English castle are shown. **Who was responsible for a castle's care and defense?**

Castle Life

When nobles were at home, they looked after their estates, went hunting and fishing, and held court. During long winter evenings, they often played chess with family members. Wandering minstrels sometimes came to entertain the nobles and their guests by singing songs and playing stringed instruments.

Noblewomen were called **ladies.** Once they married, their husbands had complete authority over them. Most marriages were planned to unite important families, and a woman had little say about who was chosen for her. The bride's family gave the groom a dowry. Most nobles looked for wives with large dowries. Women were often married by the time they were 12 years old. Those who were not married by the time they were 21 could expect to stay single for the rest of their lives.

Wives helped their husbands run their estates. When the men were away, the women had to defend the castle. The main duties of a wife, however, were to have and raise children and to

Linking Across Time

Chess After the game arrived in Europe from India about 1000 A.D., noble lords and ladies played chess (above) to pass the hours. In recent years, chess masters such as Russian expert Gary Kasparov (right) have matched their wits with chess-playing computers.
What other activities were popular in the Middle Ages?

take care of the household. She was also expected to train young girls from other castles in household duties and to supervise the making of cloth and fine embroidery. Another duty was to use her knowledge of plants and herbs to care for the poor and sick on her husband's fief.

Section 2 Assessment

1. **Define:** castles, keep, ladies.
2. What activities took place in the noble's house?
3. How did the design of a castle protect people?
4. What were the duties of a feudal noblewoman?

Critical Thinking

5. **Drawing Conclusions** What parts of castle life would you have liked? What parts would you have disliked?

Graphic Organizer Activity

6. Draw this diagram, and use it to compare the living conditions of nobles before and after the rise of castles.

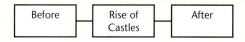

| Before | | Rise of Castles | | After |

SECTION 3 Knighthood

Almost all nobles were knights. However, knighthood had to be earned. Knights were expected to follow certain rules known as the **code of chivalry** (kōd of shiv' uhl rē). These rules stated that a knight was to obey his lord, show bravery, respect women of noble birth, honor the Church, and help people. A knight was also expected to be honest and to fight fairly against his enemies. The code of chivalry became the guide to behavior from which the western idea of good manners developed.

Training   A noble began training to be a knight when he was seven years old. He was sent away from his family to the castle of another lord. There, he learned to be a **page,** or a person who helped the knights of the castle care for their *destriers* (dā trē' uhrs), or war-horses. Pages also polished the knights' armor, some of which weighed up to 80 pounds, or 36 kilograms.

A page learned good manners and ran errands for the ladies. He was taught to ride and fight. By the age of 14, he could handle a lance and sword while on horseback.

When he was 15 years old, a page became a **squire.** Each squire was put under the care and training of one knight. The squire's duty was to go into battle with his knight. He was expected to rescue the knight if he was wounded or fell off his horse.

If the squire proved to be a good fighter, he was rewarded by being made a knight. This was done in a special ceremony

Reading Check
What was the **code of chivalry?**

Reading Check
What did a **page** hope to become?

Reading Check
What were the duties of a **squire?**

MEDIEVAL TOURNAMENT   In this painting knights on horseback joust during a tournament while other knights fight hand to hand. **Why were medieval tournaments costly events?**

> ### Reading Check
> What took place during the ceremony known as **dubbing?**

known as **dubbing.** The squire knelt before his lord with his sword suspended from his neck. He then promised to defend the Church and his lord, and to protect the weak. Then, the lord tapped the squire on his shoulder with the blade of a sword and pronounced him a knight. The knight's sword was placed in a *scabbard,* or sword holder, at the knight's side. This showed that the knight would fight by the side of his lord.

> ### Reading Check
> What was the purpose of medieval **tournaments?**

> ### Reading Check
> What was the event known as the **joust?**

Tournaments   Knights trained for war by fighting each other in **tournaments,** or special contests that tested strength, skill, and endurance. Tournaments were held in large fields. They were exciting gatherings that brought in lords, ladies, and knights who watched the events from stands. The most popular event was the **joust** (jowst). Two armored knights on horseback carrying dull lances galloped towards each other from opposite ends of the field. Each tried with all his strength and skill to knock the other to the ground with his lance.

The cost of tournaments was high. Men and horses were killed and wounded. Lances, swords, and suits of armor were damaged. The noble who gave the tournament had to feed hundreds of people. In spite of the cost, however, tournaments remained popular. In fact, it was believed that a knight who had not learned to fight in one could not fight well in battle.

Section 3 Assessment

1. **Define:** code of chivalry, page, squire, dubbing, tournaments, joust.
2. Why did noble families send their sons to other castles to work as pages?
3. How did knights train for war?

Critical Thinking

4. **Making Comparisons** How were tournaments similar to the Olympic games in ancient Greece? How were they different?

Graphic Organizer Activity

5. Draw this diagram, and use it to show the steps leading to knighthood.

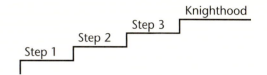

Step 1 → Step 2 → Step 3 → Knighthood

SECTION 4   The Manor

Nobles, knights, and peasants all depended on the land for everything they needed. The land was divided into **manors,** or farming communities. Manors were found on fiefs and were owned by nobles.

Daily Life   The noble chose a number of officials to run his manor. They were loyal to the noble and made sure his orders were carried out. One official was the **seneschal** (sen' uh shuhl).

Reading Check
What were **manors?**

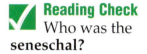

Reading Check
Who was the **seneschal?**

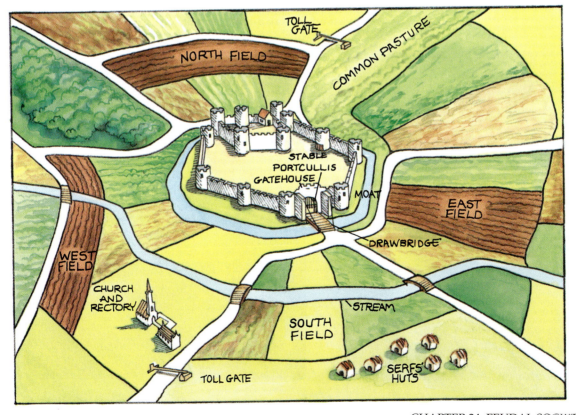

TOLL GATE
NORTH FIELD
COMMON PASTURE
STABLE
PORTCULLIS
GATEHOUSE
MOAT
EAST FIELD
DRAWBRIDGE
WEST FIELD
CHURCH AND RECTORY
STREAM
SOUTH FIELD
TOLL GATE
SERFS' HUTS

Peasant Life A typical peasant's cottage had one door that opened into a central room with a pressed dirt floor. Often a number of animals— piglets, ducklings, cats, and hens—shared the space with a married couple and their children. In cold weather, a cow might be brought inside to be near the warmth of the fire.

He looked after the noble's fiefs by visiting each fief regularly. Another official was the **bailiff** (bā' lif). He made sure the peasants worked hard in the fields. Every manor had its own court of law. The court settled differences, gave out fines and punishments, and discussed manor business.

Poor transportation and frequent fighting isolated manors from one another. The men and women of each manor produced food, clothing, and shelter for themselves and the noble. They raised sheep for wool and cattle for meat and milk. They also grew grain and vegetables, made cloth, built homes, and fashioned tools.

The noble of each manor lived in a wooden house or a castle. Nearby stood a small village of cottages in which the peasants lived. Most villages also had a church, a mill, a bread oven, and a wine press. Around the village were forests, meadows, pastures, and fields.

The cottages were crowded around an open area called the village green. They were made of wood and earth and had thatched roofs. Most had only one room. At night, family members slept there on piles of straw or on the dirt floor. Three-legged stools and a table were the only furniture. Diseases and fleas from the animals that also slept in the cottage often sickened the people.

PEASANTS AT WORK   Peasants spent long hours working in the fields of a manor. In these paintings, peasants are shown plowing the fields and doing other tasks on the manor. **What other work did the peasants do?**

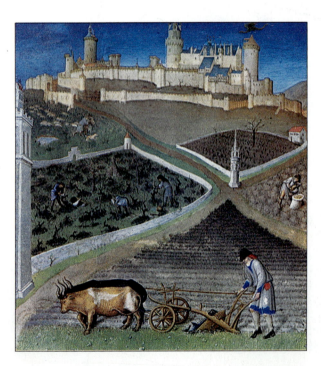

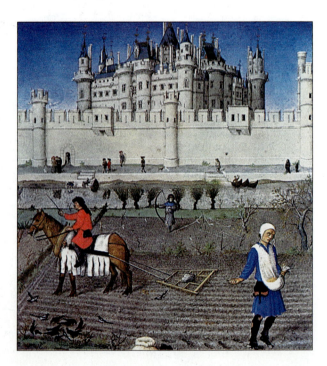

PEASANT CELEBRATION Although peasants' lives were mostly long hours of hard work, there were times for celebration. Peasants celebrated special occasions with music, dancing, and feasting. Here, the festivities at a peasant wedding are shown. **What sports did peasants enjoy?**

People in History

Trotula of Salerno
C.1097 A.D.

Doctor

Both noble and peasant women took care of the sick, but Trotula broke with tradition by becoming a trained doctor. She studied and taught at the medical school at Salerno, Italy. Trotula specialized in the health of women and wrote a book called *The Diseases of Women.* Her book influenced doctors for centuries. Today she is considered one of Europe's early women of science.

Freemen and Serfs

Two groups of peasants worked on a manor. One was the **freemen,** or peasants who paid the noble for the right to farm land. They worked only on their own strips of land and had rights under the law. They moved wherever and whenever they wished. The noble, however, had the right to throw them off the manor without warning.

The other group was the serfs. Serfs and their descendants were a noble's property. They could not move to another area, own their own property, or marry without the noble's permission. Serfs, however, could not be driven off the land and did not have to serve in the army.

It was not easy for serfs to gain their freedom. One way was to escape to the towns. If a serf was not caught and remained in town for more than a year, he or she was considered free. By the end of the Middle Ages, serfs were allowed to buy their freedom.

As in Charlemagne's time, the serfs worked long hours in the fields and performed many services for the nobles. Serfs spent three days of the week working the lord's strips of land and the rest of the week caring for their own strips. However, they had to give part of their own crops to the noble. They also paid him for the use of the village's mill, bread oven, and wine press.

In spite of the difficulties, a serf's life had some bright moments. Sunday was a day of rest from work. At Christmas, the

> **✓ Reading Check**
> How did **freemen** differ from serfs?

Serf Work A monk at Canterbury recorded an English serf's account of his day: "I work very hard. I go out at dawn, driving the oxen to the field, and I yoke them to the plough. However hard the winter, I dare not stay home for fear of my master."

lord paid for a great feast and entertainment. Certain holidays were celebrated with singing and dancing on the village green. When they could, serfs took part in such sports as wrestling, archery, and soccer.

By the 1200s, peasants began to learn better farming methods. They used the three-field system of farming and started to use a heavy iron plow. The horse collar was invented, allowing horses instead of slow-moving oxen to plow fields. All of this enabled the peasants to grow more food.

Section 4 Assessment

1. **Define:** manors, seneschal, bailiff, freemen.
2. What were some features of a manor village?
3. What rights did freemen have?
4. What did serfs contribute to a manor?

Critical Thinking

5. **Making Comparisons** What interests did nobles and serfs have in common?

Graphic Organizer Activity

6. Draw this diagram, and use it to show technological improvements in farming in the 1200s.

Chapter Summary & Study Guide

1. Following Charlemagne's death, kings began to depend on nobles for food, horses, and soldiers.
2. Some nobles began to collect their own taxes, run their own courts, coin their own money, and raise their own armies.
3. As the power of kings declined, the nobles took on the duty of defending their land and people from Viking attacks.
4. By 1000, the kingdoms of western Europe were divided into thousands of feudal territories.
5. Under feudalism, landowning nobles gave vassals land in exchange for loyalty and military service.
6. Knights followed the code of chivalry and trained for war by fighting in tournaments.
7. Fiefs were owned by nobles and worked by peasants.
8. Peasants included freemen and serfs. While freemen could leave the land if they wished, serfs were considered a noble's property.
9. By the 1200s, improvements in farming methods helped the peasants to grow more food.

Self-Check Quiz

Visit the *Human Heritage* Web site at **humanheritage. glencoe.com** and click on *Chapter 24—Self-Check Quiz* to assess your understanding of this chapter.

Using Key Terms

Imagine you are living in the late Middle Ages. Write an interview with a noble and a serf in which they describe their lives. Use the following words in your interview.

feudalism	clergy	fiefs
vassal	act of homage	knight
castles	keep	ladies
code of chivalry	page	squire
dubbing	tournaments	joust
manors	seneschal	bailiff
freemen		

Understanding Main Ideas

1. Into what three groups were people divided under feudalism?
2. Who held the political power within a feudal territory?
3. Who usually received a vassal's fief when the vassal died?
4. What was expected of a knight?
5. Why did people on a manor produce everything they needed?
6. How could serfs obtain their freedom?
7. What changes had taken place in farming by the 1200s?

Critical Thinking

1. What advantages would there be to being a vassal rather than a lord?
2. Why do you think women provided the medical care in a fief?
3. What would you have enjoyed about being a knight? What would you have disliked?
4. How do you think a serf's life would be affected by the improved farming methods of the thirteenth century?

Graphic Organizer Activity

Citizenship Create a diagram like this one, and use it to show the organization of government under feudalism. Each of these groups should appear on the chart: serfs, landowning nobles, freemen, knights.

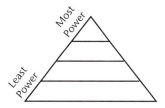

Geography in History

Environment and Society The people of the manor made good use of their natural resources to support themselves. Predict and describe how you think manor life would have changed if a plant disease had killed all the trees in an area.

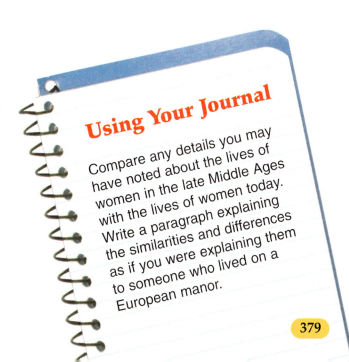

Using Your Journal

Compare any details you may have noted about the lives of women in the late Middle Ages with the lives of women today. Write a paragraph explaining the similarities and differences as if you were explaining them to someone who lived on a European manor.

CHAPTER

25

The Church
1000 A.D.–1300 A.D.

◄ Christian crusader and his wife

◄ Enameled cross

1071 A.D.
Seljuq Turks
conquer Jerusalem

1096 A.D.
Start of the
Crusades

1129 A.D.
Inquisition
begins

1212 A.D.
Children's
Crusade

1291 A.D.
Muslims win the
Crusades

Chapter Focus

Read to Discover

- How the Roman Catholic Church influenced life during the Middle Ages.
- What attempts were made to reform the Church during the Middle Ages.
- What learning was like during the Middle Ages.
- Why the Crusades took place during the Middle Ages.
- What the effects of the Crusades were.

HISTORY *Online*

Chapter Overview

Visit the *Human Heritage* Web site at **humanheritage.glencoe.com** and click on *Chapter 25— Chapter Overviews* to preview this chapter.

Terms to Learn	People to Know	Places to Locate
mass	Gregory VII	Cluny
tithes	Francis of Assisi	Palestine
cathedrals	Thomas Aquinas	Outremer
unions	Urban II	Venice
chancellor	Saladin	Acre
crusades	Richard the	
emirs	Lionheart	

Why It's Important   Leaders in the Roman Catholic Church wanted to develop a civilization in western Europe that was based on Christian ideals. By 1000, missionary monks had brought the Church's teachings to most of Europe. They converted people and built new churches and monasteries. The Roman Catholic Church united western Europeans and took the lead in government, law, art, and learning for hundreds of years. The Church helped pass on the heritage of the Roman Empire. Latin became the official language of the Church.

SECTION 1 Catholic Influence

The Roman Catholic Church had great influence during the Middle Ages. It was the center of every village and town. It played an important part in the political life of the period. At times, it even had the power of life or death over people.

Daily Life   In every village and town, daily life revolved around the Church. To become a king, vassal, or knight, a man had to take part in a religious ceremony. Most holidays were in honor of saints or religious events. On Fridays, the people obeyed the Church's rule not to eat meat. On Sundays, they went to

VILLAGE CHURCH   During the Middle Ages, the church was the religious and social center of the village. Both the local noble and the peasants contributed to the building of the church and its upkeep. **What were some daily tasks performed by the parish priest?**

Reading Check
Who usually held **mass** in medieval villages and towns?

mass, or a worship service, held by the parish priest. Church leaders ran schools and hospitals. Monks and nuns provided food and shelter for travelers. Priests recorded births, performed marriages, and conducted burials.

Political Life   The Church played an important role in the political life of the Middle Ages. Together with kings and nobles, Church officials helped govern western Europe. As large landowners, high Church leaders were both lords and vassals of other lords. They served as advisers to kings and other nobles, keeping records for the kings who could not read or write. Parish priests also played a part in government. They were chosen by local nobles and were expected to tell the people to respect the king, the nobles, and other government officials.

The Church told people to obey the king's laws unless they went against **canon laws,** or laws set up by the Church. People who disobeyed the Pope or canon laws were **excommunicated** (ek skuh myū′ nuh kā ted), or lost their membership in the Church. They also lost their political rights.

Reading Check
What are **canon laws?**
What happened to people who were **excommunicated?**

The Inquisition   Despite its power, the Church faced the problem of heresy. At first, it tried to stop the spread of heresy by preaching. Then, in 1129, a council of bishops set up the Inquisition (in kwuh zish′ uhn), or Church court, to end heresy by force.

The Church gave people it suspected of heresy one month to confess. Those who appeared in front of the Inquisition before the month ended were whipped or sent to prison for a short time. Those who did not appear were seized and brought to trial.

The reason for the trial was to get a confession. The court called only two witnesses. Based on what they said, the court decided whether or not a person was a heretic. Heretics who confessed were punished. Then, they were allowed to become Church members again. Heretics who refused to confess were often tortured. A number of people were burned at the stake.

Section 1 Assessment

1. **Define:** mass, canon laws, excommunicated.
2. What part did parish priests play in government?

Critical Thinking

3. **Making Inferences** How do you think a king might have felt about being excommunicated from the Church?

Graphic Organizer Activity

4. Draw this diagram, and use it to show examples of Church powers during the Middle Ages.

Church Powers
- Example
- Example
- Example

THE INQUISITION   The Inquisition was established to strengthen the beliefs of the Church in France, Germany, Italy, and Spain. In this painting, a heretic under trial confesses. **What punishment came to those who confessed to heresy?**

SECTION 2 Attempts at Reform

✅ **Reading Check**
What were **tithes?**

The Church became rich during the Middle Ages. Church members supported it by giving **tithes** (tīthz), or offerings equal to 10 percent of their income. Rich nobles donated money to build large churches and gave land to monasteries. The wealthier the monasteries became, however, the more careless many monks grew about carrying out their religious duties.

Monks were not the only ones to grow careless about religious duties. When a bishop died, his office and lands were taken over by the local noble. The noble often chose a close relative as the new bishop or sold the office for money or favors.

Linking Across Time

Stained-Glass Windows During the time of Charlemagne, Europeans started designing windows made from individual pieces of colored glass and held together by lead. The art form reached its peak in the church windows of the late Middle Ages (below). In the late 1800s and early 1900s, artists such as Louis Comfort Tiffany revived this art form in stained-glass windows and lamps (right). **How did church leaders raise money to pay for works of art like stained-glass windows?**

Because of this, men who were not very religious often held important Church posts. They did not keep Church rules or bother with the needs of the poor.

Before long, some western Europeans became worried about the direction in which the Church was headed. During the late 900s and early 1000s, they worked to return the Church to Christian ideals.

The Monks of Cluny

To fight corruption in the Church, *devout*, or deeply religious, nobles founded new monasteries that strictly followed the Benedictine Rule. One of the most important of these was Cluny (klū' nē) in eastern France. The monks there led simple lives, spending much time in prayer. They soon won the respect of the people. The monks of Cluny recognized only the authority of the Pope and said that the Church, not kings or nobles, should choose all Church leaders. Over time, a number of new monasteries connected with Cluny spread across Europe.

Painting of Pope Gregory VII

Pope Gregory VII

The reforms begun by the monks of Cluny were continued by Pope Gregory VII. By Gregory's time, the Pope had become a powerful political as well as religious leader. He had his own courts of justice and government offices. He ruled from Rome with the help of a group of bishops known as the College of Cardinals.

Gregory had two goals as Pope. He wanted to rid the Church of control by kings and nobles. He also wanted to increase the Pope's power over the Church officials. To reach these goals, Gregory made many changes in the Church. Church leaders who bought or sold Church offices were removed from their posts. Bishops and priests were forbidden to marry.

In a document issued in 1075, Gregory stated that the Pope was above all kings and nobles. Only the Pope had the power to choose bishops and other Church leaders. Government officials who did not obey the Pope could be removed from office. People did not have to obey officials who went against the Pope.

Some kings viewed Gregory's reforms as attacks on their power. So, they resisted his changes. In the end, however, they lost some of their power to him.

Friars

During the early 1200s, Church reforms were carried out by preachers called **friars.** Since they sold all their belongings before becoming friars, they depended on gifts of food and money from the people.

Friars were different from other monks. They did not marry and followed many monastic rules. However, they did not shut themselves off from the rest of the world. Instead, they lived in towns and worked to bring Christianity directly to the people.

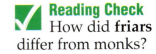 **Reading Check**
How did **friars** differ from monks?

Two well-known **orders,** or groups of friars, were the Franciscans (fran sis′ kuhns) and Dominicans (duh min′ uh kuhns). The Franciscan order was founded in 1200 by Francis of Assisi (uh sē′ zē), the son of a rich Italian merchant. Franciscans were known for their cheerfulness and confidence that God would take care of them. They had a deep love of nature. They believed it was a gift of God and should be respected.

The Dominican order was started in 1216 by a Spanish monk named Dominic. Like the Franciscans, the Dominicans lived a life of poverty. They studied different languages so they could preach everywhere. Through their words and deeds, they kept many people loyal to Church teachings.

Section 2 Assessment

1. **Define:** tithes, friars, orders.
2. What reforms did Gregory VII introduce?
3. How did the Franciscans and Dominicans try to bring Christianity directly to the people?

Critical Thinking

4. **Drawing Conclusions** Why do you think the monks of Cluny gained the people's respect?

Graphic Organizer Activity

5. Draw this diagram, and use it to show the causes and effects of the rise of Church reformers in the 900s and 1000s.

Causes	Rise of Church Reformers	Effects

SECTION 3 Learning

During the late Middle Ages, the rise of governments brought more security, and the economy grew stronger. There was more time for learning, and learning was in the hands of the Church.

Cathedral Schools   The parish clergy set up schools in **cathedrals,** or churches headed by bishops. The schools were to prepare the sons of nobles for service in the Church. Not every boy who went to school, however, wanted to be a priest or monk. So, the schools also trained students to be government workers, lawyers, and teachers. Seven subjects were taught at cathedral schools. They were grammar, rhetoric, logic, arithmetic, geometry, astronomy, and music.

Students paid a fee to attend classes held in a cold, dark hall rented by the teacher. Books were few and costly. So, students memorized the teacher's explanation.

Universities

After a while, students began to complain that teachers held few classes and did not cover enough subjects. Teachers began to complain that too many untrained people were teaching. So, students and teachers decided to make some changes by forming **unions,** or groups of people joined together for a common cause. These unions became **universities,** or groups of teachers and students devoted to learning. By the 1200s, universities had spread all through Europe.

Universities were alike in many ways. A Church official called a **chancellor** (chan' suh luhr) headed each. No one could teach without his permission. All universities had well-organized classes held at set times each day. In class, students listened to lectures on a specific subject. All students had to pass special tests. Lecturers had to be at least 21 years old and had to have studied for at least 6 years.

Students from all over Europe came to the universities. At first, they lived in boarding houses. Later, rich sponsors built special buildings in which they could live. Those who missed daily mass, disturbed the peace, or took part in gambling or sword practice were punished.

✓ **Reading Check** What led students and teachers to form **unions** in the Middle Ages? What are **universities?**

✓ **Reading Check** What was the role of a **chancellor?**

MEDIEVAL CLASSROOM Dissatisfied with earlier forms of schools, teachers and students joined together to create universities as places for serious study. In this painting a teacher at the University of Paris holds a discussion with students. **What did a scholar have to do in order to become a teacher?**

Universities In Medieval Latin, the word *universitas* meant "corporation." The earliest universities were given charters to do business by popes or emperors. Because teachers depended on their students' fees, they had to attract enough students to earn a living.

Thomas Aquinas One noted scholar of the Middle Ages was Thomas Aquinas (uh kwī' nuhs). Aquinas believed that both faith and reason were gifts of God. He saw no conflict between the two and tried to bring them together. He thought reason helped people know what the world was really like. It helped them lead a good life. He thought faith revealed religious truths to people. It helped them find life after death.

Aquinas wrote a book called *Summa Theologica* (sū' muh tā ō lō' ji kuh), or *A Summary of Religious Thought*. In it, he asked questions and presented different opinions. He then gave answers to the questions. Aquinas's teachings were later accepted and promoted by the Church.

Section 3 Assessment

1. **Define:** cathedrals, unions, universities, chancellor.
2. Why were cathedral schools started?
3. In what ways were universities alike?

Critical Thinking

4. **Demonstrating Reasoned Judgment** Why do you think that only specific subjects were taught at cathedral schools?

Graphic Organizer Activity

5. Draw this diagram, and use it to compare universities in the Middle Ages with universities today.

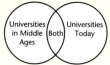

Universities in Middle Ages | Both | Universities Today

SECTION 4   The Crusades

For hundreds of years, Christians from western Europe had visited shrines in Jerusalem. Then, in 1071, a people called Seljuq (sel' juk) Turks conquered Jerusalem and took control of the Christian shrines. Traveling in Palestine became difficult for the Christians because of the trouble there.

When news of what was happening in the Holy Land reached Christians in western Europe, they were shocked and angered. The result was a series of holy wars called **crusades** (krū sāds'), which went on for about 200 years.

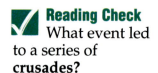

Reading Check
What event led to a series of **crusades?**

A Call to War Even after they had taken Palestine, Turkish armies continued to threaten the Byzantine Empire. The Byzantine emperor asked the Pope for military aid. Pope Urban II (er' buhn) agreed to help the Byzantines. He hoped that in return, the Eastern Orthodox Church would again unite with the Roman Catholic Church and accept him as its religious leader.

In 1095, Urban spoke before a large crowd in the town of Clermont in eastern France. He told the people that Europe's lords should stop fighting among themselves. Instead, they should fight in a crusade against the Turks.

Urban reminded the people that Europe was not producing enough food to feed its growing population. Palestine, on the other hand, had rich, fertile land on which any knight could live in comfort. The Pope promised that those who went on a crusade would be free of debts and taxes. He also promised that God would forgive the sins of those who died in battle. He encouraged soldiers to go to Palestine wearing a red cross on their tunics as a symbol of obedience to God.

The Peasants' Crusade

Urban II spent nine months journeying from one European city to another calling for a crusade. The people of Europe responded eagerly to his call. As a sign of their religious devotion, they adopted the war cry *"Deus vult"* (dā′ uhs wūlt′), which means "It is the will of God." The people felt it was their duty as Christians to win back the Holy Land. They had other reasons for being willing to fight, too. Nobles hoped to gain more land for themselves in Palestine. They also wanted the fame a crusade could bring. Peasants wanted to escape from their hard work on the land.

Urban II wanted the nobles to plan and lead the crusade. While they were drawing up their plans, however, the peasants

CALL FOR A CRUSADE   The conquest of Palestine and persecution of Christians by the Seljuq Turks angered western Europeans. A call went up to free the Holy Land from the Muslims. A church leader in this painting urges local knights to join the crusade. **What symbol did the crusaders wear?**

Evaluating a Web Site

When using the Internet as a research tool, the user must evaluate each Web site's information. This means that a person must decide if the information found on a Web site is accurate and correct.

Learning the Skill When doing research, it is important to find Web sites that present information fairly. First, you should identify the source of the information or the author of the site. Sometimes a Web site may contain the views of the person or group who supports it. The site, then, might not have information that is balanced.

Next, check the Web site for accuracy. A reliable site should contain references to other sources that support the information. A quality Web site should also be free of spelling and language errors.

Identify the purpose of the Web site. Does the site support a belief or opinion? Is the Web site meant to provide information or is it an advertisement?

You should also check to see how current the Web site is. A Web site should include information about when it was placed on the Internet and when it was last updated. A Web site should also be designed so that the user can easily locate information. Information may be hard to find if the Web site's design is cluttered and hard to read.

This chapter talks about the series of Crusades that took place in the late Middle Ages. Search for a Web site about the Crusades. Use the questions in the Skill Practice to help you evaluate the site.

Skill Practice

1. Who is the author or sponsor of the site?
2. Briefly describe the information on the site.
3. Is the information easy to find? Does the site contain links to other useful sources? Are the links up-to-date and related to the topic?
4. Are the facts on the site supported by other sources? Is there more than one source used to support information within the site?
5. When was the information last updated?
6. Is the design of the site appealing? Why or why not?
7. Overall, how reliable do you think this Web site is?

Remains of a medieval fortress in Jerusalem

grew impatient and formed their own armies. Although they lacked training in warfare, they believed God would help them.

In the spring of 1096, about 12,000 French peasants began the long journey to Palestine. At the same time, two other groups of peasants set out from Germany. As the peasant armies marched through Europe, they attacked farmers, looted cottages, and burned wheat fields. They *massacred*, or killed, all the Jews they could find. The peasants thought that since Jews were not Christians, they were enemies. Frightened villagers tried to keep the armies away from their homes. At night, the villagers often poisoned wells and attacked crusader camps.

By the time the peasant armies reached Constantinople, they had lost about one third of their number. Their clothes were in rags, and they had no money. They wandered through the streets of the city attacking passersby and stealing from markets and homes.

The Byzantine emperor had expected the Pope to send trained soldiers, not unskilled peasants. The actions of the western Europeans worried him, and he wanted to get them out of his capital. So, he gave them supplies and ships and sent them to fight the Turks in Asia Minor. There, the peasant armies were almost completely wiped out by Turkish bowmen.

The Nobles' Crusade

In 1097, the nobles set out on their crusade. Great lords led each army. They brought with them their vassals, wives, children, clerks, cooks, and blacksmiths. The crusade was very costly. Each lord had to provide his own battle gear, wagons, supplies, and horses. Nobles often had to borrow money or sell their land or jewelry to cover the costs.

About 30,000 **crusaders** arrived in Asia Minor and defeated the Turks. From there, they moved south through the desert to Syria. However, they were not prepared for the heat and did not have enough food or water. Many died of starvation or thirst. Those who survived pushed on to Palestine, capturing Syrian cities along the way.

In 1099, the 12,000 surviving crusaders reached Jerusalem. They captured the Holy City, killing Turks, Jews, and Christians alike. Then, they looted it, taking gold, silver, horses, mules, and all kinds of goods.

The Kingdom Beyond the Sea

After the crusaders captured Jerusalem, they lost much of their religious enthusiasm. Many returned to their homes in western Europe. Those who remained set up four feudal kingdoms called Outremer (ū truh mār'), or "the kingdom beyond the sea," in the areas they won.

The crusaders took over the estates of rich Turkish and Arab Muslims and divided them among themselves and their best knights. Arab peasants worked the land for them and cared for

Women in the Crusades Women responded to the call to recapture Jerusalem. A Greek historian wrote of "women dressed as men, mounted on horses and armed with lance and battle-axe." The Pope banned women from fighting in the Third Crusade (1189–1192), a decision that the kings of Europe approved. Women continued to join the crusades, however, both as soldiers and as nurses.

Reading Check What hardships did **crusaders** in the Nobles' Crusade face?

Student Web Activity
Visit the *Human Heritage* Web site at **humanheritage.glencoe.com** and click on **Chapter 25— Student Web Activities** to find out more about the Crusades.

Eleanor of Aquitaine
c. 1122-1204

French Queen

At age 15, Eleanor inherited Aquitaine, a region in southern France. As one of the largest land owners in Europe, she married a French king, Louis VII, and accompanied him on a crusade. She later married King Henry II of England and had nine children. One of them included Richard the Lionheart. While Richard headed off on a crusade, Eleanor ruled England in his absence. When Richard died, she helped put her son John on the throne. Few doubted Eleanor's power when she died at age 82.

CRUSADERS' ATTACK ON JERUSALEM   After weeks of siege warfare, the crusaders were finally able to mount a successful attack on Jerusalem. The Christians, using towers and catapults, broke through the city's walls and defeated the Muslim defenders. **What hardships did the crusaders face on their way to Jerusalem?**

the orchards and vineyards. Other Arabs served as advisers and helped them manage their estates. Friendships developed between the crusaders and the Muslims. The Muslims admired the crusaders' bravery. The crusaders discovered that many Arab scholars knew more than Europeans did about medicine, science, and mathematics.

When the crusaders were not fighting Turks, they ran their estates, went hunting, and attended the local court. Each noble built a castle in Outremer more magnificent than the one he had in Europe. This castle was more than a fortress. It was a comfortable place in which to live, with a large dining hall, living room, and bedchambers. All the rooms had marble walls and painted ceilings and were decorated with silk hangings, carpets, silver and gold objects, and beautiful furnishings.

The crusaders found that their old way of living did not suit their new surroundings. It was too hot in Palestine to wear fur and woolen clothes. Men began to wear turbans and loose, flowing silk or linen robes. However, they continued to fight in armor. Women wore jeweled tunics and gowns made with gold thread. They adopted the Muslim custom of wearing veils when they were outdoors and learned to use makeup and perfume. The heat also led the westerners to develop the habit of bathing.

The crusaders changed their eating habits, too. It was too hot to eat the heavy, solid foods they were used to. They learned to have light meals with less meat and more fruits and vegetables. They also ate new foods such as rice, oranges, figs, and melons.

The crusaders led an easier life in Palestine than they had at home. Still, they had trouble adjusting. Many died in battle against the Turks or in fights among themselves over rights and lands. Others could not survive the hot climate.

Saladin and the Crusade of Kings

In 1174, a Muslim military leader named Saladin (sal' uhd uhn) became the ruler of Egypt. He united the Muslims throughout the Near East and started a war against the Christian occupation of Palestine by western Crusaders. Saladin's armies were well organized and devoted to Islam. Groups of soldiers headed by leaders called **emirs** (i miuhrs') made up the armies. Many emirs were known for their honesty and for the consideration they showed their captives. The emirs often were shocked by the cruelty and greed of the Christian soldiers.

Saladin's soldiers rode into battle on swift ponies. Their weapons were short bows. The crusaders found it hard to fight them. The crusaders' armor was heavy, their swords were too long to handle easily, and their horses were not protected. They had to learn to depend on a new weapon called the *crossbow,* which fired an arrow with great force and speed. In 1187, Saladin's armies took Jerusalem. When he refused to massacre the city's Christians, he won the respect of many of the crusaders.

After Saladin's victory, the Church urged another crusade. This time the western armies were led by King Richard I of England, Emperor Frederick Barbarossa (bahr buh ros' uh) of Germany, and King Philip II Augustus of France. They were the three most powerful rulers in Europe.

This Crusade of Kings, as it was called, was a failure. Frederick died in Asia Minor, and many of his troops returned home without ever having fought a battle. Richard and Philip were enemies and were always quarreling. They did take a few coastal cities in Palestine together. Then, Philip returned home. Richard and his armies had to continue the crusade alone.

Richard was a brave warrior. Because of this, he was called "the Lionheart." Nevertheless, he could not defeat Saladin. After three years, he gave up and signed a truce with the Muslim leader. Although the crusaders still controlled large areas of Palestine, Jerusalem remained in Muslim hands.

The Loss of an Ideal

In 1202, Pope Innocent III called for yet another crusade. Knights from all over Europe answered the call. They decided not to take a land route to Palestine but to go by ship from the Italian port of Venice. Rich merchants there wanted

Painting of Arab Scholars

Reading Check
What were **emirs** known for?

Painting of Saladin

MAP SKILLS

Determining Exact Location

Most maps have **grids,** or patterns of horizontal and vertical lines that cross each other. Generally, the horizontal lines are lines of latitude, and the vertical ones are lines of longitude. Grids make it easier to determine the exact location of a place on Earth.

To find a place exactly, it is necessary to find what lines of latitude and longitude cross at that place. The point at which they cross is the exact location.

Exact location may be shown by a set of numbers that lists latitude first and then longitude (30°N, 60°E). Such sets are called **coordinates** (kō ōr′ din uhts).

Look at the map of "The Crusades" below. Locate the city of Marseilles on the southern coast of France. The line of latitude that passes through the city is 43°N. The line of longitude that passes through it is 5°E. This means that the exact location of Marseilles is 43°N, 5°E.

Map Practice

1. **What city is located at 32°N, 35°E?**
2. **What are the coordinates of Venice's location?**

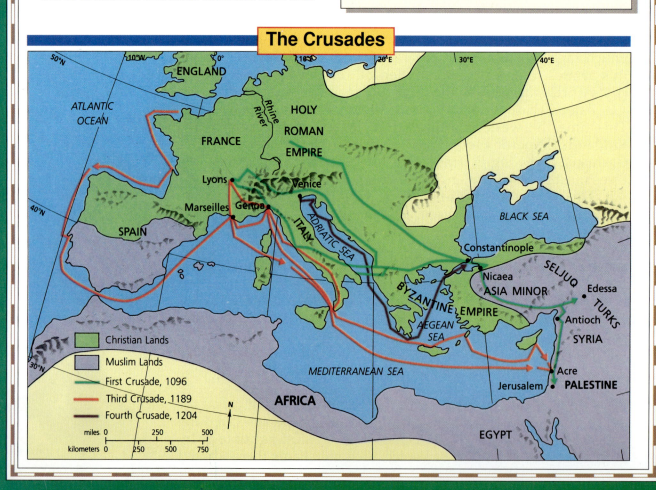

The Crusades

Christian Lands
Muslim Lands
First Crusade, 1096
Third Crusade, 1189
Fourth Crusade, 1204

miles 0 250 500
kilometers 0 250 500 750

Venice to replace Constantinople as the trading center of the eastern Mediterranean. The crusaders agreed to pay these merchants a large sum of money and to share one half of all their conquests with the Venetians. In return, the Venetians agreed to supply the crusaders with ships and equipment.

Jeweled Box

When the soldiers found they could not pay all they owed, they agreed to conquer the city of Zara for the Venetians. Then, the Venetians convinced them to capture Constantinople. For three days, the crusaders and the Venetians burned and looted Constantinople. Many priceless manuscripts and works of art were either taken to Venice, lost, or destroyed.

The crusaders finally decided not to go to Palestine. Instead, they stayed in Constantinople and divided the city with the Venetians. Their conduct shocked many western Europeans, who lost respect for the crusader ideal.

Several other crusades were fought during the 1200s, but the Europeans did not win any of them. The saddest of all was the Children's Crusade. A group of French children, led by a peasant boy named Stephen of Cloyes, set sail from Marseilles (mahr sā'), France, in 1212. Most of the children never reached Palestine. Along the way they were sold into slavery by captains of the ships on which they sailed. At the same time, another group of children set forth on foot from Germany, intending to march toward Italy. Most of them, however, starved to death or died from disease.

In 1291, the Muslims took over the city of Acre (ah' kuhr), the last Christian stronghold. The Muslims had won the Crusades. They also gained back all the land in Palestine that the crusaders had taken earlier.

Effects of the Crusades

The Crusades affected both the Near East and western Europe. The Byzantines were so angry at the actions of western Europeans that the split between eastern and western Christianity became permanent. At the same time, the Byzantine Empire was so weakened by the Crusades that it could no longer defend itself. This left Europe open to Turkish attack.

The Crusades helped to break down feudalism in western Europe. While feudal lords were fighting in Palestine, kings at home increased their authority. The desire for wealth, power, and land grew and began to cloud the religious ideals of many western Europeans.

The crusaders' contact with the cultured Byzantines and Muslims led western Europeans to again become interested in learning. At the same time, Europeans began to demand such luxuries as spices, sugar, lemons, rugs, tapestries, and richly woven cloth. To meet these demands, European merchants opened up new trade routes. As trade grew, so did the towns of western Europe.

Section 4 Assessment

1. **Define:** crusades, crusaders, emirs.
2. Why were western Europeans of all classes of society eager to go on a crusade?
3. What effect did the Crusades have on trade?

Critical Thinking

4. **Understanding Cause and Effect**
   What do you think was the most important effect of the Crusades on the entire civilized world (not just on western Europe)? Explain.

Graphic Organizer Activity

5. Draw this diagram, and use it to support a generalization about the effect of the Crusades on feudalism.

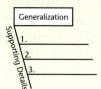

```
              Generalization
Supporting
Details      1.
             2.
             3.
```

Chapter Summary & Study Guide

1. The Roman Catholic Church was the center of life in Europe during the Middle Ages.

2. Increased wealth led many members of the clergy to grow careless about their religious duties, sparking a spirit of reform.

3. During the Middle Ages, monks and friars worked to win the respect of the people.

4. In 1075, Pope Gregory VII issued a document placing the power of the Pope above all kings and feudal lords.

5. By the 1200s, students and teachers at cathedral schools had helped form universities, which soon spread throughout Europe.

6. Scholars such as Thomas Aquinas tried to bring faith and reason together.

7. In 1071, the Seljuq Turks conquered the Holy Land and took control of the Christian shrines there.

8. In 1095, Pope Urban II agreed to help the Byzantines against the Turks and called on the people of western Europe to join in a crusade.

9. The Nobles' Crusade of 1097 succeeded in capturing Jerusalem, but the Christians could not hold on to the city.

10. Richard the Lionheart, who set out on a crusade with two other kings, could not defeat Saladin and signed a truce with him.

11. In 1202, crusaders, with the help of the Venetians, burned and looted Constantinople. This event badly damaged the crusading ideal.

12. Even though the Muslims regained all of Palestine in 1291, the Crusades brought lasting changes to Europe, including the end of feudalism.

Self-Check Quiz

Visit the *Human Heritage* Web site at **humanheritage. glencoe.com** and click on *Chapter 25—Self-Check Quiz* to assess your understanding of this chapter.

Using Key Terms

Imagine that you are a traveler in Europe during the Middle Ages. Write an article for a travel magazine describing the influence of the Roman Catholic Church. Use the following words.

mass   canon laws   excommunicated
tithes   friars   orders
cathedrals   unions   universities
chancellor   crusades   crusaders
emirs

Understanding Main Ideas

1. What role did Church officials play in the political life of the Middle Ages?
2. Why did many monks grow careless about carrying out their religious duties?
3. Why were universities started?
4. Why did Urban II encourage people to go on a crusade?
5. What effect did the climate in Palestine have on the crusaders?
6. What happened during the Children's Crusade?
7. Why did the split in the Roman Catholic Church become permanent?
8. How did the Crusades affect the power of western Europe's kings?

Critical Thinking

1. What were the advantages and disadvantages of having Church leaders run the government during the Middle Ages?
2. What would have been enjoyable about being a student in a medieval university?

3. How would you have responded to Urban II's call for a crusade?
4. How do you think crusaders felt about settling in Palestine?

Graphic Organizer Activity

Economics Create a diagram like the one below, and use it to show how the Crusades affected western Europe's economy.

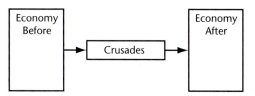

Geography in History

The World in Spatial Terms Refer to the map on page 394. Soldiers in the Fourth Crusade sailed from Venice to Constantinople. About how many miles long was their voyage? Was their voyage longer or shorter than it would have been if they had sailed to Jerusalem as planned?

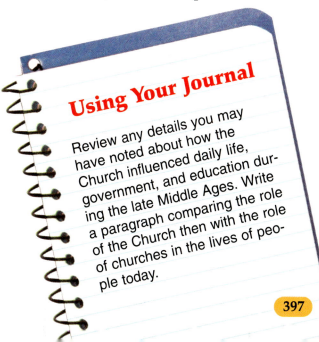

Using Your Journal

Review any details you may have noted about how the Church influenced daily life, government, and education during the late Middle Ages. Write a paragraph comparing the role of the Church then with the role of churches in the lives of people today.

Rise of Trade and Towns

500 A.D.–1400 A.D.

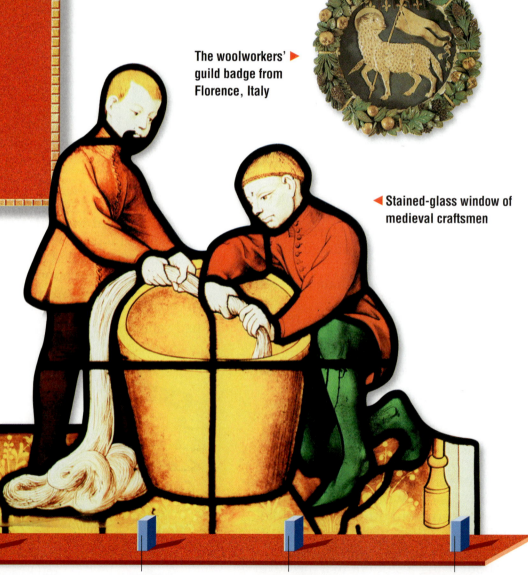

The woolworkers' ▶
guild badge from
Florence, Italy

◀ Stained-glass window of
medieval craftsmen

500s A.D.
Venice founded

1000s A.D.
Trade increases between
Europe and the Near East

1100 A.D.
Italian trading towns
drive Muslims from the
Mediterranean

1300 A.D.
Flemish develop
thriving trade
with England

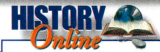

Chapter Focus

Read to Discover

- How the growth of trade led to the rise of towns in the Middle Ages.
- What living conditions were like in medieval towns.
- Why guilds were formed and why they were later opposed.
- What cultural changes to civilization took place in Europe during the 1400s.

HISTORY Online

Chapter Overview

Visit the *Human Heritage* Web site at **humanheritage.glencoe.com** and click on ***Chapter 26—Chapter Overviews*** to preview this chapter.

Terms to Learn	People to Know	Places to Locate
guilds	Dante	Venice
apprentice	Geoffrey Chaucer	Flanders
masters		
journeyman		

Why It's Important Beginning in the 1000s, the population of western Europe grew for the first time since the fall of Rome. Better ways of farming helped farmers grow more food. Many peasants left the fields to work in villages. They began to turn out cloth and metal products.

Western nobles, however, wanted such luxury items as sugar, spices, silks, and dyes. These goods came from the East. So, European merchants carried western products to the East to exchange for luxury goods.

SECTION 1 Trading Centers

The growth of trade led to the rise of the first large trading centers of the later Middle Ages. They were located on the important sea routes that connected western Europe with the Mediterranean Sea, Russia, and Scandinavia. Two of the earliest and most important trading centers were Venice and Flanders.

Venice Venice was an island port in the Adriatic (ā drē at′ ik) Sea close to the coast of Italy. It was founded in the 500s by people fleeing from the Germans.

MAP STUDY

HUMAN SYSTEMS
Trade routes tied all parts of western Europe together. **What was the most direct route merchants could take from Milan to Alexandria?**

Since the land was not very fertile, the early Venetians had to depend on the sea for a living. They fished in the Adriatic and produced salt from the seawater. They exchanged their products for wheat from towns on the mainland of Italy. They also traded wheat, wine, and slaves to the Byzantines for fabrics and spices.

During the 1100s, Venice became a leading port and many of its citizens became fulltime merchants. Venetian merchants learned to read and write, use money, and keep records. In time, they developed an effective banking system.

Venice's prosperity soon spread to other parts of Italy. Towns on the Italian mainland began to make cloth, which was sent to Venice to be shipped to other areas. Before long, other Italian towns along the seacoast became shipping centers.

The navies of the Italian trading towns drove the Muslims from the Mediterranean, making it safe for Italian seafarers. As a result, the Italians opened the Near East to Europeans.

However, the Italian trading towns quarreled among themselves over profits and trade routes. While they were quarreling,

Medieval Towns and Trade Routes

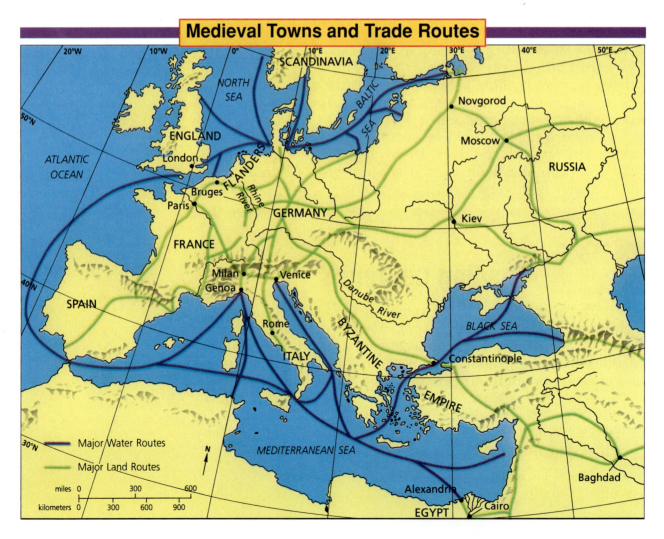

towns along Europe's Atlantic coast developed trade routes. By 1500, these towns had become more powerful than those in Italy.

Flanders Flanders, which today is part of Belgium, was an area of small towns on the northwest coast of Europe. The Flemish (flem' ish) people raised sheep and used the wool to develop a weaving industry. The cloth they produced became famous for its quality and soon was in heavy demand.

Flanders became the earliest Atlantic trading center. Its rivers joined together before they emptied into the North Sea. Where the rivers met, the Flemish built harbors. From these harbors, they shipped their valuable woolen cloth to other lands.

Flanders became an important stopping place for ships traveling along the Atlantic coast from Scandinavia to the Mediterranean. It also became an important link in the trade route between Constantinople and the North Sea.

By 1300, the most important trading partner of Flanders was England. Flemish traders set up shop in the dockyards of London. They relied on English shepherds to supply them with wool to be made into cloth. The finished cloth was then shipped back to England. In this way, the Flemish developed an international industry.

Section 1 Assessment

1. What led to the growth and development of Venice's trade?
2. How did the location of Flanders help it become an important trading center?
3. How did the Flemish develop an international industry?

Critical Thinking

4. **Demonstrating Reasoned Judgment** How effective do you think the Flemish were in using geography to benefit their economy?

Graphic Organizer Activity

5. Draw this diagram, and use it to compare the trading towns of Italy and Flanders.

	Italy	Flanders
Location		
Trade Items		
Key Trade Routes		

SECTION 2 Merchants

As sea trade grew, so did overland trade. Italian towns began sending goods across the Alps to areas in the north. Soon, an overland trade route connected Italy and Flanders. From this route, other routes developed and spread across Europe.

Merchants became an important part of European life during the late Middle Ages. The first merchants were mostly adventurers who traveled from place to place. As protection against robbers, they traveled in armed groups. They carried their goods in open wagons pulled by horses.

Fairs Merchants traveling along the chief route through eastern France stopped to trade with each other at special gatherings called **fairs.** The fairs were sponsored by nobles who collected taxes on sales. Fairs were held once a year for a few weeks at selected places. Over time, they attracted merchants from as far away as England and Egypt.

At the fairs, merchants could buy and sell goods or settle debts. They set up booths to show *wares*, or things for sale, such as pots, swords, armor, and clothing. Before long, merchants began to pay for goods with precious metals instead of bartering. Italian money changers tested and weighed coins from many different lands to determine their value. From the *banc*, or bench, at which the money changers sat comes the English word "bank."

The Growth of Towns

After awhile, merchants grew tired of moving around. They began to look for places where they could settle permanently and store their goods. They generally chose places along trade routes near waterways or road crossings. They also tried to settle close to a castle or monastery. This helped protect them from robbers and fights between nobles. The merchants surrounded their settlements with high stake

✓ **Reading Check**
Who sponsored most medieval **fairs?**

Fun Facts....

Wandering Musicians
In southern France, wandering poet-musicians called troubadours visited towns and nobles' courts, composing songs about love and the brave deeds of heroes. Some troubadours also traveled to parts of southern Spain, singing lyrics in Arabic, Hebrew, and Spanish.

MEDIEVAL MARKETPLACE During the Middle Ages merchants set up permanent shops that eventually developed into towns. Medieval merchants in this painting sell shoes, cloth, and tableware. **Why did merchants try to settle near castles or monasteries?**

fences and moats. Most towns of the Middle Ages developed from these merchant settlements.

The Germans called castles *burgs* (bergs). Towns came to be called **burgs** because they were often near castles. The new towns grew steadily and attracted people from the surrounding countryside. Markets became centers of business and social life. Once a week, nobles and peasants sold food for goods they could not make on the manor. Artisans came from the villages to find work. Often they brought their families with them. Over time, the towns became more than just centers of trade. They became communities in which people lived.

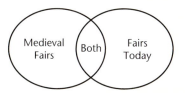

Reading Check How did **burgs** get their name?

Section 2 Assessment

1. **Define:** fairs, burgs.
2. Why did nobles sponsor fairs?
3. Where did merchants set up their marketplaces?

Critical Thinking

4. **Making Generalizations** How did merchants contribute to the growth of towns?

Graphic Organizer Activity

5. Draw the diagram below, and use it to compare the activities at medieval fairs with the activities at fairs today.

Medieval Fairs — Both — Fairs Today

SECTION 3 Living Conditions

By the 1200s, many towns were wealthy and large enough to have their fences replaced by walls and towers. Inside the walls, public buildings of stone and houses of wood were jammed close together. To save even more space, the houses had extra stories that extended over crooked narrow alleys.

The crowded conditions often made towns unhealthy places in which to live. Sewers were open, and there was little concern for cleanliness. People threw garbage out of windows onto the streets below. Rats were everywhere.

During the 1300s, diseased rats came to Europe on trading ships from the Middle East. They carried with them a plague called the "Black Death." This disease swept through Europe, killing millions of people. Experts think that one out of three Europeans died in the plague. To escape it, people fled from the towns and settled in the countryside. Trading, farming, and war came to a temporary halt.

Burgher Life   Merchants and artisans controlled a town's business and trade. They hired workers from the countryside to

Between 1348 and 1350, the Black Death claimed nearly 25 million lives. The epidemic stopped wars and slowed trade. Officials sealed off infected homes, suspended religious services, and made it illegal to meet in groups. It took almost 200 years for Europe to regain its pre-1348 level of population.

make goods for them. At first, the merchants, artisans, and workers who lived in towns were all called **burghers** (ber' guhrz). Later the title was used to refer to rich merchants.

The daily life of burghers and their families started with prayers at dawn. The burgher hurried off to the docks and market to see how his products were selling. Then, he met with his business partners.

The burgher's wife kept house, managed servants, and cared for children. The family ate two large meals a day—one at ten o'clock in the morning and another at six o'clock in the evening. A typical meal consisted of eel, roast beef, lark pastry, and curded milk. About nine o'clock in the evening, the family went to bed.

Changing Ways   Under the feudal system, the land on which towns were built was owned by kings, nobles, and bishops. They taxed the people in the towns and charged them

Linking Across Time

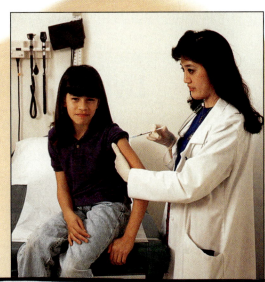

Health Care   The unhealthy, overcrowded conditions of medieval cities encouraged the rapid spread of diseases such as measles, smallpox, polio, flu, and the "Black Death" (below). Today doctors know that most diseases are caused by bacteria and viruses. Many diseases common in medieval times have been wiped out or curbed through good health practices such as washing hands or receiving vaccinations like the polio shot (right). **What carried the "Black Death" through Europe in the 1300s?**

fees to use the marketplace. The burghers did not like this or the other restrictions placed on them. They resented having to get a noble's permission to marry, move around, or own land. They also did not like serving in the noble's army.

Many nobles viewed the rise of towns as a threat to their power. They resented the wealth of the burghers and began to use feudal laws to keep them in their place. The Church was also against the rise of towns. Its leaders feared that the making of profit would interfere with religion.

The burghers, however, resented feudal laws. They thought these laws were not suited to business. The burghers now had wealth and power. Thus, they began to depend less on nobles and bishops. Instead, they developed a sense of loyalty toward their town. They worked together to build schools, hospitals, and churches. They began to demand changes.

Communes and Charters   In the 1100s, townspeople in northern Italy formed political groups called **communes** (kom' yūnz). Their purpose was to work against the nobles and bishops and for the people by establishing local self-government. The Italian communes were successful. Soon, the idea of communes spread to the towns of northern Europe. Some kings and nobles gave the townspeople **charters,** or documents allowing towns to run their own affairs.

The charters gave the townspeople the right to elect officials to run their towns. A council collected taxes and set charges for merchants who bought and sold goods in the town market. It also repaired streets, formed citizen armies, and ran hospitals, orphanages, and special homes for the poor.

The towns enforced their own laws and set up special courts. To reduce crime, the towns severely punished those who broke the law. Murderers were hanged. Robbers lost a hand or an arm. Those who committed minor crimes, such as disturbing the peace, were whipped or put in the *stocks*, or a wooden frame with holes in which a person's feet and hands were locked.

HISTORY Online

Student Web Activity

Visit the *Human Heritage* Web site at **humanheritage.glencoe.com** and click on *Chapter 26— Student Web Activities* to find out more about the towns of the Middle Ages.

Reading Check What was the purpose of **communes?**

Reading Check What did **charters** allow towns- people to do?

Section 3 Assessment

1. **Define:** burghers, communes, charters.
2. What were some of the problems faced by medieval towns?
3. What changes did burghers want to make in feudal laws?

Critical Thinking

4. **Demonstrating Reasoned Judgment** What laws or regulations would you have written to further improve condi- tions in medieval towns?

Graphic Organizer Activity

5. Draw this diagram, and use it to show characteristics of towns in the late Mid- dle Ages.

Medieval Towns

SECTION 4   The Rise of Guilds

Reading Check
Why did merchants, artisans, and workers form **guilds?**

Around the 1100s, merchants, artisans, and workers formed **guilds** (gildz). These were business groups that made sure that their members were treated equally. Each craft had its own guild, whose members lived and worked in the same area of town.

Craft guilds controlled the work of artisans such as carpenters, shoemakers, blacksmiths, masons, tailors, and weavers. Women working as laundresses, seamstresses, embroiderers, and maidservants had their own trade associations. Guild members were not allowed to compete with one another or to advertise. Each member had to work the same number of hours, hire the same number of workers, and pay the same wages.

Guilds controlled all business and trade in a town. Only members could buy, sell, or make goods there. Outsiders who wanted to sell their goods in the town market had to get permission from the guilds. The guild decided the fair price for a product or service, and all members had to charge that price. Guild members who sold poorly made goods or cheated in business dealings had to pay large fines. They could also be expelled from the guild.

Guilds were more than business or trade groups. If members became ill, other members took care of them. If members were out of work, the guild gave them food. When members died, the other members prayed for their souls, paid for funerals, and supported the families. Guilds were also centers of social life. Holy day celebrations, processions, and outdoor plays were sponsored by the guild. Close friendships often developed among guild members.

Reading Check
What was an **apprentice?** Who were the **masters** in a guild?

Job Training

It was not easy to become a member of a guild. A person had to be an **apprentice** (uh pren′ tis), or trainee, in a trade for two to seven years. Apprentices were taught their trade by **masters,** or experts. They had to live with and obey their masters until their training was finished.

Reading Check
How did a **journeyman** differ from an apprentice?

The next step was becoming a **journeyman** (jer′ nē muhn), or a person who worked under a master for a daily wage. After a certain amount of time, journeymen took a test to become masters. The test was given by guild officials. Journeymen had to make and present a "masterpiece" to prove they had learned their craft. Those who passed the test were considered masters and could make their own goods. Often, they worked in the back of their houses and sold their goods in a shop in the front of the house.

By 1400, many merchants and artisans had begun challenging the control of the guilds. They felt the guilds kept them from increasing their trade and profits. Then, too, apprentices disliked the strict rules set by guilds. It was getting harder and harder for apprentices to become masters. Many masters were grouping together and hiring unskilled workers instead of apprentices.

Section 4 Assessment

1. **Define:** guilds, apprentice, masters, journeyman.
2. What rules did guild members have to obey?
3. Why did people begin to challenge guilds in the 1400s?

Critical Thinking

4. **Analyzing Information** "The steps taken to become a master were too diffi-cult." Do you agree or disagree with this statement? Give reasons for your opinion.

Graphic Organizer Activity

5. Draw this diagram, and use it to show the steps in joining a guild.

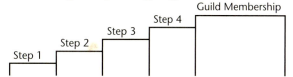

Step 1 — Step 2 — Step 3 — Step 4 — Guild Membership

SECTION 5 Cultural Changes

During the 1400s, merchants, artisans, and bankers became more important than they had been in the past. Their growing power led to the decline of feudalism.

Many townspeople were as rich as, or richer than, the nobles. Bankers lent money to kings, nobles, and church officials for wars, building repairs, and entertainment. With their new wealth, merchants turned their homes into mansions. Some even bought castles from nobles who had lost their money. They began to set fashions. Women wore furs and gowns made of *brocade* (bro kād'), or a cloth woven with raised designs on it. Men dressed in colorful jackets, stockings, and feathered caps.

The townspeople had more leisure time and money to spend on their interests. Many hired private teachers to educate their sons. The sons later went to universities to study law, religion, and medicine. There was time to enjoy art and books, so townspeople began to support the work of painters and writers.

Most townspeople used such languages as German, French, and English. A scholar named Dante (dahn' tā) wrote the *Divine Comedy* in Italian. It is one of the most famous poems of the Middle Ages. Geoffrey Chaucer (jef' rē cho' suhr) wrote the *Canterbury Tales* in English. These tales are still popular today.

Townspeople began to think differently from nobles and peasants. The townspeople came to believe that they should be free to develop their talents and to improve their way of life. They wanted a strong central government. They began to look toward kings to provide leadership.

People in History

Geoffrey Chaucer
c. 1340–1400

English Poet

Chaucer's poems include the *Legend of Good Women*, an unfinished work about heroines from the past. His most famous poem is the *Canterbury Tales*, which tells the tales told by a group of travelers on their way to a shrine.

Section 5 Assessment

1. In what ways did the cultural life of townspeople change during the 1400s?
2. What did townspeople want government to do?

Critical Thinking

3. **Making Inferences** Why might nobles have disliked the success of merchants during the Middle Ages?

Graphic Organizer Activity

4. Draw this diagram, and use it to show details that support the following main idea: "The growing power of merchants, artisans, and bankers led to the decline of feudalism."

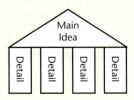

Chapter Summary & Study Guide

1. During the 1000s and 1100s, increased trade between Europe and the Near East led to the rise of trading centers, such as Venice and Flanders.
2. Venetian traders developed an effective banking system and, with the help of other Italian trading towns, drove the Muslims from the Mediterranean.
3. Flanders was the earliest Atlantic trading center, and, by 1300, it had developed a flourishing international trade with England.
4. The first medieval merchants traveled overland in armed groups and traded with each other at fairs.
5. After a while, merchants began to settle in towns known as burgs.
6. Most medieval towns were overcrowded, unhealthy places to live.
7. Artisans and rich merchants controlled the business and trade of towns.

8. Nobles and church officials viewed the rise of towns as a threat to their power and wealth.
9. Burghers resented feudal laws, and they resisted nobles and demanded charters for greater self-government.
10. Guilds set wages, prices, and working conditions, and helped members who were sick or out of work.
11. By the 1400s, many masters and artisans resented the control of guilds over profits, and they began to hire untrained workers instead of apprentices.
12. As townspeople grew richer and more powerful, they looked to kings for leadership, and feudalism declined.

Self-Check Quiz

Visit the *Human Heritage* Web site at **humanheritage. glencoe.com** and click on **Chapter 26—Self-Check Quiz** to assess your understanding of this chapter.

Using Key Terms

Imagine you are living in a town in western Europe during the late Middle Ages. Write a diary entry describing your life there. Use the following words in your diary.

fairs   burgs   burghers
communes   charters   guilds
apprentice   masters   journeyman

Understanding Main Ideas

1. What led to the development of trade between Europe and the Near East during the 1000s and 1100s?
2. What led to the decline of Italian trading centers?
3. How did fairs affect the development of banking?
4. What effects did the "Black Death" have on Europe?
5. How did a person become a master in a guild?
6. Why were nobles and church officials against the rise of towns?
7. How were the ideas of townspeople different from those of the nobles and peasants?

Critical Thinking

1. What would you have liked about being a merchant in the Middle Ages? Explain.
2. Would you have supported or opposed the position taken by Italian communes during the 1100s? Explain.
3. Would you have preferred to be a burgher or a noble during the Middle Ages? Explain.

4. Do you approve or disapprove of the rules established by the guilds? Explain.

Graphic Organizer Activity

Culture Create a diagram like the one below, and use it to compare life on a medieval manor with life in a medieval trading town.

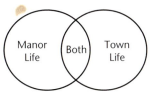

Manor Life | Both | Town Life

Geography in History

Places and Regions Refer to the map on page 400. At what places do you think European trading ships could have been attacked by pirates? How would geographic features increase the possibility of an attack? Explain.

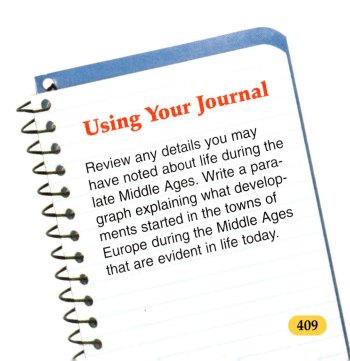

Using Your Journal

Review any details you may have noted about life during the late Middle Ages. Write a paragraph explaining what developments started in the towns of Europe during the Middle Ages that are evident in life today.

Rise of Monarchies
900 A.D.–1500 A.D.

▲ Coronation robe worn by
King Roger II of Sicily

Joan of Arc ▶

1066 A.D.	1215 A.D.	1272 A.D.	1273 A.D.	1337 A.D.	1492 A.D.
William the Conqueror invades England	Magna Carta is signed	Edward I sets up Parliament	Hapsburg dynasty is founded	Hundred Years' War begins	Ferdinand and Isabella unite Spain

Chapter Focus

Read to Discover

- How the Capetian kings strengthened the French monarchy.
- What changes took place in the English monarchy during the Middle Ages.
- What the main causes and results were of the Hundred Years' War.
- How the Holy Roman Empire was created and ruled.
- How the Catholic monarchs united Spain.

Chapter Overview

Visit the *Human Heritage* Web site at <u>humanheritage.glencoe.com</u> and click on **Chapter 27—Chapter Overviews** to preview this chapter.

 Terms to Learn

monarchies
circuit judges
grand jury
trial jury
dauphin
diet
corregidores

 People to Know

Hugh Capet
William the
  Conqueror
Joan of Arc
Frederick II
Ferdinand and
  Isabella

Places to Locate

Hastings
Orleans
Sicily
Holy Roman
  Empire
Granada

Why It's Important   The growth of trade and towns during the late Middle Ages led to many changes in western Europe. Some of these changes were political. The rise of **monarchies** (mon' uhr kēz), or countries governed by one ruler, led to the decline of feudalism.

 **Reading Check**
What are **monarchies?**

SECTION 1   France

In 987, Hugh Capet (ka pā'), a French noble, was chosen as the new king of France. At the time, France consisted of many feudal territories. As king, Capet ruled only a small area between the Seine (sān) and Loire (lwahr) rivers. Capet, who died in 996, was the first of a line of Capetian (kuh pē' shuhn) kings who ruled France for some 300 years. For 100 years after his death, however, these kings were weak and did little to increase royal power.

In 1108, Louis VI, known as "Louis the Fat," became king and increased the power of the monarchy. He got rid of disloyal nobles and put loyal persons of lower birth in their place. He stopped the raids of lawless vassals and granted charters to many towns, thus winning the loyalty of the townspeople.

The king's power was further increased under Philip II, also known as Philip Augustus. Philip, who ruled from 1179 to 1223,

LOUIS IX King Louis IX of France was known for his honesty and just dealings. After his death, he was made a saint of the Roman Catholic Church. Louis's support of the Church is expressed in this painting of the king feeding a church official. **To what line of French kings did Louis IX belong?**

made Paris the center of government. He increased the size of his kingdom through marriage and by winning back French lands held by the English. To make sure the nobles did not become too powerful while he was fighting in the Crusades, Philip II appointed royal agents to keep a close watch on them.

In 1226, Philip's grandson became King Louis IX. He brought peace to France and helped unite the French people. He ordered the nobles to stop feuding and forbade them to settle disputes by fighting duels. Most nobles minted their own money. Louis IX made it illegal to use coins made anywhere else but the royal mint. He set up a royal court to which anyone could bring disputes.

Philip IV, Louis's grandson, ruled from 1285 to 1314. Known as "Philip the Fair," Philip IV believed the interests of the state came first. So, he seized the English fortresses in France that he felt were necessary for his kingdom's security. He also went to war with the Flemish when they refused to let France control their cloth trade. Philip believed a kingdom could not exist without taxes. So, he made sure that taxes were collected regularly. He also taxed the clergy, who had not been taxed before. To help him run the country, Philip IV formed the Estates-General, an assembly of nobles, clergy, and townspeople. This marked the beginning of a national government in France. By the time Philip IV died in 1314, France was united under one ruler.

Painting of Philip the Fair

Section 1 Assessment

1. **Define:** monarchies.
2. How did Louis VI increase the power of the monarchy?
3. What did Louis IX and Philip the Fair do to help unite France?

Critical Thinking

4. **Drawing Conclusions**   Why do you think Louis IX made it illegal for nobles to coin their own money?

Graphic Organizer Activity

5. Draw this diagram, and use it to summarize the accomplishments of these French kings: Hugh Capet, Louis VI, Philip II, Louis IX, and Philip IV.

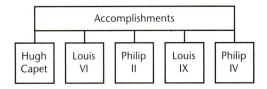

```
              ┌───────────────────────┐
              │     Accomplishments   │
              └──┬────┬────┬────┬──────┘
            ┌────┐┌────┐┌────┐┌────┐┌────┐
            │Hugh││Louis││Philip││Louis││Philip│
            │Capet││ VI ││  II  ││ IX ││  IV  │
            └────┘└────┘└────┘└────┘└────┘
```

SECTION 2   England

In 1042, the witenagemot made Edward the Confessor, an Anglo-Saxon prince, king of England. Edward gave money to the poor and sponsored the building in London of Westminster Abbey, the church in which later English kings and queens were crowned. He spent so much time in religious work, however, that he failed to carry out his royal duties. As a result, the nobles increased their hold on the country. The most powerful noble was Harold Godwinson. When Edward died in 1066 without an heir, Harold became the new king.

William the Conqueror   Harold Godwinson did not remain king for long. William, Duke of Normandy, a cousin of Edward the Confessor, claimed that before Edward died, he had promised him the English throne.

In 1066, William led an army of between 4,000 and 7,000 Norman knights across the channel to England. They met Harold's army in battle near Hastings, a town just south of London. To stop the Norman charge, English foot soldiers armed with axes formed a wall of shields on the edge of a low hill. William knew he could not break through the wall. So, he had his soldiers pretend to retreat. When the English broke formation to follow them, the Normans turned on the English. By nightfall, King Harold was dead, and the English were defeated. William the Conqueror was crowned King William I of England.

At first, the English resisted William's rule. To crush English revolts—and to keep the Normans in line—William introduced feudalism. He seized the lands of English nobles and divided them among Norman nobles. In return, they became his vassals. They promised to be loyal and to provide him with soldiers.

Then ... & Now

Language For years after the Norman conquest, the upper classes in England spoke Norman French, the lower classes Anglo-Saxon English. Modern English preserves this double heritage. Words for farm animals are mainly Anglo-Saxon: *ox, cow, pig, sheep.* Words for cooked meat, once served mainly to the upper classes, come from French: *beef, pork, mutton* (from *boeuf, porc, mouton*).

Fun Facts....

The Final Say The *Domesday Book* got this popular name because people said there was no chance of arguing with its records. That is, its determinations were as final as those of God on doomsday—the Day of Judgment.

William kept many English laws and government practices. He received advice from the witenagemot, now called the Great Council. He depended on such local officials as the sheriff. William also made many changes. In 1086, he took a census and a survey of the land in order to tax the people properly. This information was recorded in two huge volumes called the *Domesday Book.* The title comes from the Anglo-Saxon word *doom,* meaning "judgment."

William brought *continental,* or European mainland, ways to England. Under his rule, the English learned Norman customs and the French language. The wealthy built castles, cathedrals, and monasteries in the French style. The people learned new skills from Norman weavers and other artisans.

Henry II   After William died in 1087, there was confusion in England until 1154 when William's great-grandson became King Henry II. Henry ruled England, most of Ireland, Scotland, and Wales. He was also a feudal lord in France, where he owned more land than he did in England. Some of the French lands belonged to his wife, Eleanor of Aquitaine.

BATTLE OF HASTINGS   William the Conqueror took the throne of England after his army defeated the English army at the Battle of Hastings in 1066. This painting shows Norman knights on horseback attacking the English soldiers. **What title did William the Conqueror take after his victory at Hastings?**

Henry II restored order and forced the nobles to give him their loyalty. He also used the law to gain more power, and he worked to reform English courts. A central royal court was set up in London with trained lawyers as judges. **Circuit judges,** or judges who traveled throughout the country, brought the king's law to all parts of England. They made it the common law of the land, thus helping to unite the country.

Henry also set up juries to settle quarrels about land. After a while, two kinds of juries came into being. One was the **grand jury,** or a group of people who present to judges the names of people suspected of crimes. The other was the **trial jury,** or a group of people who decide whether a person accused of a crime is innocent or guilty. The trial jury took the place of the medieval trial by ordeal.

Henry II believed that everyone, even church officials, should be tried in the king's courts. Thomas à Becket, Henry's close friend and the Archbishop of Canterbury, did not agree. Becket wanted Church officials to be free of royal control. The quarrel between the king and the archbishop ultimately led to the murder of Becket by four of Henry's knights. After the murder, Henry II made peace with the Church by allowing some of the clergy to be tried in Church courts.

Magna Carta and Parliament

When Henry II died in 1189, his oldest son Richard became king. Richard, however, was more interested in his French lands than in ruling England. He spent most of his time fighting in the Near East on the Crusades.

When Richard died in 1199, his brother John became king of England. John lost most of his lands in France to the French king. When he increased England's taxes and began to ignore the law, the country's nobles became angry. They refused to obey him unless he agreed to give them certain rights. In 1215, John met the nobles in the meadow of Runnymede (ruhn' ē mēd), where they forced him to sign the *Magna Carta* (mag' nuh kar' tuh), or Great Charter.

The Magna Carta took away some of the king's power and increased that of the nobles. A king could no longer collect taxes unless the Great Council agreed. Freemen accused of crimes had the right to a trial by their *peers,* or equals. The Magna Carta was viewed as an important step toward democracy. It brought to government the new idea that even a king is not above the law.

John died in 1216, and his son became King Henry III. Henry, however, was a weak ruler who allowed the feudal lords in the Great Council to rule England. In 1264, Simon de Montfort (mahnt' fuhrt), Henry's brother-in-law, came to power. He gave the people a voice in government by letting them have representatives in the Great Council.

Reading Check How did **circuit judges** spread English law?

Reading Check What was the difference between a **grand jury** and a **trial jury?**

Constitutions Unlike the United States, the United Kingdom does not have a single written document called a "constitution." Instead, British leaders govern according to a series of laws and charters. The oldest of those is the Magna Carta.

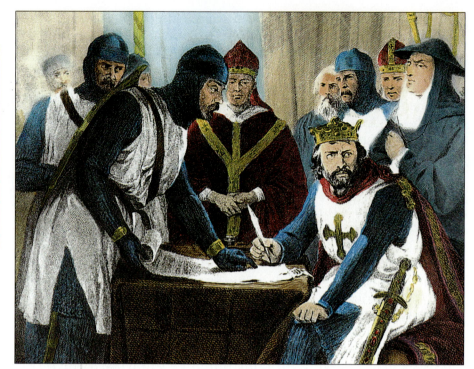

MAGNA CARTA   The Archbishop of Canterbury and merchants joined the nobles at Runnymede to force King John to sign the Magna Carta. In this painting, as the Archbishop looks on, a noble shows King John where to sign the document. **What new idea did the Magna Carta bring to government?**

Eight years later, the new king, Edward I, went even further. He called for a meeting of representatives to advise him and to help him make laws. This gathering, known as Parliament (par' luh muhnt), gave the people a greater share in the ruling of England. Parliament later broke into two separate groups. Nobles and clergy met as the House of Lords, while knights and townspeople met as the House of Commons.

Section 2 Assessment

1. **Define:** circuit judges, grand jury, trial jury.
2. How did the Normans win the Battle of Hastings?
3. Why was King John forced to sign the Magna Carta?

Critical Thinking

4. **Predicting Consequences**   How might the history of English government have been different if nobles had not forced King John to sign the Magna Carta?

Graphic Organizer Activity

5. Draw this diagram, and use it to show some of the milestones in democracy that took place in medieval England.

Milestones in English Democracy	1.
	2.
	3.
	4.

SECTION 3　The Hundred Years' War

In the early 1300s, the English still held a small part of southwest France. The kings of France, who were growing more powerful, wanted to drive the English out. In 1337, the English king, Edward III, declared himself king of France. This angered the French even more. In 1337, England and France fought the first in a long series of battles known as the Hundred Years' War.

The Hundred Years' War began when the English defeated the French fleet and won control of the sea. The English then invaded France. They defeated the French at the Battle of Crécy (krā sē') in 1346 and again at the Battle of Agincourt (aj' uhn kōrt) in 1415.

The English owed their success on land mostly to a new weapon called the *longbow,* which shot steel-tipped arrows. The French still used the shorter crossbow. The crossbow could not send arrows as far as the longbow, and the French arrows were not as sharp as the steel-tipped English arrows.

At Crécy the English forces also used the first portable firearm in European warfare—a very crude cannon. This early weapon was made of a long iron tube mounted on a pole. The weapon was difficult to carry and use, but led to the development of a more refined cannon that was a major weapon in many later wars.

Joan of Arc　By 1429, much of France was in English hands. Charles, the French *dauphin* (do' fuhn), or eldest son of the king, was fighting the English for the French throne. Then, a 17-year-old French peasant named Jeanne d'Arc (zhahn dark'), or Joan of Arc, appeared. She said that while praying, she had heard heavenly voices telling her she must save France. She went to see Charles and told him that God had sent her to help him. She said that if she had an army she would free Orleans (or lā ahn'), a city the English had been besieging for seven months. Charles gave Joan an army, a suit of armor, and a white linen banner.

Joan led an attack against the English army at Orleans. Within ten days, the city was free, and Joan became known as the "Maid of Orleans." Shortly after, with Joan at his side, the dauphin was crowned King Charles VII of France. Joan wanted to return home, but Charles convinced her to stay with the army. A few months later, a French traitor captured her and sold her to the English. After spending a year in prison, she was tried as a witch and burned at the stake. Joan died at the age of 18, a girl who could neither read nor write but who had led an army. A trial twenty-four years later proclaimed her innocence.

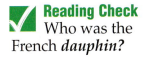

Reading Check
Who was the French *dauphin?*

Student Web Activity

Visit the *Human Heritage* Web site at humanheritage.glencoe.com and click on **Chapter 27— Student Web Activities** to find out more about Joan of Arc.

The French continued to fight after Joan's death. By 1453, they had driven the English from all of France except the seaport of Calais (ka lā´), and the war came to an end.

Results of the War

Both France and England were changed by the Hundred Years' War. By 1500, the last French feudal territories were under the king's rule, and France was unified. England, too, was unified by the war, but its monarchy was weakened. Not until 1485, when a Welshman named Henry Tudor (tū´ duhr) became king, did it become strong again.

Because of the Hundred Years' War, the common people in both England and France became more important. Many peasants had died during the war from disease or fighting. Those who remained were greatly needed as workers. The peasants knew this and began to make demands. They forced the nobles to pay them wages and allow them to move outside the manors. When the nobles tried to force them back to the old ways, they revolted. Most became farmers who rented land from the nobles.

JOAN OF ARC   Claiming that heavenly voices had instructed her to do so, Joan of Arc led a French army against the invading English and helped return the French king to the throne. She became a national heroine and a saint of the Roman Catholic Church. **How did Joan earn her nickname "Maid of Orleans"?**

Section 3 Assessment

1. **Define:** *dauphin.*
2. Why did France and England go to war?
3. How did the Hundred Years' War affect French and English peasants?

Critical Thinking

4. **Understanding Cause and Effect** What was the connection between the Hundred Years' War and the end of feudalism?

Graphic Organizer Activity

5. Draw this diagram, and use it to show facts about Joan of Arc's life. (Add more answer circles as necessary.)

SECTION 4 Germany

During the 900s, Germany was the most important country in western Europe. Over time, though, German kings lost much of their authority to powerful nobles who wanted to rule their own territories. The king, however, still had the right to remove lords who would not obey him.

Otto I   In 936, Otto I became king of Germany. He wanted to unite the country and rule without nobles. He removed lords who would not obey him and gave their estates to his family. Then, he turned to the Roman Catholic Church for help. Its leaders wanted him to set up a Christian Roman Empire in western Europe. So, Otto made many of his loyal followers bishops and abbots and gave them government posts. In return, they supplied him with money and soldiers.

Otto began expanding Germany. In 951, he marched south into Italy, where he took over the northern Italian trading cities. In 962, he led an army to Rome to free the Pope from the control of Roman nobles. In return, the Pope crowned Otto I emperor of the Holy Roman Empire, a large new state made up of Germany and northern Italy. Otto saw himself as the heir of the Roman emperors. For the next 90 years, Otto and the emperors who followed him controlled the office of Pope.

Frederick I   In 1152, Frederick I became emperor. Because of his full red beard, he was called Barbarossa, or "red beard." Frederick forced the powerful lords to promise him loyalty and to work for his government.

Frederick's attempts to control the nobles and unify the empire worked against him. The nobles grew rich from their government posts. At the same time, the Italian city-states, aided

German Crown

by the Pope, banded together and defeated Frederick's armies. Frederick had to accept a peace that recognized the independence of the city-states.

While leading the Third Crusade in 1190, Frederick drowned in a river in Asia Minor. Later, a legend about him spread among the Germans. It stated that he was not dead but under a magic spell that had put him to sleep somewhere high in the mountains. The people believed that one day he would awake and restore the glory of Germany.

Frederick II   In 1220, Frederick II, Frederick I's grandson, became emperor. Frederick II was raised in Palermo (puh luhr´ mō), Sicily, which his father had made part of the Holy Roman Empire. He ignored Germany and concentrated on ruling the people of Sicily.

Frederick was known as the best-educated monarch of his time. He spoke several languages and enjoyed doing scientific experiments. He supported many artists and scholars. He

FREDERICK II   Frederick II was greatly interested in the sciences and medicine and encouraged their study during his reign. He had a special interest in the study of birds and wrote a book on the subject. This painting of Frederick shows him with his falcon handler. **How did Frederick II aid medieval learning?**

Linking Across Time

Universities Scholarship was important to the Hapsburg family, which included Maximilian I. The Hapsburgs encouraged the growth of universities throughout the Holy Roman Empire (left). Universities spread throughout Europe and the rest of the world (below). **Why are universities important today?**

founded a university in Palermo so young men could study at home rather than in other countries. Although the Church was against it, Frederick even adopted many Muslim customs.

When Frederick began conquering land in Italy, the Pope became afraid that he would take over Church lands around Rome. To stop Frederick, the Pope excommunicated him in 1227. He also called for a crusade against Frederick. This gave the German princes the chance for which they had been waiting. They broke away from Frederick's rule and made Germany a loose grouping of states under their control.

The Hapsburgs

Whenever an emperor of the Holy Roman Empire died, the German princes met in a **diet,** or assembly. There, they elected a new emperor. In 1273, the princes elected as emperor a member of the Hapsburg (haps' berg) family named Rudolf. He and members of his family served as Holy Roman emperors for about the next 650 years.

One important Hapsburg was Maximilian I (mak suh mil' yuhn), who became emperor in 1493. He worked to extend the empire's power all through Europe. When he married Mary of Burgundy, he gained control of Flanders and other areas of what are now the Low Countries, or Belgium, the Netherlands, and Luxembourg. By marrying his children into other European

Reading Check
What was the purpose of the German **diet?**

royal families, he brought still more countries under Hapsburg control. He could not gain complete control, however, in Germany where the princes continued to have authority over their own lands.

Section 4 Assessment

1. **Define:** diet.
2. How were the German emperors able to control the office of Pope in the late 900s and early 1000s?
3. How did the Hapsburgs come to power?

Critical Thinking

4. **Drawing Conclusions** Why do you think a strong rule by a king or queen did not develop in Germany?

Graphic Organizer Activity

5. Draw this diagram, and use it to show the achievements of German rulers in the Middle Ages.

Ruler	Achievements

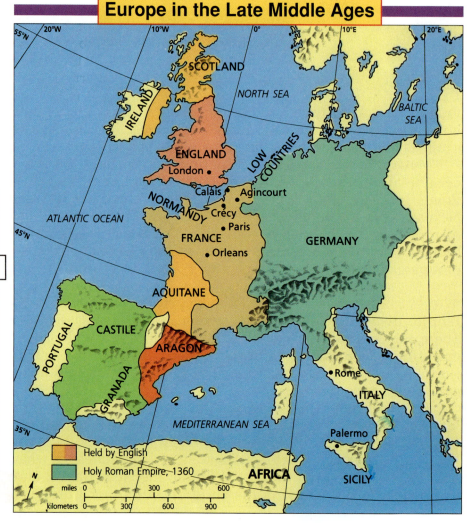

Europe in the Late Middle Ages

MAP STUDY

PLACES AND REGIONS Strong kings and queens appeared in England, France, Spain, and Portugal in the late Middle Ages. **How did the size of the Holy Roman Empire compare to other regions of western Europe during the late Middle Ages?**

Held by English

Holy Roman Empire, 1360

SECTION 5 Spain

Painting of Spanish Hero El Cid and his father

While the western European monarchies were increasing their power, Spain was under the control of the Moors. When the Moors conquered Spain in 711, they brought with them learning and luxury. Most Spaniards, however, were Christians and opposed Muslim rule. They banded together to drive the Moors out of the country. By the 1200s, the Moors controlled only the small southern kingdom of Granada (gruh nahd' uh).

The rest of Spain was made up of several kingdoms, the most powerful of which were Castile (kas tēl') and Aragon (ar' uh gahn). In 1469, Prince Ferdinand of Aragon married Princess Isabella of Castile. Within ten years, they became king and queen and united their kingdoms into one country.

Ferdinand and Isabella accomplished this in different ways. To control the nobles, the king and queen took away some of their privileges. To keep order in the land, they sent royal officials called *corregidores* (kō rā hē dō' rās) to govern the towns. They also set up special courts in the countryside.

The most important way in which they unified Spain, however, was through religion. Ferdinand and Isabella were known as the "Catholic Monarchs." They believed that to be truly united, all Spaniards should be Catholic. They turned their attention first to the Jews. The Jews had lived freely under the Moors. However, as Christians took over more of Spain, they killed thousands of Jews. To save themselves, many Jews converted.

Ferdinand and Isabella believed these new Christians were practicing their old religion in secret. So, they set up the Spanish Inquisition. The Spanish Inquisition tried and tortured thousands of people charged with heresy. More than 2,000 people were burned to death. Still, most Jews refused to change their faith. So, in 1492, Ferdinand and Isabella told the remaining Jews to convert or leave the country. Most left the country.

Next, the king and queen turned their attention to the Moors. In 1492, the last of the Moors had surrendered Granada to armies of Ferdinand and Isabella. The treaty signed at the time promised the Moors freedom of religion. Nevertheless, in 1502 the Catholic Monarchs ordered the remaining Moors to convert or leave. Most left Spain for northern Africa.

Although now a united Catholic monarchy, Spain was weaker than it had been before. This was because most of its artisans, merchants, bankers, doctors, and educators had been either Jews or Moors. After these people left, there were few trained Spaniards to take their place.

> **Reading Check**
> What was the role of the *corregidores?*

Equal Footing In 1990 Spain finally overturned the 1492 order calling for the expulsion or conversion of the Jews. Now both Judaism and Protestantism are on an equal basis with Roman Catholicism, giving all three religions the same tax breaks and privileges.

Section 5 Assessment

1. **Define:** *corregidores.*
2. How did Ferdinand and Isabella control the nobles and keep order in Spain?
3. How did Ferdinand and Isabella use religion to unite Spain?

Critical Thinking

4. **Predicting Consequences** How might Spain have been different if the Spanish king and queen had allowed freedom of religion?

Graphic Organizer Activity

5. Draw this diagram, and use it to show the causes and effects of Ferdinand and Isabella's united Catholic monarchy.

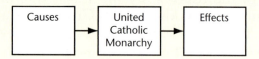

| Causes | → | United Catholic Monarchy | → | Effects |

Chapter Summary & Study Guide

1. The rise of trade and towns in western Europe led to the rise of strong monarchies.
2. The Capetian dynasty strengthened the French monarchy by granting town charters and by setting up a national court, a national currency, a tax system, and the Estates-General.
3. William the Conqueror defeated the English at the Battle of Hastings in 1066 and brought the system of feudalism to England.
4. Henry II strengthened England by imposing his law on the land and by reforming courts.
5. In 1215, English nobles forced King John to sign the Magna Carta, which established the idea that a king was not above the law.
6. In 1272, Edward I set up Parliament to help him make laws.
7. During the Hundred Years' War, fought between 1337 and 1453, Joan of Arc led armies to force the English from France.
8. Because of the Hundred Years' War, both France and England were unified and the common people became more important.
9. The Pope crowned Otto I emperor of the Holy Roman Empire in 962. However, future German emperors had a hard time uniting unruly German princes.
10. The Hapsburg family ruled the Holy Roman Empire from 1273 until the early 1900s.
11. By 1492, Ferdinand and Isabella had conquered the Moors and made Spain a united Catholic country.

HISTORY *Online*

Self-Check Quiz

Visit the *Human Heritage* Web site at **humanheritage. glencoe.com** and click on *Chapter 27—Self-Check Quiz* to assess your understanding of this chapter.

Using Key Terms

Imagine that you are a news reporter who has a chance to interview one of the kings or queens you have read about in this chapter. Identify whom you will interview, and write five questions you would like to ask that person. Use the following words in your questions.

monarchies	circuit judges	grand jury
trial jury	*dauphin*	diet
corregidores		

Understanding Main Ideas

1. How did the Estates-General help strengthen the French monarchy?
2. What changes did the Magna Carta bring about in English government?
3. Why did the position of the common people in England and France improve as a result of the Hundred Years' War?
4. How did Otto I set up a Christian Roman Empire in western Europe?
5. What did the Moors bring to Spain?
6. What was the purpose of the Spanish Inquisition?

Critical Thinking

1. If you had been King John, how would you have reacted to the demand that you sign the Magna Carta? Explain your answer.
2. If you had been Joan of Arc, what decision would you have made about attacking the English at Orleans? Explain your answer.
3. How did the Hundred Years' War both help and hurt England and France?

4. Would you have agreed or disagreed with Ferdinand and Isabella that all people in a country should follow the same religion? Explain.

Graphic Organizer Activity

Citizenship Create a diagram like the one below, and use it to compare English government in 1275 with government in the United States today.

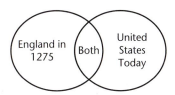

England in 1275 — Both — United States Today

Geography in History

Places and Regions Refer to the map on page 422. There were several places outside the control of either the English or the Holy Roman Empire. What geographic features do these places have in common?

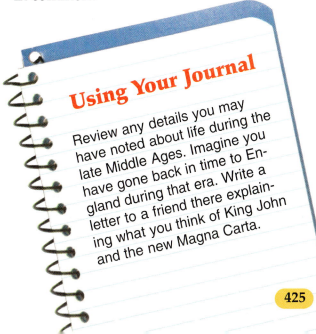

Using Your Journal

Review any details you may have noted about life during the late Middle Ages. Imagine you have gone back in time to England during that era. Write a letter to a friend there explaining what you think of King John and the new Magna Carta.

Around

FEUDAL JAPAN

From about 1000 A.D.–1600 A.D., Japan went through its own feudal age. Like the feudal age in Europe, this was a time when power belonged to military leaders, known as *samurai*, and the soldiers who served them. The most powerful samurai became *daimyo*, or local lords. The samurai, like medieval knights, pledged their loyalty and military service to the daimyo. Individual states controlled by the daimyo battled for control of Japan and the right to claim the title of *shogun*—the head of Japan's military government. The principle of *bushido*, which means "the way of the warrior," shaped life in much of feudal Japan.

Japan

130°E   140°E
44°N
SEA OF JAPAN
38°N
JAPAN
N
32°N
miles   0   150   300
kilometers 0   150   300

▲ Japan's island location helped isolate it from unwanted intruders. Its rugged terrain limited the amount of available land and increased the power of the land-owning daimyo and the samurai who served them.

▶ The Japanese considered a samurai's armor a work of art. The armor was made of horizontal rows of lacquered iron or leather held together by braided silk cords. The artisans who fashioned the armor—and the swords that went with it—were held in high regard.

the World

▲ Japanese nobles tried to include beauty and poetry in every aspect of their lives. Even everyday objects such as this tea pot were crafted with an artist's care.

▼ Swordsmiths produced beautiful—and sharp—swords.

The Japanese imported Zen Buddhism from China. Zen holds that enlightenment can be achieved by anyone who experiences a revelation, or vision, following meditation. To encourage meditation, the Japanese built Zen gardens where monks, samurai, and others came to meditate. ▼

The tales of ancient warriors and the bravery and suffering of women were told in the Noh theaters of medieval Japan. Noh theater combined music, dance, poetry, and elaborate customs. The Noh actors—all male—often wore wooden masks such as this one. ▶

▼ The samurai received land for their loyal service. They built castles to protect themselves against attacks from rival states. This castle is called the White Heron for its white plaster walls and its location high on a hill that resembles a bird protecting its nest. The castle originally belonged to samurai Toyotomi Hideyoshi.

Taking Another Look

1. How did Japan's geography help shape life in feudal Japan?

2. What was Noh theater?

Hands-On Activity

Designing a Garden Design a plan for a Zen garden. It should be simple, with wandering paths and private spots for meditation.

Standardized Test Practice

Directions: Choose the *best* answer to each of the following multiple choice questions. If you have trouble answering a question, use the process of elimination to narrow your choices. Write your answers on a separate piece of paper.

1. One reason for the growth of feudalism in western Europe was

   A an increase in the population of lords and nobles

   B the failure of kings to develop a centralized government

   C the need for many more people to work farmland

   D the desire of peasants to have a more secure future

> **Test-Taking Tip:** The key to being able to answer this question correctly is knowing what *feudalism* is. Always consult the **glossary** in the back of your book when you come across a word you are unsure of. In this case, *feudalism* was a medieval system of government by landowning nobles. Which answer choice *best* fits with this information?

2. During the Middle Ages, the Church attempted to institute reforms aimed at

   F reuniting the Roman Catholic and the Eastern Orthodox churches

   G obtaining more land and wealth for the Church

   H expanding the role of women in the Church

   J reducing the influence of kings, lords, and nobles in the Church

> **Test-Taking Tip:** Think about the meaning of the word *reform.* It means "change that leads to improvement." Usually, reforms are needed when an institution strays from its original purpose. In the Middle Ages, Church officials were often wealthy nobles who were more concerned with money than with religious ideals. Which answer choice do you think would *best* help the Church *improve,* so that it could fulfill its original *religious purposes?*

3. During the Middle Ages, universities arose

   A because there was no more classroom space in the cathedrals

   B to teach subjects not covered in cathedral schools

   C to prepare future rulers and noblemen

   D to provide the underprivileged with educational opportunity

> **Test-Taking Tip:** This question is looking for a *cause and effect* relationship. During the Middle Ages, governments were more secure, and the economy was stronger. Therefore, people had more time for—and more interest in—learning new things. Therefore, which of the answer choices would most likely have been the cause of the rise of universities?

4. **What was one important result of the Crusades?**

F Muslim and Byzantine culture was introduced to western Europe.

G The Eastern Orthodox Church accepted the Pope as its leader.

H Jerusalem came under control of the Roman Catholic Church.

J The Byzantine Empire was at last safe from the Turks.

> **Test-Taking Tip:** Always read *carefully.* Although the Crusades began as an attempt to help the Byzantine Empire, they were ultimately unsuccessful. Therefore, answer J is incorrect.

5. **Why were craft guilds created?**

A To help royalty regain control over the price of goods

B To protect the rights of people who bought goods and services

C To protect the rights of people working in these trades

D To make it easier for apprentices to become masters

> **Test-Taking Tip:** This question requires you to remember the meaning of the word *guild.* Craft guilds, like present-day unions, were business associations of artisans, such as carpenters, shoemakers, and weavers. What is the purpose of unions today?

Read the passage below, which is an excerpt from the Magna Carta, and answer the question that follows.

> We . . . have granted to all the freemen of our kingdom, for us and for our heirs forever, all the underwritten liberties, to be had and holden by them and their heirs . . .
>
> No freeman shall be taken or imprisoned, or diseased, or outlawed, or banished, or in any way destroyed, nor will we pass upon him, nor will we send upon him, unless by the lawful judgement of his peers, or by the law of the land.
>
> All merchants shall have safe and secure conduct to go out of, and to come into, England . . . without any unjust tolls. . . .

6. **The main idea of the Magna Carta was**

F to help the king further centralize his power

G to secure certain rights and liberties for noblemen

H to entitle people accused of crimes to a trial by jury

J for the Church to take on a greater role in England's government

> **Test-Taking Tip:** This question asks for the *main idea.* Remember, the main idea is a generalization about the *entire passage,* not just one detail. For example, the second paragraph does mention *the lawful judgement of peers* (a reference to trial by jury), but this is not the main idea of the *entire passage.*

9 Beginning of Modern Times

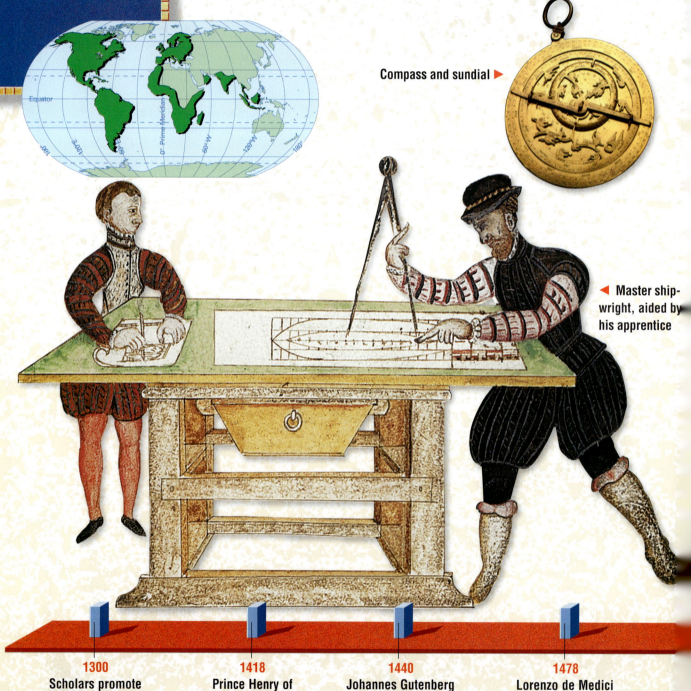

Compass and sundial ▶

◀ Master ship-wright, aided by his apprentice

1300
Scholars promote classical learning

1418
Prince Henry of Portugal starts school for navigators

1440
Johannes Gutenberg develops printing press

1478
Lorenzo de Medici rules Florence

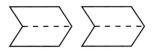

Sequencing Events Study Foldable *Make this foldable to help you sequence events that led to the Age of Discovery.*

Step 1 *Fold two sheets of paper in half from top to bottom.*

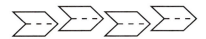

Step 2 *Turn the papers and cut each in half*

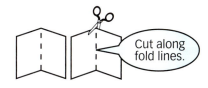

Cut along fold lines.

Step 3 *Fold the four pieces in half from top to bottom.*

Step 4 *Tape the ends of the pieces together (overlapping the edges very slightly) to make an accordion time line.*

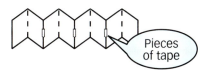

Pieces of tape

Reading and Writing *As you read the unit, sequence the events that led to European voyages of exploration by writing a date and an event on each part of the time line.*

PRIMARY SOURCES

Library

See pages 690–691 for other primary source readings to accompany Unit 9.

GO TO Read "Columbus Reaches the Americas" from the **World History Primary Source Document Library CD-ROM.**

Journal Notes

What changes took place in western Europe between 1300 and 1600? Note details about these changes as you read.

1492
Columbus lands at San Salvador

1517
Martin Luther posts 95 theses

1519
Magellan begins voyage to Pacific

CHAPTER 28

The Renaissance
1300 A.D.–1600 A.D.

A replica of a bicycle designed by Leonardo da Vinci ▼

◄ Renaissance musicians

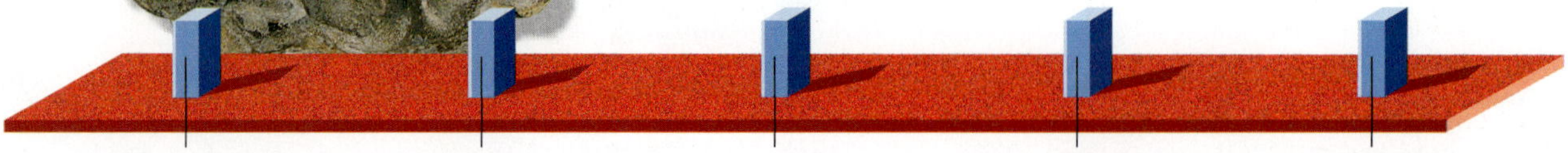

c. 1440
Johannes Gutenberg develops printing press

1478
Lorenzo de Medici becomes ruler of Florence

1485
Tudors take over the English throne

1494
The Renaissance spreads to France

1580
First English theaters built

Chapter Focus

Read to Discover

- How the Renaissance flourished in the Italian city-states.
- How France was influenced by the Italian Renaissance.
- How the Renaissance spread to Germany and Flanders.
- How the Roman Catholic Church and the government influenced the Renaissance in Spain.
- How the English monarchy promoted the Renaissance in England.

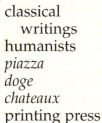

Terms to Learn

classical
  writings
humanists
piazza
doge
chateaux
printing press

People to Know

Leonardo da
  Vinci
Michelangelo
Johannes
  Gutenberg
El Greco
Henry VIII
Elizabeth I
William
  Shakespeare

Places to Locate

Florence
Venice
Papal States
Toledo

Why It's Important   Around 1300, scholars in western Europe developed a new interest in **classical writings**, or the writings of the ancient Greeks and Romans. The scholars improved their knowledge of Greek and Latin. They also began to accept some Greek and Roman ideas.

One idea that the scholars accepted was a belief in the importance of people. Because of this, the scholars were called **humanists** (hyū̄ muh nists). Their work caused a break with the thinking of the Middle Ages and led to a new age called the Renaissance (ren' uh sahns), a French word meaning "rebirth." During this age, people became less concerned with the mysteries of heaven and more interested in the world around them.

Chapter Overview

Visit the *Human Heritage* Web site at **humanheritage.glencoe.com** and click on **Chapter 28— Chapter Overviews** to preview this chapter.

Reading Check
Where did **classical writings** come from?

Reading Check
What was the main belief of the **humanists?**

SECTION 1   The Italian City-States

The first and leading center of the Renaissance was Italy, which consisted of small, independent city-states. The most important were Florence, Venice, and the Papal (pā' puhl) States. The Papal States in central Italy included Rome and were ruled by the Pope. All these city-states had grown wealthy from trade.

Painting of Leonardo da Vinci

At first, each city-state was ruled by guilds. Later, powerful individuals or families took control. They often fought each other for land and wealth. At times, they had difficulty gaining the people's loyalty and had to govern by force.

The leaders of the Italian city-states, however, were interested in more than power. They wanted to be remembered as wise, generous rulers. To be sure this would happen, they spent money on ceremonies and parades to impress and entertain the people. They ordered the building of churches and palaces. They also encouraged scholars, poets, and philosophers to set up palace schools to educate the sons of the rich. In these schools, pupils learned to develop their minds and make their bodies stronger. They spent part of the day studying classical writings and learning good manners. They spent the rest of the day wrestling, fencing, and swimming.

Art   Art was an important part of life in Renaissance Italy. City-states were proud of their artists. In fact, the city-states often competed for the services of certain painters and sculptors. The artists knew they were important and began to seek individual honor and attention. They worked hard to develop their own distinctive style.

Renaissance artists carefully studied ancient Greek and Roman art, science, and mathematics. They began to pay close attention to the details of nature. They became interested in *perspective* (puhr spek' tiv), or a way of showing objects as they appear at different distances. Above all, the artists studied the structure of the human body to learn how to draw it accurately. They began to experiment with light, color, and shade. As a result, they painted and sculpted works that were true to life and full of color and action.

Good artists were given money by the rulers of the city-states. In return, they were expected to make paintings and sculptures for the rulers' palaces and gardens. Artists often had workshops where they trained apprentices. The apprentices added backgrounds, costumes, or hands to the artists' paintings.

Many artists painted portraits for the rich. The artists tried to paint people's facial features so they showed what the people really looked like. At first, portraits were painted only to honor dead or famous people. Later, any merchant with money could have a portrait painted.

One of the greatest Renaissance artists was Leonardo da Vinci (lē uh nahr' dō dah vin' chē). He is known for the *Mona Lisa,* a portrait of an Italian noblewoman. He also painted a fresco called *The Last Supper* on the wall of an Italian monastery's dining room. It shows Christ and his disciples at their last meal before Christ's death. In these works, da Vinci tried to reveal people's feelings as well as their outward appearance.

HISTORY Online

Student Web Activity
Visit the *Human Heritage* Web site at **humanheritage.glencoe.com** and click on **Chapter 28— Student Web Activities** to find out more about Leonardo da Vinci.

Da Vinci was a scientist as well as an artist. He filled notebooks with drawings of inventions that were far ahead of the times. Da Vinci designed the first parachute and made drawings of flying machines and mechanical diggers.

Another outstanding artist was Michelangelo Buonarroti (mī kuh lan' juh lō bwah nah rō' tē). He is known for his paintings on the ceiling and altar wall of Rome's Sistine (sis' tēn) Chapel. He also sculpted the *Pietà* (pē ā' tah), which shows the dead Christ in his mother's arms. Michelangelo went farther than the ancient Greeks and Romans in presenting the human body. His figures are large and muscular and show a sense of motion.

City Life   Most Italian Renaissance cities had narrow paved streets with open sewers in the middle. Merchants and shop-keepers lived on the top floors of the buildings that housed their

RENAISSANCE ARTISTS   Michelangelo Buonarroti and Leonardo da Vinci were two leading artists of the Italian Renaissance. Michelangelo carved a very large statue of Christ and his mother known as the *Pietà* (left). Da Vinci tried to capture the personality of an Italian noblewoman in the painting known as the *Mona Lisa* (right). **What did da Vinci try to reveal in his works of art?**

shops. The rich built homes in the classical style, with rooms that were large and had high ceilings. In the center of the homes stood courtyards filled with statues, fountains, and gardens. Most people in the cities, however, were poor. They worked for low wages and lived in run-down areas.

The center of city life was the **piazza** (pē aht' suh), or central square. There, markets were set up, and merchants traded goods. People gathered to talk to friends and to carry out business dealings. On holidays, the people often watched or took part in parades and ceremonies there.

Families were close-knit. Most family members lived and worked together in the same neighborhood. Marriages were arranged as if they were business deals. Women stayed at home, ran the household, and raised children. Men spent their days at work and talking with friends on the streets and in taverns.

Most men dressed in tights and tunics. Some also wore cloaks and caps. Women dressed in simply cut, flowing dresses with tight bodices. The rich often wore brightly colored clothing made from expensive silks and velvets trimmed with fur.

Florence   The Italian Renaissance began in Florence, which was ruled by the Medici (med' uh chē) family. One of its most

Reading Check
What activities went on in the **piazza?**

RENAISSANCE MANNERS

Do not blow your nose and then open and look inside your handkerchief as if pearls or rubies had dropped out of your head.

Do not offer anyone a fruit from which you have already taken a bite.

Do not tell sad stories at parties or mealtimes. If someone starts talking this way, gently and politely change the subject and talk about something more cheerful.

Do not brag about honors, wealth, or intelligence.

Do not speak while yawning.

Do not clean your teeth with your napkin or your finger.

Do not lie all over the dinner table or fill both sides of your mouth with so much food that your cheeks stick out widely.

Do not undress, comb, or wash your hair in front of others.

Do not stick out your tongue, rub hands together, or groan out loud.

Do not talk too much, especially if your knowledge is small.

Linking Across Time

Banking   Moneylenders in Florence carried out their transactions on work areas covered with brightly embroidered cloth (below). Known as *bianchi* in Italian, these countertops gave their name to present-day banks (right), which trace their roots to the financial institutions of Florence. **Why did the Renaissance begin in Florence?**

famous members was Lorenzo de Medici, who became the ruler of Florence in 1478. He made the city a center of art and learning. Artists, poets, and philosophers flocked there to benefit from his generous support. Because of the city's prosperity and fame, Lorenzo became known as "the Magnificent."

About 1490, Florence's trade started to decline. Merchants began to complain that Lorenzo was too strict and spent too much money. The poor in Florence began to grumble about their housing and the shortages of food.

People looked for an escape from their problems. They thought they found it in a monk named Savonarola (sav uh nuh rō′ luh). Savonarola accused the Medicis of not ruling justly. He gained the people's support and overthrew the Medicis in 1494.

Savonarola did not like the gaiety and loose life of the Renaissance. He thought Renaissance ideas were hurting Florence. On his advice, the new government did away with parties, gambling, swearing, and horse-racing. Savonarola's supporters also burned paintings, fancy clothes, musical instruments, and classical books.

By 1498, the people of Florence had tired of Savonarola's strict ways, and he was hanged for heresy. The Medicis returned to power. Florence's greatness, however, had passed.

The Papal States
During the 1300s and 1400s, the power of the Popes declined. However, they wanted to show Europe's

Guidelines for Rulers
Niccolò Machiavelli wrote a handbook for rulers called *The Prince.* Here are some of Machiavelli's ideas:
• It is much safer to be feared than loved, if one must choose.
• There cannot be good laws where the state is not well armed.
• A wise leader cannot and should not keep his word when keeping it is not to his advantage.

kings that the Church was still powerful. In Rome they built large churches and palaces. Piazzas and wide streets were built in areas that had been in ruins.

Most Popes were not very religious. They acted more like political rulers than Church leaders. They sent representatives to other states and countries, collected taxes, minted money, raised armies, and fought wars.

In 1492, Rodrigo Borgia (rōd rē'gō bōr' jah) became Pope Alexander VI. He did this by bribing cardinals to vote for him. Pope Alexander's goal was to make central Italy a kingdom ruled by the Borgia family. His daughter Lucretia (lū krā' shuh) married a noble and became known for her lively parties and for poisoning her enemies.

Alexander spent a great deal of money building an army for his favorite son, Cesare (chā' sah rā). The army marched through Italy and took control of many towns. All of this territory was lost, however, after Alexander's death in 1503. By this time, Rome had replaced Florence as the center of the Renaissance.

Renaissance Italy

MAP STUDY

PLACES AND REGIONS The Renaissance began in Italy partly because Italian towns were important centers of trade during the late Middle Ages. **Why did Venice trade more with the areas outside of Italy than other Italian city-states?**

VENICE The city of Venice is famous for being built on 117 islands. About 150 canals, rather than streets, carry most of the city's traffic. Here, some of Venice's many bridges and grand palaces are shown. **Who ruled Renaissance Venice?**

Venice The Renaissance did not reach Venice until the late 1500s. This was because the Venetians had looked to Constantinople rather than to western Europe for art and literature.

Venice was different from most Italian city-states in other ways, too. The city, including its palaces and churches, was built on 117 islands linked by nearly 400 bridges. Instead of streets, Venice had canals. The largest and busiest was the Grand Canal, which was lined with brightly colored stone and marble palaces. The Rialto (rē ahl' tō), or the business area of Venice, also lay along a stretch of the Grand Canal. There, traders from Europe and the East crowded the docks to buy and sell goods.

Venice was ruled by a few merchant aristocrats. They controlled the Senate and the Council of Ten. The Council passed laws and chose the **doge** (dōj), or official ruler. The doge had little power and had to obey the Council of Ten.

The Venetians were expected to place loyalty to their city above anything else. If a neighbor did something suspicious, a Venetian was expected to report it to the Council of Ten. Citizens who wanted to accuse someone of treason placed a letter stating the charges in special boxes located throughout the city. Those charged were quickly arrested and brought before the Council. Council members then met in secret to study the evidence, listen to witnesses, and decide guilt or innocence.

Then... & Now

Venice Located on the Adriatic Sea between the Po and Piave rivers, Venice is known as the "Queen of the Adriatic." Flooding, sinking land, pollution, and age have threatened the city and its many landmarks. In recent times, the United Nations has worked to preserve the city as a world historic site.

Reading Check
Why did the **doge** have little power?

Section 1 Assessment

1. **Define:** classical writings, humanists, piazza, doge.
2. How important was art during the Renaissance? Explain.
3. What made Venice different from other Italian city-states?

Critical Thinking

4. **Demonstrating Reasoned Judgment** Do you approve or disapprove of the system of justice in Renaissance Venice? Explain.

Graphic Organizer Activity

5. Draw this diagram, and use it to show characteristics of life in Renaissance Italy. (Add more answer circles as needed.)

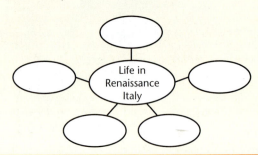

SECTION 2 France

In 1494, the French began invading Italy. French kings became fascinated by Italian architecture, art, and fashions. In the 1500s, King Francis I arranged for Italian artisans to work for him in France. He and many of his nobles hired Italian architects to design **chateaux** (sha tōz′), or castles, which were then built along the Loire River.

Francis I also encouraged French authors to model their works on those of Italian authors. Every evening, Francis and his family listened to readings of the latest books. Many were written by Rabelais (rahb′ uh lā), a physician-monk. He believed that humans were not tied down by their past and could do whatever they wished. In his most popular book, *The Adventures of Gargantua and Pantagruel,* Rabelais's main characters were two comical giants.

> ✓ **Reading Check**
> Where did King Francis I build his first **chateaux?**

Section 2 Assessment

1. **Define:** *chateaux.*
2. What did Francis I do to encourage Renaissance thought in French literature?
3. What did Rabelais believe?

Critical Thinking

4. **Making Inferences**   How do you think people of the time reacted to Rablelais's ideas? Explain.

Graphic Organizer Activity

5. Draw this diagram, and use it to show the cause and effects of the arrival of the Renaissance in France.

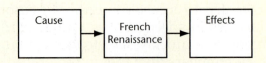

SECTION 3   Germany and Flanders

The Renaissance also spread to the rich trading centers of Germany and Flanders. There, religious scholars learned Greek and Hebrew so they could understand the earliest versions of the Bible. The German and Flemish scholars decided that over the years, many Church leaders had interpreted the Bible to suit their own needs. The scholars wanted changes that would make Church teachings simpler. One outspoken scholar, a Dutchman named Erasmus (i raz' muhs), made a new Latin translation of the New Testament. He also wrote *Praise of Folly*, a book that attacked corrupt Church leaders and practices.

At the same time, Italian traders living in the north set an example for merchants. The German merchants began to appreciate wealth, beauty, personal improvement, and other Renaissance values. This was the beginning of a new, privileged middle class.

Northern European artisans made many discoveries during the Renaissance. About 1440, a German named Johannes Gutenberg (yō' hahn gūt' n berg) developed a **printing press.** It used carved letters that could be moved around to form words and then could be used again. As a result, books could be quickly printed by machine rather than slowly written by hand. This made many more books available to people. Since printing came at a time when many townspeople were learning to read and think for themselves, new ideas spread rapidly.

Northern European artists studied Italian works of art and then developed their own styles. They painted scenes from the Bible and daily life in sharp detail. Hubert and Jan Van Eyck (van īk'), two brothers from Flanders, discovered how to paint in oils. The colors of the oil paintings were deep and rich. Soon, other artists began to use oils.

Reading Check
Who developed a **printing press** in Germany?

Section 3 Assessment

1. **Define:** printing press.
2. What Church reforms did German and Flemish scholars want to make?
3. How did the printing press change European life?

Critical Thinking

4. **Predicting Consequences**   How might life in Europe have been different without the development of Gutenberg's printing press?

Graphic Organizer Activity

5. Draw this diagram, and use it to support a generalization about the role of religion in spreading the Renaissance to Germany and Flanders.

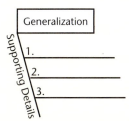

Generalization

Supporting Details
1. _____
2. _____
3. _____

SECTION 4 Spain

The Renaissance took root in Spain in the late 1400s and early 1500s. It was influenced by the close ties between the Roman Catholic Church and the government. The leading Church official, Cardinal Jiménez (hē mā' nuhs), was a loyal supporter of the monarchy. He was also a strong believer in the value of learning. He founded universities and welcomed students from other countries. He helped scholars produce a new translation of the Bible that had three columns of text side-by-side. One column was in Greek, one was in Latin, and one was in Hebrew.

In 1555, Philip II became king. He was very religious and did not trust the work of scholars. Many were charged with heresy by the Spanish Inquisition, and some were burned at the stake.

RENAISSANCE PEOPLE

Baldassare Castiglione	*1478–1529*	Italian writer; wrote book on rules of behavior for ladies and gentlemen
Benvenuto Cellini	*1500–1571*	Italian goldsmith; sculptor; wrote about his life and times
Vittoria Colonna	*1492–1547*	Italian author; wrote religious and love poems
Nicolaus Copernicus	*1473–1543*	Polish astronomer; stated that Earth moves around the sun
Albrecht Dürer	*1471–1528*	German artist; painted and made woodcuts of religious and classical subjects
Beatrice d'Este **Isabella d'Este**	*1475–1497* *1474–1539*	Italian noblewomen; sisters; honored for their learning; supported writers and artists
Galileo	*1564–1642*	Italian scientist; did experiments on the motion of objects; used telescope to discover new facts about the universe
Niccolò Machiavelli	*1469–1527*	Italian politician; writer; wrote advice to rulers on how to keep power
Thomas More	*1477–1535*	English scholar; saint; government official; refused to accept king as Church head
Petrarch	*1304–1374*	Italian poet; scholar; restored study of classics; collected manuscripts; wrote letters and poems
Raphael	*1483–1520*	Italian religious painter and architect
Andreas Vesalius	*1514–1564*	Flemish surgeon; founder of modern medicine; wrote first full description of human body

Philip had a new granite palace built just outside Madrid. Called El Escorial (el es kō rē ahl'), it served as a royal court, art gallery, monastery, church, and tomb for Spanish royalty. El Escorial soon became a symbol of the power and religious devotion of Spanish rulers.

Despite strong Church and government controls, the arts flowered. The city of Toledo (tō lā' dō) became a center for painters and poets. One artist who settled there was a Greek whom the Spanish called El Greco (el grek' ō). He painted figures with very long bodies, parts of which stretched beyond normal size. Some art experts believe that El Greco copied his style from Byzantine artists. Others insist he painted as he did because of an eye problem that distorted his vision.

The theater was also popular in Renaissance Spain. Miguel de Cervantes Saavedra (mē gel' dā suhr van' tēs suh vē druh) was one of the most noted authors of the time. He wrote many plays, short stories, and other works. His novel, *Don Quixote* (don ki hō' tā), which describes the adventures of a comical knight and his peasant squire, is still read today.

Painting of Don Quixote

Section 4 Assessment

1. What factors influenced the Renaissance in Spain?
2. Why did Philip II mistreat Spanish scholars?

Critical Thinking

3. **Making Comparisons** How did Cardinal Jiménez and Philip II differ in their attitudes toward learning?

Graphic Organizer Activity

4. Draw this diagram, and use it to summarize the contributions of Jiménez, El Greco, and Cervantes to the Spanish Renaissance.

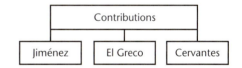

Contributions

| Jiménez | El Greco | Cervantes |

SECTION 5 England

Peace did not come to England after the Hundred Years' War. In 1455, two noble families, York and Lancaster, began a fight for the throne. The Yorkist symbol was a white rose, and the Lancastrian symbol was a red rose. For this reason, the struggles between the House of York and the House of Lancaster were called the Wars of the Roses.

When the wars ended in 1485, a family called the Tudors, who fought on the Lancastrian side, took over the English throne. The first Tudor king, Henry VII, prepared the way for the Renaissance. He made the monarchy stronger and built up trade, which made England both peaceful and rich.

Painting of English Singers

THE TUDORS These paintings of King Henry VIII of England (left) and his daughter Queen Elizabeth I (right) show members of the Tudor family, who ruled England from 1485 to 1603. Henry and Elizabeth both were strong and forceful rulers, and they were able to gain the respect and love of the English people. **How did the first Tudor king, Henry VII, pave the way for the English Renaissance?**

Henry VII's work was continued by his son, Henry VIII, who became king in 1509. He enjoyed and encouraged art, literature, hunting, and parties. He played several musical instruments and even composed his own music. Under his rule, English nobles and merchants began to look to Renaissance Italy for guidance in politics, diplomacy, and behavior.

The English Renaissance reached its height, however, during the reign of Henry VIII's daughter, Elizabeth I. She became queen in 1558 when she was 25 years old. She was shrewd and well-educated. Although she had a sharp tongue and an iron will, she won the loyalty and confidence of her people.

Elizabeth often made journeys through the kingdom so that the people could see her. During her travels, she stayed at the homes of nobles who entertained her with banquets, parades, and dances. Poets and writers praised her in their writings. The sons of merchants, lawyers, and landowners copied Italian clothes and manners and came to court to capture her attention and favor.

Poetry, music, and the theater became a part of daily life. Most nobles wrote poetry. People of all classes enjoyed singing ballads and folk songs. Many played violins, guitars, and lutes.

People in History

Henry VIII
1491–1547

English King

Henry VIII was a typical Renaissance ruler. He played tennis, liked to joust, and wrote music. He also built up the English navy and changed the course of history by convincing Parliament to declare him the head of the Church of England, splitting with the Roman Catholic Church (see Chapter 29).

The people of Renaissance England were especially fond of plays. Not since the days of ancient Greece had so many plays been written and performed. About 1580, the first theaters in England were built. Their stages stood in the open air. Most of the audience, however, sat under a roof or some sort of covering. Those who could not afford to pay for seats stood in the *pit,* or an open area in the front of the theater, and on the sides of the stage. Since there were no lights, plays were performed in the afternoon. They attracted large crowds.

One of the best known English *playwrights,* or authors of plays, was William Shakespeare (shāk' spir). He drew ideas for his tragedies and comedies from the histories of England and ancient Rome. He often used Italian scenes, characters, and tales in his plays. Some of his most famous works are *Romeo and Juliet, Macbeth, Hamlet, Julius Caesar,* and *A Midsummer Night's Dream.* Many experts consider Shakespeare the greatest playwright in the English language.

ENGLISH THEATER   The Globe Theater (left) stood near the south bank of the Thames River in the London suburb of Southwark. The Globe Theater became the home of William Shakespeare's (right) acting company in 1599. **What kind of reputation have the plays of William Shakespeare earned for him?**

Section 5 Assessment

1. What did the Tudors do to encourage the Renaissance in England?
2. What were English theaters like?
3. From what did Shakespeare draw the ideas for his plays?

Critical Thinking

4. **Understanding Cause and Effect** What was the cause of the Wars of the Roses? How did these struggles affect English history?

Graphic Organizer Activity

5. Draw this diagram, and use it to write four facts about the English Renaissance.

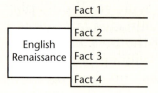

English Renaissance	Fact 1
	Fact 2
	Fact 3
	Fact 4

Chapter Summary & Study Guide

1. Around 1300, western European scholars showed a growing interest in classical writings, which in turn led to the Renaissance.

2. The Renaissance began in the Italian city-states, where the wealth from trade help fuel a burst of artistic achievement.

3. Leading figures in the Italian Renaissance included rulers such as the Medicis of Florence and artists like Michelangelo Buonarroti and Leonardo da Vinci.

4. The Renaissance moved from Florence to Rome when the Popes rebuilt the city to prove their power to the rulers of Europe.

5. In the late 1500s, the Renaissance spread from Rome to Venice.

6. After 1494, King Francis I helped bring the Renaissance to France.

7. An interest in religious reform and trading contacts with Italy helped bring the Renaissance to Germany and Flanders.

8. Development of a printing press by Johannes Gutenberg helped new Renaissance ideas to reach more people.

9. In the late 1400s and early 1500s the Renaissance spread to Spain, where it was influenced by strong ties with the Roman Catholic Church and strict government policies.

10. The Tudors paved the way for the arrival of the Renaissance in England, where it reached its peak under Elizabeth I.

11. The people of Renaissance England were very fond of plays, especially those by William Shakespeare.

Self-Check Quiz

Visit the *Human Heritage* Web site at **humanheritage. glencoe.com** and click on ***Chapter 28—Self-Check Quiz*** to assess your understanding of this chapter.

Using Key Terms

Imagine you are a drama critic writing about the literature of the Renaissance. Write a short magazine article explaining the kinds of plays being written and how they reflect the life of the times. Use the following words in your article.

classical writings   humanists   *piazza*
printing press   *chateaux*   *doge*

Understanding Main Ideas

1. Whose writings did the scholars of western Europe study during the Renaissance?
2. Why were the Renaissance scholars called humanists?
3. What did the rulers of the Italian city-states do to encourage learning and development of art?
4. Why did the people of Florence turn to Savonarola in 1494?
5. How was France introduced to the Renaissance?
6. What did Germany, Flanders, Spain, and England contribute to the Renaissance?
7. Of what did El Escorial become a well-known symbol?
8. How did the Wars of the Roses get their name?

Critical Thinking

1. How did the Renaissance differ from the Middle Ages?
2. What was the connection between trade and the start of the Renaissance?
3. Why was Lorenzo de Medici called "the Magnificent"?
4. If you could go back in time and talk with a Renaissance artist or ruler, whom would you choose? What questions would you ask? Explain your answer.

Graphic Organizer Activity

Culture Create a diagram like the one below, and use it to compare the Renaissance to the Middle Ages.

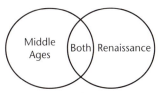

Middle Ages   Both   Renaissance

 ## Geography in History

The World in Spatial Terms Refer to the map of Renaissance Italy on page 438. This country is often compared to the shape of a boot. Describe the location of Italy by giving its latitude and longitude. Then describe its relative location.

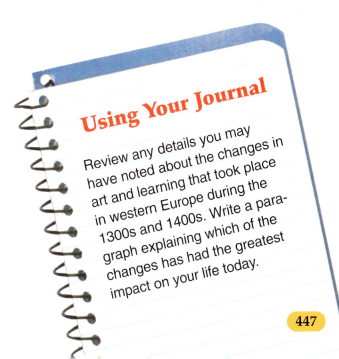

Using Your Journal

Review any details you may have noted about the changes in art and learning that took place in western Europe during the 1300s and 1400s. Write a paragraph explaining which of the changes has had the greatest impact on your life today.

The Reformation
1475 A.D.–1650 A.D.

▲ Indulgence box

Martin Luther, Church
reformer ▶

1517	1534	1545	1588	1598	1618
Luther posts 95 theses	Henry VIII heads Church of England	Council of Trent meets	England defeats the Armada	Edict of Nantes is signed	Thirty Years' War begins

Chapter Focus

 Read to Discover

- Why Martin Luther's beliefs brought him into conflict with the Roman Catholic Church.
- How Protestantism developed.
- How Catholic reformers worked to improve their Church.
- How and why the reformation of the Church of England came about.
- How the Thirty Years' War affected Europe.

Terms to Learn	**People to Know**	🌎 **Places to Locate**
reformation	Martin Luther	Wittenberg
indulgences	Pope Leo X	Geneva
theses	John Calvin	
heretic	Henry VIII	
armada	Mary Tudor	
galleons	Elizabeth I	

Why It's Important   The Roman Catholic Church did not adjust to the many changes taking place in western Europe during the 1400s and 1500s. Many Europeans began to call for a **reformation** (ref uhr mā′ shuhn), or a change, in the way the Church taught and practiced Christianity.

Church leaders, however, were too busy with their own and government affairs to make changes. They did not like the reformers' ideas, especially those that could affect their power. Because of this, the unity of the Church was threatened.

✓ **Reading Check**
Why did many Europeans call for a **reformation?**

SECTION 1   Martin Luther

One reformer who challenged the Church was a German monk named Martin Luther. Luther, born in 1483, was the son of peasants. His family wanted him to be a lawyer, but he decided to become a monk. As a monk, Luther faithfully followed Church teachings and practices. However, he could find no peace of mind. He wondered how God would judge his actions.

While studying the New Testament, Luther found the answer to the questions that had been troubling him. He decided that trusting in Jesus, rather than doing good works, would save people from their sins. Luther's ideas soon brought him into conflict with the Church. In 1517, Pope Leo X wanted money to

Reading Check
What were indulgences?

Reading Check
What did Luther state in his list of 95 theses?

rebuild St. Peter's Church in Rome. He sent out monks to sell **indulgences** (in dul' juhnt sez), or documents that freed their owners from the punishment they were due to receive for their sins. Luther believed the sale of indulgences led people to think they could buy God's forgiveness for their sins.

One night Luther posted a list of 95 **theses** (thē' sēz), or statements of beliefs, on the door of the castle church in Wittenberg (wit' uhn buhrg), Germany. In the list, Luther stated that only God could forgive sins. He challenged anyone who disagreed to debate with him.

Luther began to attack other Catholic beliefs openly. He said that Popes could make mistakes; that the only true guide to religious truth was the Bible, which every Christian had the right to read; and that every Christian had the right to pray to God without the aid of a priest.

In 1520, Pope Leo condemned Luther's teachings and excommunicated him. Leo insisted that the German emperor,

SALE OF INDULGENCES   Hoping to lessen God's punishment upon them, many Christians bought the indulgences offered by the Church. Here, indulgences are sold at the village marketplace. **Why was the Church selling indulgences?**

Charles V, try Luther as a **heretic** (her' uh tik), or person who holds a belief that is different from the accepted belief of the Church. Charles was loyal to the Church, but he relied on German princes who supported Luther. To keep their loyalty, Charles agreed to give Luther a fair trial. At the same time, he secretly promised the Pope that Luther would be condemned. In 1521, Luther was tried by the German Diet of Worms. When he refused to give up his ideas, he was condemned for heresy.

Reading Check Why did the Pope want to try Luther as a **heretic?**

Section 1 Assessment

1. **Define:** reformation, indulgences, theses, heretic.
2. Why did Luther come into conflict with the Church?
3. What happened to Luther at Worms?

Critical Thinking

4. **Identifying Central Issues** What was the central or underlying issue in the debate between Luther and Pope Leo X?

Graphic Organizer Activity

5. Draw this diagram, and use it to summarize Luther's beliefs about indulgences, the Bible, the Pope, and prayer.

SECTION 2 A New Religion

By 1524, most people in northern Germany supported Luther. They left the Roman Catholic Church and formed the Lutheran (lū' thuhr uhn) Church.

The Lutheran princes of Germany had strong armies, which Charles V could not defeat. In 1555, Charles realized he could not force the people to return to the Roman Catholic Church. He then agreed to sign a treaty known as the Peace of Augsburg (ogz' buhrg). There could be both Catholic and Lutheran churches in Germany. The Peace of Augsburg kept German Lutherans and Catholics from fighting each other for nearly 50 years.

Protestant Groups Luther's ideas soon spread to other areas of Europe. People in Scandinavia founded Lutheran churches. Preachers and merchants in Switzerland (swit' suhr luhnd) also left the Roman Catholic Church. They set up Reformed churches. Because they protested against Catholic ideas, Lutheran and Reformed churches were called Protestant (prot' uh stuhnt). Protestant church leaders were called **ministers.** They spent more time teaching from the Bible. They conducted services in the language of the area instead of in Latin. This made services easier for people to understand.

Reading Check How did Protestant **ministers** differ from Catholic priests?

John Calvin

Ulrich Zwingli was important in leading the Protestant movement in Switzerland. Zwingli lived from 1484 to 1531. Unlike Luther, however, he wanted to break completely from Catholic rituals. He ordered the removal of images from churches, and he wanted to close monasteries. Zwingli led a group of Protestants from Zurich, Switzerland, in a battle against Catholic forces in 1531 and was killed. After Zwingli's death, the Protestant church was firmly established in Switzerland.

John Calvin

The most powerful Reformed group was in the Swiss city of Geneva (juh nē' vuh). There, John Calvin set up the first Protestant church governed by a council of ministers and elected church members. Calvin also wrote books that became a guide for Protestants throughout Europe.

Calvin believed that there was nothing in the past, present, or future that God did not know about or control. He also held that from the beginning of time, God decided who would be saved and who would not. Calvin used the scriptures to support his ideas. He believed that God's will was written in the Bible, which ministers had the right to interpret. The ministers also had the right to make sure everyone obeyed God's will. Calvin had the Geneva town council pass laws to force people to follow strict rules of behavior. They could not dance, play cards, go to the theater, or take part in drinking parties. Those who refused to obey these laws were put in prison, executed, or banished.

Calvinism taught people to work hard and to save money. For this reason, many rich merchants supported Calvin. With their help, Calvin worked to improve Geneva. Streets and buildings were kept clean. New workshops opened, providing more jobs for people. Persecuted Protestants from all over Europe found safety in Geneva. Young men came to study at the school Calvin founded to train Reformed ministers. Many of them later returned to their own countries to set up Reformed churches.

Section 2 Assessment

1. **Define:** ministers.
2. What was the Peace of Augsburg?
3. Why were Lutheran and Reformed churches called Protestant?

Critical Thinking

4. **Analyzing Information**   What ideas of Calvinism do you agree with? What ideas do you disagree with?

Graphic Organizer Activity

5. Draw this diagram, and use it to compare Protestant and Catholic practices.

Protestant Practices	Catholic Practices

SECTION 3   Catholic Reform

While Protestants formed new churches, Catholic reformers worked to improve their church. Many came from Spain and Italy, the leading countries of the Catholic reform movement.

One of the best known Catholic reformers was Ignatius (ig nă′ shē uhs) of Loyola (loi ō′ luh). In 1521, he gave up his life as a Spanish noble to serve God and the Roman Catholic Church. In 1540, he founded the Society of Jesus. Its members were called Jesuits (jezh′ ū its). This group was formed to spread Roman Catholic ideas to all parts of the world. Jesuits also worked to help the people strengthen their faith. They wore black robes and lived simple lives. They set up schools, helped the poor, and preached to the people. They also taught in universities and served as advisers in royal courts. Jesuit missionaries were the first to carry Catholic ideas to India, China, and Japan.

Then...
& Now

Church Membership
Worldwide, the Roman Catholic Church is still the largest Christian church, with about 968 million people. About 466 million follow some of the many varieties of Protestantism. The next largest Christian community, with nearly 218 million, includes the different congregations of the Eastern Orthodox Church, which was once centered in Constantinople.

Linking Across Time

St. Peter's Basilica   In 1506, Donato Bramante proposed a bold design for the rebuilding of St. Peter's Basilica. Instead of medieval spires, he revived the Roman dome, as captured in a medal issued by Pope Julius II (left). Work progressed slowly, and in 1546, 71-year-old Michelangelo took over the project. Today the inner dome, built to Michelangelo's specifications, is considered one of the world's great architectural feats (right). **What other steps did Catholic reformers take to revive the Church's influences?**

COUNCIL OF TRENT   Meeting three times between 1545 and 1563, the Council of Trent helped to renew Catholic life and worship. In this painting bishops and other church leaders from throughout Europe debate an issue at a session of the Council. **Why did the Pope call for the Council of Trent?**

The Jesuits used reason and good deeds to defend the Roman Catholic Church against criticisms. They also tried to bring Protestants back to the Church. Because of their work, people in eastern European countries such as Poland, Bohemia (bō hē mē uh), and Hungary once again became loyal to the Roman Catholic Church.

During this time, the Pope also took steps to strengthen the Roman Catholic Church. He called a council of bishops to discuss reforms and to defend Catholic teachings. The council met at different times between 1545 and 1563 at Trent, Italy. The Council of Trent ended many Church practices that had been criticized for hundreds of years such as the sale of indulgences. Church leaders were ordered to follow strict rules. Each diocese was told to build a **seminary** (sem' uh ner ē), or a school to train priests.

Reading Check
What was the purpose of a **seminary**?

The Council of Trent also explained Catholic doctrine. It said that good works, as well as faith, helped people get to heaven. It also held that the Church alone decided how the Bible was to be interpreted and that mass would be said in Latin only. Together, the Council of Trent and the Jesuit missionaries helped the Pope reclaim Protestant areas.

Section 3 Assessment

1. **Define:** seminary.
2. What were the leading countries involved in the Catholic reform movement?
3. What did the Council of Trent do?

Critical Thinking

4. **Evaluating Information** "The Council of Trent was important in strengthening the Roman Catholic Church." What is your opinion of this statement? Explain.

Graphic Organizer Activity

5. Draw this diagram, and use it to describe the order of the Jesuits founded by Ignatius of Loyola.

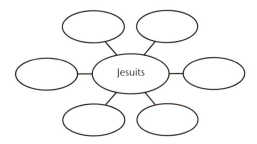

Jesuits

SECTION 4 A Middle Way

Reformation of the Church in England was led by a monarch, not by church leaders. It started as a political quarrel between the Tudor king Henry VIII and Pope Clement VII. Religious beliefs did not play a part in the struggle until later.

HENRY VIII AND ANNE BOLEYN   Henry's hopes for a son made him determined to marry Anne Boleyn and led to a political break with the Pope. In this painting Henry and Anne are shown at the home of Thomas Wolsey, the king's chief adviser. **How was Henry eventually able to marry Anne Boleyn?**

Painting of Thomas Cranmer

The Break With Rome

The trouble between Henry VIII and the Pope began in 1527. At that time, Henry was married to Catherine of Aragon, the daughter of Ferdinand and Isabella of Spain and the aunt of German emperor Charles V. Henry and Catherine had only one living child, Mary. As Catherine grew older, Henry feared she could not have any more children. This was very important to Henry because he wanted a son to succeed to the throne.

At the same time, Henry had fallen in love with Anne Boleyn (bu lin'), a young woman of the court. He wanted Pope Clement to end his marriage to Catherine so that he could marry Anne, by whom he hoped to have a son. When the Pope refused, Henry declared that the Pope no longer had power over the Church in England. Henry was then excommunicated.

In 1534, the English Parliament passed a law stating that the king was head of the Church of England. Any English church leader who did not accept the law would stand trial as a heretic. Thomas Cranmer (kran' muhr), the Archbishop of Canterbury and the most important church leader in England, supported Henry. Cranmer helped Henry end his marriage to Catherine. Henry then married Anne Boleyn, who gave him one child, a daughter named Elizabeth. A few years later, Henry had Anne executed for treason. He then married Jane Seymour (sē' mōuhr), who died shortly after giving Henry the son he wanted.

Edward and Mary

When Henry VIII died, his nine-year-old son became King Edward VI. Since Edward was too young and sick to rule, a council of nobles governed England for him. Most of the council members were Protestants, and they brought Protestant doctrines into the English Church. Thomas Cranmer supported the council. He wanted the people to have an orderly form of Protestant worship. To help achieve this, he wrote a worship service in English called the *Book of Common Prayer.* It was used in all the churches in England.

When Edward died in 1553, the council of nobles tried to bring a Protestant noblewoman to the throne. Their attempt failed, however, because the people of England refused to accept any ruler who was not a Tudor. They wanted Henry's daughter, Mary, as their monarch.

Mary was Catholic. As soon as she became queen, she accepted the Pope as head of the English Church. She then insisted that all English men and women return to the Roman Catholic Church. Many Protestants refused and were persecuted. More than 300 of them, including Cranmer, were burned at the stake for heresy. The people turned against their queen, calling her "Bloody Mary."

Mary was married to King Philip II of Spain. The English were unhappy about the marriage because Spain was England's

Painting of Edward VI

PHILIP II AND MARY TUDOR   Queen of England from 1553 to 1558, Mary I shown in this painting (right) longed to bring England back to the Roman Catholic Church. Mary married Philip II (left) of Spain, shown here, who considered himself the champion of the Roman Catholic faith. **Why did the English people object to the marriage of Mary and Philip?**

enemy and the leading Catholic power in Europe. They feared that Philip and the Pope would become the real rulers of England. The people decided that England would remain free only if it became a Protestant country. For this reason, they wanted a Protestant ruler.

Elizabeth's Church
Mary died in 1558 without a child to succeed her. Thus, her half-sister, Elizabeth, became queen. Elizabeth I was Protestant. With the help of Parliament, she ended the Pope's authority in the English Church.

Elizabeth was very popular with her subjects. She worked to set up the Church in a form that would appeal to as many people as possible. Elizabeth and Parliament decided that the Church should be Protestant. However, the Church would keep some Catholic features. The monarch would be head of the Church, which would use Cranmer's prayer book and teach Protestant beliefs.

HISTORY Online

Student Web Activity

Visit the *Human Heritage* Web site at **humanheritage.glencoe.com** and click on *Chapter 29—Student Web Activities* to find out more about English monarchs of the Reformation.

ST. TERESA OF AVILA   Another Church reformer, St. Teresa of Avila, Spain, lived from 1515–1582. As a nun she reformed convent life and wrote about religious life. **Which British monarch tried to restore the Pope as the head of the English Church?**

Most of the English people were pleased with the mix of Protestant belief and Catholic practice since many Catholic rituals remained. Those who were not pleased stayed outside the Church. Some Protestants also did not like Elizabeth's Church, but they did not leave it. Because these people wanted to purify the English Church of Catholic ways, they became known as Puritans (pyur' uh tuhnz).

Section 4 Assessment

1. What happened when Pope Clement refused to end Henry VIII's marriage?
2. What did Mary Tudor expect the people to do as soon as she became queen? How did the people feel about this?
3. What was the Church of England like under Elizabeth I?

Critical Thinking

4. **Demonstrating Reasoned Judgment** How effective do you think Elizabeth I was in establishing a new national church?

Graphic Organizer Activity

5. Draw this diagram, and use it to compare the reigns of Mary Tudor and Elizabeth I.

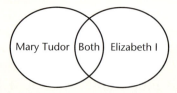

Mary Tudor | Both | Elizabeth I

SECTION 5 Wars of Religion

By the middle 1500s, most northern Europeans were Protestants, while most southern Europeans were Catholics. European monarchs had used religion to help unite their people and to build powerful nations. The ruler and people of each country were expected to belong to the same church. Those who refused were persecuted. This led to much bitterness between people of different faiths. Differences in religion also led to wars between countries. Toward the end of the 1500s, Europe entered a period of religious wars that lasted until 1648.

The Armada   Under Elizabeth I, England became the leading Protestant power in Europe. Spain, under Philip II, remained the leading Catholic power. Philip knew that if he could defeat England, Protestant Europe would be open to Catholic control. Therefore, he ordered the building of an **armada** (ar mah' duh), or a large group of warships.

After two years, the Spanish Armada, with its 130 ships, was ready. Its strength lay in its **galleons** (gal' ēuhns), or heavy ships with square-rigged sails and long, raised decks. In 1588, the Armada sailed toward England. Its main purpose was to help the Spanish armies on the continent cross over to the English shore.

✓ Reading Check Why did Philip II order the building of an **armada?**

✓ Reading Check What did Spanish **galleons** look like?

SPANISH ARMADA   In 1588, the English fleet faced the Spanish Armada in the English Channel. Here, English fire ships move toward the Armada. This action broke the curved formation of the Spanish ships and made possible a successful English attack. **What was the main strength of the Spanish Armada?**

Elizabeth I
1533–1603

English Queen

Elizabeth came to the throne at age 25. She faced a nation deeply in debt, caught up in European wars, and torn apart by religious conflicts at home. King Philip II offered to marry her, but Elizabeth rejected him—and all other suitors as well. Instead, she led England through one of its greatest eras, producing a united country, a strong navy, and a powerful European nation.

Elizabeth knew the Spanish forces were coming and prepared England for war. She had a naval commander, John Hawkins, reorganize the English fleet. He remodeled old ships and built new ones. He formed a new navy of 134 fighting ships and merchant vessels. Most of the ships were smaller than the Spanish ships, but they had larger guns and more ammunition. Expert sailors handled the English ships with much skill. One naval captain, Sir Francis Drake, was known for his overseas voyages and his capture of Spanish merchant ships.

The English knew they had to make the Spanish ships break their curved formation. Their chance came when the Spanish fleet anchored off the coast of Europe to wait for the Spanish armies to meet it. That night, the English set fire to eight small ships and sent them into the Spanish fleet. As the burning ships reached the Armada, the Spanish ships broke formation and began to drift. The English were then able to fight the Spanish ships one by one.

The Spanish naval command soon realized that the Armada was defeated. Short of food and water, it decided to return to Spain. A great storm came up, however, causing the voyage to be long and difficult. Only half the Armada reached home.

The English celebrated their victory with bonfires and parades. Although Spain was still a powerful enemy, England had shown it could defend itself. The English gained respect throughout Europe as champions of the Protestant cause. The defeat of the Armada allowed northern Europe to remain a Protestant stronghold.

The Huguenots

Most people in France during the 1500s were Catholics. Many nobles, lawyers, doctors, and merchants, however, were Protestants. These French Protestants, who were called Huguenots (hyū′ guh nots), followed Calvin's teachings.

In 1534, King Francis I, who was Catholic, forbade the Huguenots to worship freely. He wanted all French people to support the Roman Catholic Church. Catholics began to persecute Huguenots, and by 1562 a civil war broke out. By then, Charles IX had become king. Since he was too young to rule, his mother, Catherine de Medici, ruled for him.

Catherine tried to keep peace by showing favor first to one group and then to the other. She finally decided to support the Roman Catholic Church. In 1572, she allowed Catholic nobles to kill the leading Huguenots in Paris. Catholic mobs in other parts of France began to kill Protestants and burn their homes. Many Protestants left the country. The few who remained to carry on the fight were led by Henry of Navarre (nuh var′), a Huguenot prince.

In 1589, the king of France was killed. Henry of Navarre, who was next in line for the throne, became Henry IV. He wanted to gain the loyalty of the people. Since most French people were still

Drawing Conclusions

"Elementary, my dear Watson." Detective Sherlock Holmes often said these words to his assistant when he solved yet another mystery. Holmes would examine all the available evidence, or facts, and draw conclusions to solve the case.

Learning the Skill Drawing conclusions allows you to understand ideas that are not stated directly. Follow these steps in learning to draw conclusions:

- Review the facts that are stated directly.
- Use your knowledge and insight to develop some new conclusions about these facts.
- Look for information to check the accuracy of your conclusions.

GO TO Glencoe's **Skillbuilder Interactive Workbook CD-ROM, Level 1,** provides instruction and practice in key social studies skills.

Skill Practice

The excerpt on this page comes from a speech delivered to Parliament by Queen Elizabeth in 1601, just two years before her death. In it, she reviews her reign as queen. Read this excerpt, and then answer the questions that follow.

> *To be a king and wear a crown is a thing more glorious to them that see it than it is pleasing to them that bear it. For myself, I was never so much enticed with the glorious name of a king, or royal authority of a queen, as delighted . . . to defend this kingdom (as I said) from peril, dishonour, tyranny, and oppression.*

> *There will never [be a] queen sit in my seat with more zeal to my country . . . and that sooner . . . will venture her life for your good and safety than myself. . . . And though you have had, and may have many princes, more mighty and wise sitting in this state; yet you never had, or shall have, any more careful and loving.*

1. How does Elizabeth say she views the title of queen?
2. What aspect of being England's ruler has "delighted" her the most?
3. What conclusion can you draw from this speech about how Elizabeth would like to be remembered?
4. What evidence from the speech supports your conclusion?

Catholic, he decided to convert. Nevertheless, Henry ended the fighting between Protestants and Catholics. Although he made Catholicism the national religion, he also made life easier for Protestants. In 1598, he signed the Edict of Nantes (nahnts), which gave Huguenots freedom of worship. France thus became the first European country to allow two Christian religions.

The Low Countries   The Low Countries were part of the Spanish Empire. The people of the Low Countries were divided into Protestants and Catholics. Neither group liked Philip II's harsh rule. They did not like the heavy taxes imposed by Spain or the Spanish laws. Philip, however, made money from the wealth and trade of the Low Countries. He wanted to keep them under Spanish control.

Philip also wanted all his subjects to be Catholic. To achieve this, he set up an Inquisition in the Low Countries to stamp out Protestantism. In 1567, Protestants in the northern provinces revolted. Philip sent soldiers to restore order. They were joined by French Catholics from the southern provinces.

The fighting did not end until 1648. At that time, it was decided that the southern provinces, known today as Belgium, were to remain Catholic and continue under the rule of Spain. The northern provinces, known today as the Netherlands, were to be an independent Protestant country.

Section 5 Assessment

1. Define: armada, galleons.
2. How did the English defeat the Spanish Armada?
3. What led to civil war in France in 1562?

Critical Thinking

4. Identifying Alternatives   How do you think the religious wars in Europe in the 1500s and 1600s might have been avoided?

Graphic Organizer Activity

5. Draw this diagram, and use it to show the causes and effects of the Edict of Nantes.

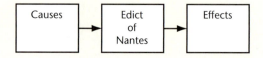

| Causes | → | Edict of Nantes | → | Effects |

SECTION 6   The Thirty Years' War

During the 1590s and early 1600s, the German states began to quarrel over the terms of the Peace of Augsburg. They formed alliances based on religion. The Catholic alliance was led by the German emperor Ferdinand II.

One Protestant state that resisted Ferdinand was Bohemia. In 1618, the Protestant nobles of Bohemia revolted. They chose a German Protestant prince as their new king. Ferdinand's armies crushed the Bohemians in a fierce battle, and Ferdinand proclaimed himself king of Bohemia. He did not allow Protestant worship. He sent Jesuits throughout the country to win the people back to the Roman Catholic Church.

The revolt in Bohemia soon grew into the Thirty Years' War. During the war, half the armies of Europe fought in Germany. First Denmark and then Sweden invaded Germany. Their kings were Protestants who wanted to stop the spread of Catholicism. They also hoped to conquer German territory. When the Swedes were finally defeated in 1634, the French became involved. Although France was a Catholic country, it entered the war on the Protestant side. This changed the nature of the war. It became

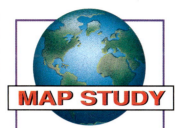

MAP STUDY

PLACES AND REGIONS By 1560 many Europeans were either Protestants or Catholic. **In which European countries did Calvinism take hold?**

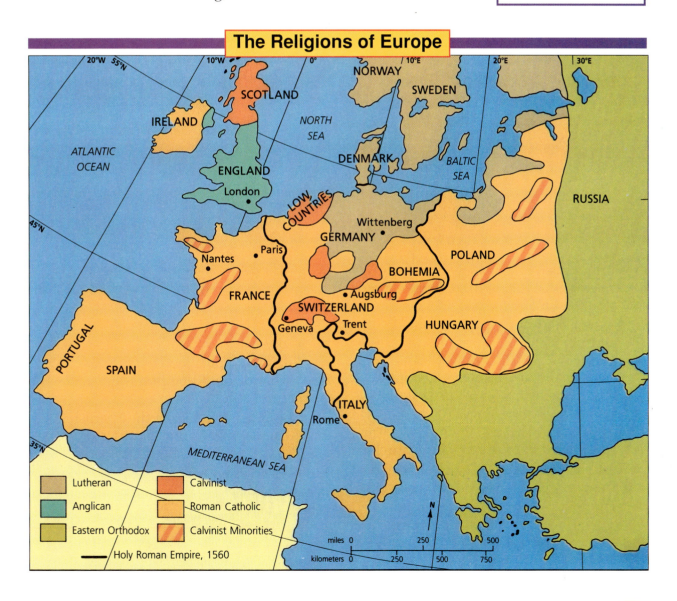

The Religions of Europe

Legend:
- Lutheran
- Anglican
- Eastern Orthodox
- Calvinist
- Roman Catholic
- Calvinist Minorities
- Holy Roman Empire, 1560

miles 0 — 250 — 500
kilometers 0 — 250 — 500 — 750

less a war over religion and more a struggle for territory and wealth.

The German people suffered great hardships during the war. Finally, in 1643, after a serious defeat, the German emperor asked for peace. In 1648, representatives of European nations signed the Peace of Westphalia (west fāl' yuh), which ended the war. The German emperor lost much of his power and France emerged as a strong nation. After this war, Europeans no longer fought over religion. Instead, nations tried to gain power through trade and expansion overseas.

Section 6 Assessment

1. What led to the Thirty Years' War?
2. What effect did the Thirty Years' War have on Europe?

Critical Thinking

3. **Drawing Conclusions** Based on the Thirty Years' War, what conclusions can you draw about the reasons nations go to war?

Graphic Organizer Activity

4. Draw this diagram, and use it to show the main events in the Thirty Years' War. (Add answer boxes as needed.)

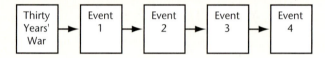

Thirty Years' War → Event 1 → Event 2 → Event 3 → Event 4

Chapter Summary & Study Guide

1. Luther posted his list of 95 theses to object to the sale of indulgences and other Church practices.

2. Luther's ideas spread, with people in northern Germany forming the Lutheran Church and people in Switzerland and elsewhere adopting what became known as Protestantism.

3. While Protestant reformers established new churches, Catholic reformers worked to improve their Church.

4. Between 1545 and 1563, the Council of Trent reformed many Catholic practices.

5. The reformation came to England when Parliament declared Henry VIII the head of the Church of England.

6. After Henry's death, advisers to his young son Edward introduced Protestant practices to the English Church.

7. Mary Tudor tried to return England to Catholicism, but failed.

8. Elizabeth I decided the Church of England should be Protestant with some Catholic features.

9. The English defeat of the Spanish Armada in 1588 kept northern Europe Protestant, but it did not prevent other religious wars.

Self-Check Quiz

Visit the *Human Heritage* Web site at **humanheritage. glencoe.com** and click on *Chapter 29—Self-Check Quiz* to assess your understanding of this chapter.

Using Key Terms

Use the following words to write a paragraph explaining the conflicts over religion among European countries during the 1500s and 1600s.

reformation   indulgences   theses
heretic   ministers   seminary
armada   galleons

Understanding Main Ideas

1. How did Protestantism get its name, and what were some of the churches that belonged to this faith?
2. What rules of behavior did John Calvin propose for his followers?
3. What organization did Ignatius of Loyola form?
4. Why did Mary Tudor become known as "Bloody Mary"?
5. How did the defeat of the Spanish Armada help the Protestant cause?
6. What was the basis of alliances formed by German states in the 1590s and early 1600s?

Critical Thinking

1. What would you have liked about living in Geneva at the time of John Calvin? What would you have disliked? Explain your answer.
2. Do you approve or disapprove of the way Elizabeth I organized the Church of England? Explain your answer.
3. Explain whether you would or would not have converted to Catholicism if you had been Henry IV.
4. If you had been a Catholic in the mid-1500s, in which European country would you have preferred to live? Why?

Graphic Organizer Activity

History Create a diagram like the one below, and use it to summarize the causes and effects of the reformation on the history of western Europe.

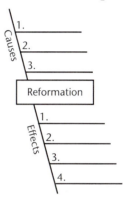

Causes
1.
2.
3.

Reformation

Effects
1.
2.
3.
4.

Geography in History

Places and Regions Refer to the location of Calvinist minorities on the map of western European religions on page 463. What connection might there be between their locations and the fact that they are minority groups (groups with fewer members than other religions)?

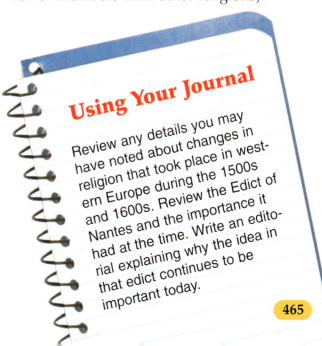

Using Your Journal

Review any details you may have noted about changes in religion that took place in western Europe during the 1500s and 1600s. Review the Edict of Nantes and the importance it had at the time. Write an editorial explaining why the idea in that edict continues to be important today.

The Age of Discovery
1300 A.D.–1620 A.D.

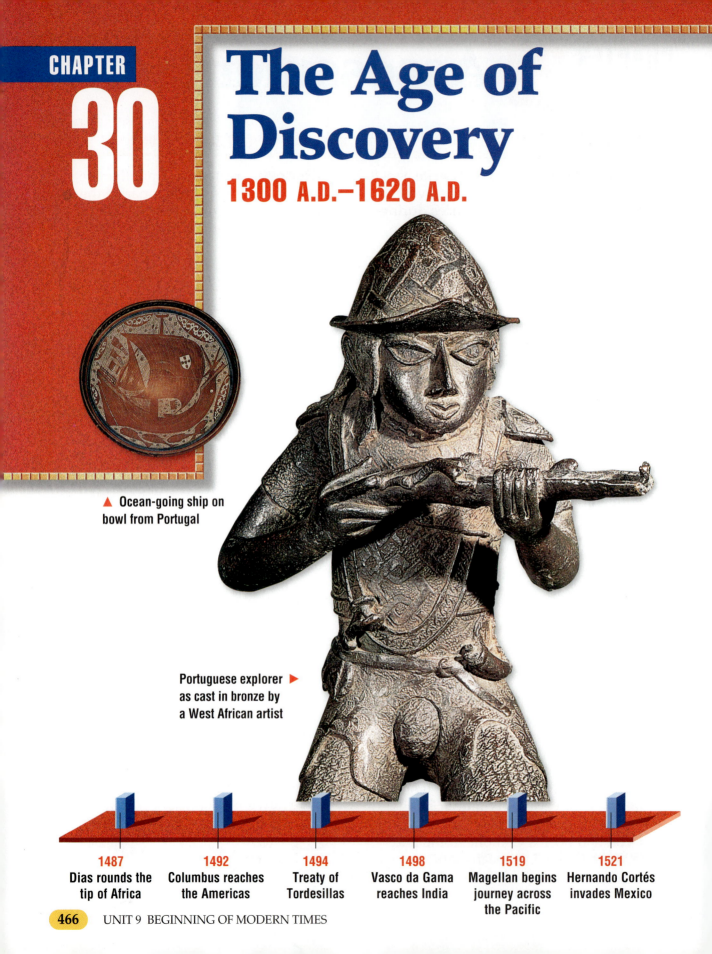

▲ Ocean-going ship on bowl from Portugal

Portuguese explorer ▶ as cast in bronze by a West African artist

1487	1492	1494	1498	1519	1521
Dias rounds the tip of Africa	Columbus reaches the Americas	Treaty of Tordesillas	Vasco da Gama reaches India	Magellan begins journey across the Pacific	Hernando Cortés invades Mexico

Chapter Focus

 ### Read to Discover

- Why the Europeans searched for a direct sea route to Asia.
- What Portuguese explorers accomplished.
- How explorers financed by Spain sailed to the Americas and beyond.
- How the search for a northwest passage affected the history of the Americas.

 **HISTORY** *Online*

Chapter Overview

Visit the *Human Heritage* Web site at **humanheritage.glencoe.com** and click on **Chapter 30— Chapter Overviews** to preview this chapter.

 Terms to Learn

compass
astrolabe
caravel
mutiny
papal line of
  demarcation
conquistadores
sea dogs

 People to Know

Henry the
  Navigator
Vasco da Gama
Christopher
  Columbus
Ponce de León
Ferdinand
  Magellan

Places to Locate

Cape of Good
  Hope
St. Lawrence
  River
Hudson River

Why It's Important   By the 1500s, Italy controlled Europe's trade with India and other parts of Asia. To break the Italian hold on trade, other European nations began to search for an all-water route to the east. They hoped their journeys would enrich their countries and spread Christianity.

A number of developments—such as more accurate maps, improved ships, and better navigation instruments—aided European explorers. One instrument was the **compass,** which has a magnetic needle that always points north. Another was the **astrolabe** (as' trō lāb), which measures the angle of the stars and helps sailors find latitude. The journeys of European explorers changed world history forever.

Reading Check
How did the **compass** and the **astrolabe** help explorers chart direction?

SECTION 1   The Portuguese

The desire for new trade routes led to a great age of exploration in the 1400s. Information from such early explorers as Marco Polo was very helpful. The Portuguese were among the first to travel beyond the Mediterranean Sea. The accomplishments of Prince Henry the Navigator and the discoveries of Bartolomeu Dias (bahr thol' uh myū dē ahs) and Vasco da Gama (vas' kō duh gah' muh) opened the way for later explorations.

Linking Across Time

Maps   Mapmakers often went on voyages of exploration so they could draw more accurate maps of the world, such as this map of Africa (below). In 1972 the United States launched its first Landsat, or land satellite, to beam back even more accurate maps of the earth, such as this image of Africa and the Indian Ocean (right). **What country took the lead in exploration in the early 1400s?**

Prince Henry   Prince Henry the Navigator, son of the king of Portugal, had heard from African merchants about discoveries of gold there. Europe's supplies of *bullion* (būl′ yuhn), or gold and silver for making coins, were running out. Prince Henry became eager for Portuguese sailors to explore the west coast of Africa. He also hoped they would find a new route to the Far East. He saw this as a way to extend Portugal's trade and power. The demand for spices such as ginger, cloves, and pepper, which he could obtain there, was great.

In the early 1400s, Henry set up the first European school for navigators in Sagres (sag′ rēsh), Portugal. Prince Henry was fascinated by all information concerning sailing, navigation, and astronomy. Although he never sailed on a single ocean voyage himself, Henry organized a way for others to learn the most skilled way to sail. He gathered together Portuguese, Spanish, Jewish, Arab, and Italian mathematicians, chartmakers, astronomers, and sea captains. They taught Portuguese sailors all they knew and helped Henry make better charts, improve navigational instruments, and put together more detailed astronomical tables.

At the same time, Henry worked with others to design and build better ships. The result was the Portuguese **caravel** (kar′ uh vel). It combined the heavy, square-rigged European ship

✔ **Reading Check**
What improvements did the **caravel** bring to sailing?

with the light, slim Arab one to produce a ship that was faster and easier to handle.

Henry sent parties of explorers south along Africa's west coast. There, they discovered the Gold Coast and Cape Verde (vuhr′ dē), as well as the Azores (ā′ zōrz), Madeira (muh dir′ uh), and Canary Islands. These islands were used as supply stations for further explorations.

In Africa, the Portuguese explorers found gold dust, ivory, and people whom they enslaved. Some explorers soon began to take more interest in trade than in discovery. Trading forts were set up along the west coast of Africa and contacts were established with African leaders. This trade brought new wealth to Portugal, and Henry saw his country become powerful. When he died in 1460, however, Portuguese caravels had gone only part of the way down the west coast of Africa.

Bartolomeu Dias   Exploration went on after Prince Henry's death, but more slowly. In 1473, the Equator was crossed. Europeans discovered that the sea did not boil and was not the

Student Web Activity

Visit the *Human Heritage* Web site at **humanheritage.glencoe.com** and click on ***Chapter 30— Student Web Activities*** to find out more about Prince Henry the Navigator.

PRINCE HENRY THE NAVIGATOR   Prince Henry's school for navigators helped make possible the great new discoveries of lands and water routes in the 1400s. In this painting Henry watches for his ships to return. **Why did Prince Henry hope to find a new route to the Far East?**

Painting of Vasco da Gama

home of great monsters as had once been believed. Gradually and carefully, Portuguese explorers made their way south along the African coast.

In 1487, Bartolomeu Dias readied ships for a long, hard voyage. Included for the first time was a supply ship with enough water and food for an extended trip. Dias touched at several points on Africa's west coast before strong winds blew him southward. After the storm ended, Dias went on to reach Africa's east coast, without knowing his ships had been blown around the tip of the continent. On the return home, Dias named what he now knew to be the southern tip of Africa the Cape of Storms. The king of Portugal later renamed it the Cape of Good Hope because the Portuguese now knew they could reach the Far East by sailing around Africa.

Vasco da Gama

In the summer of 1497, a Portuguese noble named Vasco da Gama led a *convoy* (kon' voi), or group, of four ships down the Tagus (tā' guhs) River from Lisbon, Portugal. The ships had been designed by Bartolomeu Dias. Dias, in fact, accompanied da Gama as far as Cape Verde. Da Gama had orders from the king to "proclaim the Christian faith" and to "wrest kingdoms and new states from the hands of the barbarians."

After four months at sea, da Gama's convoy rounded the Cape of Good Hope. By then, many of the crew were sick. Their water smelled, and their food was spoiling. Still, the convoy continued on, sailing north along the east coast of Africa toward the island of Mozambique (mō zam bēk'). This island was a Muslim trading center. There, the Portuguese sailors saw ships loaded with cargoes of cloves, pepper, gold, silver, pearls, and precious stones. For the first time, they saw a coconut, which they described as "fruit as large as a melon, of which the kernel is eaten." When the Muslims found out that da Gama and his party were Christians, they forced the Europeans to leave.

The next stop was Malindi (mahl in' dē) in present-day Kenya. There, the crew took on supplies and learned to make rope from coconut fiber. The king of Malindi sent da Gama an Arab pilot to lead him to his final destination of Calicut (kal' i kuht), a port and trading center on the southwest coast of India.

On May 20, 1498, da Gama's ships landed at Calicut. His arrival alarmed the Arab and Persian merchants there. They feared that Portugal would take over the trade between Africa and India. An attempt was made to kill da Gama. In August, da Gama decided to leave. He and his crew loaded what spices they could and started home.

The trip back to Lisbon took 11 months for one ship and 13 months for the ship that da Gama was sailing. During that time, the convoy was threatened by storms, and many of the men died of *scurvy* (sker' vē), a disease caused by the lack of vitamin C.

Goa Goa, on the southwest coast of India, was a Portuguese colony from 1510 until 1961, when it became part of India. Catholic and Hindu traditions blended there. Today the people of Goa celebrate festivals such as Carnival in much the same way as people in Brazil, also once a Portuguese colony.

When the ships finally reached Lisbon in 1499, da Gama was greeted with great rejoicing and rewards. His voyage opened the way for later explorations and for an era of increased trade. Before long, Lisbon became one of the major trading centers of Europe.

Section 1 Assessment

1. **Define:** compass, astrolabe, caravel.
2. Why was Dias's trip important?
3. What were the results of da Gama's voyage to India?

Critical Thinking

4. **Predicting Consequences** How do you think the lives of African Americans today might be different if Prince Henry the Navigator had not sent explorers to West Africa?

Graphic Organizer Activity

5. Draw this diagram, and use it the show the accomplishments of Portuguese leaders in exploration.

Accomplishments		
Prince Henry	Dias	da Gama

SECTION 2 The Spanish

The Spanish were as interested as the Portuguese in the wealth that could be obtained from India and the Far East. Until the late 1400s, however, they were too busy trying to gain their freedom from the Moors. By 1492, Spain had become a Christian country united under King Ferdinand and Queen Isabella. It was now ready to enter the race for new trade routes.

Christopher Columbus   Christopher Columbus, the son of a weaver, was a skilled navigator from Genoa (jen' uh wuh), Italy. Like most educated people of his time, Columbus believed the world was round, not flat. Therefore, he believed he could reach Asia by sailing west. He tried for eight years to convince rulers from different nations to finance an expedition. The Portuguese, French, and English monarchs all turned him down. Finally, in 1492, Queen Isabella of Spain agreed to support his plan, the enterprise (en' tuhr prīz) of the Indies.

Columbus set sail from Spain in August, 1492, with three small ships—the *Niña*, the *Pinta*, and the *Santa Maria*—and a crew of about 90 sailors. At first, the voyage went well. The longer they were at sea, however, the more afraid Columbus's crew became. They urged their captain to turn back. When he refused,

Painting of Santa Maria

Reading Check

Why did Columbus's crew threaten **mutiny**?

Fun Facts . . . .

Looking to the Sea

Columbus's interest in seafaring may have been shaped by the geography of his birthplace, the Republic of Genoa. Since the city lacked fertile land and was surrounded by powerful rival cities like Milan and Florence, many Genoans looked to the Mediterranean Sea to find their fortunes.

they threatened **mutiny** (myūt' nē), or an overthrow of officers. Columbus then promised to turn back if land was not sighted within three days. The night of the second day, a lookout on the *Pinta* spotted land. In the morning, Columbus landed at an outer island in the Bahamas (buh hah' muhs), probably Watling Island. Because he thought he had reached the Indies, Columbus called the people living on the islands Indians. For this reason, Native Americans are sometimes referred to as Indians.

Columbus spent several months sailing around the Bahamas, Cuba, and Hispaniola (his puhn yō' luh), an island that today consists of Haiti (hā' tē) and the Dominican Republic. In Cuba, he found Native Americans smoking cigars. This was the first European contact with tobacco.

On Christmas Eve, the *Santa Maria* ran aground on a reef and was wrecked. Columbus had his crew use the wood from the *Santa Maria* to build a fort. This was the first European settlement in the Americas.

In January 1493, Columbus boarded the *Niña* and headed back to Spain. He took with him gold, parrots, cotton, other plants and animals, and a few Native Americans. In Spain, he was

CHRISTOPHER COLUMBUS   Upon his return from the Americas, Columbus was greeted as a hero. In this painting he is being received by King Ferdinand and Queen Isabella. At the bottom of the steps are Native Americans and riches from the Americas. **What did Columbus hope to prove by sailing westward to Asia?**

received with great honors. Six months later, he was leading a fleet of 17 ships and 1,500 men on another search for Asia.

Columbus made four voyages in all. He explored the coasts of Venezuela and Central America. He returned from his last voyage in 1504. Two years later, he died still convinced he had found the way to Asia. He never realized he had explored the Americas.

The Treaty of Tordesillas   The Spanish monarchs were worried that Portugal might try to take from Spain the riches Columbus had discovered. So, they asked Pope Alexander VI for help.

In 1493, the Pope drew a **papal line of demarcation** (dē mahr kā′ shuhn), or an imaginary line from the North Pole to the South Pole, some 300 miles, or 480 kilometers, west of the Azores Islands. Spain was to have the non-Christian lands west of the line, and Portugal the non-Christian lands east of the line.

The Portuguese, however, did not like the way the lands were divided. They protested and called for a meeting. In 1494, the Treaty of Tordesillas (tord uh sē′ yuhs) was drawn up. It moved the line about 500 miles, or 800 kilometers, farther west. Because of this, Portugal was able to claim Brazil.

Other countries, like England, France, and the Netherlands, paid no attention to the Pope's rulings. They explored and claimed land where they wished.

The Conquistadores   The Spanish were eager to learn more about their new possessions. Over the next few years, Spanish *conquistadores* (kon kē stuh dōr′ āz), or conquerors, set out to find the gold Columbus had talked about and to explore new lands.

In 1513, Ponce de León (pahn′ suh de lē on′) sailed north from the island of Puerto Rico (pwer′ tō rē′ kō) to explore Florida. That same year, Vasco Núñez de Balboa (vas′ kō nū′ nyāth dā bal bō′ uh) crossed the isthmus of Panama and became the first European to see the Great South Sea. Between 1519 and 1521, Hernando Cortés (her nan′ dō kōr tes′) invaded Mexico. With the help of guns and the spread of smallpox, he destroyed the Native American empire ruled by the Aztec king Montezuma. Cortés and his troops took large amounts of gold from the Native Americans to send back to Spain.

In 1532, Francisco Pizarro (fran sis′ kō puh zahr′ ō) invaded Peru. Within five years, he conquered the Inca Empire. Like Cortés, Pizarro took great treasures of gold and silver from the Native Americans. Pizarro and his men then headed for the coast, where they built Lima (lē′ muh), the "City of Kings."

In 1539, Hernando de Soto (duh sō′ tō) sailed from Cuba to Florida and explored westward from there. He found no gold but explored the Mississippi River. In 1540, Francisco Coronado

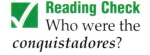

Reading Check
What was the **papal line of demarcation?**

Reading Check
Who were the *conquistadores*?

Then... & Now

Seeds Across the Sea
Did you have orange juice for breakfast? If you did, it may be because of Columbus's second voyage to the Americas in 1493. The citrus seeds that he brought to the West Indies took root in the islands and later were grown in Mexico and Florida.

Ferdinand Magellan
c. 1480–1521

Portuguese Navigator

Born a noble, Magellan sailed on early Portuguese voyages to India. However, when he sought permission to look for a new western route to this region, Portuguese rulers turned him down. He moved to Spain, where he received funding for his voyage. Sailing as a Spanish citizen, Magellan charted a journey that proved what the Greeks had guessed—that the world was round and that the continents of the earth were linked by bodies of water.

PONCE DE LEÓN   While governing Puerto Rico, Ponce de León heard stories of an island to the north that held great riches. Setting out to find this island, Ponce de León discovered Florida instead. He is shown in this painting landing on the Florida coast. **From which two Native American civilizations did the Spaniards acquire much gold?**

(kōr uh nahd′ ō) led an army overland from Mexico into the present-day United States. He reached the Grand Canyon but returned without finding any treasure. Thus, between 1492 and 1550, Spain explored an area from North America through Central America and the West Indies to South America.

Ferdinand Magellan   In 1517, Portugal controlled the eastern route to the Indies. As a result, Portugal was growing rich. This angered the Spanish king. So, when a Portuguese explorer named Ferdinand Magellan (muh jel′ uhn) offered to find Spain a western route to the Indies, the king accepted the offer. He wanted Spain to become as wealthy as Portugal.

In 1519, Magellan set sail from Spain. He commanded a fleet of five ships and a crew of 256. In October of the following year, he sailed through a stormy strait at the tip of South America. The trip took one month. Today, the strait bears Magellan's name.

From the strait, Magellan sailed on into the Great South Sea. He renamed it the Pacific Ocean from the Spanish word *pacifico*, meaning peaceful. By this time, Magellan had lost two of his ships. He continued on, however. Conditions were terrible. The drinking water was spoiled, and the biscuits were full of worms. The crew was forced to eat rats, sawdust from ship boards, and leather soaked in the sea and grilled on wood coals. By the time the fleet reached the Mariana (mar ē an′ uh) Islands three months

Reviewing Map Legends

Legends, as explained in the map skill on page 75, are used to identify information shown on maps. Legends provide the key to the meaning of an unlimited number of symbols and colors that can be used on maps.

Sometimes, however, one legend may be used in several ways. For example, on the "European Voyages of Discovery" map below, five colors are used in the legend. On this particular map, these colors are used to show two different things. First, they point out the five European countries that took part in the voyages of discovery. Second, the colors show the different routes taken by explorers from these countries. For example, Portugal is shown in yellow. The routes that the Portuguese explorers took are also shown in yellow.

Map Practice

1. **What two countries had explorers sail around the world?**
2. **What country did not send any explorers south of 25°N latitude?**

European Voyages of Discovery

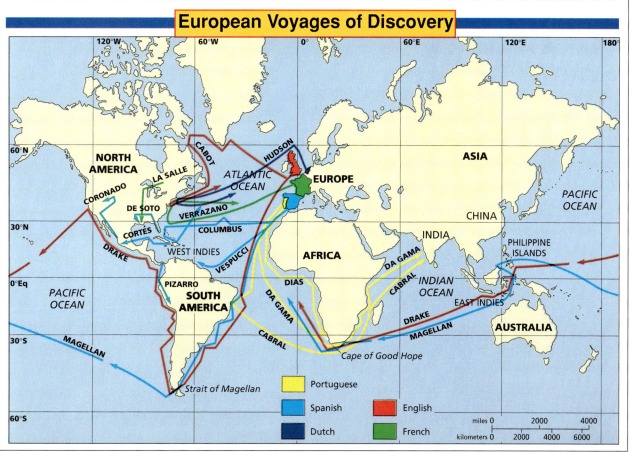

Painting of Ferdinand Magellan

later, it was almost helpless. The crew was suffering from scurvy and had no food of any kind.

After they had eaten and rested, Magellan and his crew set a southwest course for the Philippine (fil uh pēn') Islands. There, Magellan became involved in a local war and was killed. Shortly after, more crew members were killed, and two more ships were lost. The one remaining ship continued on into the Indian Ocean and around Africa. It finally arrived in Seville (suh vil'), Spain, in 1522 with 18 men and a load of spices.

The voyage was a great accomplishment. By *circumnavigating,* or sailing completely around the world, it proved that Earth is indeed round. The voyage opened the Pacific Ocean to European ships. It also proved that Columbus did not land in Asia but in the Americas.

Section 2 Assessment

1. **Define:** mutiny, papal line of demarcation, *conquistadores.*
2. What were some discoveries made by the Spanish between 1513 and 1540?
3. What did Magellan's voyage prove?

Critical Thinking

4. **Making Comparisons** Which of Spain's explorers do you think advanced knowledge of the world the most? Explain.

Graphic Organizer Activity

5. Draw this diagram, and use it to show some of the effects of Columbus's voyages.

Columbus's Voyages	Effect
	Effect
	Effect

SECTION 3 Northwest Passage

Even after the Americas were reached, the English, French, and Dutch continued to look for another route to the Far East. Since the Portuguese and the Spanish controlled the southern sea lanes, the others looked for a northwest passage.

English merchants persuaded their king to send John Cabot (kab' uht), an Italian navigator, to the Far East by a northwest route. In 1497, Cabot set sail with a handful of men. He explored the coasts of Newfoundland and Nova Scotia (nō' vuh skō' shuh) and established claims for England in the Americas.

In 1523, the French hired Giovanni da Verrazano (jē uh vahn' ē dah ver rah tsah' nō), another Italian navigator, to find a northwest passage. He sailed along the Atlantic coast from North Carolina to New York. Eleven years later, Jacques Cartier (zhahk kahr tyā′), a French navigator, sailed up the St. Lawrence River as far as present-day Montreal (mahn trē ahl′). This gave the French a claim to eastern Canada.

In 1576, Sir Martin Frobisher (frō′ bi shuhr), an English **sea dog,** or sea captain, sailed the coast of Greenland and fought a storm that almost wrecked one of his three ships. Frobisher finally discovered the bay that today bears his name.

In 1609, the Dutch sent Henry Hudson, an English navigator, to locate the passage. He explored the Hudson River and sailed to what is today Albany, New York. In 1610 he set out on a second voyage. He became lost in a storm and was never seen again. Nevertheless, his first voyage gave the Dutch their claim in the Americas.

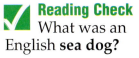

Reading Check
What was an English **sea dog?**

EXPLORERS

Name	Country	Achievements
Amerigo Vespucci	*Spain Portugal*	explored Atlantic coast of South America, 1497–1504; one of first to believe he had reached a new world
Pedro Alváres Cabral	*Portugal*	discovered Brazil and sailed east to India, 1500–1501
Vasco Núñez de Balboa	*Spain*	first European to sight eastern shore of Pacific Ocean, 1513
Alvar Núñez Cabeza de Vaca	*Spain*	explored Florida and Gulf region from Texas to Mexico, 1528–36
Juan Rodríguez Cabrillo	*Spain*	explored Pacific coast to Drake's Bay near San Francisco, 1542
Richard Chancellor	*England*	reached Moscow in search of northeast passage to Asia; opened trade with Russia, 1553–54
John Davis	*England*	explored west coast of Greenland in search of northwest passage to Asia, 1585
Sir Francis Drake	*England*	first Englishman to sail around the world, 1577–80
Father Jacques Marquette Louis Jolliet	*France*	explored Mississippi Valley to mouth of Arkansas River, 1673
Vitus Bering	*Russia*	explored coasts of Alaska and northeast Asia; discovered Bering Strait and Bering Sea, 1728, 1741

All of these voyages failed in their search to find a northwest passage to the Far East. They did, however, establish claims in the Americas for England, France, and the Netherlands.

Section 3 Assessment

1. **Define:** sea dog.
2. How did English, French, and Dutch explorers plan to reach Asia?
3. What lands in the Americas were claimed by England? By France? By the Netherlands?

Critical Thinking

4. **Demonstrating Reasoned Judgment** What characteristics or kinds of personalities do you think the English, French, and Dutch explorers had to have to achieve what they did?

Graphic Organizer Activity

5. Draw this diagram, and use it to show the causes and effects of the search for a northwest passage.

Chapter Summary & Study Guide

1. During the 1500s, Europeans tried to break the Italian hold on trade by searching for an all-water route to India and beyond.
2. The development of better maps, ships, and navigational instruments helped Europeans in their search.
3. In the early 1400s, Prince Henry of Portugal opened the first school in Europe for navigators.
4. By 1473, Portuguese ships had crossed the equator. By 1498, they had reached India.
5. Between 1492 and 1504, Columbus made four voyages to what he thought was Asia but was really the Americas.
6. In 1494, the Treaty of Tordesillas divided non-Christian lands between Spain and Portugal, but other nations ignored the agreement.
7. In the first half of the 1500s, Cortés and Pizarro conquered the Aztec and Inca empires, encouraging other explorers to search for other empires in the Americas.
8. Between 1519 and 1522, Magellan's expedition sailed around the world, proving that Columbus did not land in Asia.
9. Between 1497 and 1609, England, France, and the Netherlands sent explorers to find a northwest passage through the Americas.
10. Early English, French, and Dutch voyages paved the way for future claims in North America.

Self-Check Quiz

Visit the *Human Heritage* Web site at **humanheritage. glencoe.com** and click on *Chapter 30—Self-Check Quiz* to assess your understanding of this chapter.

CHAPTER 30 Assessment

Using Key Terms

Imagine you are writing a newspaper column entitled "Great Explorer Achievements." Use each of the following words in a description of what you think some of these achievements were.

compass   astrolabe   caravel
mutiny   papal line of   *conquistadores*
sea dog   demarcation

Understanding Main Ideas

1. What were some of the problems that European explorers faced on their voyages of discovery?
2. What was the first European settlement in the Americas?
3. What are three bodies of water named after European explorers?
4. How long did it take Magellan's ship to sail around the world?
5. What did voyages in search of a northwest passage to Asia accomplish?

Critical Thinking

1. Why do you think Queen Isabella of Spain agreed to support Columbus when others had turned him down?
2. How do you think Native Americans felt about the *conquistadores*?
3. How did competition between nations affect European voyages of exploration?

Graphic Organizer Activity

History Create a chart like the one on this page, and use it to write a headline for an important event that occurred in each of the years shown.

Year	Headline
1473	
1487	
1492	
1494	
1497	
1499	
1521	
1522	
1532	
1609	

Geography in History

The World in Spatial Terms Refer to the map on page 475. Whose voyage from Portugal to India was longer in miles (or kilometers)—da Gama's or Cabral's? How many miles (or kilometers) longer was it?

Using Your Journal

Review any details you may have noted about the changes that took place in western Europe between 1300 and 1600. Imagine you are a peasant living in London, England, in 1550. Write a diary entry describing what you have learned about the world in recent years.

THE SWAHILI CULTURE

Between 1000 and 1700 A.D., the harbor towns of East Africa blossomed. Like other trading centers, they attracted a variety of influences. More than 1,200 years ago, Arab traders came to the area, bringing the Muslim religion with them. Other influences came from Persia, India, and China. Later, Portuguese explorers edging their way along the East African coast brought yet another influence to the area.

By far the strongest influence, however, was that of the African peoples who already lived in the region. The blending of their cultures with the cultures of other regions produced the Swahili culture, which is still alive and vibrant today.

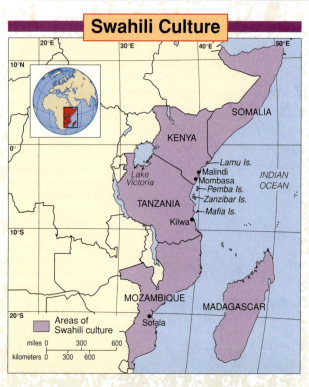

Swahili Culture

▲ The term *Swahili* comes from an Arab word meaning "coastal people." The Swahili culture includes African Muslims who live on African islands and lands bordering the Indian Ocean.

▶ In the early 1400s, Chinese explorer Zheng He made several voyages to East Africa. On his fourth voyage, the sultan of Malindi presented him with a giraffe—a gift to the Chinese emperor. The Chinese called the giraffe a "celestial unicorn" and saw it as a sign of good luck.

the W🌐rld

From the 100s to the early 1900s, Swahili merchants used a ship known as the *mtepe* to sail the coastal waters. Built without nails, the timbers of the boats were held together by rope woven from coconut husks and powered by sails made from the leaves of coconut trees. The Arabs introduced the *dhow* and its triangular cotton sail to the region around the 800s. Arab *dhows* can still be seen along the Swahili coast today. ▼

▲ Trade goods from China made their way to the Swahili coast as early as the 800s A.D. Pottery, such as this bowl made during the Ming dynasty, has been uncovered up and down the coast.

▼ This present-day market shows the blend of people that make up the Swahili culture and the many goods, particularly spices, that have made the region famous.

Gold coins found on Pemba, an island off the coast of Kenya, prove that Swahili merchants traded all over the Arab world in the 1000s. These coins come from Tunisia, Egypt, and Syria. The Swahili towns also minted their own coins. ▶

Taking Another Look

1. Where are the Swahili peoples located?
2. What evidence proves that Swahili merchants traded with the Arab world? With China?

Hands-On Activity

Writing Diary Entries Imagine you are a Portuguese ship captain visiting a Swahili town for the first time. Write several diary entries describing the experience.

481

Standardized Test Practice

Directions: Choose the *best* answer to each of the following multiple choice questions. If you have trouble answering a question, use the process of elimination to narrow your choices. Write your answers on a separate piece of paper.

1. **Which of the following Renaissance contributions was most helpful in spreading new ideas?**

   A   The creation of piazzas in the center of cities

   B   The use of perspective in artists' work

   C   The invention of the printing press

   D   The generosity of Lorenzo de Medici toward artists, poets, and philosphers

   > **Test-Taking Tip:** Always read the question and *all* the answer choices carefully. Notice that all of the answer choices are examples of Renaissance contributions to European culture. Although Lorenzo de Medici's generosity (answer D) probably helped people *create* new ideas, there is another choice that was more helpful in *spreading* these ideas to many people.

2. **Leonardo da Vinci was**

   F   a scholar and a Church leader

   G   an artist, scientist, and inventor

   H   the founder of modern medicine

   J   a philosopher and historian

   > **Test-Taking Tip:** Eliminate answers that are incorrect. Leonardo da Vinci was not a Church leader, so answer F can be eliminated.

3. **Why was Martin Luther charged with heresy?**

   A   He worshiped more than one god.

   B   He worked to secure rights for Spanish Jews.

   C   He declared himself the one true voice of God.

   D   His theses challenged the Pope and the Catholic Church.

   > **Test-Taking Tip:** This question requires you to remember a *fact* about Martin Luther. Reading all the answer choices carefully may help you remember information about this important religious leader.

4. **Which of the following was most responsible for the spread of the Protestant church through Europe?**

   F   Services were not conducted in Latin, but rather in local languages.

   G   Women were given a greater role in the Protestant church.

   H   Church members could buy indulgences to free themselves from punishment.

   J   The Protestant church was recognized by the Roman Catholic Church.

   > **Test-Taking Tip:** Again, read carefully. Lutheran and Reformed churches were known as *Protestant* because they *protested* against Catholic ideas, such as the sale of indulgences. Therefore, answer H can be eliminated.

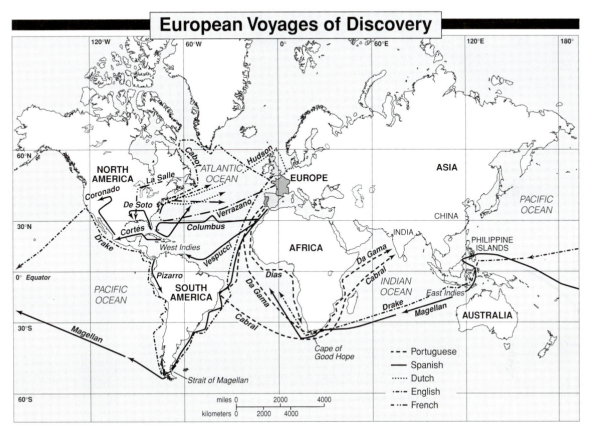

European Voyages of Discovery

5. **According to the map above, which nations' explorers sailed around the Cape of Good Hope?**

   A Portugal and Spain
   B Portugal, France, and England
   C Spain, England, and France
   D Portugal, Spain, and England

   Test-Taking Tip: Use the *map legend*, or *key*, to help you understand how the map is organized. How does this map show the routes of different countries' explorers?

6. **Which countries had explorers whose routes crossed the equator?**

   F England, Spain, and Portugal
   G England, Spain, and France
   H Spain, France, and Portugal
   J Spain, Portugal, and Holland

   Test-Taking Tip: Make sure that you do not confuse the *equator* with the *Prime Meridian*. Although both are indicated by 0°, the equator is a line of latitude, and the Prime Meridian is a line of longitude. Do you remember which is which?

The Changing World

◄ **Early microscope, which revolutionized science**

Model of the *Rocket*, one of England's first steam locomotives ▼

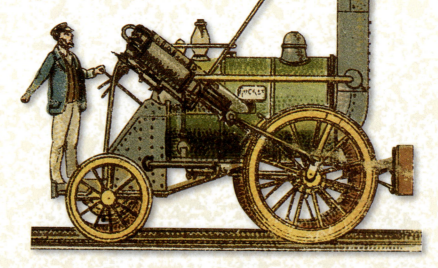

1500
Cabral claims Brazil for Portugal

1607
First permanent English settlement at Jamestown

1619
Virginia House of Burgesses meets

1688
Glorious Revolution in England

FOLDABLES™
Study Organizer

Organizing Information Study Foldable *Make this foldable to help you organize what you learn about the changes that occurred in western Europe and the Americas during the 1800s.*

Step 1 *Fold a sheet of paper into fourths from top to bottom.*

This forms four columns.

Step 2 *Open the paper and refold it into fourths from side to side.*

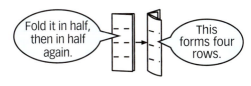

Fold it in half, then in half again.

This forms four rows.

Step 3 *Unfold, turn the paper, and draw lines along the folds.*

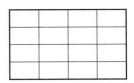

Step 4 *Label as shown.*

Unit 10	Terms	People	Places
Expansion			
Revolution			
Industry			

Reading and Writing *Complete your table foldable as you read the unit. Your foldable should contain main ideas about the political and economic developments of the 1800s.*

PRIMARY SOURCES
Library

See pages 692–693 for other primary source readings to accompany Unit 10.

Read "Life at the Mill: Memoirs of a Child Laborer" from the **World History Primary Source Document Library CD-ROM.**

Journal Notes

What changes took place in the world between the 1500s and the 1800s? Note details about these changes as you read.

1769
James Watt perfects steam engine

1776
U.S. Declaration of Independence

1847
Samuel Colt develops the assembly line

485

Expansion Into the Americas
1500 A.D.–1700 A.D.

▼ Mural from the University of Mexico

◄ Rosary beads from a Spanish mission in New Spain

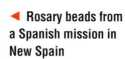

1500	1607	1608	1619	1624
Cabral claims Brazil for Portugal	English settle at Jamestown	French found Quebec	First enslaved Africans brought to Jamestown	Dutch found New Amsterdam

 Terms to Learn

colonize
viceroy
peninsulares
mestizos
indentured
  servants

 People to Know

Cabral
Sir Francis Drake
Sir Walter Raleigh
John Smith
John Rolfe
William Penn

Places to Locate

Brazil
Peru
Roanoke Island
Jamestown
Plymouth
New France

Why It's Important   From the early 1500s to the 1700s, several western European countries set out to **colonize,** or build permanent settlements in, the Americas. Europeans wanted the riches of the Americas, which they thought would bring them power. They also wanted to spread Christianity.

Reading Check
How did western Europeans **colonize** the Americas?

SECTION 1 Portugal

By 1512, the Portuguese had claimed all of Brazil. They had also established trading posts in Africa, India, Southeast Asia, and the Moluccas (muh luhk' uhz), or Spice Islands. They took most of the Asian coastal cities by force.

Portugal found it difficult to rule its new territories. One reason was that it did not have a large enough population to send settlers to all its territories. Also, most of Portugal's territories already had large populations. Then, too, the hot, wet climate of the trading posts was too uncomfortable for most Portuguese. As a result, Portugal had to depend on sea power and the cooperation of defeated leaders to protect its interests.

Brazil   In 1500, the Portuguese explorer Pedro Alváres Cabral (pā' dr ō al vah' rez kah brahl') claimed Brazil for Portugal. Since no precious metals were found, Portugal paid little attention to the discovery. Then, other countries started to take *brazilwood,* or a red wood used to make dyes. When the Portuguese realized the value of the wood, they became more interested in Brazil.

Reading Check
How did the Portuguese use **captaincies** to colonize Brazil?

In 1532, the Portuguese established their first permanent settlement in Brazil. The king of Portugal divided the area into 15 territorial strips called **captaincies** (kap' tuhn sēz). Each strip was given to a different Portuguese family who could establish towns, give out land, and raise armies. In return, they promised to colonize and protect their captaincies.

Portugal sent large numbers of settlers to Brazil. Portuguese sailors landed there and decided to stay. Criminals were sent to work off their sentences. Soldiers and officials came to protect royal interests. Ranchers arrived with herds of cattle. Missionaries came looking for converts to Christianity.

The Portuguese set up plantations in Brazil. Most plantations grew sugarcane, which was used to make sugar, molasses, and rum. About 2 million Native Americans were living in Brazil when Portugal claimed the land. The Portuguese settlers enslaved them to work the land. Most of the Native Americans, however, either ran away or died from diseases brought by the Europeans.

Before long, the Portuguese settlers began bringing over enslaved Africans. The number of Africans grew until, in some places, there were at least 20 enslaved Africans for each Portuguese settler. The Africans brought their religions with them. They also brought African music and dance to Brazil. They told folktales about their African history and carved wooden figures for churches. They also added many new words to the Portuguese language.

By the end of the 1600s, there was less demand for sugar. *Bandeirantes* (ban duh ran' tās), or fortune-hunters, looking for precious stones and escaped enslaved people began to appear. Bandeirantes were the frontiersmen of Brazil. Traveling in bands of fifty to several thousand men, they followed the rivers into the jungle. They established Portugal's claim to the far western and southern areas of Brazil.

Reading Check
Who were the *bandeirantes*, and how did they increase Portuguese land claims?

Royal interest in Brazil grew when gold was discovered in the 1690s. The king sent government clerks to check the mineral resources and make sure the monarchy received one fifth of each miner's gold. Gold brought still more people to Brazil and more wealth to Portugal. The growing of coffee, which was introduced in the early 1700s, made Portugal richer.

In many ways, Brazil was a tolerant society. It welcomed people of different countries and religions. Many men of part-African ancestry rose to high positions in the Church and the government. Women, however, were allowed little freedom or power, and hardly anyone knew how to read and write.

Early Map of Brazil

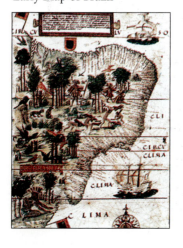

The Loss of Empire

By the middle of the 1500s, Portugal began losing its empire. The colonial government was not well organized and the economy was in poor shape. Another reason was that the conquered peoples disliked the Portuguese for forcing Christianity on them. By the time the Portuguese king died in 1580, Portugal was very weak. The king left no heirs, and the throne was claimed by Philip II of Spain. Portugal was ruled by Spain until 1640. Then, Portugal regained its independence. During that time, the English and the Dutch took over most of the Portuguese trading centers, including those in Southeast Asia.

Section 1 Assessment

1. **Define:** colonize, captaincies, *bandeirantes.*
2. What kept Portugal from colonizing settlements?
3. What happened to the Native Americans who lived in Brazil when the Portuguese claimed the land?

Critical Thinking

4. **Making Inferences** How do you think the Native Americans felt about the Portuguese settlement of Brazil?

Graphic Organizer Activity

5. Draw this diagram, and use it to show the causes of the decline of the Portuguese empire.

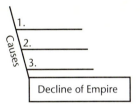

Causes
1. _____
2. _____
3. _____

Decline of Empire

BRAZILIAN PLANTATION   Early Portuguese settlers established plantations in Brazil. At first, Native American populations were enslaved to provide the needed labor. Most of the Native Americans, however, proved too rebellious or too sickly to perform the hard work required. Enslaved Africans were then brought to work on the plantations. **For what was the sugarcane grown on plantations used?**

Carnival The Brazilian capital of Rio de Janeiro is known for its annual Carnival. Celebrated just before the beginning of Lent, the Christian holy season that comes before Easter, Carnival runs for four days.

Colonial Vase

✅ **Reading Check**
What were the **viceroyalties?** What was the role of the **viceroy?**

✅ **Reading Check**
How did the *peninsulares* and *mestizos* differ from each other?

SECTION 2   Spain

By 1535, Spain had established the largest colonial empire in the Americas. Spain's colonies reached from southern North America through Central America and the West Indies to South America. Spain also had trade interests in the Philippines.

Unlike Portugal, Spain had a fairly large population. This allowed it to send thousands of people to its colonies in the Americas. Spain also had a strong, centralized colonial government.

Mexico and Peru   In the early 1500s, Spain conquered the Native American empires of Mexico and Peru. They set the example for other Spanish colonies. They were governed by the Council of the Indies, which met at the Spanish court. This council made laws, acted as a court of final appeal, and chose officials to send to the Americas. It even took charge of religious matters.

The colonies were divided into two **viceroyalties** (vīs' roi uhl tēz), or districts—New Spain, or Mexico, and New Castile, or Peru. Each viceroyalty was ruled by a **viceroy** (vīs' roi), or person who represented the king.

The colonists in the viceroyalties sent large amounts of gold and silver back to Spain. They also ran plantations that produced cocoa, coffee, tobacco, tea, and sugar. They forced Native Americans to do all of the heavy work in mines and on plantations. Most of the Native Americans were badly treated. Many died of overwork, starvation, or such diseases as measles and smallpox.

After a time, the Spanish, like the Portuguese, brought enslaved Africans to the Americas. Most of these enslaved people worked on sugar plantations located on the islands of the Caribbean. There were still far more Portuguese-owned enslaved people in Brazil, however, than Spanish-owned enslaved people in the Caribbean.

By the middle 1500s, colonists in the Americas were divided into clear-cut social groups. At the top were *peninsulares* (puh nin sū la' rās), or Spaniards born in Spain. Then came Creoles (krē' ōlz), or those of Spanish descent born in the Americas. Next were *mestizos* (me stē' zōz), or people of mixed European and Native American ancestry. They were followed by Native Americans. At the lowest level were blacks. Each group held certain jobs. Peninsulares served as viceroys or important church leaders. Mestizos were mostly artisans and merchants.

The way in which colonial cities developed also reflected this social structure. Most cities centered on a square. On one side of the square was the cathedral. On the other three sides stood the government headquarters and the houses of peninsulares. Farther out were the houses of Creoles and mestizos.

The Roman Catholic Church played a large role in Spanish colonization. It controlled most of the best land in the Spanish colonies. Although the Church itself did not pay taxes, it charged the people who rented or farmed its land a 10 percent income tax.

The Church worked to improve conditions in the colonies. Leaders, such as Bartholomé de Las Casas (bar tol uh māʹ dā lahs kahʹ sahs), tried to improve life for the Native Americans. The Church built schools, hospitals, and *asylums* (uh sīʹ luhms), or places for the mentally ill, and staffed them mostly with nuns. It established the first two universities in the Americas. One was the University of Mexico. The other was San Marcos (marʹ kuhs) University at Lima.

The Decline of an Empire

Spain received a great deal of wealth from the colonies, but it did not hold on to that wealth. The Spanish Inquisition had driven out most of the Jews and Muslims who had been the backbone of Spanish industry. As a result, much of the gold and silver sent to Spain ended up going to northern Europe to pay for goods made there.

Fun Facts....

Laziness In Inca times, anyone entering the city of Cuzco was greeted by the phrase *Ama Sua, Ama Quella, Ama Lulla*—Don't Lie, Don't Steal, Don't Be Lazy. To the Incas, laziness was such a serious offense that it was punishable by death.

Linking Across Time

Music The enslaved Africans brought to the Americas contributed to the development of the region's culture. They crafted drums (below) and other instruments similar to those in their homeland and shaped our musical heritage. Today the rhythms of Africa can be heard in the music of the steel drummers in the Caribbean (right) and in the sounds of reggae, calypso, salsa, rap, and other types of music. **What cultural contributions did Spanish settlers make?**

The Spanish also had trouble getting gold and silver from their colonies to Spain. Ships loaded with the precious metals were robbed at sea by English, French, and Dutch pirates. English sea dogs attacked Spanish treasure ships with the blessing of their queen, Elizabeth I. One of the most successful sea dogs was Sir Francis Drake. When the Spanish Armada was defeated by the English in 1588, Spain lost its power in the Atlantic. This opened the Americas to colonization by England, the Netherlands, and France.

Section 2 Assessment

1. **Define:** viceroyalties, viceroy, *peninsulares*, *mestizos*.
2. What role did the Roman Catholic Church play in the Spanish colonies?
3. Why did the Spanish have trouble transporting gold and silver from the Americas to Spain?

Critical Thinking

4. **Predicting Consequences** What do you think might have happened if Spain had used the gold and silver to develop industries in the Americas?

Graphic Organizer Activity

5. Draw this diagram, and use it to show the structure of Spanish society from the most powerful to the least powerful groups.

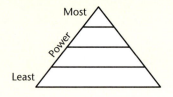

SECTION 3 England

Like Portugal and Spain, England looked to the Americas for wealth. English nobles and merchants saw it as a place to get raw materials as well as gold and silver. With enough gold, silver, and raw materials, the English could establish a favorable **balance of trade.** This meant England would be able to sell more products to other countries than it would have to buy from them. The English would no longer have to depend on other countries for their needs.

The English had other reasons for wanting colonies in the Americas. England had such a large population that jobs were becoming hard to find. New colonies meant more jobs. Then, too, the Anglican (ang' gluh kuhn) Church had become England's official church and the English people were expected to follow Anglican beliefs. Because of this, Catholics and groups of Protestants called Separatists (sep' uhr uh tists) were looking for a place where they could have religious freedom. They believed that in the Americas they would be able to worship freely.

Reading Check
How did the English try to establish a favorable **balance of trade?**

In 1585, a group of colonists financed by Sir Walter Raleigh (rahl′ ē) sailed for North America. There, they founded a colony on Roanoke (rō′ uh nōk) Island off the coast of North Carolina. After six years, however, the colonists disappeared. No one knows for certain what happened to them. For this reason, Roanoke Island became known as the "Lost Colony."

The English did not try again to found colonies in the Americas for more than 20 years. However, in 1600, English merchants formed the East India Company to trade with the East Indies. The company set up trading posts in India, Malaya (muh lā′ uh), and some islands in both the East and West Indies.

Jamestown   In 1607, a group of English nobles and merchants formed the Virginia Company of London. The following year the company sent about 100 settlers to the Americas to search for gold and silver. They founded the first permanent English settlement in America. It was located near the mouth of Chesapeake (ches′ uh pēk) Bay. The settlers named it Jamestown after their king, James I.

The area in which the colony was founded had long been home to Native Americans. By the time Christopher Columbus arrived in the Americas, there were more than 1 million Native Americans scattered across the North American continent. They were divided into some 500 different groups.

Each group of Native Americans had its own language, religion, and way of life. Some, like the Pima (pē′ muh), Papago (pap′ uh gō), Creeks, and Cherokee (cher′ uh kē), were farmers. Others, like the Comanche (kuh man′ chē), Blackfoot, Sioux (sū), Apache (uh pach′ ē), and Navaho (nav′ uh hō), were hunters and warriors who traveled in bands.

The Native Americans who lived in the area near Jamestown were the Powhatan (pau uh tan′). Their chief, whom the settlers called Powhatan, controlled 128 Native American villages.

Life in Jamestown was hard. The land was swampy and filled with mosquitoes that carried disease. Winters were colder in Jamestown than in England. The colonists burned parts of their houses as fuel. Many became sick and died.

Captain John Smith kept the settlement from total failure. He made it clear that those who did not work would not eat. He also convinced the Powhatan to supply the colonists with corn and beans. When Smith returned to England in 1609, however, many of the colonists starved to death. Those still alive a year later were ready to go back to England. When an English fleet arrived with supplies, the colonists decided to stay.

The settlers worked the land, but they did not own it. It belonged to the Virginia Company. Then, in 1618, the company began granting land to individuals. All colonists who paid their own way to America were given 50 acres, or about 20 hectares, of

John Smith

NATIVE AMERICANS

REGION	WAY OF LIFE
Arctic	fished and hunted whales, seals, walruses, and caribou; lived in wood and stone houses or igloos in winter and animal skin tents in summer
Subarctic	hunted and gathered food; built wood-frame houses; traveled by snowshoes, canoe, and toboggan
Northwest Coast	fished and hunted; built cedar wood houses and sea-going canoes; carved totem poles to honor ancestors; held potlatches, or ceremonial feasts
Plateau	hunted bison, fished, and gathered food; lived in multifamily lodges; bred the Appaloosa horse
Great Basin	hunted and gathered food; traveled over territory; wove reed baskets decorated with beads, feathers, and shells
California	hunted, fished, and gathered food; settled in communities; used acorns to make bread
Southwest	farmed corn, beans, and squash; built pueblos of stone and adobe; wove straw and reed baskets and cotton cloth
Great Plains	farmed and hunted; lived in log houses or cone-shaped tepees; communicated with other tribes by hand signals
Eastern Woodlands	fished and hunted; lived in longhouses and birch lodges; women owned property, chose chief, and passed on family name
Southeast	farmed and hunted; built towns with open squares; women owned houses and land; counted descent through mothers

land. In order to attract more colonists, the company began giving each settler an additional 50 acres, or 20 hectares, for each person that settler brought to the Americas. Soon, the number of people coming to the Americas increased tremendously.

Most of the newcomers were **indentured** (in den' chuhrd) **servants.** These were people who agreed to work for four to seven years after their arrival to pay for their passage. At the end of that time, they were free and could obtain land of their own.

The settlers saw the Native Americans using tobacco and began to use it themselves. People in Europe also started using tobacco. At first, they used it as a medicine. Later, they smoked it in clay pipes. About 1612, a settler named John Rolfe (rahlf) began planting tobacco. It soon became Virginia's most important crop. Most of the tobacco grown was exported to England because people there were willing to pay a good price for it.

The settlers brought English laws and government with them to the Americas. They were far from England, however, and travel was slow. Soon, it became necessary for them to make their own laws. In 1619, they elected 22 **burgesses** (ber' jis ez), or representatives, from among landowning males over 17 years old. The burgesses met to decide laws for the colony. This House of Burgesses set an important example of self-government.

Plymouth

Another company, the Virginia Company of Plymouth (plim' uhth), was formed in England in 1606. In 1620, it was reorganized as the Council for New England. It gained the right to grant land to settlers for colonies in New England.

That same year, a group of Separatists called Pilgrims sailed for Virginia on the *Mayflower.* They had received grants of land from the Virginia Company. Strong winds blew the *Mayflower* off course, causing the Pilgrims to land in New England just north of Cape Cod in present-day Massachusetts.

The lands in New England belonged to the Council for New England, and the Pilgrims had not been given the right to govern in them. Therefore, they signed an agreement to set up a civil government. This agreement was called the Mayflower Compact. The majority of free men would govern. Neither women nor indentured servants could vote.

The Pilgrims named their settlement Plymouth after the English town from which they had sailed. Their first winter in the Americas was hard. About one half of the settlers died. In the spring, those who remained cleared the fields for farming. The Native Americans taught them how to fertilize their crops and how to hunt and fish in the wilderness.

The people of Plymouth governed themselves for 70 years with almost no outside control. Then, in 1691, Plymouth became part of the Massachusetts Bay Colony.

Reading Check How did **indentured servants** pay for their passage to the Americas?

Reading Check Who were the **burgesses,** and how did they encourage self-government?

Baptized Indentured Servants The first Africans in Virginia, who arrived at Jamestown in 1619, were indentured servants. Among them were a couple named Antoney and Isabella, who had probably been baptized by Spanish traders. In 1623 or 1624, Isabella gave birth to a son, the first African American born in the English colonies. The baby was named William and was baptized in the Church of England.

Painting of Lord Baltimore

The Growth of an Empire

Jamestown and Plymouth were not the only English settlements in the Americas. In fact, by 1733 Great Britain had 13 colonies along the Atlantic coast of America. One of these colonies was founded in 1630, when a group of Puritans seeking religious freedom sailed to New England. There, they formed several settlements of the Massachusetts Bay Colony in the area around present-day Boston.

In 1634, the English settled in Maryland. King Charles I had granted the land to his friend Cecilius Calvert (se sēl' yuhs kal' vuhrt), the second Lord Baltimore. Calvert wanted a place in America where English Catholics could live in peace.

In 1681, William Penn, the leader of a religious group called the Quakers (kwā' kuhrz), founded a colony in Pennsylvania. King Charles II had granted Penn the land in payment for a debt he owed Penn's father.

Section 3 Assessment

1. **Define:** balance of trade, indentured servants, burgesses.
2. Why did colonists set up the House of Burgesses?
3. What group founded the Massachusetts Bay Colony? Why did they establish it?

Critical Thinking

4. **Making Inferences** Why would the Americas be a likely place for people to settle who were unhappy in their own countries?

Graphic Organizer Activity

5. Draw this diagram, and use it to compare the English colonies at Jamestown and Plymouth.

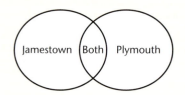

Jamestown Both Plymouth

SECTION 4 The Netherlands

The Dutch also established colonies in the Americas. In 1602, Dutch merchants founded the Dutch East India Company to trade in Africa and the East Indies. The Dutch had a fleet of more than 10,000 merchant ships. One by one, they seized Portuguese trading posts in the East Indies and soon controlled most of the East Indies. In addition, they became the first Europeans to reach Australia and New Zealand. They also founded a colony named Capetown at the southern tip of Africa. Many Dutch colonists, called Boers (borz), settled there.

In 1621, the Dutch formed another company called the Dutch West India Company to establish colonies in the Americas. Colonists were sent first to islands in the West Indies and along the coast of South America. In 1624, the Dutch founded the city of New Amsterdam (am' stuhr dam) on the island of Manhattan (man hat' n). They bought the island from the Native Americans for goods worth about $24. The Dutch called the colonies they established in North America "New Netherlands." New Amsterdam was the capital.

Later in the 1600s, rivalry between the Dutch and the English led to a series of wars, which the Dutch lost. The English took over most of the Dutch colonies, including New Amsterdam, which they renamed New York.

Section 4 Assessment

1. Why were the Dutch East India Company and the Dutch West India Company formed?
2. To what nation did the Dutch lose most of their colonies?

Critical Thinking

3. **Drawing Conclusions** Do you think the Dutch purchase of Manhattan was fair or unfair to the Native Americans? Explain.

Graphic Organizer Activity

4. Draw this diagram, and use it to show some of the areas that the Dutch explored or colonized.

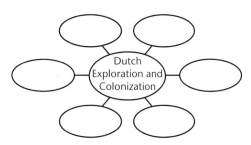

Dutch Exploration and Colonization

SECTION 5 France

In 1608, Samuel de Champlain (sham plān'), a French explorer, founded the first permanent French colony in the Americas at Quebec (kwi bek'). Soon after, the French established other settlements around the Great Lakes. They also established settlements at the northern end of the Mississippi River and along the rivers and streams that flowed into it.

Most of these settlements resembled villages in France. Houses stood side by side along a lake or river bank. Behind each house stretched a long, narrow farm. The settlements were small, because few people wanted to leave France.

Most of the French in the Americas were fur traders. On foot or by canoe, they visited various Native American tribes. They gave the Native Americans blankets, guns, knives, and wine in

Painting of Robert de La Salle

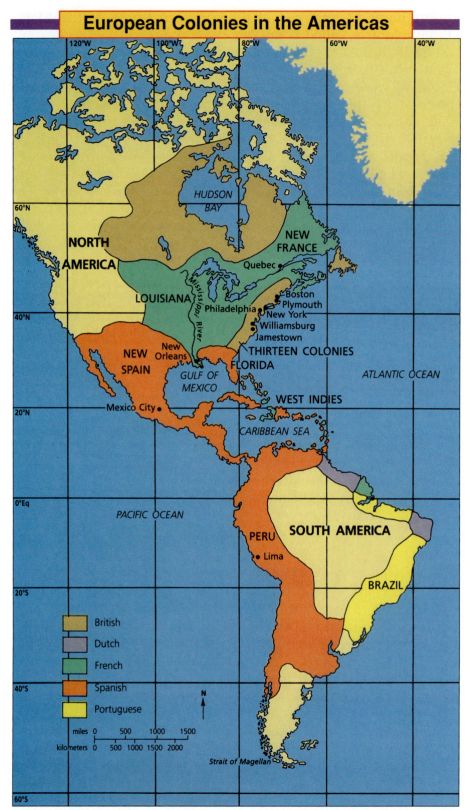

European Colonies in the Americas

NEW FRANCE

NORTH AMERICA

HUDSON BAY

Quebec

LOUISIANA

Mississippi River

Boston
Plymouth
Philadelphia
New York
Williamsburg
Jamestown

THIRTEEN COLONIES

New Orleans

NEW SPAIN

FLORIDA

GULF OF MEXICO

ATLANTIC OCEAN

Mexico City

WEST INDIES

CARIBBEAN SEA

PACIFIC OCEAN

SOUTH AMERICA

PERU

Lima

BRAZIL

British
Dutch
French
Spanish
Portuguese

N

miles 0 500 1000 1500
kilometers 0 500 1000 1500 2000

Strait of Magellan

MAP STUDY

PLACES AND REGIONS By the mid-1700s, France, England, Portugal, and the Netherlands had extended their American claims. **In what parts of the Americas were the British claims located?**

exchange for beaver and other animal skins. Beaver hats for gentlemen became very fashionable in Europe, and the fur trade brought France much wealth.

In 1682, René-Robert Cavelier (ka ve lyā′), Sieur de La Salle (sjoer dā la sal), claimed the Mississippi River valley for France. He named the area Louisiana in honor of the French king, Louis XIV. The French called Louisiana and their other lands in the Americas "New France."

The French also established settlements in the West Indies and in India. In time, the French and the English became great rivals. They clashed in Europe, the Americas, and India. After a series of four wars, the French finally were defeated. In 1763, they signed the Treaty of Paris. Under the treaty, the French lost their North American colonial empire and almost all of their settlements in India.

People in History

Robert de La Salle
1643–1687

French Explorer

Robert de La Salle moved in 1666 to what is now Canada. His explorations in the Mississippi River valley led to French claims in North America.

Section 5 Assessment

1. What was the first permanent French colony founded in the Americas?
2. Why did France's established settlements in the Americas remain small?
3. How did the French lose their lands in North America?

Critical Thinking

4. **Making Inferences**   Why do you think so few French people wanted to settle in the Americas?

Graphic Organizer Activity

5. Draw this diagram, and use it to write at least three facts about French settlements in North America.

French Settlements	Fact 1
	Fact 2
	Fact 3

SECTION 6   The Influence of Empires

Empires in the Americas helped make the nations of western Europe richer and more powerful. These empires also introduced western Europeans to many new foods. Among them were avocados, lima beans, peanuts, pineapples, tomatoes, and turkeys. Farmers in Spain, Portugal, and Italy began to grow corn, while farmers in Germany and Ireland started to specialize in potatoes. Both corn and potatoes were nourishing and easy to grow. As a result, fewer western Europeans died because of famine, and Europe's population increased.

Another popular product from the Americas was a drink made by roasting dry cocoa beans over a fire and pounding them into a paste. The chocolate paste was then mixed with water,

Fun Facts....

Chocolate Hernando Cortés may have been the first European to taste chocolate. At Montezuma's court in Mexico, he had sampled a bitter drink made from cocoa beans. He then brought the drink back to Spain. There people drank it hot, sweetened, and flavored with vanilla or cinnamon.

sugar, vanilla, and cinnamon, and shaken up and down until it bubbled. The people in London, Paris, and other cities in western Europe became so fond of the chocolate drink that they opened cafes where they could sip the drink and talk about events of the day.

Section 6 Assessment

1. What did the empires in the Americas do for the nations of western Europe?
2. What were some of the new foods the empires introduced to western Europeans?
3. What crop did Germany and Ireland specialize in raising?

Critical Thinking

4. **Synthesizing Information** Which of the foods introduced to western Europeans from the Americas are part of your diet today?

Graphic Organizer Activity

5. Draw this diagram, and use it to support this generalization: Contact with the Americas improved life for western Europeans.

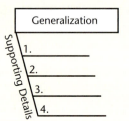

Generalization

Supporting Details
1.
2.
3.
4.

Chapter Summary & Study Guide

1. By 1532, Portugal had a colony in Brazil and trading posts in Africa, India, and Southeast Asia.
2. A poorly organized government and a weak economy allowed Spain and other nations to take over many Portuguese lands.
3. English defeat of the Spanish Armada in 1588 weakened Spain's grip on the Americas and opened the door to colonization by other nations.
4. In 1607, the English founded their first successful settlement in the Americas at Jamestown.
5. Settlers at Jamestown established the House of Burgesses, which set the example of self-government in the English colonies.
6. In 1620, the Pilgrims established England's second permanent settlement at Plymouth in New England.
7. The Dutch and French also established settlements in North America, but the English seized most Dutch holdings.
8. Empires in the Americas gave western European nations wealth and power and introduced people to many new foods.

HISTORY Online

Self-Check Quiz

Visit the *Human Heritage* Web site at **humanheritage.glencoe.com** and click on **Chapter 31—Self-Check Quiz** to assess your understanding of this chapter.

Using Key Terms

Write a paragraph as if you were a Spanish person of the 1500s who has decided to go to the Americas. Explain what you have heard that has influenced your decision. Use the following words in your paragraph.

colonize
bandeirantes
viceroy
mestizos
indentured servants

captaincies
viceroyalties
peninsulares
balance of trade
burgesses

Understanding Main Ideas

1. Why did western European nations want to colonize the Americas?
2. Why did the Portuguese settlers in Brazil bring over enslaved Africans?
3. What happened to most of the gold and silver Spain received from its colonies?
4. In what ways did Native Americans help the settlers at Jamestown? At Plymouth?
5. What kind of trade did the French establish with the Native Americans?

Critical Thinking

1. What changes did European colonization cause in the lives of Native Americans? Explain.
2. "Working as an indentured servant for several years to pay for a trip to the Americas was fair." What is your opinion of this statement? Explain.
3. What was the most difficult problem Europeans faced in the Americas?

4. What would you have liked about being a Jamestown settler? What would you have disliked?

Graphic Organizer Activity

Culture Create a chart like the one below, and use it to compare the colonies established by Portugal, Spain, England, the Netherlands, and France.

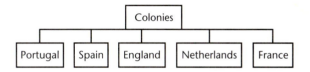

Colonies

Portugal | Spain | England | Netherlands | France

 ## Geography in History

Human Systems Refer to the map on page 498. The European colonies stretched from Hudson Bay in the north to the Strait of Magellan in the south. What is similar about the places where most colonial cities were established? Write a paragraph explaining the reasons for this similarity.

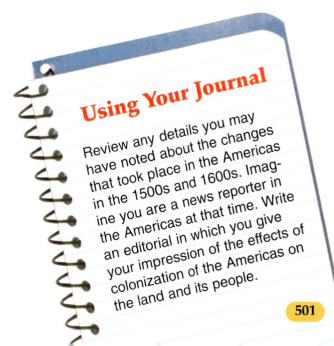

Using Your Journal

Review any details you may have noted about the changes that took place in the Americas in the 1500s and 1600s. Imagine you are a news reporter in the Americas at that time. Write an editorial in which you give your impression of the effects of colonization of the Americas on the land and its people.

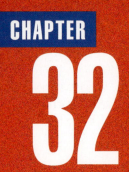
Political Revolutions
1600 A.D.–1800 A.D.

◀ Badge worn by French revolutionaries

French women march on the Palace of Versailles ▼

1622
English Civil
War begins

1688
Glorious Revolution
takes place in England

1776
U.S. issues
Declaration of
Independence

1789
U.S. Constitution
is adopted

Chapter Focus

Read to Discover

- How revolution in England began during the 1600s.
- What British policies led to the American Revolution of the late 1700s.
- How the French Revolution came about in the late 1700s and what its results were.

Chapter Overview

Visit the *Human Heritage* Web site at **humanheritage.glencoe.com** and click on ***Chapter 32— Chapter Overviews*** to preview this chapter.

Terms to Learn	**People to Know**	🌐 **Places to Locate**
revolution	James I	Concord
mercantilism	Charles I	Lexington
monopoly	Oliver Cromwell	Yorktown
direct tax	Charles II	Bastille
boycott	John Locke	
estates	Voltaire	

Why It's Important   By the 1700s, people in the western world had new ideas about government. They were less willing to be ruled without having a voice in politics. They also wanted equal justice under the law. They did not believe that monarchs or the Church had the right to tell them what to do. Thinkers and writers began spreading ideas about freedom and the right of people to change the government to meet their needs. The 1700s came to be known in Europe and the Americas as the Age of Enlightenment, or a time of increased knowledge.

SECTION 1 Revolution in England

In England, there was a struggle for power between the king and Parliament. After a civil war and a **revolution,** or an attempt to overthrow or change the government, Parliament won. From that point on, the monarch ruled in the name of the people.

Conflict with Parliament   In 1603, the last Tudor monarch, Queen Elizabeth I, died. Since she had never married, the Crown, or royal power, passed to a distant relative. This was James VI of Scotland, a member of the Stuart family. He became James I of England.

The Tudors had enjoyed great power. They had been careful, however, to get Parliament's opinion on their actions. James I, on the other hand, believed in rule by divine right. When Parliament

Reading Check
What is the goal of a political **revolution?**

objected to some of his actions, he dismissed it and ruled without a legislature for ten years.

Religious differences also caused trouble between the king and Parliament. James I wanted to force the Anglican Church on the people. Many members of Parliament, however, were Puritans. They wanted to be able to worship as they pleased. They believed in hard work and plain living and did not like the Crown's free-spending ways. They wanted a say in how the government raised and spent taxes. With the help of other groups, they worked against what they felt was the king's unjust power.

Although James I did not agree with many of his subjects about religion, it was his idea to have a new translation of the Bible. He appointed a committee of church officials who put together the King James version. Its style has greatly influenced English speech and literature. Many English-speaking Protestant churches today still use the King James version.

When James I died in 1625, his son became King Charles I. He held the same beliefs about the monarchy as his father.

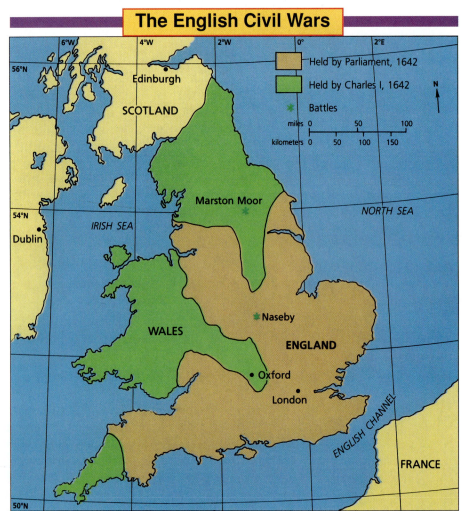

The English Civil Wars

- Held by Parliament, 1642
- Held by Charles I, 1642
- ✳ Battles

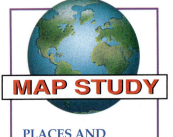

MAP STUDY

PLACES AND REGIONS The English civil war was both a religious and a political war. From what part of England did Parliament draw its support? From what part did Charles I draw his support?

In 1628, Charles I was forced to call a meeting of Parliament to approve new taxes to pay for wars with France and Spain. Parliament saw a chance to limit the Crown's power and gain more for itself. It drew up the Petition of Right. This said that the king could not declare **martial** (mar' shuhl) **law,** or rule by the army instead of by law. It also said that the Crown could not pass tax laws without Parliament's consent. In addition, people could not be put in prison just because the king wanted them out of the way. At first, Charles I agreed to the petition. Then, in 1629, he broke his word and dismissed Parliament.

In 1640, however, Charles I needed money to build a larger army to fight the Scots. He had tried to force the Anglican Church on the Presbyterian Scots, and they had revolted, taking over part of northern England. So, he called a meeting of Parliament.

Parliament again saw a chance to limit Charles's power. It passed a law abolishing taxes collected by the Crown without Parliament's consent. It also passed a law to set up regular meetings of Parliament and to do away with the Star Chamber. This was a royal court that tried people without a jury.

Civil War
Once again, Charles I accepted the laws Parliament passed and then disregarded them. In 1642, civil war broke out between the Crown and Parliament.

Those who backed the Crown were called Cavaliers (kav uh lirz'). They wore their hair shoulder length, often in curls. They were mostly rich Roman Catholics and Anglicans. Those who backed Parliament were called Roundheads because they wore their hair short. They were mostly middle- and lower-class Puritans and other Calvinists.

Oliver Cromwell (krahm' wel), a Puritan leader who backed Parliament, formed a New Model Army. It drilled hard and followed strict rules against drinking, swearing, and robbing. It chose its officers because they were good fighters and leaders, not because they were of high birth. In 1646, the New Model Army defeated the king's forces and ended the war.

Most English leaders still believed that monarchy was the best form of government. They did not, however, trust Charles I and were afraid to allow him to return to the throne. Cromwell and his supporters put Charles I on trial for treason. The court found him guilty, and he was beheaded in 1649.

Oliver Cromwell
After the king's death, Cromwell took over the rule of England, now called the Commonwealth. The Commonwealth was overwhelmed with troubles from the start. The Irish and the Scots both looked to Charles I's son as the true ruler of England. Cromwell had to put down their rebellion. He also had trouble balancing the English who felt enough changes had been made with those who wanted more. He finally did away

Reading Check
What is **martial law?**

Religion Persecution of the Puritans under Charles I led to the Great Migration—the exodus of thousands of Puritans to America between 1630 to 1640. The Puritans founded the Massachusetts Bay Colony and later became known as the Congregationalist Church.

OLIVER CROMWELL AND KING CHARLES I   Oliver Cromwell shown in this painting (left) organized the New Model Army that defeated the army of King Charles I shown in the painting (right) in 1646. This ended the four-year civil war between the Crown and Parliament. After Charles was beheaded, Cromwell took over the rule of England, which was then called the Commonwealth. **What problems did Cromwell face as he came to power?**

with Parliament and governed as a military dictator for the Puritan minority.

Many Puritans were very strict. They disapproved of dancing, theater-going, sports, and other popular amusements. They believed people should spend their free time praying and reading the Bible. Despite this, Puritan rule was not completely gloomy. Cromwell himself was fond of music and horses, and allowed women to act on stage for the first time. After Cromwell died, his son Richard took over. By 1660, however, Parliament decided that England again needed a monarch.

The Return of the Stuarts

Parliament's choice was Charles I's son, who became Charles II. Charles II had spent most of the previous 15 years in France. He brought French dances, food, and clothing styles with him to London. Soon, the English court was a center of gaiety and fashion. Men copied the fashions of Paris and wore silks and velvets and huge wigs. The wealthy ate large meals. One meal might include rabbit and chicken stew, a leg of mutton, a side of lamb, roasted pigeons, lobsters, tarts, anchovies, and wine. The English nobility was ready for this kind of living, and Charles II became very popular.

In September 1666, a great fire destroyed two-thirds of London's buildings. Charles II put Sir Christopher Wren, an architect, in charge of rebuilding the city. Wren designed St. Paul's Cathedral and 52 other churches. He also had most new houses and shops built of brick and stone instead of wood.

As king, Charles II tried to work with Parliament and not anger it. He refused, however, to consult with it about **foreign policy,** or relations with other countries. Parliament was worried by his friendship with the Roman Catholic king of France.

✔ **Reading Check** Why did Parliament worry about the **foreign policy** of Charles II?

The Glorious Revolution

In 1685, Charles II died and his brother James became king. Openly Roman Catholic, James II named many Roman Catholics to high posts in the army and the government. This went against a law passed by Parliament under Charles II. James II also tried to have the Act of Habeas Corpus (hā′ bē uhs kōr′ puhs) **repealed,** or abolished. That act had also been passed under Charles II. It stated that a person could not be put in jail unless charged with a specific crime.

The leaders of Parliament did not like James II. They did not move against him, however, until 1688 when his second wife, who was Roman Catholic, had a son. Fearing the ultimate establishment of Roman Catholic rule, they offered the throne to Mary, James's Protestant daughter by his first wife. Mary's husband William landed in England in 1688 with a large army, and James II fled to France. William and Mary were then named joint rulers. Because the change in monarchs took place without a shot being fired, it came to be called the "Glorious Revolution."

✔ **Reading Check** What would have happened if James II had **repealed** the Act of Habeas Corpus?

After becoming the new rulers of England in 1689, William and Mary accepted Parliament's Declaration of Rights. This made Parliament stronger and protected the rights of the English people. The declaration stated that the Crown could not tax people or keep an army in peacetime without Parliament's consent. Parliament had the right to debate openly, meet often, and be freely elected. People had the right to a fair and speedy trial by a jury of their peers. People could also petition the Crown without fear of being punished.

The Writings of John Locke

Many of the ideas behind the Glorious Revolution were explained in a book called *Two Treatises of Government.* It was written in 1690 by an English philosopher named John Locke. He believed that people are born with certain natural rights. Among them are the right to life, liberty, and property. Locke believed that the purpose of government is to protect these rights. If it fails to do so, then the people can revolt and set up a new government. Locke thought the best kind of government was a representative one. His writings were widely read, and his ideas became a basis for the American Revolution and, later, the French Revolution.

Painting of Queen Mary II

Section 1 Assessment

1. **Define:** revolution, martial law, foreign policy, repealed.
2. Why did civil war finally break out between the Crown and Parliament in 1642?
3. Why did Parliament remove James II from the throne?

Critical Thinking

4. **Identifying Central Issues** What was the central issue addressed by England's Declaration of Rights?

Graphic Organizer Activity

5. Draw this diagram, and use it to summarize the key ideas of John Locke's *Two Treatises of Government.*

Two Treatises of Government	Key Idea
	Key Idea
	Key Idea
	Key Idea

SECTION 2 The American Revolution

At first, England and its American colonies got along well. Over time, however, things changed. The colonists became angry over English controls. This led to revolution and the forming of a new country.

Mercantilism

In 1660, when Charles II became king of England, most European leaders believed in an economic system called **mercantilism** (mer' kuhn tēl iz uhm). Under it, colonies served as a source of raw materials and as a market for finished products. England's colonies in America were supposed to send goods to England that were scarce or could not be grown there, such as furs, lumber, tobacco, and cotton. The colonists were supposed to buy only goods made in England so that English merchants could make money. These goods could be carried only in ships built in England or in the colonies. The ships also had to be sailed by English crews. This was to make the shipbuilding industry and merchant marines stronger in case of war.

Mercantilism worked well until the 1700s. There were not enough skilled people in the American colonies to produce many goods. The colonists also enjoyed a **monopoly** (muh nop' uh lē), or sole right, on the sale of several major crops. In addition, their ships were protected against pirates by the English navy.

Then, things changed. With the population in the colonies growing, the colonists wanted to make their own manufactured goods, such as iron products and beaver hats. Also, people in northern colonies were not able to sell as much to England as

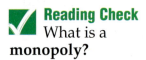
Reading Check
How did the system of **mercantilism** work?

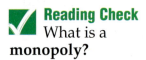
Reading Check
What is a **monopoly?**

people in southern colonies did. Yet, they needed money to buy English goods. So, they began smuggling goods to and from the West Indies. Soon, a triangular, or three-way, trade grew up. The colonists shipped in sugar and molasses from the West Indies. They made rum and traded it for enslaved Africans. Then, they brought the enslaved Africans to the West Indies, where they traded them for sugar and molasses.

Stamp

Changes in British Policy

Although England, now known as Great Britain, regulated colonial trade, the colonists handled local affairs. Their legislatures generally passed tax laws. Since colonial officials were paid out of taxes, they had to do as the colonial legislatures wished. This gave the legislatures a great deal of power.

In the middle of the 1700s, this changed. The French, who also had colonies in America, built a fort on the site of present-day Pittsburgh, Pennsylvania. The French and their Native American allies wanted to keep the British out of northern and western America. Great Britain, however, had already claimed the area for itself. The dispute led to the French and Indian War. By the time it ended in 1763, the British controlled nearly all of North America east of the Mississippi River.

The war left the British government deeply in debt. It wanted the colonies to pay a large share of the money owed. After all, the war had been fought partly to protect their western frontier. So, Great Britain moved to raise money by tightening its control over the colonies.

In 1765, Parliament passed the Stamp Act. It called for a tax on all newspapers, legal documents, calendars, and playing cards. All these items had to bear a stamp showing that the tax had been paid. This was the first **direct tax** Parliament placed on the colonies. That is, it was a tax paid directly to the government, not included in the price of the goods.

The Stamp Act hurt merchants, lawyers, and people in the newspaper business. These groups were among the most able to lead the colonists in a fight against British control. Angry mobs formed in many cities. Tax officials were threatened, and stamps were destroyed. People throughout the colonies decided to **boycott,** or refuse to buy, British goods.

In October 1765, delegates from 9 of the 13 colonies met in New York to discuss the Stamp Act. They sent a letter to the British government. It stated that the colonies had not been taxed before by anyone except their own legislatures. It also said that Parliament had no right to tax them because they did not have representatives in Parliament.

In March 1766, Parliament finally voted to repeal the Stamp Act. At the same time, however, it passed the Declaratory Act, which stated that Parliament had the right to make laws on all

✓ **Reading Check**
Why was the Stamp Act considered a **direct tax?**

✓ **Reading Check**
What action did the colonists take when they organized a **boycott?**

matters concerning the colonies. This showed that Parliament was not going to give in completely to the demands of the American colonists.

The Road to Revolution

In 1767, Parliament passed a series of laws known as the Townshend Acts. These acts placed a tax on such goods as paper, paint, glass, lead, and tea that were shipped to the colonies. Part of the tax money was to be used to pay colonial officials. This took away the colonial legislatures' main source of power. The following year, the British sent soldiers to Boston to make sure the colonists obeyed the new laws. The colonists called the soldiers "redcoats" because of their bright red uniforms.

The Townshend Acts made the colonists angry. Soon, there were incidents of violence. One of the worst of these took place in Boston in 1770. A crowd of colonists began insulting British soldiers and throwing stones at them. The soldiers fired into the crowd. Five people were killed. This incident came to be called the Boston Massacre. Shortly after, all the Townshend taxes were repealed except the one on tea. The Boston Massacre itself would probably have been forgotten had not some colonists used it to stir up feelings against British rule.

Three years later, Parliament passed the Tea Act. It allowed the British East India Company to sell tea directly to the colonists rather than to colonial merchants, who took part of the profits. This hurt the merchants. The act also further angered those colonists already tired of British tax policies. In Massachusetts, a group of colonists dressed as Native Americans boarded a British ship in Boston harbor and dumped its cargo of tea into the water. This event is known as the Boston Tea Party.

To punish the colonists, Parliament, in 1774, passed the Coercive (kō er′ siv) Acts. These acts closed Boston harbor and put the government of Massachusetts under military rule. These acts also said that British troops in the colonies should be *quartered,* or given a place to live, in private homes. Next, Parliament passed the Quebec Act, which extended the boundaries of Quebec west of the Appalachians and north of the Ohio River. This took in land that Massachusetts, Connecticut, and Virginia claimed as their own. The colonists called these laws the Intolerable Acts, or laws they could not bear.

The Coercive Acts only made the colonists more determined than ever to fight for their liberties. In September 1774, delegates from 12 of the colonies met in Philadelphia. They called themselves the First Continental Congress. The Congress spoke out against the Coercive Acts and called for their repeal.

Colonial leaders, however, were divided about what to do. Some, like George Washington of Virginia, hoped to settle the differences with Great Britain. Others, like Samuel Adams of

Painting of Boston Tea Party

Reading a Military Map

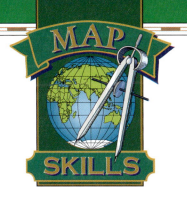

MAP SKILLS

Maps that contain information about wars are called **military maps.** They show troop movements, battle sites and dates, and battle victories.

Look at the legend for the two maps below. Notice that different symbols and colors stand for American and British advances, retreats, and battle victories.

For example, the map has a solid red line to show that the British advanced to New York City, where they won a battle in August 1776. This victory is indicated by a red star. The Americans then retreated to Trenton, New Jersey, as shown by a dashed blue line.

Map Practice

1. Which army won the battle at Saratoga, New York?
2. Which army advanced to Camden, South Carolina, after the Battle of Charleston?
3. Where did the British retreat to after the Battle of Guilford Courthouse?

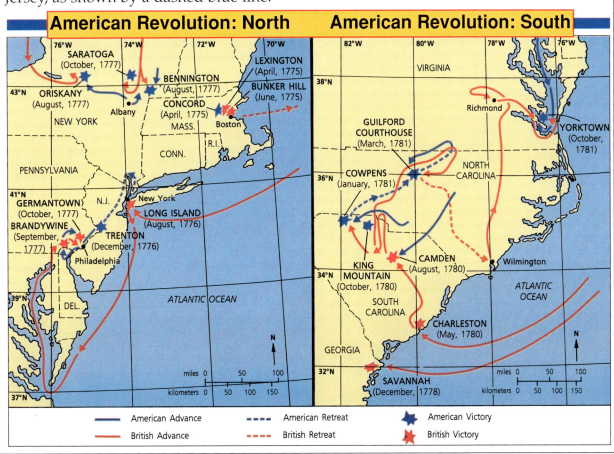

American Revolution: North

American Revolution: South

Legend:
— American Advance
---- American Retreat
★ American Victory
— British Advance
---- British Retreat
★ British Victory

Massachusetts and Patrick Henry of Virginia, wanted the colonies to become independent.

The Outcome

Before anything was decided, fighting broke out in Massachusetts between the colonists and British soldiers. The British set out to destroy a store of weapons at Concord. On the way there, they met the colonists at Lexington and fought the first battle of the American Revolution.

In May 1775, the Second Continental Congress met. George Washington was named head of the colonial army. The colonists then tried again to settle their differences with Great Britain. They appealed to King George III, who refused to listen.

On July 4, 1776, Congress issued the Declaration of Independence. Written mostly by Thomas Jefferson of Virginia, it stated that all men are created equal and have certain God-given rights. In the Declaration, the colonies broke away from Great Britain and declared themselves the United States of America.

War between the British and Americans dragged on. In 1778, the French, who were old enemies of Great Britain, agreed to help the Americans. In 1781, the Americans and French forced the British to surrender at Yorktown, Virginia. This ended the fighting. Two years later, the Treaty of Paris ended the war.

Fun Facts....

Peace Treaties Many peace treaties have been signed in Paris, France. In addition to the treaty ending the American Revolution, they include those that ended the French and Indian War (1763), the European allies' war with Napoleon (1814), and U.S. involvement in the Vietnam War (1973).

UNITED STATES CONSTITUTION   In 1787, representatives from 12 states met in Philadelphia and drew up a constitution for the United States. George Washington is shown in this painting addressing the delegates. In 1789, Washington became the first President of the United States. **What are some principles of American government expressed in the Constitution?**

In 1789, the United States adopted a constitution that set up a new form of government. The Constitution set forth certain principles of government. One of these is **popular sovereignty** (sov' ruhn tē), or the idea that a government receives its powers from the people. Another is **limited government,** or the idea that a government may use only the powers given to it by the people.

Later, ten **amendments,** or formal changes, known as the Bill of Rights were added. The Bill of Rights guarantees all American citizens such rights as freedom of speech, press, and religion; the right to trial by jury; and freedom from unreasonable searches and seizures.

✓ **Reading Check**
What is the principle of **popular sovereignty?**
What is the principle of **limited government?**
What are the first ten **amendments** to the U.S. Constitution called?

Section 2 Assessment

1. **Define:** mercantilism, monopoly, direct tax, boycott, popular sovereignty, limited government, amendments.
2. Why were colonial legislatures powerful?
3. How did the Townshend Acts affect the power of the colonial legislatures?

Critical Thinking

4. **Evaluating Information** "The Bill of Rights is an important addition to the U.S. Constitution." What is your opinion of this statement? Explain.

Graphic Organizer Activity

5. Draw this diagram, and use it to show the causes and effects of the American Revolution.

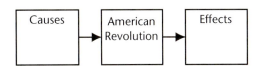

| Causes | American Revolution | Effects |

SECTION 3 The French Revolution

The events in America influenced people in France. The American example pointed to the need for political change and helped bring about a revolution.

Old Regime   During the 1600s and early 1700s—the time of the Old Regime (ri zhēm')—France was a divine-right monarchy. French society was divided into three **estates** (e stāts'), or classes. The First Estate was the clergy. Although they made up less than 1 percent of the people, they owned 10 percent of the land. They were not only *exempt,* or free, from taxes, but they also received income from church lands. Church income was not divided evenly, however. Most went to high church officials, who were generally nobles. They wore robes of purple and scarlet velvet

✓ **Reading Check**
Into how many **estates** was French society divided?

trimmed with lace. Parish priests lived simply and served people's religious needs.

The Second Estate was the nobility. They made up about 2 percent of the people and also owned large areas of land. Nobles, too, were free from taxes. They lived off grants from the royal treasury and rents paid by the peasants. Some nobles spent their time at the royal court, dancing, hunting, and gambling. Others filled the highest posts in the government and the army.

The Third Estate was everyone else in France. At the top of this class was the **bourgeoisie** (bur zhwah zē')—bankers, merchants, lawyers, doctors, manufacturers, and teachers. They controlled much of France's wealth and trade. Next were the city workers—artisans, day laborers, and servants. At the bottom were the peasants, who made up more than 80 percent of the French people.

Members of the Third Estate had no power in the government, but they paid the country's taxes. They paid taxes on income, personal property, land, and crops. They paid sales taxes on salt, tobacco, and wine. Parents even paid a tax when a child was born. In addition, the peasants still paid feudal dues.

The Estates-General

By the 1780s, the French government was in trouble. Educated French writers and thinkers called *philosophes* (fē luh zofs'), or philosophers, wrote articles pointing out the country's political problems. One of the most widely read philosophes was Francois Marie Arouet (fran' swah muh rē' ah rwe'), known as Voltaire (vōl tair'). Voltaire favored free speech, a free press, freedom of religion, and equal justice for everyone. One of his favorite sayings was: "I do not agree with a word you say, but I will defend to the death your right to say it."

The major problem facing the French government, however, was a lack of money. The French government had given so much help to the colonies during the American Revolution that it was almost bankrupt. King Louis XVI and his wife added to the problem by spending money on jewels, hunting parties, horse races, and balls. In fact, Queen Marie-Antoinette (muh rē an twuh net') spent so much that she was accused of increasing France's *deficit,* or shortage of money. For this reason, the French people called her Madame Deficit. The king wanted the clergy and nobles to give him money. They, however, had never paid taxes and saw no reason to start.

Finally, Louis XVI called a meeting of the French legislature to help decide how to raise money. It was the first time that this body, known as the Estates-General, had met since 1614. In the past, each of the estates had met separately, with each casting one vote. This meant the nobles and clergy together could outvote the Third Estate and protect themselves from change.

Reading Check
What groups made up the French **bourgeoisie?**

Reading Check
Who were the *philosophes?*

Painting of Louis XVI and Family

The Third Estate, however, wanted a bigger voice in government. "What is the Third Estate?" one of their leaders wrote in a pamphlet. "Everything. What has it been until now? Nothing. What does it demand? To become something." The members of the Third Estate wanted the Estates-General to meet as a single body with each representative having a vote. They also wanted to have the same number of representatives as the other two estates together.

In May 1789, the Estates-General met. The Third Estate was granted more representatives, but the other two estates refused to meet with it. So, the Third Estate and a small number of parish priests and nobles met as a separate body. They called themselves the National Assembly. When Louis XVI threatened to break up the National Assembly, its members swore not to do so until they had written a constitution for France. At last, the king gave in and ordered the First and Second Estates to meet with the National Assembly.

Uprisings in City and Country
Meanwhile, a series of uprisings took place throughout most of France. When the Estates-General was called to meet, most French people had high hopes for change. Before long, however, they began to fear that nothing would improve. The fall harvests had been poor, and

TENNIS COURT OATH Members of the Third Estate met on a tennis court to write a new French constitution. **What was the Third Estate?**

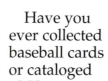

TECHNOLOGY SKILLS

Building a Database

Have you ever collected baseball cards or cataloged the CDs in your collection? Have you ever kept a list of the names and addresses of your friends and relatives? If you have collected information and kept some sort of list or file, then you have created a database.

Learning the Skill An electronic database is a collection of facts that are stored in files on a computer. The information is organized in fields.

A database can be organized and reorganized in any way that is useful to you. By using a database management system (DBMS)—special software developed for record keeping—you can easily add, delete, change, or update information. You give commands to the computer telling it what to do with the information, and it follows your commands. When you want to retrieve information, your computer searches through the files, finds the information, and displays it on the screen.

food was scarce and expensive. A loaf of bread cost more than a day's pay. The winter was so cold that water froze in front of fireplaces. Hundreds of thousands of city workers were unemployed.

In Paris, mobs began to form. On July 14, 1789, a mob in search of weapons attacked and captured the Bastille (ba stēl'). This was an old fort used as a prison. To the mob, it was a symbol of the **tyranny** (tir' uh nē), or unjust use of power, of the monarchy. The mob then killed the mayor of Paris and set up a new city government.

Reading Check
What is **tyranny?**

News of what happened in Paris spread. In the countryside, there were rumors that the nobles were planning to hire *brigands* (brig' uhndz), or roving bandits, to destroy the peasants' homes and crops. So, the peasants attacked and burned the houses of the nobles and destroyed all records of feudal dues.

The National Assembly   The uprisings caused the National Assembly to act. To calm the people, it did away with the privileges of the clergy and nobles.

On August 27, 1789, the Assembly issued the Declaration of the Rights of Man and the Citizen. It said that people "are born equal and remain free and equal in rights." It said that the government's right to rule came from the people, not from the

FRENCH PEASANTS   Farmers of the French countryside worked hard to raise their crops. They were tired of paying most of their earnings to the nobles. **What did peasants in the countryside do to show their unhappiness when they heard about the riots in Paris?**

The March of Women
In October 1789, a mob of women walked to Versailles, a few miles outside Paris. Armed with sticks and farm tools, the "March of Women" stopped first at the National Assembly and demanded lower prices for bread. They then burst into the royal palace and forced Louis XVI, Marie-Antoinette, and their son—whom they called "the baker, the baker's wife, and the baker's little boy"—to return to Paris as prisoners of the people.

Then... & Now

The Tricolor The French revolutionaries adopted a red, white, and blue flag called the tricolor. France still uses this flag.

✓ **Reading Check**
What kind of government is established under a **constitutional monarchy?**

✓ **Reading Check**
Who were the *sans-culottes,* and how were they kept from voting?

✓ **Reading Check**
Who were the French *émigrés,* and what did they want other rulers to do?

✓ **Reading Check**
What was the **guillotine?**

Crown. It gave everyone freedom of speech and the right to share in government. The ideas of equal rights and individual freedoms came mostly from the philosophes and from the English and American revolutions.

For the next two years, the National Assembly worked to write a constitution. At the same time, to pay off what the government owed, it began selling church lands to peasants. Although many peasants now owned land for the first time, the Roman Catholic Church was angered. It was further angered when the National Assembly declared that the clergy should be elected and should swear an oath to the government. The Church did not like being brought under state authority.

In 1791, a constitution was finished. It established freedom of religion and made France a **constitutional monarchy.** Under this kind of government, the ruler's power is limited by written law. The Crown and the legislature would govern together. Both representatives and voters had to have a certain amount of wealth. This pleased the bourgeoisie because it gave them the power they wanted. It did not please most peasants and the *sans-culottes* (san skū lahts'), or city workers, because they did not have enough money to vote. (The word "sans-culottes" means "without knee breeches." Wealthy men wore knee breeches and silk stockings. Workers wore long pants.)

The End of the Monarchy   Many of the ideas of the French Revolution spread to other countries. Rulers throughout Europe were afraid that these ideas would weaken their own power. French *émigrés* (em' uh grāz), or political exiles, encouraged the rulers to march into France and help Louis XVI take back control of the government. Many of the French revolutionary leaders also wanted war because it would unite the French people. Before any country could act, in the spring of 1792 France declared war on Austria, where the queen's brother ruled.

At first, the war did not go well for France. By August 1792, Austrian and Prussian armies were marching toward Paris. Meanwhile, in the city, the sans-culottes took over. They set up a new government called the National Convention. It made France a republic. The following year, Louis XVI and Marie-Antoinette were executed. As a result, more European countries joined the war against France.

Threats from outside and inside the country made the new French government take drastic action. Although another constitution was written, it was never put into force. Instead, the Committee of Public Safety, led by a lawyer named Maximilien de Robespierre (mak suh mil' yuhn duh rōbz' piuhr), took over the government. Thousands of people suspected of being against the Revolution lost their lives to the **guillotine** (gil' uh tēn). This was a machine with a heavy blade that fit between two wooden posts. When it was released, the blade came crashing down and cut off the victim's head. The wave of killing came to be known as the "Reign of Terror." Because of it, the people began to turn against Robespierre. In 1794, government leaders had him executed.

The following year, a third constitution was written. It set up a government known as the Directory. Besides the legislature, there was an executive branch with five directors. Only people who owned land could vote.

Under the new government, most reforms of the Revolution came to an end. The people of France had grown more conservative. The Directory spent its time trying to handle food shortages, rising prices, government bankruptcy, and attacks by other countries.

One reform that did remain was the idea that all French people had the right to choose their government. Another was a standard system of weights and measures known as the metric

Linking Across Time

The Metric System After France adopted use of the metric system in 1791, the government attempted to educate people about its many uses (below). Today the metric system is followed in most technological nations in the world, except the United States. It is so widespread that the metric system is used for measurement at the Olympics. **What other lasting reform grew out of the French Revolution?**

system, which the National Assembly adopted in 1791. Metrics, a system of numbers that is based on powers of ten, helped scientists carry out experiments and made international trade easier. Today, metrics are used by all major countries in the world except the United States.

Section 3 Assessment

1. **Define:** estates, bourgeoisie, *philosophes*, tyranny, constitutional monarchy, *sans-culottes*, *émigrés*, guillotine.
2. What groups made up the three French estates?
3. What did the National Assembly do about the uprisings in 1789?
4. Why did most reforms of the French Revolution come to an end under the Directory?

Critical Thinking

5. **Understanding Cause and Effect** How did the storming of the Bastille help trigger the French Revolution?

Graphic Organizer Activity

6. Draw this diagram, and use it to compare the French Declaration of the Rights of Man and the Citizen to the U.S. Declaration of Independence.

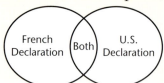

French Declaration — Both — U.S. Declaration

Chapter Summary & Study Guide

1. As a result of new ideas about freedom and government, the 1700s are known as the Age of Enlightenment.
2. England's political revolution began in the 1600s when the Crown and Parliament disagreed over issues of divine right and religion.
3. In 1689, Parliament passed the Declaration of Rights, which made Parliament stronger and protected the rights of the people.
4. In 1776, disagreements between the American colonies and Great Britain led to the Declaration of Independence, which defended the right to self-government.

5. In 1789, the United States adopted a new constitution based on the principles of popular sovereignty and limited government.
6. The French Revolution, which began in 1789, ended as a result of the Reign of Terror. However, two lasting reforms survived—use of the metric system and the idea that people had a right to choose their government.

HISTORY *Online*

Self-Check Quiz

Visit the *Human Heritage* Web site at **humanheritage. glencoe.com** and click on **Chapter 32—Self-Check Quiz** to assess your understanding of this chapter.

Using Key Terms

Sort these words describing the revolutions in England, America, and France by the country to which each applies. (Words may be used more than once.) Use the words in each group to write a sentence or two about each country's revolution.

revolution
mercantilism
direct tax
boycott
bourgeoisie
martial law
guillotine

constitutional
  monarchy
monopoly
popular sovereignty
estates
tyranny

Understanding Main Ideas

1. What were some Puritan beliefs?
2. Why was the Glorious Revolution called "glorious"?
3. How did Great Britain tighten its control over the American colonies?
4. How did the British colonists respond to the Stamp Act?
5. Who had the most power in the French government before the French Revolution? After the Revolution?
6. Why were European rulers afraid of the ideas of the French Revolution?

Critical Thinking

1. What economic questions played a part in the American Revolution? In the French Revolution?
2. What were the most important political issues that played a part in England's Glorious Revolution? Explain your answer.
3. Do you agree with the idea that people have the right to rule themselves? Explain.

4. Why are the 1700s known as the Age of Enlightenment?

Graphic Organizer Activity

Citizenship Create a diagram like the one on this page, and use it to compare the reforms and rights sought by the leaders of the English, American, and French revolutions.

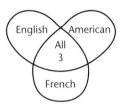

Geography in History

The World in Spatial Terms Look at the maps of the American Revolution on page 511. The advances and retreats of both armies are shown. About how many miles (or kilometers) did the British advance from the battle at Long Island, New York, to the battle at Brandywine, Pennsylvania?

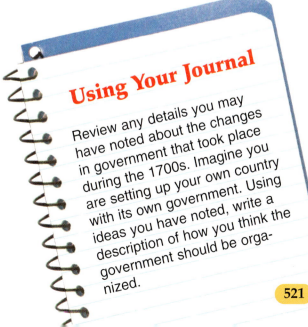

Using Your Journal

Review any details you may have noted about the changes in government that took place during the 1700s. Imagine you are setting up your own country with its own government. Using ideas you have noted, write a description of how you think the government should be organized.

CHAPTER 33

Rise of Industry
1500 A.D.–1880 A.D.

▲ Parts of a
steam engine

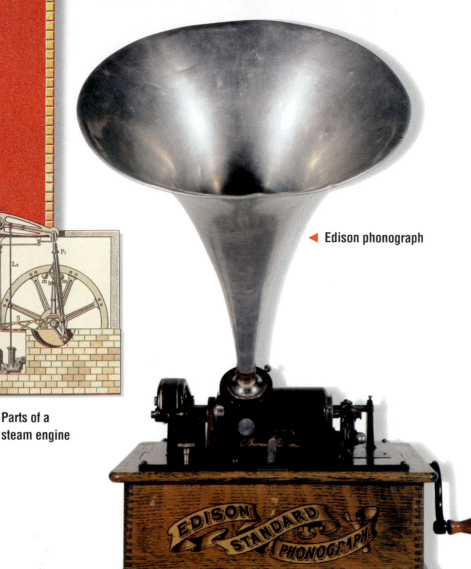

◄ Edison phonograph

1543	1733	1769	1847	1879
Copernicus proposes sun-centered solar system	John Kay invents the flying shuttle	James Watt perfects the steam engine	Samuel Colt develops assembly line	Thomas Edison develops electric light

Chapter Focus

Read to Discover

- What inventions and discoveries marked the Scientific Revolution.
- How the Agricultural Revolution contributed to the Industrial Revolution.
- How the Industrial Revolution developed.
- What the effects of industrialization were.
- How industrialization continued and spread.

 **Terms to Learn**

enclosure
textile
factory system
cotton gin

 People to Know

Galileo Galilei
Sir Isaac Newton
Robert Fulton
Samuel F.B. Morse

Why It's Important By the 1700s, people in the western world had new ideas about science. These led to new forms of power and ways of making goods. Industry and ways of living changed so much that historians call these changes the Industrial Revolution.

The Industrial Revolution involved the shift from animal and human power to machine power. This meant that society became less agricultural and more industrial. During the early years of the Industrial Revolution, Great Britain took the lead. Later, other countries rose to challenge Great Britain.

HISTORY Online

Chapter Overview
Visit the *Human Heritage* Web site at **humanheritage.glencoe.com** and click on *Chapter 33— Chapter Overviews* to preview this chapter.

SECTION 1 Scientific Revolution

Many of the changes that occurred during the Industrial Revolution grew out of changes in scientific thinking. Beginning in the 1400s, scientists started to break away from old ideas. They used the scientific method to form and test their own hypotheses. This became known as the Scientific Revolution.

Nicolaus Copernicus (kuh per' nuh kuhs) was one of the first people to use the scientific method. Copernicus was a Polish astronomer who studied the motion of the planets. What he saw proved to him that Ptolemy was wrong and that Earth was not the center of the universe. In 1543, Copernicus published a book explaining his idea that planets revolve around the sun rather

SCIENTISTS

NAME	FIELD	ACCOMPLISHMENTS
Johannes Kepler *Germany*	*Astronomy*	announced laws of movement of planets, 1609
William Harvey *England*	*Medicine*	published theory on human blood circulation, 1628
Sir Isaac Newton *England*	*Physics*	stated laws of motion and theory of gravitation, 1687
Antoine-Laurent Lavoisier *France*	*Chemistry*	discovered nature of combustion, 1777
John Dalton *England*	*Chemistry*	announced atomic theory, 1803
Maria Mitchell *United States*	*Astronomy*	discovered new comet, 1847
Charles Darwin *England*	*Biology*	advanced theory on development of plants and animals, 1858
Gregor Mendel *Austria*	*Botany*	discovered principles of heredity, 1866
Louis Pasteur *France*	*Medicine*	advanced germ theory of disease, 1876; developed a rabies vaccine, 1885
Pierre Curie **Marie Curie** *France*	*Chemistry*	discovered radium and polonium, 1898

than around Earth. This book began a complete change in scientific thinking.

Another important scientist was the Italian astronomer Galileo Galilei (gal uh lē' ō gal uh lā' ē). He invented a telescope and began to study the stars and planets. He learned that the moon's surface is not smooth but has mountains and craters. He learned that the Milky Way holds a vast number of stars and that the sun rotates on its axis. Galileo was strongly criticized by the Roman Catholic Church for teaching that Earth revolves around the sun. Even so, Galileo's ideas spread throughout Europe.

In 1642, the same year Galileo died, another important scientist, Sir Isaac Newton (ī' zuhk nūt' n), was born in England. It was Newton who explained the theory of gravitation and how objects move through space. The technology for today's rockets and space satellites is based on his work.

It was at this time that scientists in Great Britain and France formed organizations in which they could discuss their ideas and research. In this way, scientific information began to spread more quickly. Soon, thousands of people were using the scientific method to add to their knowledge and improve their lives.

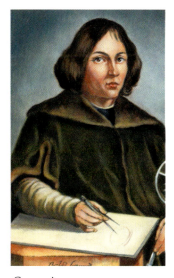

Copernicus

Section 1 Assessment

1. What scientific discoveries were made by Galileo Galilei?
2. Why were Sir Isaac Newton's theories important?

Critical Thinking

3. **Making Generalizations** Why were the early 1400s known as the Scientific Revolution?

Graphic Organizer Activity

4. Draw this diagram, and use it to show some of the new ideas developed during the Scientific Revolution. (Add circles as needed.)

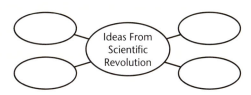

Ideas From Scientific Revolution

SECTION 2 Agricultural Revolution

As changes were taking place in science, there were new developments in farming. These changes were called the Agricultural Revolution. It set the stage for the Industrial Revolution.

By the 1700s, a system of land division called **enclosure** (en klō' zhuhr) was in use in Great Britain. Landowners combined the many small strips of land worked by tenant farmers into large areas closed in by fences, hedges, or ditches. Enclosure allowed landowners to make more money. Whole areas could grow the same crop, which meant larger harvests and greater profits. Landowners also needed fewer workers.

Reading Check
How did the system of **enclosure** work?

The tenant farmers had two choices. They could stay on as paid workers, or they could look elsewhere for jobs. Most left to find work in other places. They moved to cities and became industrial workers.

Enclosure was just part of the revolution in agriculture. New ways of growing crops and breeding animals were also developed. These changes led to greater production of food. More food meant better health and longer life spans. Population increased, and the demand for manufactured goods grew.

Section 2 Assessment

1. **Define:** enclosure.
2. How did landowners use the enclosure system?
3. How did the growth of population influence the Industrial Revolution?

Critical Thinking

4. **Making Comparisons** Do you think agriculture was more or less important in the 1700s than it is today in Great Britain?

Graphic Organizer Activity

5. Draw this diagram, and use it to show some of the effects of the enclosure system.

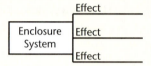

SECTION 3 Industrial Revolution

The Industrial Revolution began in the early 1700s. It was a long, slow process at first. However, as one development led to another, the revolution moved faster and faster. Much of the world changed. By the 1850s, the changes had become so widespread that people realized they were entering a new age.

The Textile Industry   The Industrial Revolution began in Great Britain in the **textile** (tek′ stuhl), or woven cloth, industry. In the 1600s and early 1700s, cloth was made by the **domestic system.** Under this system, most work was done in workers' cottages, where families worked together. Merchants went from cottage to cottage, bringing the workers raw wool and cotton. Using hand-powered spinning wheels and looms, the workers would spin the thread and weave it into wool and cotton cloth. The merchants then picked up the finished cloth to sell.

The domestic system could not meet the strong growing demand for cloth. Before long, people started looking for ways to make more cloth in less time. The first major breakthrough came in 1733 when a British inventor named John Kay invented the

✓ Reading Check
What did the **textile** industry produce? What was the **domestic system?**

flying shuttle. It was mounted on rollers, and one weaver could send it rapidly from one side of a loom to the other. It cut in half the time needed to weave cloth. Now, however, spinners could not keep up with the weavers. Then, in 1764, James Hargreaves (hahr′ grēvz), a British carpenter, invented the **spinning jenny.** It had a number of spindles fastened to a single wheel. The jenny made it possible for one person to spin many threads at the same time.

More progress was made when ways were found to use the power of falling water instead of hand power to run textile machines. This meant, however, that the machines had to be near a large water supply. Accordingly, factories were built next to rivers that could supply the necessary water power. This was the beginning of the **factory system,** which brought workers and machines together in one place to make goods. Workers still lived in their cottages, but they went to factories to work. In time, towns grew up around these factories.

Water power did not work very well with heavy machinery. So, people began looking for still another source of power. In 1769, a Scottish mechanic named James Watt perfected the steam engine. Steam soon replaced water as the major source of power. Factories of all kinds could now be set up near raw materials and town markets.

Cotton farmers in America and in India could not supply enough raw cotton to meet the needs of British textile factories. Eli Whitney (ē′ lī hwit′ nē), an American inventor, found a way to solve this problem. While visiting a cotton plantation in Georgia, he learned that it took a great deal of time to clean the seeds out of cotton by hand. In 1793, with the help of Catherine Littlefield Greene, he invented the **cotton gin,** or cotton-cleaning machine. It could clean cotton 50 times faster than a person working by hand. If it were driven by water power, it could clean cotton 1,000 times faster.

Organizing Production

About five years later, Whitney developed a new way of organizing production. This was the system of **interchangeable parts,** which means that a certain part of a product is the same size and shape as that same part in another product. Whitney first used interchangeable parts in the making of guns. Until that time, each gun was made individually, and no two guns were alike. Broken parts had to be specially made by a skilled worker in order to fit a specific gun. Whitney's use of parts of identical size and shape made it possible for less-skilled workers to make or fix guns much faster.

Other Americans also developed new ways of organizing production. In the late 1700s, a shopkeeper-mechanic named Oliver Evans was the first to use **automation,** or the process in which machines instead of people do much of the labor. Evans's

Reading Check
Why was the **flying shuttle** important? Who invented the **spinning jenny?**

Reading Check
How did the **factory system** differ from the domestic system?

Reading Check
Who invented the **cotton gin,** and what did this machine do?

Reading Check
What changes did the use of **interchangeable parts** bring to production?

Reading Check
What is **automation?**

automated flour mill was water-powered and cut by four-fifths the number of workers needed to run it.

In 1847, Samuel Colt used Whitney's idea of interchangeable parts to develop the **assembly line.** On an assembly line, each worker adds a part of the product and passes it on to the next worker, who also adds a part, until the entire product has been put together. Colt used the assembly line to produce the Colt revolver. Before assembly lines, a skilled worker had to make one product at a time from start to finish. With the assembly line, work could be divided, and many products could be put together at one time by unskilled workers. All of these discoveries and new techniques greatly increased production.

Iron, Coal, and Steel   To build machine parts, iron was needed. To fire steam engines, coal was needed. Without iron, coal, and steel, which replaced iron, the Industrial Revolution could not have continued.

By the early 1700s, ironmaking had become expensive. To smelt iron, the British used *charcoal,* a fuel that is made by burning wood. The British, however, were running out of

People in History

Robert Fulton
1765–1815

American Inventor

Born near Lancaster, Pennsylvania, Robert Fulton had many talents. He was an expert gunsmith and an accomplished landscape painter. He also designed torpedoes and early submarines. Fulton is best known for launching the *Clermont,* the first commercially successful steamboat in America.

SEWING MACHINE   Isaac Singer oversees a demonstration of his first sewing machine. **What invention benefited the textile industry during the early 1800s?**

forests, which made wood scarce and costly. In 1753, a way was found to use coal instead of charcoal for smelting. As a result, iron became cheaper, iron production grew, and coal mining became a major industry.

Iron, however, was too brittle for rails, bridge supports, and heavy equipment. In 1856, a British inventor named Henry Bessemer (bes' uh muhr) found a cheap way of removing the impurities from iron to make steel, which was harder and stronger than iron. The Bessemer Process lowered the cost of making steel from $200 a ton to $4 a ton. Seven years later, in 1863, Pierre-Emile Martin of France and William Siemens of England invented the **open-hearth process,** which used a special kind of furnace to make steel. It was even cheaper than the Bessemer Process and could turn out many different kinds of steel. Soon, mining towns and steel centers grew up in areas with supplies of iron ore and coal.

Transportation

Raw materials and finished products had to be moved quickly and cheaply. Before this could happen, transportation had to be improved. Until the 1700s, the chief means of transportation over land was by horse or horse-drawn wagon. Roads were no more than rough and narrow dirt paths. Travel was slow and uncomfortable. It was even worse when rain made the roads muddy.

Late in the 1700s, the British began to improve their roads. A Scottish engineer named Thomas Telford (tel' fuhrd) designed roadbeds so that water would drain off the roads. Another Scottish engineer, John L. McAdam, developed what became known as the **macadam** (muh kad' uhm) **road.** It had a surface made of layers of crushed stone. This surface allowed horse-drawn wagons to use the roads in all kinds of weather and to travel faster.

The British also made their rivers wider and deeper and built canals to connect navigable rivers to factory and mining centers. Horses walked beside canals and pulled barges. The barges were slow but could carry 50 times the amount of goods that horse-drawn wagons could. By 1830, Great Britain had a complete system of inland waterways.

The biggest improvement in land transportation was the railroad. For years, donkeys had pulled carts over wooden rails inside coal mines. Then, the production of iron grew. The wooden rails were replaced by iron ones that could carry heavier loads. Inventors began to build locomotives to run on iron rails. In 1829, George Stephenson (stē' vuhn suhn), a British mining engineer, won a contest to see who could build the best locomotive. Stephenson's locomotive, the *Rocket*, could pull a train about 36 miles, or 58 kilometers, an hour. The *Rocket* started a railroad-building boom in Great Britain and around the world.

✔ Reading Check What was the **open-hearth process?**

✔ Reading Check How did the **macadam road** improve transportation?

Then . . . & Now

A High Railway In 1870, an American engineer named Henry Meiggs built what is still the world's highest railroad—the Central Railway—across the Andes Mountains in Peru. At its highest point, the Central Railway reaches an altitude of nearly 16,000 feet, or 4880 meters, higher than the tallest peak in the Alps.

Railroads changed daily life as well as transportation. People started using such phrases as "keeping on track" and "tooting your own whistle." They also collected autographs of railway engineers. When American railroads adopted standard time zones in 1883, everyone else in the United States did too. The next year, time zones were established all over the world.

The biggest improvement in water transportation was the steamboat. The first practical one was developed by Robert Fulton (fūhl' tuhn), an American inventor. In 1807, Fulton's *Clermont*, powered by a British steam engine, set a record by making the trip from Albany to New York City in 32 hours. Soon, steamboats were carrying passengers and goods along the inland waterways of the United States and Europe. Steamboats, however, did not replace sailing ships in trans-oceanic travel until the late 1800s, when fuel-efficient engines were developed.

Section 3 Assessment

1. **Define:** textile, domestic system, flying shuttle, spinning jenny, factory system, cotton gin, interchangeable parts, automation, assembly line, open-hearth process, macadam road.
2. What effect did the assembly line have on the type of workers needed for production?
3. Why did transportation have to be improved during the Industrial Revolution?

Critical Thinking

4. **Predicting Consequences**   Suppose the steam engine was never invented.

Do you think the Industrial Revolution would have still occurred? Why or why not?

Graphic Organizer Activity

5. Draw this diagram, and use it to weigh the pros and cons of using an assembly line to produce goods.

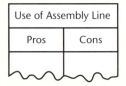

Use of Assembly Line	
Pros	Cons

Student Web Activity

Visit the *Human Heritage* Web site at **humanheritage.glencoe.com** and click on **Chapter 33— Student Web Activity** to find out more about inventors who lived during the Industrial Revolution.

SECTION 4 Industrial Impact

The Industrial Revolution brought many changes in people's lives. These changes showed up first in Great Britain. They then spread to other countries.

Changes in Society
In England, until the Middle Ages, there had been two major social classes—the nobles, who were the upper class, and the peasants, who were the lower class. Then, a middle class of rich merchants developed.

During the Industrial Revolution, the middle class increased in numbers and grew richer. Many factory, railroad, and mine owners became as wealthy as the nobles. They began to keep servants and to dress like members of the upper class. Women wore lacy petticoats and hooped skirts with stiff linings. Men wore dark suits, with top hats in winter and *boaters,* or stiff straw hats, in summer. Members of the middle class had iron ranges for cooking and gave huge dinner parties. Middle-class families began spending their weekends at seaside resorts, which were easy to reach now that railroads were common. Middle-class children went to upper-class schools.

In time, the middle class gained political power. In Great Britain, its male members gained the right to vote and to be represented in Parliament.

The Industrial Revolution also created an industrial working class. Most members of this class were peasants who could no longer support themselves by farming. Since they had no property of their own to sell, they had to sell their labor in order to live.

Members of the working class did not benefit from the Industrial Revolution in its early years. They worked 12 to 16 hours a day, six days a week, for low wages. They had to work at the pace set by machines and factory owners and were fined or

Linking Across Time

Automation The development of automation reduced the number of workers needed to produce goods. One person, for example, could run a machine that spun rows and rows of spindles of thread (below). Today the use of robots has eliminated the use of humans entirely on some jobs (right). **How did the use of machines affect the lives of workers in the Industrial Revolution?**

beaten if they did not keep up. Working conditions were difficult, dirty, and dangerous. Many people were killed or injured by unsafe machinery. The working class did not have job security. Factory and mine owners hired and fired whenever they wanted.

Most children of the working class did not have time to go to school or to play. Instead, they worked in factories and mines along with men and women. Employers often preferred to hire children since they could be paid even less than adults. Another reason was that in mines, children could crawl through narrow tunnels into which adults could not fit. Children sometimes were crippled by this difficult work.

The Growth of Cities

Another change brought by the Industrial Revolution was the growth of cities. Before the Industrial Revolution, less than 10 percent of the people in Great Britain lived in cities. By 1900, the number had reached 75 percent. Indeed, 10 percent of the people in the whole country lived in the city of London.

Some cities grew up around factories or mines that had been built in rural areas. Most factories, however, were built in existing cities, which grew rapidly as people moved there to find jobs. Soon, the cities became overcrowded. Houses could not be built fast enough. Sometimes, a dozen people had to live in one room. Many moved into damp basements or rooms with no windows. Garbage floated in the streets because sewers had not yet been built. Water supplies became polluted. Epidemics of cholera (kol' uhr uh), typhoid, and tuberculosis were common. The death rate

INDUSTRIAL CITIES The development of industry in England led to the growth of large cities. English industrial cities were located near coal or iron deposits. This painting shows a nineteenth-century steel factory in the city of Sheffield. **Why could workers in the city do nothing about their working or living conditions?**

among the working class was more than twice that of the middle and upper classes.

Workers had little economic or political power. It was against the law to form **trade unions,** or workers' associations. Workers did not have the right to vote. For these reasons, they could do nothing about their working or living conditions.

✓ **Reading Check** What were **trade unions?**

Reform　Most people in the middle and upper classes paid little attention to the suffering of the workers. Factory owners, for example, felt that raising wages and improving working conditions would raise the cost of goods and lower profits. Some, however, believed that higher wages and better working conditions could produce good profits. They began to work for reform.

The reformers started schools, orphanages, and hospitals for the poor. They also worked to change laws. In 1824, trade unions were made legal. During the 1830s and 1840s, children under ten years old and women were prohibited from working underground in mines. The workday was cut to ten hours.

The reformers also worked to improve living conditions. New laws required public sewer systems and the building of better houses. Every room had to have at least one window, and every house had to have piped-in water. Over time, life became better for the working class. There were fewer epidemics. Clothing, food, and other products became cheap enough for the workers to buy.

Section 4 Assessment

1. **Define:** trade unions.
2. What problems were caused by the rapid growth of cities?
3. Why were some people against reform?

Critical Thinking

4. **Demonstrating Reasoned Judgment** What reforms would you have worked for if you had lived during the Industrial Revolution?

Graphic Organizer Activity

5. Draw this diagram, and use it to support this generalization: The Industrial Revolution brought many changes to people's lives. (Add answer lines as needed.)

Generalization

Supporting Details
1.
2.
3.
4.
5.

SECTION 5　Spread of Industry

Meanwhile, the Industrial Revolution spread from Great Britain to other countries. These countries, aided by technology, soon **industrialized,** or built up industry. The expansion of railroads and transportation were also important factors.

✓ **Reading Check** What happened when countries **industrialized?**

Other Countries

At the beginning of the Industrial Revolution, Great Britain tried to keep its inventions secret. Machines or plans for machines were forbidden to be taken out of Great Britain. Skilled workers were forbidden to leave the country. By the 1800s, however, many workers had ignored the law and left. Other nations welcomed these **immigrants,** or people who settle permanently in a different country, because they brought British industrial secrets to their new homelands.

These countries used what they learned to build their own industries. Belgium, with its rich deposits of iron and coal, was the first country after Great Britain to industrialize. The next country was France. There, the process began in the 1700s but was slowed by war and revolution. The United States, with its many natural resources, soon followed France.

Then came Germany. Although Germany was well supplied with coal and iron, it was divided into more than 30 separate states. These states were not willing to cooperate in economic matters. Germany, therefore, did not make much industrial progress until after it was unified in 1871. It then matched the others as a leading industrial power.

Reading Check

Why did other nations welcome skilled British **immigrants?**

Then... & Now

Weights and Measures As industrialization spread, people needed a common system of weights and measures. Most countries adopted the metric system, first developed in France in the 1790s. Its basic measurement, the meter, equals one ten-millionth of the distance along a meridian from the North Pole to the Equator.

WORLD'S FAIR In 1851, Great Britain held the first World's Fair in London to celebrate its industrial achievements. Other countries then began to hold similar fairs. This painting shows the royal family attending opening day. **How did the Industrial Revolution spread from Great Britain to other countries?**

THOMAS EDISON   Although best known for the electric light, Thomas Edison had numerous other important inventions. These include the first successful phonograph, an electric railroad, and an electric battery. This photograph shows Edison in his laboratory. **What advances in communications were powered by electricity?**

Technological Advances   The development of new kinds of power helped continue the Industrial Revolution. One of these was electricity. In 1837, two Americans, Samuel F. B. Morse and Alfred Vail, built the first successful electric telegraph. It made quick communication possible. Some years later, Alexander Graham Bell, also an American, invented the telephone. Communications took another step forward. In 1895, an Italian physicist, Guglielmo Marconi (gū yel′ mō mahr kō′ nē), built the wireless telegraph, or radio. Six years later, he was able to send a message across the Atlantic Ocean.

Meanwhile, there were other advances in electricity. By 1879, Thomas Alva Edison, an American, developed the electric light. It would soon illuminate factories and homes all over the world.

Another new source of power was the **internal combustion engine,** or an engine that is fueled by gasoline. It was invented around 1885 by German engineer Gottlieb Daimler (gōt′ lēb dīm′ luhr). Daimler's engine was used to drive the first automobile as well as other machines. Another German engineer, Rudolf Diesel, developed an oil-burning internal combustion engine that could run large industrial plants, locomotives, and ocean liners. These developments helped open a whole new era in transportation.

Inspiration Guglielmo Marconi, inventor of the wireless telegraph, was inspired to experiment with science after reading a biography of Benjamin Franklin.

Reading Check
What fueled the **internal combustion engine?**

Section 5 Assessment

1. **Define:** industrialized, immigrants, internal combustion engine.
2. How did the Industrial Revolution spread?
3. What were the first countries to industrialize after Great Britain?

Critical Thinking

4. **Drawing Conclusions** Which of the advances in technology made during the Industrial Revolution do you consider the most important? Explain.

Graphic Organizer Activity

5. Draw this diagram, and use it to show inventions that advanced communication and the use of new forms of energy or power.

New Inventions	
Communication	Energy/Power

Chapter Summary & Study Guide

1. In 1543, Copernicus triggered the Scientific Revolution with his idea of a sun-centered solar system.
2. The Scientific Revolution helped lead to the Agricultural Revolution—a new system of land division, animal breeding, and growing crops.
3. The invention of new machines helped workers produce more goods in less time.
4. Perfection of the steam engine replaced the use of water power and allowed factories to be built near sources of raw materials.
5. Eli Whitney and Catherine Littlefield Greene invented the cotton gin in 1793. Whitney also developed the principle of interchangeable parts.
6. Automation and the assembly line increased production and reduced the need for skilled workers.
7. The development of inexpensive ways to smelt iron and make steel provided cheaper building materials for industry.
8. Improvements in transportation—better roads, canal systems, railroads, and steam boats—helped speed industrialization.
9. The Industrial Revolution increased the size of the middle class and created a new industrial working class, many of whom suffered poor living conditions in industrial cities.
10. During the 1800s, the Industrial Revolution spread from Great Britain to other countries, where inventors developed even more new ideas such as electricity and the internal combustion engine.

Self-Check Quiz

Visit the *Human Heritage* Web site at **humanheritage. glencoe.com** and click on *Chapter 33—Self-Check Quiz* to assess your understanding of this chapter.

Using Key Terms

Imagine that you are having a conversation with Thomas Jefferson about the most important ideas and innovations of the Industrial Revolution. Write out the dialogue using the following words.

enclosure	textile
domestic system	flying shuttle
spinning jenny	factory system
cotton gin	interchangeable parts
automation	assembly line
open-hearth process	macadam road
trade unions	industrialized
immigrants	internal combustion engine

Understanding Main Ideas

1. In what ways did ideas about science change in the 1400s, 1500s, and 1600s?
2. What effect did the Agricultural Revolution have on population growth?
3. How did the development of the macadam road affect transportation?
4. What benefits did people in the working class eventually receive from the Industrial Revolution?
5. What new sources of power helped spread the Industrial Revolution?

Critical Thinking

1. How did changes in agriculture influence the beginning of the Industrial Revolution?
2. Why did Great Britian want to keep its inventions secret from the rest of the world?
3. What things are necessary for a country to be able to industrialize?

4. Do you believe the Industrial Revolution was good or bad for most workers? Explain.

Graphic Organizer Activity

Economics Create a diagram such as the one shown, and use it to compare economic activities before and after the Industrial Revolution. (Tip: Think back to how people earned a living in the Renaissance and Middle Ages.)

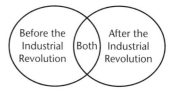

Before the Industrial Revolution | Both | After the Industrial Revolution

 ## Geography in History

Environment and Society Progress that came about during the Industrial Revolution was caused by people interacting with their environment. What geographic features were involved in this progress? Explain.

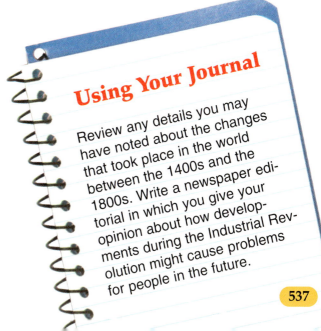

Using Your Journal

Review any details you may have noted about the changes that took place in the world between the 1400s and the 1800s. Write a newspaper editorial in which you give your opinion about how developments during the Industrial Revolution might cause problems for people in the future.

Around

RUSSIA

While western European nations pushed into the Americas, Russian czars expanded their borders both in the east and in the west. By the 1800s, Russia covered one-sixth of the earth's surface. It extended from the Baltic Sea in the west to Alaska in the east and from the Arctic Ocean in the north to central Asia in the south. The greatest czars—rulers like Peter the Great and Catherine the Great—worked tirelessly to modernize Russia. No matter how hard they tried, however, Russia remained a mostly rural nation, with nearly all of its vast population working as serfs or living in remote villages.

Russian Empire

ARCTIC OCEAN

Siberia

Alaska

RUSSIA

Bering Strait

St. Petersburg

URAL MOUNTAINS

Moscow

Kiev

OTTOMAN EMPIRE

PACIFIC OCEAN

Russian Empire at Its Height

CHINA

miles 0   1250   2500
kilometers 0   1250   2500

▼ Both nobles and serfs loved the folktales that formed part of Russia's oral history. These tales drew an audience everywhere, whether it be in a peasant's cottage or a czar's palace. Russian artists captured scenes from these stories on beautiful lacquered boxes such as this one.

▲ Most of the Russian empire stretched east of the Ural Mountains—the traditional boundary between Europe and Asia. Even so, the heart of the empire always lay west of the Urals—the place where the states of Rus and Muscovy were born. It was here that Russian rulers built their greatest cities and set up governments to rule their sprawling lands.

▶ Peter the Great founded St. Petersburg on the Baltic Sea in the early 1700s. Peter tried to "westernize" Russia. He even worked to ban beards on Russian men.

By the end of the 1700s, Russia reached some 6,000 miles from east to west. The larger it grew, the more diverse its population became. Peoples ranged from the hunters of the Tungus region in eastern Siberia (right) to the peasant women of the St. Petersburg area (left). ▶

▲ Russian serfs farmed the land, worked as servants, and generally served the nobles who owned the land on which they lived. In this painting, serfs escort a noble family through the winter countryside in a carriage.

◀ The skill of Russian artisans is shown in this fur-lined gold crown set with precious jewels. Crafted in the mid-sixteenth century, the crown is in a museum in the Kremlin today.

Taking Another Look

1. What was the size and location of the Russian empire at its height?

2. How did expansion affect the population makeup of Russia?

Hands-On Activity

Writing a Letter to the Editor Write a letter to the editor of a Russian newspaper commenting on the decision to ban all beards.

539

Standardized Test Practice

Directions: Choose the *best* answer to each of the following multiple choice questions. If you have trouble answering a question, use the process of elimination to narrow your choices. Write your answers on a separate piece of paper.

Spanish Colonies in the Americas

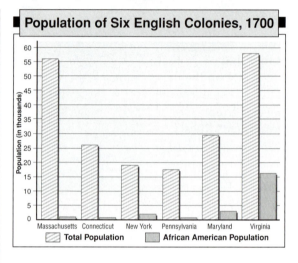

Population of Six English Colonies, 1700

1. According to the map above, what colony was located at approximately 29°N and 82°W?

   A Cuba

   B Gulf of Mexico

   C St. Augustine

   D Cajamarca

   Test-Taking Tip: Look at the map's labels carefully. How does it show which labels belong to *continents?* To *islands?* To *colonies?*

2. According to the graph above, which colonies had the largest and smallest total populations in 1700?

   F Virginia and Pennsylvania

   G Massachusetts and New York

   H New York and Pennsylvania

   J Connecticut and Maryland

   Test-Taking Tip: Notice that the question asks for *total population*. This graph shows two different bars for each colony. Do you need to add the bars together to get the total population? Why or why not?

3. Native Americans in the Subarctic, Great Basin, and California areas relied on hunting, fishing, and gathering food. Native Americans in the Eastern Woodlands, Southwest, and Southeast became farmers. What might explain this difference?

A Native Americans in the Eastern Woodlands, Southwest, and Southeast learned how to farm from the colonists.

B Native Americans in the Subarctic, Great Basin, and California did not have farming tools.

C Native Americans in the Eastern Woodlands, Southwest, and Southeast were allowed to own land, so they could establish permanent farms.

D The climate and soil in the Subarctic, Great Basin, and California areas were not good for farming.

> **Test-Taking Tip:** Since the "hunters" and the "farmers" came from different geographic regions, it is likely that the answer has something to do with geography. Which answer choice fits *best* with this information?

4. The civil war in England was fought between

F the government and serfs

G the monarchy and the feudal lords

H the king and Parliament

J England and France

> **Test-Taking Tip:** Eliminate answers that do not make sense. A *civil war* is a type of war fought *within one country*. Therefore, answer J can be eliminated.

5. In *Two Treatises of Government*, John Locke wrote about certain natural rights with which all people are born. These rights did NOT include

A life

B liberty

C education

D property

> **Test-Taking Tip:** It may be helpful to remember that Locke's ideas helped form the basis for the Declaration of Independence. What rights did the colonists *most* want to protect?

6. Like the English and American revolutions, the French Revolution was fought over

F the power of the monarchy

G the role of the Church

H the right to own property

J the rights of taxpaying citizens

> **Test-Taking Tip:** This question asks you to make a *comparison.* What did *all three* revolutions have in common? For instance, did the American Revolution have anything to do with the role of the Church? No. Therefore, you can eliminate choice G.

7. The Agricultural Revolution led to

A a decrease in farm productivity

B more people moving to farms to work

C better farming technologies

D many bloody wars between farmers and the government

> **Test-Taking Tip:** This question asks about a *different* type of revolution. Remember that the Agricultural Revolution set the stage for the Industrial Revolution a hundred years later. However, neither of these revolutions involved warfare. In this case, the word *revolution* refers to a change in the system of farming. Therefore, you can eliminate choice D.

11 Nations and Empires

Yoruba carving of Catholic missionary ▶
arriving in West Africa, late 1800s

▲ Medicines to conquer
the diseases that
hindered colonization
of Africa

1784
Russian settlement
of Kodiak Island

1804
Haiti becomes
independent

1822
Mexico becomes
independent

1839
Opium War in China

Organizing Information Study Foldable *Make the following foldable to help you organize what you learn about the nation and empire building during the 1800s.*

Step 1 *Collect 2 sheets of paper and place them about 1 inch apart.*

Keep the edges straight.

Step 2 *Fold up the bottom edges of the paper to form 4 tabs.*

This makes all tabs the same size.

Reading and Writing *As you read the unit, write the main ideas presented in each of the three chapters under the tabs of your foldable. Note details that support the main ideas.*

Step 3 *When all the tabs are the same size, crease the paper to hold the tabs in place and staple the sheets together. Label each tab as shown.*

Staple together along the fold.

Nations & Empires
The Americas
Unrest in Europe
Rise of Imperialism

PRIMARY SOURCES

Library

See pages 694–695 for another primary source reading to accompany Unit 11.

GO TO

Read "Victory at Waterloo" from the **World History Primary Source Document Library CD-ROM.**

Journal Notes

How did world governments and ideas about democracy change during the 1800s? Note details about these changes as you read.

1846
War between U.S. and Mexico begins

1900
Boxer Rebellion breaks out in China

1910
Union of South Africa formed

The Americas
1800 A.D.–1875 A.D.

◀ Native American dress

Covered wagons carrying U.S. settlers westward ▼

1803
U.S. buys the Louisiana Territory

1804
Haiti becomes first independent country in Latin America

1822
Mexico wins independence

1861
U.S. Civil War begins

Chapter Focus

 Read to Discover

- What kind of government developed in the newly formed United States.
- How and why the United States expanded its boundaries during the 1800s.
- What led to the Civil War in the United States.
- What cultural changes took place in the United States during the late 1800s and early 1900s.
- How colonies in Latin America won their independence.
- Why democracy did not develop in Latin America.

Chapter Overview

Visit the *Human Heritage* Web site at <u>humanheritage.glencoe.com</u> and click on ***Chapter 34— Chapter Overviews*** to preview this chapter.

 Terms to Learn
federal
manifest
   destiny

 People to Know
Abraham
   Lincoln
Simón Bolívar

 Places to Locate
Alamo
Rio Grande
Haiti

Why It's Important   Many changes took place in the Americas from 1800 to the early 1900s. The United States more than doubled in size, and its government was set on a firm base. This allowed the country to grow industrially and to become a world power. Latin America, which is made up of Mexico, Central America, the Caribbean islands, and South America, won independence from European rule. However, colonial traditions remained strong. So, despite many efforts, democracy did not develop in most of Latin America.

SECTION 1   The United States

In the years after winning independence, the Americans set up a democratic government and expanded the boundaries of their country. They fought each other in a civil war and then worked to reunite the nation after the war ended. Industry grew and brought about many changes in daily life. By 1900, the United States had become a powerful country.

Government   One thing that helped the United States become powerful was its government. Americans developed a tradition of **stable government,** or a government that rules from year to year without great changes.

Reading Check
Why was a **stable government** important to the future of the United States?

Reading Check
What two **political parties** had formed by 1800? What is the **federal** government?

By 1800, two **political parties,** or groups with different ideas about government, had come into being. One was the Federalist (fed' uhr uh list) party. It favored a strong **federal,** or national, government. Most Federalists believed that only people of wealth and education should hold office. They thought the economy should be based more on industry than on trade or agriculture. The other political party was the Democratic-Republican party. It favored more power for the states. Most Democratic-Republicans believed that average people should lead the country. They thought the economy should be based more on agriculture than on industry or trade.

Although in other countries wars were often fought when political power changed hands, in the United States the government changed hands through peaceful elections. For example, in 1800, Thomas Jefferson, who was a Democratic-Republican, was elected President. He took the place of John Adams, who was a Federalist. This was the first peaceful passing of power from one political group to another in the United States.

Reading Check
How are officials chosen in a **representative government?**

The United States also had a tradition of **representative government.** This is a government in which officials are elected by the people. In 1800, however, only white males who owned property could vote. This changed over the next 30 years. New states in the West began to allow all adult white males to vote. Other states soon followed. By 1830, the number of voters had greatly increased. Although women, enslaved people, and Native Americans were not allowed to vote, the United States government was one of the most democratic in the world at the time.

With the growing number of voters, election campaigns changed. They became filled with entertainment and advertising. People sang songs and wore ribbons to show which candidates they supported. Political parties held parades, rallies, and dinners. Presidential races in particular were noted for slogans and symbols. For example, Andrew Jackson, who became President in 1829, was known as "Old Hickory." So, during his campaign, the newly formed Democratic party planted hickory trees in town squares and gave out hickory brooms and canes.

The Westward Movement

At the end of the American Revolution, the United States claimed most of the land east of the Mississippi River. Soon, thousands of Americans were putting their belongings into farm wagons and traveling across the Appalachian Mountains to find new homes. When they came to the Ohio River and other water routes, they loaded their goods and animals on flatboats and floated downstream.

The settlers were careful about choosing a spot for their new home. It had to be near a stream for water. It also had to be near a large settlement or fort for safety. After choosing a place, the settlers would clear the land of trees and build a log cabin. It usually had one room, with a dirt-packed floor and a door made of wood planks. Each cabin had one or two tiny windows covered with deerskin. There was a fireplace that supplied heat for warmth and cooking.

The settlers' way of life was generally different from that of the Native Americans in the area. The settlers were farmers, while most Native Americans were hunters. The settlers claimed land for themselves. The Native Americans believed land belonged to everyone.

The Native Americans and the settlers did learn from one another, however. Many of the settlers wore Native American clothing, such as moccasins and deerskin leggings. They used Native American herbs as medicine and paddled Native American canoes. Many of the Native Americans used rifles, iron pots, and woolen blankets that were made in Great Britain.

The Native Americans tried to defend their lands against the settlers. However, there were many more settlers than Native Americans. Also, many Native Americans died from such diseases as measles and smallpox brought by the whites. Over time, the Native Americans were slowly pushed farther and farther west. In the 1830s, the United States government began forcing the Native Americans to live on reservations.

Territorial Expansion   Many settlers chose land newly acquired by the United States. In 1803, the United States doubled its size by buying the Louisiana Territory from France for $15 million. The Louisiana Purchase, as it was called, provided an

NATIVE AMERICAN LIFE   Many Native Americans west of the Mississippi were nomadic and hunted the great migrating herds of buffalo. The Native Americans depended on the buffalo's meat for food and its hide for clothing and shelter. **Why were the Native Americans unable to stop the movement of the settlers?**

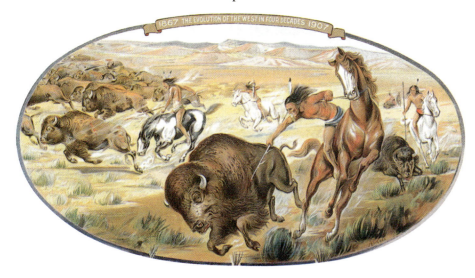

THE ALAMO   The Alamo was a Catholic mission in San Antonio, Texas. In 1836, during the war for Texan independence, 187 Texans used the Alamo as a fortress and held out for several days against nearly 4,000 Mexican soldiers before being defeated. **What conditions had the Mexicans placed on Americans settling in Texas?**

Manifest Destiny The spirit of manifest destiny was captured in this 1821 speech by Francis Baylies, a Massachusetts Congressman. "Our natural boundary is the Pacific Ocean. The swelling tide of our population must and will roll on until that mighty ocean . . . limits our territorial empire."

Reading Check
What was the principle of **manifest destiny?**

area rich in farmland, minerals, and forests. It also gave the United States control of the Mississippi River and the important seaport of New Orleans.

In 1819, the United States and Spain signed a treaty. This treaty, called the Adams-Onís Treaty, gave Florida to the United States and set the boundary between the Louisiana Purchase and the Spanish lands to the south and west.

One of the Spanish lands was Mexico. It became independent in 1821. The Mexicans wanted more people to settle in their territory, especially in Texas. So, they offered people from the United States large areas of free land if they would swear loyalty to Mexico and become Catholic. By the early 1830s, there were 30,000 Americans living in Texas. Most were from the South, and many owned enslaved people.

Enslavement and other issues soon led to quarrels between the Americans who moved to Texas and the Mexican government. Mexico had outlawed enslavement in 1824, and it objected to Texans enslaving people. It also began wondering whether American settlers were loyal to Mexico or to the United States. So, the Mexican government tried to stop more Americans from entering Texas. The Texans then asked for more control over their local affairs. Finally, in 1835, the Texans revolted. The following year, they declared their independence.

Many Americans believed in the **manifest destiny** (man' uh fest des' tuh nē) of the United States, or the idea that it was the fate of the United States to stretch from the Atlantic Ocean to the Pacific Ocean. They wanted the federal government to allow the annexation of Texas. **Annexation** (an ek sā′ shuhn) is the act of taking over a territory and combining it with an existing country or state. In 1845, the United States annexed Texas. This greatly angered Mexico. A dispute over the Texas-Mexico boundary caused more trouble. By the following year, the two countries were at war. American soldiers invaded California, which was part of Mexico. They also marched into Mexico City.

In 1848, Mexico signed the Treaty of Guadalupe Hidalgo (gwah dl ū′ pā huh duhl′ gō). It gave the United States almost one half of Mexico's land. It also set the Rio Grande (rē′ ō gran′ dā) as the boundary between Texas and Mexico.

Five years after the treaty, in 1853, the United States bought a piece of land from Mexico in order to build a railroad to the Pacific. This was called the Gadsden (gadz′ duhn) Purchase after James Gadsden, the American who arranged the purchase.

Meanwhile, the United States acquired the Oregon Territory. During the 1840s, thousands of American settlers made the long, hard trip over the Rocky Mountains to Oregon, which both the United States and Great Britain claimed. The presence of these settlers gave the United States control of much of the area. In 1846, the two countries agreed to divide the Oregon Territory at the 49th parallel.

Reading Check
How did the **annexation** of Texas affect U.S. relations with Mexico?

MAP STUDY

PLACES AND REGIONS The Louisiana Purchase eventually formed parts of 13 states. **What geographic features marked the western and eastern boundaries of the Louisiana Purchase?**

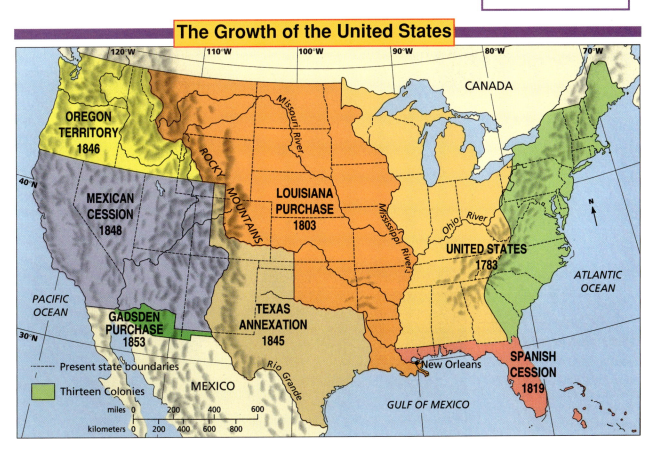

The Growth of the United States

OREGON TERRITORY 1846

MEXICAN CESSION 1848

GADSDEN PURCHASE 1853

ROCKY MOUNTAINS

LOUISIANA PURCHASE 1803

TEXAS ANNEXATION 1845

Missouri River

Mississippi River

Ohio River

CANADA

UNITED STATES 1783

ATLANTIC OCEAN

New Orleans

SPANISH CESSION 1819

PACIFIC OCEAN

MEXICO

Rio Grande

GULF OF MEXICO

- - - - Present state boundaries

Thirteen Colonies

miles 0 200 400 600

kilometers 0 200 400 600 800

40°N

30°N

120°W 110°W 100°W 90°W 80°W 70°W

Later, another large area of land, Alaska, was added to the United States. In 1784, Russian fur hunters had established a permanent settlement at Kodiak (kōd' ē ak) Island off the Alaskan coast. From there, they set up hunting and trading settlements as far south as California. After a time, however, Russia lost interest in Alaska and sold the territory to the United States in 1867.

Civil War and Reunion

As the United States expanded westward, different ways of life developed in the northern and southern states. The northern states were industrialized. They had most of the nation's factories, railroads, and canals. Labor in the North was done by hired workers. About 20 percent of the people lived in cities. Education was widespread, and immigration brought in all different kinds of people. Northern leaders wanted a strong national government. They also wanted the government to aid industry and improve transportation. They believed that enslavement should not be allowed in new areas of the country.

The southern states depended on agriculture. Tobacco, rice, sugar cane, and especially cotton were important. These crops

ABRAHAM LINCOLN As President during the Civil War, Abraham Lincoln led the United States through one of the most critical periods in the nation's history. Lincoln was assassinated by a southern sympathizer shortly after the North and South were reunited. **What did the southern states that seceded call their new government?**

Student Web Activity
Visit the *Human Heritage* Web site at **humanheritage.glencoe.com** and click on *Chapter 34—Student Web Activities* to find out more about the Civil War.

were grown on large plantations that used enslaved labor. Enslaved people made up about one third of the South's population. Only 10 percent of the people lived in cities. There were few immigrants. Southern leaders believed that the rights of the states were more important than those of the federal government. They also believed that as the country grew, enslavement should be allowed in new areas.

In 1860, Abraham Lincoln was elected President. Southerners feared he would try to do away with enslavement and destroy their way of life. Seven southern states announced that they were **seceding** (si sēd′ ē ng), or withdrawing, from the nation. They formed a new government called the Confederate States of America or the Confederacy (kuhn fed′ uhr uh sē). Soon, four more states seceded and joined the Confederacy. Northerners did not think the southern states had a right to secede. By 1861, the North and the South were fighting a civil war. In 1865, the North won, and the country was once more politically united.

The Civil War settled the question of whether or not states have the right to secede. It also led to freedom for nearly 4 million enslaved African Americans. The country began to build itself up again. By 1870, it was on its way to becoming a strong industrial country and a world power.

Cultural Changes

As the United States expanded and industrialized, many cultural changes took place. The rise of industry led to **urbanization,** or the growth of cities. During the late 1800s and early 1900s, many Americans left the farm and moved to the city. At the same time, a large number of immigrants came to America. Most settled in cities. City life provided jobs, education, and new ways for people to enjoy themselves.

Not everyone lived in the same way in the cities. The lives of the lower, middle, and upper classes differed greatly from one another. One way in which people's lives differed was in housing. The lower class, which included most immigrants, lived in old houses or commercial buildings that had been made into apartments. These were called **tenements** and were generally run-down. Areas with large numbers of tenements were called **slums.**

The middle class lived in various types of housing. One was the apartment house. It was often six to eight stories high, with at least two apartments on each story. Another kind of house was the row house. It was a private house that shared its side walls with its neighbors. Some members of the middle class lived in homes built for two families or in single-family residences. The upper class generally lived in huge homes staffed with servants.

Another way in which people's lives differed was in jobs. Lower-class men, women, and children worked in factories. Middle- and upper-class men held business and professional jobs, and their wives rarely worked outside the home.

Reading Check Why did seven southern states announce that they were **seceding** from the nation in 1861?

Reading Check What were some of the reasons for **urbanization** in the United States?

Reading Check Which groups of people generally lived in **tenements?** What were **slums?**

People's lives also differed in education. By the late 1800s, there were tax-supported public schools that all children could attend. However, it was generally middle- and upper-class children who benefited. Lower-class children, who had to work, rarely went past elementary school.

Technological advances changed daily life during the late 1800s and early 1900s. For example, the invention of the refrigerator ended the need for daily shopping. Labor-saving machines gave many Americans time to read books, newspapers, and magazines. They also enjoyed music and the theater. City governments began to set aside land for parks.

Section 1 Assessment

1. **Define:** stable government, political parties, federal, representative government, manifest destiny, annexation, seceding, urbanization, tenements, slums.
2. How did election campaigns change by the 1830s?
3. What were two results of the Civil War?

Critical Thinking

4. **Demonstrating Reasoned Judgment** Do you agree with the settlers' or the Native Americans' ideas about land ownership? Explain.

Graphic Organizer Activity

5. Draw this diagram, and use it to show the causes and effects of the war between Mexico and the United States.

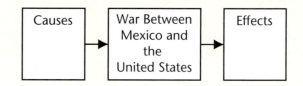

| Causes | → | War Between Mexico and the United States | → | Effects |

Painting of Toussaint-L'Ouverture

Painting of Toussaint-L'Ouverture

SECTION 2 Latin America

While the United States was expanding and settling its internal differences, the European-ruled colonies of Latin America were moving toward independence. The American and French Revolutions stirred the people of Latin America to action. Everywhere, colonists tried to take charge of their own affairs.

The First Revolt The first major successful revolt against European rule took place in the French West Indies on Saint Domingue (san duh manj'), the western part of the island of Hispaniola. There, a few French plantation owners used the labor of 500,000 enslaved Africans to grow sugarcane, coffee, cotton, and *indigo* (in' duh gō), or a kind of plant that yields a blue dye.

Then, Pierre Dominique Toussaint-L'Ouverture (pē auhr' dom uh nēk' tū san' lū vuh tyuhr') appeared on the scene. The grandson of an African chief, Toussaint was born enslaved around 1743. His white slaveholder, however, taught Toussaint to read and write and, in 1777, gave him his freedom. When news of the French Revolution reached Saint Domingue, Toussaint was inspired. In 1791, he led a revolt of enslaved people. In 1794, the French government agreed to abolish enslavement. Toussaint became governor-general of Saint Domingue in 1801. Two years later, he issued a constitution. The French then tried to regain control of Saint Domingue but were unsuccessful. In 1804, Saint Domingue became the first free country in Latin America. It changed its name to Haiti, a Native American word meaning "mountainous."

Revolution Spreads

The fight for independence in South America was led by the Creoles. They were well educated and had enough power to make changes. The Creoles resented the peninsulares, who held the most important government posts.

Soon after the French Revolution began, a Creole named Antonio Nariño (ahn tō' nē ō nah rēn' yō) translated into Spanish the Declaration of the Rights of Man and the Citizen. This helped spread French democratic ideas throughout the Spanish colonies. Before long, the people there began to revolt.

In the northern part of South America, Simón Bolívar (sē mōn' bō lē' vahr), another Creole, led the fight for freedom. Known as "the Liberator," Bolívar was the son of a rich family in New Granada, or what is today Colombia and Venezuela. In 1805, he went to Europe. There, he learned about the French Revolution and its ideas. He then returned home, vowing to free his people.

In 1810, Bolívar and other leaders of New Granada organized a **junta** (hun' tuh), or political committee, to take over the government. Spanish officials soon crushed the movement, however. Bolívar then went into exile where he formed and trained an army. In 1817, he successfully invaded what is today Venezuela. In August 1819, he defeated the Spanish in what is today Colombia (kuh lum' bē uh). Later that year, he became the first president of Gran Colombia, Ecuador (ek' wuh dor), and Panama. In 1824, Bolívar freed Peru from Spanish rule. He also sent one of his generals to free a Spanish colony called Upper Peru. After declaring its independence in 1825, the new nation was named Bolivia (buh liv' ē uh).

While Bolívar was fighting for freedom in the north, another Creole, José de San Martín (hō sā' dā san mahr tēn'), was fighting for freedom in the south. In 1810, Creole leaders in La Plata (luh plaht' uh) organized a junta to take over the government. In 1812, San Martín joined the struggle for independence. A professional

People in History

Toussaint-L'Ouverture
c. 1743–1803

Haitian Patriot

A self-educated grandson of an African chief, Toussaint-L'Ouverture led the battle to free enslaved people in what is now Haiti. With the help of generals Jean Jacques Dessalines and Henri Christophe, he forced the British to withdraw from the island, and he also resisted a French invasion. He later was seized by the French and died in a prison in 1803. His battle for freedom made Toussaint a symbol for the fight for liberty.

Reading Check
Why did Simón Bolívar form a **junta** in 1810?

soldier, San Martín organized an army. He was aided by his wife, who persuaded the women of Buenos Aires (bwā′ nuhs er′ ēz) to give their jewels to help buy supplies for her husband's troops. He was also aided by Father Luís Beltrán (lū ēs′ bel trahn′), who melted down church bells to make guns and bullets. In 1816, the part of La Plata that is now Argentina (ahr juhn tē′ nuh) won its independence.

In 1817, San Martín led his army across the Andes Mountains into what is now Chile. The crossing was difficult, and many soldiers died from the cold and the lack of oxygen. Most of their horses and pack mules also died. However, San Martín was able to take the Spanish forces in Chile by surprise. He and another soldier, Bernardo O'Higgins (ber nahrd′ ō ō hig′ enz), defeated the Spanish. Chile became independent a year later.

Mexico, Central America, and Brazil

A fight for independence went on in Mexico as well. Father Miguel Hidalgo y Costilla (mē gel′ ē dahl′ gō ē kahs tē′ yuh) played an important part in this struggle. He had long been upset about the way the Native Americans were treated. Now, he urged his congregation not to submit any longer to Spanish rule.

Led by Hidalgo, the Native Americans revolted in 1810. Frightened by the Native Americans, the Creoles joined with the peninsulares to crush the revolt. Hidalgo himself was caught and put to death. Three years later, another priest, Father José María Morelos y Pavón (hō sā′ mah rē′ ah mō rā′ lōs ē pah vōn′), led a second revolt. It was no more successful than the first. Morelos, like Hidalgo, was caught and put to death.

In 1820, there was a revolt in Spain. The rebels there wanted to stop forced labor in Mexico and divide the land among the peasants. This greatly upset the Creoles, church leaders, and army officers. So, they joined together and revolted against Spanish rule in Mexico. Two years later, Mexico was declared to be independent. It was ruled by Agustín de Iturbide (ah gūs tēn′ dā ē tur bē′ thā), a Creole army officer, who served as emperor. Iturbide, however, refused to share power with the Mexican legislature. He was also a poor administrator. The Mexicans soon tired of his rule and in 1823, they overthrew him. In 1824, after a new constitution was written, Mexico became a republic.

Moved by what had happened in Mexico, the people of Central America also revolted. In 1821, they declared their independence and two years later joined together to form the United Provinces of Central America. Not long after, the United Provinces split into the present-day countries of Costa Rica (kos′ tuh rē′ kuh), El Salvador (el sal′ vuh dor), Guatemala, Honduras (hon dūr′ uhs), and Nicaragua (nik uh rah′ gwuh).

A struggle for independence also took place in Brazil. Many Brazilians could see no reason to remain a part of the Portuguese

Painting of Father Hidalgo

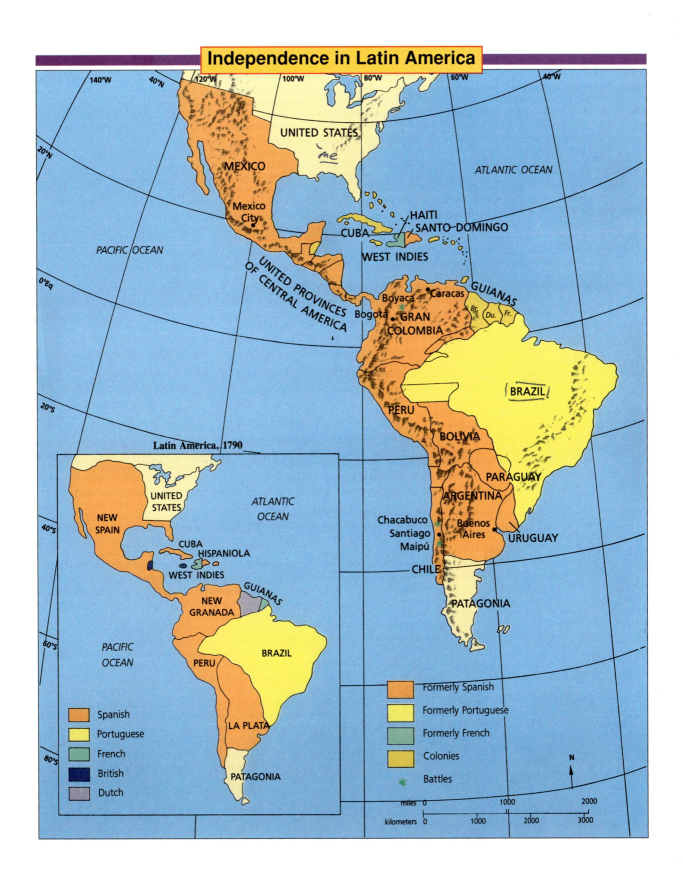

Independence in Latin America

140°W · 40°N · 120°W · 100°W · 80°W · 60°W · 40°W

20°N

UNITED STATES

MEXICO

Mexico City

PACIFIC OCEAN

ATLANTIC OCEAN

0°Eq

HAITI
SANTO DOMINGO
CUBA
WEST INDIES

UNITED PROVINCES OF CENTRAL AMERICA

Boyaca · Caracas
Bogota · GRAN COLOMBIA
GUIANAS
Br. Du. Fr.

20°S

PERU

BRAZIL

BOLIVIA

PARAGUAY

ARGENTINA

Chacabuco
Santiago
Maipú

Buenos Aires

URUGUAY

CHILE

PATAGONIA

Latin America, 1790

UNITED STATES

ATLANTIC OCEAN

NEW SPAIN

CUBA
HISPANIOLA
WEST INDIES

40°S

GUIANAS
NEW GRANADA

PACIFIC OCEAN

PERU

BRAZIL

60°S

LA PLATA

PATAGONIA

Spanish
Portuguese
French
British
Dutch

80°S

Formerly Spanish
Formerly Portuguese
Formerly French
Colonies
* **Battles**

N

miles 0 · 1000 · 2000
kilometers 0 · 1000 · 2000 · 3000

✓ **Reading Check**
Which groups of people generally backed a Latin American **caudillo?**

Empire. They were angry that Portugal tried to control their trade. They also did not like the way the Portuguese parliament treated Brazilian representatives. In 1822, the Brazilians declared their independence from Portugal. Pedro (pā' drō), their Portuguese ruler, agreed to accept a constitution and became their emperor. Brazil was the only country in South America to become a monarchy after independence.

Rule by Caudillos

Most people in Latin America hoped the newly independent countries would become democratic. Spanish rule had given the people little training in self-government, however. The mestizos, Native Americans, and African Americans had received no opportunity for education. Also, the Creoles were not willing to share power with other groups.

A new kind of leader called a **caudillo** (kau thē' yō), or strong man, rose to power. Caudillos were backed by the army. Most were also backed by large landowners and church leaders, who did not want their lands divided among the peasants.

Generally, a caudillo took over a government by force. He ruled until he was overthrown by another caudillo. With each change in government, there was a violent revolution and much bloodshed. Because of this, most Latin American countries did not have stable governments.

Most caudillos ruled as dictators. They did not care about improving the lot of the people. One such caudillo was Antonio López de Santa Anna (ahn tō' nyō lō' pās da san' tuh an' uh) of Mexico, who had been a commander in Iturbide's army. One historian described Santa Anna as "a fortune hunter and a glory

BRAZILIAN INDEPENDENCE   Brazil gained its independence from Portugal in 1822. Here, Pedro I, Brazil's first emperor, is shown raising his sword and crying out "Independence or death." **What was unusual about Brazil's independence?**

hound." In 1833, Santa Anna led his troops into Mexico City and had himself elected president. He ruled Mexico six times between 1833 and 1855. During his rule Mexico lost almost one half of its land to the United States through the Treaty of Guadalupe Hidalgo.

A different type of caudillo eventually took Santa Anna's place. Benito Juárez (ba nē' tō hwahr' ez) proved that a caudillo could care about the people. A lawyer, Juárez was the first Native American to rule Mexico since the fall of the Aztec. Juárez was officially elected president in 1861, after several years of civil war. At the time, Mexico owed money to several countries, including France. Juárez asked these countries to wait two years for their money. France refused. Instead, it sent troops and made a European prince named Maximilian emperor. Juárez refused to give up, and finally defeated the French.

Juárez was again elected president in 1867. He held office until his death in 1872. As president, he worked to hold democratic elections. He reduced the power of the Roman Catholic Church by selling its land to the peasants. He started free schools to educate Native American children.

Linking Across Time

Symbol of Mexico According to legend, the Aztec were to settle where they saw an eagle perched on a cactus. The eagle and cactus symbol appeared on the coat of arms adopted by the first ruler of an independent Mexico (left). It also appears on the flag of Mexico today (right). **What reforms did Benito Juárez bring to Mexico?**

Section 2 Assessment

1. **Define:** junta, caudillo.
2. What inspired the people of Latin America to move toward independence?
3. Why did caudillos rule most of the newly independent nations of Latin America?

Critical Thinking

4. **Making Inferences** Why do you think Simón Bolívar was known as "The Liberator"?

Graphic Organizer Activity

5. Draw this diagram, and use it to show the accomplishments of key leaders in the Latin American struggle for independence.

Independence Leader	Accomplishment

Chapter Summary & Study Guide

1. A stable, independent government helped the United States grow in power.
2. In 1800, political power in the United States passed from one party to another through a peaceful election, rather than through war.
3. In 1830, most adult white males in the United States were able to vote, making it one of the world's most democratic governments at the time.
4. As settlers moved westward, they came into conflict with the Native Americans, who eventually were forced to live on reservations.
5. By 1867, the United States had acquired the Louisiana Territory, Florida, the Oregon Territory, almost half of Mexico's land, and Alaska.
6. Different ways of life in the northern and southern states led to the Civil War in the United States between 1861 and 1865.
7. The Civil War resulted in freedom for enslaved African Americans and the preservation of the Union.
8. Urbanization changed life in the United States in the late 1800s and early 1900s.
9. The American and French revolutions inspired the people of Latin America to fight for independence.
10. In 1804, Haiti became the first independent nation in Latin America. Other Spanish colonies and Brazil soon followed its example.
11. The newly independent Latin American nations lacked a tradition of self-government. As a result, most were ruled by caudillos.

HISTORY *Online*

Self-Check Quiz

Visit the *Human Heritage* Web site at **humanheritage. glencoe.com** and click on ***Chapter 34—Self-Check Quiz*** to assess your understanding of this chapter.

Using Key Terms

Write a newspaper article that gives an overview or summary of the major changes in government that took place in the United States and Latin America during the 1800s. Use the following words in your article.

stable government
political parties
federal
representative government
manifest destiny
annexation

seceding
urbanization
tenements
slums
junta
caudillo

Understanding Main Ideas

1. What was important about the American election of 1800?
2. What did the United States gain by the Louisiana Purchase?
3. What happened to Native Americans as the United States expanded its borders?
4. How did city life differ for lower-, middle-, and upper-class Americans?
5. How did Antonio Nariño help spread French democratic ideas throughout the Spanish colonies?
6. Why did Father Hidalgo revolt against Spanish rule?

Critical Thinking

1. What do you think are some ways the creation of public schools changed American life?
2. If you lived in Brazil in 1822, would you have supported the Portuguese government or the monarchy? Explain your answer.

3. How did the revolution in Brazil compare to the revolution in Mexico? Explain your answer.

Graphic Organizer Activity

Citizenship Create a diagram like the one shown, and use it to compare voting rights in the United States in 1830 with voting rights today. (Think of the groups who can vote today but could not vote in 1830.)

Voting Rights
1830   2000s

 ## Geography in History

Places and Regions Refer to the map of Latin America on page 555. The three battle sites marked show that they were all fought near large cities. What other things do these battle sites have in common? Describe them in a paragraph.

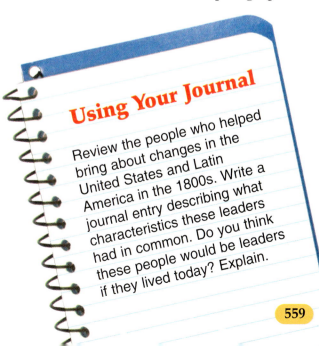

Using Your Journal

Review the people who helped bring about changes in the United States and Latin America in the 1800s. Write a journal entry describing what characteristics these leaders had in common. Do you think these people would be leaders if they lived today? Explain.

Unrest in Europe
1755 A.D.–1875 A.D.

▲ An urn from Napoleon's time

1804
Napoleon crowned

1814
Congress of Vienna meets

1815
Napoleon defeated

1848
Universal male suffrage begins to spread

1867
Dual monarchy of Austria-Hungary

Chapter Focus

 Read to Discover

- How Napoleon influenced France and formed the Grand Empire.
- How the Congress of Vienna established a balance of power and brought peace to Europe.
- How liberals, nationalists, and socialists led revolutions that threatened the Congress System.
- What effects nationalism had on Italy, Germany, and Austria.

Chapter Overview
Visit the *Human Heritage* Web site at humanheritage.glencoe.com and click on **Chapter 35— Chapter Overviews** to preview this chapter.

 Terms to Learn

plebiscite
abdicate
proletariat

 People to Know

Napoleon
Bonaparte
Karl Marx

🌐 **Places to Locate**

Waterloo
Vienna
Sardinia

Why It's Important   In the early 1800s, Napoleon occupied the center of the European stage. He came closer than anyone else to unifying Europe politically. In so doing, he spread revolutionary ideas. After his downfall, there was a return to the old order. However, the ideas of the Napoleonic (nuh pō lē ahn' ik) era had taken hold, and from 1820 to 1848, revolutions took place in country after country. The years after 1848 saw the breakup of the old order and the formation of new nations.

SECTION 1 The Age of Napoleon

By 1799, France had experienced ten years of revolution and war. The people longed for a return to peace and order. They were ready for a strong leader to take charge. It was during this time that Napoleon rose to power. His rule started a chain of events that affected not only France, but all of Europe.

Napoleon   When the French Revolution began, Napoleon Bonaparte, who had come to France from Corsica (kōr' si kuh), was a lieutenant in the French army. By the time he was 24 years old, he had become a general. He was not satisfied, however. He wanted more power.

In 1796, Napoleon was chosen to lead French troops into Italy. There, the French defeated the Austrians, who ruled Italy at

Student Web Activity

Visit the *Human Heritage* Web site at **humanheritage.glencoe.com** and click on *Chapter 35— Student Web Activities* to find out more about Napoleon.

Example of Napoleonic Dress

that time. As a result of this victory, France acquired Belgium from Austria. France also acquired hundreds of art treasures from Italy, which were placed in the Louvre (lūv), the French national museum.

Two years later, Napoleon sailed for Egypt, where British forces were stationed. He won a great land victory there, but the British fleet destroyed the French fleet. Nevertheless, the French succeeded in establishing their influence in Egypt. Another important outcome of the French campaign was that soldiers accompanying Napoleon discovered the Rosetta Stone.

Meanwhile, Austria, Russia, and Great Britain defeated French forces in Europe. When Napoleon learned of this, he saw his chance to gain more power. He left his troops in Egypt and returned to Paris. There, he and two members of the Directory plotted to take over the government. On November 9, 1799, they put their plan into effect and met with success.

Napoleon set up a new government called the Consulate (kon' suh luht). He placed himself at its head and took the title of First Consul. By this time, Russia was no longer at war with France. However, Austria and Great Britain were. In 1801, Napoleon led French forces to victory over Austria. In 1802, he arranged a peace treaty with Great Britain.

Affairs at Home   Once France was at peace, Napoleon turned his attention to affairs at home. The Directory had been weak and in debt. Napoleon set out to make the Consulate strong and rich. He took away the people's right to choose their own local officials and gave that power to the national government. He prohibited local governments from collecting taxes and assigned all tax collection to the national government. Because Napoleon's system was better organized, the French government was able to collect more taxes. In a few years, France's debt was paid, and its economy had improved. Napoleon also used some of the tax money to set up a system of public education.

Napoleon also set to work to bring order to the French legal system. The French Revolution had swept away most laws and the different revolutionary governments had never been able to agree on new ones. As a result, different laws were followed in different parts of the country. To correct this, Napoleon appointed a committee of lawyers and told them to write a new code of law for the whole country. The laws they wrote were divided into five parts and were called the Napoleonic Code.

The Napoleonic Code preserved the most important rights won in the French Revolution. Serfdom was ended. People were made equal before the law. Anyone charged with a crime was guaranteed a public trial by jury. Freedom of religion was also guaranteed. However, some rights the people had won in the revolution were taken away. No one was allowed to criticize the national government. There was no freedom of speech or of the press. A large police force kept watch on anyone suspected of being against Napoleon. Many people were put in jail.

Napoleon tried to make both Paris and France more beautiful. He had a huge marble arch, called the Arc de Triomphe (ahrk deh trē ahmf'), built as a monument to his campaigns. He named Jacques-Louis David as court painter. David designed furniture that looked like that of ancient Greece and Rome. Soon, the "Empire" style spread throughout Europe. This style affected clothes as well as furniture. Women wore narrow white cotton or muslin dresses with low square necklines and short puffed sleeves. They also fixed their hair like the women of ancient Rome.

Photograph of Arc de Triomphe

Napoleon also worked to improve transportation. Under his direction, French workers dug canals and improved roads. Fourteen new bridges were built across the Seine River, which runs through Paris.

Because Napoleon brought peace and order, he was very popular. In 1802, he asked the people to elect him First Consul for life. They did so in a **plebiscite** (pleb' uh sīt), or popular vote. Two years later, the French made Napoleon emperor of France. His coronation was held in the Notre Dame (nō' truh dahm) Cathedral. The Pope came from Rome for the crowning but did not have a chance to place the crown on Napoleon's head. Instead, Napoleon took the crown from the Pope's hands and crowned himself.

Reading Check
What is a **plebiscite?**

The Grand Empire

Being emperor of France was not enough for Napoleon. He wanted to build a Grand Empire that would take the place of the Holy Roman Empire. He had the advantage of an army whose soldiers worshiped their emperor and whose officers were chosen because they were able in battle, not just because they were aristocrats.

In 1803, Great Britain, threatened by Napoleon's actions, declared war on France. Great Britain and its allies, however, were not able to stop Napoleon and his soldiers. In 1805, Napoleon had himself crowned king of Italy. In 1806, he formed the Confederation (kuhn fed uhr ā' shuhn) of the Rhine, which consisted of a group of conquered German states. In 1808, he invaded Spain and Portugal. The following year, he made the Papal States part of France and put the Pope in prison. France's boundaries now included much of Europe.

Painting of a Napoleonic Officer

The countries in Napoleon's Grand Empire were strongly influenced by France. French citizens, including relatives of Napoleon, took over the government of many conquered areas. The French rulers made the Napoleonic Code law. Thus, Napoleon's conquests helped spread the ideas of the French Revolution throughout Europe.

MAP STUDY

PLACES AND REGIONS Napoleon had power over most of the European continent in 1812. **What bodies of water helped to protect Great Britain from Napoleon's armies?**

Only Great Britain and Russia remained undefeated by Napoleon. Since the French could not defeat the British navy, Napoleon tried to obtain victory in a different way. He forbade the countries in his empire to trade with Great Britain, which he called a "nation of shopkeepers." His order, however, was hard to enforce, and it proved unsuccessful.

Napoleon then decided to take on Russia. He organized a Grand Army of about 600,000 soldiers of different nationalities. It was the largest army the world had yet seen. In the summer of 1812, the Grand Army invaded Russia. Except for one battle, though, the Russians did not fight. Instead, they retreated, drawing the French deeper into Russia. As the Russians retreated, they burned their villages and food supplies, leaving nothing for the advancing French. This tactic is called a **scorched-earth policy.**

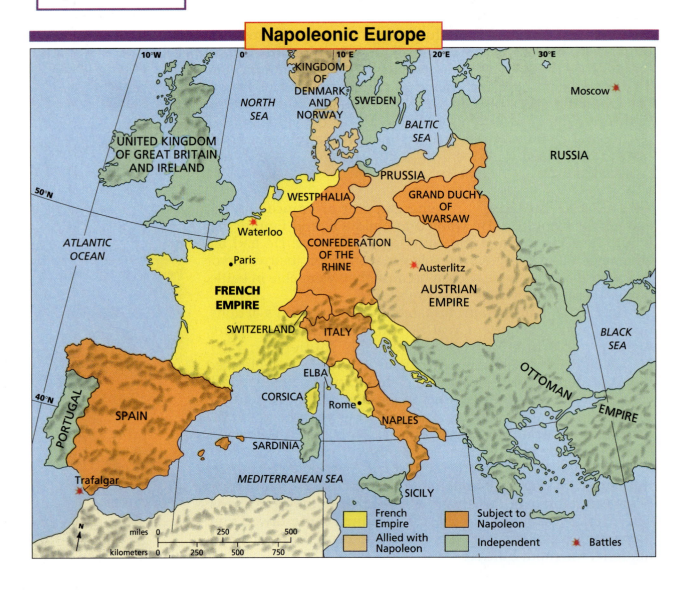

Napoleonic Europe

In September, Napoleon reached Moscow, which had been abandoned by the Russians. Shortly after the French arrived, the city caught fire and three fourths of it was destroyed. The French army now had neither food nor shelter. Napoleon sent several peace proposals to the Russians, which they ignored. He finally gave the order to withdraw. By then the bitter Russian winter had started. Hundreds of thousands of French soldiers froze to death as temperatures fell to 40 degrees below zero. Thousands more died from disease and lack of food. In the end, fewer than 100,000 soldiers made it back to France.

Napoleon quickly raised another army, but the new soldiers were not well trained. They were defeated by the allied forces of Austria, Prussia, Russia, and Great Britain. This was the first time the four countries had joined together to fight Napoleon.

In 1814, the allies took Paris, and Napoleon was forced to **abdicate** (ab' duh kāt), or give up the throne. He was sent into exile to the small island of Elba off the coast of Italy. He managed to escape, however, and gathered together enough troops to invade France. For 100 days, Napoleon again reigned as emperor. The allies, under the British leadership of the Duke of Wellington, finally defeated him in 1815 at the Battle of Waterloo. This time, Napoleon was sent to the island of St. Helena (huh lē' nuh) off the west coast of Africa, where he died in 1821.

Reading Check
How did the Russians use a **scorched-earth policy** to defeat the French?

Reading Check
Where did Napoleon go when he was forced to **abdicate** his throne?

Section 1 Assessment

1. **Define:** plebiscite, scorched-earth policy, abdicate.
2. What was the Grand Empire?
3. Why did Napoleon's invasion of Russia fail?

Critical Thinking

4. **Understanding Cause and Effect**
   How did weaknesses of government under the Directory help pave the way for the rise of Napoleon?

Graphic Organizer Activity

5. Draw this diagram, and use it to summarize Napoleon's accomplishments in the areas of government, education, law, transportation, and the arts.

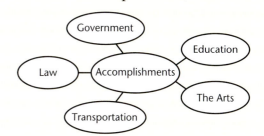

SECTION 2 Revolution and Reform

After Napoleon's defeat, representatives from Austria, Prussia, Russia, and Great Britain met in Vienna (vē en' uh) to decide what to do about France and the rest of Europe. Although the settlement they agreed upon brought peace to Europe for a time, it also set the stage for revolution in many countries and reform in others.

Painting of Metternich

Reading Check
Why did the Congress of Vienna want to achieve a **balance of power?**

The Congress of Vienna

The Congress of Vienna was sometimes called the "Waltzing Congress." This was because the representatives spent much of their time at dinners, dances, and fox hunts. However, decisions were made by a few leaders. They included Prince Klemens von Metternich (met' uhr nik), the Austrian foreign minister; Czar Alexander I of Russia; King Frederick William III of Prussia; and Viscount Castlereagh (vī' kownt kas' uhl rā), the British foreign secretary. Charles-Maurice de Talleyrand (tal' ē ran) decided matters for France.

The leaders did not want to punish France too harshly. At the same time, they wanted to build a peaceful and stable Europe. They believed the best way to do this was by establishing a **balance of power,** or equal strength among countries. They hoped that a balance of power would prevent any single country from starting another war.

To accomplish this, the leaders divided Napoleon's Grand Empire. Russia got Finland and most of Poland. Sweden got Norway. Austria got part of northern Italy. Great Britain got the islands of Malta (mahl' tuh) and Ceylon (sā lahn'), as well as the Dutch Cape Colony in South Africa. Belgium and Holland were made into a single nation. In addition, the 39 German states were combined into a loose confederation headed by Austria.

The leaders of the Congress of Vienna were against democracy. Hoping to crush revolutionary ideas, they brought back divine-right monarchy. They had already put Louis XVIII, younger brother of Louis XVI, on the French throne. Now, they brought back the monarchy in Spain and Portugal. The Pope was again made ruler of the Papal States.

Political Movements

The balance of power in Europe was maintained for a number of years. However, the revolutionary ideas that had been spread by Napoleon's Grand Empire did not die. Several groups were against the Congress System, or the political plan and division of Europe set up by the Congress of Vienna.

Reading Check
What changes did the **liberals** support?

One group was the **liberals.** They wanted political reform based on the ideals of the French Revolution. These included individual freedom, equal rights under the law, and freedom of thought and religion. Most liberals were members of the middle class. They also wanted changes that would improve their own lives. Among these changes were voting rights for landowners and the protection of private property. Some liberals wanted a constitutional monarchy. Others wanted a republic. The liberals were strongest in Great Britain and France.

Reading Check
Why did the **nationalists** oppose the Congress System?

Another group that was against the Congress System was the **nationalists** (nash' uh nuh lists). They wanted political independence for areas where people shared the same language, customs, and history. The Congress of Vienna had paid no

Comparing Historical Maps

A comparison of historical maps can reveal the changes that occur in the political features of an area over time.

Look at the map on page 564. Now, look at the map below. Note that both show about the same area, but at different times. The map on page 564 shows Europe's political divisions during Napoleon's rule. The map below shows Europe after the Congress of Vienna.

To compare historical maps, first look at both maps to make sure the same region is being illustrated. Then, study the boundaries and note any changes. Study also the names of the countries to see if they have changed.

For example, note that the Grand Duchy of Warsaw was subject to Napoleon. After the Congress of Vienna, however, both its boundaries and its name changed.

Compare both maps and answer the following questions.

Map Practice

1. **How was the French Empire divided after the Congress of Vienna?**
2. **What countries were not directly affected by either Napoleon's rule or the Congress of Vienna?**

Europe After the Congress of Vienna

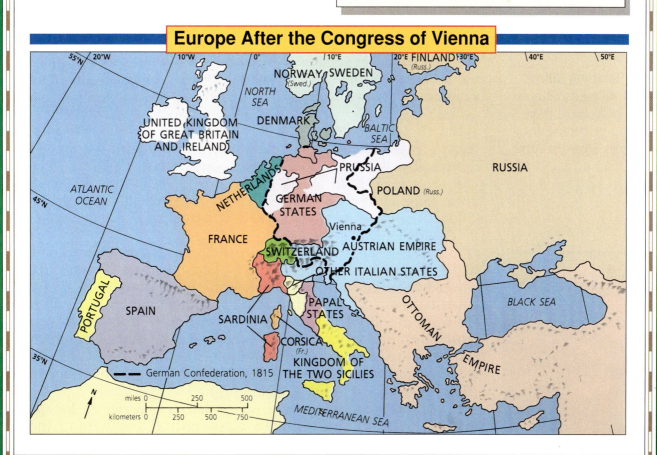

attention to nationalist feelings when it divided the Grand Empire. For example, the Belgians did not want to be part of Holland. The northern Italians did not want to be ruled by Austria.

A third group that was against the Congress System was the **socialists.** They wanted to end private ownership of land and factories. They believed the state, or the people as a whole, should own all means of production. In this way, the socialists believed, everyone would be treated fairly and the workers' lives would improve.

Some socialists tried to set up ideal communities based on economic cooperation. They thought these communities would show that theirs was a better way of life. Such socialists were known as **utopian socialists** (yū tō′ pē uhn sō′shuh lists).

Other socialists believed the only way to bring about reform was by revolution. One such socialist was Karl Marx, a German. He believed the **proletariat** (prō luh tār′ ē uht), or industrial working class, would rise up and take power. "The workers have nothing to lose . . . but their chains," he wrote in his book *The Communist Manifesto* (kahm′ yū nist man uh fes′ tō). "They have a world to gain. Workers of the world, unite!"

Marx believed that after the workers' revolution, there would be no hunger or poverty. Everyone would become equal. Governments would not even be needed. People would work because they wanted to give something to society. In return, they would be able to develop their own interests and talents. Marx called his kind of socialism **communism** (kahm′ yu‾ niz uhm). He believed the workers' revolution would be led by his new Communist party.

An Era of Revolution

Beginning in 1820, liberals, nationalists, and socialists led revolutions against the Congress System. The earliest of these took place in Spain, Portugal, Italy, and Russia. They all failed. However, Greek nationalists were given hope by these attempts. In 1821, they rebelled against the Ottoman Empire. After eight years of fighting, Greece gained its independence.

In 1830, there was another revolution in France. After Louis XVIII died, his brother Charles X had taken the throne. He wanted to bring back the Old Regime. Just a few weeks after being crowned, Charles did away with the National Assembly. He took the right to vote away from the middle class and returned control of the schools to the Roman Catholic Church. In response to Charles's actions, middle-class liberals, helped by students and unemployed workers, overthrew the government. After three days of fighting, Charles X fled.

The July Revolution, as it was called, was a victory for the middle class. Members of this class, unlike members of the working class, wanted a constitutional monarchy rather than a

Reading Check How did the **socialists** feel about private property?

Reading Check Who were the **utopian socialists?** What did Karl Marx expect the **proletariat** to do?

Reading Check What did Marx believe would happen to government under **communism?**

Karl Marx

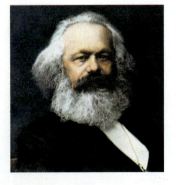

Linking Across Time

Universal Suffrage   English author and teacher Mary Wollstonecraft (left) believed all people should vote, regardless of gender. In 1792, she published a widely read book defending the rights of women. Her book helped spark the start of the woman's suffrage movement, which eventually made it possible for Margaret Thatcher (right) to become Great Britain's first female Prime Minister. She held the office from 1979 to 1990. **What reforms helped increase suffrage in Great Britain in the 1830s?**

republic. So, they gave the throne to Charles X's cousin, Louis-Philippe (lū′ ē fi lēp′). Under Louis-Philippe's rule, the number of people who could vote increased. However, of the middle class, only its richest members could vote. This angered other members of the middle class. Working-class people were also angry. They had wanted not only a republic but also **universal male suffrage** (suhf′ rij), or the right of all adult males to vote.

News of the July Revolution touched off rebellions in other countries. In 1831, Belgian nationalists won independence from Holland. The Poles fought against Russia but were defeated. Uprisings in several German and Italian states also were put down and ended quickly.

In Great Britain, however, liberal reforms were made by gradual change instead of revolution. In 1832, the British government passed a law that lowered the amount of land a man had to own in order to vote. This increased by one half the number of voters. It also gave the new industrial towns more representation in Parliament. As a result, the British middle class had more say in the government.

Reforms also helped the working class. Labor unions gained the right to **strike,** or stop work, in order to obtain shorter hours,

> ✓ **Reading Check**
> What group fought for **universal male suffrage** in France?

> ✓ **Reading Check**
> Why did workers want the right to **strike?**

higher wages, and better working conditions. By 1890, working-class males also obtained the right to vote.

The Revolutions of 1848

In 1848, another series of revolutions broke out. All over Europe, governments were overthrown. Once again, the rebellion started in France.

Louis-Philippe had tried to be a "citizen-king." He walked through the streets of Paris without any servants to show that he was a bourgeois rather than an aristocrat. He wore a frock coat and trousers like the men of the middle class. He was very rich himself, however, and his government served only the rich. Industrial workers and middle-class liberals became increasingly unhappy. At the same time, the economy was bad throughout Europe, including France. Many people did not have jobs. Then, in 1845 and 1846, the potato and wheat crops failed. There was not enough food to feed everyone.

In February of 1848, riots broke out in the streets of Paris. Louis-Philippe fled, and the revolutionary leaders declared the Second French Republic. They set up a temporary government to rule until a new National Assembly could be elected. Louis Blanc (lū ē blahnk), a socialist, was one of the leaders. He persuaded the other leaders to set up **national workshops**, or factories run by the workers but paid for by the government. The national workshops provided jobs for thousands of people. However, the number of people out of work grew faster than jobs could be created. Before long, the French government was supporting over 100,000 people.

When the new National Assembly was finally elected in April, it did away with the workshops. The workers revolted, fighting violently for three days. They were defeated by the army, but not before over 10,000 people were killed.

The National Assembly then drew up a constitution. It called for a strong president to be elected by universal male suffrage. Napoleon's nephew, Louis-Napoleon Bonaparte, was elected president of the Second French Republic. He believed, however, that he had inherited his uncle's destiny. So, in 1851 he did away with the constitution. A year later, the people voted him Emperor Napoleon III. At the same time, the Second French Republic was renamed the Second French Empire. Louis-Napoleon remained on the throne until 1870.

The revolution in France was followed by revolutions in other parts of Europe. The Hungarians (hung ger' ē uhns), the Italians, and the Germans all rebelled. Their revolts failed. Even so, the revolutions of 1848 led to some important changes. In time, universal male suffrage spread to most northern and western European countries. Workers, who felt they had been cheated, began to form political parties. Soon, there was a socialist party in almost every European country.

Reading Check
What was the purpose of the **national workshops,** and why did they fail?

Painting of Louis-Napoleon

Predicting Consequences

Did you ever wish you could see into the future? Predicting future events is very difficult. You can, however, develop skills that will help you identify the logical consequences of decisions or actions.

Learning the Skill Follow these steps to help you accurately predict consequences.

- Review what you already know about a situation by listing facts, events, and people's responses. The list will help you recall events and how they affected people.

- Analyze patterns. Try to determine what the patterns show.

- Use your knowledge and observations of similar situations. In other words, ask yourself, "What were the consequences of a similar decision or action that occurred in the past?"

- Analyze each of the potential consequences by asking, "How likely is it that this will occur?"

- Make a prediction.

Louis-Philippe fled France in 1848

GO TO Glencoe's **Skillbuilder Interactive Workbook CD-ROM, Level 1,** provides instruction and practice in key social studies skills.

Skill Practice

Historians often make predictions about the future based on patterns from the past. Imagine you are a historian at the start of 1849. Use the information in the chart below to make predictions about what lies ahead for the 1850s and 1860s.

Events of the Early 1800s	Results and Reactions
Napoleon is defeated at the Battle of Waterloo.	The Congress of Vienna seeks to restore divine-right monarchy to Europe.
The July Revolution of 1830 returns constitutional monarchy to France.	Rebellions erupt in other European nations.
Worker riots in France lead to revolution and the Second French Republic.	The revolution in France is followed by revolutions in other parts of Europe.
The revolutions of 1848 fail to overturn the Congress System.	?

The following questions will serve as a guide.

1. Review the information on the chart. What patterns do you notice? What do the facts tell you about political affairs in Europe during the early 1800s?

2. Suppose one of the leaders who took part in the Congress of Vienna asked you to predict what to expect in the mid-1800s. What would you say? Was the Congress System safe from future threats? Explain.

Section 2 Assessment

1. **Define:** balance of power, liberals, nationalists, socialists, utopian socialists, proletariat, communism, universal male suffrage, strike, national workshops.
2. What were two goals of the Congress of Vienna?
3. What were some of the results of the revolutions of 1848?

Critical Thinking

4. **Making Comparisons** Which one of the three groups—liberals, nationalists, or socialists—would you have supported in the 1800s? Why?

Graphic Organizer Activity

5. Draw this diagram, and use it to show predictions made by Karl Marx.

Marx's Predictions

SECTION 3 Growth of Nationalism

After the revolutions of 1848 failed, the Congress System seemed stronger than ever. However, this was not the case. Before long, the growth of nationalism would destroy the balance of power that had been established at Vienna. Three countries that were affected by the growth of nationalism were Italy, Germany, and Austria.

Italy   In 1848, eight of the nine Italian states were under Austrian control. Only Sardinia (sahr din′ ē uh) was independent. Ever since Napoleon's time, the Italians had been unhappy about this state of affairs. They remembered that Rome had once ruled the ancient world and that Italian city-states had led the Renaissance. They wanted to become a unified nation.

Many nationalists in Italy looked to Sardinia to take the lead. This was because of Sardinia's prime minister, Count Camillo di Cavour (kont kuh mē′ lō dē kuh vuhr′). Cavour believed in industrialization and favored a constitutional monarchy. He also realized that Sardinia needed help to drive the Austrians out of Italy. To this end, he made an agreement with Napoleon III. It stated that if the Austrians attacked Sardinia, the French would help the Sardinians. When Austria declared war on Sardinia in 1859, Napoleon III kept his word. Austria was defeated, and the Italian state of Lombardy (lahm′ bahr dē) was united with Sardinia. By 1860, the other northern Italian states also revolted against Austria and united with Sardinia.

That same year, an Italian nationalist named Giuseppe Garibaldi (jū zep′ ā gār uh bahl′ dē) led another revolution in

Charcoal and Freedom *Carbonari,* which means "charcoal burners" in Italian, was the name of one of the first secret societies formed to overthrow foreign rule in Italy. Charcoal is black, but it glows brightly when burning. Italian rebels associated the glow with the light of freedom and liberty.

GIUSEPPE GARIBALDI   Giuseppe Garibaldi led the fight for Italian unification in southern Italy. He was skilled in guerrilla warfare, having fought in other revolutionary wars. In this painting, Garibaldi leads his Red Shirts in an attack on troops from Naples. **Who became king of the united Italy?**

southern Italy. Garibaldi had spent much of his life in exile in Brazil and Uruguay (yūr' uh gwī). There, he had learned how to lead small bands of soldiers behind enemy lines. The bands would hide in forests and on hillsides. They would make surprise attacks on the enemy and then go back into hiding. This kind of fighting is called **guerrilla warfare** (guh ril' uh wōr fär). In guerrilla warfare, a small group of soldiers can often defeat a much larger army.

Garibaldi taught guerrilla warfare to his followers. They were called "Red Shirts" because they, like their leader, wore red shirts. They also wore loose grey trousers, silk handkerchiefs around their necks, grey cloaks, and black felt hats. In 1860, Garibaldi's Red Shirts conquered Sicily within three months. Then, they sailed to the Italian mainland and conquered the state of Naples.

In 1861, the northern and southern nationalist groups combined. The Kingdom of Italy was formed as a constitutional monarchy. Victor Emmanuel II (ē man' yū el) of Sardinia became king. The Pope, who wanted to keep control over the Papal

Reading Check
Why might rebels such as the "Red Shirts" engage in **guerrilla warfare?**

Germany Bismarck fought three wars to unify Germany, but another war—World War II— left Germany divided for 45 years. In 1990, West Germany and East Germany were reunited as one country.

Reading Check
What was a **junker?**

States, fought against Italian unity and lost. In 1870, the Papal States became part of Italy, and Italian unification was complete. The balance of power in Europe, however, was weakened.

Germany

Nationalist feelings were also strong in the 39 German states. German poets and writers, like Johann Wolfgang von Goethe (ger' tuh) and Friedrich von Schiller (shil' uhr), wrote about German nationalism. German composer Richard Wagner (vahg' nuhr) wrote operas based on German folk tales. In 1834, many of the German states signed a trade agreement. In it, they promised not to tax goods coming from other German states. Soon, the economy of these states improved. However, many of the rulers of the smaller states were not willing to give up their political power. Austria was also against any attempt to unify Germany.

These obstacles were overcome by the Kingdom of Prussia. In 1862, King William I named Count Otto von Bismarck (biz' mahrk) prime minister of Prussia. Bismarck was a **junker** (yung' kuhr), or rich landowner, who believed in divine-right monarchy. He said that he would unite Germany, not "by speeches and majority votes—but by blood and iron." He also believed that war against a common enemy would bring the German states closer together.

In 1864, Bismarck joined with Austria to defeat Denmark and to gain territory. Two years later, he used a dispute over this territory as an excuse to go to war against Austria. Prussia won the war in seven weeks. It had superior weapons, as well as an excellent railroad system that moved troops quickly from one battlefield to another. The resulting peace treaty ended the loose German Confederation. The North German Confederation, led by Prussia, was set up in its place.

In 1870, Bismarck found an excuse to go to war against France, Germany's oldest enemy. As Bismarck had hoped, the southern German states joined the northern German states in the struggle. Well-trained and well-equipped, the German army easily defeated the French army. Bismarck then laid siege to Paris. The city held out for four months. Food became so scarce that the people were forced to eat the animals in the zoo. The trees that Napoleon III had planted along the streets of Paris were cut down and used for fuel. At last, on January 28, 1871, the city surrendered.

Meanwhile, at Versailles (vuhr sī'), William I of Prussia was named **kaiser** (kī' zuhr), or emperor, of the new German Empire. This included both the northern and the southern German states, as well as the rich mining and manufacturing lands of Alsace (al' sas) and Lorraine (luh rān'), which had been won from France. A unified Germany, however, meant a further weakening of the balance of power.

Reading Check
Who was the **kaiser** of the new German Empire?

THE GERMAN EMPIRE   The struggle for a united Germany was led by Count Otto von Bismarck, prime minister of Prussia. In this painting, Bismarck (center) proclaims King William I of Prussia (on platform) the emperor of a new German empire. **What effect did a unified Germany have on Europe?**

Austria   Nationalists in Italy and Germany wanted to unify their nations. Nationalists in Austria, on the other hand, threatened the unity of the Austrian Empire.

The Austrian Empire was made up of many nationalities. Although its emperor, Francis Joseph, was German, four out of five people were not. Other nationalities included the Czechs, the Slovaks, the Poles, the Croats, the Slovenes, and the Magyars (mag' yahrs), the largest group in Hungary. Each had its own language and history and wanted self-rule.

By 1866, Austria had been defeated by both Sardinia and Prussia. Magyar nationalists saw their chance to become independent. They revolted. In 1867, a weakened Austria agreed to create a dual monarchy. Now, the emperor ruled over two separate kingdoms—Austria and Hungary. Each had its own official language, parliament, and laws. Although they were separate politically, the two countries needed each other economically. Austria supplied manufactured goods to Hungary. In return, Hungary supplied Austria with food products.

The Magyars were satisfied with the situation of having separate countries, but other nationalities in Austria-Hungary were not. Their unhappiness presented a continuing threat to the dual monarchy and the peace of Europe.

Section 3 Assessment

1. **Define:** guerrilla warfare, junker, kaiser.
2. What did Garibaldi do to further nationalism in Italy?
3. How was Austria-Hungary formed? How did most of its citizens feel about this?

Critical Thinking

4. **Drawing Conclusions** Why do you think the Italian city-states wanted to be a unified nation? Explain.

Graphic Organizer Activity

5. Draw this diagram, and use it to describe the importance of these dates in the drive for German unification: 1834, 1862, 1864, 1870.

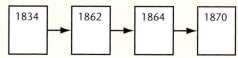

| 1834 | → | 1862 | → | 1864 | → | 1870 |

Chapter Summary & Study Guide

1. In 1804, Napoleon became emperor of France. He then set out to conquer the rest of Europe—a plan that nearly succeeded.
2. Although Napoleon created a strong central government and a new code of laws, the people of France still lost certain rights.
3. After Napoleon's defeat, the Congress of Vienna tried to establish a balance of power in Europe and to restore divine-right monarchy.
4. Liberals, nationalists, and socialists opposed the Congress System.
5. A series of revolutions broke out in many European countries in 1820, 1830, and 1848.
6. Liberal reforms were made in Great Britain without a revolution.
7. The revolutions of 1848 failed to overthrow the Congress System, but they still had lasting results, including the spread of universal male suffrage and the rise of socialism among workers.
8. The rise of nationalism led to the unification of Italy between 1859 and 1870 and the unification of Germany between 1862 and 1871.
9. In the Austrian Empire, nationalism led to the Empire's division into two separate kingdoms—Austria and Hungary—each of which had many different national groups that wanted independence.

HISTORY Online

Self-Check Quiz

Visit the *Human Heritage* Web site at **humanheritage.glencoe.com** and click on **Chapter 35—Self-Check Quiz** to assess your understanding of this chapter.

Using Key Terms

Imagine you are a writer in Europe in the 1800s. You have been asked to prepare a brief introduction to a revolutionary handbook—a book telling people how to bring about change or to resist unfair governments. Use the following words in your introduction.

plebiscite	scorched-earth policy
abdicate	balance of power
liberals	proletariat
communism	strike
guerrilla warfare	kaiser

Understanding Main Ideas

1. Why did the representatives at the Congress of Vienna try to bring back divine-right monarchy?
2. Why did the temporary French government of 1848 set up national workshops?
3. How did Napoleon III help Italian nationalists?
4. How did the German states become unified?
5. What were some of the results of the war between Prussia and France?
6. Why were national groups in Austria-Hungary unhappy in the 1860s?

Critical Thinking

1. What did Napolean reveal about himself at his crowning as emperor?
2. Do you think Napoleon's conquests were good or bad for Europe? Explain your answer.
3. How important was nationalism in Europe during the second half of the 1800s? Explain.

4. "Liberal reforms can only be made with a revolution." Do you agree or disagree with this statement? Explain.

Graphic Organizer Activity

History Create a diagram like the one shown, and use it to give details that support the following generalization: The Congress of Vienna failed in its goal to return Europe to the old order.

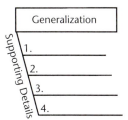

Generalization

Supporting Details
1.
2.
3.
4.

Geography in History

The World in Spatial Terms Refer to the map on page 564. During Napoleon's time, as during other historical eras, Paris was an important city. What is the latitude of Paris? What is the longitude? Describe its relative location.

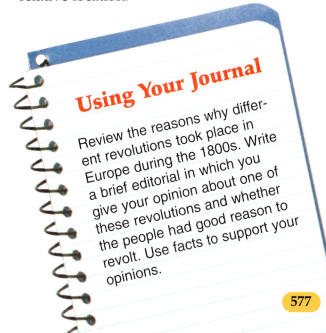

Using Your Journal

Review the reasons why different revolutions took place in Europe during the 1800s. Write a brief editorial in which you give your opinion about one of these revolutions and whether the people had good reason to revolt. Use facts to support your opinions.

Rise of Imperialism
1840 A.D.–1916 A.D.

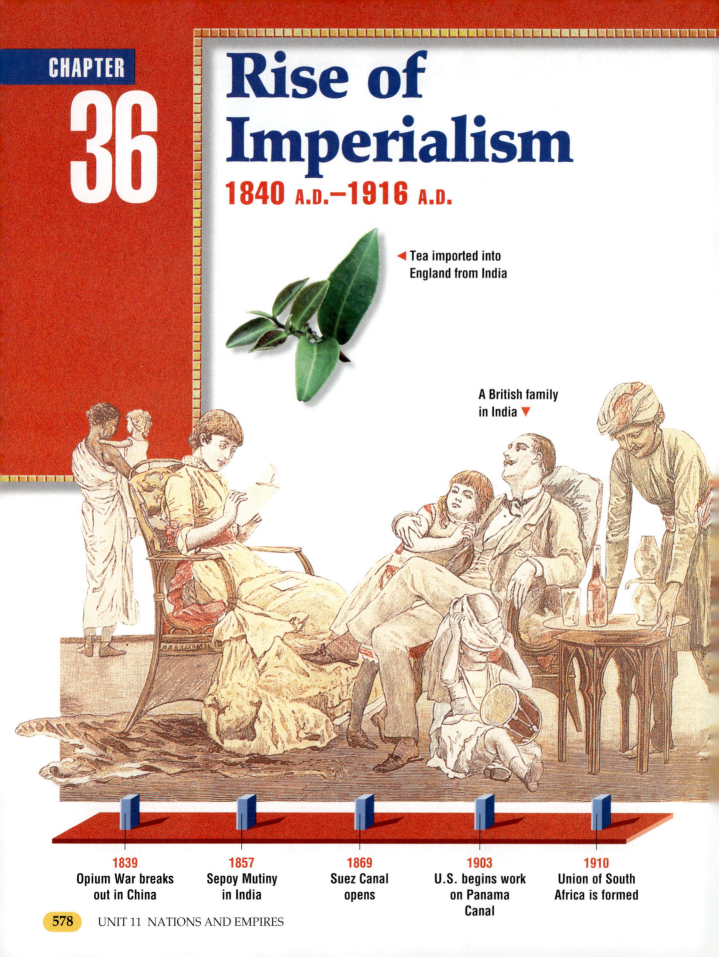

◀ Tea imported into England from India

A British family in India ▼

1839
Opium War breaks out in China

1857
Sepoy Mutiny in India

1869
Suez Canal opens

1903
U.S. begins work on Panama Canal

1910
Union of South Africa is formed

Chapter Focus

Chapter Overview

Visit the *Human Heritage* Web site at **humanheritage.glencoe.com** and click on ***Chapter 36—Chapter Overviews*** to preview this chapter.

📖 Read to Discover

- What caused the move toward imperialism.
- How Great Britain and other European powers established colonies in Africa.
- How Asian countries were affected by imperialism.
- Why the United States became involved in Latin America.
- What the effects of imperialism were.

 Terms to Learn

imperialism
protectorate

 People to Know

Leopold II
Cecil Rhodes
Matthew Perry

 Places to Locate

Suez Canal
Indochina
Panama Canal

Why It's Important   In the late 1800s, an interest in colonies rose again. Many countries rushed to take over parts of the world that had not been claimed during the Age of Discovery and the expansion of the Americas. New colonial powers were added. Among these new powers were Belgium, Germany, Italy, Japan, and the United States. Those countries in Africa, Asia, and Latin America who were colonized had little say in how their nations developed.

SECTION 1 Growth of Imperialism

There were many reasons for the rise of **imperialism** (im pir´ ē uh liz uhm), or the policy of setting up colonies and building empires. One was the Industrial Revolution. Factories in the industrialized countries needed such raw materials as rubber, cotton, oil, tin, and copper. There was also a growing demand for tea, sugar, and cocoa. Both raw materials and food products could be found in areas that were not industrially developed, such as Africa, Asia, and Latin America.

Then, too, industries needed new markets for their products. Factories were turning out more goods than people at home could afford to buy. Many leaders believed new markets could be found in areas that were not industrially developed.

Also, many factory owners had grown rich during the Industrial Revolution. They could not find enough places in their

Reading Check
What was **imperialism**?

Cocoa Pods

own countries in which to invest. Even when they did invest, they thought the profits were too small. Investments in undeveloped areas, however, generally brought large profits.

Another reason for imperialism was nationalism. Many people thought colonies would add to their country's power. The newly formed countries of Italy and Germany wanted to catch up with Great Britain, France, and other established colonial powers. Japan and the United States wanted to become as important as the colonial powers of western Europe.

Still another reason for imperialism was the belief that western countries had a duty to "civilize" the "backward" peoples of the world. To many westerners, any people whose way of life and religion were different from their own were "backward." These westerners believed they had a mission to spread Christianity and the Industrial Revolution everywhere. The British author Rudyard Kipling (ruhd' yuhrd kip' lēng) called this mission "the white man's burden."

Section 1 Assessment

1. **Define:** imperialism.
2. How did the Industrial Revolution lead to imperialism?
3. How did nationalism lead to imperialism?

Critical Thinking

4. **Demonstrating Reasoned Judgment** If you had lived during the late 1800s, would you have supported or opposed imperialism? Why?

Graphic Organizer Activity

5. Draw this diagram, and use it to show characteristics of imperialist nations.

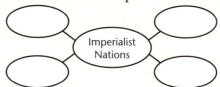

SECTION 2   Africa

Before 1870, European powers had few holdings in Africa. Those they did have were mostly seaports and trading stations along the coast. The only major exceptions were the Cape Colony at Africa's southern tip and Algeria in northern Africa. Great Britain had received the Cape Colony from the Dutch at the Congress of Vienna. Algeria was held by France. Before long, however, most of Africa belonged to European powers.

The Opening of Africa   At first, most Europeans stayed along the African coast because they were safer there from tropical diseases and other dangers. Little was known about Africa's interior. Then, missionaries and explorers opened up these areas.

In 1840, a Scottish medical missionary named David Livingstone (liv' ing stuhn) went to Africa to convert the people to Christianity. During his years in Africa, Dr. Livingstone worked hard to end the Arab trade of enslaved Africans and explored much of the continent's interior. He wrote about his journeys in letters that appeared in newspapers in Great Britain and the United States. These letters aroused a great deal of interest in Africa.

Suddenly, the letters stopped. A New York newspaper decided to find out what had happened to Dr. Livingstone. It assigned reporter Henry Stanley to the story. After two years of searching, Stanley found Dr. Livingstone in a small Arab village on the shores of Lake Tanganyika (tan guhn yē' kuh). Stanley then became an explorer himself. Between 1874 and 1889, he explored the Congo and wrote about his adventures.

In 1879, Stanley was hired by King Leopold II of Belgium to obtain African lands for him. Stanley signed many treaties with African chiefs in the Congo Basin. Most of the chiefs could not

STANLEY AND LIVINGSTONE   This painting shows Henry Stanley (center left) who found David Livingstone (center right) living in the tiny village of Ujiji on Lake Tanganyika. Stanley greeted him with the now famous words, "Dr. Livingstone, I presume?" **Why had Dr. Livingstone gone to Africa?**

✔️ **Reading Check**
Why did Great Britain make Egypt a British **protectorate**?

Charles G. Gordon, Military Governor of the Sudan

read or write English and did not realize what they were signing away. In return for their lands, many of which were rich in minerals and rubber, the chiefs received cloth, beads, and sometimes guns. The signing of such treaties became a common way of gaining colonial territory.

Leopold II wanted to make a lot of money as quickly as possible. He had his soldiers force the Africans to collect rubber for him. Anyone who resisted was shot. However, missionaries and other Europeans protested so much that the king finally turned the Congo over to the Belgian government. The government did away with forced labor.

In northern Africa, the Suez (sū ez') Canal was opened in 1869. Built by Egyptian workers and paid for with French funds, it connected the Mediterranean and Red seas. The Suez Canal made possible a shorter all-water route to India and the Far East. In 1875, however, the Egyptian ruler needed money. So, he sold his shares in the canal to Great Britain. Great Britain and France then took over Egypt's finances. This made many Egyptians angry. When they rebelled in 1882, British troops moved in. Egypt became a British **protectorate** (pruh tek' tuhr it), or a country under the control and protection of a larger, stronger nation.

From the Cape to Cairo   Soon after Great Britain made Egypt a protectorate, the British began moving south. After several years of fighting, they conquered the Sudan. There, Great Britain set up a joint government with Egypt.

At the same time, the British began moving north from the Cape Colony. The Boers, or Dutch farmers in South Africa, did not like British rule. They did not want to speak English, and they disagreed with Great Britain's doing away with enslavement. In 1836, many Boers decided to leave the Cape Colony. They traveled northward and finally settled in the grasslands of the interior. There, they set up two independent states, the Transvaal (trans vahl') and the Orange Free State.

In the late 1800s, gold and diamonds were discovered in the Boer states. Thousands of adventurers began pouring into the area. The Boers were soon outnumbered. Afraid of losing control of their government, the Boers would not allow the newcomers, who were mostly British, to vote. However, the newcomers had to pay heavy taxes.

This angered Cecil Rhodes (rōdz), the prime minister of the Cape Colony. Rhodes had a dream of an English-speaking empire that would stretch from the Cape to Cairo (kī rō), the capital of Egypt. The British already controlled land to the south and west of the Boer states. So, Rhodes built a railway line into land to the north of the Boer states. As soon as the railroad was completed, British settlers began moving into this area, which was called Rhodesia (rō dē' zhuh).

Linking Across Time

South Africa The labor of black South Africans, such as these 1906 diamond miners (left), helped make South Africa rich. Even so, they lost their rights to the Afrikaners, a white minority who dominated government. The Afrikaners held on to power until 1994, when South Africa held its first all-race election (right) and selected Nelson Mandela as president. **How did South Africa come under British control?**

At this point, Germany, jealous of Great Britain's growing power, offered the Boers its best artillery. The Boers promptly attacked British outposts, and the Boer War began. At first the Boers defeated the British. Then, the British captured the Boer capital. The Boers, however, refused to surrender and carried on guerrilla warfare for more than two years. Finally, the British destroyed Boer farms and imprisoned Boer women and children. When that happened, the Boers gave up. In 1910, the Transvaal and the Orange Free State were joined with the Cape Colony and one other British colony to form the Union of South Africa.

The British gained other African possessions besides Egypt, the Sudan, Rhodesia, and the Union of South Africa. Between 1890 and 1914, Zanzibar (zan' zuh bahr), Uganda (yū gan' duh), British East Africa, and Nigeria all came under British control. Except for one German colony, Cecil Rhodes's plan of an English-speaking empire in Africa came true.

Painting of King Menelik II

Other European Empires Leopold's actions in the Congo and the British takeover of Egypt spurred other European powers into action. Over the next few years, they divided the African continent among themselves.

Spain and Portugal kept their original possessions. Angola (an gō′ luh), founded in 1648 by the Portuguese, was the oldest colony in Africa. In 1885, Portugal also made Portuguese East Africa, or Mozambique, a protectorate.

The French moved out from Algeria to establish the largest European empire in Africa. This empire included Tunisia, Morocco, French West Africa, French Equatorial Africa, and Madagascar (mad uh gas′ kuhr).

The Italians conquered Eritrea (er uh trē′ uh), an area on the east coast, and took over part of Somaliland (sō mahl′ ē land). However, when they tried to take Ethiopia in 1896, they were defeated by the troops of King Menelik II. In 1911, the Italians acquired two Turkish provinces from the Ottomans. The Italians combined the two and renamed the area Libya. The Germans set up protectorates over Togoland and the Cameroons (kam uh rūnz′) in 1884. They later added German Southwest Africa and German East Africa.

By 1914, only two areas in Africa remained independent. One was Ethiopia. The other was Liberia (lī bir′ ē uh), which had been founded in the 1830s by former enslaved African Americans from the United States.

Section 2 Assessment

1. **Define:** protectorate.
2. Why did many Boers leave the Cape Colony?
3. What plan did Cecil Rhodes have for Africa? How successful was he in helping Great Britain achieve this plan?

Critical Thinking

4. **Making Inferences** Why do you think the Suez Canal was so valuable to Egypt?

Graphic Organizer Activity

5. Draw this diagram, and use it to show the causes and effects of what is known as the Boer War.

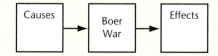

SECTION 3 Asia

The British and the Dutch started trading with Asia in the 1600s. However, Chinese and Japanese rulers allowed only limited contact with the West. So, western European countries turned their attention to India.

India   By the middle 1700s, the Mogul Empire of India was breaking up. This allowed Great Britain and France to set up trading stations along the Indian coast. Then, in 1763, France lost the Seven Years' War, also known in the Americas as the French and Indian War. As a result, the French left India, and the British East India Company took over.

The British East India Company stayed in power for almost 100 years. During that time, it brought many changes to India.

Not everyone was happy with British rule, however. Many Indians felt the British were trying to change their culture. In 1857, the **sepoys** (sē′ pois), or Indian soldiers in the British army, mutinied. The immediate cause was a new rifle. Its cartridges were greased, and one end had to be bitten off before loading. The Hindus thought the grease was beef fat. The Muslims thought it was pork fat. Hindus are not allowed by their religion to eat beef, while Muslims are not allowed to eat pork.

Although the Sepoy Mutiny failed, the British government realized that changes were needed. It took control of India away from the British East India Company and gave it to the Crown.

Great Britain wanted to protect its Indian empire from other countries, especially Russia. From 1865 to 1884, most of the central Asian centers of Muslim civilization fell to Russia. To guard India's northwest frontier, the British made Afghanistan (af gan′ uh stan) a protectorate. In Persia, both Great Britain and Russia set up **spheres of influence,** or areas within a country in which another country has special rights.

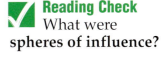
Reading Check
Who were the **sepoys,** and why did they mutiny?

Reading Check
What were **spheres of influence?**

THE BRITISH IN INDIA   British settlers in India kept many Indian servants. In this painting, Indians unload a newly arrived British family and their luggage. **How did Great Britain try to protect its Indian Empire from Russia?**

China From the early 1500s, all trade between China and the West was limited to the city of Guangzhou (gwong jō′). The Chinese looked upon westerners as barbarians.

The Chinese people were divided into two classes. The upper class were mostly government officials, scholars, and landowners. They knew how to read and write, and looked down upon people who worked with their hands. The lower class were usually farmers and artisans who did not know how to read and write.

Both classes, however, had certain things in common. They followed the teachings of Confucius and believed that the family was most important. Marriages were arranged to benefit families. When a son married, he and his wife lived with his parents. The Chinese greatly respected their ancestors. On New Year's Day they would burn incense and place an offering of food on the family altar. Then they would tell the ancestors what had happened to the family in the past year.

The Chinese followed their way of life until the 1800s. Then came the Industrial Revolution. Western factory owners and merchants became interested in increasing overseas trade. They were no longer satisfied with the amount of business the Chinese allowed them.

CHINESE SOCIETY Here an upper-class Chinese family is shown receiving gifts for a wedding. **Where will the new husband and wife probably live?**

OPIUM WAR   The British and Chinese battled over the selling of opium in China. **From what natural source does opium come?**

About this time, British traders discovered that they could make large profits selling *opium* (ō pē uhm), or a drug made from the dried juice of certain poppies, to the Chinese. The traders took cotton cloth made in Great Britain to India, where they traded it for opium. They then took the opium to China, where it was exchanged for tea and silk to be shipped to Great Britain.

At first, the Chinese government paid little attention to the opium trade. When it saw how much damage the drug was doing, the government declared the trade illegal. When a government official in Guangzhou seized and publicly burned a large shipment of opium, British traders became angry. In 1839, what became known as the Opium War broke out between the British and the Chinese.

Although they greatly outnumbered the British, the Chinese had neither cannon nor steam-driven warships. In 1842, they were defeated and forced to sign a treaty that opened more ports and gave Great Britain the island of Hong Kong. The treaty also gave British citizens in China the **right of extraterritoriality** (rīt of ek struh ter uh tōr ē al' uh tē). This meant that British citizens accused of breaking Chinese laws could be tried only in British courts.

✓ Reading Check
How did the **right of extra-territoriality** weaken the power of the Chinese government?

China lost even more power in the late 1800s. In 1894, Japan and China went to war over Korea. The Japanese won easily and took Chinese territory. Great Britain, France, Germany, and Russia rushed to get *concessions* (kuhn sesh' uhns), or special rights, from the Chinese government. These included the rights to develop mineral resources and build railroads and naval bases. Several countries also got leases on Chinese port cities.

The United States did not want China divided up by foreign powers or kept from trading with American merchants. In 1899, the American government asked countries to approve the Open Door policy. This gave everyone equal trading rights in China.

The Open Door Policy did not please the Chinese because it meant that foreign powers were still trying to control them. So, the Chinese began a movement to drive all foreigners from their country. The movement was called the Boxer Rebellion because it had been started by a Chinese secret society called Boxers. In the spring of 1900, the Boxers began attacking foreigners, including

THE BOXER REBELLION   The Boxers were a secret society dedicated to removing all foreign influences from China. British, French, Russian, American, German, and Japanese troops were sent to put down the revolt. In this painting foreign troops attack the rebels in Beijing. **What was the outcome of the Boxer Rebellion?**

the diplomats in Beijing (bā jing'), the capital of China. The foreign powers joined forces and sent an army to China. In 1901, the rebellion was put down. China had to pay heavy penalties, and foreign powers gained almost total control of the country.

Japan   Like China, Japan allowed only limited trade with the West at first. The Japanese government even refused to provide shelter to shipwrecked sailors. In the middle 1800s, however, this changed.

In 1853, the American government sent a naval force under Commodore Matthew Perry to Japan. Perry was able to negotiate a treaty to open up trade and to protect shipwrecked American sailors. Soon after, Japan signed similar treaties with Great Britain, France, Russia, and the Netherlands.

The military strength and industrial accomplishments of the West impressed most Japanese leaders. They felt that in order to survive, Japan must modernize. To this end, in 1868, several Japanese lords overthrew the shogun and restored the power of the emperor. The new emperor moved the capital of Japan from Kyoto (kyō' tō) to Tokyo. He called his rule Meiji (mā' jē), which means "enlightened peace." The changes that came about during this time are known as the Meiji Restoration.

The new government did away with feudalism. Common people were now allowed to take a family name. They also could live and work where they wished. The government ordered all Japanese males to cut off the topknots worn in their hair. Western-style clothing and a new calendar were introduced.

The Meiji government took away the special position of the samurai. Instead, all Japanese men were expected to serve for a certain amount of time in the armed forces. The government also set up a modern army and navy.

In 1889, Japanese leaders wrote Japan's first constitution. Public schools were opened, and education was required for all. Japanese leaders also began a push to industrialize. To help reach this goal, they gave certain privileges and protection to the *zaibatsu* (zī' bah tsū'), or the rich and powerful families who controlled many industries.

By the end of the 1800s, Japan was fully industrialized. However, Japan needed raw materials and markets for its manufactured goods. In addition, because of modern sanitation and medicine, its population was growing rapidly. Japan did not have enough fertile land to grow food for all its people.

To help find answers to these problems, the Japanese began a program of imperialism. Japan gained control of the island of Formosa (for mō' suh), or present-day Taiwan (tī wahn'), and part of Manchuria (man chūr' ē uh) after a war with China. Ten years later, Japan went to war with Russia and got control of the

Painting of Matthew Perry

✔ **Reading Check**
Why did Japanese leaders feel they needed the help of the *zaibatsu?*

MAP STUDY

THE WORLD IN SPATIAL TERMS

By the early 1900s, Europeans had spread their rule throughout the world. **Which country's empire included territories in the greatest number of continents?**

southern half of the island of Sakhalin (sak' uh lēn). It also won a sphere of influence in Korea. Five years later, Japan annexed Korea.

Southeast Asia and the Pacific   Europeans first entered Southeast Asia in the 1500s in search of spices. By the 1600s, Portugal, Spain, and the Netherlands all had colonies there. Although there was an active trade with the islands in the area, no one paid much attention to the mainland.

In the late 1800s, the European powers changed their minds. The mainland of Southeast Asia was a source of cash crops, such as coffee and tea. It also had raw materials, such as petroleum, rubber, and tin.

Great Britain and France competed in Southeast Asia. The British took control of Burma, Ceylon, the Malay States, and Singapore. The French set up protectorates in Cochin-China

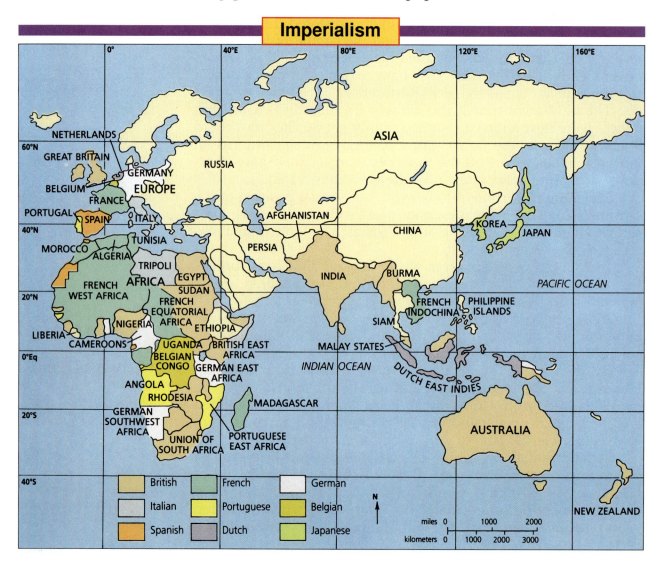

Imperialism

(kō′ chuhn chī nuh), Kampuchea, and Annam (a nam′). They then took over Laos (lah′ ōs) and combined the four colonies into Indochina. Only Siam, or present-day Thailand, remained independent.

During this period, Great Britain, France, Germany, and the United States were also trying to win control of islands in the Pacific. Some of the islands had rich soil that could be used for sugar and pineapple plantations. Others had minerals. Still others could be used as bases for refueling and repairing ships.

Great Britain, which had the largest navy in the world, already held Australia and New Zealand. Now, it took the Fiji, Solomon, and Gilbert Islands, along with parts of New Guinea (gin′ ē) and Borneo (bor′ nē ō). France claimed Tahiti, the Marquesas (mahr kā′ zuhz), and several other islands. Germany took part of New Guinea and the Marshall, Caroline, and Mariana Islands. Later, Germany divided the Samoan (suh mō′ uhn) Islands with the United States. The United States also controlled the Hawaiian and Philippine Islands and Guam (gwahm).

Section 3 Assessment

1. **Define:** sepoys, spheres of influence, right of extraterritoriality, *zaibatsu*.
2. Why did the Japanese start a program of imperialism?
3. Why did many European countries in the 1800s want to control territory in Southeast Asia?

Critical Thinking

4. **Identifying Central Issues** What was the central issue in the Boxer Rebellion?

Graphic Organizer Activity

5. Draw this diagram, and use it to show the steps leading to the takeover of India by the British Crown.

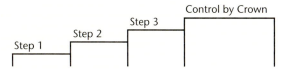

SECTION 4 Latin America

The imperialist powers were also interested in Latin America. The countries there that had gained their independence in the early 1800s faced many problems. Most Latin Americans were poor and had no land of their own. The new leaders had little government experience. There were many revolutions. These shaky conditions seemed to invite outside interference.

To stop this, President James Monroe issued the Monroe Doctrine in 1823. It said that any attempt to gain colonies in Latin America would be considered an unfriendly act toward the United States. Most of the European powers went along with the Monroe Doctrine, largely because the British navy supported the American position. The French made Prince Maximilian of Austria the emperor of Mexico.

By the late 1800s, Spain had colonies in Cuba and Puerto Rico. The Cubans, eager to be independent, had revolted in 1868 and again in 1895. Some Americans, who had large amounts of money invested there, wanted the rebels to win. In 1898, an American battleship, the U.S.S. *Maine,* blew up in the harbor of Havana, Cuba. People in the United States blamed the Spanish. Before long, Congress declared war on Spain.

In less than a year, the United States won the Spanish-American War. The resulting peace treaty gave the United States Puerto Rico, Guam, and the Philippine Islands. Cuba became an American protectorate.

The United States was now a world power. As such, it became even more involved in Latin America.

The United States needed a way to protect its new territories. Its fleet had to be able to sail quickly between American islands in the Caribbean Sea and those in the Pacific Ocean. President

PANAMA CANAL   The building of the Panama Canal took over eight years and the labor of more than 40,000 persons. About 5,600 workers died from accidents and disease. Here, the digging of the Gaillard Cut is shown. **How was the United States able to gain rights to the land for a canal?**

Theodore Roosevelt wanted to build a canal across Panama, a province of Colombia. The United States, however, could not come to terms with Colombia.

In 1903, the United States supported a revolution by people in Panama against Colombia. The revolution was a success. The United States and Panama then signed a treaty in which Panama leased land to the United States to be used for building a canal. In 1914, the Panama Canal was opened. It shortened the route between the two oceans by nearly 7,000 miles, or 11,200 kilometers. The Colombians, however, were angry that the United States had interfered in their affairs.

The United States' interest in Latin America continued. Some countries there had financial and political troubles that led to riots. The United States wanted to protect its business investments. So, between 1912 and 1916, the government sent American soldiers to Nicaragua, the Dominican Republic, and Haiti to restore order.

Student Web Activity

Visit the *Human Heritage* Web site at **humanheritage.glencoe.com** and click on **Chapter 36— Student Web Activities** to find out more about U.S. colonies.

Section 4 Assessment

1. Why did President Monroe issue the Monroe Doctrine?

2. Why did the United States want a canal through Panama?

Critical Thinking

3. Predicting Consequences What might have happened if most European powers had not gone along with the Monroe Doctrine?

Graphic Organizer Activity

4. Draw this diagram, and use it to show some of the effects of the Spanish-American War.

Spanish-American War

Effects

1. _____
2. _____
3. _____
4. _____

SECTION 5 Effects of Imperialism

By 1914, European colonial powers, Japan, and the United States had brought about 85 percent of the world under their control. This had many benefits. Orderly governments were set up. Many local wars were stopped. Industry, agriculture, and transportation were developed. Hospitals and schools were built, and sanitation was improved. Western ideas about democracy and individual rights spread.

At the same time, however, imperialism brought about major problems. One was bitter feelings between colonists and colonizers. Most Europeans, North Americans, and Japanese thought they were better than the people in the colonies. Colonists were seldom allowed to hold high jobs in government, industry, or the armed forces. Often, they were not even allowed in city areas where Europeans and North Americans lived.

The colonists resented this. They blamed the colonial powers for the loss of their land and for being forced to work on plantations and in factories. They disliked the colonial powers for trying to change their customs, languages, and religions. These feelings helped nationalism to grow.

There was yet another problem. The scramble for colonies led to a great deal of competition among colonial powers. This, in turn, led to disputes that caused future wars.

Section 5 Assessment

1. What percent of the world was colonized by 1914?
2. What problems did the scramble for empires create for the colonial powers?

Critical Thinking

3. **Identifying Alternatives**   If you were a colonist in the early 1900s, would you have tried to get a job in the colonial government or would you have tried to rebel? Explain.

Graphic Organizer Activity

4. Draw this diagram, and use it to weigh the benefits and drawbacks of imperialism.

Benefits	Drawbacks

Chapter Summary & Study Guide

1. Imperialism developed in the 1800s because of the growth of nationalism; the need for raw materials, new markets, and investment opportunities; and the belief among Europeans that they should spread their way of life.

2. By the early 1900s, European nations had carved up Africa, with only Ethiopia and Liberia remaining independent.

3. By the late 1800s, Great Britain controlled India, Russia was moving into central Asia, and foreign powers were competing for control of China.

4. By the early 1900s, Japan had become industrialized and was a powerful imperialist nation.

5. By 1900, Great Britain, France, Germany, and the United States controlled most of Southeast Asia and many islands in the Pacific.

6. In 1823, the United States issued the Monroe Doctrine to keep European nations from expanding their control into Latin America.

7. The United States became an imperialist power after winning Puerto Rico, Guam, and the Philippines from Spain in 1898 and building the Panama Canal in 1903.

8. While imperialism led to the development of orderly governments, industry, and social reforms, it also increased nationalism and dangerous competition for empires.

Self-Check Quiz

Visit the *Human Heritage* Web site at **humanheritage.glencoe.com** and click on *Chapter 36—Self-Check Quiz* to assess your understanding of this chapter.

Using Key Terms

Imagine it is the late 1800s. Write a newspaper advertisement to encourage more British citizens to settle in colonies in Africa or Asia. Use the following words in your ad.

imperialism

sepoys

right of
  extraterritoriality

protectorate

spheres of influence

zaibatsu

Understanding Main Ideas

1. What were the main reasons for the rise of imperialism?
2. How did some Europeans get colonial territory from African chiefs?
3. What caused settlers to move into Transvaal after 1885?
4. How did the British gain control over India?
5. What was the purpose of the Open Door Policy?
6. Why did Commodore Perry go to Japan in 1853?
7. Why was the United States interested in Latin American countries in the early 1900s?
8. How did imperialism increase nationalism in the colonies?

Critical Thinking

1. Do you think nations would be as interested or less interested today in gaining control of the Suez Canal? Why?
2. If you had lived in the United States in 1823, how would you have felt about the Monroe Doctrine? Explain your answer.

3. Do you think attitudes about imperialism have changed from the 1800s to today? Explain.

Graphic Organizer Activity

Economics Create a diagram such as the one shown, and use it to demonstrate the pattern of trade that developed between imperialist nations and their colonies.

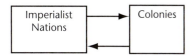

Imperialist Nations → Colonies

Geography in History

Environment and Society Changes took place in nations when colonial powers took them over. What specific changes in the growing of crops took place in India and China when they were colonized? Draw a poster showing how the growing of typical crops likely changed.

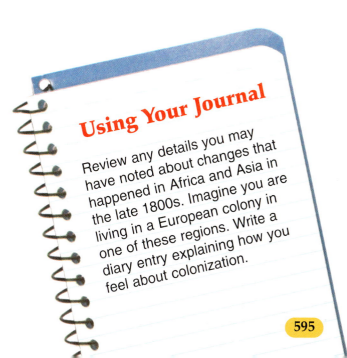

Using Your Journal

Review any details you may have noted about changes that happened in Africa and Asia in the late 1800s. Imagine you are living in a European colony in one of these regions. Write a diary entry explaining how you feel about colonization.

Around

TIBET

Bordered by towering mountains and dry plains, the Tibetan Plateau is the highest and one of the most isolated regions on Earth. With an average elevation of 12,000 feet, people sometimes call it the "Rooftop of the World." For much of its 2,000-year history, Tibet's geography helped protect its independence. In the late 1800s and early 1900s, however, it became the target of Russian, British, and Chinese imperialism. To block Russian expansion, Great Britain recognized Chinese rights in Tibet. The agreement, signed in 1906, began a long struggle for Tibetan freedom. Tibetans resisted Chinese rule from the start and continue to resist it today.

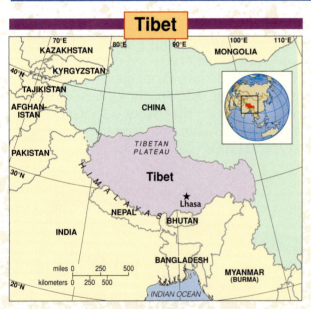

▲ Tibet covers an area roughly the size of western Europe. For China, it has long represented a land of untapped natural resources and a thinly populated region where some of China's huge population might settle.

▲ Outside of Lhasa, nomads have occupied Tibet for much of its history. In remote areas, many Tibetans still live as their ancestors did, herding livestock such as horses, sheep, and goats. They load trade goods–salt, cheese, rugs, and other items–onto horses or yaks and travel along caravan routes as old as Tibet itself.

the World

▼ Until 1959, the Dalai Lama, the religious and political leader of Tibet, lived in the Potala. Built in the 1600s, this huge palace continues to dominate Lhasa with its size and beauty.

When communist troops took over China in 1949, the new government tightened its control of Tibet. When the Tibetans rebelled in 1959, Chinese troops brutally put down the rebellion. More than 100,000 Tibetans fled into Bhutan, Nepal, and India. The present-day Dalai Lama lives in Dharamsala, India, where he leads the fight for Tibetan independence. ▶

◀ Missionaries from India introduced Buddhism to Tibet around 620 A.D. and developed an alphabet for the Tibetan language. Legend says this Buddhist statue was brought to Lhasa, the capital of Tibet, in the early 600s by the bride of a Tibetan king.

Over time, Tibet developed into a *theocracy*, or government run by religious leaders. In the early 1900s, an estimated 500,000 Buddhist *lamas*, or monks, lived in Tibet. When the last Chinese dynasty fell in 1911, monks such as the ones in this photo led the fight to push the Chinese from Tibet—an effort that succeeded for a short time. Today monks continue their religious studies. ▶

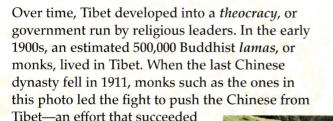

▼

Taking Another Look

1. How did Tibet's geography help protect its independence?

2. How did imperialism change the history of Tibet?

Hands-On Activity

Creating a Poster Design a poster that a group of Tibetan children living in Nepal might create in defense of Tibetan freedom.

597

Standardized Test Practice

Directions: Choose the *best* answer to each of the following multiple choice questions. If you have trouble answering a question, use the process of elimination to narrow your choices. Write your answers on a separate piece of paper.

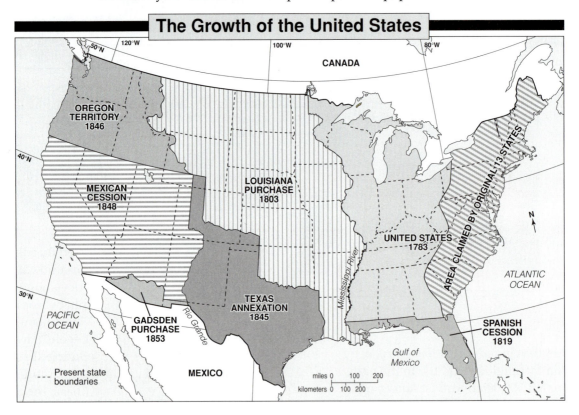

The Growth of the United States

1. According to the map above, in what year was the territory that includes present-day Utah acquired by the United States?

   A 1846
   B 1848
   C 1803
   D 1845

   Test-Taking Tip: This map uses *labels* as well as *symbols* to show the United States during different time periods. How are present state boundaries shown? (Make sure that you can identify all the state names on a map.)

2. The western movement of people in the United States after the American Revolution led to all of the following EXCEPT

   F new states being added to the Union
   G declining populations in east coast cities
   H the relocation of Native Americans to reservations
   J more tension between slave and non-slave states

   Test-Taking Tip: Be careful—overlooking the words NOT or EXCEPT on a multiple choice test is a common error.

3. A difference between the American Revolution and the fight for independence in Haiti was that

A Haiti's revolution was led by slaves

B the revolution in Haiti did not involve fighting

C Haiti was not seeking freedom from a European nation

D the Haitian revolution was not successful

> *Test-Taking Tip:* Eliminate answers that you know are incorrect. For example, Haiti *was* seeking freedom from a European nation and the revolution *was* successful, so you can eliminate answers C and D.

4. Even though Napoleon took away many rights from the French citizens, they made him emperor of France. Why?

F The citizens of France feared Napoleon.

G The French no longer wanted a monarch.

H The Pope approved of making Napoleon emperor.

J Napoleon brought peace and order to France.

> *Test-Taking Tip:* This question requires you to remember a *fact* about Napoleon. Napoleon was a strong leader who preserved some rights (trial by jury, freedom of religion) but took away others (freedom of speech and the press). Remember, more than one answer may seem correct. Choose the answer that *best* fits the question. For instance, although Napoleon jailed many people whom he considered to be his enemies, he was still a very popular figure in France. He was not made emperor out of fear. Therefore, you can eliminate choice F.

5. Socialists believe that equality among people can only be achieved by

A giving all adults the right to vote

B letting the poor own land

C making all land and factories publicly owned

D electing a strong monarch

> *Test-Taking Tip:* *Socialism* is one of the many political movements that arose in Europe after the end of Napoleon's Grand Empire. As you study this time period, you may want to make a chart to compare these movements. They include: *liberalism, nationalism, socialism, utopian socialism*, and *communism*.

6. In the late 1800s, European nations began to set up colonies in foreign lands again. All of the following were reasons for imperialism EXCEPT the

F need for more raw materials

G desire of nations to gain more power

H supposed duty to spread Christianity

J need to bring more workers to Europe

> *Test-Taking Tip:* Remember, three of the answer choices for this question will be *true*. Look for the *exception*. For instance, would setting up colonies probably increase or decrease a nation's power? Most likely it would increase it. Therefore, you can eliminate choice G.

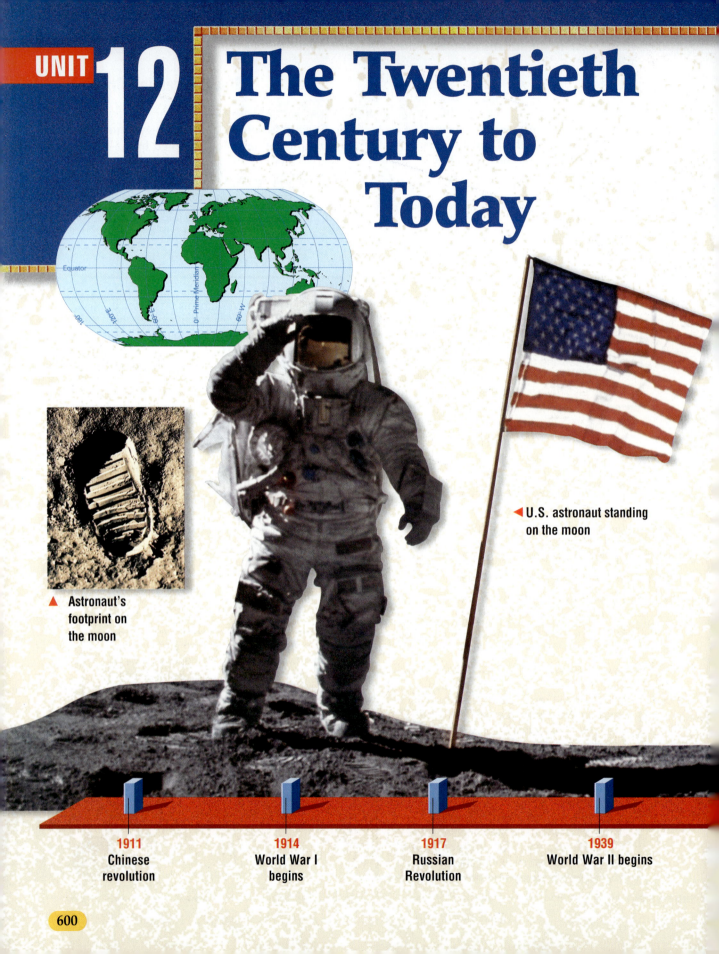

12

The Twentieth Century to Today

Equator

0° Prime Meridian

▲ Astronaut's footprint on the moon

◄ U.S. astronaut standing on the moon

1911
Chinese revolution

1914
World War I begins

1917
Russian Revolution

1939
World War II begins

FOLDABLES
Study Organizer

Evaluating Information Study Foldable *Make this foldable to help you learn about the major global events of the twentieth century to the present.*

Step 1 *Fold the paper from the top right corner down so the edges line up. Cut off the leftover piece.*

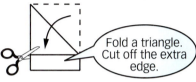

Fold a triangle. Cut off the extra edge.

Step 2 *Fold the triangle in half. Unfold.*

The folds will form an X dividing four equal sections.

Reading and Writing *As you read, ask yourself why many of the major events of the 1900s and early 2000s occurred. Write your questions under each appropriate pyramid wall.*

Step 3 *Cut up one fold line and stop at the middle. Draw an X on one tab and label the other three.*

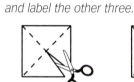

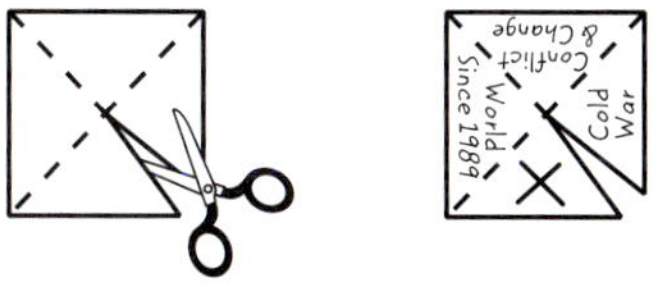

Step 4 *Fold the X flap under the other flap and glue together.*

This makes a three-sided pyramid.

PRIMARY SOURCES
Library

See pages 696–697 for other primary source readings to accompany Unit 12.

 Read "A Day in Space" from the **World History Primary Source Document Library CD-ROM.**

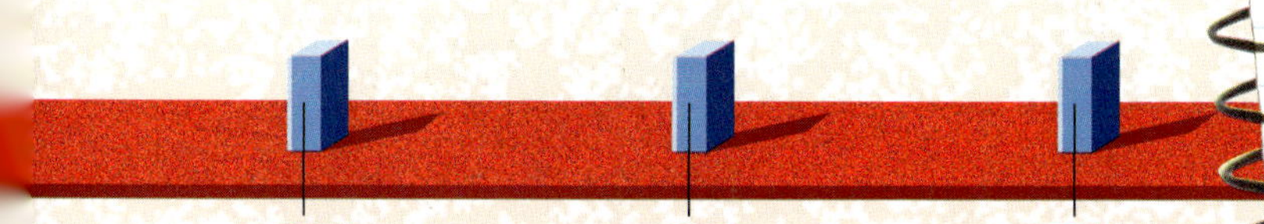

Journal Notes

What world changes and challenges took place in the 1900s? Note details about these changes as you read.

1960
"Year of Africa"

1991
Soviet Union breaks up

2001
World responds to terrorist attacks on U.S.

Conflict and Change

1900 A.D.–1945 A.D.

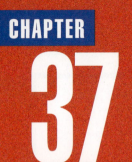

▲English poster

◄ Allied soldiers from World War I

1914	1917	1929	1939	1945
World War I begins	Russian Revolution	Worldwide depression	World War II begins	First atomic bomb dropped on Japan

Chapter Focus

 Read to Discover

- What the causes, events, and results of World War I were.
- How communism developed in Russia.
- Why Italy and Germany became dictatorships.
- What the causes, events, and results of World War II were.

Chapter Overview

Visit the *Human Heritage* Web site at **humanheritage.glencoe.com** and click on *Chapter 37— Chapter Overviews* to preview this chapter.

 Terms to Learn

mobilize
armistice
soviets
dictatorship
appeasement
genocide
Holocaust

 People to Know

Franz Ferdinand
Woodrow Wilson
Nicholas II
Vladimir Lenin
Joseph Stalin
Adolf Hitler
Winston
  Churchill

 Places to Locate

Sarajevo
Pearl Harbor
Hiroshima
Nagasaki

Why It's Important   The first half of the 1900s was a period of turmoil throughout the world. In 1914, a war broke out in Europe that turned into World War I. Although it ended in 1918, anger over the peace settlement and poor economic conditions following the war led to World War II. The same period also saw the rise of communism in Russia and neighboring countries.

SECTION 1 World War I

For almost 100 years after Napoleon's defeat, no long, general European war developed. By the early 1900s, however, rivalries among the countries of Europe were causing trouble.

Background   By the early 1900s, tension grew between several countries. France was jealous of Germany because it was industrializing rapidly. Great Britain did not like Germany expanding its navy. Russia involved itself with the problems of the Slavic peoples in Austria-Hungary.

Each European country built up its armed forces and made alliances with other nations. They each promised to help the others in their alliance if they were attacked. Thus, trouble between any two nations of different alliances could draw in many countries. A small war could easily grow into a large one. All that was needed was a spark.

The spark for World War I occurred in Sarajevo (sahr uh yē vō), a small town in Austria-Hungary. There, in June 1914, a teenager named Gavrilo Princip shot and killed Archduke Franz Ferdinand, heir to the throne of Austria-Hungary. Princip belonged to a secret nationalist group called the Black Hand. This group wanted the Serbs ruled by Austria-Hungary to be ruled by Serbia (ser' bē uh).

Austria-Hungary blamed the Serbian government for the Archduke's death and declared war on Serbia. Russia, an ally of Serbia, began to **mobilize,** or call up its troops, to go to Serbia's aid. Germany then showed its support of Austria-Hungary by declaring war on Russia. Shortly after, France and Great Britain entered the war on the side of Russia. So did Japan and, later, Italy and China. The Ottoman Empire, on the other hand, decided to support Germany and Austria-Hungary. Together, Germany, Austria-Hungary, the Ottoman Empire, and Bulgaria were called the Central Powers. Russia, Serbia, France, Great Britain, Japan, Italy, and China were called the Allied Powers.

From 1914 to 1918 World War I, also called the Great War, was different from any earlier war. It was the first war where **civilians** (suh vil' yuhnz), or people who are not soldiers, were also attacked. The war grew so large that 31 countries, with 65 million soldiers, took part. Although most land fighting took place in Europe, the Middle East, and Africa, naval warfare took place throughout the world.

There were also new, more powerful weapons being used. Machine guns fired bullets one after another at a rapid speed. Huge guns fired shells more than 75 miles, or 120 kilometers, away. Airplanes carried bombs behind enemy lines and dropped them on enemy cities. Submarines attacked ships at sea. Poison gases were used. Tanks and flame throwers were introduced.

Much of the fighting took place on the western front, the zone between France and Germany. There, opposing armies dug themselves into the ground in trenches protected by barbed wire. This kind of fighting is called **trench warfare.** To get at the enemy, each side had to climb out of its trenches and cross open land under **artillery** (ar til' uhr ē), or mounted gun, fire. The casualties were enormous. One battle alone cost 900,000 lives. In another area, French and German soldiers engaged in trench warfare for ten months.

On the eastern front, the Russian Empire suffered heavy losses. Some 3.8 million soldiers were killed in just the first ten months of the war. In 1918, after two revolutions, Russia withdrew from the war and signed a separate peace treaty with Germany, having recognized Ukraine as an independent country. The Russians gave up large areas of land previously conquered by them. Located to the

✓ Reading Check
Why did Russia **mobilize** for war?

✓ Reading Check
Why was World War I different from other wars for **civilians?**

✓ Reading Check
What is **trench warfare?**
Why did **artillery** fire claim so many lives?

TRENCH WARFARE   Much of the fighting of the First World War was carried out from trenches. Men had to charge across "no man's land," the open area in front of the enemy's trenches, in order to attack. Machine guns made these attacks especially dangerous. **Where was the western front located?**

HISTORY Online

Student Web Activity

Visit the *Human Heritage* Web site at **humanheritage.glencoe.com** and click on ***Chapter 37— Student Web Activities*** to find out more about World War I.

west of Russia, these lands included one third of their farmland, one third of their population, and almost all of their resources of coal, iron, and oil.

In the meantime, German submarines tried to stop supply ships to Great Britain and France. In 1917, after the submarines sank American ships with civilians on board, the United States declared war on Germany. Until then, the United States had tried to stay out of the conflict.

The United States sent 2 million fresh troops to Europe to aid the tired Allied forces. The Americans helped to bring a quick end to the war, in favor of the Allied Powers. On November 11, 1918, Germany and its allies agreed to an **armistice** (ar´ muh stis), or a stop in the fighting.

The Great War was over. Over 13 million soldiers and 17 million civilians lost their lives. Another 20 million soldiers had been wounded, and there was billions of dollars in damage to property.

Making the Peace   Woodrow Wilson, the President of the United States, had drawn up a peace plan called the Fourteen Points. Wilson believed that national groups in Europe should have the right to form their own countries. He wanted to reduce **armaments** (ar´ muh muhnts), or equipment for war. Above all,

Reading Check
How did the arrival of American troops help bring about an **armistice?**

Reading Check
What did Woodrow Wilson want nations to do with their **armaments?**

Then ... & Now

Remembering Veterans November 11, 1918—the day World War I ended—is a time when members of the armed services are honored in many of the former Allied countries. Once called Armistice Day, since 1954 it has been called Veterans Day in the United States. It is Remembrance Day in Canada and Armistice Day in Britain.

he wanted a world association of nations to keep the peace. The British, French, and Italian leaders, however, had other plans. They wanted repayment for their losses during the war from the defeated countries.

The peace treaty that Germany signed after World War I was called the Treaty of Versailles (vuhr sī'). This treaty put most of the blame for the war and the financial repayment on Germany, for which the Germans were very angry. Under this treaty, Germany lost land in Europe and overseas. Alsace and Lorraine, which Germany had taken from France in 1870, were returned to France. Some of Germany's eastern territory became part of the reestablished nation of Poland. Germany's African colonies were divided between France and Great Britain, while its Pacific colonies were given to Japan.

Under the Treaty of Versailles, Russia lost even more territory than Germany did. Part of the Russian territory was lost to Poland and Romania, and part of it became the new nations of Finland, Estonia, Latvia, and Lithuania. Ukraine's desire for independence, however, was ignored.

The treaty did not deal with the needs of some other countries. India and people in Southeast Asia who had supported the Allied Powers wanted independence from Great Britain and France. Their wishes were ignored. Over the next 30 years, serious troubles developed in all these areas.

The other Central Powers were dealt with in separate treaties. Austria-Hungary was broken up, and four new countries—Austria,

Reading Check
What is a **mandate?**
What type of policy does an **isolationist** country follow?

TREATY OF VERSAILLES   The Treaty of Versailles was signed in June, 1919, at the palace of Versailles outside Paris. Only the Allied Powers took part in the negotiations. Germany was not allowed to participate. Here, the Allied leaders meet in the Hall of Mirrors. **How was Germany affected by the Treaty of Versailles?**

Hungary, Czechoslovakia, and Yugoslavia—were created. France received a **mandate** (man'dāt), or right to rule, in Syria and Lebanon. Great Britain received mandates in Iraq and Palestine.

For the most part, President Wilson's peace plan was not followed. However, one point was kept. An organization called the League of Nations was established so the countries of the world could come together to talk over their troubles. Most hoped the League could help prevent future wars. But the League had a serious weakness—it had no army of its own. If a country did not want to obey the League, it could not be forced to do so. The League was also weak because the United States refused to become a member. Many Americans disagreed with the World War I treaties. After 1919, the United States became an **isolationist** country. It decided to stay out of European affairs and world problems.

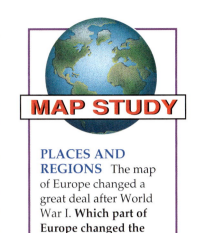

MAP STUDY

PLACES AND REGIONS The map of Europe changed a great deal after World War I. **Which part of Europe changed the most?**

Europe After World War I

Newly-Formed Nations

Under French Control

Under British Control

Central Powers During the War

Section 1 Assessment

1. **Define:** mobilize, civilians, trench warfare, artillery, armistice, armaments, mandate, isolationist.
2. What made World War I different from earlier wars?
3. Why did the United States refuse to join the League of Nations?

Critical Thinking

4. **Identifying Central Issues** Why do you think many Americans opposed United States membership in the League of Nations?

Graphic Organizer Activity

5. Draw this diagram, and use it to show the new nations created by the treaties ending World War I. (Add more answer circles as needed.)

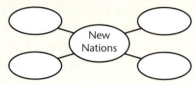

New Nations

SECTION 2 Between the Wars

The 1920s and 1930s were a difficult time for people everywhere. Most were trying to recover from the damage caused by World War I. Then, in 1929, a **depression,** or a sudden slowdown in business, began. People in many countries started to question their forms of government. In Germany, the people turned to a leader who would soon threaten world peace. People in Russia had overthrown their government and set up the world's first Communist nation.

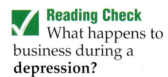

Reading Check What happens to business during a **depression?**

Emerging Russia   In Muscovy, the years following the death of Ivan the Terrible in 1584 were called the "Time of Troubles." There was much disorder in the country. The troubles ended in 1613 with the crowning of seventeen-year-old Michael Romanov (rō' muh nahf) as czar. The Romanov dynasty ruled Russia until 1917.

The first great Romanov ruler was a grandson of Michael's, Peter the Great, who came to the throne in 1682. Determined to make Muscovy strong and modern, Peter disguised himself as a sailor and visited the capitals of various European countries. There he learned all he could of western ways.

When Peter returned home, he began reforming the country he named Russia. He started textile factories, built canals, and encouraged mining. He ordered a new capital, St. Petersburg, built on the Baltic Sea. Since St. Petersburg was an ice-free port, the country's trade by water with western Europe continued

Painting of Peter the Great

even in winter. Peter revised the alphabet and set up schools for the upper class. He trained a powerful army and also built the country's first navy. He even changed people's appearance. He ordered men to shave their beards and to wear European-style short jackets instead of long coats.

The next great Romanov ruler was Catherine the Great, who came to the throne in 1762. At first Catherine wanted to improve the condition of the peasants. She even considered abolishing serfdom. Then peasants in a newly conquered area of Ukraine rebelled. Soon after, the French Revolution broke out. These two events so frightened Catherine that she gave up her ideas of reform.

Catherine did not help the peasants, but she did make Russia much larger. In a number of wars, the country's borders were pushed farther east, west, and south.

Painting of Catherine the Great

The Road to Revolution

During the 1800s, there was a great deal of discontent in the Russian Empire. About 30 million serfs, one half of whom were owned by the czar, labored to support about one-half million nobles and clergy. The czar controlled what industry there was. All society suffered and students protested, peasants revolted, and workers staged strikes. In 1825, a group of army officers, inspired by the ideas of the French Revolution, rose up against the czar. The rebellion, however, was put down.

A period of strong government controls followed. Writers who ridiculed government leaders were not published. Some writers were exiled. Even so, ideas about freedom and reform spread.

In 1861, Czar Alexander II, who was trying to modernize the country and appear to be a fair ruler, freed the serfs. However, he did not give them land of their own. As a result, most became tenant farmers.

In 1905, another uprising took place. It began when thousands of workers appeared in the square before the czar's palace. They carried petitions asking for a national assembly, freedom of speech and religion, and better conditions for workers and peasants. Government soldiers fired on the crowd, killing hundreds of unarmed people. A general strike then broke out. Finally, Czar Nicholas II agreed to some of the workers' demands. He ignored the national assembly, however, and its plans for reform.

World War I only made Russia's problems worse. The country did not have enough factories to produce guns and ammunition or enough railroads to carry supplies to the front. As a result, it suffered higher casualties than any other country. Nearly 9 million soldiers were killed or wounded in battle. Civilians suffered from lack of food and fuel.

Photograph of Nicholas II

LENIN   Lenin was a powerful speaker and was able to rally much support for the Communist cause. He ruled the Soviet Union until his death in 1924. **What did the Bolsheviks promise in order to gain support?**

> ✓ **Reading Check**
> What action did the military **garrison** in St. Petersburg take toward striking workers?

At last the Russian people could stand no more. In March 1917, they revolted. Striking workers, led by women textile laborers, jammed the streets of St. Petersburg, which had been renamed Petrograd (pet′ ruh grad). They demanded bread and peace. The workers were soon joined by the city's **garrison** (gar′ uh suhn), or military group stationed in the area. Within a few days, the revolt spread throughout the country. Peasants took over the lands of nobles. Soldiers left the front and began walking home. The czar was forced to abdicate, and a temporary government was set up.

Lenin   There was much confusion in the months following the overthrow of Nicholas II. A revolutionary group called Bolsheviks (bol′ shuh viks) took advantage of this. Led by Vladimir Lenin (len′ in), they gained the support of the **soviets,** or committees that represented workers and soldiers. The Bolsheviks promised land to the peasants and bread to the workers. They also promised to get Russia out of the war.

> ✓ **Reading Check**
> What were the **soviets?**

In November 1917, the Bolsheviks seized power from the temporary government. Lenin was chosen to lead the new government. Soon after, he signed a peace treaty with Germany that ended Russia's part in World War I. The treaty, however, did not end the troubles at home.

From 1918 to 1920, Russia was divided by a civil war between the majority Bolsheviks—now known as Communists—and the minority Mensheviks (men' chuh viks) and other groups who were non-Communists. The Communists were also called Reds, because red had been the color of revolution since the French Revolution. The non-Communists were called Whites.

The Whites received soldiers and supplies from other countries, including the United States. These countries were afraid that if the Reds won, communism would spread throughout Europe. The Russian people as a whole did not like the Communists. However, because they did not want to return to old ways, most of them supported the Reds, and by 1921, the Whites had been defeated.

In 1922, the Union of Soviet Socialist Republics, or the Soviet Union, was formed. It was made up of four republics, the largest of which was Russia. By 1924, the Soviet Union was completely under the control of the Communist party.

Lenin died that same year. His body was embalmed and placed in a glass coffin inside a red marble tomb near the wall of Moscow's Kremlin. In his honor, Petrograd was renamed Leningrad.

Stalin   After Lenin died, there was a struggle for power in the Soviet Union which lasted until 1928. In that year, Joseph Stalin (stah'lin) took control of the government. He also controlled the Communist party, which was the only political party allowed in the country.

Stalin wanted the Soviet Union to industrialize as quickly as possible. So, he set up a series of Five-Year Plans. Their major goal was to build up **heavy industry,** or the manufacture of basic materials and machines. Under these plans, steel mills, power plants, oil refineries, and chemical plants were built and kept under government control. Workers were paid according to how much they produced. Factory managers had to turn out a certain quantity of goods. By 1939, the Soviet Union was a major industrial power. The people paid a price for industrialization. Workers labored long hours for low wages. Consumer goods, such as clothing and household goods, were poorly made and hard to find, and housing shortages were common.

Another goal of the Five-Year Plans was **collectivization** (kuh lek ti vuh zā' shuhn), or combining small farms into large ones controlled by the government. On a collective, farmers were paid according to the number of days they worked. Collectivization allowed them to share tractors and other farm machinery. The government bought their crops at fixed prices and sold them abroad to buy machinery for factories.

Many peasants wanted to keep working on their own farms. They resisted collectivization by killing their horses, cows, and

pigs. Those who refused to move were either shot or sent to labor camps in Siberia (sī bir' ē uh), a frozen wilderness in the northeast. In Ukraine, Stalin caused famine to control the people. By 1936, most farms in the Soviet Union were collectivized.

The World Economy

The worldwide depression that began in 1929 did not affect the Soviet Union. However, it affected most of the other industrialized countries. For this reason, it was called the Great Depression. Factories closed and millions of people lost their jobs. By 1932, one out of four Americans and British and two out of five Germans were out of work. Banks failed and people lost their savings. People who had been put out of their homes lived in shacks built out of cardboard or tin. In Germany, prices skyrocketed. Money bought so little that people lit their stoves with it instead of using firewood.

Democracy or Dictatorship

Some western countries, such as the United States and Great Britain, had a long tradition of stable, democratic government. Voters in these countries wanted to keep their governments but felt that the governments should do more to help the people.

Linking Across Time

News Media   The invention of motion pictures with sound brought the news into the movie theaters of the 1930s and 1940s (below). Before the start of each "picture show," as movies were called, many theaters played *newsreels*—short movies showing current events from around the world. Today, thanks to communication satellites, live coverage of the news can be sent directly into people's homes via television (right). **How did the Depression shape economic news in the 1930s?**

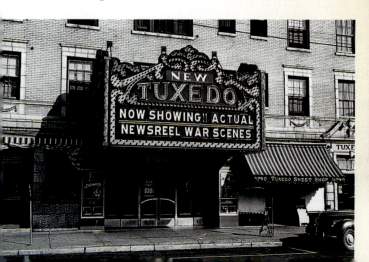

In the United States, President Franklin D. Roosevelt (roo' zuh velt) set up a program known as the New Deal. Two of its chief aims were relief and reform. To provide relief and put people back to work, the federal government set up several different agencies. One of these, the Civilian Conservation Corps (CCC), gave jobs mostly to young people. They planted trees and built small dams all over the United States. The Works Progress Administration (WPA) paid unemployed people to build roads, airports, bridges, and hospitals. It also provided work for artists and writers. The Tennessee Valley Authority (TVA) built dams that provided cheap electric power.

The federal government also planned long-range reform. Congress passed **social security laws** that provided money for elderly people and orphaned children. Many people, however, were not covered by these laws and did not receive help.

Other western countries, such as Germany and Italy, did not have a long tradition of stable, democratic government. Germany had only had an elected government since World War I. Many Germans thought their elected representatives spent too much time debating issues. They wondered if it might not be better to have one strong leader who could act quickly.

Italy was the first nation to become a **dictatorship** (dik tā' tuhr ship), or a country ruled by a single person with absolute authority. In 1922, Benito Mussolini (buh nēt' ō moo suh lē' nē), leader of the Fascist (fash'ist) Party, took over the Italian government.

✔ Reading Check
What groups were helped by passage of **social security laws?**

✔ Reading Check
What type of government is set up under a **dictatorship?**

UNEMPLOYMENT   The Great Depression caused many people who had lost their jobs to wait in long lines, hoping to get another one. **What programs did the U.S. government offer to help the unemployed?**

A Party Theme When Franklin D. Roosevelt ran for president in 1932, he adopted the song "Happy Days Are Here Again" as his campaign theme. The Democrats still play the song at their party's national convention.

Anne Frank Anne Frank, a Jewish teenager, kept a diary during the two years she and her family spent hiding from the Nazis in an attic room in Amsterdam. She was arrested in 1944 and sent to the Nazi death camp at Bergen-Belsen, where she died at age 15. Millions of people have read her account, *The Diary of a Young Girl,* first published in 1952.

NAZI RALLY Adolf Hitler was an excellent speaker, and he used this skill to unite and gather support from the German people. The Nazis made impressive spectacles of huge rallies at which thousands of Germans would gather to listen to Hitler speak. **What political steps did Hitler take once he was in power in Germany?**

Reading Check How did Hitler change German government once he became **chancellor?**

Reading Check What did the **swastika** symbolize?

In 1933, Adolf Hitler became **chancellor,** or prime minister, of Germany. Before long, he did away with the German republic and set himself up as dictator. He called himself *Der Fuhrer* (dār fyū′ uhr), which means "the leader." He called Germany the Third Reich (rīk), which means the "third empire." Hitler was supported by a violent political group called the National Socialist Party, or Nazis (nah′ tsēz). The Nazi symbol of identity was the **swastika** (swos′ tuh kuh), or hooked black cross. Many citizens of Germany were angry over the Treaty of Versailles. They saw Hitler as a leader who would make their country economically and politically strong.

Once Hitler was in power, he did away with all political parties except the Nazis. He had books about democracy burned. He took over the courts and set up a secret police. He took over the radio and the press and abolished trade unions. He fought against the Christian churches.

Hitler blamed many of Germany's troubles on the Jews and others. The Nazis believed the Germans were a "master race." Jews were not part of the "master race." So the Nazis took away the Jews' businesses and jobs. Jews could not go to school or get medical care. They were no longer allowed to vote or to walk along the streets after eight o'clock. They had to wear a yellow six-pointed star on their clothing. The lives of the Jews would continue to worsen.

The Road to War

Soon Germany and its allies, Italy and Japan, began to threaten world peace. In 1935, the Italians, bitter about not getting enough land after World War I, invaded Ethiopia. The League of Nations was not able to stop them. Hitler announced that his goal was to unite all the German people. He sent German troops into the Rhineland, a disputed area, in 1936. Then, in March 1938, his army marched into Austria. Then he demanded that the Germans living in Czechoslovakia be placed under German rule. The British and the French were afraid of another war. So they decided to follow a policy of **appeasement,** or giving in to demands. They did nothing while Czechoslovakia was first divided and then made a part of Hitler's Germany in March 1939.

In Japan, the military that ran the country felt that Japan needed more land and natural resources to make its economy stronger. In 1931 Japan invaded Manchuria, in northern China. In 1937, Japanese troops invaded the main part of China. That same year, Japan signed a friendship treaty with Germany and Italy.

In August 1939, Germany and the Soviet Union signed a treaty agreeing not to attack each other. Now Hitler felt safe to take more land. On September 1, 1939, the German army attacked Poland. German troops overran the western part of the country, while the Soviets occupied the rest. The British and the French realized they had made a mistake in not resisting Hitler's aggression, or attacks, earlier. Both France and Great Britain declared war on Germany.

✓ Reading Check
What is a policy of **appeasement?**

Photograph of Adolf Hitler

Section 2 Assessment

1. **Define:** depression, garrison, soviets, heavy industry, collectivization, social security laws, dictatorship, chancellor, swastika, appeasement.
2. How did Peter the Great reform Russia?
3. What were the goals of Stalin's Five-Year Plans?
4. Why did Great Britain and France declare war on Germany?

Critical Thinking

5. **Understanding Cause and Effect** How did the policy of appeasement contribute to the start of World War II?

Graphic Organizer Activity

6. Draw this diagram, and use it to write a headline showing the importance of each of these dates in Russian history: 1613, 1682, 1762, 1825, 1861, 1905, 1917, 1921.

Date	Headline
1613	
1682	
1762	
1825	
1861	
1905	
1917	
1921	

SECTION 3   World War II

For the second time during the 1900s, the world was at war. World War II caught the Allied Powers—including Great Britain, France, and, later, the Soviet Union and the United States—unprepared. The Axis Powers—Germany, Italy, and, later, Japan—were prepared. The war would end with the Allied Powers victorious, but not before a terrible cost was paid.

Early Axis Victories

Germany had developed a new way of fighting called **blitzkrieg** (blits' krēg), or "lightning war." German airplanes would first bomb enemy cities, roads, and airfields. Then soldiers and civilians alike would be machine-gunned from the air. Finally, armored tanks would roll through the countryside, wiping out all defenses.

Using the blitzkrieg, Germany crushed Poland in three weeks. In 1940, German forces overran most of western Europe, except for Great Britain. Hitler tried to bomb the British into surrendering. The British, however, under the leadership of Prime Minister Winston Churchill, fought back for 10 months. Finally, British pilots and anti-aircraft guns shot down so many German planes that Hitler gave up the idea of invading Great Britain. In the meantime, however, German and Italian troops overran much of southeastern Europe and North Africa.

Reading Check
How did the German **blitzkrieg** change warfare?

Fun Facts....

Radar Radar, invented by physicist Robert Watson-Watts in 1935, gave the British a powerful new weapon against the German air force during the Battle of Britain. By 1939, a chain of radar stations had been built along England's southern and eastern coasts, detecting incoming aircraft and providing an early-warning system.

BLITZKRIEG   Germany's bombing of European cities was a devastating new method of attack in World War II. Many parts of London, as shown here, were destroyed. **Why was Germany's blitzkrieg of Great Britain unsuccessful in allowing Germany to invade that country?**

At the same time, the Japanese made conquests in Asia. They took over much of China and Southeast Asia. Then they turned their attention to the United States, which had military forces in the Pacific. On December 7, 1941, the Japanese made a surprise air attack on Pearl Harbor, the American naval base in the Hawaiian Islands. The United States, followed by most of Latin America, immediately entered the war on the side of the Allied Powers.

War in Europe

The entry of the United States helped the Allies win the war in Europe. The United States was the greatest

Axis Expansion in Europe and Africa

[Map showing Europe and Africa with labels including:]

ICELAND, SWEDEN, NORWAY, FINLAND, SOVIET UNION, GREAT BRITAIN, NORTH SEA, ESTONIA, LATVIA, Moscow, DENMARK, LITHUANIA, BALTIC SEA, NETH., IRELAND, London, Berlin, GERMANY, POLAND, CZECHOSLOVAKIA, ENGLISH CHANNEL, BELG., AUSTRIA, HUNGARY, ROMANIA, NORMANDY, Paris, SWITZERLAND, FRANCE, ITALY, YUGOSLAVIA, ATLANTIC OCEAN, SPAIN, BULGARIA, BLACK SEA, PORTUGAL, Rome, TURKEY, ALBANIA, GREECE, SP. MOROCCO, SICILY, SYRIA, Suez Canal, IRAN, MOROCCO, TUNISIA, IRAQ, ALGERIA, LIBYA, EGYPT, TRANS-JORDAN, RIO DE ORO, ANGLO-EGYPTIAN SUDAN, SAUDI ARABIA, OMAN, RED SEA, FRENCH WEST AFRICA, YEMEN, GAMBIA, EQUATORIAL AFRICA, NIGERIA, ERITREA, SOMALILAND, PORT. GUINEA, SIERRA LEONE, ETHIOPIA, LIBERIA, GOLD COAST, TOGO, CAMEROONS, BR. EAST AFRICA, CASPIAN SEA

Coordinates: 20°W, 0°, 20°E, 40°E, 60°N, 40°N, 20°N, 0°Eq

Legend:
- Axis Powers
- Area Controlled by Axis Powers, 1942
- Allied Territory
- Neutral Territory

miles 0 400 800 1200
kilometers 0 400 800 1200 1600

industrial power in the world. Soon its factories were turning out thousands of planes and tanks. Ships were built in large numbers. Other supplies the Allies were lacking were provided by the United States.

Earlier, Hitler had decided that Germany needed the resources of the Soviet Union. He ignored the treaty he had signed and attacked the Soviet Union in 1941. However, Hitler had underestimated the size of the Soviet Union, the bitterness of its winters, and the Russian people's fighting spirit.

In defense, Soviet troops used a scorched-earth policy. They burned cities, destroyed their own crops, and blew up dams that produced electric power. Though the Russians sustained great losses, the tide of battle turned in 1943. The Red Army surrounded German forces at Stalingrad (stah' lin grad) and forced them to surrender. From then on, Soviet forces kept pushing the Germans back all along the eastern front. That same year, American and British armies drove the Axis forces out of North Africa and invaded Italy.

In 1944, under the command of American General Dwight D. Eisenhower, Allied troops crossed the English Channel from Great Britain and landed on the beaches of Normandy in France. About 155,000 Allied soldiers landed on the first day, June 6, known as D-Day. Another 2 million landed later. By August the Allied forces had retaken Paris and were moving eastward.

German armies were now caught between the Soviets in the east and the Americans, British, French, and Canadians in the west. In April 1945, the Allied forces joined together at the Elbe

Fun Facts . . .

PLUTO After D-Day, the Allies installed PLUTO— Pipe-Line Under the Ocean. The pipeline ran under the English Channel and supplied 700 tons of gasoline a day for Allied trucks and tanks advancing across Europe.

NORMANDY   Landing craft and supply ships crowded the Normandy coast when Allied troops landed on June 6, 1944. **What name was given to this date?**

(el' buh) River in Germany. Hitler and the Germans realized they could not win. Hitler killed himself, and on May 7, Germany surrendered. The next day, the war in Europe was officially over.

War in Asia and the Pacific The war in Asia and the Pacific was fought at the same time as the one in Europe. At first the Japanese were victorious everywhere. They captured the Philippines and various other islands in the Pacific, including three islands off the coast of Alaska. They also captured Indochina (now Laos, Vietnam, and Cambodia), Malaya, Singapore, Hong Kong, Burma, Thailand, and the Dutch East Indies (now Indonesia). Then, in June 1942, a great sea and air battle took place at Midway Island. The battle changed the course

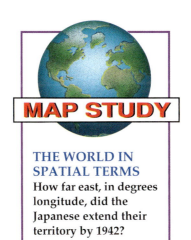

MAP STUDY

THE WORLD IN SPATIAL TERMS
How far east, in degrees longitude, did the Japanese extend their territory by 1942?

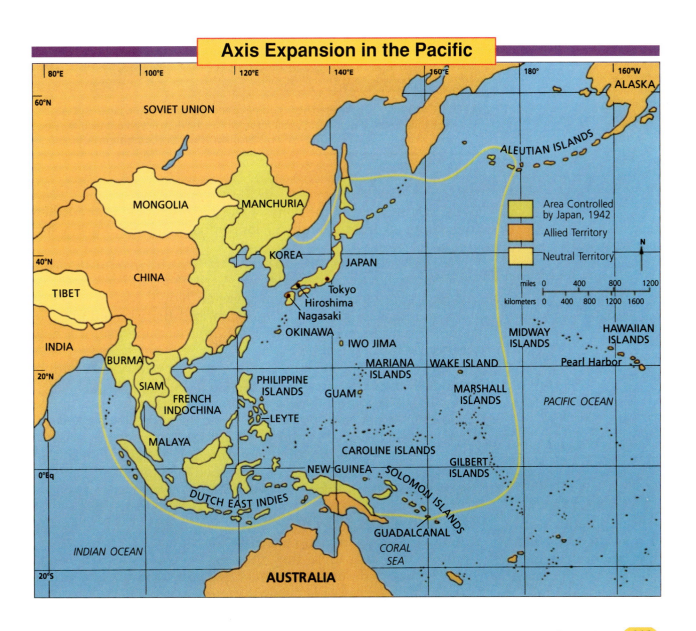

Axis Expansion in the Pacific

ATOMIC BOMB The United States dropped the atomic bomb on Japan in 1945. The huge mushroom cloud (left) from it formed over the destruction of much of Nagasaki, shown here. **Why did President Truman allow the bombing?**

of the war in favor of the Allies. Over the next three years, Allied forces moved from island to island, pushing their way toward Japan.

President Harry S Truman (tru' muhn), who became President after Roosevelt died in April 1945, did not want to invade Japan. He knew that an invasion would cost the lives of hundreds of thousands of American and British soldiers. So, hoping for a Japanese surrender, he approved the use of a new weapon — the atomic bomb.

On August 6, 1945, the bomb was dropped on Hiroshima (hir ō she' muh), Japan. It destroyed most of the city and killed about 100,000 people. Thousands more died later from radiation poisoning. When the Japanese refused to surrender, a second atomic bomb was dropped on Nagasaki (nah guh sah' kē), Japan. About 75,000 people were killed. On August 14, Japan surrendered. The peace treaty was signed on September 2 aboard the USS *Missouri* in Tokyo Bay. World War II was over.

Reading Check
What did Allied armies discover when they entered German **concentration camps?** What is **genocide?**

The Aftermath of War
After the war ended, Allied armies in Europe found German **concentration camps,** or camps where Germans had kept those they thought were enemies. There the Nazis had carried out a program of **genocide** (jen' uh sīd), or the mass murder of a people, against the Jews and others. This pro-

gram became known as the **Holocaust** (hol' uh kahst). At the start of World War II, German forces shot hundreds of thousands of Jews in Poland and the Soviet Union. However, Hitler felt that Jews were not being killed fast enough. So he ordered six concentration camps to be equipped with poison gas chambers and **cremation** (kri mā' shuhn) **ovens,** or places to burn dead bodies. The Nazis then rounded up all the Jews in the areas of Europe they controlled and shipped them in sealed cattle cars to the camps. There, most of the Jews were gassed to death. By the end of World War II, the Nazis had killed more than 6 million Jews. About 1.5 million of them were children under the age of six.

The Jews were not the only ones who died at the hands of the Nazis. The Nazis used the people they conquered as slave laborers in German factories and on German farms. Poles, Ukrainians, Russians, gypsies, and those people considered mentally ill or whom the Germans thought were inferior were treated worst of all. By the end of the war, about 6 million had died from starvation, overwork, and torture. More than 3 million of these were Soviet prisoners of war.

The Japanese, too, had killed men, women, and children in the countries they conquered. Many Allied prisoners of war, both soldiers and civilians, died because of poor treatment from the Japanese army.

The Allied governments felt that the cruel acts of the Nazis and the Japanese could not be excused as normal occurrences of war. So the Allied governments put German and Japanese leaders on trial for war crimes.

Making the Peace   One result of World War II was the formation of the United Nations (UN), an organization like the League of Nations. In 1945, the United Nations was approved by 50 countries. UN responsibilities were to prevent war, lend money to poor countries, and provide them with medical care and better education.

Following the war, Germany was divided into four zones. Each was occupied by one of the major Allied powers—the United States, Great Britain, France, and the Soviet Union. The German capital of Berlin, located in the Russian zone, was also divided. In addition, German territory in the east was given to Poland. This was in exchange for the Soviet Union's acquiring western Ukraine, which had been occupied by Poland since 1923. In fact, the Soviet Union acquired most of the land it had lost after World War I, including Estonia, Latvia, and Lithuania.

Japan was occupied by the United States for nearly seven years. Under American General Douglas MacArthur, the Japanese military lost power in the government and Japan became a democracy. Laws were passed giving women the right to vote and allowing trade unions. The secret police was abolished.

Reading Check What was the **Holocaust?**

Reading Check What did the **cremation ovens** reveal about the horror of Nazi Germany?

Photograph of Holocaust Victim

Large farms were divided and sold to farm workers at low prices. Loans were made to help rebuild the economy. Japan turned its efforts to building a strong economy rather than a strong military.

Section 3 Assessment

1. **Define:** blitzkrieg, concentration camps, genocide, Holocaust, cremation ovens.
2. Why did Germany attack the Soviet Union in 1941?
3. Why did the United States decide to drop atomic bombs on Hiroshima and Nagasaki?

Critical Thinking

4. **Demonstrating Reasoned Judgment** If you were living in 1945, would you have supported or opposed the use of the atomic bomb against Japan? Why?

Graphic Organizer Activity

5. Draw this diagram, and use it to show some of the results of World War II for Germany, Japan, and the Soviet Union.

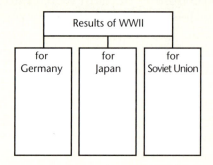

Chapter Summary & Study Guide

1. In 1914, a conflict between Serbia and Austria-Hungary began World War I.
2. World War I involved more nations, used more technological weapons, and resulted in more deaths than any other earlier war.
3. The United States entered the war in 1917 and helped defeat Germany and its allies.
4. President Woodrow Wilson was unable to prevent the passage of treaties aimed at punishing Germany.
5. Despite efforts by Peter the Great and Catherine the Great to modernize Russia, Russian serfs and workers continued to suffer, leading to a series of revolts against the czars and the final overthrow of the government in 1917.
6. Under the leadership of Lenin and then Stalin, Russia became a Communist nation known as the Soviet Union.

7. A worldwide depression aided the rise of dictatorships and paved the way for a second world war.
8. World War II began in 1939 when Germany broke an agreement and invaded Poland. The United States entered the war in 1941 after Japan bombed the U.S. naval base at Pearl Harbor, Hawaii.
9. World War II ended after the United States dropped two atomic bombs on Japan.
10. After World War II, the United Nations was formed, Germany was divided into four zones, and the United States occupied Japan.

Self-Check Quiz

Visit the *Human Heritage* Web site at **humanheritage. glencoe.com** and click on *Chapter 37—Self-Check Quiz* to assess your understanding of this chapter.

Using Key Terms

Sort the following list of words into three columns under one of the following headings: World War I, Between Wars, or World War II. Then write a descriptive paragraph about something in each period using all the words.

mobilize	trench warfare
artillery	armistice
mandate	soviets
collectivization	dictatorship
appeasement	genocide
Holocaust	

Understanding Main Ideas

1. How did nationalism contribute to World War I?
2. What kind of peace plan did European Allied leaders want after World War I?
3. What happened to the world economy in 1929?
4. Why did the British and French give in to Hitler's demands at first?
5. What major events led to the defeat of Germany in World War II? To the defeat of Japan?
6. Why was the United Nations formed?

Critical Thinking

1. What do you think might have happened if the United States had not entered World War I?
2. Why do you think so many Soviet peasants resisted collectivization?
3. What do you think could have been done to stop Hitler from invading neighboring countries?

4. Do you think the United States would have entered World War II if Japan had not bombed Pearl Harbor? Explain.

Graphic Organizer Activity

Citizenship Create a diagram like the one on this page, and use it to compare President Wilson's Fourteen Points with the Treaty of Versailles.

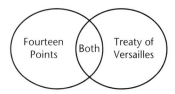

Geography in History

The World in Spatial Terms Refer to the map on page 619. Several small island groups in the Pacific Ocean were the sites of battles between the United States and Japan. Why do you think the battles occurred on these islands rather than on the Japanese mainland?

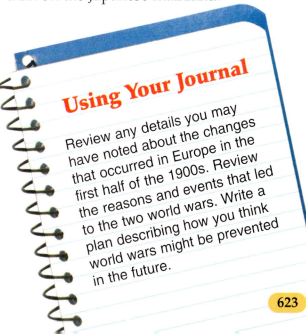

Using Your Journal

Review any details you may have noted about the changes that occurred in Europe in the first half of the 1900s. Review the reasons and events that led to the two world wars. Write a plan describing how you think world wars might be prevented in the future.

The Cold War Era

1945 A.D.–1989 A.D.

▼ Children protesting nuclear buildups

THERE IS NO SHELTER IN NUCLEAR WAR

I WANT TO GROW UP

▲ Geiger counter from a 1950s fallout shelter

1948	1950	1959	1960	1989
Berlin airlift	Korean War begins	Cuban Revolution	"Year of Africa"	China crushes student protest in Tiananmen Square

Chapter Focus

 Read to Discover

- How relationships between Western and Communist powers have changed since World War II.
- What changes have occurred in the Soviet Union.
- What life has been like in the People's Republic of China.
- How countries in Africa, South Asia, and Latin America have struggled with political and economic problems.

 Terms to Learn

cold war
satellite nations
glasnost
perestroika

 People to Know

Fidel Castro
Ho Chi Minh
Mao Zedong

🌎 **Places to Locate**

Berlin
Tiananmen
Square

Why It's Important   Soon after World War II ended, a split occurred between the Soviet Union and other Allied Powers. At issue was the Soviet threat to spread communism beyond its borders. Gradually, a **cold war**, or state of hostility without fighting, developed. Tensions were so high that people feared the outbreak of the world's first all-out nuclear war.

Chapter Overview

Visit the *Human Heritage* Web site at **humanheritage.glencoe.com** and click on **Chapter 38— Chapter Overviews** to preview this chapter.

✅ **Reading Check**
Why did a **cold war** develop?

SECTION 1   An Uneasy Peace

After World War II, Europe began its recovery. Tension between the United States and the Soviet Union grew over problems in Berlin, Korea, Cuba, and Vietnam (vē et nahm′).

Western Europe   When World War II ended, most of Western Europe was in ruins. To help rebuild areas, the United States started a loan program in 1948. It was named the Marshall Plan after George Marshall, the U.S. Secretary of State. Under the Marshall Plan, factories were rebuilt, coal mines were reopened, and roads were repaired or replaced. The economies of Western Europe soon began to grow.

In 1957, six Western European nations formed an economic union called the European Common Market. The six nations were Belgium, France, Italy, Luxembourg (luk′ suhm borg), the Netherlands, and West Germany. They agreed to remove all trade barriers among them. This meant that manufacturers could sell their goods in other member nations without paying tariffs.

AIRLIFT   The children in this photograph watch as an American plane brings food to Berlin during the Soviet blockade. **Why did the Soviet Union block off land and water traffic to the city of Berlin?**

Workers from one nation could take jobs in any other member nation. Between 1957 and 1986, Denmark, Great Britain, Greece, Ireland, Portugal, and Spain also joined the European Common Market. Trade among the nations increased. Today, this economic union is known as the European Union.

The Start of the Cold War

Toward the end of World War II, the Soviet Union set up Communist governments in Bulgaria, Czechoslovakia, Hungary, Poland, and Romania. By 1948, these countries were Soviet **satellite nations,** or countries controlled by a stronger neighboring country. Yugoslavia, although Communist, refused to let itself be put under Soviet control.

The Soviet leader, Stalin, had originally promised the other Allies that he would allow free elections in these countries. When he broke his promise, the cold war began.

Berlin

The first cold war crisis took place over Berlin. In 1948, Great Britain, France, and the United States decided to unite their zones in Germany to encourage peace. The Soviet Union disagreed. It distrusted a united Germany because that nation had invaded the Soviet Union twice in 40 years. In June 1948, the Soviets **blockaded,** or closed off, all land and water traffic into Berlin. They hoped this would force the western powers to leave the city.

In response, the United States and Great Britain began an **airlift,** or a system of carrying supplies by airplane into Berlin.

Reading Check
What **satellite nations** fell under Soviet control?

Reading Check
What was the reason that the Soviets **blockaded** Berlin? What nations organized an **airlift** to break the blockade?

Each day planes flew in tons of food, fuel, and raw materials to the city. In May 1949, the Soviets finally lifted their blockade of Berlin. That same year, two separate governments were set up—a democratic one for West Germany and a Communist one for East Germany. East Germany became a Soviet satellite nation.

The Berlin blockade convinced the western powers that the Soviets wanted to control Europe. In 1949, the United States, Great Britain, and France joined with nine other countries to form the North Atlantic Treaty Organization (NATO). All 12 countries agreed to help one another if attacked. Six years later, the Soviet Union and its satellites formed a similar organization called the Warsaw Pact.

Meanwhile, many people in East Germany were unhappy under Communist rule. About three million fled into West Berlin in search of political freedom and better living conditions. Because many of those who fled were well-educated professionals, the East German government wanted to stop these escapes. So in August 1961, it built a wall between East and West Berlin. The Berlin Wall, with Soviet soldiers guarding it, became a symbol of the split between Communist and non-Communist Europe. Many East Berliners continued to try to escape through the wall, risking their lives.

Korea

After World War II, Korea was also geographically divided. A Communist government was set up in North Korea and a non-Communist government was organized in South Korea. In 1950, North Korea invaded South Korea in an attempt to take over that country. Both the Soviets and the Chinese sent the North Koreans military aid. The United Nations sent soldiers—mostly Americans— to help South Korea.

General Douglas MacArthur, the United Nations commander, suggested that dropping atomic bombs on Chinese bases and supply lines would gain a quick victory. However, President Harry S Truman refused. Truman did not want the Korean War to turn into World War III. In 1953, North Korea and South Korea signed a truce calling for the two countries, and their governments, to remain separate.

Cuba

In 1955 Fidel Castro (fē del' kas trō) launched an unsuccessful revolution in Cuba against dictator Fulgencio Batista (fūl hen' sē ō buh tēs' tuh). In 1959, Castro tried again and finally succeeded—Batista was overthrown.

Castro at first promised free elections and social and economic reforms in Cuba. Many countries, including the United States, supported him. Most of the promises he made, however, were not kept. Cubans who had opposed Castro were jailed or executed. Thousands fled to the United States. Before long, Castro announced that his government would be Communist. He

Photograph of Fidel Castro

NATO Growth Although the Warsaw Pact ended in 1991, NATO continues to grow. In the late 1990s, NATO members voted to invite several former Soviet satellites—the Czech Republic, Hungary, and Poland—to join the organization. In addition, Russia and other members of the former Soviet Union, which dissolved in 1991, were accepted as partner nations.

Student Web Activity
Visit the *Human Heritage* Web site at **humanheritage.glencoe.com** and click on ***Chapter 38—Student Web Activities*** to find out more about the cold war.

Photograph of Vietnam War Protesters

developed close ties with the Soviet Union, which continued to send him economic aid.

In 1961, Cuban refugees who had been trained in the United States invaded Cuba. Their mission was to force Castro out of power. The invasion, in the area known as the Bay of Pigs, failed. Castro then asked the Soviet Union for more military aid. In 1962, Soviet nuclear missile bases were built on the island. The United States blockaded Cuba and insisted the Soviets remove the missiles. The Soviets finally agreed, and another world war was avoided.

Vietnam   In 1941, Vietnam was a French colony and part of a larger region known as French Indochina. Japan invaded Vietnam in 1941, but pulled out of the country in 1945 at the end of World War II. At that time, the Vietnamese hoped to be independent, but they were invaded again by the French. As a result, Communists and non-Communist Vietnamese nationalists joined together in a guerrilla war against the French. The guerrillas were led by a Communist named Ho Chi Minh (hō chē min'), a Vietnamese nationalist.

In 1954, the French were defeated and the country was temporarily divided into two parts—North and South Vietnam. North Vietnam became a Communist country headed by Ho Chi Minh. South Vietnam became a non-Communist country. A 1956 election meant to unite the two countries was never held. It was protested by the South Vietnamese government who feared it would show Ho's strength.

A war for the control of the country erupted between South Vietnam and North Vietnam. Guerrillas, known as the Vietcong, and the Soviet Union aided North Vietnam. The United States had already been sending military supplies to South Vietnam. It began sending combat troops there in 1965. Altogether, more than 3.3 million Americans fought in the Vietnam War. Eventually 58,000 of them lost their lives, and almost $200 billion was spent.

The Vietnam War deeply divided the American people. Many believed the United States should fight to help South Vietnam and prevent the spread of communism. Many others believed the fight was a civil war that the Vietnamese should settle themselves.

In 1973, an agreement between North Vietnam, South Vietnam, and the United States was reached. American troops pulled out of the country. Then, in 1975, troops from North Vietnam moved into South Vietnam and it came under Communist control.

The Space Race   Part of the cold war between the Soviet Union and the United States involved the race to explore space. The Soviets took the first lead. In 1957, they launched *Sputnik I*, the first spacecraft to circle the earth. Four years later, Soviet

Satellite view of Venus

astronaut Yuri Gagarin (yū rē guh gahr' uhn) became the first human being to circle the earth.

Then the United States took the lead. In 1969, American astronaut Neil Armstrong became the first person to walk on the moon. During the 1970s, the first landings on Venus and Mars were made by U.S. unmanned space vehicles. Later, these spacecraft explored Jupiter and Saturn.

Section 1 Assessment

1. **Define:** cold war, satellite nations, blockaded, airlift.
2. Why did Western European nations form the European Common Market?
3. Why did East Germany build the Berlin Wall?
4. Why did Castro have the support of the United States during his revolution? Why did he lose that support?

Critical Thinking

5. **Demonstrating Reasoned Judgment** If you were living during the Vietnam War, would you have supported or opposed the war? Why?

Graphic Organizer Activity

6. Draw this diagram, and use it to summarize the issues during the cold war: Soviet blockade of Berlin, construction of the Berlin Wall, Korean War, Cuban revolution, Vietnamese civil war, launch of *Sputnik I.*

Crisis	Issue Involved

SECTION 2 Communist Powers

After World War II, China became a Communist nation. Later, however, both China and the Soviet Union made changes to the type of communism they practiced.

Revolution in China   While the Soviet Union and the United States were competing in the cold war, communism was gaining support in China. The conditions that led to China's acceptance of communism developed over a long time.

Before the 1900s, there had been several revolts over control of the government. All had failed. In 1911, however, a revolt led by Sun Yat-sen (sun' yaht sen') overturned the government. He formed the Nationalist party, which wanted China to be a free, democratic republic. He was ousted, and Chinese warlords divided the country.

INVASION   Japananese troops invaded the streets of Shanghai, China, in 1937. Chinese soldiers united to fight the attack. **What major Chinese parties cooperated in this effort to fight the Japanese?**

Taiwan Taiwan was named Formosa, meaning "beautiful," by Portuguese explorers. In the 1600s, the island was controlled by the Dutch and then the Spanish. Still later it was acquired by China, then Japan, then China again. China, which regards Taiwan as a province, has strongly resisted Taiwanese moves toward independence.

After Sun died in 1925, Chiang Kai-shek (chyang kī shek') became the leader of the Nationalist party. He tried to unite China and wipe out the Communists. However, in 1927, the Chinese Communists who opposed the Nationalists began a movement to gain control of the country. Their leader was Mao Zedong (mow' dzuh dung').

The struggle between the two parties was interrupted by the Japanese invasion of China in 1937. The Nationalists joined the Communists to fight the Japanese. After the war, however, the struggle between them continued. In 1949, the Communists gained the support of the peasants with promises of land and forced the Nationalists to leave the Chinese mainland and go to the island of Taiwan (tī wahn'). There, Chiang set up a Nationalist government claiming it ruled China. The Communists set up their own government on mainland China headed by Mao Zedong. They called it the People's Republic of China.

China Under Mao

Mao's main goal was to make China a strong, modern country. In 1953, the Chinese began a series of plans to improve the country's economy. By the middle of the 1960s, the Chinese had more food and better health care. Many people had learned how to read and write. Also, under Mao the position of women in China changed. Women were now allowed to choose their own husbands, enter any occupation they chose, and receive equal pay. Men, however, continued to hold the highest positions in government and the best-paying jobs.

Then Mao began to fear that the Chinese had lost their revolutionary spirit. As a result, in 1966 he carried out **purges** (per′ juhs), or removals of undesirable members, of the Communist party. He also purged the country's *intellectuals* (in tuh lek′ chū uhls), or scholars. This purge was called the Cultural Revolution. Students and young adults known as Red Guards attacked politicians, teachers, and others accused of not supporting communism. The purge soon got out of control, however, and there were battles between Red Guards and other citizens. The Red Guards were later broken up.

China After Mao

After Mao died in 1976, a group led by Deng Xiaoping (duhng′ syow ping′) came into power in China. Deng cared more about economic growth than about

Reading Check
Who were some of the victims of Mao Zedong's **purges?**

CHINESE LEADERS   From 1928 to 1949, General Chiang Kai-shek (shown left) was a powerful leader in China. In 1949, the Communists, led by Mao Zedong (shown right), overthrew Chiang's government. Mao proclaimed the People's Republic of China on the Chinese mainland, while Chiang set up the Nationalist government on the island of Taiwan. **How did the Communists gain the support of the Chinese peasants?**

POLITICAL PROTEST   As crowds of Chinese demonstrators filled Tiananmen Square in 1989, government officials decided to attack them. **What were the demonstrators protesting against?**

Tibet Human rights are an issue in Tibet, seized by China in 1951. Eight years later, Tibetans waged an unsuccessful rebellion against Chinese control. Since then, the Dalai Lama, the religious leader of Tibet, has led a worldwide movement in support of Tibetan rights from his home in India. In 1989, the Dalai Lama received the Nobel Peace Prize.

✓ **Reading Check**
Who were the Soviet **hard-liners?**

revolutionary spirit. He encouraged foreign countries to invest money in China. He let many factory managers decide what goods to produce and what prices to charge. As a result of such changes, economic conditions in China improved greatly.

Political conditions, however, remained the same and many people were unhappy. They wanted the same control over politics that they had been given over the economy. Then, beginning in April of 1989, a demonstration took place in Tiananmen (tyen' ahn men) Square in Beijing. For seven weeks, about one million Chinese people, mostly students, gathered in the square and demanded democracy.

The demonstration was peaceful, but it frightened many Communist leaders. So Deng sent Red Army soldiers into Tiananmen Square to break up the gathering. Between 500 and 1,000 civilians were killed. Other students and labor leaders were imprisoned or executed. Since then, there have been changes in economic balance and trade in China, but not in human rights. Chinese leaders do not acknowledge that the people's human rights are being ignored.

Changes in the Soviet Union
Two groups of Communists existed in the Soviet Union after Stalin's rule. **Hard-liners,** or people who stick to the rules regardless of the circumstances, made up one group. They wanted to keep the Soviet Union as it

was. Reformers made up the other group of Communists. They were interested in economic growth, even if that meant introducing capitalism into the country. Under **capitalism,** most production is privately owned rather than owned by the government. After Stalin died in 1953, there was a Communist struggle for control.

In 1955, a reformer, Nikita Khrushchev (nuh kēt′ uh krūsh chof′), became the leader of the Soviet Union. The following year, he began a program of **de-Stalinization** (dē stahl uh nuh zā′ shuhn), or an attack on the policies established by Stalin. Many labor camps were shut down, and the secret police became less violent. More apartment houses were built, and consumer goods became more available.

In 1964, Leonid Brezhnev (lā uh nid brezh′ nef) became the Soviet ruler. Under Brezhnev, life once again became less free for the Soviet people. In 1985, however, a reformer, Mikhail Gorbachev (mēk′ hī el gōr′ buh chahf), came to power. Gorbachev adopted two policies to try to improve the growth of the economy in the Soviet Union.

Under Gorbachev's policy of *glasnost* (glaz nōst), or openness, the Soviet people could say and write what they thought without fear of being punished. Free elections were held in which many non-Communist officials gained office. Under the policy of *perestroika* (per uhs troi kuh), which means restructuring, Gorbachev changed the structure of the Soviet government and moved the country's economy toward capitalism.

As the Soviet Union continued moving toward democracy and capitalism, tensions within the country increased. Some people thought Gorbachev was moving too quickly with reform. Others thought he was not moving fast enough. At the same time, many ethnic groups within the country were demanding independence.

Reading Check
Who owns production under **capitalism?**

Reading Check
What changes took place under **de-Stalinization?**

Reading Check
What was the policy of *glasnost?*

Reading Check
What was the economic goal of *perestroika?*

Section 2 Assessment

1. **Define:** purge, hard-liners, capitalism, de-Stalinization, *glasnost, perestroika.*
2. What was Mao Zedong's main goal for China?
3. Why did some people oppose the ideas of *glasnost* and *perestroika?*

Critical Thinking

4. **Predicting Consequences** Based on recent changes, do you think China will become a democracy or remain under strict Communist control? Explain.

Graphic Organizer Activity

5. Draw this diagram, and use it to compare the People's Republic of China under Mao Zedong and Deng Xiaoping.

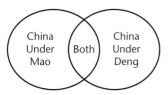

SECTION 3 Developing Nations

Most of the countries in South Asia and Africa gained their independence after World War II. The majority of countries in Latin America gained independence in the early 1800s. All of these countries are considered to be **developing nations.** They generally have little industry and most of the people are poor, uneducated, and make their living from the land.

A great number of developing nations also have rapidly growing populations. They cannot produce enough food to feed their people and must buy it elsewhere. As a result, they do not have enough money to provide decent housing, health care, and education for their citizens.

India's Independence

India, originally under British rule, was one of the first colonial countries of Asia in which nationalism grew. At first, several problems in India had to be dealt with. There were two major religions—Hinduism and Islam—many of whose followers did not like each other. The people also spoke hundreds of different languages. However, they had one thing in common—opposition to British rule.

In 1885, a political party called the Indian National Congress was formed. Its members called for more Indian self-government.

About that time, an Indian leader named Mohandas Gandhi (mah hahn' dahs gahn' dē) began a protest movement against British rule. Gandhi was a lawyer and a member of the upper class, but he identified himself with the common people. He went from village to village talking about self-government. The people called him Mahatma (muh haht' muh), which means Great Soul.

Gandhi did not believe in violence. He believed in **civil disobedience,** or refusing to obey laws considered unjust. He convinced millions of Indians to show their resistance to British rule through peaceful demonstrations and boycotts.

In 1947, Great Britain finally granted independence to its Indian colony. Instead of one country, however, two were formed. India, the larger country, had a majority of Hindus. A separate country, Pakistan, was created that had a majority of Muslims.

During the *partition,* or dividing, of India, fighting broke out between Hindus and Muslims. Many Hindus in Pakistan fled to India, while many Muslims in India fled to Pakistan. Of the more than 12 million people who changed homelands, nearly 1 million were killed in the fighting.

Reading Check
What were most **developing nations** like right after independence?

Reading Check
How did Gandhi use **civil disobedience** to win independence from Great Britain?

INDUSTRIAL INDIA Industry has grown rapidly in India since the nation became independent in 1947. The government has encouraged the establishment of heavy industry in hopes of improving India's economy. Here, workers are employed at an automobile plant. **How do most of India's people make their living?**

In 1971 a civil war broke out between the eastern and western parts of Pakistan. Three years later, Pakistan recognized East Pakistan as the independent nation of Bangladesh.

India Since 1947
After independence, India's leaders worked to set up a stable government. In 1950, a democratic constitution was adopted. Under prime ministers Jawaharlal Nehru (juh wu' har lul nā' rū) and later Indira Gandhi (in dēr' uh gahn' dē), democracy advanced.

Since that time the Indian government has worked to improve people's living conditions. It has encouraged such industries as electric power, iron and steel manufacturing, and textiles. About 70 percent of the Indian people, however, still make their living by farming. Although some have small farms, most work on the estates of large landowners for low pay. Families in Indian villages are generally large although the government has encouraged people to have smaller families.

Many of India's large cities have two sections. One is modern with tall apartment and office buildings. The other section has narrow, twisting, crowded streets. These narrow avenues are lined with two- and three-story, old apartment buildings and hundreds of small businesses.

TECHNOLOGY SKILLS

Using an Electronic Spreadsheet

People use electronic spreadsheets to manage numbers quickly and easily. You can use a spreadsheet any time a problem involves numbers that you can arrange in rows and columns.

Learning the Skill A spreadsheet is an electronic worksheet. All spreadsheets follow a basic design of rows and columns. Each column (vertical) is assigned a letter or a number. Each row (horizontal) is assigned a number. Each point where a column and row intersect is called a cell. The cell's position on the spreadsheet is labeled according to its corresponding column and row—Column A, Row 1 (A1); Column B, Row 2 (B2), and so on.

Spreadsheets use standard formulas to calculate the numbers. You create a mathematical equation that uses these standard formulas, and the computer does the calculations for you.

Skill Practice

Suppose you want to compare the number of births in the three most highly populated nations—China, India, and the United States—over the past five years. Use these steps to create a spreadsheet that will provide this information:

1. In cells B1, C1, and D1 respectively, type the name of each of the three countries listed above. In cell E1, type the term *total*.
2. In cells A2–A6, type each year, starting with the most recent year for which statistics are available.
3. In row 2, enter the number of births that occurred in each nation for the year listed in A2. Repeat this process in rows 3 through 6.
4. Create a formula to calculate the number of children born for the first year on the spreadsheet. The formula for the equation tells what cells (2B + 2C + 2D) to add together.
5. Copy the formula down in the cells for the other four years.
6. Use the process in steps 4 and 5 to create and copy a formula to calculate the total births for each of the three countries over a five-year period.

Malaysia   Malaysia is another developing Asian country that has gone through revolution and successfully built a cooperative government since World War II. Following riots in 1969 between the Malay and the Chinese, the country has become peaceful. With a prospering economy, it lies in a major shipping crossroads of the Pacific Ocean. Muslims, Christians, Buddhists, and Hindus live together, giving Malaysia its cultural richness. The three major ethnic groups of the country—Malays, Chinese, and Indians—cooperatively share power and resources.

Independence in Africa   World War II helped African nationalism grow. During the war, many Africans served in the armies of the European colonial powers. They were sent to fight in many different places around the world. The soldiers saw new sights and learned new skills. When they returned to Africa, they were not content with conditions there and wanted self-rule.

Nationalism grew quickly among educated Africans who worked for independence in different ways. They formed politi-

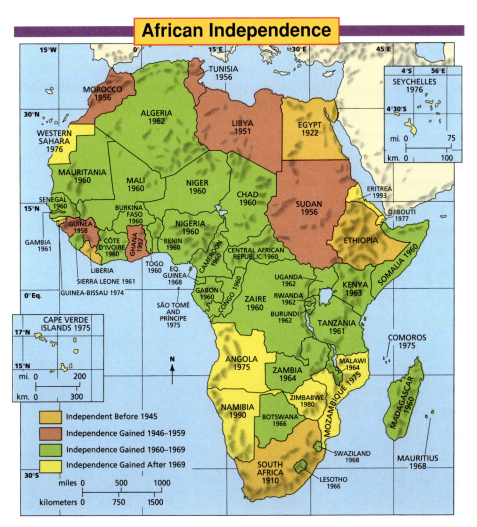

African Independence

Independent Before 1945
Independence Gained 1946–1959
Independence Gained 1960–1969
Independence Gained After 1969

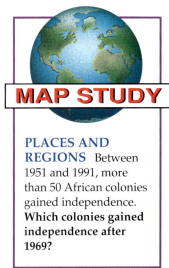

MAP STUDY

PLACES AND REGIONS Between 1951 and 1991, more than 50 African colonies gained independence. **Which colonies gained independence after 1969?**

Then... & Now

Meaningful Names

Once they won freedom, many African nations took new names with deep historical meaning. Zimbabwe, for example, refers to the 1,000-year-old city of Great Zimbabwe. Massive, protective stone walls gave the city its name, which means "stone enclosure."

Reading Check

What type of farming is done by **subsistence farmers?** What are some of Africa's most important **cash crops?**

cal parties and bargained with government leaders. They also boycotted goods from colonial countries. In some cases, violence broke out.

In 1960, 17 African countries became independent. The year became known as the "Year of Africa." Other African colonies freed themselves from European rule in following years.

At first most newly independent African countries set up democratic governments. Many did not last, however, and today most have one-party governments or are ruled by a military leader.

Many African countries—including Angola, Ethiopia, Mozambique (mō zam beek'), Nigeria, Rwanda (roo ahn' duh), Somalia, Sudan, Zaire (zīhr), and Zimbabwe (zim bahb' wā)—have suffered from civil war since they became independent. When Europeans originally drew colonial boundaries in Africa, they often put groups that had been fighting one another for hundreds of years in the same colony. Fighting often broke out among these groups.

Farming   About 70 percent of all African workers make their living from farming. In the past, most farmers were **subsistence farmers.** They produced only enough food for their families. Today much of the land is used to grow **cash crops,** or crops that are sold in regional or world markets. In fact, more than half of Africa's income results from selling such crops as cacao (kuh kā' ō), coffee, cotton, peanuts, rubber, and tea.

Rural and Urban Africa   Many Africans still live in small rural villages, such as the one in Zaire shown here (left), and hold onto their traditional ways. Africa also has many large, modern cities. **What differences face villagers who move to the city?**

In recent years, because of poor farming methods, drought, disease, lack of fertilizer, and the increased growth of cash crops, there have been food shortages in Africa. Many African nations must buy food from other countries. Often this food is expensive and not plentiful. African governments have begun to teach farmers better farming methods, but progress is slow. The United States has sent advisers also.

Large parts of Africa, however, are rich in energy resources. Coal, natural gas, oil, and hydroelectric power are plentiful. The continent also has large mineral deposits, such as copper, tin, iron, manganese, gold, and diamonds. To make full use of these resources, however, more money and skilled workers are needed. More roads and railroads are also needed to move the resources to market.

Ways of Life   Life has been changing in Africa since the 1960s. Most people still live in rural villages, where they belong to **extended families.** These are made up of parents, children, and other close relatives who live together in one house. Most houses in Africa consist of several buildings surrounded by a wall or fence. Rural village houses are often made of mud, clay, or tall grasses and might not have running water, electricity, or indoor plumbing. Large African cities, however, are modern, active centers of growth and progress.

Children in rural areas may receive little or no formal schooling, but they have knowledge of and pride in their group's culture. Many leaders of emerging African nations have encouraged the pride each group within a nation shows in its heritage. Writers, musicians, artists, and scholars of African nations are recognized all over the world for their talent and achievements.

African heritage is also seen in the special body markings and certain colors and kinds of clothing and jewelry African groups display. For example, the Fulani (fū lah' nē) of West Africa wear royal blue, red, and yellow. The Masai (mah' sī) women of Kenya wear huge collars of brightly colored beads.

In recent years, many Africans have left their home villages and moved to the cities in search of jobs and better housing and education. Some high schools and colleges in the cities offer training in higher-level occupations and technology. They hope trained young people will return to the villages to improve their way of life. Lack of education, however, is a serious problem.

Foreign Influence in Latin America   Even after gaining independence, most Latin American countries remained under foreign control. Industrial nations such as Great Britain, France, Germany, and the United States organized businesses there. They produced such goods as bananas, sugar, coffee, metals, and oil which were sold in markets overseas.

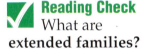

Reading Check
What are **extended families?**

Photograph of Housing in Rio de Janeiro, Brazil

LATIN AMERICAN FARMING   Although Latin America is primarily an agricultural region, wealthy landowners hold much of the land in large ranches. These haciendas are worked by peasants with few modern techniques or tools. Here, a Mexican farmer plows behind a team of oxen. **Why do most hacienda owners have little or no desire to modernize their farms?**

Latin American nations benefited from foreign investments. Wages rose, and there were more jobs. Foreign business interests also built roads, railroads, and ports. They set up telephone systems and electric plants.

Still, there were problems. The economies of most of the countries depended on only one or two products. If the price of these products dropped, their incomes did too. Also, food, clothing, household goods, and other such items had to be brought in from other countries at high cost. In addition, Latin American nationalists who wanted their countries to be free of outside influence resented foreigners.

Domestic Changes in Latin America   Since World War II, most Latin American countries have been trying to industrialize. They have greatly increased their production of such goods as steel, chemicals, oil, and automobiles. Argentina, Brazil, and Mexico are now fairly well-industrialized. Yet even they do not produce enough to meet the needs of their growing populations.

The Latin American economy depends on farming. Most land is held in *haciendas* (ah sē en′ duhz), or large ranches. These are owned by a few very rich families. Most work on the *haciendas* is done by peasants known as *campesinos* (kam puh sē′ nos).

Reading Check
What are *haciendas?* How do the *campesinos* earn a living?

Campesinos usually live in villages. Their small houses are made of wood, mud, sun-dried brick, or stone. Larger villages have a church and a few stores and hold open-air markets once a week. People meet there to exchange news as well as to buy and sell food and hand-made goods.

The *campesinos* farm the land in the same way their parents and grandparents did. They are not encouraged to learn new ways. Peasant labor is cheap, so most *hacienda* owners have no wish to modernize or reform the economic system. Often the result is that the land is poorly managed and crops are small.

The *hacienda* system holds back economic progress. Many Latin Americans would like to end it. They believe that farm production will rise if *campesinos* are allowed to own land and learn new ways of farming. In recent years, peasants in several Latin American countries have started revolutions for land reform. This reform has been opposed by the governments and wealthy landowners. Some of the worst violence has taken place in El Salvador, Nicaragua, and Peru. The demand for a voice in their governments by Latin American people, however, has increased.

Latin American cities have also grown larger in recent years. Poor farming methods, drought, warfare, or drops in farm prices have forced millions throughout Latin America off the land and into the cities. There are not enough jobs in the cities to go around, however, for all of these people.

Linking Across Time

Rain Forests   Rain forests once covered much of Central America. However, the clearing of land for ranches and farmland and the cutting of timber for export (right) reduced the rain forests of some nations by almost half. Starting in the late 1970s, Costa Rica set an example for other nations by creating parks and preserves to protect its remaining rain forests (left). **What other problems have resulted from Latin American dependence on cash crops?**

Section 3 Assessment

1. **Define:** developing nations, civil disobedience, subsistence farmers, cash crops, extended families, *haciendas*, *campesinos*.
2. How did Gandhi show his resistance to British rule?
3. Why is 1960 called the "Year of Africa"?
4. How does the *hacienda* system hold back economic progress in Latin America?

Critical Thinking

5. **Drawing Conclusions** How do you think civil wars have affected African nations in recent years?

Graphic Organizer Activity

6. Draw this diagram, and use it to show supporting details for this generalization: World War II helped spark the independence movement in Africa.

```
           ┌─────────────────────┐
           │   Generalization    │
           └─────────────────────┘
Supporting  1. _____
Details     2. _____
            3. _____
            4. _____
```

Chapter Summary & Study Guide

1. After World War II ended, a cold war developed between the United States and the Soviet Union, with the first crisis taking place during the 1948 blockade of Berlin.
2. The cold war turned hot when North Korean soldiers invaded South Korea, and U.N. troops led by the United States became involved in the conflict.
3. The 1959 Cuban revolution led by Fidel Castro brought a communist government to Cuba.
4. Vietnam was the site of a war between the North Vietnamese and South Vietnamese that lasted until 1975.
5. Led by Mao Zedong, the Communists defeated Chinese Nationalists in 1949 and formed the People's Republic of China.
6. Although Deng Xiaoping relaxed some of China's economic policies, he limited political freedoms.
7. Under Mikhail Gorbachev, the policies of *glasnost* and *perestroika* moved the Soviet Union toward capitalism and greater freedom.
8. Most of the developing nations of South Asia, Africa, and Latin America have struggled with their lack of industry and their dependence on cash crops.
9. Since independence, Indian leaders have tried to set up a stable government and improve living conditions for the poor.
10. The nationalism triggered by World War II led African nations to seek independence. However, imperialism left these nations with numerous problems.

HISTORY Online

Self-Check Quiz

Visit the *Human Heritage* Web site at **humanheritage. glencoe.com** and click on *Chapter 38—Self-Check Quiz* to assess your understanding of this chapter.

Using Key Terms

Imagine you are a newspaper reporter looking back on events in the world since World War II. Write a newspaper article describing the changes in the world since the war. Use the following words in your article.

cold war
blockaded
purges
glasnost
developing nations
haciendas

satellite nations
airlift
capitalism
perestroika
cash crops
campesinos

Understanding Main Ideas

1. How did the United States propose to rebuild Western Europe following World War II?
2. Why did the Soviet Union blockade Berlin in 1948?
3. What changes did Castro make once he came to power in Cuba?
4. Why did Mao Zedong order the Cultural Revolution?
5. What were the demonstrators at Tiananmen Square demanding?
6. What problems do most African nations face today?

Critical Thinking

1. Why do you think Chinese leaders restrict political freedom? Explain your reasoning.
2. What do you think might have happened if Mikhail Gorbachev had not introduced the policies of *glasnost* and *perestroika*?

3. If you were the leader of a developing Latin American country, what actions would you take to industrialize your country?

Graphic Organizer Activity

History Create a time line like the one shown, and use it to describe important events that occurred in each of the following years of the cold war: 1948, 1949, 1950, 1954, 1957, 1959, 1961. (Some years may have more than one event.)

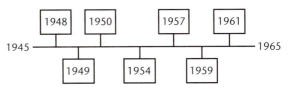

Geography in History

Human Systems Refer to the map tracing African independence on page 637. Note the locations of countries that gained their independence before 1945. Why might you expect revolutions for freedom to develop in coastal countries?

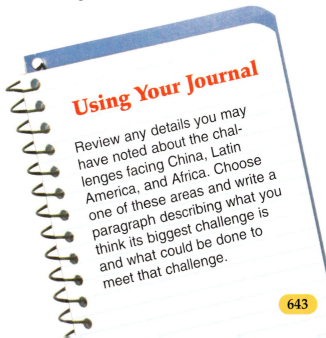

Using Your Journal

Review any details you may have noted about the challenges facing China, Latin America, and Africa. Choose one of these areas and write a paragraph describing what you think its biggest challenge is and what could be done to meet that challenge.

The World Since 1989

1989–Present

▲ iMac computer,
a symbol of global
communication

The International Space Station, 2002 ▶

1989
The cold
war ends

1991
The Soviet Union
breaks up

1994
South Africa holds its
first all-race election

2001
World responds
to terrorist
attacks on U.S.

2003
U.S. and British
forces invade
Iraq

Chapter Overview

Visit the *Human Heritage* Web site at **humanheritage.glencoe.com** and click on *Chapter 39— Chapter Overviews* to preview this chapter.

Chapter Focus

Read to Discover

- How independence came to the nations of Eastern Europe.
- What changes came to Russia after the breakup of the Soviet Union.
- How nations responded to issues of war and peace after the cold war ended.
- What challenges the world faces in the 2000s.

 Terms to Learn

aggression
coup
sovereign
secede
autonomous
apartheid
terrorism
euro

 People to Know

Boris Yeltsin
Lech Walesa
Saddam Hussein
Nelson Mandela
George W. Bush
Osama bin
    Laden

 Places to Locate

Berlin
Chechnya
Persian Gulf
Kosovo
Northern Ireland
Hong Kong
Taiwan
East Timor
Afghanistan
Iraq

Why It's Important   The 1980s and 1990s saw the end of the cold war and the collapse of the Soviet Union. People looked forward to a new era of peace. However, national and ethnic rivalries soon erupted around the world. Regional conflicts forced leaders to develop new rules for stopping **aggression,** or warlike acts, and intervening in the affairs of other nations.

As the 2000s opened, another threat came from groups that used violence against ordinary citizens to achieve political aims. It had become clear that nations needed to work together to solve these and other problems.

 **Reading Check**
What is **aggression**?

SECTION 1   # The End of the Cold War

The 1990s saw the collapse of communism in Eastern Europe and the breakup of the Soviet Union. Freed from Communist control, independent nations throughout the region struggled to develop new economic and political systems.

A Spirit of Democracy   The Communist hold on government weakened under Soviet premier Mikhail Gorbachev. Earlier Soviet rulers had refused to publicly discuss problems facing the Soviet

Student Web Activity

Visit the *Human Heritage* Web site at **humanheritage.glencoe.com** and click on ***Chapter 39— Student Web Activities*** to find out more about the fall of the Berlin Wall.

Union. Gorbachev, however, believed the only way to solve these problems was to talk about them freely.

As Gorbachev introduced his new policy of glasnost, or openness, to the Soviet Union, he urged leaders in the Soviet satellites to do the same. He indicated that the Soviet Union would no longer use troops and tanks to support Communist governments, as had been done in Hungary in 1956 and in Czechoslovakia in 1968.

The first successful challenge to Communist rule came in Poland. In January 1989, the Polish government lifted its ban on Solidarity, a labor union that had been calling for reform since 1980. In June, Polish voters elected Solidarity members to two-thirds of the seats in the Polish legislature. For the first time, a Communist government in Eastern Europe had lost power as a result of an election.

Fall of the Berlin Wall   In East Germany, Communist leader Erich Honecker ignored the people's call for reform. In 1989, however, Hungary started reforms and opened its borders with Austria. Thousands of East Germans—mostly young people—took this chance to show their rejection of communism by fleeing through Hungary into western Europe. Meanwhile, thousands of other East Germans held protest marches against the government.

In October 1989, Honecker resigned. On November 9, at the stroke of midnight, officials in East Berlin threw open the main gate in the Berlin Wall—a 28-mile-long, steel-and-concrete symbol of the

Linking Across Time

Collapse of Communism   The collapse of communism in Eastern Europe was symbolized by the destruction of the Berlin Wall in 1989 (below). Today pieces of the wall can be found on display in the United States (right) and in other places around the world. **When did Germany become reunited?**

cold war. A roar went up as people from both East and West Berlin climbed on top of the wall and danced with joy.

The next morning, a gigantic headline in a West Berlin newspaper declared "BERLIN IS BERLIN AGAIN!" That day, soldiers began to knock down the wall. Civilians joined them, whacking away with hammers, axes, and chisels. By December, the entire wall had disappeared.

The Last Satellites

East German demands for freedom sparked changes in other Eastern European nations. A week after officials opened the Berlin Wall, Bulgaria's hard-line Communist boss resigned. A little later, popular elections overturned Communist rule in Hungary and Czechoslovakia. When the Communist leader of Romania tried to crush the reform movement, rebels tried him and then executed him for crimes against the people.

As one Communist government after another collapsed in Eastern Europe, Gorbachev astounded the world by refusing to interfere. Throughout 1989, he worked with leaders in Europe and the United States to promote peace in the region.

In early 1990, East Germany held its first democratic election since the rise of Adolf Hitler in the 1930s. On October 3, it was reunited with West Germany. That December, Germans elected Helmut Kohl as the first chancellor of the reunited nation. The cold war, which had begun with the division of Germany after World War II, was over.

Conflict Within the Soviet Union

As former Soviet satellites celebrated their independence, trouble brewed within the Soviet Union. The new spirit of openness introduced by Gorbachev allowed **dissent**, or criticism, against the government for the first time since the 1917 Communist takeover.

Although widely popular in Europe and the United States, Gorbachev found himself attacked at home by both hard-liners and reformers. Hard-liners blasted Gorbachev for "giving up" Eastern Europe. They resisted reform, fearing both the loss of their jobs and the weakening of Soviet power. Because the hard-liners included many military leaders, Gorbachev moved carefully to avoid a takeover of the government. The slow pace of change provoked criticism from reformers led by Boris Yeltsin.

Yeltsin's outspoken comments caused a break with Gorbachev, who dismissed him from important positions within the Communist party. Yeltsin responded by taking his case to the Soviet people. In May 1990, he won election as president of Russia, the largest of the 15 Soviet republics. For the first time, a Russian head of state had been elected by the people. Two months later, Yeltsin surprised hard-liners by publicly quitting the Communist party.

Meanwhile, people in the other 14 Soviet republics talked openly of independence. In March 1990, Lithuania—a Baltic state

Fun Facts . . . .

East Germany
On October 7, 1989, East Germany celebrated its 40th anniversary. When Gorbachev showed up to speak in East Berlin, thousands of protestors shouted, "Gorbi, help us!" They then started chanting a popular political slogan, "We are the people!"

Reading Check
What is **dissent**?

Boris N. Yeltsin

Commonwealth of Independent States map showing Russia, Ukraine, Belarus, Moldova, Lithuania, Latvia, Estonia, Georgia, Armenia, Azerbaijan, Kazakhstan, Uzbekistan, Turkmenistan, Kyrgyzstan, Tajikistan with capitals including Tallinn, Riga, Vilnius, Minsk, Moscow, Kiev, Chisinău, Tbilisi, Yerevan, Baku, Astana, Tashkent, Ashgabat, Dushanbe, Bishkek. Includes Arctic Ocean, Pacific Ocean, Black Sea, Caspian Sea, Aral Sea.

• Republic capital

miles 0 — 500 — 1000
kilometers 0 — 750 — 1500

MAP STUDY

PLACES AND REGIONS What geographic factors made it easier for Russia to have power over the other former Soviet republics?

Reading Check

Why did Communist hard-liners attempt a **coup** in 1991?

occupied by Russia at the beginning of World War II—proclaimed its freedom. Instead of stopping the revolt, Gorbachev negotiated Lithuania's independence. The other Baltic states—Latvia and Estonia—declared their freedom in the following year.

Hard-liners exploded at the breakup of what they called the "Soviet empire." In August 1991, the military and secret police arranged a **coup** (koo), or forced takeover of the government. They placed Gorbachev under house arrest and vowed to rebuild the Communist state.

In a tense, three-day struggle known as the "Second Russian Revolution," Yeltsin stepped in to restore order. He condemned the leaders of the revolt, who then lost the support of the military. On August 24, Gorbachev returned to Moscow. The next day, he shut down the Communist party, thus ending 74 years of Communist rule.

Popular anger at the Communist party and secret police now boiled over. People tore down statues of Communist leaders such as Vladimir Lenin and Joseph Stalin. They rejected names given to cities to honor Communists. Leningrad, for example, returned to its pre-1924 name of St. Petersburg.

Independence and Ethnic Rivalries   By the end of 1991, all 15 Soviet republics had proclaimed their independence. In December, Gorbachev—a ruler without a country—resigned. Under the leadership of Yeltsin, 11 former Soviet republics formed the Commonwealth of Independent States (CIS)—a loose confederation of **sovereign**, or self-governing, nations.

The growth of independence went hand-in-hand with a spirit of nationalism among the many ethnic and religious groups in Eastern Europe and the former Soviet Union. Starting in 1991, Yugoslavia—a confederation of six individual republics—began to split apart as ethnic rivalries erupted in war. Two years later, Czechoslovakia peacefully split into the Czech Republic and the Republic of Slovakia. That same year, two republics quit the CIS, while Russia acted increasingly on its own.

Within Russia, rebels in the state of Chechnya tried to **secede**, or withdraw, to form their own government. Yeltsin responded by sending in troops and tanks. The drawn-out battle lasted throughout the Yeltsin presidency of the 1990s. The use of force and the failure to resolve the conflict weakened Yeltsin's reputation as a reformer.

Economic Hardships   Perhaps no single issue troubled the new governments more than the economy. In the effort to win the cold war, Communist leaders had neglected economic development. As a result, the new governments inherited outdated industries and a shortage of consumer goods, such as household appliances.

For many years, Communist governments had controlled prices, wages, and the production of goods. With the collapse of communism, however, the principle of supply and demand went into effect. In most places, consumer goods remained in short supply throughout the 1990s. This situation created a high demand, which in turn pushed up prices. Because governments no longer employed workers in state-owned businesses, unemployment soared and wages dropped.

Governments moved to **privatize**, or allow the private ownership of, state-owned stores, businesses, and factories. However, few people had enough money or experience to run businesses based on free competition—the cornerstone of capitalism.

By the mid-1990s, about 30 percent of the Russian population had fallen into poverty. Strikes shook Poland as workers demanded wage increases. Throughout the region, interest rates skyrocketed as investment money remained scarce.

Political Challenges   At first, citizens expressed a willingness to endure the economic hardships. But as the excitement over independence cooled, the pains of poverty tested people's faith in democracy. Open elections allowed political parties to challenge the supporters of independence. In some nations, including Russia, the

✓ **Reading Check**
What are **sovereign** nations? How did Yeltsin respond when Chechnya tried to **secede?**

Chechen rebel

✓ **Reading Check**
What obstacles slowed Russian efforts to **privatize** businesses, shops, and factories?

Lech Walesa, the leader of Solidarity

Communists reminded people of a time when the government put wages in their pockets and bread on their tables.

In 1994, Hungary elected a number of former Communists to the legislature. In 1995, a former Communist defeated Lech Walesa—the leader of Solidarity—in his bid for reelection as the president of Poland. In 1996, a half dozen candidates in Russia, including a Communist, tried to take the presidency away from Boris Yeltsin.

By the end of the 1990s, however, none of those nations had returned to communism. In 1997, a coalition of groups led by Solidarity overwhelmingly defeated Communist candidates to the legislature. That year, the North Atlantic Treaty Organization (NATO) felt secure enough in the political future of Poland, Hungary, and the Czech Republic to admit all three former Soviet satellites as members.

Suddenly, on December 31, 1999, Russian president Boris Yeltsin resigned. Vladimir Putin was named acting president, later winning the presidency in elections held in 2000. This peaceful transfer of power showed how much the political climate had changed since the days of Communist rule.

Perhaps the most important change in Russia was in the attitudes of young people who grew up during the 1980s and 1990s. They lived at a time when Russians won the right to make their own decisions and to vote freely. As one Russian exchange student in the United States put it: "Let me tell you how Russia has changed. I'm not a Communist. My mother is not a Communist. My father is not a Communist. Do you think I could have said that in the old days?"

POLITICAL CHANGE   Teenagers in Russia have more social and political freedom than their parents or grandparents. **What political and economic challenges did Russia face after the fall of communism?**

Reading a Demographic Map

In order to show information about where people live on the earth, mapmakers use **demographic maps.** Among other things, these maps can show population density, or the average number of people per square mile, or square kilometer, of land.

Some parts of the world have many people living in each square mile, or square kilometer. People generally live in areas with good physical environments. Other parts of the world have few people, and there are even some areas in which no people live. These are known as *uninhabited* areas.

For example, on the "World Population" map below, the green color indicates areas, such as Southeast Asia, with more than 250 people per square mile, or more than 100 people per square kilometer. This is the highest population density shown. The light brown color indicates areas, such as Antarctica, that are uninhabited.

Map Practice

1. **What color represents 60-125 people per square mile (25-50 per sq. km)?**
2. **What areas in South America have densities of 2-60 people per square mile (1-25 per sq. km)?**

World Population

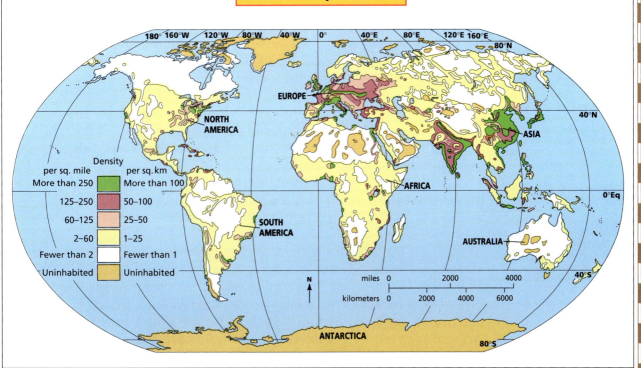

Section 1 Assessment

1. **Define:** aggression, dissent, coup, sovereign, secede, privatize.
2. What changes took place in Eastern Europe as a result of reforms introduced by Mikhail Gorbachev?
3. Why did hard-liners in the Soviet Union try to take control of the government?

Critical Thinking

4. **Making Predictions** Do you think the world has seen the last of communism in Russia? Why or why not?

Graphic Organizer Activity

5. Draw a diagram like this one, and use it to show some of the problems faced by former Soviet satellites.

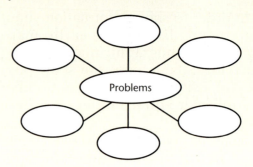

Problems

SECTION 2   World Challenges

With the collapse of the Soviet Union, world peace was within reach. There were problems, though, with achieving this peace. During the cold war, the United States and the Soviet Union competed against each other to control events in other nations. After the cold war ended, however, new problems developed. Long-standing issues between nations and groups of people erupted into violence and confusion. World leaders also had to deal with scattered but well-organized groups that used violence to achieve their goals.

In the 1990s, world leaders struggled to find new ways to bring about peace. United States leaders looked for the help of other countries before stepping in alone to deal with certain problems. Violence in the Middle East, the Balkans, and elsewhere made solving problems difficult. At times, global organizations such as the United Nations (UN) seemed unable to have any effect on the violence. Peace, though, seemed possible in South Africa, Ireland, and other places.

Iraq   One of the greatest challenges after the cold war was dealing with the Middle Eastern country of Iraq. In August 1990, Iraq's leader, dictator Saddam Hussein, ordered the invasion of his oil-rich neighbor Kuwait. He also moved Iraqi troops close to the border of Saudi Arabia, which is the site of the world's largest known oil reserves. United States leaders were concerned about the safety of the countries in the Middle East. It used the United

Nations as a **forum,** or meeting place. A *coalition*, or a temporary union of nations, was put together to free Kuwait. A coalition army attacked Iraq in January 1991, after Hussein ignored a UN deadline to remove his troops. The United States supported the coalition army. This action was named the Persian Gulf War because of Kuwait's location along the Persian Gulf. By late February, Kuwait had been freed.

The Persian Gulf War had mixed results. Although Iraq was forced to leave Kuwait, Hussein was still the country's leader. He continued to abuse the rights of people who did not support him, such as the Kurds. The Kurds are a people living in northern Iraq. Also, UN inspectors were not allowed to check areas in Iraq where they thought dangerous weapons were being stored or built. The inspectors were supposed to make sure Iraq had stopped producing deadly weapons, which included poison gas and bombs that spread dangerous germs that could hurt adults and children.

During the early 2000s, the weapons inspections issue was still a problem. Leaders in the United States believed that as long as Hussein stayed in power, Iraq would develop deadly nuclear weapons. In December 2002, the UN sent experts back into Iraq to search for nuclear and other deadly weapons. The United States did not believe Hussein was fully cooperating, however. In March 2003, U.S. and British forces invaded Iraq. About a month later, Hussein was overthrown and fled Baghdad, the capital. He was captured by a U.S.-led coalition in December 2003. American forces began helping to rebuild the country's schools, roads, hospitals, and power plants. The Iraqi people faced the daunting task of creating a democratic government.

Reading Check
What is a **forum?**

GULF WAR   As Allied forces put an end to Saddam Hussein's invasion of Kuwait, retreating Iraqi troops set fire to hundreds of oil wells. **What actions did Saddam Hussein take after the Gulf War?**

Oil Production Kuwait and Saudi Arabia are believed to possess more than 50 percent of the world's known oil reserves. Kuwait has about 20 percent, while Saudi Arabia has 33 percent.

KOSOVO CONFLICT   Reports of fighting and hardship for the people of Kosovo spread throughout the world. **How did NATO react to the fighting in Kosovo?**

Balkan Wars   Yugoslavia was a war-torn area located in Europe's Balkan Peninsula. Yugoslavia's problems developed in 1980, the year Communist leader Josip Broz Tito died. Since World War II, Tito had held Yugoslavia's six republics together with his iron-fisted rule. When Tito died, however, different ethnic groups struggled for power.

The republic of Serbia tried to rule all of Yugoslavia. Four other republics, though, opposed Serb control and declared their independence. These republics included Slovenia, Croatia, Bosnia-Herzegovina, and Macedonia.

Different groups were struggling for power within each republic in the late 1980s and early 1990s. Fighting in Croatia and Bosnia-Herzegovina was the heaviest. Many people died or fled their homes, becoming refugees. Countries around the world sent food, medical supplies, and warm clothing to help the refugees.

With UN support, NATO carried out air strikes in order to force the different groups to take part in peace talks. The United States supported these peace talks. In 1995, the leaders of Bosnia-Herzegovina, Yugoslavia, and Croatia met in Dayton, Ohio. They signed the Dayton Accords. This peace agreement divided Bosnia into Croat-Muslim and Serb regions. NATO troops stayed in Bosnia to prevent the spread of more violence.

Meanwhile, Serb pride was still strong in Yugoslavia. The Serbs decided to try to remove Muslim Albanians from Kosovo. Kosovo had been an **autonomous,** or self-governing, province of Yugoslavia. Albanians formed about 90 percent of Kosovo's

Reading Check
What did it mean that Kosovo was an **autonomous** province of Yugoslavia?

people, and many of them wanted independence. As many Albanian refugees left Kosovo in 1999, NATO bombed Serbian military targets. The Serbs finally allowed a NATO peacekeeping force to enter Kosovo. In the fall of 2000, a new democratic government emerged in Serbia.

Arabs and Israelis   The conflict in the Middle East between Arabs and Israelis has deep roots. During World War I, many Arabs sided with Great Britain and France against the Turks of the Ottoman Empire. The Arab countries thought that this would help them gain their independence. By 1947, a number of Arab territories had won their freedom.

At the same time, the situation in Palestine was different. Jews and Arabs lived in Palestine. In 1947, the UN voted to divide Palestine into a Jewish state and an Arab state. The Arabs in Palestine and in neighboring countries did not support this plan. In 1948, when the British withdrew, the Jews established the nation of Israel in their part of Palestine.

Most Arabs opposed the creation of Israel, and five Arab nations waged war on the new nation. The war was difficult for both the Israeli and Arab people. Many lost relatives and friends in the fighting. The war ended with Israel's victory.

Between 1948 and 1993, Arab nations and Israel fought more wars. As a result, Israel won control of some neighboring lands. An Arab group known as the Palestine Liberation Organization (PLO) opposed Israel and wanted an entirely Palestinian state, rather than the state of Israel. The PLO continued to carry out

MIDDLE EAST CONFLICT   Attempts to solve the problems between Jews and Palestinians in the Middle East have failed. **When was the nation of Israel established?**

attacks on Israel. Throughout the 1990s, there were times of peace and times of war.

Although many Arabs and Israelis supported peace efforts, hatred and fears ran deep on both sides. In 2000, violence erupted between the Israelis and Arabs after peace talks failed. Observers believed that ending violence and restoring trust would be necessary before any new peace talks could begin.

Toward Peace in Ireland   In the late 1990s, the world saw progress in settling a European conflict that dated back hundreds of years. Historically, Ireland has been controlled by Great Britain. The people of Northern Ireland were mostly Protestants and were satisfied to be ruled by Great Britain. The people of southern Ireland, however, were mostly Catholic and wanted to be independent. In 1922, Catholic southern Ireland finally became self-governing, while the largely Protestant north remained a part of Great Britain.

Beginning in the 1960s, violent fighting broke out between the Catholics and Protestants in British-ruled Northern Ireland. Both groups wanted to control the government. This fighting continued for years.

In 1998, a peace agreement was reached that went into effect the following year. Catholics and Protestants in Northern Ireland agreed to share power in the government. Both groups agreed to end the violence. Continuing distrust between the two sides, however, has made achieving peace very difficult.

NORTHERN IRELAND   After nearly 30 years of violence, Gerry Adams (center), a Catholic leader, joins with the people of Belfast in celebrating the peace agreement. **What were the terms of peace agreed upon in 1998?**

Changes in China

During the 1990s, the future of the world's remaining Communist nations was in doubt. The Soviet Union—formerly a strong Communist country—had collapsed. Without Soviet aid, governments in Cuba and North Korea had severe economic problems. China, however, seemed to be moving toward capitalism.

Chinese leaders in the 1990s set up policies to change the economic system of communism. They began to allow some people to own their own businesses. The Communist party, however, was still in control of the government.

Hong Kong, a busy port on the south China coast, was returned to China in 1997. Until that time, it had been under British rule. Hong Kong had become one of the world's largest financial and trade centers. The Chinese government agreed to allow Hong Kong to keep its capitalist system for 50 years. Many Hong Kong citizens, though, worried about their future under Chinese rule.

Fears over the future of Hong Kong grew worse because of Chinese actions toward Taiwan. Taiwan is an independent country located near China. Non-Communist Chinese leaders have ruled the island since 1949, when the Communists took control of the mainland. China claims Taiwan as its territory. People living on Taiwan, however, do not want to be under Chinese Communist rule. The people are Chinese but have been independent from the mainland for many years. Taiwan also has a free press and democratic elections.

By 2000, the United States had developed a closer trading relationship with China. Charges that the Chinese government did not respect the human rights of its people set off a debate within the United States. Supporters of trade between the two nations claimed that the only way to bring change to China was to speed up the development of capitalism there.

Port of Hong Kong

Indonesia

For much of the past century, Indonesia has had many problems. Indonesia is made up of more than 17,000 islands. It stretches along the Equator from the Malay Peninsula toward Australia. Indonesia is one of the world's most populated countries. It is also the largest Muslim country and one of the world's leading oil producers.

In 1949, Indonesia won its independence after centuries of Dutch rule. Indonesia's first president tried to unite the country's islands under one government. However, he faced two challenges. Some of the islands wanted greater self-rule, while the Indonesian Communist party wanted to gain control of the country.

In 1965, the communists tried to take over Indonesia's government. Army forces quickly put down the uprising. The government continued to maintain strict control of its people.

This government approved the takeover of East Timor, a nearby island colony that, until 1975, had been Portuguese. The people of East Timor organized an independence movement. Over the next

Macao On December 20, 1999, Portugal returned Macao—a peninsula and two islands on the south coast of China—to the People's Republic. Founded in 1557, the port was the oldest European outpost in China. As with Hong Kong, Chinese officials promised to respect Macao's way of life for 50 years after the start of Chinese rule.

INDONESIA   A mosque rises above a modern street in Indonesia. **What were the two problems that Indonesia faced after it won its independence from the Dutch?**

25 years, nearly 200,000 East Timorese died from famine, disease, and fighting.

By the late 1990s, falling oil prices and government corruption had deeply affected Indonesia. As a result of student protests, the strict government was replaced in 1999. The new Indonesian government agreed to hold a **referendum,** or popular vote, for the independence of East Timor. As expected, most East Timorese voted to form their own nation. Fighting broke out among people who did not want East Timor to be separate from Indonesia. In 2002, peace and independence finally came to East Timor.

Meanwhile, Indonesia established a democratic government. In 2001, its new president faced a weakened economy and uprisings in islands that also wanted to separate from Indonesia.

Struggles and Progress in Africa   As you know, Africa is made up of many different countries. As the 2000s began, most nations in Africa had been free for less than 50 years. Lack of experience in self-government led to **authoritarian rule**, or government in which one ruler of one political party holds power, for many of these countries. Like other parts of the world, differences that date back hundreds of years also deeply divided some African nations.

During the 1990s, Somalia, Rwanda, Sierra Leone, the Democratic Republic of the Congo, and Liberia suffered bloody wars. Many Africans lost their lives, and large numbers of refugees fled to neighboring countries.

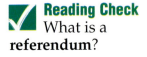
Reading Check
What is a **referendum**?

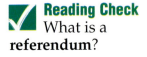
Reading Check
Why did **authoritarian rule** develop in many African countries?

Even with the conflicts in many places, some experts feel that progress can still be seen. Today there are fewer civil wars in Africa than in the past. Democratic elections have been carried out in some nations. In 2002, African leaders formed the African Union to deal with the problems of the continent.

Perhaps the most remarkable changes, however, have taken place in South Africa. In 1948, South Africa passed into law a system of **apartheid**, or forced separation of races. Apartheid allowed for a small group of whites to have power over the much larger group of black South Africans. To end apartheid, the United States and other nations placed trade restrictions on South Africa in the 1980s.

In 1989, the white South African government led by President F. W. de Klerk gave in to world opinion. It lifted the long-standing ban on the African National Congress (ANC). The ANC was a political group that spoke for most black South Africans. In 1990, Nelson Mandela, the head of the ANC, was released from prison after 27 years. By 1992, most of the laws that made apartheid legal had been thrown out. All South Africans of voting age, regardless of race, won the right to vote.

In 1994, the nation held its first democratic election open to blacks and whites alike. Many stood in lines for hours to exercise their right to vote. The ANC won a majority in the legislature, and Nelson Mandela later became president. During his term of office, Mandela reached out to all black and white South Africans. In 1999, South Africa held its second all-race democratic election.

Reading Check
What was **apartheid**?

Nelson Mandela
1918–PRESENT

South African Statesman

Born of royal parents, Nelson Mandela experienced apartheid while working in a South African gold mine. He went on to study law and to help form the ANC. Imprisoned in 1964 for his opposition to apartheid, he emerged in 1990 to help F.W. de Klerk end the hated system. In 1993, the two men shared the Nobel Peace Prize.

SOUTH AFRICA   Nelson Mandela congratulates Thabo Mbeki on his victory in South Africa's second all-race election. **When was South Africa's first all-race democratic election held?**

Section 2 Assessment

1. Define: forum, autonomous, referendum, authoritarian rule, apartheid.

2. What type of economic system did China move toward in the 1990s?

Critical Thinking

3. Making Predictions What role do you think South Africa will play in world affairs during the next 100 years?

Graphic Organizer Activity

4. Draw this chart, and use it to summarize the responses of the world community to these global issues.

Global Issue	World Response
Invasion of Kuwait	
Fighting in Bosnia	
Fighting in Kosovo	
Apartheid in South Africa	

SECTION 3 The World Today

Today, the world faces many challenges that require cooperation among nations. The threat of war and other forms of violence continues to grow. Tensions have developed between industrial and developing nations over the use of limited resources, readily available health care, and other issues. Continued global progress depends on solving these and other problems.

Reading Check
What is **terrorism**?

Global Terrorism

The use of violence to reach a political goal—**terrorism**—has become a major global concern. Terrorists—either as individuals or groups—act on their own, usually without formal government support. In 2001, the United States government identified nearly 30 terrorist groups operating in Asia, Europe, the Americas, and Africa.

United States leaders believe that the most dangerous of these terrorists is the Islamic group al-Qaeda (al KY duh), or "the Base." In the late 1990s, al-Qaeda leader Osama bin Laden told Muslims to work toward removing U.S. influence from the Middle East. Bin Laden stated that any action—such as the killing of American citizens—would be acceptable in order to achieve this goal. This view, however, does not follow the beliefs of the religion of Islam.

Al-Qaeda is believed to have been responsible for the bombings of two American embassies in Africa in 1998. The

TERRORISM   The 1998 terrorist bombing of the U.S. embassy in Nairobi, Kenya, killed or injured hundreds of civilians and government workers. **What did Osama bin Laden say Muslims should work toward?**

terrorist group is also believed to have been behind the attack on a United States Navy destroyer, the USS *Cole,* in 2000. This attack took place off the coast of Yemen. Al-Qaeda, however, is most widely known for its link to the attacks on the United States that took place on September 11, 2001.

On September 11, 2001, terrorists took control of four American passenger planes. Two planes were deliberately flown into New York City's World Trade Center. At about the same time, a third plane was flown into the Pentagon, the U.S. military headquarters outside Washington, D.C. A fourth plane was seized, but the passengers heroically resisted the terrorists. Their attack caused the plane to crash in a field in Pennsylvania. The results of these attacks shocked people around the world. In New York City, firefighters, police officers, and rescue workers rushed to help victims. However, many of these brave people lost their lives when the World Trade Center towers collapsed. In all, thousands died on that tragic day.

The United States reacted to the September 11 attacks with strength and courage. People from all parts of the country responded quickly to aid the victims of the New York City tragedy. To show their unity, people displayed American flags and held prayer services. The U.S. government acted swiftly, too. President George W. Bush called for steps to organize government efforts more efficiently in order to protect Americans

REMEMBERING THE VICTIMS   In Las Vegas, Nevada, and around the world, people gathered at candlelight services to remember the victims of the terrorist attacks of September 11, 2001. **How did the United States government respond to the terrorist attacks?**

from further terrorist attacks. Congress passed a law to help police track down terrorists. In November 2002, Congress approved a new cabinet department, the Department of Homeland Security. According to President Bush, the Department's primary mission is "to help prevent, protect against, and respond to acts of terrorism on our soil." The Department is responsible for coordinating the nation's defenses against terrorist attacks.

The September 11 attacks alarmed other countries. Many of these countries also lost citizens in the World Trade Center. As a result, the United States won much support for a global struggle to end terrorism. President Bush warned that the struggle would not end "until every terrorist group of global reach has been found, stopped, and defeated."

The first military action against terrorism began in the Southwest Asian nation of Afghanistan. Afghanistan's rulers, known as the Taliban, strictly controlled the Afghan people, especially women and children. The Taliban also protected the suspected terrorists. Even with American pressure, the Taliban refused to hand over those accused of planning the attacks. President Bush then ordered the United States military to attack Afghanistan and find the al-Qaeda terrorists.

In October 2001, American and British warplanes began bombing Afghan military targets. The United States also sent special troops to help the Afghan people who were already fighting the Taliban. The military forces captured major cities and scattered the Taliban. Within three months, the Taliban government had fallen. The UN then worked with local leaders to create a new government for Afghanistan.

Afghanistan, 2001

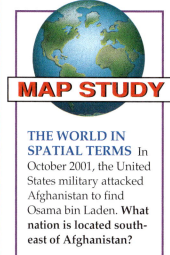

MAP STUDY

THE WORLD IN SPATIAL TERMS In October 2001, the United States military attacked Afghanistan to find Osama bin Laden. **What nation is located southeast of Afghanistan?**

Dangerous Weapons and Terrorism   By the 1990s, many nations had developed **weapons of mass destruction.** These weapons include nuclear bombs, poisonous chemicals, and biological weapons that spread disease. At the same time, some nations, including Iraq, Iran, Syria, and North Korea, were believed to be supporting terrorist groups. World leaders feared these nations might give weapons of mass destruction to terrorists.

As you read in Section 2, U.S. and British forces invaded Iraq in 2003, believing that Saddam Hussein held weapons of mass destruction and supported terrorists. For the United States and its partners, rebuilding Iraq was more difficult than winning the war. Hussein's supporters and terrorists battled coalition forces in an attempt to defeat American efforts to rebuild Iraq's economy and to create a democracy. In June 2004, the United States handed control of Iraq to a temporary Iraqi government. The new government's goal was to prepare Iraq for free elections.

Reading Check What are **weapons of mass destruction?**

Crowded street in India—a nation with over 1 billion people

✓ **Reading Check**
What conditions help spread **communicable diseases**?

✓ **Reading Check**
Why has the possibility of **pandemics** increased in recent years?

✓ **Reading Check**
How does the **greenhouse effect** endanger our planet?

A Growing Population

As the 2000s began, a different kind of explosion occurred on the earth—a population explosion. In a 100-year period, the earth's population quadrupled, or became four times greater. In August 2004, the world's population had reached almost 6.4 billion. Only 15 years had passed since it had reached the 5-billion mark.

A number of factors are responsible for this growth. These factors include increased food production, improved medical care, and better living conditions.

Improving Health Care

Overcrowding in cities, polluted water, and poor methods of removing waste can spread disease. In many developing nations, millions of people still die from **communicable diseases,** or diseases passed along from an infected person or animal to another person. In 2004, tuberculosis and malaria alone—curable diseases—claimed more than 3 million lives a year.

Increased contact among nations through travel has increased the possibility of **pandemics,** or epidemics spread over a wide region. The Black Death in the Middle Ages is an example of a pandemic. Germs once limited to certain regions now can spread quickly to all parts of the world.

No disease has made the world more aware of the importance of improving health care than Acquired Immune Deficiency Syndrome, or AIDS. In 1981, scientists found the virus that causes the disease, known as the Human Immunodeficiency Virus, or HIV. As the 2000s began, however, researchers had not yet discovered a cure for AIDS.

Protecting the Environment

In recent years, people have become aware of the importance of protecting the environment. In 1995, UN-sponsored scientists sounded an alarm. They believed that there was a buildup of carbon dioxide in the atmosphere. This buildup of carbon dioxide was trapping heat released from the earth's surface, much like the glass in a greenhouse. The scientists stated that this **greenhouse effect** was increasing the earth's temperature to dangerous levels.

The scientists feared that the rising temperatures might reduce the number of crops that could be farmed around the world. They predicted that polar ice caps might even melt, causing severe flooding in coastal regions. By the 2000s, most of the UN member nations had signed a series of agreements to cut down on the production of greenhouse gases.

In 2002, government leaders met at a UN-sponsored conference in South Africa to discuss environmental and economic issues. They agreed to provide clean drinking water and basic sanitation to more of the world's poor.

Economic Interdependence

Progress in the twenty-first century depends upon global cooperation. Issues that affect many, such as water shortages, cannot be solved by one nation alone. In addition, few countries can fully meet all the needs of their people without global trade. Because of this, the world's countries have become increasingly interdependent. Interdependence exists when countries depend on one another for goods, raw materials to make goods, and markets in which to sell goods.

Events around the world have a rippling effect because of interdependence. For example, war or drought may cause crop failure in a country. Other nations that trade with that country are also affected because now there are no crops to buy.

Some nations have joined together to strengthen trade. In 1993, for example, 12 western European countries formed the European Union (EU). Three more countries joined in 1995, and another 10—including many nations from eastern Europe—joined in 2004. One of the goals of the EU was the political unity of Europe. Another goal was to help Europe become an economic superpower like the United States. Citizens of EU countries hold common passports and can travel anywhere in the EU to work and shop. In January 2002, most EU members began using a common currency, the **euro**, to replace their national currencies. This means that they use the same type of money to buy goods and services.

Trade agreements were also made among the countries of North America. In 1993, the United States, Canada, and Mexico reduced trade barriers under the North American Free Trade Agreement (NAFTA). In 1995, blocs of nations in South America signed similar trade agreements.

Globalization

Contact among nations has increased because of new forms of communication technology. Satellites surrounding the earth in space receive radio, television, and other signals. People almost everywhere in the world can now contact others by phone, fax, or computer. The result has been the rise of what some experts call a *global culture*, or globalization.

Many people perceive cultures in developing countries as backward because they do not have the same level of technology as industrialized countries. Others, however, appreciate the diverse cultures that exist in many developing countries. Some fear that globalization might erase the traditions of smaller groups.

Still, the speed at which goods, ideas, and people move is expected to increase in the years ahead. Cultures around the world will change as they become more interdependent. The most important force in bringing about the change, say some experts, is teenagers. They travel, watch television, buy things, and most of all, talk. As future leaders, today's teens will be able to work together with better communication tools and more shared knowledge than any previous generation.

Reading Check How does the **euro** help create economic ties among the nations of Europe?

The Global Culture

Section 3 Assessment

1. **Define:** terrorism, weapons of mass destruction, communicable diseases, pandemics, greenhouse effect, euro.
2. What serious events occurred in the United States on September 11, 2001?
3. What environmental challenges must be solved in the years ahead?

Critical Thinking

4. **Identifying Alternatives** Do you think the United States should try to reduce the gap between the rich and poor nations in the world? Explain your answer.

Graphic Organizer Activity

5. Draw this diagram, and use it to show the way your own life has been touched by increased contact and communication with other nations.

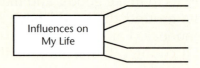

Influences on My Life

Chapter Summary & Study Guide

1. Between 1989 and 1991, communism collapsed in Eastern Europe and the cold war came to an end.
2. By late 1991, the Soviet Union had formed into 15 independent republics.
3. Differences among people and economic hardships created many challenges for nations formerly under Soviet control.
4. In 1997, NATO offered membership to Poland, Hungary, and the Czech Republic.
5. Following Iraq's invasion of Kuwait, a coalition of nations attacked Iraq. Saddam Hussein was overthrown in 2003.
6. Ethnic conflicts in Bosnia and Kosovo led to NATO air strikes against Serbia.
7. In the Middle East, Israel and several Arab nations took steps toward peace, but conflict remained between Israelis and Palestinians.
8. In 1999, Catholics and Protestants agreed to joint rule of Northern Ireland.
9. Hong Kong was returned to China in 1997.
10. East Timor gained freedom, while a democratic government was established in Indonesia.
11. The September 11, 2001, attacks on the United States encouraged a global struggle against terrorism.
12. Population growth and health and environmental issues challenge the global community.

Self-Check Quiz

Visit the *Human Heritage* Web site at **humanheritage.glencoe.com** and click on **Chapter 39—Self-Check Quiz** to assess your understanding of this chapter.

Using Key Terms

Imagine you are a historian in 2100. You have been asked to write an essay in which you describe the major challenges facing the world as the century opened. Use the following words in your essay.

aggression
sovereign
authoritarian
   rule
terrorism
apartheid
euro
dissent

secede
forum
communicable
   diseases
greenhouse
   effect
coup

privatize
autonomous
referendum
weapons of
   mass
   destruction
pandemics

Understanding Main Ideas

1. What was the symbolic importance of destroying the Berlin Wall?
2. What problems did Russia face in reforming its government and economy?
3. Why did American and British forces invade Iraq?
4. What was the role of NATO in Bosnia and Kosovo?
5. What obstacles to peace exist in Africa?
6. What forms of communication link nations in the 2000s?

Critical Thinking

1. Do you agree that trade is linked to the growth of democracy in the People's Republic of China? Why or why not?
2. Do you support the United States giving financial help to peacekeeping forces in places like Bosnia and Kosovo? Explain.
3. How do you think the events of September 11, 2001, changed the world?

Graphic Organizer Activity

Culture Create a diagram like this one, and use it to show some of the causes and effects of increased contact among the diverse cultures of the world.

Causes → Increased Contact → Effects

Geography in History

Places and Regions Look at the population map on page 651. Scientists are predicting great increases in the world's population by the year 2050. In what regions would you expect the most growth to take place? Explain.

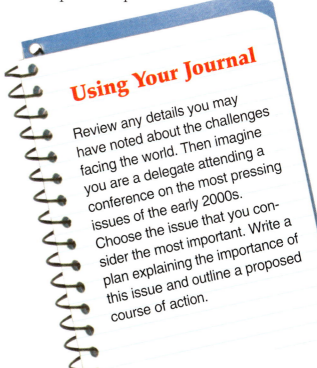

Using Your Journal

Review any details you may have noted about the challenges facing the world. Then imagine you are a delegate attending a conference on the most pressing issues of the early 2000s. Choose the issue that you consider the most important. Write a plan explaining the importance of this issue and outline a proposed course of action.

Around

OUR SHRINKING WORLD

People today can talk across an ocean as easily as across a backyard fence. This is what is meant when you hear people say that the world is "shrinking." The technology that allows such communication includes telephone cables, satellites, and computers. Through their personal computers, people are now able to go on the Internet. This is a huge web of linked computer networks. The Internet has made global communications—and cooperation—almost instant.

Worldwide Internet Use

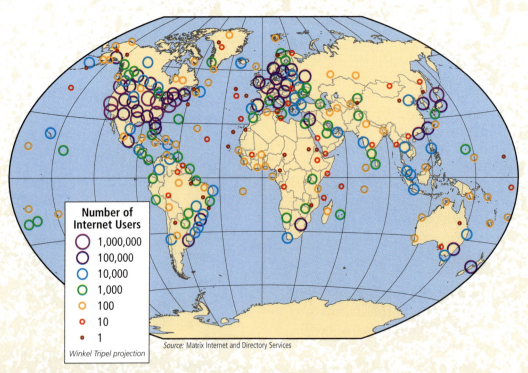

Number of Internet Users

○ 1,000,000
○ 100,000
○ 10,000
○ 1,000
○ 100
○ 10
· 1

Winkel Tripel projection

Source: Matrix Internet and Directory Services

▲ The map above shows the geographic locations of the number of computers linked to the Internet. In 2000, the Internet was commonly used throughout North America, Europe, and East Asia. (Each purple circle represents more than 1 million Internet users.) The rest of the world was quickly catching up, however.

the W🌍rld

◀ A Yagua (right) takes part in an Internet poll in the rain forests of Peru. The Internet has also allowed people in developing countries to line up buyers for their products.

A man wearing a traditional headdress chats on a cellular phone in the Israeli desert. Scenes like this one are most common in countries with oil- or industry-based economies. ▼

Students in Moscow School 1173 are linked by the Internet to students in more than 1,000 U.S. schools and 27 schools in other countries. Increased communication results in increased understanding. ▶

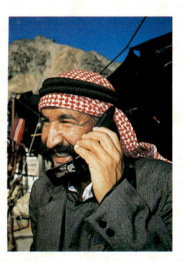

A Pakistani soldier searches a car in Karachi, Pakistan. Governments have begun sharing intelligence information about terrorist groups in order to prevent more attacks. ▼

Taking Another Look

1. Based on the map, what generalization can you make about the countries that have Internet access?

2. How has communication technology affected cooperation among governments?

Hands-On Activity

Making a Poster In a web diagram, list ways in which the Internet is used. In the middle of the web, summarize how technology is "shrinking" the world.

Standardized Test Practice

Directions: Choose the *best* answer to each of the following multiple choice questions. If you have trouble answering a question, use the process of elimination to narrow your choices. Write your answers on a separate piece of paper.

1. **Why was World War I different from earlier wars?**

   A It was the first war fought on European soil.

   B It was the first time the United States fought in a war.

   C New weapons made it the deadliest war up to that time.

   D The war resulted in many political reforms.

   > **Test-Taking Tip:**   This question asks for a *comparison*. Although the war did result in political reforms (answer D), this fact does not make it *different* from other wars.

2. **The Russian Revolution was different from the French and American revolutions in which of the following ways?**

   F The Russian Revolution was not fought because the poor wanted more equality.

   G The Russian Revolution relied on trench warfare.

   H The people of Russia did not support the Russian Revolution.

   J The goal of the Russian Revolution was not to put a democratically elected government in power.

   > **Test-Taking Tip:**   This question also asks you to find a *difference* by *comparison*. Ask yourself, how is *communism* different from *democracy*?

3. **In which of the following ways did Hitler unite Germany?**

   A He gave voting rights to all males over the age of 18.

   B He enacted a law requiring religion in Germany.

   C He united the people of Germany against what he thought was a common enemy.

   D He used various tactics from Soviet communism to improve the economy.

   > **Test-Taking Tip:**   Always read the question and all of the answer choices *carefully*. You may be tempted to choose answer D, since Hitler did promise to improve the economy. However, these tactics were not borrowed from Soviet communism—and they were not his most *significant* unifying action.

4. **President Truman avoided sending American troops to invade Japan by**

   F signing a peace treaty with the emperor of Japan

   G convincing other Allied nations to fight in Japan

   H limiting the war to a fight for Midway Island

   J ordering atomic bombs to be dropped on Hiroshima and Nagasaki

   > **Test-Taking Tip:**   This question asks you to remember an important event in World War II. President Truman did not limit the fighting just to Midway Island, though an important battle did take place there. Therefore, you can eliminate answer H.

5. The United Nations was formed at the end of World War II. The activities of the United Nations include all of the following EXCEPT

    A providing medical care to people in poor countries

    B preventing the spread of communism to western nations

    C negotiating and keeping peace between nations

    D lending money to poor countries

> **Test-Taking Tip:** Think about what you know about the United Nations. It is an organization made up of countries with many different types of governments. Which answer choice best fits this information? Remember, the question is asking for the EXCEPTION.

6. Why is Mohandas Gandhi considered a great leader?

    F He convinced the Indian people to boycott British goods.

    G He gained the respect of both the upper class and the common people.

    H He believed in achieving peace without violence.

    J He traveled through India convincing people to support democracy.

> **Test-Taking Tip:** Always read the question and *all* of the answer choices carefully. Even if you do not remember the answer to a fact-based question such as this one, it is usually a good idea to eliminate answers that you know are incorrect and then guess from the remaining choices.

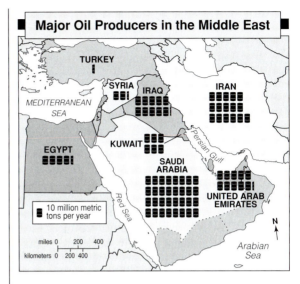

Major Oil Producers in the Middle East

7. According to this map, how much oil does Kuwait produce annually?

    A 6 metric tons

    B 60 metric tons

    C 6 million metric tons

    D 60 million metric tons

> **Test-Taking Tip:** Use the map *legend*, or *key*, to understand the symbols used on the map. On this map, each barrel symbolizes a larger number to save space (and make them easier to count!). Make sure you double-check all the answer choices—this type of question can be tricky. However, all the information you need is on the map: you just need to *interpret* it.

WORKING WITH PRIMARY SOURCES

Suppose that you have been asked to write a report on changes in your community over the past 25 years. Where would you get the information you need to begin writing? You would draw upon two types of information— primary sources and secondary sources.

Definitions

Primary sources are often first-person accounts by someone who actually saw or lived through what is being described. In other words, if you see a fire or live through a great storm and then write about your experiences, you are creating a primary source. Diaries, journals, photographs, and eyewitness reports are examples of primary sources. Secondary sources are second-hand accounts. For instance, if your friend experiences a fire or storm and tells you about it, or if you read about a fire or storm in the newspaper and then you write about it, you are creating a secondary source. Textbooks, biographies, and histories are secondary sources.

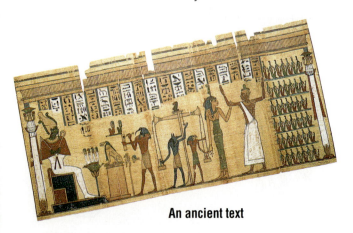

An ancient text

Checking Your Sources

When you read primary or secondary sources, you should analyze them to figure out if they are dependable or reliable. Historians usually prefer primary sources to secondary sources, but both can be reliable or unreliable, depending on the following factors.

Time Span

With primary sources, it is important to consider how long after the event occurred the primary source was written. Generally, the longer the time span between the event and the account, the less reliable the account is. As time passes, people often forget details and fill in gaps with events that never took place. Although we like to think we remember things exactly as they happened, the fact is we often remember them in a way that we wanted them to occur.

Reliability

Another factor to consider when evaluating a primary source is the writer's background and reliability. First, try to determine how this person knows about what he or she is writing. How much does he or she know? Is the writer being truthful? Is the account convincing?

Opinions

When evaluating a primary source, you should also decide whether the account has been influenced by emotion, opinion, or exaggeration. Writers can have reasons to distort the truth to suit their personal purposes. Ask yourself: Why did the person write the account? Do any key

Opera glasses,
late 1800s

words or expressions reveal the author's emotions or opinions? You may wish to compare the account with one written by another witness to the event. If the two accounts differ, ask yourself why they differ and which is more accurate.

Interpreting Primary Sources

To help you analyze a primary source, use the following steps:

- **Examine the origins of the document.**
  You need to determine if it is a primary source.

Classifying Primary Sources

Primary sources fall into different categories:

Printed Publications

Printed publications include books such as autobiographies. Printed publications also include newspapers and magazines.

Personal Records

Personal records are accounts of events kept by an individual who is a participant in or witness to these events. Personal records include diaries, journals, and letters.

Oral Histories

Oral histories are chronicles, memoirs, myths, and legends that are passed along from one generation to another by word of mouth. Interviews are another form of oral history.

- **Find the main ideas.**
  Read the document and summarize the main ideas in your own words. These ideas may be fairly easy to identify in newspapers and journals, for example, but are much more difficult to find in poetry.
- **Reread the document.**
  Difficult ideas are not always easily understood on the first reading.
- **Use a variety of resources.**
  Form the habit of using the dictionary, the encyclopedia, and maps. These resources are tools to help you discover new ideas and knowledge and check the validity of sources.

Songs and Poems

Songs and poems include works that express the personal thoughts and feelings or political or religious beliefs of the writer, usually using rhyming and rhythmic language.

Artifacts

Artifacts are objects such as tools or ornaments. Artifacts present information about a particular culture or a stage of technological development.

GO TO For additional primary sources, use the **World History Primary Source Document Library CD-ROM.**

UNIT 1

AFRICAN ORIGINS

The work of one family—the Leakeys—helped uncover some of the earliest chapters in human history. Louis B. Leakey, born in Kenya in 1903, started the work. He believed that human history began in Africa. He also believed that this history was far older than anyone had ever imagined. His wife, Mary Nicol Leakey, joined him in his work, along with the couple's son, Richard. Together they made some of the most exciting archaeological and anthropological discoveries of the past 100 years.

■ Reader's Dictionary

petrified ash volcanic dust that has turned into stone

hominid member of a group that includes human beings and early human-like creatures

retained kept

bipedal walking on two feet

tuff pieces of volcanic rock

relief contrast with the surrounding area

haunt to reappear constantly

trek a long journey, usually by foot

perilous dangerous

Printed Publications

Footprints in Time

The death of Louis Leakey in 1972 did not stop Mary and Richard Leakey from digging into the past. In 1978, Mary Leakey discovered a set of ancient footprints south of the Olduvai Gorge in present-day Tanzania. In a 1979 article for *National Geographic*, she describes a trail that carried her back in time.

This article . . . will cause yet another upheaval in the study of human origins. For in the gray, petrified ash . . . we have found hominid footprints that are remarkably similar to those of modern man. . . . Prints that were laid down an incredible 3,600,000 years ago! . . .

Two individuals, one larger, one smaller, had passed this way. . . . We have measured their footprints and the length of their stride. Was the larger one a male, the smaller one a female? Or was one mature, the other young? It is unlikely that we will ever know with certainty. . . .

The closeness of the two sets of prints indicates that their owners were not walking [side by side]. Other clues suggest that the hominids may have passed at different times. For example, the imprints of the smaller individual stand out clearly. The crispness of definition and sharp outlines convince me that they were left on a damp surface that retained the form of the foot.

On the other hand, the prints of the larger are blurred, as if he had shuffled or dragged his feet. In fact, I think that the surface when he passed was loose and dusty, hence the collapsed appearance of his prints. Nonetheless, luck favored us again; the bigger hominid left one absolutely clear print, probably on a patch of once damp ash.

What did these footprints tell us? First, they demonstrate once and for all that at least 3,600,000 years ago, in Pliocene times, what I believe to be man's direct ancestor walked fully upright with a bipedal, freestriding gait. Second, that the form of his foot was exactly the same as ours.

Sometimes, . . . I go out and watch the dust settle over the gray tuff with its eerie record of time long past. The slanting light of evening throws the hominid prints into sharp relief, so sharp that they could have been left this morning.

I cannot help but think about the distant creatures who made them. Where did they come from? Where were they going? We simply do not know. It has been suggested that they were merely crossing this scorched plain toward the greener ridges to the north. Perhaps so.

In any case, those footprints out of the deep past, left by the oldest known hominids, haunt the imagination. Across the gulf of time I can only wish them well on that prehistoric trek. It was, I believe, part of a greater and more perilous journey, one that . . . culminated in the emergence of modern man.

▲ Mary Leakey

Interpreting Primary Sources

1. What effect does Mary Leakey think her article will have?
2. Why does she feel this way?
3. How might a geographer describe the landscape at the time the footprints were made?
4. What does Mary Leakey mean when she says the footprints "haunt the imagination"?
5. What one important thing do you think the footprints revealed?

ACTIVITY

Writing a News Bulletin   Write a 30-second news bulletin that a television or radio reporter might have given upon learning of Mary Leakey's discovery.

675

Printed Publications

UNIT 2

THE PURSUIT OF JUSTICE

Hammurabi's gift to civilization was his code of laws. Other rulers had enacted laws in the past, but Hammurabi was the first to collect them into a single written code. The code included nearly 300 legal decisions. Some were harsh—even brutal—by today's standards. However, the code made the state responsible for their enforcement. This was a great advance over a system in which people often took justice into their own hands. Under the Hammurabi Code, society began its long journey toward the ideal of "equal justice for all."

■ Reader's Dictionary

justified proven
commoner someone not of noble birth
thirtyfold thirty times (its value)
render pay
tenfold ten times (its value)
creditor person who has made a loan
interest fee charged on a loan
mina an ancient unit of weight
traffic trade
gored pierced with horns
plumbed tested or examined

The Hammurabi Code

The Hammurabi Code touched on almost every aspect of life. The purpose of the code, said the prologue, was "to cause justice to prevail in the land, to destroy the wicked and the evil, that the strong may not oppress the weak." Here are some of the laws intended to achieve that goal.

1. If a man . . . bring a charge of murder against another man and has not justified himself, the accuser shall be put to death.

8. If a man has stolen ox or sheep . . . or pig or ship, whether from the temple or from the palace, he shall pay thirtyfold; if he stole from a commoner, he shall render tenfold. If the thief cannot pay, he shall be put to death.

15. If a man has helped a male or female palace slave, or a commoner's slave to escape out of the city gate, he shall be put to death.

21. If a man has broken into a house, he shall be killed . . . and walled in it.

48. If a man has a debt upon him and . . . the grain has not grown for lack of water, in that year he shall make no return of grain to his creditor . . . and he shall not pay interest for that year.

104. If a merchant has lent a trader corn, wool, or oil or any sort of goods to traffic with, the trader shall write down the price and pay it back. . . .

195. If a man has struck his father, his hand shall be cut off.

200. If a man has made the tooth of a man that is his equal fall out, they shall take his tooth out.

201. If a man has made the tooth of a commoner fall out, he shall pay one third of a mina of silver.

229. If a builder has built a house and not made his work strong and the house he built has fallen and so has caused the death of the owner of the house, that builder shall be put to death.

250. If a wild bull in his charge has gored a man, and caused him to die, that case has no remedy.

▲ Hammurabi

Artifacts

In December 1910, a team of French archaeologists working in Iran discovered three pieces of black stone covered with inscriptions. The stones fit together in a block nearly eight feet long. At the top, a king speaks with a seated god. The king introduces himself as a "god among kings," "a fighter without peer," and "the one who plumbed the depths of wisdom." The archaeologists had found the Hammurabi Code.

Interpreting Primary Sources

1. What do the pictures and inscriptions on the stone block reveal about Hammurabi's ideas about kingship?

2. How do you think discovery of the Hammurabi Code affected the way people viewed ancient Mesopotamia?

3. Which of the code's laws were intended to discourage theft?

4. Which were intended to promote fair business dealings?

5. Based on these laws, what social classes do you think made up Babylonian society?

6. Which, if any, of these laws would probably be upheld under our Constitution?

ACTIVITY

Design a code of laws that you think should be enforced in your school. To be just, the code must take into account those rights guaranteed to defendants by the United States Constitution. (Study the Bill of Rights closely.) Present your code to the student government in your school.

UNIT 3

THE EMPIRE OF MALI

Mali owed its success to two great conquerors—Sundiata Keita and Mansa Musa I. They helped build one of the largest empires in the world and by far the richest Africa has ever known. People from all over Africa and the Middle East traveled to see Mali. Generations of African storytellers have sung its praises.

■ Reader's Dictionary

eloquence beautiful speech
vanquished defeated
taboos forbidden acts
Keitas African people from which Sundiata came
ebony a type of dark wood
arms weapons
quiver case for holding arrows
score twenty
page a boy servant or attendant
sovereign all-powerful ruler
mitgals type of gold coin

Oral Histories

The Father of Mali

A modern-day *griot*, or West African storyteller, celebrates the accomplishments of Sundiata Keita.

I am a griot, . . . master in the art of eloquence. . . . I teach kings the history of their ancestors so that the lives of the ancients might serve them as an example, for the word is old, but the future springs from the past.

My word is pure and free of all untruth; it is the word of my father; it is the word of my father's father. . . .

Listen, then, sons of Mali, . . . for I am going to tell you of Sundiata, . . . the master of a hundred vanquished kings. . . .

Sundiata was unique. In his own time no one equalled him, and after him no one had the ambition to surpass him. He left his mark on Mali, for all time, and his taboos still guide men in their conduct. . . .

Men of today, how small you are beside your ancestors. . . . Sundiata rests, . . . but his spirit lives on, and today the Keitas still come and bow before the stone under which lies the father of Mali.

Personal Records

The Sultan of Mali

An Arab scholar named Ibn Fadl Allah al Omari describes the court and army of Mansa Musa. He refers to Mansa Musa as *sultan*, the Arab word for "king."

The sultan of this kingdom presides in his palace on a great balcony, called *bembe*, where he has a seat of ebony that is like a throne fit for a large and tall person: on either side it is flanked by elephant tusks turned toward each other. His arms stand near him, being all of gold—saber, lance, quiver, bows, and arrows. He wears wide trousers made of about twenty pieces [of cloth], of a kind only he can wear.

Behind him stand a score of Turkish or other pages which are bought for him in Cairo. . . . His officers are seated in a circle about him, in two rows, one to the right and one to the left; behind them sit the chief commanders of his cavalry. . . .

Others dance before their sovereign, who enjoys this, and make him laugh. Two banners are spread behind him. Before him they keep two saddled and bridled horses in case he should wish to ride.

Arab horses are brought for sale to the kings of this country, who spend considerable sums in this way. Their army numbers 100,000 men of whom there are about 10,000 horse-mounted cavalry: the others are infantry having neither horses nor any other mounts. . . .

The officers of this king, his soldiers, and his guard receive gifts of land and presents. Some among the greatest of them receive as much as 50,000 *mitgals* of gold a year, besides which the king provides them with horses and clothing. He is much concerned with giving them garments and making his cities into capitals.

▲ An early map of North Africa showing Mansa Musa

Interpreting Primary Sources

1. Why does the griot say he is telling the story of Sundiata?

2. Why was Sundiata unique?

3. What conclusions can you draw about Mansa Musa's power?

4. Why do you think Mansa Musa treated his soldiers so well?

5. If you had the chance to meet one of these two leaders, whom would you choose—Sundiata Keita or Mansa Musa? Explain.

ACTIVITY

Storytelling   Write an account of Mansa Musa that a West African griot might tell to a group of children. (For more information on Mansa Musa, see pages 133–134.)

UNIT 4

GREEK SOCIETY

Each of the Greek city-states had its own ideas on the rights of citizens. None of the city-states, however, gave women an equal voice in society or government. Even in Athens, which claimed to be a democracy, women had few legal rights. Parents arranged the marriages of their daughters, typically at ages 13 to 15, to men at least twice their age. Once married, women rarely appeared in public and took no part in politics. The philosopher Plato saw little justice in this situation and brought it to the attention of the ancient world.

■ Reader's Dictionary

regulations rules

flocks herds of animals, especially sheep and goats

nurture upbringing

gymnastic activities involving exercise or physical strength

inference a conclusion drawn through the use of reason

gymnasia buildings or rooms used for physical exercise or training

notions thoughts

jests jokes

attainments accomplishments

Printed Publications

The Rights of Women

In *The Republic*, Plato presents his ideas on a just society in the form of dialogues, or imaginary conversations, between Socrates and his students. In this dialogue, Socrates has just finished questioning his student about the type of men who might make the best "watchdogs" of Athenian government. He surprises his student by turning to the subject of women.

Let us suppose further the birth and education of our women to be subject to similar or nearly similar regulations [as men]. . . .

What do you mean?

What I mean may be put into the form of a question. . . . I said: Are dogs divided into hes and shes, or do they both share equally in hunting and in keeping watch and in the other duties of dogs? [O]r do we entrust to the males the entire and exclusive care of the flocks, while we leave the females at home, under the idea that the bearing and . . . [feeding of] their puppies is labour enough for them?

No, he said, they share alike; the only difference between them is that the males are stronger and the females weaker.

But can you use different animals for the same purpose, unless they are . . . [raised] in the same way?

You cannot.

Then, if women are to have the same duties as men, they must have the same nurture and education?

Yes.

The education which was assigned to the men was music and gymnastic.

Yes.

Then women must be taught music and gymnastic and also the art of war, which they must practise like the men?

That is the inference, I suppose.

I should rather expect, I said, that . . . our proposals, if they are carried out, being unusual, may appear ridiculous.

No doubt of it. . . .

Yes, and the most ridiculous thing of all would be the sight of women . . . exercising with the men . . . [who] frequent the gymnasia.

Yes, indeed, he said, according to present notions the proposal would be thought ridiculous.

But, then, I said, . . . we must not fear the jests . . . which will be directed against this sort of innovation; how they will talk of women's attainments both in music and gymnastic, and above all about their wearing armour and riding upon horseback!

Very true, he replied. . . .

Artifacts

Paintings on fifth-century vases give an inside look at Greek society. These vases took so much effort to make that an ancient Greek expression for working hard was "to make pottery." Careful studies of vase paintings show that at least some women managed to escape a world that said that they should "see as little, hear as little, and ask as few questions as possible."

Interpreting Primary Sources

1. What does Plato think will help to make men and women more equal?
2. How does he think most Athenians will react to this suggestion?
3. Based on this selection, what conclusions can you draw about the education of women in ancient Greece?
4. How do you think Plato might react to the role of women in government in the United States today? Explain.

ACTIVITY

Illustrating Ideas   Design a vase painting illustrating Plato's ideas for the reform of Athenian society.

UNIT 5

ERUPTION OF MOUNT VESUVIUS

Early in August of 79 A.D., a series of small earthquakes shook the countryside around Mount Vesuvius, a volcano located along the Bay of Naples in southern Italy. On the morning of August 24, a cloud of ash formed over the volcano. Later that afternoon, Vesuvius exploded. Streams of molten rock shot upward as high as 17 miles. Then it rained back down on cities along the bay. The eruption lasted for about two days and formed one of the great natural disasters in Roman history.

■ Reader's Dictionary

posterity future generations
implored begged
inquiry search for knowledge
helmsman person who steers a ship
Fortune good luck
allay calm

Personal Records

A Heroic Rescue Attempt

Pliny the Elder—a Roman admiral and well-known author and scientist— died attempting to rescue people trapped at the foot of Vesuvius. His nephew, Pliny the Younger, recorded his uncle's death in a letter written to a Roman historian named Tacitus. The letter forms an eyewitness account of the eruption and expresses Roman views of courage and duty.

Thank you for asking me to send you an account of my uncle's death so that you can leave an accurate account of it for posterity. . . .

On 24 August, in the early afternoon, my mother drew his attention to a cloud of unusual size and appearance. . . . It was not clear at the distance from which mountain the cloud was rising (it was afterwards known to be Vesuvius). . . . My uncle . . . saw at once that it was important enough for a closer inspection, and he ordered a boat to be made ready. . . .

As he was leaving the house he was handed a message from Rectina, . . . whose house was at the foot of the mountain, so that escape was impossible except by boat. She was terrified by the danger threatening her and implored him to rescue her. . . . He changed his plans, and what he had begun in a spirit of inquiry he completed as a hero. He gave orders for the warships to be launched and went on board himself with the intention of bringing help to many more people than Rectina. . . . He hurried to the place which everyone else was hastily leaving, steering his course straight for the danger zone. . . .

Ashes were already falling, hotter and thicker as the ships drew near. . . . For a moment my uncle wondered whether he should turn back, but when the helmsman advised this he refused, telling him that Fortune stood by the courageous. . . . The wind was . . . in my uncle's favor, and he was able to bring the ship in.

Meanwhile on Mount Vesuvius broad sheets of fire and leaping flames blazed at several points. . . . My uncle tried to allay the fears of his companions. . . . They debated whether to stay indoors or take their chances in the open, for buildings were now shaking with violent shocks, and seemed to be swaying. . . .

My uncle decided to go down to the shore and investigate on the spot the possibility of any escape by the sea, but he found the waves still wild and dangerous. A sheet was spread on the ground for him to lie down, and he repeatedly asked for cold water to drink. Then the flames and smell of sulfur which gave warning of the approaching fire drove the others to take flight. . . . He stood . . . and then suddenly collapsed, I imagine because the dense fumes choked his breathing. . . . When daylight appeared on the 26th—two days after the last day he had been seen—his body was found, . . . looking more like sleep than death. . . .

I will say no more, except to add that I have described in detail every incident which I either witnessed myself or heard about immediately after the event, when reports were most likely to be accurate.

Artifacts The mud and lava that poured out of Vesuvius buried entire cities. When archaeologists uncovered the city of Pompeii, they got a firsthand look at life at the height of Roman power. The art and artifacts found at Pompeii reveal some of the comforts and pleasures enjoyed by its citizens.

Interpreting Primary Sources

1. Why did Pliny the Elder originally want to sail toward Vesuvius?
2. Why did he change his plans?
3. Why did Pliny the Younger consider his uncle a hero? Do you agree? Explain.
4. Why do you think historians consider Pompeii an important source of information about daily life in the Roman Empire?

ACTIVITY

Writing an Obituary Write an obituary for Pliny the Elder that might have appeared in a Roman newspaper. (Pliny the Elder was born around 23 A.D.)

UNIT 6

THE AGE OF VIKING CONQUEST

The early Middle Ages was a time of disorder in Europe. Scattered communities throughout the region struggled to survive the hardships of daily life. In these unsettled times, the Vikings embarked on an age of conquest. They sailed out of Scandinavia and headed into lands that stretched from what is now Russia in the east to present-day Newfoundland in the west. They explored, traded, and set up colonies. They also attacked and robbed villages, earning a reputation as some of the most fearsome invaders of the early Middle Ages.

■ Reader's Dictionary

plundered robbed
booty stolen goods
heathen barbarian
famine time of great hunger
fodder food for livestock
entrenched well-established
razed leveled
hither and yon here and there
Flemings people from Flanders, a medieval country along the North Sea
kinsmen relatives

Personal Records

Plundering Europe

After the death of Charlemagne, central government again collapsed in western Europe. Records kept by a monastery near what is now Cologne, Germany, reveal the suffering caused by a new round of invasions by the Vikings, or the Northmen, as they were known at the time.

(846) According to their custom the Northmen plundered Eastern and Western Frisia and burned the town of Dordrecht, with two other villages. . . . The Northmen, with their boats filled with immense booty including men and goods, returned to their own country. . . .
(852) The steel of the heathen glistened; excessive heat; a famine followed. There was not fodder enough for the animals. . . .
(882) The Northmen in the month of October entrenched themselves at Condé and horribly devastated the kingdom of Carloman. . . .

They destroyed houses, and razed monasteries and churches to the ground. . . . They killed the dwellers in the land and none could resist them.

Abbot Hugo . . . gathered an army and came to aid the King. When the Northmen came back from a plundering expedition . . . he, in company with the King, gave them chase. They, however, . . . scattered hither and yon, and finally returned to their ships with little loss. . . .
(883) In the spring the Northmen left Condé and . . . forced the Flemings to flee from their lands and raged everywhere, laying waste to the country with fire and sword.

Artifacts The Vikings valued captured treasures. However, they also created their own beautiful works of art, including jewelry fashioned from precious metals seized in raids. This brooch shows the complicated designs for which the Vikings became famous.

Songs and Poems

Words of Praise

The Vikings celebrated their conquests in songs and verses written by *skalds*—professional poets hired by kings and nobles throughout Scandinavia.

Cattle die, kinsmen die,
one day you die yourself;
but the words of praise will not perish
when a man wins fair fame.

Interpreting Primary Sources

1. Why did the Vikings raid the villages and towns surrounding the monastery?
2. How did the Vikings avoid capture by the army raised by Abbot Hugo and the king?
3. In addition to Viking raids, what other problems did people living around the monastery face?
4. What do the lines written by a *skald* promise Vikings who win "fair fame"?
5. How did the Vikings use some of their plunder?

ACTIVITY

Writing a Song Imagine you are a *skald*. Write a song about a Viking expedition to explore the waters and lands to the west of Scandinavia.

685

UNIT 7

BYZANTINE WOMEN

The Byzantines valued intelligence, whether in a man or a woman. An emperor or noble might marry a woman as much for her education or political skills as for her royal birth. As a result, the women who belonged to the royal courts of the Byzantine Empire had a great deal of influence. Rarely did women elsewhere in the world exercise more power than the imperial women of Byzantium.

■ Reader's Dictionary

concealed kept hidden
confidant close friend
monastery religious community
endowed gifted
aptitude ability
sovereign ruler
reserved kept
ravaged damaged
undaunted fearless

Printed Publications

A Woman on the Throne

In 1081, an able general named Alexius Commenus captured Constantinople. As Emperor Alexius I, he defended the Byzantine Empire against attacks from invaders in both the east and the west. His daughter, Anna Commena, retold the story of his reign in a book called the *Alexiad* (uh lek' sē uhd). She begins her account by describing Alexius's decision to turn the government over to his mother Anna Dalassena. (The story refers to the Byzantine Empire as the Roman Empire.)

It was his desire that his mother should govern rather than himself, but . . . the plan had been concealed for fear that she, if she knew of it, might leave the palace. (Alexius was aware that she considered withdrawal to a monastery.) Nevertheless, in all matters however ordinary he did nothing without her advice: she became his confidant and co-partner in government. Gradually . . . he involved her more and more in state affairs; on occasions he even declared openly that without her brains and good judgement the Empire would not survive. . . .

The truth is that Anna Dalassena was in any case endowed with a fine intellect and possessed besides a really first-class aptitude for government. . . . For my grandmother had an exceptional grasp of public affairs, with a genius for organization and government; she was capable, in fact, of managing not only the

Roman Empire, but every other empire under the sun as well. . . .

But, as I was saying, once he seized power my father reserved for himself the struggles and hard labour of war, while . . . he made her the sovereign. . . . I can sum up the whole situation thus: he was in theory the emperor, but she had the real power. She was the legislator, the complete organizer and governor. . . .

Such were the events that marked the beginning of the reign. . . . Alexius knew the Empire was almost at its last gasp. The east was being horribly ravaged by the Turks; the west was in bad condition. . . . The emperors before him, having little knowledge of war and military affairs, had reduced Roman prestige to a minimum. Indeed, I have heard it said by men who were soldiers themselves, and by some of the older men, that no other state in living memory had reached such depths of misery. Conditions were desperate then for the emperor. . . . However, being not only a courageous man and undaunted, but having excellent experiences in war, he wanted to restore his Empire. . . .

Artifacts Some empresses were not handed power—they took it. This detail from an altar shows Empress Irene, the Byzantine Empire's first woman ruler. Supported by the generals, she seized the throne from her only son and ruled from 797 to 802. Although she held power for only five years, Irene put in place much-needed financial reforms.

Interpreting Primary Sources

1. Why did Alexius conceal his plans to turn government over to his mother?
2. How did Anna Dalassena help her son to strengthen the Byzantine Empire?
3. What do these two sources of information—the *Alexiad* and the altar artifact—tell you about the role of women in the Byzantine Empire?

ACTIVITY

Writing a News Bulletin Write a short news bulletin announcing Alexius's decision to put his mother in charge of government while he fought invaders along the Byzantine borders.

UNIT 8

THE MEDIEVAL MANOR

During medieval times, nobody had an easy life. However, nobles and knights enjoyed more benefits than the peasants who worked the land. In exchange for protection, peasants kept a lord's castle well supplied with food, while they themselves lived on little or went hungry.

■ Reader's Dictionary

alms gifts for the poor

coffers treasury

whence from which

sup eat dinner

pullets young chickens

curds solid substance formed when milk sours; used to make cheese

hovels small, dirty, poorly built houses

charged made responsible for

spare save

meal powder made from grain

porridge hot cereal

Personal Records

A Noble Household

Nobles often threw open their castles to travelers, who sought safety and a place to rest. In this passage, a French traveler describes his stay with a count, a high-ranking noble with close ties to the king.

I shall now tell you several particulars respecting the count and his household. . . . He had, every day, distributed, as alms at his gate, . . . small coin, to all comers. He was liberal and courteous in his gifts, and well knew how to take and how to give back. He loved dogs above all other animals; and during summer and winter amused himself much with hunting. . . . He chose twelve of his most able subjects to receive and administer his finances. . . . He had certain coffers in his apartment, whence he took money to give to different knights, squires, or gentlemen, . . . for none ever left him without a gift. . . . When he quitted his chamber at midnight for supper, twelve servants bore each a lighted torch before him. The hall was full of knights and squires, and there were plenty of tables laid out for any who chose to sup. No one spoke to him at table unless he first began the conversation. He ate heartily . . . [and] had great pleasure in hearing minstrels. . . . In short, . . . though I had before been in several courts, I never was at one which pleased me more. . . .

Songs and Poems

A Peasant's Life

The following selection comes from *The Vision of Piers Plowman,* written by English poet William Langland. The lines describe what it was like to be a medieval serf.

"I have no penny," said Piers, "to buy pullets,
No geese nor pigs, but two green cheeses,
A few curds of cream, a cake of oatmeal,
Two loaves of beans and bran, baked for my
    children;
And, by my soul, I swear I have no salt bacon,
But I have parsley and pot herbs and a plenty
    of cabbages,
And a cow and a calf, and a cart mare. . . .

The needy are our neighbors, if we note rightly;
As prisoners in cells, or poor folks in hovels,
Charged with children and overcharged by
    landlords.
What they spare in spinning they spend on
    rental,
On milk, or on meal to make porridge
To still the sobbing of the children at meal
    time."

▲ A peasant harvesting crops

Interpreting Primary Sources

1. What did the French traveler admire about the count?
2. Why do you think the count treated his knights and squires so well?
3. What hardships did serfs such as Piers Plowman face? Why do you think serfs were willing to bear such hardships?

ACTIVITY

Writing a Poem Imagine you are a medieval poet. Write a poem about life on a medieval manor from the point of view of a noble, knight, or peasant.

UNIT 9

THE FALL OF THE AZTEC EMPIRE

According to Aztec legend, a light-skinned god named Quetzalcoatl sailed across the sea in ancient times. He promised to return in the year One Reed on the Aztec calendar and reclaim his land. When Hernando Cortés and his army arrived in Mexico, the year was One Reed. Emperor Montezuma—spelled Motecuhzoma by some scholars—believed Cortés to be the returning god Quetzalcoatl, and so he invited the invaders into the Aztec capital of Tenochtitlán. The decision helped end his empire.

■ Reader's Dictionary

finery fancy clothes and jewelry worn on special occasions
installed placed
plunder stolen goods, usually taken in war
Mexicanos people of Mexico; term used by the translator to refer to the Aztec
shied avoided out of fear

Personal Records

Arrival of the Spaniards

Aztec accounts of the Spanish conquest of Mexico is recorded in *The Broken Spears*, edited and translated by Miguel Leon-Portilla. This selection describes the meeting of Motecuhzoma and Cortés. It also shows the role of La Malinche, a woman who came from a people conquered by the Aztec and who served as an interpreter for Cortés.

The Spaniards arrived . . . near the entrance to Tenochtitlán. That was the end of their march, for they had reached their goal.

Motecuhzoma now arrayed himself in his finery, preparing to go out to meet them. . . . Then he hung the gold necklaces around their necks and gave them presents of every sort as gifts of welcome.

When Motecuhzoma had given necklaces to each one, Cortés asked him: "Are you Motecuhzoma? Are you the king? . . ."

And the king said: "Yes, I am Motecuhzoma." Then he stood up to welcome Cortés; he came forward, bowed his head low and addressed him in these words: "Our lord, you are weary. The journey has tired you, but now you have arrived on the earth. You have come to your city, Mexico. You have come here to sit on your throne. . . ."

When the Spaniards were installed in the palace, they asked Motecuhzoma about the city's resources. . . . They questioned him closely and then demanded gold.

Motecuhzoma guided them to it. . . . When they entered the hall of treasures, it was as if they had arrived in Paradise. . . . All of

Motecuhzoma's possessions were brought out: fine bracelets, necklaces with large stones, ankle rings with little gold bells, the royal crowns and all the royal finery—everything that belonged to the king. . . . They seized these treasures as if they were their own, as if this plunder were merely a stroke of good luck. And when they had taken all the gold, they heaped up everything in the middle of the patio.

La Malinche called the nobles together. She climbed up to the palace roof and cried: "Mexicanos, come forward! The Spaniards need your help! Bring them food and pure water. They are tired and hungry; they are almost fainting from exhaustion! Why do you not come forward? Are you angry with them?"

The Mexicans . . . shied away . . . as if the hour were midnight on the blackest night of the year. Yet they did not abandon the Spaniards to hunger and thirst. . . . They delivered the supplies to the Spaniards with trembling hands, then turned and hurried away.

▲ An Aztec double-headed serpent charm

Songs and Poems

The Fall of Tenochtitlán

Aztec writers recorded the loss of their empire in a series of poems known as "songs of sorrow." This excerpt from a poem entitled "The Fall of Tenochtitlán" recalls their loss.

How can we save our homes, my people?
The Aztecs are deserting the city:
the city is in flames, and all
is darkness and destruction. . . .
Weep, my people:
know that with these disasters
we have lost the Mexican nation.
The water has turned bitter,
our food is bitter!
These are the acts of the Giver of Life. . . .

Interpreting Primary Sources

1. What gifts did Motecuhzoma give to Cortés?

2. Why do you think Motecuhzoma took Cortés to his personal treasury?

3. What does the poet tell you about the fate of the Aztec capital?

4. What do these two sources reveal about how the Aztec viewed the arrival of the *conquistadores* in what is now Mexico?

ACTIVITY

Writing Letters Write a letter that Cortés might have sent to the king of Spain describing his conquest. The letter should predict what this event means for the future of Spain.

THE IRON HORSE

Invention of the railroad brought a revolution to transportation. The British led the way, with the first steam-powered railroads appearing in the early 1800s. However, like the Industrial Revolution itself, the idea soon spread. In the United States, inventors tried to replace the horse with one of the new steam-powered locomotives. Not surprisingly, the new type of locomotive won the nickname "iron horse."

■ Reader's Dictionary

pistons metal cylinders that slide up and down, causing an internal combustion engine to work

laden heavily loaded

facility ease

Printed Publications

Riding the Railroad

In 1830, actress Frances Kemble took a ride on the Liverpool-Manchester Railway, the second passenger line in England. She had the pleasure of riding with George Stephenson, the railroad pioneer who invented the *Rocket* (see page 529). In *Record of a Girlhood*, Kemble describes the trip.

She [the engine] . . . consisted of a boiler, a stove, a small platform, a bench, and . . . a barrel containing enough water to prevent her being thirsty for fifteen miles. . . . She goes upon two wheels which are her feet and are moved by bright steel legs called pistons; these are propelled by steam. . . . This snorting little animal, which I felt rather inclined to pat, was then harnessed to our carriage, and Mr. Stephenson having taken me on the bench of the engine with him, we started at about ten miles an hour. . . . You can't imagine how strange it seemed to be journeying on thus, without any visible cause of progress other than the magical machine, with its flying white breath. . . . I felt as if no fairy tale was ever half so wonderful as what I saw. . . .

When I closed my eyes this sensation of flying was quite delightful and strange beyond description; yet strange as it was, I had a perfect sense of security and not the slightest fear. At one time, to exhibit the power of the engine, having met another steam carriage which was unsupplied with water, Mr. Stephenson caused it to be fastened in front of ours; moreover, a wagon laden with timber was also chained to us, and thus propelling the idle steam engine and dragging the loaded wagon . . . and our own carriage full of people behind, this brave little she-dragon of ours flew on. Farther on she met three carts, which being fastened in front of her she pushed on before her without the slightest delay or difficulty; when I add that this pretty little creature can run with equal facility either backwards or forwards, I believe I have given you an account of all her capacities.

A Horse Race

In 1829, American inventor Peter Cooper tested his new steam-powered locomotive—the *Tom Thumb*—on some track laid down by the Baltimore and Ohio Railroad. The following year, a horse-drawn railcar challenged the *Tom Thumb* to a race. An observer later recalled the scene in a history of railroads compiled by the Baltimore and Ohio Railroad.

The horse was perhaps a quarter of a mile ahead before the engine started. The blower whistled, the steam blew off in vapory clouds, and the pace increased. Then the engine passed the horse, and a great hurrah hailed the victory. But it was not repeated. The engine began to wheeze and pant. Although the steam again did its best, the horse was too far ahead to be overtaken. But the real victory was with Mr. Cooper.

Interpreting Primary Sources

1. What impressed Frances Kemble about the new steam-powered locomotive?
2. What clues in the reading show that she viewed the engine as an "iron horse"?
3. What was the outcome of the race between the horse-drawn railcar and the *Tom Thumb*?
4. What do you think the observer meant by the remark that the "real victory was with Mr. Cooper"?

ACTIVITY

Writing a Diary Entry   Imagine you are one of the passengers aboard the Liverpool-Manchester Railway shown in the picture on this page. Describe your trip in the form of a diary entry. Be sure to indicate whether you are a first-class or a second-class passenger and how you feel about your choice of railcar.

UNIT 11

BRITISH INDIA

The British brought many things to India, including a unified government and a railroad system that spanned a subcontinent. They made it possible for Indians to receive a British education and trained Indians as *civil servants*—the name given to people who work for the government. For the most part, however, the British looked down on Indian culture and denied Indians positions of importance. This attitude would be the undoing of British rule in India.

■ Reader's Dictionary

feeble weak

natives people born and raised in a place; in this case, the people of India

excluded left out

sent out graduated

aught all

material physical

convulsion upheaval

despotism cruel use of power

Printed Publications

Stirrings of Nationalism

An early Indian nationalist named Dadabhai Naoroji admired British self-government. He feared, however, that colonial policies might prevent this system from ever coming to India. In 1880, he described these policies and their effect on India in a strongly worded memo to British officials.

Europeans occupy almost all the higher places in every department of government. . . . While in India they acquire India's money, experience, and wisdom, and when they go they carry both away with them, leaving India so much poorer. . . . Thus India is left without, and cannot have, those elders in wisdom and experience who in every country are the natural guides of the rising generations. . . .

Every European is isolated from the people around him. . . . For any . . . guidance or sympathy with the people, he might just as well be living in the moon. The people know not him, and he knows not nor cares for the people. Some honorable exceptions do now and then make an effort to do some good, . . . but in the very nature of things, these efforts are always feeble . . . and of little permanent effect. . . .

The Europeans are not the natural leaders of the people. They do not belong to the people. They cannot . . . sympathize with their joys or griefs. . . . There may be very few social institutions started by Europeans in which natives, however fit and desirous to join, are not deliberately and insultingly excluded. The Europeans . . . make themselves strangers in every way. . . .

. . . The thousands [of Indians] that are being sent out by the universities every year find themselves in a most [difficult] position. There is no place for them in their motherland. They may beg in the streets or break stones on the roads, for aught the rulers seem to care. . . .

. . . If the present material and moral destruction of India continues, a great convulsion must inevitably arise by which either India will be more and more crushed under the iron heel of despotism and destruction, or may succeed in shattering the destroying hand and power [that holds it down]. Far, far is it from my earnest prayer and hope that such should be the result of the British rule.

Artifacts Like most visitors to a foreign land, the British sent postcards and bought souvenirs that reminded them of India. The postcard on the left from the 1890s shows a British traveler in India. The photo below shows the Victoria Memorial, built by the British in Calcutta.

A Tonjon, or Ladies' Carriage

Interpreting Primary Sources

1. What things does Naoroji say the British are taking from India?
2. Why does he feel the British are not the "natural leaders" of India?
3. What prediction does he make for the future if Great Britain does not change its policies?
4. What do the postcard and photograph show about the benefits and drawbacks of British rule?

ACTIVITY

Designing a Postcard Design a postcard that an Indian artist might create to capture some aspect of life in British India.

UNIT 12

EQUALITY AND PEACE

On June 11, 1964, a South African judge sentenced Nelson Mandela and seven others to life in prison. They opposed apartheid, the system that denied black South Africans their rights. South Africa bowed to world pressure and freed Mandela on February 11, 1990. By the end of the century, a new South African government would be organized based on freedom and equality.

Like Nelson Mandela, Aung San Suu Kyi has become a symbol of peaceful resistance against oppression. Since 1988, she has worked to bring peace and democracy to her homeland of Myanmar (formerly Burma), a Southeast Asian country currently ruled by the military.

■ Reader's Dictionary

domination authority over others
tantamount equivalent or equal
passivity lacking energy or will
security freedom from fear or anxiety
obstacles something that gets in the way of progress

Printed Publications

"I Am Prepared to Die"

The following is a portion of a speech that Nelson Mandela delivered in his own defense before being sentenced to life in prison. It is considered one of the great democratic speeches in world history.

During my lifetime I have dedicated myself to this struggle of the African people. I have fought against white domination, and I have fought against black domination. I have cherished the ideal of a democratic and free society in which all persons live together in harmony and with equal opportunities. It is an ideal which I hope to live for and to achieve. But if needs be, it is an ideal for which I am prepared to die.

Oral Histories

Peace Is Life

Aung San Suu Kyi has won numerous international awards, including the Nobel Peace Prize in 1991, for her attempts to bring democracy to Myanmar (Burma). She was unable to personally receive these awards, however. The Burmese military government has kept her under house arrest for nine of the last fifteen years. The following speech reveals her views on peace.

A conference on peace is tantamount to a conference on one of the basic necessities of life. In fact one could say that peace is life itself because a life without peace is hardly a life worth living. But by peace I do not mean a life of passivity, I do not mean a life without action because sometimes we have to act a lot to bring about peace. What do we mean actually by peace? I suppose basically we mean a sense of inner security that will give us the strength to work for others and for the community, to work for progress and development. Without a sense of inner security we cannot work for progress.

There are so many obstacles in the way of development without peace. Peace, development and justice are all connected to each other. We cannot talk about economic development without talking about peace. How can we expect economic development in a battlefield? It would not be possible. But there is more than one kind of battlefield in this world. A battlefield is not necessarily a place where people are shooting each other. In a civil society, where basic human rights are ignored, where the rights of the people are violated every day, it is like a battlefield where lives are lost and people are crippled, because people can lose their lives. And the development of their lives can be crippled by a lack of basic human rights. So when we talk about peace, we cannot avoid talking about basic human rights, especially in a country like Burma where people are troubled constantly by a lack of human rights and a lack of justice and a lack of peace.

In our country, there are many races living together, but we have not been able to live together in peace because the situation does not exist where we can trust each other. So trust is a basic element for peace. Unless we can trust each other, unless we can be sure that we will receive justice, and that we also have to give justice, we cannot achieve peace. I very much hope that this conference on peace will deal with the close connection between peace, justice and development, and that development will be seen in human rather than in economic terms.

I wish you all success and I hope that the day will come when Burma will be able to contribute to more peace in this world.

May 23, 2003

▲ Aung San Suu Kyi

Interpreting Primary Sources

1. What kind of government did Nelson Mandela say he wanted in 1964?

2. How does Aung San Suu Kyi define "peace"?

3. According to Aung San Suu Kyi, with what is peace connected?

ACTIVITY

Writing a Speech   Write your own speech in which you describe what equality and peace mean to you.

REFERENCE ATLAS

NATIONAL GEOGRAPHIC

The World: Political	700	Europe: Political	710
The World: Physical	702	Asia: Political	712
North America: Political	704	Middle East: Physical/Political	714
South America: Political	705	Africa: Political	716
United States: Political	706	Polar Regions: Physical	717
Middle America: Physical/Political	708	Pacific Rim: Physical/Political	718

ATLAS KEY

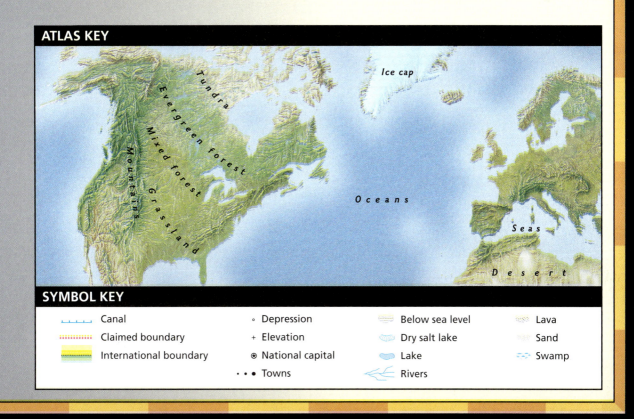

SYMBOL KEY

Canal	∘ Depression	Below sea level	Lava
Claimed boundary	+ Elevation	Dry salt lake	Sand
International boundary	⊗ National capital	Lake	Swamp
• • ● Towns		Rivers	

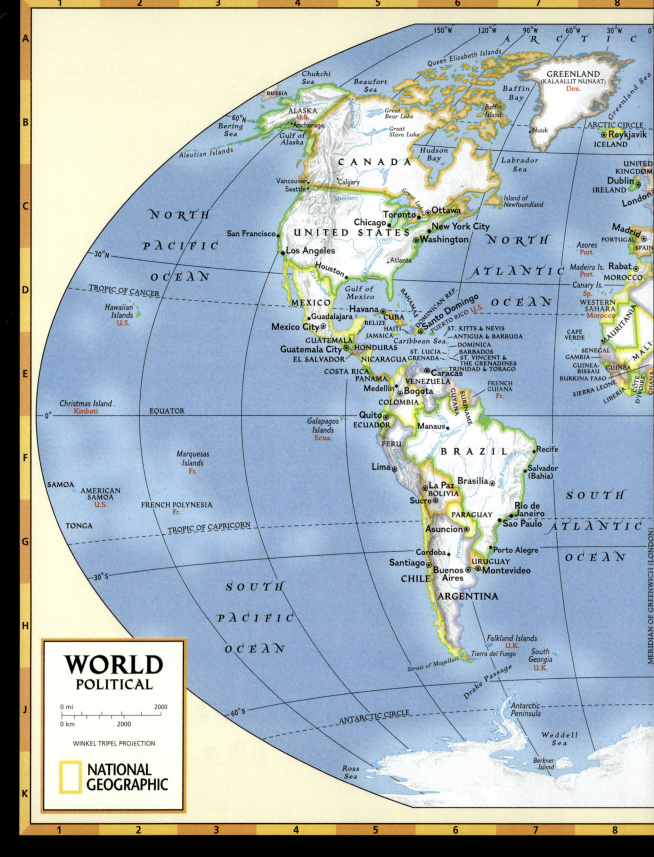

WORLD
POLITICAL

0 mi   2000

0 km   2000

WINKEL TRIPEL PROJECTION

NATIONAL GEOGRAPHIC

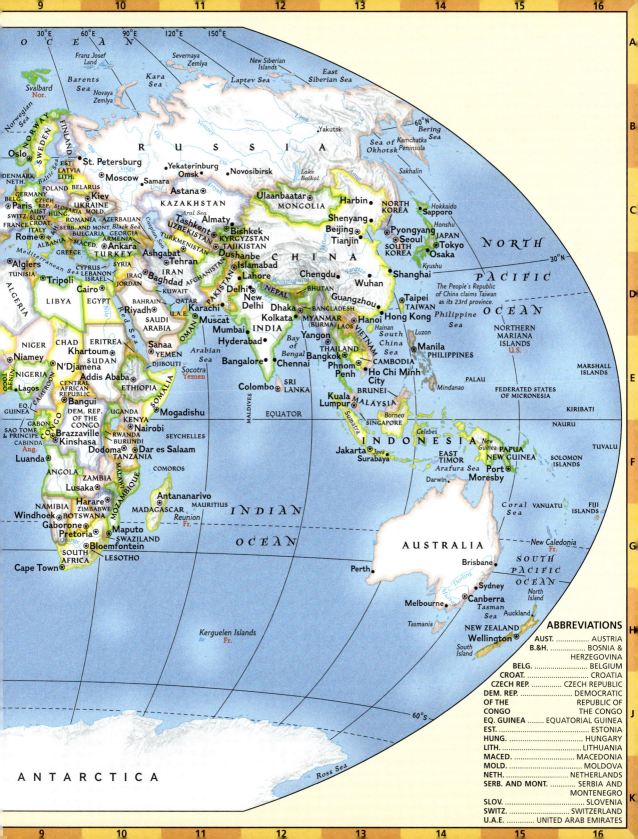

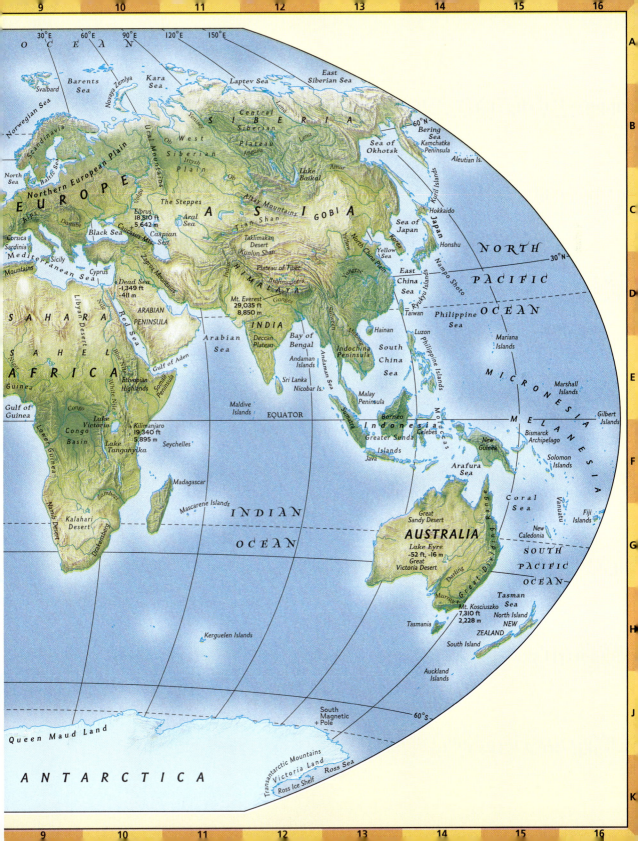

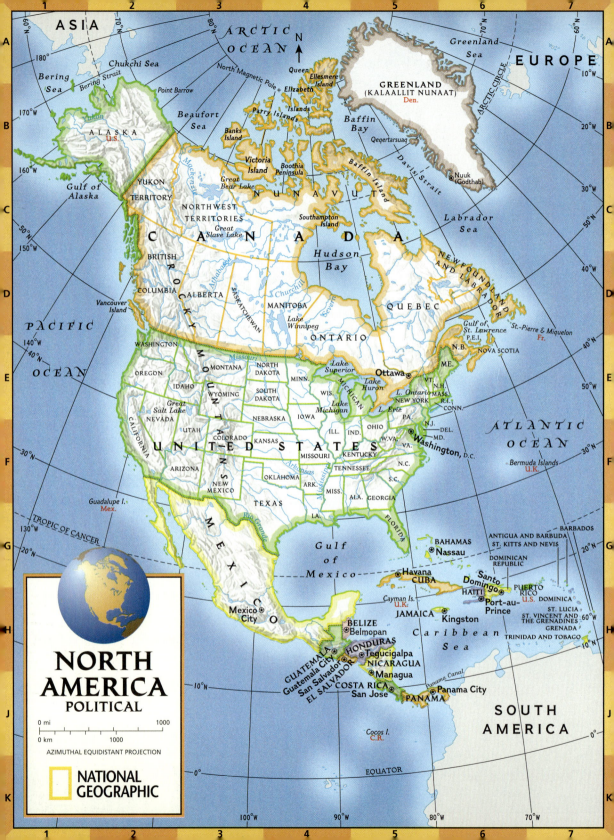

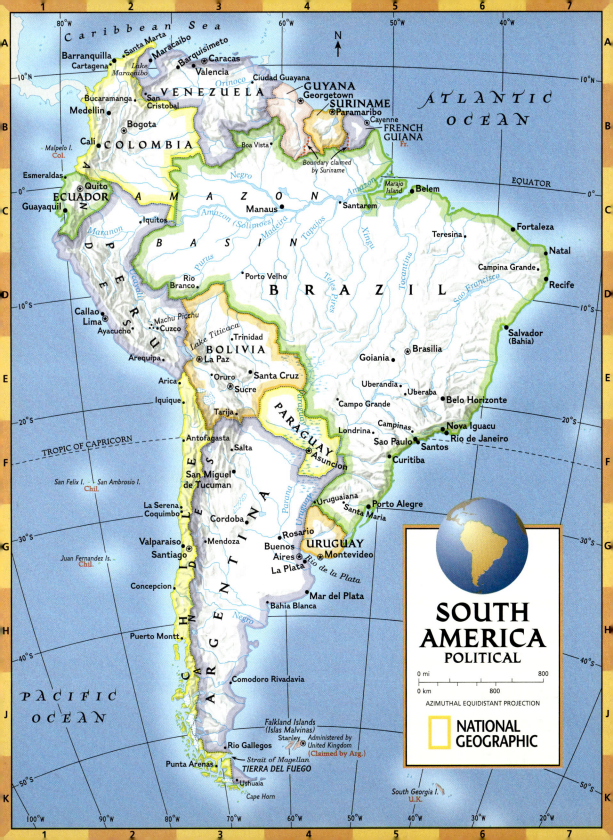

SOUTH AMERICA
POLITICAL

AZIMUTHAL EQUIDISTANT PROJECTION

NATIONAL GEOGRAPHIC

UNITED STATES
STATES
POLITICAL

0 mi 600
0 km 600

OBLIQUE AZIMUTHAL EQUIDISTANT PROJECTION

NATIONAL GEOGRAPHIC

GREENLAND
(KALAALLIT NUNAAT)
Den.

ARCTIC CIRCLE

C A N A D A

MONTANA
Helena
Billings
NORTH DAKOTA
Bismarck
MINNESOTA
MICHIGAN
Lake Superior
Lake Huron
MAINE
Augusta
Montpelier
Portland
Concord, N.H.
NEW YORK
VT.
Boston, MASS.
Lake Ontario
Albany
Providence, R.I.
Hartford, CONN.

SOUTH DAKOTA
Pierre
WISCONSIN
Minneapolis
St. Paul
Milwaukee
Madison
Lansing
Detroit
Buffalo
PA.
Cleveland
New York City

WYOMING
Casper
Cheyenne
IOWA
Sioux City
Des Moines
Chicago
L. Michigan
L. Erie
Toledo
Harrisburg
Pittsburgh
Trenton, N.J.
Philadelphia
Dover, DEL.

NEBRASKA
Lincoln
Omaha
ILLINOIS
IND.
Columbus
OHIO
Dayton
W. VA.
Annapolis, MD.
Washington, D.C.

Denver
COLORADO
Indianapolis
Cincinnati
Charleston
Richmond
Virginia Beach

Santa Fe
Topeka
KANSAS
Kansas City
MISSOURI
Jefferson City
Springfield
St. Louis
Frankfort
Louisville
VIRGINIA
KENTUCKY
Raleigh
NORTH CAROLINA

Albuquerque
Oklahoma City
OKLAHOMA
Tulsa
ARKANSAS
Nashville
TENNESSEE
Memphis
Charlotte
SOUTH CAROLINA
Columbia
Little Rock

El Paso
NEW MEXICO
Fort Worth
Dallas
Birmingham
MISS.
ALABAMA
GEORGIA
Atlanta
Charleston
Savannah

T E X A S
LOUISIANA
Jackson
Montgomery
Jacksonville

Austin
San Antonio
Baton Rouge
Houston
New Orleans
Tallahassee
FLORIDA

Rio Grande

M E X I C O

Gulf of Mexico
Tampa
Miami

Straits of Florida

Bermuda Is.
U.K.

BAHAMAS

A T L A N T I C   O C E A N

CUBA

Caribbean Sea
JAMAICA
HAITI
DOMINICAN REPUBLIC
PUERTO RICO
U.S.
San Juan
DOMINICA

ANTIGUA & BARBUDA
ST. KITTS & NEVIS

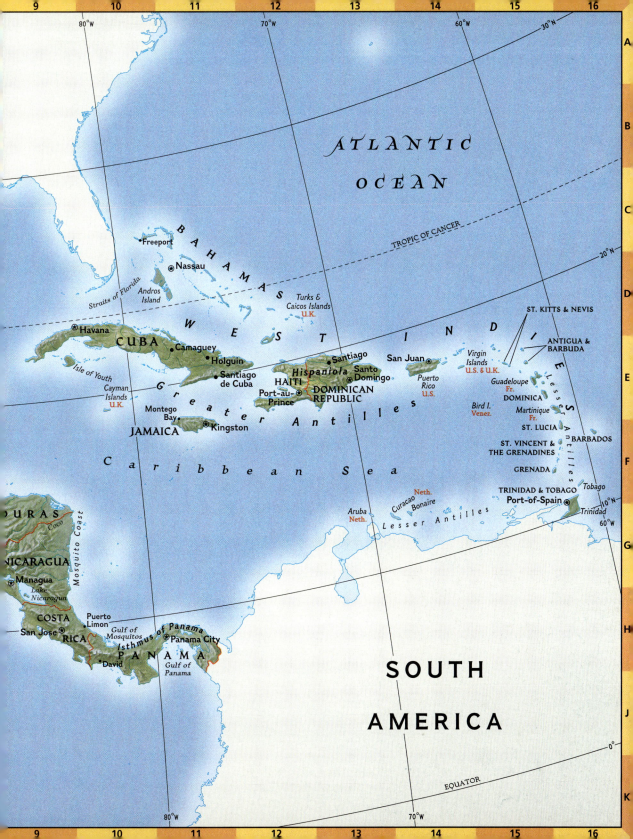

A commonly accepted division between Asia and Europe—here marked by a gray line—is formed by the Ural Mountains, Ural River, Caspian Sea, Caucasus Mountains, and the Black Sea with its outlets, the Bosporus and the Dardanelles.

Barents Sea

Tobseda

Pechora•

•Murmansk

Kirovsk•

Kola Peninsula

•Umba

White Sea

•Syktyvkar

•Archangel
Severodvinsk•

Kiruna•

Ivalo

•Kemi

•Lulea

•Oulu

Imea

Bothnia

•Vaasa

•Kuopio

Lake Onega

R U S S I A

U R A L   M O U N T A I N S

70°E

80°E

60°N

80°E

Europe-Asia boundary

A S I A

•Pori

•Tampere

Lake Ladoga

•Perm

70°N

•Turku

•Helsinki

•St. Petersburg

•Kirov

•Ufa

50°N

ESTONIA

Tallinn⊛

Velikiy Novgorod•

•Yaroslavl

•Kazan

•Riga

Moscow⊛

•Tver

•Nizhniy Novgorod

•Samara

•Orenburg

LATVIA

•Daugavpils

•Ryazan

•Penza

K A Z A K H S T A N

LITHUANIA

•Vitsyebsk

•Smolensk

•Saratov

•Oral

USSIA

•Vilnius

Kaunas

⊛Minsk

•Bryansk

Volga

Ural

60°E

BELARUS

Homyel•

•Kursk

•Volgograd

•Warsaw

Chernihiv•

•Astrakhan

•Krakow

Sumy•

•Kharkiv

Carpathian Mts.

•Lviv

Kiev⊛

•Poltava

•Donetsk

U K R A I N E

•Vinnytsya

•Dnipropetrovsk

•Rostov

Dniester

•Stavropol

MOLDOVA

⊛Chisinau

Sea of Azov

•Groznyy

60°E

40°N

•Odesa

•Kerch

Crimea

Caucasus Mountains

Caspian Sea

ROMANIA

•Simferopol

GEORGIA

AZERBAIJAN

•Belgrade

•Bucharest

•Yalta
Sevastopol•

•Baku

ERBIA
ND
ONTENEGRO

Danube

Constanta•

B l a c k   S e a

Balkan Mts.

•Varna

BULGARIA

•Sofia

OSOVO

⊛Skopje

MACED

Bosporus

•Istanbul

•Thessaloniki

T U R K E Y

GREECE

Dardanelles

Sea of Marmara

Aegean Sea

⊛Athens

Peloponnesus

Crete

•Iraklio

Rhodes

•Nicosia⊛

C Y P R U S

Sea

30°N

50°E

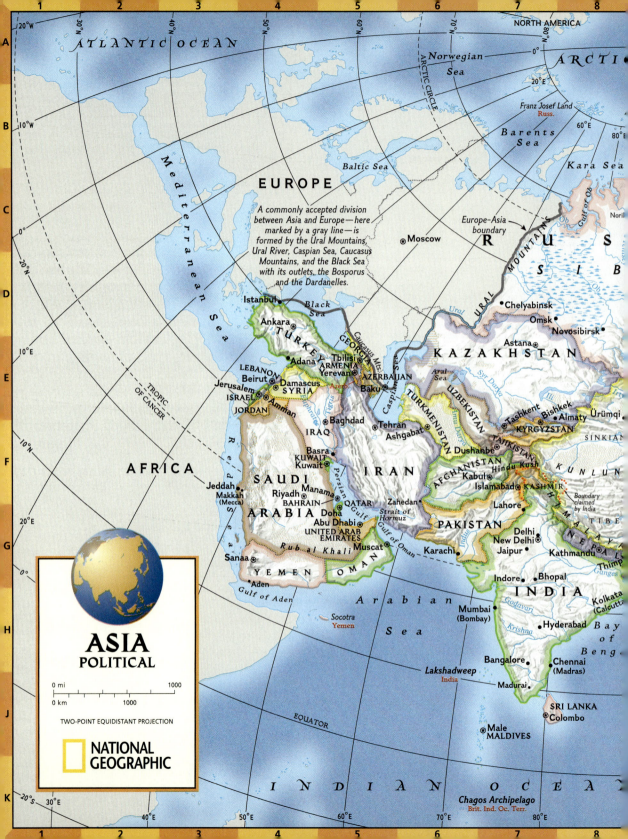

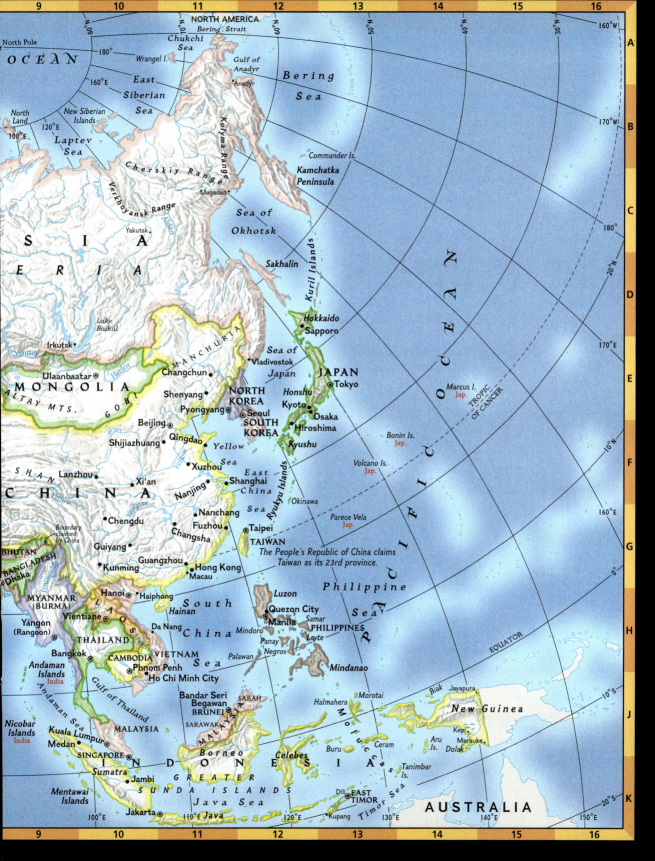

EUROPE

Black Sea

Sea of
Marmara

Istanbul

ANATOLIA

Ankara

TURKEY

Tunis

TUNISIA

Mediterranean Sea

Tripoli

LIBYA

Taurus Mountains

Aleppo

CYPRUS   SYRIA
LEBANON   Damascus
Beirut   Syrian
ISRAEL   Desert
Jerusalem
Alexandria   Amman
Cairo   JORDAN
El Giza
Sinai
Pen.
See inset below

EGYPT

Nile R.

Hejaz

Aswan
High Dam

Red Sea

Boundary claimed
by Sudan

SAHARA

SUDAN

AFRICA

Khartoum

Eastern Mediterranean Area

TURKEY

N

Aleppo

CYPRUS   SYRIA

Mediterranean
Sea

LEBANON

Beirut

Damascus

Sea of Galilee   Golan Heights
Jordan River
Tel Aviv–Yafo   West Bank
Jerusalem   Amman
Gaza Strip
Dead Sea

ISRAEL

JORDAN

Suez Canal

El Giza   Cairo

EGYPT

SAUDI
ARABIA

Nile River

Gulf of Suez

Gulf of
Aqaba

Red Sea

0 mi   100
0 km   100

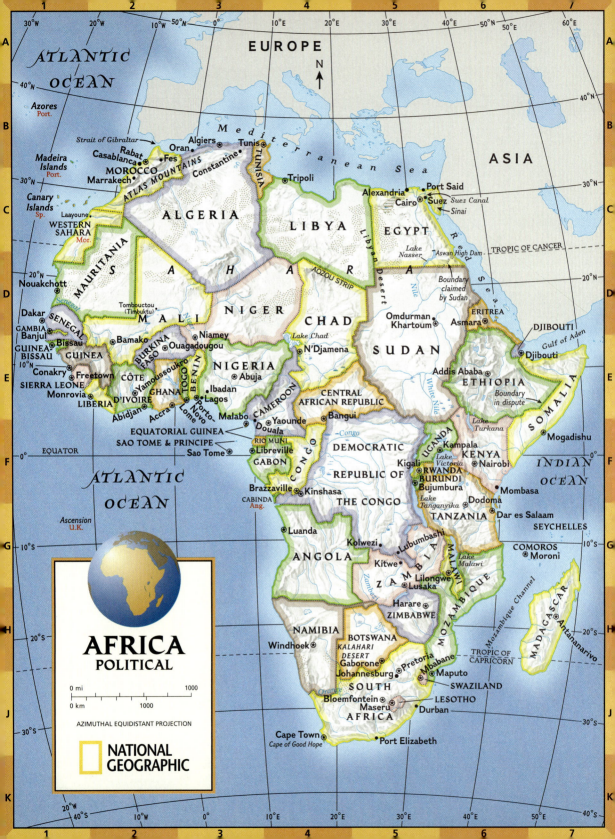

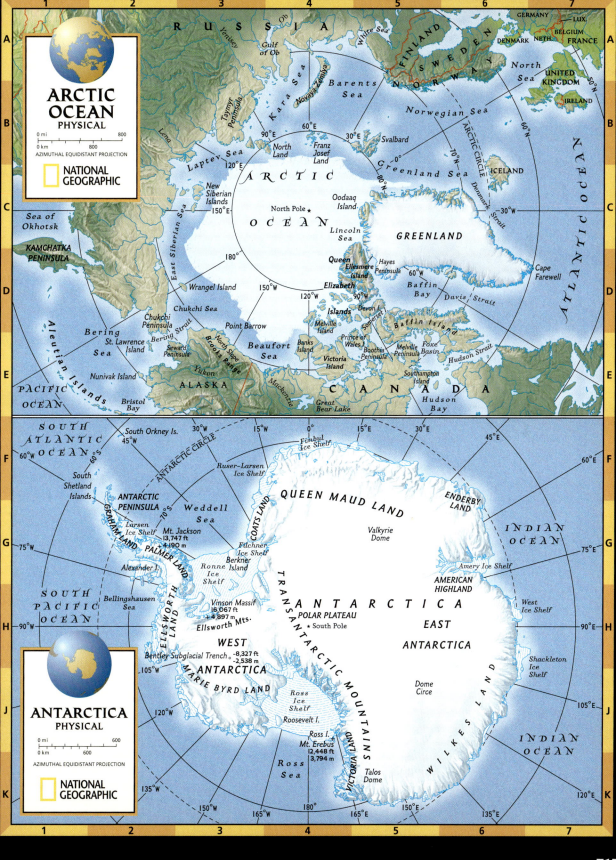

ARCTIC OCEAN
PHYSICAL

0 mi 800
0 km 800
AZIMUTHAL EQUIDISTANT PROJECTION

NATIONAL GEOGRAPHIC

ANTARCTICA
PHYSICAL

0 mi 600
0 km 600
AZIMUTHAL EQUIDISTANT PROJECTION

NATIONAL GEOGRAPHIC

RUSSIA
GERMANY
LUX.
BELGIUM
FRANCE
DENMARK
NETH.
FINLAND
NORWAY
SWEDEN
North Sea
UNITED KINGDOM
IRELAND
ARCTIC CIRCLE
Ob
Yenisey
Gulf of Ob
White Sea
Barents Sea
Norwegian Sea
Taymyr Peninsula
Kara Sea
Novaya Zemlya
Svalbard
Franz Josef Land
Greenland Sea
Lena
North Land
ICELAND
Laptev Sea
ARCTIC
OCEAN
Denmark Strait
GREENLAND
New Siberian Islands
North Pole ★
Oodaaq Island
Lincoln Sea
East Siberian Sea
Wrangel Island
Queen
Ellesmere Island
Hayes Peninsula
Cape Farewell
Elizabeth
Chukchi Sea
Devon Island
Baffin Bay
Davis Strait
Sea of Okhotsk
Chukchi Peninsula
Point Barrow
Islands
Melville Island
Somerset
Baffin Island
KAMCHATKA PENINSULA
Bering Strait
Beaufort Sea
Banks Island
Prince of Wales
Foxe Basin
Bering Sea
St. Lawrence Island
North Slope
Boothia Peninsula
Melville Peninsula
Hudson Strait
Seward Peninsula
Brooks Range
Victoria Island
Aleutian Islands
Nunivak Island
Yukon
ALASKA
Mackenzie
CANADA
Southampton Island
PACIFIC OCEAN
Bristol Bay
Great Bear Lake
Hudson Bay
ATLANTIC OCEAN

SOUTH ATLANTIC OCEAN
South Orkney Is.
ANTARCTIC CIRCLE
Finbul Ice Shelf
Ruser-Larsen Ice Shelf
ENDERBY LAND
South Shetland Islands
ANTARCTIC PENINSULA
Coats Land
QUEEN MAUD LAND
INDIAN OCEAN
GRAHAM LAND
Larsen Ice Shelf
Mt. Jackson 13,747 ft 4,190 m
Weddell Sea
Valkyrie Dome
Alexander I.
Filchner Ice Shelf
Berkner Island
Amery Ice Shelf
PALMER LAND
Ronne Ice Shelf
AMERICAN HIGHLAND
West Ice Shelf
SOUTH PACIFIC OCEAN
Bellingshausen Sea
Vinson Massif 16,067 ft 4,897 m
Ellsworth Mts.
ANTARCTICA
POLAR PLATEAU
★ South Pole
EAST ANTARCTICA
ELLSWORTH LAND
Bentley Subglacial Trench -8,327 ft -2,538 m
WEST ANTARCTICA
TRANSANTARCTIC MOUNTAINS
Dome Circe
Shackleton Ice Shelf
MARIE BYRD LAND
Ross Ice Shelf
Roosevelt I.
WILKES LAND
INDIAN OCEAN
Ross I.
Mt. Erebus 12,448 ft 3,794 m
Ross Sea
VICTORIA LAND
Talos Dome

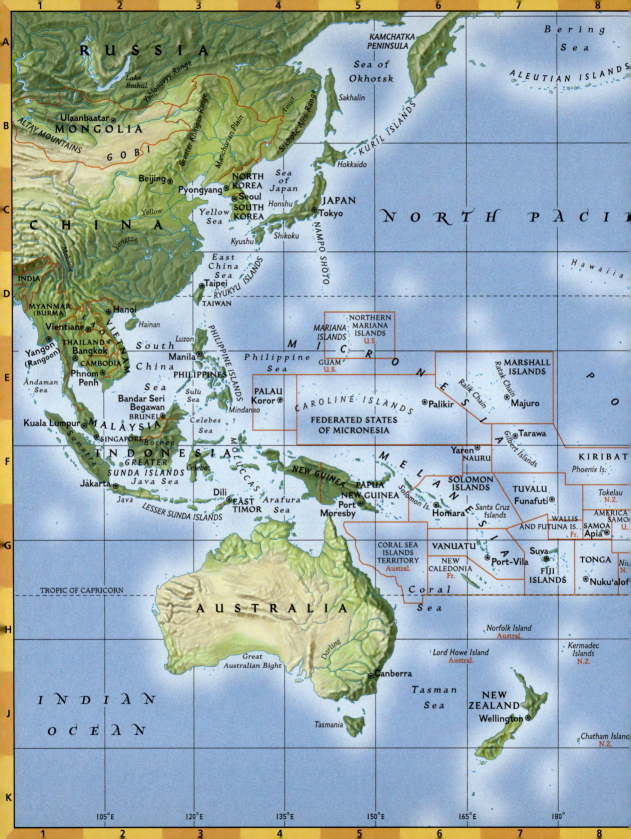

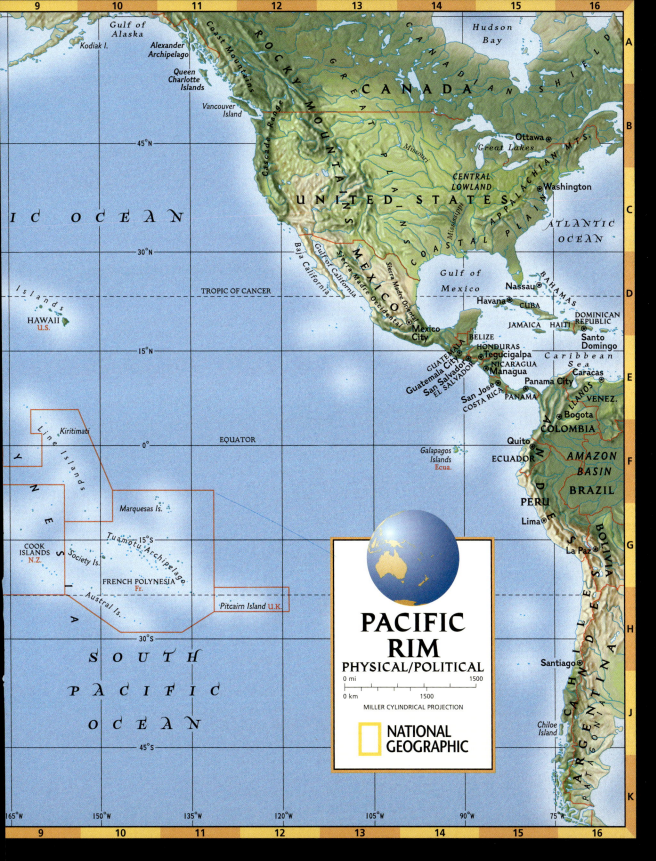

Glossary

Pronunciations are indicated in parentheses.

A

abbot (ab' uht) Monastery head. (p. 255)

abdicate (ab' duh-kāt) Give up the throne. (p. 565)

absolute location (ab sō lūt lō kā shun) Exact location of a place on the Earth's surface. (p. 5)

acropolis (uh krop' uh lis) Fortified hill in ancient Greek cities. (p. 163)

act of homage (akt of om' ij) Ceremony in which a vassal promises loyalty to a lord. (p. 368)

ages (ā' juhs) Time periods. (p. 27)

aggression (uh greh' shuhn) Warlike acts. (p. 645)

agora (ag' uh ruh) Ancient Greek marketplace. (p. 163)

airlift (ār' lift) System of carrying supplies into an isolated area by airplane. (p. 626)

alchemists (al'kuh mists) Scientists who try to turn metals into gold and silver. (p. 343)

alliances (uh lī' uhn siz) Agreements between people or countries. (p. 195)

amendments (uh mend' muhntz) Law changes. (p. 513)

ancestors (an' ses terz) Family members from past generations. (p. 89)

annexation (an ek sā shuhn) Incorporating an area into an existing state. (p. 549)

anointed (uh noin' tuhd) Blessed with holy oil. (p. 279)

anthropologists (an thruh pol' uh jists) People who study human beings. (p. 24)

apartheid (uh pahr' tāt) Separation of the races. (p. 659)

apostles (uh pos' uhls) Men chosen by Jesus to teach his beliefs to others. (p. 253)

appeasement (uh pēz' muhnt) Giving in to demands. (p. 615)

apprentice (uh pren' tis) Person who is learning a craft or trade. (p. 406)

archaeology (ar kē ol' uh jē) Study of remains of past human cultures. (p. 25)

archaeologists (ar kē ol' uh jists) People who study ruins and artifacts. (p. 24)

archbishops (arch' bish uhps) Bishops at the head of churches in large cities. (p. 253)

aristocrats (uh rist' ō kratz) Members of the upper class. (p. 164)

armada (ar mah' duh) Fleet of warships. (p. 459)

armaments (ar' muh muhnts) Military supplies. (p. 605)

armistice (ar' muh stis) Agreement to stop fighting. (p. 605)

artifacts (ar' tuh fakts) Products of human skill. (p. 25)

artillery (ar til' uhr ē) Mounted guns. (p. 604)

artisans (art' uh zuhnz) Skilled workers. (p. 57)

assembly line (uh sem' blē līn) Work system in which each worker adds one part to a product until it is assembled. (p. 528)

astrolabe (as' truh lāb) Navigational instrument used to determine latitude. (p. 467)

astronomers (uh stron' uh muhrs) People who study the heavenly bodies. (p. 122)

authoritarian rule (aw thōr uh tār' ē uhn rūl') Government in which one ruler or political party holds power. (p. 658)

automation (aw tuh mā' shuhn) Process in which machines replace workers. (p. 527)

autonomous (aw tah' nuh muhs) Self-governing. (p. 654)

B

bailiff (bā' lif) Medieval official who saw that peasants did their work. (p. 376)

balance of power (bal' uhnts of pau' uhr) Equal strength among countries. (p. 566)

balance of trade (bal' uhns of trād) Difference between the amount of goods a country brings in and sends out. (p. 492)

bandeirantes (ban duh ran' tās) Fortune hunters in colonial Brazil. (p. 488)

bands (bandz) Prehistoric groups that gathered food and lived together. (p. 34)

barbaroi (bar' buh roi) People who did not follow Greek customs. (p. 197)

barter (bar' ter) To exchange goods without using money. (p. 241)

berserkers (ber zerk' erz) Viking warriors. (p. 301)

bishop (bish' uhp) Diocese head. (p. 253)

blitzkrieg (blits' krēg) Lightning war. (p. 616)

blockaded (blok' ād uhd) Closed off. (p. 626)

blood feuds (bluhd fyūds) Longstanding quarrels between families. (p. 269)

bourgeoisie (bur zhwah zē) Middle class. (p. 514)

boyars (bō yahrs') Members of the wealthy class in czarist Russia. (p. 350)

boycott (boi' kot) Refuse to pay. (p. 509)

bull leaping (būl lēp' ēng) Minoan bullfighting. (p. 152)

burgesses (ber' jis ez) Elected representatives in colonial Virginia. (p. 495)

burghers (ber' guhrz) Freemen or wealthy merchants who lived in medieval towns. (p. 404)

burgs (bergs) Medieval towns. (p. 403)

C

caliph (kā' lif) Muslim ruler. (p. 336)

campesinos (kam puh sē' nōz) Latin American farmers and peasants. (p. 640)

canon laws (kan' uhn lahs) Church laws. (p. 382)

capitalism (ka pih tuhl izm) An economic system where most production is privately owned. (p. 633)

captaincies (kap' tuhn sēs) Land in Brazil given to Portuguese nobles. (p. 488)

caravans (kar' uh vans) Groups who traveled together for safety. (p. 121)

caravel (kar' uh vel) Portuguese ship. (p. 468)

cash crops (kash krops) Crops sold in the market. (p. 638)

castles (kas' uhlz) Large, fortified houses. (p. 370)

catacombs (kat' uh kōmz) Underground cemeteries. (p. 214)

cathedrals (kuh thē' druhlz) Churches headed by bishops. (p. 386)

caudillo (kau dē' yō) Latin American military dictator. (p. 556)

census (sen' suhs) Population count. (p. 234)

chancellor (chan' suh luhr) English university head. (p. 387); Prime minister. (p. 614)

charters (char' tuhrz) Documents that enabled towns to control their affairs. (p. 405)

chateaux (sha tōz') French castles. (p. 440)

chieftain (chēf' tuhn) Clan leader. (p. 267)

churches (cher' chez) Groups of people who share the same religious beliefs. (p. 252)

circuit judges (ser' kit juj' iz) Judges who travel throughout a country. (p. 415)

citadel (sit' uh duhl) Fortress. (p. 85)

city-states (sit' ē stāts) Cities and the surrounding territories. (p. 57)

civil disobedience (siv' uhl dis uh bē' dē uhns) Refusal to obey government demands. (p. 634)

civilians (suh vil' yuhnz) Non-soldiers. (p. 604)

civilization (siv' uh luh zā shuhn) Society with a developed knowledge of farming, trade, government, art, and science. (p. 33)

civil wars (siv' uhl wōrz) Wars between citizens of one nation. (p. 159)

clans (klans) Groups based on family ties. (p. 267)

classical writings (klas' i' kuhl rī tēngs) Ancient Greek and Roman writings. (p. 433)

clergy (kler' jē) Religious leaders. (p. 367)

climate (klī' mit) Average weather condition at a place over a period of years. (p. 14)

code of chivalry (kōd of shiv' uhl rē) Rules knights had to live by. (p. 373)

cold war (kōld wōr) Non-fighting hostility between nations. (p. 625)

collectivization (kuh lek ti vuh zā' shuhn) Uniting small farms into large ones controlled by the government. (p. 611)

colonies (kol' uh nēz) Permanent settlements. (p. 105)

colonize (kol' uh nīz) Permanently settle in an area. (p. 487)

communes (kom' yūnz) Political groups formed by townspeople in medieval Italy. (p. 405)

communicable diseases (kah mū ni kah bl dis ē zez) Diseases that are passed from an infected person or animal to another person or animal. (p. 664)

compass (kum' puhs) Instrument used to tell direction. (p. 467)

concentration camps (kon suhn trā shuhn kamps) Prison camps for political enemies. (p. 620)

conquistadores (kon kē stuh dōr' ēz) Spanish conquerors in the 1500s. (p. 473)

constitution (kon stuh tū' shuhn) Written laws used to govern a state. (p. 169)

constitutional monarchy (kon stuh tū' shuh nuhl mon' uhr kē) Monarchy limited in its powers by a constitution. (p. 518)

consuls (kon' suhlz) Heads of the ancient Roman Republic. (p. 219)

continental drift (kon tuh nen' tl drift) Theory that the continents move. (p. 10)

convents (kon' vents) Communities of nuns. (p. 255)

converted (kuhn ver' tuhd) Changed. (p. 277)

coracles (kor' uh kuhls) Small Irish boats. (p. 290)

core (kōr) Central part of the earth. (p. 10)

corregidores (kō rā hē dō' rās) Spanish royal officials. (p. 423)

cotton gin (kot' n jin) Cotton-cleaning machine. (p. 527)

counts (kounts) French law court officials. (p. 281)

coup (koo) Forced takeover of government. (p. 648)

cremation ovens (krē mā' shuhn uh' vuhns) Furnaces that burn bodies to ashes. (p. 621)

crusades (krū sāds') Wars fought to regain the Holy Land from Muslims. (p. 388)

crust (krust) Outer layer of the earth. (p. 10)

culture (kuhl' chuhr) Way of life. (p. 61)

cuneiform (kyū nē' uh form) Sumerian writing made up of wedge-shaped signs. (p. 58)

czar (zahr) Russian ruler. (p. 355)

D

dauphin (do' fuhn) Eldest son of the king of France. (p. 417)

defensive league (di fen' siv lēg) Protective group formed by Greek city-states. (p. 173)

democratic (dem uh krat' ik) Favoring the equality of all people. (p. 169)

depression (di presh' uhn) Economic decline. (p. 608)

descendants (di sen' duhnts) Offspring. (p. 107)

de-Stalinization (dē stahl uh nuh zā' shuhn) Attack on Stalin's policies. (p. 633)

developing nations (duh vel' uh pēng nā shuns) Countries advancing in production, technology, and standard of living. (p. 634)

dictator (dik' tā tuhr) Absolute ruler of a state. (p. 228)

dictatorship (dik tā' tuhr ship) Government ruled by a dictator. (p. 613)

diet (dī' uht) Formal assembly. (p. 421)

diocese (dī' uh sis) Area under the control of a bishop. (p. 253)

direct tax (duh rekt' taks) Tax paid directly to a government. (p. 509)

dissent (dih sent') Criticism. (p. 647)

doge (dōj) Ruler of Renaissance Venice. (p. 439)

domesticated (duh mes' tuh kāt uhd) Tamed. (p. 42)

domestic system (duh mes' tik sis' tuhm) Manufacturing done in workers' cottages. (p. 526)

domus (dō' muhs) Roman house. (p. 236)

dowry (dow' rē) Wealth brought by a woman when she marries. (p. 322)

dubbing (dub' ēng) Ceremony in which a squire is made a knight. (p. 374)

dynasty (dī nuh stē) Series of rulers from the same family. (p. 88)

E

earthquake (erth' kwāk) Shaking or sliding of a portion of the earth's crust. (p. 11)

Eddas (ed' uhz) Written poems based on stories of Viking gods. (p. 303)

elevation (el uh vā' shuhn) Altitude. (p. 9)

embalming (em bahm' ēng) Process used to keep dead bodies from decaying. (p. 73)

emigrated (em' uh grāt ed) Left one's country. (p. 200)

émigrés (em' uh grāz) French political exiles. (p. 518)

emirs (i miuhrs') Muslim army leaders. (p. 393)

emperor (em' phur uhr) Ruler of an empire. (p. 233)

empire (em' pīr) Territories governed by a single ruler or nation. (p. 61)

enclosure (en klō' zuhr) Fencing off common land for individual use. (p. 525)

erosion (i rō' zuhn) Wearing away by wind, water, and ice. (p. 12)

estates (e stāts') French social classes. (p. 513)

euro (yur' ō) Currency used by members of the European Union. (p. 665)

excavate (ek' skuh vāt) Uncover by digging. (p. 27)

excommunicated (ek skuh myū nuh kā ted) Barred as a member of the Roman Catholic Church. (p. 382)

extended families (ek sten' duhd fam' uh lēs) Parents, children, and other relatives living together in one house. (p. 639)

F

factories (fak' tuhr ēz) Buildings where goods are manufactured. (p. 200)

factory system (fak' tuh rē sis' tuhm) Workers and machines in one place to make goods. (p. 527)

fairs (fāuhrz) Medieval gatherings for trade. (p. 402)

fasces (fas' ēz) Rods tied around an ax. (p. 215)

federal (fed' uhr uhl) National government. (p. 546)

feudalism (fyū' dl iz uhm) Medieval political system based on the relation of lords to vassals. (p. 367)

fiefs (fēfs) Pieces of land given to vassals by their lords. (p. 367)

flying shuttle (flī' ēng shut' l) Weaving device that carries thread quickly back and forth across the piece being woven. (p. 527)

foreign policy (fōr' uhn pol' uh sē) Relations with other countries. (p. 507)

forum (fōr' uhm) Meeting place. (p. 653)

Forum (fōr' uhm) Roman public square. (p. 215)

freemen (frē' muhn) Peasants who paid the lord for the right to farm their own land. (p. 377)

freedmen (frēd' muhn) Former enslaved people. (p. 234)

friars (frī uhrs) Preachers. (p. 385)

G

galleons (gal' ē uhns) Spanish ships. (p. 459)

garrison (gar' uh suhn) Military force stationed in an area. (p. 610)

genocide (jen' uh sīd) Deliberate destruction of an entire people. (p. 620)

gentiles (jen' tīls) Non-Jews. (p. 249)

geography (jē ahg ruh fē) Study of the earth and the ways people live and work on it. (p. 5)

glaciers (glā' shuhrz) Great ice sheets. (p. 13)

gladiatorial games (glad' ē uh tōr ē uhl gāmz) Roman games in which gladiators fought. (p. 215)

gladiators (glad' ē ā tuhrz) Fighters in gladiatorial games. (p. 238)

glasnost (glaz nōst) Russian policy allowing openness. (p. 633)

grand jury (grand jūr' ē) Jury that examines accusations and advises criminal charges. (p. 415)

Greek fire (grēk fīr) Chemical weapon used by the Byzantines. (p. 324)

greenhouse effect (grēn hows uh fekt) Carbon dioxide traps heat from the Earth's surface. (p. 664)

guerrilla warfare (guh ril' uh wōr' fār) Hit-and-run fighting. (p. 573)

guilds (gildz) Medieval craft organizations. (p. 406)

guillotine (gil' uh tēn) Machine that cuts off a victim's head. (p. 518)

H

haciendas (ah sē en' duhz) Large ranches. (p. 640)

hajj (haj) Muslim journey to Makkah. (p. 336)

hard-liners (hahrd līnuhrz) People who stick to their ideas regardless of circumstances. (p. 632)

heavy industry (hev' ē in' duhs trē) Industry that manufactures machines. (p. 611)

helots (hel' uhts) Enslaved people owned by city-states. (p. 164)

heresy (her' uh sē) Religious belief at odds with church doctrine. (p. 253)

heretic (her' uh tik) Church member who disagrees with official doctrine. (p. 451)

hieroglyphic (hī uhr uh glif' ik) Egyptian writing system based on pictures. (p. 77)

Holocaust (hol' uh kahst) Nazi program of genocide against the Jews. (p. 621)

holy of holies (hō' lē of hō' lēs) Innermost and most sacred chamber of a temple. (p. 104)

home territory (hōm ter' uh tōr ē) Area where hunters and food gatherers lived. (p. 35)

hostage (hos' tij) Person held by another until certain promises are carried out. (p. 193)

humanists (hyū' muh nists) Philosophers who believe that people are important. (p. 433)

hypothesis (hī poth' uh sis) Possible explanation for a problem. (p. 188)

I

icons (ī konz) Sacred pictures of Eastern Orthodoxy. (p. 325)

imam (i mam') Muslim prayer leader. (p. 335)

immigrants (im' uh gruhnts) People who settle permanently in a different country. (p. 534)

imperialism (im pir' ē uh liz uhm) Establishing colonies and building empires. (p. 579)

indentured servants (in den' chuhrd ser' vuhntz) Settlers who pledged labor for their passage to the Americas. (p. 495)

indulgences (in dul' juhnt sez) Church pardons that lessen punishment for sins. (p. 450)

industrialized (in dus' trē uh līzd) Developed industry. (p. 533)

inflation (in flā shuhn) Period when prices go up and money value goes down. (p. 240)

interchangeable parts (in tuhr chān juh buhl parts) Machine parts made to a uniform size so they can be easily replaced. (p. 527)

internal combustion engine (in tuhr' nuhl kuhm buhs' chuhn en' juhn) Engine that is fueled by gasoline. (p. 535)

isolationist (ī sō lā shun ist) A country that stays out of the affairs of other countries. (p. 607)

izbas (iz' bahs) One-room wooden cabin built by Eastern Slavs. (p. 348)

J

jarls (yahrlz) Viking military leaders. (p. 301)

journeyman (jer' nē muhn) Person who works under a master for a daily wage. (p. 406)

joust (jowst) Contest on horseback between two knights. (p. 374)

judge (juj) Hebrew tribe leader. (p. 112)

junker (jung' kuhr) Rich Prussian landowner. (p. 574)

junta (hun' tuh) Committee organized to take over a government. (p. 553)

juris prudentes (jū' ruhs prū' duhntz) Roman lawyers. (p. 236)

K

kaiser (kī' zuhr) German emperor. (p. 574)

keep (kēp) Strongest part of a castle. (p. 371)

khan (kahn) Mongol leader. (p. 353)

king's peace (kings pēs) Protection extended to any area an Anglo-Saxon king visited. (p. 295)

knight (nīt) Warrior on horseback. (p. 369)

kremlin (krem' luhn) Russian fortress. (p. 354)

L

labyrinth (lab' uh rinth) Maze. (p. 153)

ladies (lā' dēz) Noblewomen. (p. 372)

landforms (land' forms) Physical features of the earth's surface. (p. 9)

latifundias (lat uh fuhn' dē uhs) Large Roman estates. (p. 225)

latitude (lat' uh tūd) Distance north or south of the Equator. (p. 14)

legends (lej' undz) Folktales or stories passed down from generation to generation. (p. 22)

legionaries (lē' juh ner ēz) Roman soldiers. (p. 221)

legions (lē juhnz) Divisions of Roman soldiers. (p. 221)

liberals (lib' uhr uhls) People who favor political reforms. (p. 566)

limited government (lim' uh tid guv' uhrn muhnt) Government has only powers given to it by the people. (p. 513)

lords (lordz) Medieval nobles. (p. 283)

M

macadam road (muh kad' uhm rōd) Road made of layers of crushed rock. (p. 529)

manifest destiny (man' uh fest des' tuh nē) Belief that the United States should extend from coast to coast. (p. 548)

mandate (man' dāt) Authority to govern. (p. 607)

manors (man' uhrz) Medieval estates with a lord and tenants. (p. 375)

mantle (man' tl) Part of the earth beneath the crust and above the core. (p. 10)

martial law (mar' shuhl lah) Rule by the army instead of by civil government. (p. 505)

mass (mas) Worship service. (p. 382)

masters (mas' tuhrz) Experts. (p. 406)

megaron (meg' uh ron) Square room in the center of a Mycenaean palace. (p. 155)

mercantilism (mer' kuhn tēl iz uhm) System in which colonies provide wealth to their parent country. (p. 508)

mercenaries (mer' suh nār ēz) Men hired to be soldiers for a foreign country. (p. 175)

messiah (muh' sī' uh) Savior. (p. 248)

mestizos (me stē' zōz) People of mixed European and Native American ancestry. (p. 490)

metropolitans (met ruh pol' uh tuhns) Eastern Orthodox Church officials in charge of large cities. (p. 325)

migrate (mī' grāt) To move from one place to another. (p. 34)

minerals (min' uhr uhls) Nonliving substances found beneath the earth's surface. (p. 19)

ministers (min' uh stuhrz) Protestant religious leaders. (p. 451)

minstrels (min' struhlz) Medieval traveling poets and singers. (p. 285)

missionary (mish' uh ner ē) Person who tries to convert nonbelievers. (p. 250)

mobilize (mō' buh līz) Prepare troops for action. (p. 604)

monarchies (mon' uhr kēz) Countries ruled by a king or queen. (p. 411)

monasteries (mon' uh ster ēz) Places where monks live. (p. 255)

monks (mungks) Men who live in a religious community. (p. 255)

monopoly (muh nop' uh lē) Total control. (p. 508)

monsoons (mon sūnz) Seasonal winds that change direction. (p. 16)

mosaics (mō zā' iks) Colorful pictures made of stone or glass. (p. 323)

mosque (mosk) Muslim house of worship. (p. 335)

mummy (mum ē) Wrapped body of a preserved dead person. (p. 73)

mundus (muhn' duhs) Meeting point of the worlds of the living and the dead for the Romans. (p. 216)

municipal (myū nis' uh puhl) Relating to a city. (p. 215)

mutiny (myūt' n ē) Revolt against officers. (p. 472)

N

nationalists (nash' uh nuhl ists) People in favor of national independence. (p. 566)

national workshops (nash' uh nuhl wuhrk' shops) Factories run by workers but paid for by the government. (p. 570)

natural resources (nach' uhr uhl rē' sōr sez) Materials found in nature. (p. 19)

necropolis (nek rop' uh luhs) Etruscan cemetery. (p. 214)

nobles (nō' buhlz) People having high rank in a kingdom. (p. 90)

nomadic (nō mad' ik) Wandering. (p. 106)

nonrenewable resources (non ri nū' uh buhl rē sōr sez) Irreplaceable natural resources. (p. 20)

nuns (nunz) Women belonging to a religious order. (p. 255)

O

oath-helpers (ōth help' erz) Germans who swore an accused person was telling the truth. (p. 269)

ocean current (ō' shun kur' uhnt) Water that flows in the ocean in a steady stream. (p. 16)

oligarchy (ol' uh gahr kē) Government in which a few people rule. (p. 169)

omens (ō' muhnz) Signs believed to indicate the future. (p. 214)

open-hearth process (ō' puhn hahrth prah' ses) Process that uses a special kind of furnace to make steel inexpensively. (p. 529)

oracles (ōr' uh kuhlz) Greeks through whom the gods spoke. (p. 179)

oracle bones (ōr' uh kuhl bōnz) Bones used by the Shang to receive messages from ancestors. (p. 90)

orator (ōr' uh ter) Public speaker. (p. 195)

ordeal (ōr dēl) Painful test used by the Germans to decide innocence or guilt. (p. 269)

orders (ōr' duhrs) Groups of friars. (p. 386)

P

page (pāj) Person who helped knights care for their horses and armor. (p. 373)

pancratium (pan krā' shē uhm) Olympic event that combined boxing and wrestling. (p. 183)

pandemics (pan dem' icks) Epidemics spread over a wide region. (p. 664)

papal line of demarcation (pā' puhl līn ov dē mahr kā' shuhn) Line drawn in 1493 dividing Spanish and Portuguese land claims. (p. 473)

papyrus (puh pī' ruhs) Egyptian paper. (p. 78)

parchment (parch' muhnt) Material made from thin animal skin used for windows and as paper. (p. 153)

parish (par' ish) Area assigned to a local church. (p. 253)

patriarchs (pā' trē arks) Most important bishops in the early Christian church. (p. 253)

patricians (puh trish' uhnz) Powerful upper-class citizens of ancient Rome. (p. 219)

peninsulares (puh nin sū la' rās) Colonials born in Spain who later came to the Americas. (p. 490)

pentathlon (pen tath' luhn) Olympic game made up of five events. (p. 183)

perestroika (pār uhs troi kuh) Russian system of restructuring. (p. 633)

perioeci (pār ē ē' sī) Merchants and artisans in Spartan villages. (p. 166)

phalanx (fā' langks) Greek infantry formation. (p. 194)

pharaoh (fār' ō) Egyptian ruler. (p. 70)

philosophes (fē luh zofs') French philosophers of the 1700s. (p. 514)

philosophia (fi la sō fē' ya) The love of wisdom, according to the Greeks. (p. 185)

piazza (pē aht' suh) Italian city square. (p. 436)

pilgrimage (pil' gruh mij) Religious journey to a shrine or holy place. (p. 133)

pilgrims (pil' gruhms) People who travel to a holy place to worship. (p. 332)

pillars of faith (pil' uhrs of fāth) Five Muslim duties as described in the Quran. (p. 335)

planned communities (pland kuh myū′ nuh tēz) Cities built to a definite plan. (p. 85)

plebeians (pli bē uhnz) Poor and lower-class citizens of ancient Rome. (p. 219)

plebiscite (pleb′ uh sīt) Popular vote. (p. 563)

polar zone (pō′ luhr zōn) Climate zone more than 60° north or south of the Equator. (p. 15)

polis (pah′ lis) Greek city-state. (p. 163)

political parties (puh lit′ uh kuhl par′ tēz) Groups with set ideas about government. (p. 546)

political science (puh lit′ uh kuhl sī′ uhns) Study of government. (p. 187)

popular sovereignty (pop′ yuh luhr sov′ ruhn tē) Idea that government derives its powers from the people. (p. 513)

population (pop ū lā shuhn) Number of living things in a particular area. (p. 42)

population explosion (pop ū lā′ shuhn ek splō′ zhuhn) Sudden growth in the number of people. (p. 136)

precipitation (prē sip uh tā shuhn) Falling moisture such as snow or rain. (p. 16)

prehistory (prē′ his tuh rē) Time before people began to keep written records. (p. 33)

prevailing winds (pri vā′ lēng winds) Winds that blow mostly from one direction. (p. 16)

priest (prēst) Religious leader, usually Roman Catholic or Eastern Orthodox. (p. 253)

priest-king (prēst king) Sumerian governmental and religious leader. (p. 59)

printing press (prin′ tēng pres) Machine for printing books, using movable type. (p. 441)

privatize (prī vuh tīz) Allow ownership by private citizens. (p. 649)

proletariat (pro luh tār′ ē uht) Industrial working class. (p. 568)

prophecy (prof′ uh sē) Statement of what might happen in the future. (p. 179)

prophets (prof′ its) People claiming to have messages from God. (p. 112)

protectorate (pruh tek′ tuhr it) Country that gives up foreign policy to an imperial authority. (p. 582)

provinces (prah′ vins uhs) Political districts. (p. 119)

psalms (sahms) Sacred songs. (p. 112)

publicans (pub′ luh′ kuhnz) Ancient Roman tax collectors. (p. 225)

purges (per′ juhs) Removals of undesirable members. (p. 631)

pyramids (pir′ uh midz) Large Egyptian tombs. (p. 71)

Q

quipus (k′ pūz) Inca counting devices. (p. 142)

R

referendum (ref ah ren′ duhm) Popular vote. (p. 660)

reformation (ref uhr mā′ shuhn) Change. (p. 449)

reform (rē form) Change that leads to improvement. (p. 61)

reign (rān) Period of power. (p. 63)

relative location (rel uhtiv lō kā shun) Location of a place in relation to other places. (p. 6)

relics (rel′ iks) Sacred objects from the past. (p. 319)

relief (ri lēf′) Differences in height between a region′s summits and lowlands. (p. 9)

renewable resources (ri nū′ uh buhl rē sōr sez) Replaceable natural resources. (p. 20)

repealed (ri pēld′) Abolished or called back. (p. 507)

representative government (rep ri ent′ uht iv guv′ uhrn muhnt) System of ruling in which officials are elected. (p. 546)

republic (ri pub′ lik) Government in which citizens choose their leaders. (p. 219)

revolution (rev uh lū′ shuhn) Activity designed to overthrow a government. (p. 503)

right of extraterritoriality (rīt ov ek struh ter i tōr ē al′ uh tē) Right of an accused person in a different country to be tried in a court of his or her own nation. (p. 587)

river system (riv′ uhr sis tuhm) River and all streams that flow into it. (p. 14)

rule by divine right (rūl bī duh vīn′ rīt) Rule based on the theory that a monarch′s right to rule comes from God. (p. 243)

runes (rūnz) Letters of the Viking alphabet. (p. 303)

S

sabbath (sab′ uhth) Day of the week used for rest and worship. (p. 113)

sans-culottes (san skū′ lahts) French city workers and peasants in the 1700s. (p. 518)

satellite nations (sat′ l īt nā shuhns) Countries controlled by another, stronger country. (p. 626)

scientific method (sī uhn tif′ ik meth′ uhd) Process used by scientists for study. (p. 188)

scorched-earth policy (skōrchd uhrth pahl' uh sē) Tactic of destruction used by a retreating army. (p. 564)

scribe (skrīb) Sumerian writer. (p. 58)

scriptures (skrip' churz) Sacred writings. (p. 247)

sea dog (sē dahg) Veteran sea captain in Tudor England. (p. 477)

seceding (si sēd' ēng) Withdrawing. (p. 551)

seminary (sem' uh ner ē) School for training priests. (p. 454)

seneschal (sēn' uh shuhl) Medieval official who looked after the noble's fiefs. (p. 375)

sepoys (sē' pois) Indian soldiers in the British army. (p. 585)

serfs (serfz) Medieval poor people bound to the land. (p. 285)

shadoof (shuh dūf') Egyptian machine used to raise water. (p. 68)

sheriff (sher' if) English government official in charge of a shire. (p. 295)

shires (shīrz) Districts in England. (p. 295)

shrines (shrīns) Sacred places to worship. (p. 154)

silent barter (sī luhnt bahr' ter) Method of exchanging goods without talking; used in the middle kingdoms of Africa. (p. 132)

slums (slumz) Run-down city areas. (p. 551)

smelting (smel' tēng) Heating iron or metals to remove impurities. (p. 118)

social justice (sō' shuhl jus' tis) Fair treatment of all people in a society. (p. 110)

social order (sō' shuhl ōr' der) Social divisions according to wealth and other factors. (p. 213)

social security laws (sō shuhl si kyūr' uh tē lahz) United States laws that provided for people's welfare. (p. 613)

Socratic method (sō krat' ik me' thuhd) Form of questioning developed by Socrates. (p. 186)

soothsayers (sūth' sā uhrz) People who are believed to be able to fortell the future. (p. 214)

sovereign (sah' vuh ruhn) Independent and self-governing. (p. 649)

soviets (sō' vē ets) Communist committees that represent workers and soldiers. (p. 610)

specialization (spesh uh luh zā' shuhn) Development of occupations. (p. 45)

spheres of influence (sfērs of in' flū uhns) Areas in one country in which another country has special rights. (p. 585)

spinning jenny (spin' ēng jen' ē) Machine for spinning that uses many spindles. (p. 527)

spirits (spēr' itz) Supernatural beings. (p. 89)

squire (skwīr) Young noble under the care and training of a knight. (p. 373)

stable government (stā' buhl guv' uhrn muhnt) Firmly established government. (p. 545)

strike (strīk) Stop work. (p. 569)

subsistence farmers (suhb sis stuhns far muhrs) People who produce only enough food for their own use. (p. 638)

swastika (swos' tuh kuh) Hooked black cross used as a Nazi symbol. (p. 614)

syllogism (sil' uh jiz uhm) Form of reasoning developed by Aristotle. (p. 188)

T

tariffs (tar' ifz) Taxes placed on goods entering one country from another. (p. 235)

tectonic plates (tek ton' ik plāts) Slow-moving sections of the earth. (p. 10)

temperate zone (tem' puhr it zōn) Climate zone between 30° and 60° north or south of the Equator. (p. 15)

tenants (ten' uhnts) People who live and work on someone else's land. (p. 155)

tenements (ten' uh muhnts) Apartments that meet minimum standards. (p. 551)

terrorism (tār' ōr izm) Violence to achieve a political goal. (p. 660)

textile (tek' stuhl) Woven cloth. (p. 526)

theology (thē ol' uh jē) Study of religion. (p. 320)

theses (thē' sēz) Statements written by Luther criticizing Church practices. (p. 450)

tithes (tīthz) Payments to the church. (p. 384)

tournaments (tur' nuh muhnts) Contests to test the skill of knights. (p. 374)

trade unions (trād yū' nyuhns) Associations of workers. (p. 533)

treaties (trē' tēz) Formal agreements between nations. (p. 103)

trench warfare (trench wōr' fāuhr) Warfare in which opposing forces attack from a system of trenches. (p. 604)

trial jury (trī uhl jūr' ē) Group of people that decides whether a person accused of a crime is innocent or guilty. (p. 415)

tribunes (trib' yūnz) Roman officials elected to protect the lower class. (p. 220)

triremes (trī' rēmz) Greek warships. (p. 172)

triumph (trī' uhmf) Parade to welcome home a Roman hero. (p. 215)

triumvirate (trī um' vuhr it) Group of three people who rule with equal power. (p. 228)

tropical zone (trop' uh kuhl zōn) Climate zone between 30° north and 30° south of the Equator. (p. 15)

tyranny (tir' uh nē) Unjust use of power. (p. 517)

U

unions (yūn' yuhns) Groups of people joined together for a common cause, especially medieval students and teachers. (p. 387)

universal male suffrage (yū nuh ver' suhl māl suhf' rij) Right of all men to vote. (p. 569)

universities (yū ni ver' suh tēs) Institutions of higher learning. (p. 387)

urbanization (uhr buh nuh zā' shuhn) Growth of cities. (p. 551)

utopian socialists (yū tō' pē uhn sō' shuh lists) People who want to set up ideal communities based on economic cooperation. (p. 568)

V

vassal (vas' uhl) Medieval noble who served a lord of higher rank. (p. 368)

veche (ve' chuh) Russian town assembly. (p. 350)

veto (vē' tō) Refuse consent. (p. 219)

viceroy (vīs roi) Ruler of a viceroyalty. (p. 490)

viceroyalties (vīs' roi uhl tēz) Districts in Spain's colonies in the Americas. (p. 490)

vizier (vi zir') Chief adviser to the caliph of the Abbasids. (p. 338)

volcano (vol kā' nō) Opening in the earth's crust through which, when active, steam, ashes, and magma are forced. (p. 11)

W

weapons of mass destruction (we pons ov mas di struk shuhn) Weapons such as nuclear bombs, poisonous chemicals, and biological weapons that spread disease. (p. 663)

wergeld (wuhr' geld) Fine paid by the family of a German who committed a crime. (p. 269)

witan (wi' tuhn) Member of the witenagemot. (p. 295)

witenagemot (wit uhn uh' guh mōt) Anglo-Saxon council that advised the king. (p. 295)

Z

zaibatsu (zī bah tsū) Industrialist families in Japan. (p. 589)

zakah (zuh kah') Muslim charitable giving. (p. 335)

ziggurat (zig' uh rat) Mesopotamian temple. (p. 57)

Spanish Glossary

A

abbot / abad jefe de monasterio. (pág. 255)

abdicate / abdicar dejar al trono. (pág. 565)

absolute location / localización absoluta posición exacta de un lugar en la superficie de la tierra. (pág. 5)

acropolis / acrópolis colina fortificada en las ciudades de la antigua Grecia. (pág. 163)

act of homage / acto de homenaje ceremonia en la cual un vasallo promete lealtad a su señor. (pág. 368)

ages / épocas períodos de tiempo. (pág. 27)

aggression /agresión actos violentos (pág. 645)

agora / ágora plaza pública en las ciudades de la antigua Grecia. (pág. 163)

airlift / puente aéreo sistema de transportar provisiones por avión a un área aislada. (pág. 626)

alchemists / alquimistas científicos que trataron de cambiar los metales a oro y plata. (pág. 343)

alliances / alianzas acuerdos entre pueblos o países. (pág. 195)

amendments / enmiendas cambios de ley. (pág. 513)

ancestors / antepasados miembros de la familia de generaciones pasadas. (pág. 89)

annexation / anexión incorporación de áreas dentro de un estado existente. (pág. 549)

anointed / ungido untado con aceite bendito. (pág. 279)

anthropologists / antropólogos personas que se dedican al estudio de los seres humanos. (pág. 24)

apartheid / *apartheid* separación de las razas. (pág. 659)

apostles / apóstoles hombres escogidos por Jesús para enseñar sus creencias a otros. (pág. 253)

appeasement / apaciguamiento cederse a demandas (pág. 615)

apprentice / aprendiz persona que está aprendiendo una artesanía u oficio. (pág. 406)

archaeology / arqueología estudio de los restos de culturas humanas antiguas. (pág. 25)

archaeologists / arqueólogos personas que se dedican al estudio de ruinas y artefactos. (pág. 24)

archbishops / arzobispos obispos titulares en las iglesias de las grandes ciudades. (pág. 253)

aristocrats / aristócratas miembros de la clase alta. (pág. 164)

armada / armada flota de buques de guerra. (pág. 459)

armaments / armamentos equipo militar. (pág. 605)

armistice / armisticio acuerdo para suspender peleas. (pág. 605)

artifacts / artefactos productos de habilidades humanas. (pág. 25)

artillery / artillería armas montadas. (pág. 604)

artisans / artesanos trabajadores expertos. (pág. 57)

assembly line / línea de montaje sistema de trabajo en el cual cada trabajador agrega una parte a un producto hasta que está ensamblado. (pág. 528)

astrolabe / astrolabio instrumento de navegación usado para determinar la latitud. (pág. 467)

astronomers / astrónomos personas que estudian los cuerpos celestes. (pág. 122)

authoritarian rule / régimen autoritario gobierno en que una persona o partido político tiene todo el poder. (pág. 658)

automation / automatización proceso en el cual las máquinas reemplazan a los trabajadores. (pág. 527)

autonomous / autónomo que se gobierna por sí solo. (pág. 654)

B

bailiff / mayordomo oficial medieval que vigilaba que los campesinos hicieran su trabajo. (pág. 376)

balance of power / equilibrio de poder fuerza igual entre países. (pág. 566)

balance of trade / equilibrio de comercio diferencia entre la cantidad de mercancía que un país exporta a la que importa. (pág. 492)

***bandeirantes* / bandeirantes** aventureros de fortuna del Brasil colonial. (pág. 488)

bands / bandas grupos prehistóricos que colectaban comida y vivían juntos. (pág. 34)

barbaroi / barbaroi personas que no seguían las costumbres griegas. (pág. 197)

barter / trocar cambiar artículos sin el uso de dinero. (pág. 241)

berserkers / berserkers guerreros vikingos. (pág. 301)

bishop / obispo jefe de diócesis. (pág. 253)

blitzkrieg / *blitzkrieg* guerra relámpago. (pág. 616)

blockaded / bloqueado cerrado. (pág. 626)

blood feuds / enemistad hereditaria pleitos antiguos entre familias o clanes. (pág. 269)

bourgeosie / burguesía clase media. (pág. 514)

boyars / boyardos miembros de la clase rica en la Rusia zarista. (pág. 350)

boycott / boicotear rehusar a pagar. (pág. 509)

bull leaping / salto de toros tauromaquia minoica. (pág. 152)

burgesses / diputados representantes elegidos de Virginia en la época colonial. (pág. 495)

burghers / burgueses hombres libres o adinerados que vivían en pueblos medievales. (pág. 404)

burgs / burgos pueblos pequeños medievales. (pág. 403)

C

caliph / califa gobernante musulmán. (pág. 336)

campesinos / **campesinos** paisanos y granjeros latinoamericanos. (pág. 640)

canon laws / leyes canónicas leyes de la iglesia. (pág. 382)

capitalism / capitalismo sistema económico donde la mayoría de la producción es de propiedad privada. (pág. 633)

captaincies / capitanías territorios de Brasil dados a los nobles portugueses. (pág. 488)

caravans / caravanas grupos que viajaban juntos para la seguridad. (pág. 121)

caravel / carabela embarcación portuguesa. (pág. 468)

cash crops / cultivo comercial cosecha vendida en el mercado. (pág. 638)

castles / castillos grandes casas fortificadas. (pág. 370)

catacombs / catacumbas cementerios subterráneos. (pág. 214)

cathedrals / catedrales iglesias dirigidas por obispos. (pág. 386)

caudillo / caudillo dictador militar latinoamericano. (pág. 556)

census / censo escrutinio de la población. (pág. 234)

chancellor / rector director de universidad inglesa. (pág. 387); primer ministro. (pág. 614)

charters / cartas documentos que permitían a las ciudades el control de sus asuntos. (pág. 405)

chateaux / *chateaux* castillos franceses. (pág. 440)

chieftain / cacique jefe de clan. (pág. 267)

churches / iglesias grupos de personas que comparten sus mismas creencias religiosas. (pág. 252)

circuit judges / jueces de distrito jueces que viajan a través de un país. (pág. 415)

citadel / ciudadela fuerte. (pág. 85)

city-states / ciudades estados ciudades y los territorios de sus alrededores. (pág. 57)

civil disobedience / desobediencia civil el negar a obedecer las demandas del gobierno. (pág. 634)

civilians / civiles que no son soldados. (pág. 604)

civilization / civilización sociedad con conocimiento desarrollado de agricultura, comercio, gobierno, arte, y ciencia. (pág. 33)

civil wars / guerras civiles guerras entre los ciudadanos de una nación. (pág. 159)

clans / clanes grupos fundamentados en sus lazos familiares. (pág. 267)

classical writings / obras clásicas escrituras de la antigua Grecia y Roma. (pág. 433)

clergy / clero líderes religiosos. (pág. 367)

climate / clima promedio de las condiciones del tiempo en un lugar a través de un período de años. (pág. 14)

code of chivalry / código de caballerosidad reglamentos que tenían que seguir los caballeros. (pág. 373)

cold war / guerra fría hostilidad entre naciones sin pelear. (pág. 625)

collectivization / colectivización la unión de granjas pequeñas en granjas grandes controladas por el gobierno. (pág. 611)

colonies / colonias poblaciones permanentes. (pág. 105)

colonize / colonizar establecerse permanentemente en un lugar. (pág. 487)

communes / comunes grupos políticos formados por ciudadanos en la Italia medieval. (pág. 405)

communicable diseases / enfermedades contagiosas enfermedades que son transmitidas de una persona o animal infectado a otra persona o animal. (pág. 664)

compass / brújula instrumento usado para determinar direcciones. (pág. 467)

concentration camps / campos de concentración prisiones para enemigos políticos. (pág. 620)

conquistadores / **conquistadores** vencedores españoles en los años 1500. (pág. 473)

constitution / constitución leyes escritas usadas para gobernar un estado. (pág. 169)

constitutional monarchy / monarquía constitucional monarquía limitada en sus poderes por una constitución. (pág. 518)

consuls / cónsules jefes de la antigua República Romana. (pág. 219)

continental drift / deriva continental teoría de que se mueven los continentes. (pág. 10)

convents / conventos comunidades de monjas. (pág. 255)

converted / convertido cambiado. (pág. 277)

coracles / barcos de cuero pequeños barcos irlandeses. (pág. 290)

core / núcleo parte central de la tierra. (pág. 10)

corregidores / **corregidores** oficiales de la realeza española. (pág. 423)

cotton gin / desmotadora de algodón máquina para limpiar el algodón. (pág. 527)

counts / condes oficiales del tribunal de justicia francés. (pág. 281)

coup / golpe de estado toma del gobierno por la fuerza. (pág. 648)

cremation ovens / hornos de cremación hornos para quemar los cuerpos y quedarlos reducidos en cenizas. (pág. 621)

crusades / cruzadas guerras hechas para recuperar de los musulmanes la Tierra Sagrada. (pág. 388)

crust / corteza terrestre capa exterior de la tierra. (pág. 10)

culture / cultura modo de vida. (pág. 61)

cuneiform / cuneiforme escritura sumeria hecha con signos en forma de cuña. (pág. 58)

czar / zar soberano ruso. (pág. 355)

D

dauphin / *dauphin* hijo mayor del rey de Francia. (pág. 417)

defensive league / liga defensiva grupo protector formado por las ciudades estados griegas. (pág. 173)

democratic / democrático que favorece la igualdad de toda la gente. (pág. 169)

depression / depresión decadencia económica. (pág. 608)

descendants / descendientes progenitura. (pág. 107)

de-Stalinization / de-Stalinización ataque a las políticas de Stalin. (pág. 633)

developing countries / países en desarrollo países progresando en la producción, la tecnología, o la norma de vida. (pág. 634)

dictator / dictador gobernante absoluto de un país. (pág. 228)

dictatorship / dictadura gobierno manejado por un dictador. (pág. 613)

diet / dieta asamblea formal. (pág. 421)

diocese / diócesis área bajo el control de un obispo. (pág. 253)

direct tax / impuesto directo impuesto pagado directamente a un gobierno. (pág. 509)

dissent / disensión crítica. (pág. 647)

doge / *doge* gobernante de la Venecia del Renacimiento. (pág. 439)

domesticated / domesticado sumiso. (pág. 42)

domestic system / sistema doméstico fabricación hecha en las casas de los trabajadores. (pág. 526)

domus / *domus* casa romana. (pág. 236)

dowry / dote riqueza que lleva la mujer cuando se casa. (pág. 322)

dubbing / armar ceremonia en la cual un escudero se hace caballero. (pág. 374)

dynasty / dinastía sucesión de soberanos de la misma familia. (pág. 88)

E

earthquake / terremoto temblor o deriva de una porción de la corteza terrestre. (pág. 11)

Eddas / *Eddas* poemas escritos basados en las historias de los dioses vikingos. (pág. 303)

elevation / elevación altitud. (pág. 9)

embalming / embalsamar proceso usado para mantener los cuerpos muertos sin que se descompusieran. (pág. 73)

emigrated / emigrado haber dejado el país de uno. (pág. 200)

émigrés /*émigrés* exiliados políticos franceses. (pág. 518)

emirs / *emirs* jefes del ejército musulmán. (pág. 393)

emperor / emperador gobernante de un imperio. (pág. 233)

empire / imperio territorios gobernados por un solo gobernante o nación. (pág. 61)

enclosure / cercado encierro de terrenos comunes para uso individual. (pág. 525)

erosion / erosión desgaste de la tierra por el viento, el agua, y el hielo. (pág. 12)

estates / estados clases sociales francesas. (pág. 513)

euro / euro moneda usada por los países miembros de la Unión Europea. (pág. 665)

excavate / excavar dejar al aire libre por medio de remover tierra. (pág. 27)

excommunicated / excomulgado excluido como miembro de la Iglesia Católica. (pág. 382)

extended families / familia extendida padres, hijos, y otros parientes viviendo juntos en un mismo hogar. (pág. 639)

F

factories / fábricas edificios donde artículos son manufacturados. (pág. 200)

factory system / sistema de fábricas trabajadores y maquinarias en un lugar para elaborar la mercancía. (pág. 527)

fairs / ferias recaudaciones medievales para el comercio. (pág. 402)

fasces / fasces varas atadas alrededor de un hacha. (pág. 215)

federal / federal gobierno nacional. (pág. 546)

feudalism / feudalismo sistema político medieval basado en la relación de los señores y sus vasallos. (pág. 367)

fiefs / feudos terrenos dados a los vasallos por sus señores. (pág. 367)

flying shuttle / lanzadera aparato tejedora que lleva el hilo rápidamente hacia adelante y de regreso a través de la pieza que se está tejiendo. (pág. 527)

foreign policy / política exterior relaciones con otros países. (pág. 507)

forum / foro lugar para reuniones. (pág. 653)

Forum / Foro plaza pública romana. (pág. 215)

freedmen / libertos antiguos esclavos. (pág. 234)

freemen / hombres libres campesinos que pagaron a su señor por el derecho de sembrar su propia tierra. (pág. 377)

friars / frailes predicadores. (pág. 385)

G

galleons / galeones barcos españoles. (pág. 459)

garrison / guarnición fuerza militar estacionada en un área. (pág. 610)

genocide / genocidio destrucción deliberada de toda una población. (pág. 620)

gentiles / gentiles que no son judíos. (pág. 249)

geography / geografía estudio de la tierra y las maneras en que viven y trabajan en ella la gente. (pág. 5)

glaciers / glaciares grandes mantos de hielo. (pág. 13)

gladiatorial games / juegos de gladiadores juegos romanos en los cuales luchaban los gladiadores. (pág. 215)

gladiators / gladiadores luchadores en los juegos de gladiadores. (pág. 238)

glasnost / glasnost política rusa para permitir franqueza. (pág. 633)

grand jury / gran jurado jurado que examina las acusaciones y aconseja los cargos criminales. (pág. 415)

Greek fire / fuego griego arma química usada por los bizantinos. (pág. 324)

greenhouse effect / efecto invernadero el bióxido de carbono retiene el calor de la superficie de la tierra. (pág. 664)

guerrilla warfare / guerra de guerrillas peleas de asaltar y esconderse. (pág. 573)

guilds / gremios organizaciones medievales de artesanos. (pág. 406)

guillotine / guillotina aparato que quita la cabeza de una víctima. (pág. 518)

H

haciendas / haciendas grandes ranchos. (pág. 640)

hajj / hajj jornada musulmana hacia la Meca. (pág. 336)

hard-liners / extremistas personas que se apegan a sus ideas sin preocuparse de las circunstancias. (pág. 632)

heavy industry / industria pesada industria que fabrica la maquinaria. (pág. 611)

helots / ilotas esclavos que eran propiedad de las ciudades estados. (pág. 164)

heresy / herejía creencias religiosas en contra de la doctrina de la iglesia. (pág. 253)

heretic / hereje miembro de la iglesia que no está de acuerdo con la doctrina oficial. (pág. 451)

heiroglyphic / jeroglífico sistema de escritura egipcia basada en figuras. (pág. 77)

Holocaust / Holocausto programa nazi de genocidio en contra de los judíos. (pág. 621)

holy of holies / santo de santo la cámara más profunda y más sagrada de un templo. (pág. 104)

home territory / territorio de hogar lugar donde vivían los cazadores y recolectores de comidas. (pág. 35)

hostage / rehén persona detenida por otra hasta que se cumplan ciertas promesas. (pág. 193)

humanists / humanistas filósofos que creen que la gente es importante. (pág. 433)

hypothesis / hipótesis explicación posible para un problema. (pág. 188)

I

icons / iconos dibujos sagrados del ortodoxo oriental. (pág. 325)

imam / imam guía musulmán de oración. (pág. 335)

immigrants / inmigrantes personas que se quedan a vivir permanentemente en un país diferente al suyo. (pág. 534)

imperialism / imperialismo establecer colonias y construir imperios. (pág. 579)

indentured servants / sirvientes escriturados colonos que prometían trabajar a cambio de su viaje a las Américas. (pág. 495)

indulgences / indulgencias perdones de la iglesia que disminuyen el castigo por pecados. (pág. 450)

industrialized / industrializado industria desarrollada. (pág. 533)

inflation / inflación período cuando se suben los precios y se baja el valor de dinero. (pág. 240)

interchangeable parts / partes intercambiables partes maquinarias hechas de un tamaño uniforme para que puedan ser reemplazadas fácilmente. (pág. 527)

internal combustion engine / motor de combustión interna motor que trabaja con gasolina. (pág. 535)

isolationist / aislacionista país que se mantiene afuera de los asuntos de otros países. (pág. 607)

izbas / izbas cabañas de un cuarto construidas por los eslavos orientales. (pág. 348)

J

jarls / jarls jefes militares vikingos. (pág. 301)

journeyman / oficial persona que trabaja bajo un maestro por un salario diario. (pág. 406)

joust / justa combate en caballo entre dos caballeros. (pág. 374)

judge / juez líder de tribu hebrea. (pág. 112)

junker / junker terrateniente rico prusiano. (pág. 574)

junta / junta comité organizado para tomar posesión de un gobierno. (pág. 553)

juris prudentes / juris prudentes abogados romanos. (pág. 236)

K

kaiser / káiser emperador alemán. (pág. 574)

keep / torre de homenaje la parte más fuerte de un castillo. (pág. 371)

khan / khan líder mongol. (pág. 353)

king's peace / paz del rey protección extendida en cualquier área que visitara un rey anglosajón. (pág. 295)

knight / caballero guerrero a caballo. (pág. 369)

kremlin / kremlin fuerte ruso. (pág. 354)

L

labyrinth / laberinto caminos que entrecruzan, de manera que es difícil orientarse. (pág. 153)

ladies / damas mujeres de la nobleza. (pág. 372)

landforms / formas de tierra características físicas de la superficie de la tierra. (pág. 9)

latifundias / latifundios grandes estados romanos. (pág. 225)

latitude / latitud distancia al Norte o al Sur del ecuador. (pág. 14)

legends / leyendas cuentos o historias populares que se han pasado de generación en generación. (pág. 22)

legionaries / legionarios soldados romanos. (pág. 221)

legions / legiones divisiones de los soldados romanos. (pág. 221)

liberals / liberales personas que están a favor de las reformas políticas. (pág. 566)

limited government / gobierno limitado gobierno que tiene solamente los poderes otorgados por la gente. (pág. 513)

lords / señores nobles medievales. (pág. 283)

M

macadam road / calle de macadán camino hecho de capas de roca triturada. (pág. 529)

mandate / mandato autoridad para gobernar. (pág. 607)

manifest destiny / destino manifiesto creencia que los Estados Unidos deberían extenderse de costa a costa. (pág. 548)

manors / feudos estados medievales con un señor y habitantes. (pág. 375)

mantle / capa terrestre parte de la tierra debajo de la corteza y arriba del núcleo. (pág. 10)

martial law / ley marcial dominio del ejército en lugar de mando del gobierno civil. (pág. 505)

mass / misa servicio de alabanza. (pág. 382)

masters / maestros artesanos expertos. (pág. 406)

megaron / megaron sala cuadrada al centro de un palacio micénico. (pág. 155)

mercantilism / mercantilismo sistema en el cual las colonias proveían de riquezas a su país patrón. (pág. 508)

mercenaries / mercenarios hombres pagados para servir de soldados de parte de un país extranjero. (pág. 175)

messiah / mesías salvador. (pág. 248)

mestizos / mestizos personas de ascendencia mixta europea e indígena americana. (pág. 490)

metropolitans / metropolitanos oficiales de la Iglesia Ortodoxo Oriental a cargo de ciudades grandes. (pág. 325)

migrate / migrar trasladarse de un lugar a otro. (pág. 34)

minerals / minerales substancias no vivas encontradas bajo la superficie de la tierra. (pág. 19)

ministers / ministros líderes religiosos protestantes. (pág. 451)

minstrels / trovadores poetas y cantores ambulantes medievales. (pág. 285)

missionary / misionero persona que trata de convertir a los que no creen. (pág. 250)

mobilize / movilizar preparar a las tropas para acción. (pág. 604)

monarchies / monarquías países gobernados por un rey o una reina. (pág. 411)

monasteries / monasterios lugares donde viven monjes. (pág. 255)

monks / monjes hombres que viven en una comunidad religiosa. (pág. 255)

monopoly / monopolio control total. (pág. 508)

monsoons / monzones vientos estacionales que cambian de dirección. (pág. 16)

mosaics / mosaicos dibujos llenos de color hechos de piedra o vidrio. (pág. 323)

mosque / **mezquita** casa de alabanza musulmana. (pág. 335)

mummy / momia cuerpo envuelto y preservado de una persona muerta. (pág. 73)

mundus / *mundus* para los romanos, el lugar donde se reúnen el mundo de los vivos y el mundo de los muertos. (pág. 216)

municipal / municipal tocante a una ciudad. (pág. 215)

mutiny / motín rebelión en contra de los oficiales. (pág. 472)

N

nationalists / nacionalistas personas a favor de la independencia nacional. (pág. 566)

national workshops / talleres nacionales fábricas dirigidas por los obreros pero pagadas por el gobierno. (pág. 570)

natural resources / recursos naturales materiales encontrados en la naturaleza. (pág. 19)

necropolis / necrópolis cementerio etrusco. (pág. 214)

nobles / nobles personas de clase alta en un reino. (pág. 90)

nomadic / nómada ambulante. (pág. 106)

nonrenewable resources / recursos no renovables recursos naturales irreemplazables. (pág. 20)

nuns / monjas mujeres que pertenecen a una orden religiosa. (pág. 255)

O

oath-helpers / colaboradores de juramento alemanes que prestaron juramento de que una persona acusada estaba diciendo la verdad. (pág. 269)

ocean current / corriente oceánica agua que fluye en el océano en un chorro constante. (pág. 16)

oligarchy / oligarquía gobierno en el cual varias personas gobiernan. (pág. 169)

omens / presagios signos que se creen indicar el futuro. (pág. 214)

open-hearth process / proceso de hogar abierto proceso que usa una clase especial de horno para producir económicamente el acero. (pág. 529)

oracle bones / huesos del oráculo huesos usados por el Shang para recibir mensajes de los antepasados. (pág. 90)

oracles / oráculos griegos por los cuales hablaron los dioses. (pág. 179)

orator / orador uno que habla públicamente. (pág. 195)

ordeal / prueba muy dura prueba dolorosa usada por los alemanes para determinar la inocencia o la culpa. (pág. 269)

orders / órdenes grupos de frailes. (pág. 386)

P

page / paje persona que ayudaba a los caballeros en cuidar sus caballos y sus armaduras. (pág. 373)

pancratium / pancracio evento olímpico que combinaba el boxeo y la lucha. (pág. 183)

pandemics / pandemias epidemias que se propagan por una región extensa. (pág. 664)

papal line of demarcation / línea papal de demarcación línea trazada en 1493 dividiendo las tierras demandadas por España y Portugal. (pág. 473)

papyrus / papiro papel egipcio. (pág. 78)

parchment / pergamino material hecho de pieles delgadas de animales usado para ventanas y papel. (pág. 153)

parish / parroquia área designada para una iglesia local. (pág. 253)

patriarchs / patriarcas los obispos más importantes de la iglesia cristiana antigua. (pág. 253)

patricians / patricios ciudadanos poderosos de la clase alta de la Roma antigua. (pág. 219)

peninsulares / **peninsulares** colonos nacidos en España que vinieron luego a las Américas. (pág. 490)

pentathlon / pentatlón juego olímpico con cinco eventos. (pág. 183)

perestroika / *perestroika* sistema ruso de reestructuración. (pág. 633)

perioeci / *perioeci* mercaderes y artesanos de pueblos espartanos. (pág. 166)

phalanx / falange formación de infantería griega. (pág. 194)

pharaoh / faraón gobernante egipcio. (pág. 70)

philosophes / *philosophes* filósofos franceses de los años 1700. (pág. 514)

philosophia / *philosophia* el amor a la sabiduría, según los griegos. (pág. 185)

piazza / *piazza* zócalo italiano. (pág. 436)

pilgrimage / peregrinaje jornada religiosa a un santuario o lugar santo. (pág. 133)

pilgrims / peregrinos personas que viajan a un lugar santo para alabar. (pág. 332)

pillars of faith / pilares de fe cinco deberes musulmanes descritos en el Corán. (pág. 335)

planned communities / comunidades planeadas ciudades construidas según un plan definido. (pág. 85)

plebeians / plebeyos ciudadanos pobres y de baja clase de la Roma antigua. (pág. 219)

plebiscite / plebiscito voto popular. (pág. 563)

polar zone / zona polar zona atmosférica a más de 60° al norte o al sur del ecuador. (pág. 15)

polis / *polis* ciudad estado greco. (pág. 163)

political parties / partidos políticos grupos con ideas establecidas sobre el gobierno. (pág. 546)

political science / ciencia política estudio del gobierno. (pág. 187)

popular sovereignty / soberanía popular la idea de que el gobierno saca sus poderes de la gente. (pág. 513)

population / población número de habitantes que viven en una zona en particular. (pág. 42)

population explosion / explosión demográfica crecimiento inesperado del número de personas. (pág. 136)

precipitation / precipitación humedad cayendo tal como la lluvia o la nieve. (pág. 16)

prehistory / prehistoria la época antes de que las personas empezaron a mantener historias escritas. (pág. 33)

prevailing winds / vientos predominantes vientos que soplan principalmente de una dirección. (pág. 16)

priest / sacerdote líder religioso, generalmente católico romano u ortodoxo oriental. (pág. 253)

priest-king / rey sacerdote líder religioso y gubernamental sumerio. (pág. 59)

printing press / prensa máquina para imprimir libros usando tipos movibles. (pág. 441)

privatize / privatizar permitir que particulares sean dueños de negocios. (pág. 649)

proletariat / proletariado clase industrial trabajadora. (pág. 568)

prophecy / profecía declaración de lo que podría suceder en el futuro. (pág. 179)

prophets / profetas personas que pretenden tener mensajes de Dios. (pág. 112)

protectorate / protectorado país que deja su política exterior a cargo de una autoridad imperial. (pág. 582)

provinces / provincias distritos políticos. (pág. 119)

psalms / salmos cantos sagrados. (pág. 112)

publicans / publicanos colectores de impuestos de la Roma antigua. (pág. 225)

purges / purgas despidos de miembros indeseables. (pág. 631)

pyramids / pirámides grandes tumbas egipcias. (pág. 71)

Q

quipus / quipos artefactos con que contaban los inca. (pág. 142)

R

referendum / referéndum plebiscito o voto popular. (pág. 660)

reformation / reforma cambio. (pág. 449)

reform / reforma cambio que se hace para mejorar. (pág. 61)

reign / reinado período de poder. (pág. 63)

relative location / localización relativa localización de un lugar en relación a otros lugares. (pág. 6)

relics / reliquias objetos sagrados del pasado. (pág. 319)

relief / relieve diferencias de altura entre las cimas y las tierras bajas de una región. (pág. 9)

renewable resources / recursos renovables recursos naturales reemplazables. (pág. 20)

repealed / anulado revocado. (pág. 507)

representative government / gobierno representativo sistema de gobierno en el cual los oficiales son elegidos. (pág. 546)

republic / república gobierno en el cual los ciudadanos escogen a sus dirigentes. (pág. 219)

revolution / revolución actividad planeada para derrocar un gobierno. (pág. 503)

right of extraterritoriality / derecho extraterritorial derecho de una persona acusada en diferente país de ser procesada en un tribunal de su propia nación. (pág. 587)

river system / sistema de río un río y todas las corrientes que desembocan en él. (pág. 14)

rule by divine right / dominio por derecho divino mando basado en la teoría de que el derecho de gobernar de un monarca viene de Dios. (pág. 243)

runes / runas letras del alfabeto vikingo. (pág. 303)

S

sabbath / sábado día de la semana usado para descansar y venerar. (pág. 113)

sans-culottes / sans-culottes trabajadores municipales y campesinos franceses en los años 1700. (pág. 518)

satellite nations / naciones satélites países controlados por otro país más poderoso. (pág. 626)

scientific method / método científico proceso usado por los científicos para estudiar. (pág. 188)

scorched-earth policy / política de tierra quemada (táctica de avance) táctica de destrucción usada por un ejército al retroceder. (pág. 564)

scribe / escribiente escritor sumerio. (pág. 58)

scriptures / libros sagrados escrituras sagradas. (pág. 247)

sea dog / lobo de mar veterano del mar en Tudor, Inglaterra. (pág. 477)

seceding / separándose retirándose. (pág. 551)

seminary / seminario escuela para el entrenamiento de sacerdotes. (pág. 454)

seneschal / senescal oficial medieval que vigilaba los feudos de un noble. (pág. 375)

sepoys / cipayos soldados indios al servicio del ejército inglés. (pág. 585)

serfs / siervos gente pobre medieval vinculada a la tierra. (pág. 285)

shadoof / cigoñal maquinaria egipcia usada para levantar el agua. (pág. 68)

sheriff / gobernador civil oficial del gobierno inglés a cargo de un condado. (pág. 295)

shires / condados distritos de Inglaterra. (pág. 295)

shrines / capillas lugares sagrados para la veneración. (pág. 154)

silent barter / cambio silencioso método de cambiar artículos sin hablar; usado en los reinos medios de África. (pág. 132)

slums / barrios bajos áreas arruinadas de la ciudad. (pág. 551)

smelting / fundición calentamiento del hierro o de metales para remover impurezas. (pág. 118)

social justice / justicia social tratamiento justo a toda la gente de una sociedad. (pág. 110)

social order / orden social divisiones sociales de acuerdo a la riqueza y otros factores. (pág. 213)

social security laws / leyes de seguridad social leyes de los Estados Unidos proporcionadas para el bienestar de la gente. (pág. 613)

Socratic method / método socrático forma de cuestionamiento desarrollado por Sócrates. (pág. 186)

soothsayers / adivinos gente que se creen habilitados para predecir el futuro. (pág. 214)

sovereign / soberano país independiente que se gobierna a sí mismo. (pág. 649)

soviets / soviéticos comités comunistas que representan a trabajadores y soldados. (pág. 610)

specialization / especialización desarrollo de profesiones. (pág. 45)

spheres of influence / esferas de influencia áreas en un país en los cuales otro país tiene derechos especiales. (pág. 585)

spinning jenny / máquina de hilar máquina para hilar algodón que utiliza muchos ejes. (pág. 527)

spirits / espíritus seres sobrenaturales. (pág. 89)

squire / escudero noble joven bajo el cuidado y entrenamiento de un caballero. (pág. 373)

stable government / gobierno estable gobierno establecido firmemente. (pág. 545)

strike / huelga paro laboral. (pág. 569)

subsistance farmers / agricultores de subsistencia personas que solamente producen comida suficiente para su propio consumo. (pág. 638)

swastika / esvástica cruz negra ganchuda usada como símbolo nazi. (pág. 614)

syllogism / silogismo forma de razonamiento desarrollado por Aristóteles. (pág. 188)

T

tariffs / tarifas impuestos exigidos para mercancía al entrar de un país a otro. (pág. 235)

tectonic plates / tectónica de placas secciones de la tierra que se mueven lentamente. (pág. 10)

temperate zone / zona templada zona climatológica entre 30° y 60° al norte y al sur del ecuador. (pág. 15)

tenants / arrendatarios personas que viven y trabajan en la tierra de otra persona. (pág. 155)

tenements / casas de vecindad apartamentos que cumplen con los mínimos requisitos para vivir. (pág. 551)

terrorism / terrorismo uso de violencia para llevar a cabo metas políticas. (pág. 660)

textile / textil tela de tejido. (pág. 526)

theology / teología estudio de la religión. (pág. 320)

theses / tesis declaraciones escritas por Lutero criticando las prácticas de la Iglesia. (pág. 450)

tithes / diezmo pagos a la iglesia. (pág. 384)

tournaments / torneos concursos para examinar las destrezas de los caballeros. (pág. 374)

trade unions / gremios asociaciones de trabajadores. (pág. 533)

treaties / tratados acuerdos formales entre naciones. (pág. 103)

trench warfare / guerra de trincheras guerra en la cual fuerzas enemigas atacan desde un sistema de trincheras. (pág. 604)

trial jury / jurado grupo de personas que deciden entre la inocencia o la culpabilidad de una persona acusada de un crimen. (pág. 415)

tribunes / tribunos oficiales romanos elegidos para proteger a las clases bajas. (pág. 220)

triremes / trirremes buques de guerra griegos. (pág. 172)

triumph / triunfo desfile de bienvenida a casa para un héroe romano. (pág. 215)

triumvirate / triunvirato grupo de tres personas que gobiernan con igualdad de poderes. (pág. 228)

tropical zone / zona tropical zona climatológica entre 30° al norte y 30° al sur del ecuador. (pág. 15)

tyranny / tiranía uso injusto de poder. (pág. 517)

U

unions / sindicatos grupos de personas unidas por

una causa común, especialmente estudiantes y maestros en la época medieval. (pág. 387)

universal male sufferage / sufragio universal masculino derechos de todo hombre para votar. (pág. 569)

universities / universidades instituciones de la educación superior. (pág. 387)

urbanization / urbanización crecimiento de las ciudades. (pág. 551)

utopian socialists / socialistas utópicos personas que quieren establecer comunidades ideales basadas en la cooperación económica. (pág. 568)

V

vassal / vasallo noble medieval que servía a un señor de rango más alto. (pág. 368)

veche / veche asamblea en un pueblo ruso. (pág. 350)

veto / vetar rehusar permiso. (pág. 219)

viceroy / virrey gobernante de un virreinato. (pág. 490)

viceroyalties / virreinatos distritos de las colonias de España en las Américas. (pág. 490)

vizier / visir primer consejero al califa de los abasidas. (pág. 338)

volcano / volcán una abertura en la corteza terrestre por la cual están forzados vapor, cenizas y magma, cuando está activa. (pág. 11)

W

weapons of mass destruction / armas de destrucción masiva armas como bombas nucleares, sustancias químicas tóxicas y armas biológicas que transmiten enfermedades. (pág. 663)

wergeld / wergeld multa pagada por la familia de un alemán que cometió un crimen. (pág. 269)

witan / *witan* miembro de la *witenagemot*. (pág. 295)

witenagemot / *witenagemot* concilio anglosajón que aconsejaba al rey. (pág. 295)

Z

zaibatsu / zaibatsu familias industriales en el Japón. (pág. 589)

zakah / zakah dádivas caritativas musulmanas. (pág. 335)

ziggurat / ziggurat templo mesopotámico. (pág. 57)

Index

A

Aachen, 281
Abbasids, 314, 338–40
Abraham, 98, 107
Adrianople, Battle of, 243, 262, 271
Aegeans, 159–60
Afghanistan, 662–63, 669
Africa, 11, 23, 33–34, 468–70, 580–84, 637–42, 658–59
 ancient kingdoms, 129–31
 East African civilizations, 136–37
 Middle Kingdoms, 132–34
 independence, 637–39, 658
 prehistoric peoples, 48–49
African National Congress, 659
Agincourt, Battle of, 417
Agricultural Revolution, 525–26
Ahmose, prince of Egypt, 74
AIDS, 664
Airplanes, 604, 612
Akhenaton, 77
Akkad, 61
Aksum, 131
Alaric, 244, 271
Al-Qaeda, 660–61
Alaska purchase, 550
Alexander I (Russia), 566
Alexander II (Russia), 609
Alexander VI, Pope, 438, 473
Alexander the Great, 195–99
Alexandria, Egypt, 197–98
Alfred the Great, 293–95, 307
Allah, 331–33, 335
Allied Powers, 604–5
 World War II, 616–22
Alphabet, 98, 105–6, 210, 215, 267, 303, 325, 351, 609
Amenhotep IV, 77–78
Americas, 137–42, 472–73, 486–500
Amon–Re, 76–77
Anasazi, 362–63
Anglican Church, see Church of England
Anglo Saxons, 289, 292–97, 299, 413
Angola, 638
Antonius, Marcus (Mark Antony), 229
Apartheid, 659, 696
Apostles, 253
Apprentice system, 406
Aquinas, Thomas, 388
Arab Empire, 331, 336–42
Arab-Israeli conflict, 655–56
Arabian Peninsula, 55, 331
Arabic numerals, 343
Arabs, 338–39, 342–44
Aragon, 423
Archaeologists, 24–30
 dating remains, 27–28, 30

Aristophanes, 184
Aristotle, 188, 195–96
Armada, Spanish, 459–60
Aryans, 86, 122
Ashurbanipal, 119–20
Assyria, 78, 116–20, 130
Astrolabe, 467
Astronomers, 122, 139, 343, 523–525
Athens, 149, 164, 168–69, 171–75, 183, 185–86, 195, 198
Atomic bomb, 620
Augsburg, Peace of, 451, 462
Augustine, a father of the Church, 254
Augustine, missionary, 292
Augustus Caesar (Octavian), 229–30, 233–34
Aung San Suu Kyi, 696–97
Aurelius, Marcus, 240
Austria-Hungary, 575–76, 603–5
Austrian Empire, 575
Axis Powers, 616–19
Aztecs, 99, 139–40, 473

B

Babylon, 61, 63, 112–13, 117, 120–22
Babylonia, 112–13
Baghdad, 111, 338–40
Balboa, Vasco Núñez de, 473
Basilian Rule, 254–55
Bastille, storming of, 502, 517
Batista, Fulgencio, 627
Becket, Thomas à, 415
Bedouins, 331
Belgium, 462, 534, 625
Benedictine Rule, 255, 385
Beowulf, 292
Berlin blockade and airlift, 626
Berlin Wall, 627, 646–47
Bible, 59, 101, 113, 253–54, 441–42, 450, 452, 454
Bin Laden, Osama, 660–62, 696–97
Bismarck, Otto von, 574–75
Black Death, 403
Boer War, 582–83
Bohemia, 463
Bolívar, Simón, 553
Bolsheviks, 620
Bonaparte, Napoleon, 561–67
 invades Russia, 18, 564–65
Borgia family, 438
Bosnia-Herzegovina, 654
Brazil, 8, 473, 484, 554–56, 573
Brezhnev, Leonid, 633
Bronze Age, 28
Buddhism, 310–311, 596–597
Bulgaria, 626
Buonarroti, Michelangelo, 435

Bush, George W., 645, 661–63
Byzantine Empire, 240, 314–29, 388
 influence, 317, 326–27, 351–52, 443
Byzantium, 305, 349
 see also Constantinople

C

Cabot, John, 476
Cabral, Pedro Alváres, 475, 477, 484
Caesar, Julius, 207, 228–29, 289
Calendar, 64, 79, 122, 139, 229, 292, 333
Caliphs, Rightly Guided, 336–38
Calvin, John, 452, 460
Canaan, 98, 101, 105–12
Canals, 140, 529
Canute, 307
Capet, Hugh, 411
Capitalism, 633
Carthage, 105, 222–24
Cartier, Jacques, 477
Castile, 423
Castles, 370–73
Castro, Fidel, 627–28
Catal Hüyük, 43, 45
Catherine de Medici, see Medici
Catherine the Great, 609
Cavour, Camillo di, 572
Celts, 289–91
Central America, 473, 554–57, 639–42
Central Powers, 604
Chaldeans, 117, 120–22
Charlemagne, 275, 279–85, 326, 368, 377
 education program, 281–82, 291, 295
Charles I (England), 504–6
Charles II (England), 506–8
Charles Martel, see Martel
Charles V (Germany), 451, 455
Charles VII (France), 417
Charles X (France), 568–69
Chaucer, Geoffrey, 407
Chechnya, 645, 649
Chiang Kai-shek, 630
China, 12, 20, 22, 88–93, 600, 615, 657
 ancient, 88–93
 Boxer Rebellion, 543, 588–89
 Communist, 629–32
 Hong Kong, 657
 Open Door policy, 588
 Taiwan, 657
 trade, 125, 586–89, 657
Cholera, 532, 664
Christ, see Jesus
Christianity, 131, 207, 246–57, 279–82, 290–93, 319
 fathers of the Church, 253–54
 break between East and West, 253, 326, 395

Church, Middle Ages, 253, 281, 324–26, 381–95, 423
  Inquisition, 382–83
  learning, 254–56, 386–88
  see also Roman Catholic Church
Churchill, Winston, 616
Church of England, 455–58, 504
Circumnavigation of world, 476
City–states, 103, 136, 327, 419–20
  Greece, 13, 162–76, 193, 195, 199–200, 222, 224
  Renaissance, 433–39
  Sumer, 55–57, 61, 63–64
Clovis, 275, 277, 284
Cluny, 385–86
Coins, 126, 167, 174, 338, 402, 412
Cold war, 624–29, 632–33, 645–47
College of Cardinals, 385
Columbus, Christopher, 471–73, 476
Commonwealth of Independent States, 648–49
Communists, 568, 601, 611, 624–33, 645–50, 657
Communist Manifesto, 568
Compass, 467
Concentration camps, 620
Confucianism, 145, 586
Confucius, 145, 586
Conquistadores, 473–74
Conquerors, eastern, 341
Constantine I, 241, 243, 252, 317, 318
Constantinople, 243, 314, 317–19, 395, 439
Constitution, French, 518–19
Constitution, U.S., 512–13
Continental Congresses, 510, 512
Copernicus, Nicolaus, 523, 525
Coronado, Francisco, 473–74
Cortés, Hernando, 466, 473
Cranmer, Thomas, 456
Crécy, Battle of, 417
Crete, 151–52, 157
Critical Thinking Skills
  bias, 170
  cause and effect, 29
  comparing, 111
  conclusions, 461
  fact and opinion, 60
  predicting, 571
  generalizations, 321
  main idea, 242
Croatia, 654
Cro-Magnons, 33, 37, 39–40
Cromwell, Oliver, 505–6
Crossbow, 393, 417
Crusades, 364–65, 388–95, 412, 420
  Children's, 395
  Kings', 393, 420
  Nobles', 391
  Peasants', 389, 393
Cuba, 472, 627–28
Cultural Revolution, 631
Czechoslovakia, 601, 607, 615, 626, 646–47, 649
Czech Republic, 649–50

D

Danelaw, 294, 307
Danes, 293–94, 307–8
Dante, 407
Darius, 98, 123–24, 171
Da Gama, Vasco, *see* Gama
David (Israel), 112
Da Vinci, Leonardo, *see* Vinci
Dayton Accords, p. 654
Declaration of Independence, U.S., 485, 512
Declaration of Rights, 507
Declaration of the Rights of Man and the Citizen, 517–518, 553
Declaratory Act, 509–10
De Klerk, Frederick W., 659
Delian League, 173–74
Democracy, 169, 415, 610, 635, 645
Demosthenes, 194–95
Deng Xiaoping, 631–32
Denmark, 299, 463
Department of Homeland Security, 662
De Soto, Hernando, 473
Developing nations, 634–42
  Africa, 637–39, 658–59
  India, 634–35
  Indonesia, 657–58
  Latin America, 639–42
  Malaysia, 637
Dias, Bartolomeu, 467, 469–70, 475
Diet, German, 421, 451
Diocletian, 241, 243
Discovery, Age of, 466–78
Domesday Book, 414
Domestic system, 526
Dorians, 159
Draco, 169
Drake, Sir Francis, 460

E

Eastern Orthodox Church, 253, 255, 324–26, 350–55, 388
  conflict with Pope, 253, 326
  icons, 325–26, 351
Eastern Slavs, 347–49
East Frankish Kingdom, 285
East Goths, 270–72
East India Company, 510, 585
East Timor, 660–61
Education, 351, 407, 434, 552, 557, 562
  see also Learning, Schools
Edward I (England), 416
Edward III, 417
Edward VI, 456
Edward the Confessor, 413
Egypt, 25, 66–81, 83, 582
  hieroglyphics, 26–27, 77–78, 105, 130
  invasions, 53, 73–74, 78, 130
  Middle Kingdom, 73–74
  New Kingdom, 53, 74, 76–78, 129
  Old Kingdom, 52, 69–73
  pyramids, 71–72
Eleanor of Aquitaine, 392, 414

Elizabeth I, 444, 457–58, 503
  Armada, 459–60
El Salvador, 554
England, 288–97, 443–46
  Anglo-Saxons, 289–96, 413
  Danish invasion, 293–94, 307
  expansion, 489, 508–9, 582–83
  monarchy, 295, 413–16, 418, 518–20
  Revolution, 503–7, 518
  see also Great Britain
English language, 295, 407
Enlightenment, Age of, 503
Enslavement, 134, 139, 213, 580
  Americas, 484, 509
  Athens, 168
  Latin America, 553
  Nazi Germany, 614–15
  Roman Empire, 236, 238
  Rome, 219–20, 224–25, 236, 238, 251, 270
  Sparta, 164, 166–67
  trade, 470, 580
  triangular, 509
  United States, 548, 551
Environment, 664
Erasmus, 441
Eratosthenes, 197–98
Eriksson, Leif, 302, 305
Estates-General, 412, 514–15
Ethiopia, 131, 638
Etruscans, 206, 210–16
Euclid, 197
Euphrates River, 27, 53, 55, 106
Euripides, 183–84
European Common Market, 625–26
European Union (EU), 626, 665

F

Factory system, 527
Farming, 20, 41–42, 56, 84, 98, 225, 283, 285, 339, 525–26, 611, 638–42
Fascists, 610
Ferdinand (Aragon), 365, 423, 471
Ferdinand II (Germany), 462–63
Feudalism, 285, 364–79, 395, 403, 405, 407–8, 414
Fire, discovery, 33, 36
Flanders, 401, 441
Florence, 433, 436–37, 438
Fourteen Points, 605
France, 9, 307–8, 411–13, 440, 509, 513–15, 517–20, 534, 561–69, 604–6, 625
  expansion, 563–65
  government, 562–63
  July Revolution (1830), 568–69
  monarchy, 411–12, 518–19
  revolution, 508, 513–15, 517–20, 552–53, 561
  three estates, 513–14
Francis I, 440, 460
Francis of Assisi, 386
Franks, 274–87
Franz Ferdinand, 604
Frederic I (Barbarossa), 365, 393, 419–20
Frederick II (Germany), 420–21

French and Indian War, 509, 585
French Empire, 563–65
    Second, 570
French language, 277, 407, 414
French Revolution, *see* France, revolution
Fulton, Robert, 530

G

Galilei, Galileo, 525
Gama, Vasco Da, 467, 470–71, 475
Gandhi, Indira, 635
Gandhi, Mohandas, 634
Garibaldi, Giuseppe, 572–73
Gaul, 223, 243–44, 271
Genghis Khan, 360–61, 461
Genocide, 620–21
Geography and history, 4–31
Geometry, 79, 197
George III, 512
German Empire, 574
German language, 267, 407
Germans, 243–44, 264–73, 279
Germany, 441, 534–35, 574–75, 603–6,
    625–27
    anti-Semitism, 611, 620
    concentration camps, 620
    monarchy, 419–22
    reunification, 646–47
    Third Reich, 614
    World War II, 616–22
Ghana, 99, 132, 276
Gilgamesh of Uruk, 59
Glaciers, 13
Gladiators, 215, 238–39
Glasnost, 633, 646
Global culture, 665
Goethe, Johann Wolfgang von, 574
Gorbachev, Mikhail S., 633, 645–49
Goths, 270, 275
    see also East and West Goths
Government, central, 45, 367–68, 407, 412
Gracchus, Gaius Sempronius, 227
Gracchus, Tiberius Sempronius, 227
Granada, Moors, 423
Great Britain, 523, 525, 529–34, 569,
    603–8, 615–22
    Germanic invasions, 290
    Gulf War, 653–54
    Ireland, 658
    Roman invasion, 289
    see also England
Great Depression, 612
Greece, ancient, 13, 25, 28, 148–201
    beginnings, 150–61
    Golden Age, 180, 183
    influence, 131, 178–91, 199, 210, 212,
        317, 339, 381, 433–34
    language and literature, 180–85, 193,
        319, 321, 441–42, 445
    see also Hellenes, Hellenistic
Greece, modern, independence, 568
Gregory I, Pope, 292
Gregory VII, Pope, 385
Guangzhou, 586–87

Guilds, 406, 434
Gulf War, *see* Persian Gulf War
Guptas, 310–11
Gutenberg, Johannes, 441

H

Hagia Sophia, 316, 322–23, 351
Hammurabi, 53–54, 61, 63, 120
    code of law, 61, 63
Hannibal Barca, 223–24
Hapsburgs, 421–22
Harappans, 83–88
Hastings, Battle of, 364, 413–14
Hatshepsut, 74
Hawaiian Islands, 11, 591
Hebrew language, 248, 441–42
Hebrew prophets, 113
Hebrews, 94, 101, 106–7, 109–10, 112–14
Hellenes, 160, 163, 193
Hellenistic Period, 192–201
Henry II (England), 390, 414–15
Henry III (England), 415
Henry IV (France), 460, 462
Henry VII (England), 418, 443–44
Henry VIII (England), 444, 455–56
Henry of Navarre, *see* Henry IV (France)
Henry, Patrick, 512
Henry the Navigator, 468–69
Henry Tudor, see Henry VII (England)
Herodotus, 183
Hidalgo y Costilla, Father Miguel, 554
Hieroglyphics, *see* Writing
Himalayas, 9, 11, 170
Hinduism, 634
Hippocratic Oath, 190
Hiroshima, atomic bomb, 620
Hitler, Adolf, 18, 614–22
Hittites, 94–95, 118
Ho Chi Minh, 628
Holocaust, 621
Holy Roman Empire, 411, 419, 421–22
Homer, 148, 158–59, 171
Hong Kong, 657
Huang Ho, 12, 83, 88–93
Hudson, Henry, 477
Huguenots, 460, 462
Humanists, 433
Hundred Years' War, 365, 411, 417–18, 443
Hungary, 603, 606–07, 626, 646–47, 650
Huns, 243, 270
Hussein, Saddam, 652–53
Hyksos, 73–74

I

Ice Ages, 13
Iceland, 303, 305
Icons, 325–26
Imperialism, 578–94
Incas, 16, 140–42
India, 11, 83, 461, 584–85, 634–36
    ancient, 83
    independence, 601, 634–35
    trade, 467, 470, 584–85

Indies, western route to, 474, 476
Indochina, 591, 619, 628
Indonesia, 659–61
Indus River, 82–87
Industrial Revolution, 523, 526–35, 579,
    586
Industry, rise of, 21, 503–15, 517–20,
    522–35
Innocent III, Pope, 393, 395
Inquisition, 382–83, 423
    Low Countries, 462
    Spanish, 423, 442
Interdependence, 665
Internet, 668–69
Inventions, 526–530
    assembly line, 528
    atomic bomb, 620
    automation, 527–28
    cotton gin, 527
    electric light, 535
    flying shuttle, 526–27
    interchangeable parts, 527
    internal combustion engine, 535
    printing press, 441
    radio, 535
    railroad, 529–30
    spinning jenny, 527
    telegraph, 535
    telephone, 535
    wheel, 63
Ionia, 159, 171
Iran, 122, 663
Iraq, 55, 652–653, 663
Ireland, 289–93, 656
Iron Age, 28
Isabella (Castile), 423, 471
Islam, 279, 335, 342–44, 660
    spread of, 330–45
    see also Muslims
Israel, 43, 101, 655–56
    ancient, 110, 112
Italy, 209, 572–74, 604, 625
    dictatorship, 613
    invades Ethiopia, 615
Ivan III (the Great), 355
Ivan IV (the Terrible), 315, 355, 355–56, 608

J

James I (England), 503–505
James II, 507
James VI (Scotland), *see* James I
Jamestown, 484
Japan, 589–90, 606, 616
    attacks China, 615, 630
    attacks Pearl Harbor, 617
    feudal, 426–27
    World War II, 616–22
Jerusalem, 112–13, 388–89, 391–95
Jesuits, *see* Society of Jesus
Jesus, 247–49
Jews, 113, 248–49, 340, 391, 655–656
    Nazi Germany, 614
    Spain, 340, 423
    see also Hebrews

Joan of Arc, 417–18
Jordan, 656
Juárez, Benito, 557
Judah, 112
Judaism, 106
Julius Caesar, *see* Caesar, Gaius
Justinian I, Emperor, 314, 320, 322–24
    law code, 322

K

Ka'bah, 332–33
Kampuchea, 591
Kenya, 5–6, 8, 470, 639
Khrushchev, Nikita S., 633
Kiev, 349
Kievan Rus, 349–352
King James Bible, 504
Knights, 373–74
Knossos, 152–55
Koran, *see* Quran
Korean War, 627
Kosovo, 654–55
Kublai Khan, 362–63
Kurds, 653
Kush, 129–31
Kuwait, 652–53

L

Land bridge, Asia to America, 34, 137
Laos, 591
La Salle, Rene-Robert Cavalier, Sieur
    de, 499
Latin America, 552–57, 591–93, 639–42
Latins, 206, 209–10, 213, 215
Latitude, 14–15, 135
Law, 235–36, 405, 412, 562–63
    canon, 382
    common law's origins, 268–69
    England, 294–95, 414–15, 505
    feudal, 377
    German, 268–69
    Roman, 220, 235–36, 268–69
League of Nations, 607, 615, 621
Leakey, Mary Nicol, 28
Lebanon, 101
Legends, 22–24, 57–59, 88, 103–5, 155,
    158–59, 209–10, 292, 332
Lenin, Vladimir Ilyich, 610–11
Leningrad, 611
Leo III, Byzantine Emperor, 326
Leo X, Pope, 449–51
León, Ponce de, 473–74
Leopold II (Belgium), 581–82
Liliuokalani, 591
Lithuania, 606, 648
Livingstone, David, 580–81
Locke, John, 507
Lombards, 279
London, 294, 507, 532
Longbow, 417
Longitude, 156
Lothair, 285
Louis VI (the Fat), 411

Louis VII, 390
Louis IX, 412
Louis XVI, 514–15, 518–19
Louis XVIII, 566, 568
Louisiana Purchase, 547–48
Louis-Philippe, 569–70
Louis the Pious, 285
Loyola, Ignatius of, 453
Lucy, 35
Luther, Martin, 448–51
Lutheran Church, 451
Luxembourg, 625
Lydia, 126, 210

M

Macedonia, 176, 193–94, 654
Madina, 333–34, 336–37
Magellan, Ferdinand, 474–76
Magna Carta, 365, 415–16
Makkah, 332–36
Malaria, 664
Malaysia, 637
Mali, 99, 132–34
Mamelukes, 341
Mandela, Nelson, 659, 696–97
Manor, 375–78
Mansa Musa I, 133–34
Mao Zedong, 630–31
Map Skills, 467–68
    demographic, 651
    direction, 44
    grids, 394
    historical, 306, 356, 567
    inset, 284
    latitude, 135
    legends, 75, 475
    location, 41, 394
    longitude, 156
    mercator, 13
    military, 511
    physical, 62, 165
    political, 211
    projections, 17
    scale, 108
Marathon, Battle of, 171–72
Marcus Aurelius, *see* Aurelius
Marie-Antoinette, 514, 518–19
Marius, Gaius, 227–28
Marshall Plan, 625
Martel, Charles, 277–79, 367
Marx, Karl, 568
Mary I, 456–57
Maximilian I, Holy Roman Emperor,
    421–22
Maximilian, Emperor (Mexico), 557, 592
Mayas, 99, 138–39
Mayflower Compact, 495
Mayors of the Palace, 278
Mbeki, Thabo, 659
Mecca, *see* Makkah
Medici, Catherine de, 460
Medici, Lorenzo de, 436–37
Medicine, 79–80, 111, 190, 343, 373, 392

Medina, *see* Madina
Mercantilism, 401–3, 508–9
Mesoamerica, 138–40
Mesopotamia, 53–65, 83, 94, 101, 117
Mexico, 12, 42, 139–40, 548–49, 554, 557
Michelangelo Buonarroti, *see* Buonarroti
Middle East, 55, 655–56, 660
Minoans, 148, 151–55, 157
Missionaries, Roman, 250, 292
Moche, 260–61
Mogul Empire, 585–86
Mohenjo-daro, 85–86
Monarchy, rise of, 410–25
Mongols, 315, 341, 353–54
Monks, 255–56, 282, 290–92, 325–26, 351,
    353, 381, 384–86
Monroe Doctrine, 592
Montezuma II, 140, 466, 473
Moors, 340, 423, 471
Moscow, rise, 315, 354–55
Moses, 109–10
Mozambique, 638
Muhammad, 331–37, 342
Muscovy, 354, 608
Muslims, 262, 278–79, 327, 332, 391–93,
    400, 461, 470, 634, 660
    Shi'ah, 338
    Sunni, 338
    see also Islam
Mussolini, Benito, 613
Mycenaeans, 148, 151, 155, 157–60

N

NAFTA, *see* North American Free Trade
    Agreement
Nagasaki, atomic bomb, 620
Nantes, Edict of, 462
Napoleon Bonaparte, *see* Bonaparte
Napoleon III, 570, 572, 574
Napoleonic Code, 562–63
Narmer, king of Egypt, 69
National Assembly, France, 517–18, 520
National Socialist party (Nazis), 614–15
Nationalism, 566, 568, 572–76, 580, 634
Native Americans, 305, 472–73, 493–94
NATO, *see* North Atlantic Treaty
    Organization
Natural resources, 19–21, 639
Neanderthals, 33, 37–38
Nicaragua, 554
Nebuchadnezzar, 120–21
Nehru, Jawaharlal, 635
Neolithic Age, 33, 41–43, 45–46
Netherlands, 462
Newton, Sir Isaac, 525
New Zealand, 538–541
Nicaragua, 554
Nicholas II (Russia), 609–610
Nigeria, 638
Nile River, 67–69, 79, 129
Normans, 308, 413–14
Norse gods, 304
Norsemen, 298–309

North American Free Trade Agreement (NAFTA), 665
North Atlantic Treaty Organization (NATO), 627, 650
  Bosnia, 654
  Kosovo, 654–55
North Korea, 627, 663
Northwest Passage, 476–78
Norway, 299, 303
Novgorod, 349
Nubians, 202–203
Nuclear weapons, 653, 663

O

Odoacer, 264, 272
Old Stone Age, *see* Paleolithic Age
Olduvai Gorge, 29, 36
Oleg, 349
Olmecs, 138–39
Olympic Games, 181–83
Olympus, Mount, 180
  gods and goddesses, 181
Ostrogoths, *see* East Goths
Otto I (Holy Roman Emperor), 419
Ottoman Empire, 568, 584, 604

P

Pacific Ocean, 11, 474, 476
Paleolithic Age, 33–40
Palestine, 655–56
Palestine Liberation Organization (PLO), 655–56
Panama, 473, 593
Panama Canal, 592–93
Pangaea, 10–11
Papal States, 433, 437–38, 563, 566, 573–74
Parliament, 416, 456, 503–7, 531
Paul, 249–50
Pax Romana, 207, 234–36, 240, 250
  emperors, 241
  empire, 123–26, 171–73, 195–96
  see also Seleucid Empire
Pearl Harbor, Japan attacks, 617
Peloponnesian War, 149, 175
Pepin, 279
Perestroika, 633
Pericles, 174–75
Perry, Commodore Matthew, 589
Persepolis, 123–24
Persian Gulf War, 652–53
Persians, 117, 122–26, 340
  empire, 123–26, 171–73, 195–196
  see also Seleucid Empire
Persian Wars, 149, 171–73, 183, 193
Peru, 140, 473, 553
Petersburg, St., 18, 608–9
  see also Petrograd, Leningrad
Peter the Great, 608
Petrograd, 610
Philip II (Macedonia), 176, 193–95
Philip II (Augustus), 393, 412
Philip II (Spain), 442–43, 456–57, 459–60, 462

Philip IV (the Fair), 412–13
Philistines, 101
Philosophes, 514, 518
Phoenicians, 98, 100–106, 222, 300
Pilgrims, 495
Pizarro, Francisco, 473
Plato, 187–88
Poland, 347, 350, 454, 606, 616, 621, 626, 646, 650
Polis, *see* City-states
Polo, Marco, 19–20, 467
Pompeii, 26
Pompeius, Gnaeus (Pompey), 229
Ponce de León, *see* León
Popes, 279, 326, 385, 419, 437–38, 451
Portugal, 467–71, 473, 563
Prehistoric people, 32–47
Princeton Review, 50–51, 96–97, 146–47, 204–05, 260–61, 312–13, 362–63, 428–29, 482–83, 540–41, 598–99, 670–71
Protestantism, 451–54, 462, 504
Ptolemy, 198, 523
Punic Wars, 206, 222–24
Puritans, 458, 504, 505–506
Putin, Vladimir, 650, 669
Pyramids, 71–72, 130–31

Q

Quebec, 8, 510
Quran, 334–36, 342

R

Railroads, 529–30
Rain forests, 641
Referendum, 658
Reformation, 448–65
  Bible, 450–52, 454
  Society of Jesus, 453–54
  wars, 459–60, 462–64
Regions, 7
Religion, 45–46
  Byzantine Empire, 319, 324–26
  Egypt, 72–77
  Germanic, 267–68
  Greece, 171, 179–85
  Hebrews, 106, 107, 109–10, 112–14
  Ireland, 290–92, 658
  Minoan, 154
  Rus, 348, 350–52, 353–54
  see also Buddhism, Christianity, Hinduism, Islam, Judaism
Renaissance, 432–47
Revolutions of 1848, 570, 572
Rhodes, Cecil, 582–83
Rhodesia, 582
  see also Zimbabwe
Richard I (the Lionheart), 390, 393, 415
Robespierre, Maximilien de, 518
Roman Catholic Church, 253–55, 277, 281, 291, 381–95, 419, 449–60, 462–64, 518, 525
  internal reform, 384–86, 453–54

Roman Empire, 232–45, 381
  attacks, 243–44, 290
  decline, 240–41, 243–44, 271–72
  peace, *see* Pax Romana
Roman Republic, 206, 218–31, 233
  decline, 225–26, 229–30
  government, 219–20, 227–30
Romania, 23–24, 626
Rome, 206–45, 247, 438–39
  ancient, 25–26, 149
  banquet menu, 239
  beginnings, 208–17
  city invaded, 223–24, 244, 271
  effects of conquest, 224–26
  fall of, 240–41, 243–44, 262, 272, 317
  influence, 272, 289, 318, 433–35
  learning and literature, 256
  Punic Wars, 222–24
  trade with China, 235, 258–59
Romulus, 210
Rosetta Stone, 25–27
Rubáiyát, 343
Rumanians, 23–24
Runnymede, 415
Rurik, founds Russia, 305, 349
Russia, 9, 18, 315, 347–58, 608–10, 637
  civil war, 610–11
  early, 305, 347–58
  imperial, 540–41
  Mongol conquest, 353–54
  new economic policy, 649
  1917 Revolution, 610–11
  Post-Soviet Union, 647–49
  secret police, 357
  World War I, 603–7
  see also Soviet Union
Rwanda, 658

S

Sagas, 303
St. Paul's Cathedral, London, 507
Saladin, 393
Salamis, Battle of, 172
Samurai, 589
Santa Anna, Antonio López de, 556–57
Sargon I, 52, 61, 95
Saudi Arabia, 652
Saul (Israel), 112
Saxons, 279–80, 289
Scientific Revolution, 523–25
Sepoy Mutiny, 585
September 11, 2001, 661–63, 668–69, 696–97
Serbia, 604, 654–55
Seven Years' War, 509, 585
Shakespeare, William, 445
Shang Dynasty, 53, 88–92
Slavs, 325, 346–59
Slovakia, 649
Slovenia, 654
Socialists, 568
Society of Jesus, 453, 463
Socrates, 185–86

Solidarity, 646, 650
Solomon, King of Israel, 112
Solon, 168–69
Somalia, 638
Songhai, 134
Sophocles, 183–84
South Africa, *see* Union of South Africa
South America, 10, 140–42, 639–42
Southeast Asia, 12, 590–91, 627, 628
South Korea, 627
Soviet Union, 611–12, 616, 618, 621
 breakup, 645–50
 First Five-Year Plan, 609
 see also Russia, Commonwealth of
  Independent States
Space exploration, 628–29
Spain, 224, 271, 423–24, 442–43, 563
 anti-Semitism, 423–24
 Armada, 459–60
 expansion, 471–76
 Golden Age, 340
 Jews, 340, 423
 Low Countries, 462
 Moors, 279, 340, 423
 Muslim, 280, 340
Spanish-American War, 592
Sparta, 164–67, 172, 175–76, 182, 199
Sputnik I, 628
Stalin, Joseph, 611
Stalingrad, Battle of, 618
Stamp Act, 509
Stanley, Henry, 581
Stone Age, 28
Stuarts, 503, 506–7
Submarines, 604–5
Sudan, 638
Suez Canal, 582
Sumer, 52, 55–64, 83
Sun Yat-sen, 629
Swahili, 136–37
 Swahili culture, 480–81
Sweden, 299, 303, 463
Syria, 43, 120, 663

T

Taiwan, 657
Taliban, 662–63, 669, 696–97
Tanzania, 29
Tarquinius, Lucius, 215
Technology Skills
 database, 516
 electronic spreadsheet, 636
 multimedia presentations, 276
 Web site, 390
Ten Commandments, 109
Terrorism, 660–63, 668–69, 696–97
Textile industry, 526–28
Thailand, 591
Theater, 181, 183–85, 445–46
Thebes, 176, 193, 195
Theodora, Byzantine Empress, 320, 322–23

Theodoric, 267, 272
Thermopylae, Battle of, 172–73
Theseus, 155
Thirty Years' War, 462–64
Thutmose III, 74
Tiananmen Square, 632
Tiber River, 209
Tibet, 596–97
Tigris River, 27, 53, 55, 106, 117, 338
Timbuktu, 134
Toledo, Spain, 443
Torah, 113
Tordesillas, Treaty of, 473
Tours, Battle of, 278–79
Toussaint L'Ouverture, Pierre
 Dominique, 553
Towns, 42–43, 395, 399, 402–8, 412
Townshend Acts, 510
Trade, 63, 74, 102–3, 121, 125–26, 131,
 136, 349, 467–74, 659, 661, 665
 Greek, 199
 and growth of towns, 300–1, 364, 395,
  398–409
 medieval centers, 399–401
 routes, 132, 317, 401, 468–74
Trent, Council of, 454
Trojan War, 148, 158–59
Trotula of Salerno, 377
Troy, 158–59
Tudor Dynasty, 443–44, 503
Tudor, Henry, *see* Henry VII
Tudor, Mary, *see* Mary I
Turks, 315, 328, 341, 388, 391–93, 641
Tutankhamen, 66, 77, 78

U

Umayyad Dynasty, 337–38
Union of South Africa, 543, 583
 apartheid, 661–62
United Nations (UN), 621, 652–55, 664
United States, 512, 545–52
 Bosnia, 654
 Civil War, 550–51
 government stability, 545–46
 Gulf War, 653
 slavery, 548, 551
 terrorist attacks, 660–63, 668–69,
  696–97
 urbanization, 551
 westward movement, 546–50
 World War I, 605
 World War II, 617
Universities, 387–88, 407, 421
Upper Egypt, 69
Ur, 57, 106–7
Urban II, Pope, 388–89, 391
USS *Cole,* 661

V

Vandals, 262, 271, 275
Varangian Route, 305–6, 349

Venezuela, 138, 473, 553
Venice, 19–20, 327, 395, 399–401, 433, 439
Verdun, Treaty of, 285
Verrazano, Giovanni da, 476–77
Versailles, Treaty of, 606
Vienna, Congress of, 542, 566, 572
 balance of power, 566
Vietnam War, 628
Vikings, 298–309, 327, 349, 367–68
Vinci, Leonardo da, 434–35
Vinland, 305
Visigoths, *see* West Goths
Vladimir I (Kiev), 350–52
Volga River, 347–48, 352, 357
Voltaire, 514

W

Walesa, Lech, 650
Wars of the Roses, 443
Warsaw Pact, 627
West Africa, 132–34, 639
West Frankish Kingdom, 285
West Goths, 270–71, 340
West Indies, 474, 552
Westphalia, Peace of, 464
William I (England), 413
William I (Prussia), 574
William and Mary (England), 507
William the Conqueror, *see* William I
 (England)
Wilson, Woodrow, 605–7
Women's status, 59, 90, 124, 167, 184,
 213, 237–38, 242, 266, 302, 322, 342,
 354, 361, 372–73, 404, 426, 481, 624
World War I, 600, 603–6
World War II, 600, 612–15
Worms, Diet of, 451
Writing, 58, 86, 90, 94, 105–6, 117, 130,
 157, 282, 311, 427
 alphabet, 105–6
 cuneiform, 58, 61, 63
 hieroglyphics, 67, 77–78, 105, 130, 139
 runes, 303
Wu, 91

X

Xerxes, 172
Xia, 88

Y

Yahweh, 107, 109, 112
Yaroslav the Wise (Kiev), 352
Yeltsin, Boris, 647–50
Yugoslavia, 607, 649, 654

Z

Zaire, 638
Zhou Dynasty, 53, 91, 144–45
Zimbabwe, 136, 638
Zoroaster, 124–25

Photo Credits

Abbreviation key: **AA** = The Art Archive; **AAA** = Ancient Art & Architecture; **AR** = Art Resource, NY; **BAL** = Bridgeman Art Library; **CB** = Corbis; **CS** = Corbis Sygma; **EL** = Erich Lessing; **MH** = Michael Holford; **LA** = Liaison Agency; **LOC** = Library of Congress; **ME** = Mary Evans Picture Library; **NGS** = National Geographic Society Image Collection; **NWPA** = North Wind Picture Archives; **PR** = Photo Researchers; **RH** = Robert Harding Picture Library; **RS** = Ronald Sheridan; **SM** = Stock Montage; **SPL** = Science Photo Library; **SS** = SuperStock; **TSM** = The Stock Market; **WC** = Woodfin Camp & Associates; **WF** = Werner Forman Archive

Front cover Scala/AR, (bkgrd)Cyberphoto; back cover EL/AR; **iii** RS/AAA; **iv** (t)MH, (b)Walters Art Gallery, Baltimore; **v** WF/AR; **vii** Steve Liss/Timepix; **2** (l)Pat L. Filed/Coleman, (r)Lauros-Giraudon/AR; **4** (t)WF/AR, (b)Tom Till/DRK Photo; **6** RH; **7** David R. Frazier Photolibrary; **8** (l)RS/AAA, (r)Alan Schein/TSM; **12** Mike Maple/WC; **16** Steve McCurry/Magnum; **18** Robert Francis/RH; **20** (l)Conoco, Inc., (r)courtesy Gulf Oil Corp.; **21** Ohio Dept. of Natural Resources/Dept. of Reclamation; **25** (l)Smithsonian Institution, (r)file photo; **26** (l)Kenneth Garrett/NGS, (r)Scala/AR; **28** (l)Gerry Clyde/MH, (r)Ira Block; **32** RS/AAA; **34** Zdenek Buriam; **35** American Museum of Natural History; **36** John Reader/SPL/PR; **37** American Museum of Natural History; **38** (t)Belinda Wright/DRK Photo, (bl)Tom Till/DRK Photo, (br)Peter Skinner/PR; **39** Rene Burri/Magnum; **41** file photo; **42** Zdenek Buriam; **43** Wolfgang Kaehler; **48** David Coulson/Robert Estall Photo Library; **49** (tl)A. DeWildenberg/LA, (tr)Betsy Blass/PR, (c)EL/AR, (b)David Coulson/Robert Estall Photo Library; **52** (l)Ali Meyer/BAL, (r)EL/AR; **54** (l)Scala/AR, (r)MH; **56** (l)MH, (r)John T. Wong/Index Stock Imagery/PNI; **58** Oriental Institute Museum, U. of Chicago/Victor Boswell/NGS; **61** AKG Photo; **63** Hirmer Verlag; **66** (l)Victor Boswell/NGS, (r)Egyptian National Museum, Cairo/SS; **68** Vladimir Bibic; **69** Giraudon/AR; **70** (l)Gianni Dagli Orti/CB, (r)Caroline Penn/CB; **71** Dallas & John Heaton/Corbis Los Angeles; **72** (c)British Museum; **73** Smithsonian Institution; **74** Metropolitan Museum of Art, Rogers Fund and Edward S. Harkness Gift,1929 (29.3.3); **76** SEF/AR; **77** (l)Smithsonian Institution, (r)Egyptian National Museum, Cairo/SS; **79** Courtesy Parke Davis & Co.; **82** (l)Archivo Iconografico, S.A./CB, (r)Angelo Hornak/CB; **85** Vision International; **86** Borromeo/AR; **87** Smithsonian Institution; **88** SM; **90** (l)AA, (r)Wan-Go Weng, Collection of Academia Sinica, Taipei, Taiwan, ROC; **91** (l)Arthur M. Sackler Museum, Harvard University, Bequest of Grenville L. Winthrop/BAL, (r)Ed Lallo/LA; **94** EL/Archaeological Museum, Istanbul, Turkey/AR; **95** (t)Gianni Dagli Orti/CB, (cl)MH, (cr)Metropolitan Museum of Art, Gift of Norbert Schimmel Trust, 1989 (1989.281.12). Photo by Schecter Lee, (b)EL/AR; **98** (l)AA, (r)Gianni Dagli Orti/CB; **100** EL/AR; **102** (l)Louvre, Paris/BAL, (r)Beghin Thierry/LA; **104 106** file photos; **107** Tom Lovell/NGS; **109** NWPA; **110** (l)AKG Photo, (r)file photo; **116** (l)AKG London, (r)Bill Lyons; **118** MH; **121** S. Fiore/SS; **123** (l)American Numismatic Society, (r)US Mint/LA; **124** George Holton/PR; **128** (l)RS/AAA, (r)WF/AR; **130** Timothy Kendall/Museum of Fine Arts, Boston; **131** WF/AR; **132** Geoff Renner/RH; **133** (l)Lee Boltin, (r)AA; **136** Mike St. Maur Sheil/Susan Griggs Agency; **138** O'Neill/AR; **139** (l)Nicholas M. Hellmuth/NGS, (r)SS; **140** Courtesy Department of Library Services, American Museum of Natural History; **144** LA; **145** (tl)file photo, (tr)Asian Art & Archaeology/CB, (c)Seattle Museum of Art/Laurie Platt Winfrey, (b)file photo; **148** (l)Smithsonian Institution, (r)Jack Fields/CB; **150** RS/AAA; **152** C.M. Dixon; **153** Eugene Gilliom; **154** Bettmann/CB; **157** (l)Gianni Dagli Orti/CB, (r)Wolfgang Kaehler; **158** (l)Louvre, Paris/SS, (r)Bettmann/CB; **159** (c)British Museum; **162** (l)AA, (r)Foto Marburg/AR; **166** Bettmann/CB; **167** MH; **168** S. Vidler/SS; **171** MH; **172** Peter Connolly; **174** (l)British Museum/BAL, (r)SS; **175** MH; **178** (l)Araldo de Luca/CB, (r)AAA; **180** (l)ME, (r)Photri; **182** Tom Lovell/NGS; **184** (l)SS, (r)The Purcell Team/CB; **186** Metropolitan Museum of Art, Wolfe Fund,1931, Catharine Lorillard Wolfe Collection (31.45); **187** Vatican Museum; **188** Scala/AR; **192** (l)RH, (r)Fitzwilliam Museum, U. of Cambridge, UK/BAL; **194** file photo; **197** Bettmann/CB; **198** Tom Lovell/NGS; **199** (l)Vanni Archive/CB, (r)Aaron Haupt; **202** Museum of Fine Arts, Boston; **203** (tl)Museum of Fine Arts, Boston, (tr)Giraudon/AR, (bl)courtesy Museum of Fine Arts, Boston, (br)Oriental Institute Museum, U. of Chicago; **206** (l)BAL, (r)Giraudon/AR; **208** (l)Metropolitan Museum of Art, Fletcher Fund, 1924. (24.97.21ab), (r)Archivo Iconografico, S.A./CB; **210** file photo; **212** (l)Scala/AR, (r)Richard Pasley/SS; **213** Archiv/PR; **215** Vatican Museum; **218** (l)Francis G. Mayer/CB, (r)SM; **220** Scala/AR; **221** (l)EL/AR, (r)Mark Richards/PhotoEdit; **222** Smithsonian Institution; **223** Pinacoteca Capitolina, Palazzo Conservatori, Rome/BAL; **225** MH; **226** Stanley Seaberg; **227** Scala/AR; **229** NWPA; **232** (l)MH, (r)EL/AR; **237** 1994 Board of Trustees, National Gallery of Art, Washington/Sir Peter Paul Rubens, *Tiberius and Agrippina*; **238** (l)Nimatallah/AR, (r)Robert Essel/TSM; **243** BAL; **246** (l)Elio Ciol/CB, (r)Scala/AR; **248** (t)MH, (b)Scala/AR; **249** Doug Martin; **252** North Carolina Museum of Art/CB; **254** (l)Galleria dell' Accademia, Florence, Italy/BAL, (r)Miklos Szabo/LA; **255** Giraudon/AR; **258** Nathan Benn/CB; **259** (tl)Gianni Dagli Orti/CB, (tr)Charles & Josette Lenars/CB, (bl br)Nathan Benn/CB; **262** (l)WF/AR, (r)Pierpont Morgan Library/AR; **264** (l)Walters Art Gallery, Baltimore, (r)SS; **266** SM; **267** RS/AAA; **268** (l)NWPA, (r)Kevin Jacobs/Image Works; **274** (l)Scala/AR, (r)Giraudon/AR; **278** file photo; **280** Scala/AR; **282** SM; **283** (l)Archive Photos, (r)Aaron Haupt; **285** file photo; **288** (l)BAL, (r)MH; **291** file photo; **292** Stapleton Collection/BAL; **293** (l)Bettmann/CB, (r)A. Ramey/PhotoEdit; **298** (l)WF/AR, (r)York Archaeological Trust; **300** Lennart Larsen/Frances Lincoln Publishers; **302** (l)(c)British Museum, (r)BAL; **303** Charles & Josette Lenars/CB; **305** (l)(c)British Museum, (r)Randall Hyman/Stock Boston; **307** (l)Tom Lovell/NGS, (r)RS/AAA; **310** Burstein Collection/CB; **311** (t)Borromeo/AR, (c)Scala/AR, (b)Charles & Josette Lenars/CB; **314** (l)Basilica di Sant'Apollinare Nuovo, Ravenna/Explorer, Paris/SS, (r)Scala/AR; **316** (l)WF/British Museum/AR, (r)AAA; **318** (l)Capitoline Museum, Rome/SS, (r) Michael Hampshire/NGS; **319** Dumbarton Oaks; **320** Andre Durenceau/NGS; **321** MH; **325** (l)AA, (r)David Ball/TSM; **326** C.M. Dixon; **330** (l)EL/AR, (r)MH; **333** Robert Azzi/WC; **335** (l)ARAMCO, (r)Pablo Koch/Vision International; **339** (l)AA, (r)Jeff Greenberg/PR; **340** Pablo Koch/Vision International; **342** Freer Gallery of Art, Smithsonian Institution, Washington, D.C. (29.9), *Jug with a bottle neck*, Persia, Seljuk, early 13th century, glazed clay, 18.0x14.8cm; **343** Bodleian Library, Oxford; **346** (l)Christie's Images/SS, (r)Harald Sund/Image Bank; **348** Eugene Gilliom; **349** (t)Scala/AR, (b)Tretyakov Gallery, Moscow; **351** (l)1994 Board of Trustees, National Gallery of Art, Washington, Byzantine 13th century, *Enthroned Madonna and Child*, Gift of Mrs. Otto H. Kahn, (r)Pablo Koch/Vision International; **352** file photo; **353** (l)Statens Historiska Museum, Stockholm, Sweden, (r)Kremlin Museums, Moscow/BAL; **354** file photo; **355** SM; **357** Nationalmuseet, Copenhagen/BAL; **360** Arthur Tilley/FPG; **361** (tl, bc)Dewitt Jones/CB, (tr)George Ranalli/PR, (bl)Tim Davis/PR, (br)Richard A. Cooke/CB; **364** (l)EL/AR, (r)Malcolm Gibson/FPG; **366** Ashmolean Museum/BAL; **366** Pierpont Morgan Library/AR; **370** Scala/AR; **371** Norma Brenneman; **372** (l)Pierpont Morgan Library/AR, (r)Jeff Christensen/LA; **374** BAL; **376** SS; **377** file photo; **380** EL/AR; **382** Don Nieman; **383** Borromeo/AR; **384** (l)MH, (r)Cooper-Hewitt Museum, Smithsonian Institution/AR; **385 387** Bettmann/CB; **389** SM; **390** Lance Nelson/TSM; **392** (l)SM, (r) Robert W. Nicholson/NGS; **393** (t)Library of Istanbul University, (b)file photo; **395** 1994 Board of Trustees, National Gallery of Art, Washington, French 12th century, *Reliquary chasse*, Widener Collection; **398** (l)Archivo Iconografico, S.A./CB, (r)Scala/AR; **402** Giraudon/AR; **404** (t)David Young-Wolfe/PhotoEdit, (b)NWPA; **410** (l)EL/AR, (r)A. Woolfitt/WC/PNI; **412** (t)file photo, (b)Bibliotheque Nationale, Paris/BAL; **414** Tom Lovell/NGS; **416** file photo; **418** Musees Nationaux; **419** SM; **420** Archiv/PR; **421** (l)Biblioteca Trivulziana, Milan/BAL, (r)Bernard Annebicque/CS; **423** BAL; **426** MH; **427** (tl)Victoria & Albert Museum, London/AR, (tr)Tony Stone Images, (cl)Scala/AR, (cr)WF/AR, (b)Michael S. Yamashita/CB; **430** (l)Pepys Library, Magdalene College, Cambridge, (r)Michael Freeman/CB; **432** (l)Scala/AR, (r)Il Museo Leonardo da Vinci; **434** Scala/AR; **435** (l)file photo, (r)Louvre, Paris/AR; **437** (l)Scala/AR, (r)Chuck Savage/TSM; **439** Bodleian Library, Oxford, fol.218r (Venice); **443** (t)file photo, (b)Folger Shakespeare Library; **444** (l)LOC, (r)Folger Shakespeare Library; **445** (l)SM, (r)Folger Shakespeare Library; **448** (l)Sammlungen des Stiftes, Klosterneuburg, Austria/EL/AR, (r)SS; **450** Michael Hampshire/NGS; **452** Museo del Castello Sforzesco, Milan, Italy/BAL; **453** (l)Giraudon/Art Resource, (r)Toyohiro Yamada/FPG; **454** Giraudon/AR; **455** SM; **456** (t)National Portrait Gallery, (b) (c)Reserved to Her Majesty Queen Elizabeth II; **457** (l)MH, (r)Scala/AR; **458** Scala/AR; **459** National Maritime Museum; **460** National Portrait Gallery, London/SS; **461** Victoria & Albert Museum, London/BAL; **466** (l)Victoria & Albert Museum, London/BAL, (r)MH; **468** (l)Archivo Iconografico, S.A./CB, (r)NASA; **469** Bettmann/CB; **470** SM; **471 472** file photos; **474** (l)SM/SS, (r)file photo; **476** Collection of The New-York Historical Society; **480** Philadelphia Museum of Art/CB; **481** (tl)Tanzania National Museum, Dar es Salaam/WF/AR, (tc)RS/AAA, (tr)Hugh Sitton/Tony Stone Images, (bl)David Butz/FPG, (bc br)RS/AAA; **484** (t)Science & Society Picture Library/Science Museum, London, (b)ME; **486** (l)courtesy Pecos National Historic Park, (r)Paul Almasy/CB; **488** Bibliotheque Nationale, Paris; **489** file photo; **490** (c)British Museum; **491** (l) (c)British Museum, (r)Wolfgang Kaehler; **493** Bettmann/CB; **496** Courtesy Enoch Pratt Free Library, reprinted by permission; **497** Culver Pictures/PNI; **502** (t)PR, (b)SM; **506** (l)BAL, (r)National Gallery of Art; **507** (c) Reserved to Her Majesty Queen Elizabeth II; **509** file photo; **510** LOC; **512** Virginia Museum of Fine Arts, Junius Brutus Stearns, *Washington Addressing the Constitutional Convention* (detail), oil on canvas, 37.5' x 54'; **514 515** Giraudon/AR; **516** Aaron Haupt; **517** Huntington Library Art Collections & Botanical Gardens, San Marino, CA/SS; **519** (l)ME, (r)Christie Linford/LA; **522** (l)ME, (r)Bettmann/CB; **525** Bettmann/CB; **528** (l)New York State Historical Association, Cooperstown, NY. Photo by Richard Walker, (r)NWPA; **531** (l)LOC, (r)Greg Girard/TSM; **532** Courtesy Sheffield City Museums; **534** Victoria & Albert Museum, London/AR; **535** file photo; **538** Scala/AR; **539** (tl)Hermitage, St. Petersburg, Russia/BAL, (tr)Bibliotheque Nationale, Paris/BAL, (cl, cr)AAA, (b)Kremlin Museums, Moscow/BAL; **542** (l)Science & Society Picture Library/Science Museum, London, (r)Royal Pavilion Libraries & Museums, Brighton & Hove; **544** (l)Christie's Images, (r)LOC; **547** LOC; **548** George Schneegass/Tom Stack & Assoc.; **550** National Portrait Gallery, Smithsonian Institution/AR; **552** AKG Photo; **554** Organization of American States; **556** Museu Paulista, Universite de Sao Paulo; **557** (l)Flag Research Center, Winchester, MA, (r)Gary A. Conner/PhotoEdit; **560** Peter Harholdt/SS; **562** Leonard de Selva/CB; **563** (t)Jules Talon/FPG, (b)SEF/AR; **566** SM; **568** Bettmann/CB; **569** (l)Tate Gallery, London/AR, (r)Mike King/CB; **570** Giraudon/AR; **573** Archivo Iconografico, S.A./CB; **575** file photo; **578** (t)Hans Georg Roth/CB, (b)E.K. Johnson/ME; **580** David L. Perry; **581** NWPA; **582** Michael Nicholson/CB; **583** (l)NGS, (r)A. Ramey/PhotoEdit; **584** SM; **585** MH; **586** Laurie Platt Winfrey; **587** Metropolitan Museum of Art/Laurie Platt Winfrey; **588 589** LOC; **592** CB; **596** Keren Su/AllStock/PNI; **597** (tl)Lindsay Hebberd/CB, (tr)Julia Waterlow, Eye Ubiquitous/CB, (cl)Ruth Kimpel, (cr)Fred Ward, (b)NGS; **600** NASA; **602** (l)Hulton-Deutsch Collection/CB, (r)Roger-Viollet/LA; **605** Courtesy Director, National Army Museum, London; **606** file photo; **608** Archivo Iconografico, S.A./CB; **609** (t)Archivo Iconografico, S.A./CB, (b)Bettmann/CB; **610** Sovfoto/Eastfoto; **611** Sovfoto/Eastfoto/PNI; **612** (l)Image Bank, (r)courtesy CNN; **613** FPG; **614** Bettmann/CB; **615** FPG; **616** Hulton-Deutsch Collection/CB; **618** U.S. Coast Guard Photo, National Archives; **620** (l)US Air Force Photo/FPG, (r)George Silk/Life Magazine/Time Warner; **621** Bettmann/CB; **624** (l)Photodisc, Inc., (r)Bettmann/CB; **626** UPI/Bettmann/CB; **627** Zadora/Sygma; **628** (t)Dennis Brack/Black Star, (b)Sygma; **630** UPI/Bettmann/CB; **631** (l)Bettmann/CB, (r)Tom Stack/Tom Stack & Assoc.; **632** Peter Turnley/Black Star; **635** (l)Jehangir Gazdar/WC, (r)Topham/Image Works; **636** Ron McMillan/LA; **638** (l)James Sugar/Black Star, (r)Abbas/Magnum; **639** Paulo Fridman/CS; **640** Robert Frerck/Odyssey; **641** (l)Farrell Grehan/FPG, (r)Natsuko Utsumi/LA; **644** (l)Courtesy Apple Computer, Inc., (r)CB; **646** (l)R. Bossu/CS, (r)Lee Snider/ImageWorks; **647** Ivo Lorenc/CS; **649** A. Gyori/CS; **650** (l)Chip Hires/LA, (r)Les Stone/CS; **653** S. Compoint/CS; **654** Alexandra Soulat/Sipa; **655** Amit Shabi/Reuters/STR/Archive Photos; **656** Sion Touhig/CS; **657** Carol Havens/CB; **658** Vince Streano/CB; **659** Jean-Marc Bouju/Wide World Photos; **661** Liz Gilbert/CS; **662** Steve Liss/Timepix; **664** Ch. Simonpietri/CS; **665** Pierre Toutain-Dorbec/CS; **669** (t) Garwood & Ainsile, Planet Project/TIME, (cl) Klaus Reisinger/Black Star, (cr) Sylvain Grandadam/Stone, (b) Zia Mazhar/AP/Wide World Photos; **672** Louvre, Paris/SS; **673** Courtesy Oakland Museum of California; **675** John Reader/SPL/PR; **677** Gianni Dagli Orti/CB; **679** AA; **681** Cummer Museum of Art & Gardens, Jacksonville, FL/SS; **683** AA; **685** Universitetets Oldsaksamling, Oslo/WF/AR; **687** St. Mark's Cathedral, Venice/WF/AR; **689** Archivo Iconografico, S.A./CB; **691** WF/AR; **693** ME; **695** (l)ME, (r)Earl Kowall/CB; **697** Apichart Weerawong/Reuters/CORBIS.